D1127438

p 7
p 105
p 18
p 204

# THE OPPENHEIMER CASE: SECURITY ON TRIAL

# THE OPPENHEIMER

# CASE: *SECURITY ON TRIAL*

BY Philip M. Stern

WITH THE COLLABORATION OF Harold P. Green

*with a special commentary by* LLOYD K. GARRISON,
*Chief Defense Counsel for Dr. Oppenheimer*

HARPER & ROW  PUBLISHERS

1817    NEW YORK, EVENSTON, AND LONDON

*This book is dedicated to my mother, with love.*

# ACKNOWLEDGMENTS

Let me begin with an effort to correct one of the major injustices of this world: the lack of recognition that is the usual lot of book editors. Such an injustice would be particularly heinous in this instance, for to a considerable extent, this book owes its very existence to the courage and enthusiasm of Thomas B. Congdon. The reader cannot know how much this manuscript has benefited from his many hours of painstaking, skilled and sensitive editing; nor can others know at what sacrifice to himself and his family. But I do. And I am fortunate to have him both as editor and as new-found friend.

As the extensive Notes and Sources suggest, this book involved a prodigious amount of research, far more than one person could ever have done. At the outset, Anne Allen helped, with characteristic skill and dispatch. When her husband George claimed her to accompany him on a reportorial stint in Saigon, Elaine Buller stepped in, and it would not be possible to describe or acknowledge fully her contribution to the completeness and accuracy of this work. No fact or figure seemed too obscure for her sleuthing skill. With incomprehensible patience, tenacity and consistent good cheer, she questioned and checked every statement in this long manuscript. How she managed to do so while running a family (not to mention maintaining her sanity) is a source of wonderment, admiration and profound gratitude on my part.

Her patience and fortitude were equaled by my most loyal secretary, Gertrude Callander (and by her husband, Charles), who was unfailingly supportive in so many ways during the many ups and downs of this book, who steadfastly typed the various drafts of this long work, and who could always, somehow, find that priceless paper or bit of information I *knew* I had—but, of course, couldn't locate. She has been an indispensable part of this work.

Michael E. Tigar, that walking West Reporter, never tired of my long series of queries on the legal and procedural aspects of the book, and never failed to produce an apposite legal precedent or example (often with full numerical citation, miraculously stored in a mind that is as perceptive as it is retentive).

Mr. Tigar's standing would suffer (and I would be an ingrate) if I did not also acknowledge the guidance and help received from his senior, Edward Bennett Williams, whose personal credo, instincts and courtroom experience make him uniquely familiar with the ingredients of a fair hearing. These he generously shared with me in person, as well as through his excellent book, *One Man's Freedom*. Allan B. Ecker, who lived through the Oppenheimer case at Lloyd Garrison's side, also shared valuable insights into the requirements of fair trial procedures.

I am indebted to my close friend Anthony Lewis, not only for moral support and friendship but also for comments on portions of the manuscript that were as helpful as I knew they would be; to another valued friend, Marcus Raskin, not only for persevering through an early draft of the manuscript, but for guiding and stimulating me to enlarge the scope of the work; to Richard Barnet, for his helpful reading of the manuscript; to Mary Clynes, for her everlasting and uncanny knack of unearthing just the right fact at just the right time; to historian Richard Hewlett of the Atomic Energy Commission, not only for the richness of his exceptionally well-written history of the early atomic years, *New World*, but for his patience and thoroughness in answering the many factual queries that were put to him; to Kimbell Johnson of the Civil Service Commission for his generous help and counsel on matters relating to the Federal loyalty program; to Gordon

Arneson, for sharing his unique knowledge about governmental atomic matters and for permitting me to use facts from his unpublished accounts of these events; to Edith Cohen, for furnishing otherwise unobtainable material as well as for her unending kindness and solicitude; to Richard E. Passmore, for the care and good taste with which he ministered to the manuscript and notes; to Edna Evans, for her painstaking and able travail on the index; and to Joseph Iseman, Louis Oberdorfer and Max Truitt for their friendship as well as their wise counsel.

Particular thanks are due Jerome B. Wiesner, not only for his comments and guidance on portions of the manuscript but for his generous efforts to lead me to authoritative source material.

I owe a special debt of gratitude to Dorothy and Ben Burch, the most hospitable and understanding neighbors a writer of eccentric habits could ever hope to have.

I am deeply grateful to Lloyd K. Garrison for the many hours he devoted to the preparation of the special commentary in this book. I think I appreciate the anguish and tribulations which the Oppenheimer case brought into his life. I understood fully his initial reluctance to become involved in any reopening of the subject, which makes me appreciate his contribution all the more. I consider him one of the very noble men of this world.

Finally, words cannot acknowledge my debt to the five greatest rewards of my life—my children, Henry, Michael, Holly, David and Eve, not only for putting up with outrageous absenteeism on the part of their father during the three and a half years this book has been in process, but for the joy and gratification they bring to every day of my life. Nor can words wholly convey my thanks to and love for their mother, whose sure instincts and unquenchable capacity to grow and learn have made this a larger and far better book, and me a far better man.

P.M.S.

# CONTENTS

# PREFACE

This began as a book about a security case. It ended as a book about the security system. The case is now history. The system is still with us.

Initially, this book was to show how the Federal Government used its power to bring one man, J. Robert Oppenheimer, to his knees. But the more that story unfolded, the more the Oppenheimer case seemed to lay bare the vices of the security system itself and their malign effects on American society.

Indeed, in many respects the Oppenheimer affair offers the most graphic illustration of the system's defects. It is the only security case whose hearing record has been made public. Its voluminous transcript displays both the procedural injustices of the system and the extent to which security investigations often intrude into the most intimate details of a man's life. The origins of the Oppenheimer case—in the white-hot policy debates, the animosities—demonstrate the system's susceptibility to being exploited for political (if not for personal) ends. And the consequence of the case—the loss to the nation of Oppenheimer's talents and services—shows the costliness of the obsession with "security."

Finally, the case highlights one of the most invidious aspects of the security system: its encouragement of citizens to inform on one another. Most security cases involve unknown career civil servants, whose livelihoods depend on the favor of the Federal Government. Robert Oppenheimer was a world-renowned figure and enjoyed great independence. Yet even he permitted himself to become the instrument of the security system. If such a man would yield, how many can be expected to resist?

The idea for this book was originally suggested to me by Harold P. Green, and the book began as a co-authorship venture. For many years Mr. Green has maintained an acute interest in the Oppenheimer case and in matters of government security generally, and has held, as a major goal, the writing of a definitive book on the case, especially its legal and procedural aspects. He is especially well qualified to write such a book: not only has he been a student of the Oppenheimer case itself; he is also extremely knowledgeable in the law of personnel security.

But since he was engaged full time in the teaching and practice of law, it was apparent that he would be unable to complete his book within any finite period of time. Accordingly, in the fall of 1965, he invited me to join in the venture. The case had long fascinated me, and I readily agreed.

As I began my researches on the case, aided by Mr. Green's special knowledge both of the case and of the legal framework within which it took place, I developed interests that were complementary to his—in the political, the historical and the personality aspects of the case. As time went on, the focus of my attention shifted, as I have said, from the case itself to the security system as a whole and its effects on the United States.

The book that finally emerged represents primarily my interests, research, views and conclusions rather than those of Mr. Green. He and I both recognized that his analyses and insights were being unduly submerged and that they merited exposition in his own book on the Oppenheimer case. That book, which Mr. Green intends writing, will, I feel sure, illuminate a very important aspect of the case.

Chapter II ("The Oppenheimer Story"), which occupies nearly half of this book, presents in chronological form the evidence heard by Oppenheimer's hearing board. Part of its

purpose is to give the reader a basis for arriving at his own judgment about the case and the verdicts.* Thus Chapter II represents, in essence, a report of the proceeding itself. It also seeks
to help the reader cope with a problem that severely hampers
the security system—the problem of perspective. When Oppenheimer's case was heard in 1954, the atmosphere of the Cold War
and of the McCarthy era could not help but pervade the hearing
room. This made it all the harder for the physicist's judges to
evaluate his behavior during the depression-ridden Thirties and
the wartime Forties, when Russia was a staunch ally. It was as
if the judges were peering at those earlier days through the
wrong end of a telescope. Chapter II attempts to correct that
distortion by interleaving among the events recounted at Oppenheimer's hearing some incidents that suggest the mood of the
times.

The researching and writing of this book have required three
and a half years, fifteen thousand miles of travel, and interviews
with 150 persons, from California to Paris and London. In general, those with whom I sought interviews granted them willingly. The few who were unwilling to see me were at the extreme
ends of the spectrum: those most opposed to and those closest to
Dr. Oppenheimer. I naturally sought to interview Dr. Oppenheimer, but he declined, explaining:

> I have thought that I should not interpose my judgment as
> to whether [this] will be a helpful book. Indeed, I do not
> know. But I am clear that the book will be better for having
> been written totally without my collaboration, suggestions, or
> implied approval. The subject of the book is one on which I
> do not have a total sense of detachment, and on which I have
> very large and central areas of ignorance. I cannot think of a
> more poisonous brew.

I also sought an interview with Mrs. Oppenheimer, after her
husband's death. She likewise declined, citing the above letter
from Dr. Oppenheimer.

* It is impossible to put the reader on a completely equal footing with the
hearing board members, who had before them some three thousand pages of
investigative reports that were not made part of the public record.

Although I never met J. Robert Oppenheimer, I have, in one sense, felt his presence keenly while writing this book. For more than two years the remarkable photograph on the dust jacket has stared from the wall of my writing room, and I have been haunted by those extraordinary Oppenheimer eyes, particularly by the pain, the hurt I find in them. There is certainly reason for hurt, for here was a man, called upon to advise his government, who counseled a course of action about the hydrogen bomb that he deeply believed would be in his country's best interests; yet his views were interpreted (by men who disagreed with him) as ill-motivated. And his judges, in finding him unworthy of his government's trust, in effect agreed.

J. Robert Oppenheimer is dead, but the power that was invested in his judges—the power to pronounce upon another's loyalty, to appraise his motives—lives on. That fact has greater meaning and potentially affects more people now than it did in 1954. The debate about the H-bomb was supersecret, confined for the most part to the top councils of government. Today, vastly larger numbers of people are engaged in the controversies over the Vietnam war, the draft, the military—and, in fact, all the premises of the established order. Feelings are intense, expression is vehement. Are the dissenters less loyal, less motivated by conscience than are those who, say, support the war and the draft, convinced that their country must be protected against the spread of Communism? There are those, both in and out of government, who seem to feel so (see pp. 484–88). But who can know—who has the right to probe and appraise—the inner motives of another?

The government continues to assert that right, through the security system. As Chapter XIV shows, it is still using that system—and, more disturbingly, other governmental powers and programs as well—to punish or discourage those whose opinions are in official disfavor.

And so this is not a book about yesterday. It is, to a distressing extent, a book about today.

PHILIP M. STERN

*Washington, D.C.*
*July, 1969*

THE OPPENHEIMER CASE: SECURITY ON TRIAL

# I   THE TRIGGER

On the evening of Saturday, November 7, 1953, a registered letter (return receipt requested) was posted at the main post office in Pittsburgh. It was addressed to J. Edgar Hoover, Director, Federal Bureau of Investigation, Washington, D.C. "Dear Mr. Hoover," it began. "This letter concerns J. Robert Oppenheimer. . . .

"The purpose of this letter," it went on, "is to state my own exhaustively considered opinion, based upon years of study of the available classified evidence, that more probably than not, J. Robert Oppenheimer is an agent of the Soviet Union."*

Having posted the letter, William Liscum Borden, former executive director of Congress' powerful Joint Atomic Energy Committee and then an executive of the Westinghouse Corporation, was satisfied at last that he had fully discharged his duty to his country regarding his deep concern about the nation's most celebrated atomic scientist.

If any informed member of the general public had learned of Borden's drastic accusation, he would have been flabbergasted,

* The source of this and numerous other facts and quotations may be found in the Notes and Sources section, pages 567–601.

for J. Robert Oppenheimer enjoyed an unexceptionable reputation. Not only was he a universally respected leader of the scientific and intellectual community; more than any other man he had been responsible for America's achievement of the first atomic bomb. It was almost unthinkable that such a man could possibly be "an agent of the Soviet Union."

On what evidence, then, did Borden base his grave charge? Where had he obtained that evidence? His information came from the government's massive investigative dossier on Oppenheimer. This file, a four-and-a-half-foot stack of reports, had been amassed in the course of eleven years' minute surveillance of the scientist's life, private as well as public. Oppenheimer's telephone had been tapped. His office and home had been bugged. His mail had been opened. Even so intimate an event as a night spent with a former fiancée had not escaped the watchful eyes of government agents.

From these detailed reports, Borden had learned:

• That in the years before World War II, as a physics professor in Berkeley, California, Oppenheimer had been intimately and actively involved with the radical left and with numerous Communists.

• That his wife, Katherine, had formerly been married to a Communist and had herself been a party member.

• That Oppenheimer's brother and sister-in-law had been Communist Party members until 1941.

• That Oppenheimer himself had reportedly once attended a closed Communist meeting in his own home in Berkeley.

• That he had made cash contributions to (or through) the Communist Party. Significantly, to Borden, these contributions had continued right up to the moment of Oppenheimer's entry into government atomic research, in April, 1942.

The dossier also reported a brief conversation in the kitchen of the Oppenheimer home between the physicist and a close friend, Haakon Chevalier. It took place in early 1943, after Oppenheimer had been named director of the supersecret nuclear weapons laboratory at Los Alamos. Chevalier told Oppenheimer about a scientist who had claimed he could transmit secret technical information to the Soviets. Oppenheimer emphatically told Chevalier he would have no part of such an activity. But (and for Oppenheimer it was to be a fateful "but") for eight months he failed to report the conversation to security officials. And when he did report it, he lied.

The surveillance reports showed that in the postwar years Oppenheimer had kept up his close friendship with Chevalier. There had been, for example, exchanges of letters about intimate family matters and a weekend visit by the Oppenheimers to the Chevalier oceanside home near San Francisco. The government dossier also stated that many of the scientists recruited by Oppenheimer for wartime atomic work were believed by security officers to have been Communists or Communist sympathizers. In fact, at one point during the war, concerned security officials had urged Oppenheimer's immediate dismissal not only from the directorship of the Los Alamos laboratory but from all government service.

Although on its face it was a serious bill of particulars that William Borden recited in his letter to the FBI, the information about Oppenheimer's leftist connections was far from new to the government. Some of it had been known as much as eleven years earlier, during the war, when Oppenheimer was first cleared for secret atomic work. Most of the balance had been reviewed in detail by the Atomic Energy Commissioners themselves in 1947, when they unanimously recleared Oppenheimer for an important advisory post. Thus, by 1951, when William Borden first saw the file, Oppenheimer's prewar radical background and his wartime brushes with security officers had been known to high government officials for at least four years. Yet this knowledge had prompted no one to seek to bar Oppenheimer from the innermost secrets and councils of government.

In William Borden's eyes, Oppenheimer's conduct in those very councils constituted additional evidence of the scientist's suspect character, evidence that postdated the AEC clearance in 1947. As Borden viewed it, Oppenheimer had consistently opposed efforts to strengthen America's nuclear arsenal after the war. Not only that; his prestige and charisma had persuaded other scientist-advisers to follow his lead. Borden was particularly alarmed by Oppenheimer's stand on the question of whether the United States should make an all-out effort to develop a new "superweapon"—a hydrogen bomb thousands of times more powerful than the original Hiroshima A-bomb. Borden was among the most zealous advocates of the "Super," while Oppenheimer had opposed the "crash program" for the new weapon. Even after 1950, when President Truman had authorized an H-bomb program, Oppenheimer's opposition had persisted, and Borden was persuaded that the physicist had gone so far as to discourage other scientists from working on the H-bomb project. To Borden, convinced that the Soviets were embarked on a headlong quest for the "Super," Oppenheimer's stance was utterly incredible. This, together with Oppenheimer's seeming opposition to the expansion of other nuclear programs, reinforced Borden's conviction that the physicist had been a "hardened Communist" in prewar years, that he had merely "gone underground" during the war, and that he had, in fact, never ceased to be a loyal "agent of the Soviet Union."

Even though the Borden letter contained no evidence that had not been officially recognized (and apparently accepted) for years, it triggered a whole chain reaction of improbabilities:

• President Eisenhower ordered a "blank wall" placed between the nation's atomic secrets and J. Robert Oppenheimer, the man who had been instrumental in creating many of those very secrets and who therefore continued to hold them in his head, despite the "blank wall."

• Even though Oppenheimer's connection with the government and its secrets had all but ended, the Atomic Energy Commission ordered a full-scale security proceeding against him in which it played an eager and often savage prosecutory role. The government went so far as to use electronic devices to eavesdrop on a private conference between Oppenheimer and his attorney.

• The man who was also to be the chief appellate judge in the matter, AEC Chairman Lewis L. Strauss, took an unusual personal interest in the prosecution of the case. Strauss' apparently hostile role seemed contradictory for a man who a few years earlier had carefully reviewed the physicist's dossier and had voted to clear him for supersecret atomic work. Moreover, it was Strauss who had offered Oppenheimer the directorship of the prestigious Institute for Advanced Study at Princeton.

• The AEC expended substantial time, funds and energy on the case; a special three-man panel sat for nearly four weeks, heard forty witnesses, took nearly three-quarters of a million words of testimony. All of this could have been avoided simply by waiting a few months and allowing Oppenheimer's consultant's contract to expire.

• At the security hearing, former associates of Oppenheimer —including, most poignantly, his once intimate intellectual colleague, Edward Teller—appeared and testified against him.

• In the end Oppenheimer's judges found the physicist not only loyal but *unusually* discreet with secrets—but nonetheless ruled that "the father of the A-bomb" was a "security risk," no longer entitled to his government's trust.

If the Borden letter contained no substantial evidence that had not been long known and accepted in official circles, why did it suddenly prompt the government to move against Oppenheimer? Why was it so important to shut the doors of secrecy that had been open to him for eleven years? What compelled the AEC to mount a full-dress security proceeding when a few months' delay could have spared both Oppenheimer and the government the agony and the expense? And, if Oppenheimer's opposition to the H-bomb was one basis for charging that he was a "security risk," couldn't similar questions have been raised against other scientists who had opposed the "Super" more vigorously and far more publicly than he? Since, on the H-bomb question, Oppenheimer had been standing in a crowd, why did the lightning single him out?

These questions involve motive, the motives especially of the men aligned against Oppenheimer on the great matter of the H-bomb: AEC Chairman Lewis Strauss, physicist Edward Teller and the high command of the U.S. Air Force, which was to have the job of delivering the new superweapon.

But there are other questions of motive, the motives of Op-

penheimer himself. As the special hearing panel opened the proceeding "In the Matter of J. Robert Oppenheimer," on April 12,
1954, its three judges had before them an official statement of
charges against the physicist, which told of his prewar connections with the radical left, including the Communist Party; his
conversation with Haakon Chevalier and his delayed and men-
dacious reporting of it; the continuation of his friendship with
Chevalier in the immediate postwar years; his purported recruitment of Communist sympathizers for wartime nuclear work; and
his postwar opposition to the H-bomb, which included his alleged efforts to dissuade other scientists from working on the
bomb.

What, the judges had to decide, had been the real nature of
Oppenheimer's ties with the Communists in prewar Berkeley?
Had he been a "hardened Communist," as Borden alleged in his
letter? Or merely a temporary "fellow traveler," like so many
Americans who were deeply disaffected by the Great Depression?

How should the "Chevalier incident" be assessed? Why did
Oppenheimer fail to report the incident promptly and truthfully,
and was this failure outweighed by his immediate rejection of
whatever espionage overture may have been involved?

What of Oppenheimer's continued friendship with Chevalier?
Was it innocent or suspect? And even if innocent, did this continuing association with a man who had once talked of espionage
reflect a disregard for security?

Did Oppenheimer's occasional refusal to answer security officials' questions likewise indicate a disrespect for the security
system?

And what lay behind Oppenheimer's opposition to the hydrogen bomb? Was it genuine fear of an unbridled arms race that
could end with the obliteration of civilization? Or were there
other, more suspect motives?

But all those questions were subsidiary to the core issue for, as
Oppenheimer's staunchest defender and his severest detractor*
were later to agree, there was really only one question facing his
judges as they heard and weighed the evidence: Was Oppenheimer sufficiently loyal and sufficiently discreet to be entrusted

* AEC Commissioner Henry Smyth and Chairman Strauss.

with his country's secrets? Or was there a substantial danger that he might divulge those secrets, wittingly or unwittingly?

The evidence on which the hearing panel was to judge J. Robert Oppenheimer consisted, in essence, of an unfolding of his life, from the year 1936.

# II   THE OPPENHEIMER STORY

## 1. *The Prewar Years*

In 1936, at the age of thirty-two, a brilliant but somewhat abstracted professor of theoretical physics at the University of California at Berkeley emerged from what had been, politically speaking, a cocoon of oblivion and began to look at the world around him. A bachelor, he had lived in near-seclusion in an apartment tucked away in the Berkeley hills, with neither telephone nor radio. He had never read newspapers or magazines. So complete had been his isolation from events, he later recalled, that he was not even aware of the 1929 stock market crash until long after the fact.

Nor had the world yet heard of Julius Robert Oppenheimer.*

* There is some disagreement about the "J" in Oppenheimer's name. Official communications by FBI Director J. Edgar Hoover, as well as a 1968 book, *Lawrence & Oppenheimer*, by Nuel Pharr Davis, referred to him as "Julius Robert Oppenheimer." In a review of the Davis book, Jeremy Bernstein, a close friend of Oppenheimer, objected that "the 'J' doesn't stand for anything." This conforms with what Oppenheimer himself is known to have told associates. However, the Bureau of Records and Statistics, Department of Health, City of New York, advises that the city's records "contain a birth certificate for a Julius R. Oppenheimer [sic] born on April 22, 1904."

Outside the select community of theoretical physicists he was unknown. Yet inside that community he had already become legendary. Already his colleagues had observed those exceptional qualities that were later to raise him to international repute: a superlatively quick mind; a supreme command of the spoken word; an almost hypnotic power to captivate, inspire, persuade, stimulate. Within this same human being, however, there lived an opposite force: a capacity to belittle, wither, antagonize, alienate. In the course of the ordeal to which Oppenheimer would later be subjected, both these positive and negative aspects would contribute to his fall.

By 1936 the Oppenheimer magnetism had succeeded in attracting to Berkeley brilliant physics students from all over the country. One, for example, had been headed for an Eastern university, met Oppenheimer briefly, reversed his course and headed for Berkeley. By the end of the Thirties Oppenheimer had made Berkeley a great center of theoretical physics.

His students idolized him. It was no trick to spot "Oppie's boys," for they affected his mannerisms, even his intonations. Whenever one saw a student running his fingers through his hair as he talked or murmuring "*ja, ja*" as he listened, or assiduously jumping up to light the cigarettes of others, one could expect that the student was a disciple of J. Robert Oppenheimer. Oppenheimer's friend I. I. Rabi recalls the time he thought he heard the physicist's voice in an adjacent room; he went and looked and found it was Arnold Nordsieck, one of Oppenheimer's closest adherents. Each spring, when the master went south to Pasadena to teach at the California Institute of Technology, a retinue of devoted Berkeley students would pack their meager belongings into cars and, in a long caravan, would follow him.

The physicist's power to beguile was astounding. A particularly able Los Alamos scientist recalls that frequently, after an office appointment with Oppenheimer, he would suddenly realize that in his entrancement with the lab director's conversation he had either forgotten or been unconsciously dissuaded from the carefully considered point of his visit. His only protection, he found, was to write down the object of his appointment and consult the scrap of paper before leaving Oppenheimer's office.

Oppenheimer could be extraordinarily considerate. A student

whom Oppenheimer drew into war work, at the sacrifice of his doctorate, remembers how Oppenheimer strolled into his office and hit on the idea that the secret work the student was doing qualified as a doctoral dissertation. Oppenheimer went to some pains to persuade the physics faculty to grant the prized degree, which must have taken considerable doing inasmuch as the faculty could not even be told the *subject* of the top-secret dissertation, much less its contents.

There was, however, a harsh side to Robert Oppenheimer. If he considered a question silly, he would not even deign to answer, and many a student stayed up all night trying to work out a problem rather than admit he didn't understand it. One, in fact, usually articulate, found himself so tongue-tied before Oppenheimer that he could hardly talk without written notes before him. Some excellent students, beaten down by his personality, fled the field of theoretical physics. A former student has described Oppenheimer's tongue as, at times, "annihilating."

He could also be cruel. Once the gentle, elderly James Franck, one of Oppenheimer's former professors, came to Berkeley to present a series of lectures on which someone had bestowed the grandiose title, "The Fundamental Meaning of Quantum Mechanics." During his visit, Franck heard one of Oppenheimer's prize students deliver a particularly arcane paper. From the audience, Franck asked a question that none of Oppenheimer's students would have dared to ask in the presence of their sharp-tongued mentor. From the other side of the audience came the voice of Robert Oppenheimer. "Well," he said caustically, "I don't intend to deliver any lectures on 'The Fundamental Meaning of Quantum Mechanics,' but part of the meaning is that *that* question is a foolish one." To the former Oppenheimer student who recalled this incident, the mere retelling of it, even thirty years later, produced the same horror and embarrassment he had felt when he had been eyewitness to the scene.

James Franck was neither of a mind nor in a position to bring harm to Robert Oppenheimer. But others who in later years were humiliated by the physicist's acerbic tongue *were* in such a position, and were to play important roles in his confrontation with the United States Government.

The negative attributes of Oppenheimer's personality may have sprung from his almost freakish quickness of mind, which separated him from, and often made him seem intolerant of, less gifted persons. Even as a boy he displayed impatience with others slower than he. But, one devoted contemporary has said, this "probably stemmed from his inability to imagine that they were really trying to understand what seemed so simple to him."

Robert Oppenheimer grew up in an intellectually and aesthetically stimulating atmosphere, and in affluence. In winter the Oppenheimers lived comfortably in Manhattan, in a sunny nine-room apartment on Riverside Drive which was adorned with presciently purchased Van Goghs, Gaugins and Cézannes. In the summer they stayed at Bay Shore, Long Island. There were maids and a chauffeur. Robert's father, Julius Oppenheimer, had immigrated from Germany at the age of seventeen and was a prosperous importer of men's suit linings. A bright, somewhat peremptory man, he doted on his son. Robert's mother, Ella Oppenheimer, has been described as lovely, artistic, sensitive, gentle. She is said to have permitted the thinking of harsh or rude thoughts but not their outward expression. Robert later observed, "My life as a child did not prepare me in any way for the fact that there are cruel and bitter things."

He remembered himself as an "unctuous, repulsively good little boy" whose home life offered "no normal healthy way to be a bastard." Childhood acquaintances speak of him as conscientious—his homework was always finished on Friday afternoon; somewhat precious—he would introduce himself with exaggerated precision: "My name is J. Rob-ert Opp-en-heim-er" (even as a child he was called J. Robert by many of his peers); and of course, enormously precocious—at the age of nine or so he was challenging an older girl-cousin to "ask me a question in Latin and I will answer you in Greek."

He was, from the beginning, something of a loner. A boyhood contemporary, who spent several summers with Robert at Bay Shore, has recalled: "We were thrown together a lot and yet we were never close. He was usually preoccupied with whatever he was doing or thinking." Family members recall vividly the time when, on a shopping expedition with his father, he tried on a new suit, retired to the changing room, but failed to emerge. His father found Robert in his underwear and in the process of removing shoes and socks. He was, it seems, working out the answer to a mathematical problem and was lost to the world. A classmate has remembered him sitting morosely in class, "exactly as though he weren't getting enough to eat or drink." He was a ravenous reader, for whom small talk was difficult. He shunned team sports such as baseball and football and was often teased for not being like other boys.

Robert's parents adored him, worried about him and protected him. They were active members of the New York Society for Ethical Culture ("dedicated to the ever increasing knowledge and practice and love of the right") and sent him and his younger brother, Frank, through its school. "If there ever was an outfit where ethics and honesty and morals were stressed," a cousin has said, "that was it!"

While at various times Robert considered being an architect, a poet, a painter or classical scholar, his interest in science was not long in rising to the surface: at the age of five, his grandfather gave him a small box of minerals; at eleven he was elected a member of the New York Mineralogical Club; at twelve he delivered his first paper there. During one high school summer, he completed a year's work in chemistry and physics in six weeks' time. The daily contact in the laboratory that summer with an inspiring teacher, Augustus Klock, and with the principles of atomic theory was, he later said, "a very exciting experience."

At Harvard (whose course he completed, *summa cum laude*, in only three years) the tartness and arrogance that were to become integral parts of his later personality began to manifest themselves. During an evening visit to the home of physics professor Percy Bridgman, he noticed a photograph of a temple at Segesta, Sicily. Bridgman remarked that it had been built in 700 B.C., to which Oppenheimer commented, "I should judge from the capitals on the columns that it was built about fifty years earlier than that."

Oppenheimer was even more the loner at Harvard. Involved in no clubs and no outside activities, he spent most of his time in the library. (A legendary remark of Oppenheimer's on a sultry spring day: "It's been so hot the only thing I could do all afternoon was lie on my bed and read Jeans' *Dynamic Theory of*

*Gases.*") In his graduating yearbook, he summarized his Harvard career in the single dreary phrase: "In college three years as an undergraduate."

When Oppenheimer emerged from Harvard in 1925, Americans desiring a first-rate education in physics could not find it at home; they had no choice but to make a pilgrimage to Europe, a dependency that Oppenheimer was to be instrumental in ending. And so Robert Oppenheimer went, successively, to Cambridge (where he met the greats of physics: Bohr, Dirac, Rutherford, Born); to Germany's Göttingen, where he received his Ph.D. at the age of twenty-three; and to the University of Leyden in Holland, where he stunned faculty and students by delivering a lecture in Dutch after only six weeks, and where he gained the affectionate nickname "Opje"—pronounced "Oppie"—later used by those who considered themselves his intimates.

In Europe the intellectual competition and the demands on Robert Oppenheimer were greater than they had been in America. According to one contemporary, a professor of Oppenheimer's at Leyden "found that he lacked discipline in every sense" and "sent him [to] Zurich to learn precision of thought and expression." In some quarters, Oppenheimer's work began to be known for sloppiness; often others would have to rework his mathematics—only to discover, to their annoyance, that while his math had been faulty, his conclusions had been brilliantly correct.

Oppenheimer was considerably better off than his fellow students, although he affected frayed clothes and there were holes in his shoes. On occasion he seemed not to appreciate fully the financial straits of his friends.

In the early portion of his European stay, Oppenheimer was beset with deep depression and doubt—to such an extent that he found himself, one Christmastime, walking on the Brittany shore, "on the point of bumping myself off. This was chronic." In 1929, after four years in Europe, this man whose loyalty to his country was later questioned felt homesick for America and returned. Remarkably enough, for a man of his means and broad cultural and aesthetic interests, he was not to leave the country again for nineteen years.

Of several teaching offers, Oppenheimer, then twenty-five,

accepted a dual appointment: to lecture in the fall and winter at the University of California at Berkeley and in the spring at the California Institute of Technology in Pasadena.

Robert Oppenheimer was not a "born teacher." When he began, he had difficulty gearing the speed of his own mind to his students' and chose an unusual way of emphasizing points—lowering his voice, rather than raising it. In those initial days, his sharp tongue and his impatience with those slower to understand are said to have terrorized many of his students. Within a few years, however, the sharpness and impatience abated (although they never disappeared) and his charismatic qualities began to emerge. Most of his students would sit through his courses at least twice. "He was the first person who made physics more than a set of rules," one former student has recalled. "He made it a matter of quarrying knowledge from nature."

Over the next decade, starting with but a single graduate student, Oppenheimer fashioned a great center for theoretical physics that was to break the European monopoly of the subject and largely transform American physics. Berkeley was to attract, train and send out to other American universities the brightest of American intellectual talent. Many regard this as Oppenheimer's most enduring contribution to American science.

His relationships with his students were out of the ordinary. As one ex-student has put it, his social life was closely "intertwined" with theirs. These were Depression days, and Oppenheimer, who continued to maintain a comfortable income, enjoyed treating the young men to dinners at Jack's Restaurant in San Francisco, with good food and fine wines. For many of his students, "Oppie was introducing them to an unfamiliar way of life." Physics discussions would continue through dinner and afterward into the night at his hillside bachelor apartment. Invariably the discussion would turn to the "wider realms of the intellect, of art, music and literature."

Oppenheimer's own research and writing produced few scientific insights. Unlike many of the famous men he would later oversee as director of the Los Alamos laboratory, he neither won nor was ever a serious contender for a Nobel prize. Some attribute this to his concentration of his time and creative energies on his students, but another explanation might lie in the prodigious breadth of Oppenheimer's intellectual appetite. One long-time acquaintance has said, "Oppie couldn't bear the notion that there was one important idea he didn't know or one field with which he didn't have a pretty intimate acquaintanceship." He read hugely, and could talk with the flair of an expert on almost any subject. (At the Berkeley Faculty Club he unexpectedly broke in on two French professors' discussion of an obscure early French poet—even quoting from the poet's work in an archaic French equivalent to Chaucerian English.) Already conversant with seven languages, Oppenheimer added still another—Sanskrit—and read the Bhagavad-Gita in its original form. It was this poem that was to come to his mind at that blinding instant at Alamagordo in 1945, when the world's first atomic device was exploded.

Yet by his later acknowledgment he had, in those early years, one intellectual blind spot: the arena of politics and public affairs. "I was interested in man and his experience," he later recalled, "but I had no understanding of the relations of man to his society." By the year 1936, however, two things had eclipsed all else for Oppenheimer—the Great Depression at home and the rise of Fascism abroad.

Both phenomena touched Oppenheimer directly. He had relatives in Germany (whom he would later help to extricate), and the treatment of the Jews aroused in him what he later spoke of as a "smoldering fury." At home, the effects of the Great Depression were most directly evident to Oppenheimer through his students. The only jobs many of them could get upon graduation were wholly inadequate to their training; others could get no jobs whatever. "Through them," Oppenheimer said, "I began to understand how deeply political and economic events could affect men's lives. I began to feel the need to participate more fully in the life of the community." But he had "no framework of political conviction or experience to give me perspective in these matters." He was unusually malleable for a man his age, and leaned heavily on other people to shape his political and social activism.

Among those persons, none was closer or more important to Oppenheimer than Jean Tatlock, daughter of a noted professor of

English at Berkeley. They met in the spring of 1936. By fall Oppenheimer was courting her. They "grew close"; twice they thought of themselves as engaged. She talked rather freely about herself and, among other things, told Oppenheimer of her sporadic membership in the Communist Party, a series of on-again, off-again, never satisfactory episodes. Of the friends to whom she introduced him, many were (according to later accusations by the government) Communists or what later came to be called "fellow travelers." Some of them—Dr. Thomas Addis, Kenneth May, Rudy Lambert—later came to play an important role in Oppenheimer's ordeal.

None of his new acquaintances, though, was to affect Oppenheimer's later life as crucially as a leftist French instructor on the Berkeley campus named Haakon Chevalier. American-born, Chevalier had spent his formative years in France and Norway, the native lands of his father and mother. At the age of eighteen he had shipped out to sea for a year. He returned ultimately to America and the serious study of French literature.

When he met Oppenheimer in the fall of 1937, Chevalier had already published a book on Anatole France, had tried his hand at novel writing, and translated several of André Malraux's works, including the celebrated *Man's Fate*. Friends remember him as "charming, congenial, enthusiastic, and cultivated," a man who "knew French poetry, French wines and intelligent people." He was intelligent himself, but not brilliant ("a good translator but a bad novelist," in the view of one contemporary)—not of the intellectual caliber of many of Oppenheimer's students. Yet while Oppenheimer was inclined to show disdain for others who were not his cerebral equal, something about Chevalier evidently struck a deep responsive chord in him. Chevalier became a close and important friend.

The association sprang in important measure from Chevalier's broad connections with the activists of the left—meaningful to a physics professor like Oppenheimer with a newly awakened social conscience and seeking avenues of action. Oppenheimer became a joiner and a doer—to such an extent that he later remarked to the head of the wartime atomic bomb project that, while he had never been a Communist, he had "probably belonged to every Communist-front organization on the West Coast."*

To such "subversive" organizations as the Friends of the Chinese People, the Western Council of the Consumers Union and the American Committee for Democracy and Intellectual Freedom (which was concerned with the plight of German intellectuals), Oppenheimer lent principally his name and occasional token financial support. But two other causes commanded far more of his time and energy. One was the plight of the California farm workers, who often had to put up with low wages (twenty cents an hour in the cotton fields; two dollars for a nine-hour day in the tobacco fields) and miserable living conditions (the mushroom workers had to live among open garbage containers, had no showers, and but one cold-water basin for the male and one for the female workers). The other cause was that of the university faculty, especially that of teaching assistants, whose annual pay had been cut from $750 to $600 in 1932 and never restored. Haakon Chevalier was then president of the teachers' union. Oppenheimer joined East Bay Local 349 in the fall of 1937 and was elected recording secretary. According to Chevalier's later recollection, Oppenheimer was an extremely faithful and active member who rarely missed a meeting and was willing to do the most menial tasks (including, in one instance, addressing envelopes and licking stamps well into the night so that an urgent union notice might go out). While the teachers had a very real grievance (the assistants were receiving considerably less, on an hourly basis, than most people on WPA relief), most union meetings were spent wrangling over resolutions on national and world problems of scant relevance to their economic lot. Ultimately, in the months prior to Pearl Harbor, the union became fatally divided on the question of U.S. intervention in the European war and disbanded—a move opposed by the Communists in the union but supported by Oppenheimer.

* In an important sense, this half-joking remark was a self-inflicted injustice, for at the time he uttered it, the law contained no provision for officially labeling organizations as "Communist fronts." Only the House Un-American Activities Committee was wielding that branding iron; and although three or four of the groups in which Oppenheimer enlisted *later* won the committee's seal of disapproval, in no case was this true at the time he was alleged to have belonged to them.

If there were Communists in the teachers' union and in other of the organizations to which Oppenheimer belonged, this was no cause for eyebrow-raising in the mid-Thirties. For one thing, this was the era of the Popular Front—the result of a new policy adopted in 1935 by the Communist International whereby working-class cooperation replaced the former enmity between the Communists and the non-Communist left. In America, party discipline was loosened and in many newly formed Popular Front organizations, Communists and non-Communists worked together for a common cause.

For another, Communists were both more numerous and, in cities such as San Francisco, more commonplace than they came to be in the Fifties and Sixties. For as the Depression dragged on and the capitalist system appeared increasingly ineffectual, the political left in America grew rapidly. In the year Oppenheimer cast his first vote for President, no less than eighty thousand Americans voted in favor of having a Communist occupy the White House.

American Communists were not quarantined from the rest of society like so many lepers, as they later came to be. They and their arguments were easily seen and heard. On the Berkeley campus, where Oppenheimer was teaching, the Young Communist League was as actively and openly in evidence as the Young Republicans. The League was welcome to hold open meetings at Sather Gate (then the Hyde Park Corner of the Berkeley campus), and in a campus straw vote at the time of the 1936 presidential election, Earl Browder, the Communist candidate, polled 120 votes—up from 27 votes in 1932.*

In California and elsewhere, Democratic and Republican politicians were happy to accept Communist cooperation and support. One example was a California Democratic official named Clyde Doyle. A little more than a decade later, as a U.S. Congressman, Doyle was a member of the Communist-hunting House Un-American Activities Committee. But in 1938 he saw nothing wrong with sitting at a table with leading California Communists

---

* In that era, Browder was a widely accepted campus speaker. Twice he was an invited guest speaker at the now staid University of Virginia, and his speeches were even reproduced in college textbooks on public speaking.

to plot a common strategy for the election of Democrat Cuthbert Olson as Governor.

In the mid-Thirties, Robert Oppenheimer's father lent him a book: *Soviet Communism: A New Civilisation?*, by Sidney and Beatrice Webb. It was one of the first books on a political subject that Oppenheimer had read, and he was greatly impressed by the Webbs' enthusiastic account of the achievements of Communist Russia. But he was far from alone. Many in America looked upon Russia more as a great "social experiment" than as an expansionist and threatening nation.* Edgar B. Stern, an ardently anti-New Deal businessman from New Orleans, emerged from a visit to Russia with such lyrical comments as these: "One gasps with wonder as to how these former workers and peasants could have learned so quickly how to manufacture and operate such intricate machines as the linotype . . . one concludes that the Russians must be a people of great inherent ability, as well as of tremendous industry and giant will. . . . I shall earnestly hope that the people of our democracies will stop sneering at the Russian experiment and be willing to study it with open minds."

In 1932 an attack by three thousand unemployed workers on the Ford Motor Company plant at Dearborn, Michigan, had been observed by seventy Soviet engineers—who watched the spectacle from *inside* the plant, where they had been invited by Henry Ford to learn mass production methods. Equally striking, among those present at the Soviet Embassy's observance of the Twentieth Anniversary of the Russian Revolution was the President-General of the Daughters of the American Revolution, "wearing a black ensemble, with orchids at the shoulder."

In July, 1936, those wishing to enhance American acceptance of Russia and Communism received a windfall. Right-wing Generalissimo Francisco Franco brought his army back to Spain to overthrow the government and received prompt support from the Axis dictators. As Hitler and Mussolini tested out their shock troops, their airplanes and their bombs, only one country—the Soviet Union—came to the support of the beleaguered Loyalists.

Spain became the battlefield in the fight against Fascism. It

* "That Stalin's Russia cherishes no aggression may be taken for granted," a 1931 *New York Times* editorial had said.

became a world-wide cause: some 2,800 Americans felt moved
to fight on that battlefield as members of the Abraham Lincoln
Brigade—of these, only 1,200 returned. It produced heroes and
heroics. Who could resist the emotional appeal of a blinded
member of the Lincoln Brigade, rising to speak to a packed
rally at Madison Square Garden, while eighteen thousand voices
chanted, *"No Pasarán"* ("They Shall Not Pass")—the last words
the soldier was alleged to have heard before he was rendered
sightless?

With the European democracies insistently neutral and the
United States aloof, it seemed to many Americans that only the
Communists and the Soviet Union were seriously engaged in
combating Fascism. And if some in the far left were disturbed by
unsettling news emanating from Moscow in 1937 and 1938
about purge trials and executions of former heroes of the Revolution, there was a temptation for them to look the other way.
Writer Granville Hicks, one of the intellectuals temporarily lured
into the Communist ranks, later recalled convincing himself, at
the time of the purge trials, that he "had no right to let my
private doubts interfere with this great struggle against evil."

This setting produced a natural opportunity for American
Communists to blend with ardently anti-Fascist American liberals. They came together in many organizations dedicated to
alleviating the effects of the Great Depression or to resisting the
Axis. Thus the letterhead of the Spanish Medical Aid Committee
commingled such unexceptionable names as Mrs. H. V. Kalten-
born and Bishop G. Bromley Oxnam with such radical leftists as
Paul Robeson and Vito Marcantonio, and a 1939 San Francisco
protest against American arms shipments to Japan allied such
established groups as the American Legion and the YMCA with
the Friends of the Abraham Lincoln Brigade and the American
Friends of the Chinese People, later cited by the House Un-
American Activities Committee as subversive. If the membership
of such organizations happened to include some Communists,
this was either unnoticed or of minor concern. The Cause was
paramount.

It has been said of Robert Oppenheimer that he never did
anything by halves; that is certainly true of his emergence into

the world of radical politics. In the summer of 1937, for example, on a train trip to the East Coast, he read through the complete three volumes of Marx's *Das Kapital*. He also read all of Lenin, prompting Haakon Chevalier to note, in a diary entry of the time, that Oppenheimer was "better read than most [Communist] party members."

Better read, doubtless; yet, he later said, party membership held no attraction for him, although he had ample opportunity to see the party in action. This exposure to the party came through his younger brother Frank, eight years Robert's junior, to whom Robert had been both older brother and, in part, father. As the only two children of Julius and Ella Oppenheimer, the two had been close in earlier years: they bicycled together, sailed together, and later, united by a common love of horses, they began spending summers together on a primitive ranch they rented high in the mountains of New Mexico.

Frank had manifold interests: painting, poetry, belles-lettres and, especially, music. He became an expert flutist—Robert thought he could have become a professional—but decided to study physics instead. This, said Robert, "produced a kind of rivalry" (in which Frank was always destined to be a badly trailing second). "He worked fairly well at physics," Robert recalled, "but he was slow. It took him a long time to get his doctor's degree."* An associate of the two at the California Institute of Technology has recalled that in the early and middle Thirties Robert was always at the center of any group—smooth, articulate, captivating—while Frank stood at the fringe, shoulders hunched over, clothes mussed and frayed, fingers still dirty from the laboratory.

In 1936 Frank met and married a student at Berkeley who had connections in radical circles there. Jackie Oppenheimer did for Frank what Jean Tatlock had done for Robert: she turned his attentions to politics and introduced him to people who shared his new interest. Shortly after their marriage, they joined the Communist Party in Pasadena.

Some months later, Frank drove up to Berkeley, spent the night with Robert and told him of his party membership. Robert later recalled that while he was upset by this news, he was far

---

* He was "slow" only by Robert's standards: he got his doctorate at the normal age of twenty-seven (Robert achieved his at twenty-three).

from "shocked." In the circles in which he then moved, membership in the party was not regarded as "a matter of dishonor or shame."

Later, in Pasadena, Frank asked Robert and a friend to attend a Communist Party meeting at Frank's house—the only thing "recognizable . . . as a Communist Party meeting" Robert ever recalled attending. The meeting, mainly concerned with racial segregation at the municipal pool in Pasadena, made a rather pathetic impression on Robert. As he and his friend walked away from the meeting, the friend commented, "What a sad spectacle."

During the late Thirties, the cause that most engaged Oppenheimer's sympathies was the war in Spain. At first he contributed to various Spanish relief groups and helped organize fund-raising parties and bazaars. But sometime in the winter of 1937–38, his close friend Dr. Thomas Addis (whom he had met through Jean Tatlock) suggested that Oppenheimer channel his contributions to the war in Spain through the Communist Party rather than through the standard Spanish relief groups. In that way, Addis said, the funds would go straight to the fighting effort, to aid in manning and equipping the International Brigade.

From time to time during that winter, Addis and Oppenheimer met, sometimes in Berkeley, sometimes in Addis' Stanford laboratory, sometimes in San Francisco. Addis would bring the physicist up to date on the progress of the fighting in Spain, usually painting a desperate picture of the situation facing the Loyalists. And Oppenheimer, a bachelor with modest needs and an ample income of fifteen thousand dollars (his professor's salary was supplemented with stock dividends), responded to Addis' pleas with contributions amounting to about a thousand dollars a year. These were made in cash, partly because he didn't want to "advertise" his actions, partly because he had the impression it was illegal to give direct support to the fighting in Spain. Addis, in turn, conveyed these funds to Isaac Folkoff, later identified by Oppenheimer as a Communist Party functionary.

Oppenheimer also subscribed to the *People's Daily World*, the West Coast voice of the Communist Party. First published on New Year's Day, 1938, the paper was necessary, it proclaimed, because "the economic royalists have your daily information sewed up." It was indeed distinctive: in no other California news-paper could one have read such glowing accounts of events in the Soviet Union. "SOVIETS FACE JOYOUS YEAR; GAINS LISTED: PROMISE OF 1938 IS CONTRAST TO SLUMP IN AMERICA," declared a page-one headline. The ensuing article boasted unabashedly about such 1937 feats as the Soviet "conquering" of the North Pole and two nonstop Moscow-America flights by "brave and resourceful" Soviet pilots.

To subscribe to the *People's World* (as Robert Oppenheimer soon did) did not signify that one was either a Russophile or a hard-core party-liner. The newspaper's inaugural issue was wel-comed in advertisements by a broad cross-section of small San Francisco merchants and labor unions. Among those sending congratulatory messages were Assemblyman Sam Yorty (who became, in the Sixties, a decidedly conservative Mayor of Los Angeles) and Assemblyman Jack B. Tenney (who, just two years later, was to be chairman of the zealously Communist-hunting state Un-American Activities Committee, and who was still later to be vice-presidential candidate on Gerald L. K. Smith's anti-Semitic Christian Nationalist ticket). And the newspaper did, in fact, examine domestic and world problems to which the established newspapers gave scant attention. Asked, years later, why he had subscribed to the *World,* Oppenheimer said, "I guess I took an interest in [its] formulation of issues." Apparently he was indeed stirred. At one point that year, for example, he traveled all the way to the headquarters of Harry Bridges' Long-shoremen's Union in San Francisco to contribute one hundred dollars to the union's strike fund.

Across the continent, in Washington, D.C., a slight, blond eighteen-year-old named William Liscum Borden was preparing to graduate from a strict Episcopal school, St. Albans. Borden was completing one of the most exemplary records of achieve-ment in the school's history. In all four of his high school years he had been chosen president of his class; in his junior year he was named best all-round boy; as a senior, he was editor in chief of the school newspaper, which won three national journalism contests. Borden also played varsity football, was a leader of the Civics Club, was elected a prefect and, on top of all that, was a consistent honors student. As one of his teachers recalled, "As a boy, Liscum had the clearly defined personality and character traits of a grown young man."

These exceptional qualities Liscum Borden had perhaps inherited from his father—an extremely hard-working, exacting and prominent Washington surgeon—and from his paternal grandfather, a self-made career Army doctor of steely self-discipline, with whom Liscum had a special closeness. Like his grandfather, Liscum had a considerable gift with words and an impatience with ignorance. Like both grandfather and father, he had a rare sense of rectitude, duty and self-expectation.

As he graduated from St. Albans School in that June of 1938, Liscum Borden was the model of a model student. "Definitely, Liscum was outstanding," his headmaster said later. The picture Borden gave was certainly not that of a person who would one day make an extreme accusation against one of the nation's most distinguished citizens.

For Oppenheimer, one of the significant events of 1938 was an extended visit to his summer ranch by two scientists, Victor Weisskopf and George Placzek, for this brought about a significant transformation of Oppenheimer's view of the Soviet Union. His reading of the Webbs' laudatory book, together with the talk he had heard of the Soviet Union and its solitary stand against European Fascism, had predisposed him to make much of Russia's economic progress and little of the political tyranny of the Stalinist regime. He was inclined to discount most negative accounts of the Soviet Union as coming from sources he considered motivated by blind anti-Communism.

His two summer visitors could not be so classed. Both Weisskopf and Placzek had recently spent considerable time in Russia, and to them, the development of that country under Stalin represented the perversion of an ideal that was as close to their hearts as to Oppenheimer's: the ideal of a socialistic egalitarian reconstruction of a society that would be free of discrimination and repression. The two scientists had gone to Russia with high hopes, but they had found, instead, a Nazi-like oppression. They told Oppenheimer of concentration camps; the purge trials; the lack of personal freedom; the tight government control over science, including the purging of scientists for political unorthodoxy. To Oppenheimer, these reports seemed "so solid, so unfanatical, so true, that [they] made a great impression" and helped dissipate his uncritical faith in Stalinist Russia.

September, 1938. Munich.

The headlines that Robert Oppenheimer might have seen in the San Francisco *Examiner* tell the swift, raw story of Hitler's expansion to the East:

*September 19*

**BRITAIN AND FRANCE AGREE TO ALL OF NAZI DEMANDS**

*September 20*

**CZECHS PROTEST BETRAYAL BUT PREPARE TO GIVE IN!**

*September 21*

**NEW ULTIMATUM TO CZECHS: QUIT OR FIGHT IN 24 HOURS; FRANCE, BRITAIN WARN PRAGUE SHE MUST FIGHT ALONE**

*September 26*

**F.D.R. APPEALS FOR PEACE; ALLIES SPURN NAZI TERMS; LEAGUE MUST AID PRAGUE, SAYS RUSSIA**

*September 27*

**BRITAIN WILL FIGHT IF CZECHS ATTACKED, HITLER WARNED**

*September 28*

**HITLER MAY MARCH TODAY! NEW F.D.R. PEACE APPEAL! BRITAIN MOBILIZES NAVY**

*September 30*

**FOUR-POWER PACT GIVES HITLER HIS SUDETENS! PRAGUE MUST QUIT FRONTIER AREAS BY OCTOBER 10**

To many among Oppenheimer's political aquaintances, Munich was more than a mere sellout of the Czech Sudetenland. It was unmistakable evidence that the real target of Hitler's east-ward ambitions—the Soviet Union—could count on no help from the West and would have to fight alone for her survival. This conclusion was to have a direct bearing on the attitudes of these Oppenheimer friends (and perhaps of Oppenheimer himself) when, a year later, the San Francisco *Examiner* devoted its biggest, blackest headline type to a piece of startling news:

**RUSSIA, NAZIS IN PEACE PACT; EUROPE STUNNED! VON RIBBEN-TROP DUE IN MOSCOW TOMORROW TO SIGN NON-AGGRESSION DEAL**

The American Communist Party and its spokesmen found little difficulty in adjusting to this abrupt about-face. On the day after the pact was signed, a page-one editorial in the *People's Daily World* was proclaiming the agreement as "a triumph for Soviet Peace policy [and a] humiliation for Hitler."* Yet to most American liberals, who had been sympathetic to Russia precisely because of her enmity to Hitler, the spectacle of her suddenly climbing into bed with the Nazi dictator was perplexing, if not totally disillusioning. The abruptness of the Soviet shift—and, more strikingly, the completeness and rapidity with which the American Communists were able to fall into step—all but shattered the Popular Front. The standing of the Communist Party plummeted. Its membership dropped from 60,000 to 35,000 in just three months.

The precise nature of Oppenheimer's reaction to the Nazi-Soviet pact is not clear. His later recollection was of "hat[ing] the sudden switch they [the Soviets] made" and of "hop[ing] that they would realize that this was a mistake." On the other hand, Haakon Chevalier has strongly indicated that at the time Oppenheimer defended the pact, using his "simple, lucid way of presenting facts and arguments" to "allay" the "misgivings" of those who had been "confused and upset" by the nonaggression pact. Chevalier has recalled that Oppenheimer invoked the line of

---

* The next day, the *World* found an added reason to praise the pact. It had, said the *World*, isolated "the most rabid Japanese militarists, who were set back on their haunches by Germany coolly deserting their cherished scheme for mutual attack against the Soviet Union."

defense adopted by some intellectuals who were not necessarily hard-core party-liners: that Munich had left Russia no alternative but to buy time to arm herself to withstand, alone and without Western help, the German blitzkrieg she was sure was inevitable.

Whatever his precise reaction to the Nazi-Soviet pact, it did not mean for Oppenheimer a sharp break with his Communist friends who continued to look upon Russia with unabated admiration. He continued, for example, to see Dr. Thomas Addis and to make contributions to the Spanish cause through him.

But soon Addis suggested a change in the procedure: he would bow out as the middleman, and Oppenheimer would give his contributions directly to Communist Party official Isaac Folkoff. And so Oppenheimer began to see Folkoff from time to time. Once or twice they were joined for lunch by a friend of Jean Tatlock's by the name of Rudy Lambert, a fact that was to prove a stumbling block for Oppenheimer in his security hearing some fifteen years later.

By now the war in Spain had ended in disaster for the Loyalists, but Folkoff explained that funds were needed to resettle the thousands of Spanish refugees crowded into French camps. Sometimes Folkoff talked of other activities in which the Communist Party was interested—such as a campaign to organize migrant farm workers in California. To these Oppenheimer also lent his financial support, through Folkoff and the party.

One effect of the sudden Soviet alliance with the Nazis was to heighten the concern of American military security officials both about the danger from Federal employees with Red leanings and about the difficulty of removing them under existing Civil Service regulations.

This was a relatively new concern in the Executive Branch of the United States Government. One study observes that "the question of requiring complete loyalty to the United States Government as a condition of employment was virtually never considered prior to 1939." Until that date, the study states, "the classified Civil Service excluded only the criminal and the incompetent," and the principal concern of the Civil Service Commission during the Thirties was the mushrooming, under the New Deal, of Federal positions exempt from Civil Service regulations and open to political exploitation. Even in Congress there was comparatively little concern about the loyalty of Federal employees. In the wake of World War I there had been a flurry of interest in "Bolshevik" and German activity, but during the Twenties Congressional interest had languished. The creation in 1930 of a special House committee to investigate Communist propaganda revived the matter, but the attacks were sporadic and confined to a few legislators.

But in the military agencies, according to one student of the loyalty-security program, there had "long been [concern] with the possible danger to the national security that could result from the presence of extreme radicals, particularly Communists, in the Government service." The services had adopted their own rules for the screening of military personnel. But even within the military the interest in "security" appears to have been a limited one, judging from the testimony given, years later, by a high-ranking Army officer,* who said: "We didn't deal with matters of security in the Army until World War II. The Army as a whole didn't deal with matters of security until after the atomic bomb burst on the world. . . ."

As for employees of civilian agencies, the government had neither the authority nor the machinery to screen Federal jobholders or applicants for "loyalty." In fact, since 1884 the government had been barred by Civil Service Rule I from inquiring into the "political or religious opinions or affiliations of any applicant." A citizen's "loyalty" was simply taken for granted.

In August, 1939, however, the blanket prohibition of Civil Service Rule I was somewhat diminished when Congress enacted a provision barring Federal employment to anyone belonging to any organization that advocated the violent overthrow of the government. This provision, inserted into the so-called "Hatch Act" during consideration of the bill in the House of Representatives, without hearings or even extensive deliberation, became the seedling from which a massive program for the screening of Federal employees was later to grow.

Even this provision did not entirely satisfy some military-security officials. Spurred by the Nazi-Soviet pact, they drafted

---

* General Leslie Groves, at the Oppenheimer security hearing.

(and Congress presently passed) laws giving the War and Navy departments the right to dismiss suspected employees summarily, irrespective of ordinary Civil Service protections.

The year 1940 contained two events of great importance in Oppenheimer's life.

The first was the fall of France, in June. To Oppenheimer, a keen student of French history, language and literature, this was a profoundly affecting matter. At least three scientists who talked with him about it at a meeting of the American Physical Society in Seattle that June have distinctly recalled Oppenheimer's preoccupation with France's fate. Hans Bethe in particular, who had known of Oppenheimer's "leftist" views, was struck by the eloquence and earnestness with which he now spoke. The fall of France, Oppenheimer said, meant an end of many things he had considered precious; the values of Western civilization now hinged upon the outcome of the war. Bethe had little doubt that Oppenheimer's heart was with the Allies.

The same could hardly be said of the American Communist Party, which by now was officially and vociferously anti-interventionist. And so, during the summer and fall of 1940, with France lost and Britain under brutal air siege, Robert Oppenheimer found himself increasingly out of sympathy with the Communist policy of neutrality and disengagement.

The second important event of 1940 for Oppenheimer came in November, when Katherine Puening Dallet Harrison became Mrs. J. Robert Oppenheimer. The two had met in Pasadena in the summer of 1939 and had been immediately attracted to one another.

This was the second great romance in Kitty's life. The first had begun in Pittsburgh, during the Christmas holidays in 1933, when she was home on a college vacation. A friend, Zelma Baker, asked whether Kitty and her group would like to meet a Communist acquaintance of hers. None of them had ever met a genuine Communist before, and they decided it would be "interesting." When Zelma arrived at a New Year's party, she had on her arm a handsome young man named Joseph Dallet who had left a comfortably situated home (his father was an investment banker) for the rigors of organizing a union of steelworkers in Youngstown,

Ohio. Before the holidays were over, Joseph Dallet and Katherine Puening had fallen in love. At the end of January, 1934, she joined him in Youngstown and they were married.

Quite naturally, Joseph wanted his bride to join the Communist Party, and she loyally obliged. She even went to work in the party office, mimeographing leaflets and letters mainly in support of the embryonic steel union. Their life was Spartan. They paid five dollars a month for one bedroom in a tiny house whose sole other bedroom was occupied by John Gates and Gus Hall (later to become celebrated national leaders of the Communist Party). Their tiny stove leaked, it was impossible to cook, and food consisted of two meals a day at a grimy restaurant, where fifteen cents would buy soup, meat, potato, cabbage, a doughnut and coffee. Gradually, the poverty became more and more depressing to Kitty Dallet; she became increasingly reluctant to go to party meetings. Her waning interest in party activities created a fissure in the marriage. In mid-1936 the Dallets agreed to separate. Kitty left both Youngstown and the Communist Party, and went to join her parents in England.

But she found herself unable to forget Joe Dallet, and the following spring the two were reunited for a romantic two weeks in Paris. Dallet was on his way to the battlefields of Spain, and Kitty, hoping to save their marriage, met him in Cherbourg. After a fortnight, Dallet departed for the wars, and Kitty returned to England, hoping that arrangements would soon be made for her to join him in Spain. After months of waiting, a telegram arrived, asking her to report in Paris. But when she arrived, she was shown another telegram. Joe Dallet was dead, killed in action. So Katherine Puening Dallet found herself, at the age of twenty-seven, suddenly widowed and alone in Paris.

She was told that a friend of her husband named Steve Nelson was due in Paris in several days and had a lot to tell her about Joe. She waited until Nelson arrived, and for the next week she saw him most of the time. He was, she later recalled, sweet, gentle and completely sympathetic. For a time, Kitty wanted to go to Spain, as she and Dallet had planned, but Nelson discouraged this.

And so she decided to return to America and resume her interrupted studies. At first, in New York, she saw a good many Communist Party members, most of them friends of Joseph Dallet's who wanted to know about him. But soon she moved to Philadelphia, entered the University of Pennsylvania, and the party faded from her life.

In December, 1938, she married an English physician, Richard Harrison, who soon moved to Pasadena. There his interest in problems of radiology brought him into contact with many Caltech physicists. It was thus that Kitty met Robert Oppenheimer. Eighteen months later, after her divorce from Harrison, she married him.

Kitty Oppenheimer's strong emotional identification with the Loyalist cause in Spain made her naturally attuned to the views of her new husband and his circle of radical friends in the San Francisco Bay area. The Oppenheimers became particularly close to the Haakon Chevaliers, who showed the newlyweds "many acts of kindness," as Oppenheimer later put it, after Kitty's arrival on the Berkeley scene. The Oppenheimers were occasionally invited to gatherings that were more or less obviously left-wing—one at the home of the Haakon Chevaliers, another at that of a wealthy San Francisco left-wing sympathizer named Louise Bransten. At both the guest speaker was William Schneiderman, secretary of the California Communist Party. Schneiderman sought to explain the current Communist line, but, according to Robert's later recollection, the Oppenheimers found him unpersuasive.

At one of the parties they attended, Kitty Oppenheimer learned that Steve Nelson was in the San Francisco area. He was by now an important Communist on the West Coast. (When Robert Oppenheimer had met him in San Francisco in the fall of 1939, at a Spanish relief party, Nelson had been looked on as quite a Spanish war hero.) Nelson soon telephoned Kitty and received an invitation to a picnic lunch at the Oppenheimers'. The Nelsons arrived with their small baby. They talked about old days and about family matters.

Nelson was not an educated man, but he and Oppenheimer had, as common bonds, an affection for Kitty and an intense interest in the Spanish war, and Oppenheimer was a willing listener to Nelson's authoritative accounts of that struggle.

In January of 1941 a young officer in the Army's Counter Intelligence Corps by the name of Boris T. Pash entered the Justice Department Building in Washington to begin a special FBI course in investigative techniques. The son of a Russian immigrant, Pash had returned to his father's homeland to serve as a relief worker, then taught school in California (biology and physical education) before joining the Army in 1940. Now, at the FBI, he spent several weeks learning about espionage tactics and the means of investigating and countering them. Upon his return to the West Coast in March he was made Chief of Counter Intelligence for the Ninth Army Corps, which soon came to have jurisdiction over the West Coast atomic energy facilities in which Robert Oppenheimer was to work.

In May of that same year, John Lansdale, Jr., a Virginia Military Institute graduate with a reserve Army commission, was called away from his Cleveland law practice, ordered to Counter Intelligence in Washington and assigned the job of screening Army personnel in order to identify those of dubious loyalty or discretion. He found his superiors in G-2 (Intelligence) less concerned about Nazi supporters than about Russophiles and Communist sympathizers; they strongly believed that Russia, not Germany, would in the long run be America's real enemy. Their views prompted Lansdale to make his own independent study of Communist theory, from which he emerged impressed with the almost religious intensity of Communism's followers and deeply suspicious of American Russophiles. He feared their idolatry of Russia might prompt them to become, in effect, spies without pay, justifying acts of treachery in the name of simple friendship for the Soviet Union.

That was the apprehension that John Lansdale brought to his later assignment: General Groves' aide on security matters for the atomic bomb project, in which Robert Oppenheimer was to be a key figure.

In the same month that John Lansdale went into the Army, a son was born to Robert and Kitty Oppenheimer. They were then living in Pasadena, and Robert was teaching at Caltech. The baby, he proudly wrote Haakon Chevalier on May 15, was "pretty wee"; he was formally named Peter, but jokingly nicknamed "Pronto," since the Oppenheimers had been married only a very short time.

In mid-June, at the Oppenheimers' invitation, Haakon and Barbara Chevalier spent a week with the Oppenheimers, staying in their guest house. On Sunday, June 22, the last day of their visit, an event of great significance occurred: the Nazis invaded the Soviet Union. Instantaneously, Russia was transformed from the contemptible bedfellow of the Nazis into a noble and courageous friend of the Allies. Deep into that Sunday night the Oppenheimers and Chevaliers sought to analyze the new turn of affairs. As Chevalier has recalled the conversation, Oppenheimer regarded the Soviet invasion as Hitler's decisive blunder. A day or two later, however, as he and Chevalier drove north to Berkeley, his mood had apparently changed. Stopping off for a meal midway in the drive, the two bumped into Carey McWilliams (then Commissioner of Housing for California, later editor of *The Nation*), who has remembered being struck by the deep pessimism of both men that Russia would never be able to withstand the Nazi blitzkrieg and was headed for black days.*

In July the Oppenheimers flattered the Chevaliers by asking them to care for their newborn son while they escaped for a few weeks of rest at Perro Caliente (Spanish for "hot dog"), the Oppenheimer ranch in the New Mexico mountains.

The twenty-third day of that month was to become a controversial one in Oppenheimer's life. Where was he on that date? Was he at Perro Caliente, relaxing in the dry mountain air? Or was he, as an informant for the Department of Justice later testified, actually in Berkeley, California, playing host to a closed meeting of the Communist Party of Alameda in his own home? Nearly thirteen years after the fact, Oppenheimer would have to delve into time and establish that he left Berkeley shortly after

---

* The Communist newspaper, the *People's Daily World*, made its usual facile adjustment to the new state of affairs. Throughout the spring, the *World* had been ardently noninterventionist, chiding FDR for slipping away from his "keep-us-out-of-war" pledge of the 1940 campaign. But within days of the Nazi invasion of Russia, the newspaper was calling for "the fullest direct support under the Lend-Lease law to the one great army which is genuinely shedding its blood against Fascist aggression." Nor was the *World* in the least abashed about the sudden policy switch: "As to 'changes' [in the party line], of course, only fools never change. That is an axiom."

July 4, not to return until the end of the first week in August. Moreover, Oppenheimer's friend, fellow physicist Hans Bethe, would be sent scurrying to his own records to try to establish just when, during that summer, he had visited the Oppenheimer ranch for a day. The records of a nearby hotel would be unearthed and searched, and, finally, Bethe would establish that the date of his visit was July 24. And there could be no doubt that Robert Oppenheimer had been at the ranch that day. Why? Because he had been kicked by a horse he was trying to catch for Bethe to ride—Bethe remembered it vividly.

While at the ranch that summer, Oppenheimer negotiated for the purchase of a house in Berkeley which became known as Eagle Hill, and into which he and Kitty moved shortly after their return from New Mexico. Soon Frank Oppenheimer also moved to Berkeley, and was hired to work under the celebrated Ernest Orlando Lawrence in the Berkeley Radiation Laboratory. Robert talked with Dr. Lawrence about his brother's past involvements in left-wing activities. He did not, however, tell Lawrence of Frank's past membership in the Communist Party (by now, Frank told Robert, he was out of the party) because, as he later put it, in those days it "wasn't regarded . . . as a great state crime."

Early that fall, on September 20, there was a housewarming party, for the benefit of the *People's Daily World,* at the home of Kenneth May, a radical young member of the Berkeley faculty who had been publicly disowned by his father and fired by the university for joining the Communist Party. Oppenheimer was later alleged to have attended this party, and to have been seen in the company of two men later accused—but not convicted—of being Soviet spies. Did the Oppenheimers in fact attend? Years afterward neither he nor Kitty could summon up any special recollection of it, although, Oppenheimer said, it would have been in character for them to have gone.

As the Oppenheimers settled in at Eagle Hill, Robert began to feel restive. Many of his colleagues were leaving for war work in radar or other military research, and Oppenheimer was somewhat envious of them. But his involvement in war work was not long in coming.

Ever since the discovery of nuclear fission in 1938, the possibility of using the resulting energy to make powerful explosives had been very much in Oppenheimer's mind, as well as the minds of many other physicists. On October 21, 1941, at the General Electric Research Laboratory in Schenectady, he and other scientists met to discuss the military possibilities of atomic energy. Oppenheimer himself presented some calculations on the amount of uranium 235 required for an effective weapon. It was his first official connection with the atomic energy program. In sharp contrast to the later years of the program, no security "clearance" was required for admission to the Schenectady discussion. It was assumed that all those present were loyal to the United States.

Back in Berkeley, working on new calculations regarding an atomic bomb, Oppenheimer became increasingly excited about the prospects. Despite a heavy teaching schedule, he devoted more and more time to nuclear matters, and soon was instrumental in developing an invention later put into use in the large-scale production of fissionable A-bomb materials.

While Robert Oppenheimer was thus engaged, William Liscum Borden was launching into his senior year at Yale, pursuing his interest in journalism as avidly as he had at St. Albans. An editor of the *Yale Daily News,* Borden was custodian of a weekly column called "Straws in the Wind." If the prescience of the December 2, 1941, edition is representative, the column was aptly titled. The topic of that column, just five days before Pearl Harbor: "The Case for Immediate War on Japan."

On Saturday night, December 6, 1941, Robert Oppenheimer attended what was to be his last party for Spanish war relief. The next day, the radio brought news that Pearl Harbor had been attacked. With the nation suddenly immersed in a world war, Oppenheimer decided he had had about enough of the Spanish cause. Within a few months his contributions through the Communist Party came to an end. Precisely when this happened is not clear. The charges that triggered off his formal security proceeding twelve years later stated the contributions continued until May, 1942; the official findings of the hearing panel settled on April; Oppenheimer himself could be no more precise than to say they stopped in "early 1942."

This cutoff date was to take on importance because it seemed to coincide with another important event in Oppenheimer's life, the beginning of his full-time involvement in the government's atomic energy work. In January, 1942, Oppenheimer had attended a planning session in Chicago and emerged with a specific follow-up assignment. In the spring, Arthur H. Compton, then in charge of the atomic work, asked Oppenheimer to devote all his time to the project. On April 22, he filled out his first security questionnaire and in May began to work full time on the atomic project.

Did the Oppenheimer contributions through (or to) the Communist Party continue right up to that moment? His principal accuser, William Liscum Borden, was to point out that the Communist Party's instruction to its hard-core members was to go underground upon entering government employment. If Oppenheimer's contributions did end just at the time he entered government service, Borden concluded, it was proof that Oppenheimer was, at the moment of his entry into the war effort, "a sufficiently hardened Communist" to have conveyed "espionage information to the Soviets."

## 2. *The War Years*

On June 6, at Compton's request, Oppenheimer undertook to organize and head a group of physicists who would spend the summer of 1942 in Berkeley exploring more deeply the theoretical aspects of atomic explosions and calculating the amounts of nuclear materials needed for an A-bomb. One of those tapped by Oppenheimer was nearly barred from participating. He was a young Hungarian-born physicist teaching in Washington, D.C., who still had relatives in Nazi-dominated Hungary. For that reason security officials were reluctant to clear him for participation in the secret summer work. But Oppenheimer decided he was essential to the project and entered a special request for his clearance.

So it was Robert Oppenheimer's intervention that made it possible for Edward Teller to come to Berkeley that summer and begin his contributions to the development of American nuclear weaponry.

The summer of 1942 was one of intense work for Oppenheimer's remarkable team of physicists. Oppenheimer himself was stimulated by a challenging possibility that Teller introduced into the deliberations: that a mammoth explosion could be produced, not by *splitting* atoms but by *fusing* them—i.e., by merging, under conditions of extreme heat, the atoms of deuterium, a heavy-hydrogen isotope. This process held a dual advantage. Not only was the explosive potential vastly greater, but the ingredient, deuterium, was presumably far more plentiful than the uranium isotopes needed for the fission process.

At that moment in the history of nuclear physics, the fusion process later embodied in the H-bomb was far more intellectually challenging than the atom-splitting, or fission process, that was used in the A-bombs. Since the fission bomb seemed clearly feasible, in theory at least, and mainly involved a great deal of laborious mathematical calculation, Oppenheimer left the problem largely to the younger members of the group while he, Teller and German-born physicist Hans Bethe concentrated on the matter of fusion. Indeed, Oppenheimer became so excited by its prospects that in July he made a special trip to Arthur Compton's summer retreat in Michigan to report his findings.

That summer was the first close and prolonged contact between Oppenheimer and Teller. By all reports, the two men were delighted with each other. One ex-colleague has recalled, "Without any double meaning, of course, this started off as a kind of mental love affair. Edward liked and respected Oppie enormously. He kept . . . bringing up his name in conversation. Oppie has always been more reserved by nature, but in his quieter way, he seemed to reciprocate." Another recalled, "They started a mutual admiration society that summer. They practically became pals—buddies."

Thus in that summer of 1942 began a relationship that would profoundly affect the lives of both: two men brought intellectually together—virtually fused—by the very concept that would later split them irrevocably.

In those pioneering, groping days of the early Forties the free interchange of scientific information among allies was not frowned upon as it was to be later; indeed, such interchange was thoroughly accepted.* It was only natural, therefore, that the report prepared by Oppenheimer and his colleagues on their summer's work was promptly shared with British nuclear scientists. In postwar years Oppenheimer was to favor a similar openness in the interchange of atomic information with Britain and some other countries, and this was to bring him into sharp conflict with powerful persons in Washington—particularly Lewis Strauss—who believed such information-sharing to be dangerous. This conflict was to be a factor in Oppenheimer's security difficulties.

* As it happened, this was of crucial benefit to the United States. In the summer of 1941, when Britain was at war but America was not, British atomic scientists were pressing ahead faster in the nuclear field than were the Americans. But this did not inhibit the British from permitting Caltech physicist Charles C. Lauritsen to sit in on the deliberations of their highest technical committee. And it was Lauritsen's reports on British insights and plans that opened the eyes of Vannevar Bush and James B. Conant to new and surer ways of producing an atomic bomb. They thus were able to get President Roosevelt's approval for laying the groundwork for the massive industrial program essential to atomic success.

As the Oppenheimer group worked in Berkeley on the theoretical aspects of nuclear explosions, the government's top science administrators in Washington, Vannevar Bush and James B. Conant, increasingly aware of the enormity of the prospective atomic venture, were searching for the best mode of tying together its many elements: scientific, industrial, logistic, etc. They decided to place the project under one of the armed services. The Army was selected, and on September 17, 1942, a forty-six-year-old colonel by the name of Leslie Richard Groves presented himself to a surprised Vannevar Bush and announced that Lieutenant General Brehon Somervell, Chief of the Army Services of Supply, had named him to head the nuclear program.

Twenty-one days later, Groves met Robert Oppenheimer. Groves listened with interest as the physicist expounded his idea of a single scientific laboratory where all the theoretical and experimental work on atomic weapons could be brought together. Oppenheimer said he was concerned about the waste and frustration caused by the existing fragmentation of work among various laboratories as well as by the sometimes pointless quarantining of knowledge within laboratories. What was needed, he said, was a facility where all of the chemical, metallurgical, engineering and ordnance problems could be subjected to a concerted attack and within which there could be a maximum interchange of information. Any added danger of important information leaks which this might present could be offset by locating the laboratory at an isolated site, where contacts with the outside world could be readily controlled.

This proposal appealed to the security-conscious Groves. On a fall day in 1942, Oppenheimer led Groves to a site in the New Mexico mountains near Santa Fe, known to Oppenheimer through horseback excursions from his mountain ranch, Perro Caliente. The site was the level top of a steep-sided mesa, occupied, at the moment, by a boys' school, with a breathtaking view of the Sangre de Cristo Mountains. The General was pleased. The spot was indeed isolated; access to it could easily be governed. He moved rapidly to acquire the site and get construction under way.

But who should head the laboratory? Groves was impressed

with Oppenheimer, who had suggested the idea. But there were drawbacks: Oppenheimer was only thirty-eight and had no high scientific awards to his name. He had had little experience either in administration or in experimental physics. Would older, more eminent scientists, would Noble laureates serve and work under such a man?

There was also the matter of his left-wing background. This had been known to Arthur Compton when he first asked Oppenheimer to work full time on the atomic project back in the spring. Late in the summer, Compton had sent word to the physicist that there was a question about his security clearance because of his affiliation with left-wing groups. But, Compton later recalled, a personal investigation of Oppenheimer led him to conclude that the physicist's rejection of Communism, after his brief flirtation with it, was a factor in favor of his reliability.

Compton's confidence was not, however, universally shared. Army Intelligence officials were currently receiving disturbing reports, primarily from the Federal Bureau of Investigation, concerning Oppenheimer's associations and relatives. One officer in particular—John Lansdale, who had just been probing possible infiltration by radicals of the Berkeley Radiation Laboratory—has recalled entertaining considerable doubts about Robert Oppenheimer.

But the responsibility for recommending a Los Alamos director lay with Leslie Richard Groves. A career Army officer, Groves had spent twenty-four years working his way up from second lieutenant to brigadier general and was one of the few Americans who favored the Franco forces from the very outset of the Spanish Civil War. Had he fit the stereotype, he could hardly have been expected to risk tarnishing his career (or to offend his own political viewpoint) by naming to a post of the highest sensitivity a long-haired scientist with a suspiciously radical past that included a deep involvement on behalf of the anti-Franco Loyalists.

But in selecting a nominee for the Los Alamos directorship, Leslie Groves fit no stereotype. First of all, there were some practical considerations. For one, Oppenheimer was already deeply involved in the atomic project, and hence was privy to some of its highest secrets.* More important, no other potential laboratory directors seemed to Groves as promising as Oppenheimer. The scientists of major eminence were mostly aliens, and those with administrative experience (Ernest Lawrence, Harold Urey, Arthur Compton) were already engaged in essential high-level work and could not be spared.

Groves suggested Oppenheimer's name to the Military Policy Committee overseeing the atomic work. When committee members did not immediately respond to the suggestion, Groves invited them to propose alternatives; a few weeks of deliberation produced none, and in November, 1942, Groves asked Oppenheimer to take on the task of heading the Los Alamos laboratory.

With all the practical considerations behind the choice, the frail, ascetic, supremely cerebral and conspicuously radical physics professor remains an intriguing selection for this conservatively oriented, career Army officer to have made. Associates describe Groves as vain and blustery, with little sympathy for intellectuals. How account for his choice? Robert Oppenheimer was asked that question years later; his reply, while perhaps lacking in modesty, was perceptive: Leslie Groves, he said, "had a fatal weakness for good men."

If John Lansdale and other officers in Army Counter Intelligence were convinced, in 1942, that Soviet Russia was the real long-run enemy of the United States, their view was not generally shared by opinion-shapers around the country, as the Red Army fought off the Nazi blitzkrieg. On February 23, for example, on the occasion of its twenty-fourth anniversary, the Red Army received a congratulatory message proclaiming that "the hopes of civilization rest on the worthy banners of the courageous Russian Army," and grandiloquently portraying the "scale and grandeur" of its effort as "the greatest military achievement in all history." This was high praise, indeed, from such a student of military history as General Douglas MacArthur.

* The contrast with modern-day security-consciousness is striking, for at the time Groves named him to the directorship of the Los Alamos laboratory, Oppenheimer had been working in the atomic program for seven months, but had not yet received any formal government security "clearance"; his first such "clearance" was granted on December 8, 1942, by the Office of Scientific Research and Development.

In May of that year, Henry C. Alexander, a partner in J. P. Morgan & Co., became vice chairman of a $6,000,000 aid-to-Russia campaign. June 22 was designated as "Aid to Russia Day," a "day of tribute to the courage of the Russian Army and people." All during September and October, Americans read daily headlines of the German siege of Stalingrad, of house-to-house fighting seesawing back and forth, of the valor of the Russian Army and the people of Stalingrad. In October, *Life* Magazine placed the Russian Army "in the top class of fighters." In November, a New York lawyer by the name of Herbert Brownell, Jr., later to be a controversially anti-Communist Attorney General of the United States, agreed to serve on a "Thanks to Russia" committee. A month later, Bernard Baruch gave $100,000 to Russian War Relief.

It is not surprising, then, that about that same time a Russian War Relief party in Berkeley, California, given by a radical French professor named Haakon Chevalier, should have been sponsored by many civic leaders and even some regents of the University of California.

For Oppenheimer, there were scarcely enough hours available in the last months of 1942 and the early months of 1943 to get the Los Alamos effort under way. A key problem was to attract to the new laboratory the highest-caliber scientists and technicians needed for an assault on the many atomic unknowns. The difficulty of this recruiting may be hard to imagine today. In postwar years atomic energy has connoted mystery, urgency, challenge, promise and importance. But in the early Forties scientists knew work in that field had for years been floundering and direction-less, and the subject had no such allure. Most leading scientists were already involved in work with immediate military applica-tion—radar, underwater sound, new conventional weapons, etc. By comparison, Oppenheimer's project, with its many uncertain-ties, had all the earmarks of a gigantic boondoggle that might have no relevance to the global war at hand. Moreover, most scientists—and their families—viewed with great misgivings the prospect of disappearing for the duration of the war into an iso-lated and only vaguely described military post in the Southwest.

So Oppenheimer's persuasive gifts were fully taxed as he trav-

eled the country, expounding, cajoling, seeking to inspire enthusiasm, telling of the challenge and of the opportunity for
national service that would, hopefully, offset the prospect of isolation, censorship, restricted travel and a quasi-military life. His
success in his recruiting efforts was later attributed to what one
of his "victims" characterized as "intellectual sex appeal."

In his quest for talent, Oppenheimer sought out, as was only
natural, those whom he knew best: his students and former
students. Robert Serber, a member of the "inner-inner circle" of
Oppenheimer protégés, was an early enlistee and became a group
leader in the Theoretical Division at Los Alamos. Oppenheimer
sought the services of Bernard Peters, in part for Peters' own
talents, in part for his wife Hannah's medical skills, for he knew
that doctors would be scarce at Los Alamos. The Peterses turned
him down. He asked for the transfer of the young and gifted
David Bohm from the Radiation Lab at Berkeley, but the security
officers ruled this out. When the administrative burdens at Los
Alamos began to sponge up too much of his time and he was
urged to bring on an administrative assistant, he turned to David
Hawkins, a young professor of mathematics and philosophy at
Berkeley whom he had met through his brother Frank, and whom
he knew and liked. Philip Morrison, another Oppenheimer intimate in the prewar period, spent the early war years in the Chicago part of the atomic project (where, in Stagg Stadium, Fermi
produced the first controlled nuclear chain reaction), but he later
joined Oppenheimer at Los Alamos.

Most of these people had shared Oppenheimer's radical views
and activities in prewar Berkeley. To Oppenheimer's knowledge,
some had been members of the Communist Party.\* Eleven years
later, his recruitment of them became one basis for questioning
his loyalty.

It could not have been easy for Oppenheimer's judges, in his
1954 security proceeding, to appraise that particular charge in
the context of the wartime conditions under which Oppenheimer's recruitment activities took place. In 1954 it would have
been difficult, if not impossible, to obtain security clearance for
such alleged former Communists as Hawkins and Morrison. But

---

\* Hawkins and Morrison later told Congressional investigating committees
that they had been members of the party before World War II.

in 1942 and 1943, when Oppenheimer was doing his recruiting, the Federal security program was much less systematic than it later became. (It was 1944 before the Civil Service Commission even set up any central security index file on personnel.) Even among personnel of the military departments, dismissal on grounds of "security risk" was extremely rare—from 1942 to 1950, the Army dismissed only 115 persons on that ground.

All personnel decisions were made against the hard fact that the United States was in a global war. No person with a skill could be spared. Especially was this true in the budding nuclear program, which had to compete against other urgent war projects for the few trained physicists. To bolster his recruitment efforts, Oppenheimer was given a letter signed by both General Groves and James B. Conant, attesting to the urgent priority the government attached to the work at Los Alamos. This letter was based in large part on reports of German activity in the field of nuclear fission. An American victory in the race for the bomb was clearly of overriding importance. Thus, in 1943, if Oppenheimer found a scientist whose intellect and training would aid in the race with the Germans, such matters as past Communist connections or sympathies were not necessarily disqualifying, provided the man seemed dependable and honest.

These were the conditions under which Robert Oppenheimer gathered a staff for the Los Alamos laboratory.

In January or February of 1943—no one has been able precisely to pinpoint the date—a conversation took place in the kitchen of Eagle Hill, Berkeley, California, the residence of J. Robert Oppenheimer. There were just two participants: Oppenheimer and his close friend, Haakon Chevalier.

The Chevaliers had come over for a quiet dinner *à quatre* with the Oppenheimers. When the host went out to the kitchen to fetch the ingredients for his savored Martinis, Chevalier followed him. Precisely what was said in the ensuing minutes is not known with certainty, for only the two men were present and their recollections do not coincide completely. Their memories do jibe on the fact that the conversation dealt with a recent talk Chevalier had had with one George C. Eltenton. Eltenton was a British chemical engineer who had spent some time in the Soviet Union, and was now working for the Shell Development Corporation in Berkeley. He was a friend of Chevalier's and a mild acquaintance of Oppenheimer's, and he took an active interest in a union of scientists and technicians that was seeking members among the staff of the Berkeley Radiation Lab.

There is no dispute over the fact that Chevalier reported that Eltenton said he had means of getting technical information to the Russians. It is also agreed that Oppenheimer made it immediately clear that he would have no part in such an affair. But did Chevalier actually *ask* Oppenheimer to furnish information for transmission to the Russians, as Oppenheimer's judges, eleven years later, seem to have assumed? Both participants in the conversation have denied that he did. Chevalier has maintained that he had already turned Eltenton down flat (at which, he has said, Eltenton seemed to feel great relief) and that in the Oppenheimer kitchen he was merely reporting the conversation to his friend as something "he should know of."

Oppenheimer later portrayed Chevalier's attitude during the kitchen conversation in three slightly varying versions. First, in Congressional testimony in 1949, he hinted at some ambivalence on Chevalier's part, stating that while Chevalier had not asked him for information, he had seemed clearly embarrassed and confused by Eltenton's suggestion. Oppenheimer further recalled having told Chevalier not to be confused, and to have no connection with what Eltenton was apparently proposing. Second, in 1950, in a letter to Chevalier reporting on his 1949 testimony, he more nearly confirmed Chevalier's portrayal of the conversation as a mere warning to him, Oppenheimer, about Eltenton and his illicit interests, omitting the prior suggestion of ambivalence or confusion on Chevalier's part. Third, in 1954, at his security hearing, Oppenheimer merely said he believed that when Chevalier told him of the Eltenton suggestion, he, Oppenheimer, had exclaimed that this was "treason,"* to which Chevalier had agreed, and the conversation had ended there. But from the point of view of Oppenheimer's later security hearing, the crucial aspect is that in all the extant versions of the kitchen interlude Op-

---

* The word "treason" would not properly apply to a noncitizen of the U.S., such as Eltenton, even if he asked a U.S. citizen's aid in transmitting secret information to a foreign power.

penheimer's immediate response to the notion of turning over information to the Russians was instantaneous and negative.

In any event, "the kitchen conversation" seems to have been the briefest of exchanges, and to have been immediately swallowed up in the pleasantness of a social evening—and in the swirl of events that was engulfing Oppenheimer.

Some weeks later, the nucleus of a laboratory staff having been recruited, the Oppenheimers left Berkeley for Los Alamos. They arrived there on March 15, 1943.

One of the first issues that confronted Oppenheimer was the basic character of the lab: was it to be a military or civilian establishment? General Groves and his staff had in mind the former, a military post where the scientists would be commissioned officers. To the surprise of some, Oppenheimer at first went along with the idea. He would have been glad to be a commissioned officer (and even visited the Army's Presidio in San Francisco to take the first steps toward that end), and he thought other scientists would share his feeling. He quickly learned otherwise. In fact, he encountered such vociferous opposition that in his subsequent recruiting efforts he was obliged to carry with him the letter signed jointly by James Conant and General Groves, stipulating that in its initial stages, at least, the laboratory would be civilian-run. The responsibilities of the military commander would be confined to the maintenance of proper living conditions—and of secrecy.

The matter of secrecy was assigned the highest possible priority, by none other than the Commander in Chief himself. On June 29, 1943, President Roosevelt dispatched a letter to Oppenheimer, admonishing him that the work of his laboratory must "be even more drastically guarded than other highly secret war developments." And so Oppenheimer had to walk a thin and diplomatic line between, on the one hand, worried Army security officers and, on the other, his scientists, to whom free thought, talk and interchange were as natural (and, they thought, essential) as breath itself. Oppenheimer's sympathies were decidedly with the scientists. After all, his initial proposal of a single integrated laboratory had been predicated on a free flow of information within Los Alamos. General Groves accepted the principle, but only grudgingly. To win internal freedom, Oppenheimer and his colleagues had to pay a price in the form of "fantastic security measures" (as Oppenheimer later described them) to prevent information leaks to the outside. For example, operators listened in on telephone calls; mail, both incoming and outgoing, was opened, read and censored; travel outside the laboratory—even into Santa Fe—was rigidly limited; scientists who brought their families had to agree to keep them at Los Alamos "for the duration." Even casual conversation had to be carefully guarded; so innocent a remark as "I saw the Fermis last night" could be a breach of security, and agents mingled incognito among the employees of the lab to detect just such lapses.

These strictures placed Oppenheimer in an uncomfortable posture. He had, as he later put it, "partly the job of devising these idiotic things, and partly the job of making them welcome." Yet he delivered several speeches to Los Alamos personnel on why these various precautions were both necessary and desirable. And while some of the scientists, even the leading ones, could not seem to curb their tongues,* Oppenheimer was not among these. While he may not have observed General Groves' wishes to the letter, the General later said he could not recall a case where Oppenheimer deliberately violated what he knew Groves expected. Groves' security chief, John Lansdale, has recalled Oppenheimer as being "extremely cooperative" on security matters. And when Peer de Silva was replaced as local security officer at Los Alamos, he wrote Oppenheimer to thank him for "personally" giving "support and encouragement" to de Silva's security work.

Not that Oppenheimer enjoyed the complete trust of the security organization. Far from it. Colonel Lansdale brought to Groves' attention the fact that FBI reports about Oppenheimer were flowing into G-2. The two discussed them at length. Groves said he had concluded that Oppenheimer was both essential *and*

---

* General Groves has told of lecturing the celebrated Niels Bohr for several hours on the train trip to Los Alamos as to just what he was *not* supposed to say; but within five minutes of his arrival Bohr was saying everything he had promised he wouldn't. And even Ernest O. Lawrence said to a small group, "I know General Groves doesn't want me to say this, but . . ."

loyal, and would have to be cleared. But Lansdale was still un-easy. He ordered tight surveillance over Oppenheimer's every movement; he had his telephone calls monitored, his mail opened, and "all sorts of nasty things" done that Lansdale has never felt at liberty to disclose. A round-the-clock watchdog (in the guise of a "bodyguard") was assigned to Oppenheimer. When the physicist traveled, his movements were carefully ob-served.

Rarely were Oppenheimer's comings and goings more mi-nutely watched and recorded than during a visit he paid to Berkeley in June, 1943. The official purpose of his trip was fur-ther recruitment for Los Alamos, but his surveillants did not rest when the business day was over. Unknown to Oppenheimer, they continued their watch as he paid a visit to his old love, for-mer Communist Party member Jean Tatlock. She had urgently wanted to see him before he left for Los Alamos, but for him it had not been possible. Under security regulations, he had not even been able to tell her where he was going. She was, at the time, undergoing psychiatric treatment. She was very unhappy. She had to see him. And so, on his last evening in San Francisco, innocent of the security men who were recording his move-ments in their notebooks, he went to her home on Telegraph Hill. He did not emerge until morning. Jean Tatlock drove him to the airport. He never saw her again. Seven months later she was dead by her own hand.

The reports of Oppenheimer's surveillants added to the doubts of Lieutenant Colonel Boris T. Pash, the atomic project security officer who at the time was in charge of investigating an alleged Soviet effort to penetrate the Berkeley Radiation Laboratory. Two reports had already involved Oppenheimer. One said that a Soviet unit or "cell" was being organized by Communist official Steve Nelson, who was thought by security investigators to have asked Oppenheimer for atomic information. The other main-tained that the "cell" supposedly involved several physicists who were former students of Oppenheimer's.

On top of these came the report of Oppenheimer's visit to Jean Tatlock. Two weeks after that visit, Pash wrote a memorandum to Lieutenant Colonel Lansdale in Washington. He expressed his concern that Oppenheimer might turn scientific information over to the Communist Party for transmission to the Soviet Union and suggested that the scientist be summoned to Washington, told that military intelligence knew of his former Communist affiliations, and severely warned that the government would not tolerate any leakage of information. Pash surmised that in view of Oppenheimer's desire to "protect his own future and reputation and the high degree of honor which would be his if his present work [was] successful," it was likely he would "lend every effort to cooperating with the Government in any plan which would leave him in charge" at Los Alamos.

But Pash was unwilling to rely on a mere probability. He recommended that Oppenheimer be "removed completely from the project and dismissed from employment by the United States government."

It was against this background that in July of 1943 General Leslie R. Groves was obliged to decide the question of security clearance for his chief Los Alamos scientist. To grant clearance would mean overriding the alarmed reports of his security subordinates. Yet there were countervailing considerations: the fact, for example, that Oppenheimer was already privy to the secrets, and the risk that to deny him security clearance might "drive him over to the other side." But foremost in Groves' mind was his view that Oppenheimer was essential to the success of the project. And so, on July 20, he dispatched the following directive to the District Engineer, United States Engineer Office, Station F, New York:

IN ACCORDANCE WITH MY VERBAL DIRECTIONS OF JULY 15,
IT IS DESIRED THAT CLEARANCE BE ISSUED FOR THE
EMPLOYMENT OF JULIUS ROBERT OPPENHEIMER WITHOUT
DELAY, IRRESPECTIVE OF THE INFORMATION WHICH YOU HAVE
CONCERNING MR. OPPENHEIMER. HE IS ABSOLUTELY ESSENTIAL
TO THE PROJECT.

Back in Berkeley, Lieutenant Colonel Pash was still preoccupied with the possibility of Soviet espionage at the Radiation

Laboratory. His main clue was the report from the War Department asserting that among those involved was the Communist official Steve Nelson; another key person it mentioned was a man known only as "Joe." At first, intelligence agents thought "Joe" was a brilliant young physicist (and former Oppenheimer protégé) by the name of Giovanni Rossi Lomanitz. Intelligence reports said that Rossi Lomanitz was affiliated with many Communist front organizations. Besides, his first name, they wrongly thought, was Italian for "Joe." Although the investigators soon concluded that Lomanitz was not the "Joe" they were looking for, they believed him to be a grave danger as a Radiation Lab employee and set about getting him drafted into the Army.

Lomanitz was an Oklahoman who had graduated from high school at the age of fourteen and come to Berkeley in the fall of 1940, at age nineteen, to enroll in the graduate school of physics. A "wide-eyed boy from the sticks," he came quickly to look on Robert Oppenheimer as a god. Oppenheimer, in turn, was sufficiently impressed with the young student to ask him to take notes, for later publication, on his course in electrodynamics. In the spring of 1942 Oppenheimer worked with Lomanitz on a new method of electromagnetic separation of isotopes, which later played a major role in the atomic bomb project.

Lomanitz was outspoken on political matters, and Oppenheimer later recalled his "wild" talk about how the war was so terrible he didn't care which side won. After considerable effort, Oppenheimer persuaded Lomanitz to join the Radiation Lab, despite his misgivings about taking any part in the atomic project. Months later, when senior scientists began to be drawn off to Los Alamos, Lomanitz, then only twenty-one, took over their work. He performed well.

On Tuesday, July 27, 1943, Ernest Lawrence, the Radiation Lab director, called Lomanitz to his office. He was well pleased with Lomanitz' work, he said, and was promoting the young physicist to be a group leader and giving him an increase in salary. Then they discussed some urgent problems that Lomanitz should tackle immediately. That was on Tuesday. On Friday Lomanitz received a special-delivery notice from the draft board to appear for a physical examination the next day, Saturday. At the draft board, he was surprised to note that the doctor had instructions to rush his blood sample to the laboratory by special messenger. Baffled by the sudden turnabout since his Tuesday promotion, Lomanitz went to Ernest Lawrence. The lab director said this came as a total surprise, made an inquiry and told Lomanitz that the case would be given a second look.

That same afternoon, Lomanitz also put in a call to his former mentor, Robert Oppenheimer, at Los Alamos. Oppenheimer was aware of the concern about Lomanitz (he had talked about it with Colonel Lansdale), but he was also acutely conscious of the desperate shortage of trained scientists at the Berkeley lab. That afternoon he telegraphed the headquarters of the Manhattan District (the code name of the whole atomic project) in New York, saying he understood Lomanitz' draft deferment had been revoked:

BELIEVE UNDERSTAND REASONS BUT FEEL THAT VERY SERIOUS MISTAKE IS BEING MADE. LOMANITZ NOW ONLY MAN AT BERKELEY WHO CAN TAKE THIS RESPONSIBILITY. HIS WORK FOR LAWRENCE PREEMINENTLY SATISFACTORY. IF HE IS DRAFTED AND NOT RETURNED PROMPTLY TO PROJECT LAWRENCE WILL REQUEST THAT I RELEASE ONE OR TWO OF MY MEN. I SHALL NOT BE ABLE TO ACCEDE TO THIS. THEREFORE URGE YOU SUPPORT DEFERMENT OF LOMANITZ OR INSURE BY OTHER MEANS HIS CONTINUED AVAILABILITY TO PROJECT. . . . I REGARD [THIS] AS URGENT REQUEST. LOMANITZ DEFERMENT EXPIRES AUGUST 2.

Oppenheimer also wired Lomanitz that he had "requested in proper place reconsideration [and] support for your deferment. Cannot guarantee outcome, but have made strong request. . . . Good luck." The telegram was signed "Opje."

Nonetheless, Lomanitz promptly received orders to report for induction a scant nine days hence. He appealed. His local draft board sought to side with him, and the matter went first to the state and then to national draft headquarters. There, draft director Lewis Hershey went so far as to warn that if Lomanitz wasn't drafted, Hershey would get rid of both the state and local draft boards. Twice Lomanitz secured draft-deferrable jobs in private electronics plants; twice the employers were persuaded to withdraw their job offers. Lomanitz was inducted into the Army.

Meanwhile, at the Radiation Laboratory, it was urgent that the work he had been doing be carried forward. Replacing Lomanitz was a senior physicist, Dr. Edward U. Condon, recently transferred from Los Alamos. But Condon found that in the abruptness of his departure Lomanitz had been unable to leave any notes on his work. And so, precisely as Oppenheimer had predicted, a physicist badly needed at Los Alamos had to be temporarily detached and sent to Berkeley to educate Condon to his new assignment.

But perhaps from a "security" point of view, it was all worthwhile. Rossi Lomanitz was no longer a "danger." The brilliant, well-trained theoretical physicist was a company clerk in the Army's 44th Division.

Not long after this, Robert Oppenheimer was visited at Los Alamos by Lieutenant Colonel John Lansdale, General Groves' security aide. They talked at length, mainly about Lomanitz. Lansdale advised the physicist not to intercede further on Lomanitz' behalf since he said the young man had been guilty of "indiscretions which could not be overlooked or condoned." Lansdale also said that Lomanitz had failed to keep a promise he had made to Oppenheimer to cease his political activities after joining the Radiation Laboratory. "That makes me mad," Oppenheimer said.

Then the talk turned to the more general topic of Communist Party membership. Lansdale said that his sole concern, as a security officer, was to prevent the "unauthorized transmission" of information. A man's political or social beliefs, he said, were irrelevant.

But Oppenheimer, remarkably, demurred. He emphatically told Lansdale that he did not want any *current* member of the Communist Party working for him at Los Alamos, because the discipline imposed by the party was so stringent that there was always a "question of divided loyalty." He emphasized he was not referring to certain employees at Los Alamos whom he knew to be *former* party members, but only to present members. The conversation was interrupted before Lansdale had a chance to question Oppenheimer about the ex-Communist Los Alamosites to whom he had referred.

Mulling over the talk afterward, Lansdale had the definite impression that Oppenheimer had been trying—had, in fact, seemed almost anxious—to convey to Lansdale that he himself had been a member of the party, but had severed all connections with it upon joining the atomic project.

The talk set Oppenheimer to mulling, too. Indeed, it prompted him a few weeks later to take a step that was to prove one of the most momentous of his life.

Lansdale, referring to the possibility of Soviet espionage in Berkeley, had voiced particular concern about a newly formed union known as the Federation of Architects, Engineers, Chemists, and Technicians—FAECT. Mention of the union made Oppenheimer think of George C. Eltenton, the scientist who Haakon Chevalier, in his "kitchen conversation" with Oppenheimer eight months before, had said was interested in conveying technical information to the Soviet Union. Oppenheimer knew Eltenton to be an active member of the union, and when Lansdale spoke of FAECT, Oppenheimer decided to tell the authorities about Eltenton.

On August 25 he entered Durant Hall on the Berkeley campus and wandered into the office of Lieutenant Lyall Johnson, the atomic project's security officer for Berkeley. He told Johnson there was a man in the San Francisco area whom he thought the security officers ought to keep an eye on. His name was Eltenton, he worked for the Shell Development Corporation, and he was an active member of the FAECT union.

The conversation was a short one. Oppenheimer seemed anxious to convey what he had to say and depart, and Johnson, for his part, did not feel inclined at this juncture to detain or interrogate the scientist. For one thing, he and other security officers were already aware of Eltenton; for another, since Eltenton was beyond his Berkeley campus jurisdiction, Johnson felt the matter should be handled by Lieutenant Colonel Boris Pash. He called Pash, who agreed and directed Johnson to arrange an interview with Oppenheimer the following day.

And so on August 26 Oppenheimer found himself again in

Durant Hall, this time confronted by Pash as well as Johnson. But there was a fourth party in the room, of which Oppenheimer was not aware. In the mouthpiece of a telephone placed between Oppenheimer and Pash was a hidden microphone. In the adjacent teletype room sat a primitive version of the modern tape recorder, with a broad tape, similar to a movie film, complete with sprocket holes. All of this had been arranged overnight, on orders from Pash.

Oppenheimer sat down. The recording machine started turning. An important conversation began.

Colonel Pash began ingratiatingly, deferentially: "This is a pleasure. . . . I don't mean to take too much of your time."

Oppenheimer broke in: "That's perfectly all right. Whatever time you choose."

Pash referred to the previous day's interchange with Johnson. Oppenheimer immediately began talking about Rossi Lomanitz, but Pash said he had another, more serious interest, namely, that there might be some "groups" interested in the Radiation Laboratory and its secret information.

Oppenheimer said he thought that was true; he had no firsthand information about it, but he understood that an unnamed man attached to the Soviet Consulate had indicated he was in a position to transmit information about the Berkeley atomic project without danger of discovery. He said he was concerned lest there be indiscretions on the part of people close to the project. "To put it quite frankly," he told Pash, "I would feel friendly to the idea of the Commander in Chief informing the Russians that we were working on this problem. At least, I can see there might be some arguments for doing that, but I do not feel friendly to the idea of having it moved out the back door."

Pash pressed him to be more specific about the channels to the Soviet Consulate. Oppenheimer said that "to give more . . . than one name would be to implicate people whose attitude was one of bewilderment rather than one of cooperation," but there was one person "whose name was mentioned to me a couple of times" as an intermediary and who would bear watching. He then named Eltenton, who, he said, had "talked to a friend of his who is also an acquaintance of one of the men on the project, and that was one of the channels by which this thing went. Now

I think that to go beyond that would be to put a lot of names down, of people who are not only innocent but whose attitude was 100 percent cooperative."

There now began a polite sparring match between the security officer and the physicist. Pash sought to draw Oppenheimer out by assuring absolute anonymity in anything he might report. Oppenheimer became slightly less guarded.

He said there *had* been a contact with two of his close associates at Los Alamos, not by Eltenton but through another party. But Oppenheimer insisted it was important to understand the *flavor* of the approach, which, while technically treasonable, had not been presented in that light. Rather, it had been in the context of an American failure to convey vital military information to our Russian allies, who, after all, were "battling for their lives." That is, said Oppenheimer, the object of the approach was simply to make up for "defects of our official communication" on the part of U.S. officials who "don't feel very friendly to Russia." Since the Soviets were our allies, this was merely to implement what was "more or less a policy of the Government." Oppenheimer described the means contemplated for effecting this: George Eltenton, he said, was to arrange a contact with a reliable man from the Soviet Consulate who had had "a lot of experience in microfilm work, or whatever the hell."

Pash moved in quickly. "Well, now, could we know through whom that contact was made?"

Oppenheimer retreated. "I think it would be a mistake. That is, I think I have told you where the initiative came from." To go any further "would involve people who ought not be involved in this." Oppenheimer did go so far as to say that Eltenton's intermediary was "a member of the faculty," but stopped there.

Pash was getting restive. "I don't want to seem . . . insistent. I want to again sort of explore the possibility of getting the name of the person on the faculty . . . not for the purpose of taking him to task . . . but to try to see Eltenton's method of approach."

Oppenheimer remained firm about withholding the name of the faculty member, but he did begin to furnish some added detail: three people, in all, had been approached by Eltenton's intermediary—two of them at Los Alamos, contacted within a week of each other, but not in each other's presence, and a third in Berkeley who either had joined, or was about to join, the Oak Ridge laboratory, a facility in Tennessee engaged in producing fissionable materials.

The balance of the interrogation was rambling and inconclusive. Pash tried to keep it light (Pash: "I am not persistent (ha ha) but . . ." Oppenheimer: "You *are* persistent and it is your duty"). The Colonel also sought to identify the man in the Soviet Consulate, but Oppenheimer said he could provide no further details. How qualified was Eltenton to convey scientific information to the Soviets? Well suited, Oppenheimer felt, to pass on the kind of general information that would be most helpful. Could Pash visit Oppenheimer at Los Alamos if further information should be needed? Oppenheimer: "My motto is, God bless you."

The Colonel sought to impress on Oppenheimer the trouble his reticence was going to cause, in trying to track down the unnamed contacts ("We could work a hundred years," Pash said, "and never get this information"). But in the end the conversation ended much as it had begun—politely.

Pash: "Well, we appreciate it, and the best of luck."

Oppenheimer: "Thank you very much."

End of interview. End of tape recording.

The bulk of what Oppenheimer told Colonel Pash in that interview was later branded as a "tissue of lies" and acknowledged as such by Oppenheimer himself. But some of the scientist's judges, in later years, were not altogether persuaded of this for there was, in their minds, an unresolved question: namely, if Oppenheimer was correct in stating that the purpose of his tale was to protect an innocent Chevalier, why would he conjure up in detail a story (involving Soviet consuls and microfilm and the like) that was far more injurious to his friend and to himself than the truth? Was it not possible, they wondered, that Oppenheimer was telling Pash the truth—and that it was his later contradictions that were lies?

If anything, the Oppenheimer interview had only added to Colonel Pash's problems, by obliging him to pursue vague leads. Oppenheimer had mentioned a professor—but which one? The university staff was tremendous. Oppenheimer had also said that one of the purported Eltenton contacts either just had been or was about to be transferred to Oak Ridge. So Pash had to make a tedious search of the files "to try to find out who was going to go to site X [Oak Ridge]." (One suspect person was found and his transfer stopped.)

In one instance, Oppenheimer caused Pash not just labor but embarrassment. One of the persons Pash's agents were "tailing" suddenly, and without prior indication, boarded the *Daylight*, the crack San Francisco–Los Angeles train. In order to gain time to get his agent to Los Angeles, Pash ordered the train stopped en route. Unhappily, his order was carried out in a most peremptory and undiplomatic way. Railroad officials were outraged. They complained to the commanding general, but since Pash's project was ultrasecret, Pash had not informed his superiors of his actions; nor could they pry any information out of the Colonel even after the rude train-stopping was traced to him. The ironic footnote is that the object of Pash's pursuit turned out to have nothing whatever to do with the case.

On the day of his interview with Oppenheimer, Pash directed a special message to General Groves speculating about what had prompted the scientist to volunteer information about George C. Eltenton. Pash suggested that the controversy about the drafting of Rossi Lomanitz had triggered in Oppenheimer a fear that his own radical background was under Army investigation and suspicion. Oppenheimer, he concluded, had volunteered the Eltenton information to "retain the confidence of the Army personnel responsible for this project."

Pash was not alone in this theory. In a separate memorandum written the same day, Pash's security man at Los Alamos, Peer de Silva, offered precisely the same idea. But de Silva went further than Boris Pash. His memorandum contained by far the gravest charges yet leveled at Oppenheimer. To him, Oppenheimer's reticence in naming names meant "that J. R. Oppenheimer is playing a key part in the attempts of the Soviet Union to secure, by espionage, highly secret information which is vital to the security of the United States."

In support of this assertion, de Silva noted that Oppenheimer had "allowed a tight clique of known Communists or Communist sympathizers to grow up about him within the project" so that they comprised "a large proportion of the key personnel." De Silva concluded that Oppenheimer must either be "incredibly naïve and almost childlike in his sense of reality" (a possibility he ruled out) or "extremely clever and disloyal." He concluded by reiterating the Pash notion that Oppenheimer was "deeply concerned with gaining a worldwide reputation as a scientist, and a place in history," and by noting that "the Army is in the position of being able to allow him to do so or to destroy his name, reputation and career, if it should choose to do so." The latter possibility, "if strongly presented," would, de Silva believed, change not only Oppenheimer's attitude about security but that of "the lower echelons of employees."

The doubts of West Coast intelligence officials about Robert Oppenheimer were heightened by an additional event. This was their interception, on September 6, of a note from Joseph Weinberg,* a former Oppenheimer student whom they now believed to be the "Joe" involved in the suspected Soviet espionage attempt. The note said:

> Dear A. Please don't make any contact with me, and pass this message to S and B, only don't mention any names. I will take a walk with you when this matter is all cleared up.

To intelligence officers, this mysteriously worded note meant that Weinberg had wind that the security officers were onto him and was running for temporary cover. Coming just eleven days after the Pash-Oppenheimer interrogation, the note made them wonder if it had been Oppenheimer who had tipped off his former student.

In the early days of September, 1943, Oppenheimer shared a sixteen-hour train ride from Cheyenne to Chicago with his boss, General Groves, and with Groves' top security officer, John Lans-

* Weinberg was later to be labeled by government investigators as "Scientist X," who had allegedly obtained atomic data for a Soviet spy ring; and he was to be indicted on three counts of perjury. However, of these, the government withdrew one; the trial judge ordered acquittal on the second; and in March, 1953, Weinberg was acquitted on the third count, involving his denial of having been a member of the Communist Party.

dale. As the train moved eastward, the three had a long talk about security matters. The Lomanitz matter came up, and Oppenheimer, still angry over reports that Lomanitz had violated his promise to avoid political involvements while in the atomic program, told Groves he was sorry he had had anything to do with Lomanitz and desired no further connection with him.

They also talked about Oppenheimer's interview with Colonel Pash. The physicist told Groves he was reluctant to reveal the name of the professor whom George Eltenton had used as an intermediary, but would do so if General Groves ordered him to. Groves, however, was loath to make an issue of it with Oppenheimer. After all, hadn't the scientist volunteered the information that the Radiation Laboratory was in danger of penetration and hadn't he given the name of the most dangerous man involved (Eltenton)? If Groves rewarded Oppenheimer's initiative by extracting information he was clearly reluctant to give, would Oppenheimer ever volunteer information again? What's more, Groves reasoned, whoever "Professor X" might be, Oppenheimer had effectively discouraged him from making any further overtures.

Eleven years later, in Oppenheimer's security hearing, the "Chevalier incident" was to be portrayed as a major threat to American security. But in September, 1943, the man responsible for developing the bomb and for protecting its secret elected not to press his number one scientist for Haakon Chevalier's name.

When John Lansdale returned to Washington from the Western train trip with General Groves, the alarmist memoranda about Oppenheimer from Pash and de Silva awaited him. Lansdale decided he would do well to interrogate the recalcitrant scientist himself. On Oppenheimer's next trip to Washington, Lansdale seized the opportunity, and on September 12, 1943, in General Groves' office in the Pentagon, Robert Oppenheimer had his second confrontation over the "Chevalier incident." Again there was an unseen observer in the room: a concealed microphone.

By now Lansdale and Oppenheimer were far from strangers. They had had many long conversations; Lansdale was aware of the security concern about Oppenheimer and felt that as General

Groves' chief intelligence officer he had a duty to satisfy himself about Oppenheimer's trustworthiness. And so he had made a point of having several long and leisurely talks in Los Alamos that year, not only with Oppenheimer alone but with Kitty as well (since the FBI reports dwelt at some length on her and her former marriage with Joseph Dallet). Kitty impressed Lansdale as "a strong woman with strong convictions . . . as the type of person who could have been . . . a Communist." But now, he felt, "Dr. Oppenheimer was the most important thing in her life" and that "her strength of . . . will was a powerful influence in keeping Dr. Oppenheimer away from what we would regard as dangerous associations," for the sake of his own future. As to Oppenheimer himself, Lansdale had concluded that he was not a Communist, as Lansdale defined one (i.e., as one who would put loyalty to Russia ahead of loyalty to the United States).

But the conversation that was about to take place in Washington would be far different from the comfortable ones in Los Alamos. There was a specific item of business at hand: the identity of the professor whom George Eltenton had contacted on behalf of the Soviets. In this interview with Lansdale, Haakon Chevalier would emerge unnamed and unscathed. Other friends and associates of Robert Oppenheimer would not be so fortunate.

Lansdale began as Pash had in Berkeley—ingratiatingly ("You're probably the most intelligent man I ever met"). He proceeded to paint a serious picture of how much the Russians had already been able to find out about the atomic project, and the two talked about whether nuclear information was being fed through the Communist Party. Oppenheimer said he had been told by a prominent Midwestern Communist that it was party policy for members to drop out of the party when they entered confidential war work. Lansdale agreed that in such cases party severance was illusory only. Oppenheimer volunteered that his brother, Frank, had made a "severance in fact," although he was "not so sure about his wife," Jackie.

Soon Lansdale got to the main purpose of the talk. In a Perry Mason-style bluff, he told Oppenheimer he thought they now knew who the Eltenton contact was, but wondered "if you feel that you're in a position to tell me." But as with Colonel Pash, Oppenheimer balked at unveiling the name of Haakon Chevalier.

Again he took the position that he had given the name of the one man he thought "would persevere" (Eltenton), and that it "would be wrong" for him to give the name of the intermediary since it was his "overwhelming judgment that this guy [wasn't] involved" and since this "judgment [was not] based on hope but [on] his character."

"I don't see," said Lansdale, "how you can have any hesitancy in disclosing the name of the man who has actually been engaged in an attempt at espionage for a foreign power in time of war."

"I know," replied Oppenheimer. "It's a tough problem, and I'm worried about it a lot."

"Well," said Lansdale, "if you won't do it, you won't do it, but don't think I won't ask you again."

Now he tried a different tack. Who among the atomic project personnel, he asked, were either current or past members of the Communist Party? Lansdale's question opened before Oppenheimer the same pit of quicksand that would engulf many a hapless witness before Congressional investigating committees inquiring into the subversive activities (or perhaps merely the beliefs) of the witness' friends and associates. Robert Oppenheimer now took his first step into that pit.

"I will try to answer that question," he began. "I know for a fact . . . I learned on my last visit to Berkeley that both Lomanitz and Weinberg were members. I suspected that before, but was not sure. I never had any way of knowing."* Eleven years later, these words were to be used to question Oppenheimer's veracity.

There were other ex-party members whose names he now proceeded to convey to Lansdale after "think[ing] a minute." He named a secretary who he thought was a member, but he wasn't sure. Mrs. Charlotte Serber—the wife of his intimate friend and valued Los Alamos physicist, Robert—she had been a member . . . "and I know that my wife was a member."

* This statement is cited here because it later became an important factor in the Oppenheimer security hearing. However, as noted previously, in March, 1953, Weinberg was acquitted of a charge of perjury, involving his denial of Communist Party membership. Whether or not Lomanitz was a member has never been established in any legal proceeding. When asked about this in Congressional hearings, Lomanitz declined to answer on grounds of self-incrimination.

Lansdale: "That was a long time ago."

Oppenheimer: "Yes—you haven't found out a lot about my wife."

Lansdale asked whether Oppenheimer himself had ever been a member of the party. The reply was an unambiguous "No." Had he ever been "felt out . . . about passing a little information to the party," as Lansdale said he had reason to believe? Oppenheimer said if there had been an overture, "it was so gentle I did not know it."

Now Lansdale said he had a number of names—would Oppenheimer mind saying "yea" or "nay" as to their party membership? No, Oppenheimer wouldn't mind. There followed an interchange, quick and casual at the time, that was to be considered, eleven years later, another major test of Robert Oppenheimer's truthfulness.

Lansdale: "Do you know a fellow named Rudy Lambert?"

Oppenheimer: *"I'm not sure, do you know what he looks like?"* (Emphasis added.)

Lansdale: "No, I've never seen him. He's a member of the party."

That was all there was about Rudy Lambert. Lansdale passed on to the next name.

It was almost like blindman's buff: Lansdale was casting about without any way of knowing whether he was "hot" or "cold." He asked about Isaac Folkoff and Steve Nelson. Suddenly, he became very, very "warm" indeed:

"How about Haakon Chevalier?"

Oppenheimer: "Is he a member of the party?"

Lansdale: "I don't know."

Oppenheimer: "He is a member of the faculty, and I know him well. I wouldn't be surprised if he were a member. He is quite a Red."

No signal that Lansdale was any closer to his target than he had been. Still blindfolded, he moved away.

Now a bit of cat and mouse: knowing far more than Oppenheimer knew he knew, Lansdale asked, "How about a girl named Jean Tatlock?"

"She is a close friend of mine, and I'm certain at one time she was a member of the party." How about now? "I would rather doubt it. I know she dropped out at one time, and I rather think she probably still is."

Whatever trap there may have been had been safely skirted. A few more questions. Then:

Lansdale: "Cigarette?"

Oppenheimer: "No, I'll smoke my pipe."

More discussion—about Lomanitz; about the distinction between adherence to the "party line" and subservient loyalty to the party (Oppenheimer thought one could follow the "line" without being subservient); about whether a spy could transmit any meaningful technical information without reducing it to writing (Oppenheimer thought not).

Suddenly the scientist asked Lansdale, "Why do you look so worried?"

"Because I'm not getting anywhere."

"Well," said Oppenheimer, "except on that one point, I think you're getting everywhere that I can get you."

The ever-resourceful Lansdale again switched strategy. He began: "Well, try to put yourself in our position."

"All right, Lansdale." (Later in the interview it was to be "Colonel"; now it was just plain "Lansdale.")

Lansdale explained that he was responsible for preventing any espionage at Los Alamos, and was certain he hadn't identified all the possible spies. All he had to go on, in most cases, was past associations and activities. Then, perhaps bearing in mind the de Silva–Pash hypothesis about Oppenheimer's ambition for world recognition and his fear of an Army investigation of his own past that might tarnish his reputation, Lansdale turned to an illustration—"the case of Dr. J. R. Oppenheimer,* whose wife was at one time a member of the party anyway, who himself knows many prominent Communists, associates with them, who belongs to a large number of so-called front organizations, and may perhaps have contributed financially to the party himself, who becomes aware of an espionage attempt by the party six months ago and doesn't mention it, and who still won't make a complete disclosure."

Having set forth for Oppenheimer the remarkably complete

* The illustration, Lansdale told Oppenheimer, was "personal, but not pointed, [if] you get my distinction."

contents of the investigative dossier, Lansdale quickly became reassuring. He was using Oppenheimer as an example, he made clear, to avoid disclosing information about anyone else. Moreover, "I've made up my mind that you yourself are O.K. or otherwise I wouldn't be talking to you like this, see?"

Oppenheimer: "I'd better be—that's all I've got to say."

After a bit more discussion, Lansdale put it squarely before Oppenheimer: was he close enough to party members to get information from them? Specifically, would he be willing to become, in effect, a counterintelligence agent and "get information about who is and who isn't a member of the party"?

"Not in writing. I think that would make a very bad impression."

This was a reply that would, when made public years later, make his close friends of the Thirties wince in embarrassment.

More talk. Another try at the main quest for that missing name. Still stubborn resistance.

"Well, is there anything else that you believe you can tell me that could give us any assistance?"

"Let me walk around the room and think."

"Sure, it's getting warm, isn't it?"

On his feet, Oppenheimer was able to come up with one more name: Lansdale had mentioned Hannah Peters. Oppenheimer didn't know whether or not her husband, Bernard, was a member, but he did know he had been in prison in Germany, in Dachau, and had "always expressed a very great interest in the Communists, and I think whether he is a member or not would perhaps partly depend on whether he was a citizen or whether he was working on a war job." This was not to be the last time Oppenheimer mentioned the name of Bernard Peters to anti-Communist questioners.

On another subject: how important would atomic information be to the Russians? Earlier in the conversation, Oppenheimer had said categorically it would be a "catastrophe" if Russia were to find out about the project except through official channels.* But now he qualified that earlier position: he doubted that

* At one point in the interrogation Oppenheimer even questioned whether the relatively free sharing of atomic information with America's close ally, the British, was "the right thing to do."

Russian knowledge of the atomic project "was likely to be dynamite" because the Soviets were so "tied up" fighting the Nazis that they wouldn't be able to do anything with the information— not, at any rate, until the war was over. This did not mean he *favored* conveying information through unauthorized channels— that, he said, would be a "very serious thing," for even if it were not actually used by Russia, "we have no control over what happens to it."

The two men had now been sparring futilely for nearly two hours, and Lansdale said he had "about talked himself down." Oppenheimer said he couldn't deny he had the information the "Colonel" wanted, and wished he could give it to him. Lansdale assured Oppenheimer he liked him very much "personally," wished he wouldn't be so formal in calling him "Colonel," and warned again this would not be the last time he would ask the physicist for the undisclosed name.

Oppenheimer's closing explanation of his reticence: *"It is a question of some past loyalties. . . .* I would regard it as a low trick to involve someone where I would bet dollars to doughnuts he wasn't involved." (Emphasis added.)

Lansdale said, "O.K., sir," and Robert Oppenheimer's second confrontation on the Chevalier matter was at an end. He had not revealed the name the security officers most desired. At the same time, however, his "past loyalties" had not inhibited him from implicating some other friends and furnishing their names for the security grist mill.

Four weeks later, Army Private 39140466—Giovanni Rossi Lomanitz—wrote "Dear Opje" to report that his Army career to date (four days) had not been "half bad" and that the food was "excellent and abundant."

Lomanitz also told "Opje" that Ernest Lawrence had initiated the notion of getting the Army to ask Lomanitz back to the Radiation Lab and had further suggested it "might be quite effective" if Oppenheimer would simultaneously ask for Lomanitz to be assigned either to Berkeley or to Los Alamos. He asked Oppenheimer if he were "in sympathy" with the idea, to put in a prompt request before the Army assigned him elsewhere.

Oppenheimer had told General Groves he wanted nothing

further to do with Lomanitz. Nonetheless, upon receiving Lomanitz' letter he acted quickly, albeit more cautiously than before. On October 19 he wrote Lansdale in Washington, enclosing a copy of Lomanitz' letter, and calling attention to Lawrence's interest in having Lomanitz back at the Radiation Lab.

Since I am not in possession of the facts which led to Mr. Lomanitz' induction, *I am, of course, not able to endorse this request in any absolute way.* I can, however, say that Mr. Lomanitz' competence and his past experience on the work in Berkeley should make him a man of real value whose technical service we should make every effort to secure for the project. In particular, Lomanitz has been working on a part of Dr. Lawrence's project in which historically I have a close interest and which I know is in need of added personnel. [Emphasis added.]

For the moment, that ended Oppenheimer's contact with Rossi Lomanitz. But before closing the covers on the episode, Oppenheimer did what was for him an unusual thing: he took pains to make a special file of his correspondence with his former student, because, he later explained, Lomanitz was in "some kind of trouble" and Oppenheimer thought "that some day I might be asked about how I behaved."

At Thanksgiving, 1943, the investigation of Soviet espionage in Berkeley lost one of its major figures: Boris Pash was transferred to Europe on special assignment. He was to become the military commander of a special mission known as "Alsos," whose task was to enter Germany, find the key German scientists who were thought to be working on nuclear fission, and determine the status of German nuclear research. Before he left Berkeley, however, Pash sent to Washington a report on his efforts to identify the mysterious Professor X. Since late October, Pash said, his office had been checking the FBI records on "all professors and associates in both the physics and chemistry departments at the University of California." He thought it "entirely possible" that Professor X might be one of nine persons he proceeded to name —all physicists or chemists. It did not occur to him that the professor he was looking for was not a scientist at all, but a specialist in French literature, and so naturally his list did not include the name of Haakon Chevalier.

Even after Pash's departure, General Groves continued to be harassed by his security officers about the missing name. John Lansdale reported his futile attempt to wrest the name from Oppenheimer and said it was now up to the General to secure the identity of Professor X. On December 12, on one of his many visits to Los Alamos, Groves finally decided he must act. He called Oppenheimer to his room and told him he must now order him to divulge the name of the Eltenton contact.

This is another of the conversations in the Oppenheimer affair whose precise content later became a matter of intense controversy, and about which memories differ sharply. There is no disagreement about the fact that Dr. Oppenheimer identified the unknown professor as Haakon Chevalier. But did he also identify himself as the person whom Chevalier had contacted?

Oppenheimer himself contended that he did. According to his recollection, he told Groves that his story to Pash about *three* contacts in the atomic project had been a fabrication, a "cock and bull story"—that "there were no three people" who had been approached by the intermediary, that the incident "occurred in our house" in Berkeley and that the sole contact in the project "was me."

Questioned about that conversation twenty-five years later, General Groves had only an indistinct recollection of it, but his aide, John Lansdale, remembered clearly what General Groves told him at the time: that Chevalier had made but one contact—and that was not Robert Oppenheimer, but his brother Frank.*

The vividness of Lansdale's recollection is explainable. After General Groves mentioned Frank's name to him under an explicit injunction of strict secrecy, Lansdale did a very unmilitary thing: that very night he consciously violated General Groves' order and went to the Federal Bureau of Investigation. There he discussed Frank Oppenheimer with Director Hoover's personal assistant,

* This conformed with General Groves' long-held suspicion that one of Robert Oppenheimer's prime motives in refusing to reveal the mysterious professor's name was his desire at all costs to protect "someone"—most probably Frank Oppenheimer, in Groves' view.

Frank Tamm, and with the FBI's foremost expert on Communism, Lish Whitson.

But both Oppenheimer's and Lansdale's recollections are belied by important contemporaneous records: the telegrams dispatched by Colonel K. D. Nichols, Groves' second-in-command, to the various security offices of the Manhattan Project the day after Oppenheimer and Groves had their talk. Presumably, these are based on General Groves' report of what Oppenheimer had told him. One was addressed to Lieutenant Lyall Johnson in Berkeley, the officer to whom Oppenheimer had first gone to volunteer his information:

LANSDALE ADVISES THAT ACCORDING TO OPPENHEIMER PROFESSOR CONTACT OF ELTENTON IS HAAKON CHEVALIER. OPPENHEIMER STATES IN HIS OPINION CHEVALIER ENGAGED IN NO FURTHER ACTIVITY OTHER THAN THREE ORIGINAL ATTEMPTS. [Emphasis added.]

A second telegram went to Captain Peer de Silva, in Santa Fe:

HAAKON CHEVALIER TO BE REPORTED BY OPPENHEIMER TO BE PROFESSOR AT RADLAB [the Berkeley Radiation Laboratory] WHO MADE THREE CONTACTS FOR ELTENTON. CLASSIFIED SECRET. OPPENHEIMER BELIEVED CHEVALIER ENGAGED IN NO FURTHER ACTIVITY OTHER THAN THREE ORIGINAL ATTEMPTS.

The third went to the security officer at Oak Ridge:

ACCORDING TO OPPENHEIMER PROFESSOR CONTACT OF ELTENTON IS HAAKON CHEVALIER. OPPY STATES IN HIS OPINION BEYOND ORIGINAL THREE ATTEMPTS CHEVALIER ENGAGED IN NO FURTHER ACTIVITY. FROM LANSDALE. DE SILVA AND JOHNSON TO BE NOTIFIED BY YOU.

Thus, according to all three telegrams, which are the best contemporaneous record of the conversation, Oppenheimer did *not* reveal himself as Chevalier's contact within the atomic project, but persisted in his story that there had been three such contacts.

Which version is correct—that of the telegrams or Oppenheimer's contrary recollection, eleven years later, that he told Groves there had been but one contact: himself?

Neither version of the Oppenheimer-Groves conversation reflects well on Oppenheimer. If his own recollection was accurate, it means that he was in effect admitting to General Groves that he had been guilty of a felony under Section 80, Title 18 of the United States Code, aimed at anyone who "knowingly or willfully falsifies or conceal(s) . . . a material fact . . . in any matter within the jurisdiction or agency of the United States."* If, on the other hand, the three telegrams accurately reflect what Robert Oppenheimer said to General Groves in Los Alamos on that cold December day, he was guilty of implicating his friend while protecting his own good name by concealing his role in "the Chevalier incident." This latter was the conclusion reluctantly reached, years later, by a bitter Haakon Chevalier.

The security officers knew now that the "Professor X" for whose name they had been clamoring was Haakon Chevalier. What did they do about it?

The answer, so far as is publicly discernible, is: nothing. At any rate, security officials seem to have made no effort whatever to contact or question Haakon Chevalier for nearly three years, by which time the war was over. Nor, so far as Chevalier was aware, was any effort made to place him under surveillance.

This in itself raises a question about the three telegrams dispatched the day after the Groves-Oppenheimer conversation. If the security officials really believed that Chevalier had contacted *three* people in the atomic project, how could they be content to permit the three to remain unidentified? (Besides, if Oppenheimer really told General Groves there were three contacts, why didn't Groves order him to reveal the identity of all three?) And why did no security or intelligence official question George C. Eltenton until 1946?

One explanation for the failure to contact and question Chevalier and Eltenton until after the war is that to have done so might merely have confirmed to the Soviets the existence of our atomic project, and thus done more harm than good. Some support for

* This statement is taken directly from General Nichols' opinion in the Oppenheimer case. (Princ. Docs. 45.)

this is found in the fact that General Groves did, for a time, consider a *secret* prosecution of Chevalier and Eltenton, but was dissuaded from this by a lawyer on his staff, who told him that even in wartime a secret conviction was out of the question.*

At the time of the Groves-Oppenheimer conversation, Haakon Chevalier was in New York City, awaiting clearance for a job with the Office of War Information. By his account, he received definite—and negative—word on the matter in January, 1944, one month after Robert Oppenheimer revealed his name to General Groves. According to Chevalier, he was called in by a New York OWI official who had just returned from Washington, where he had seen Chevalier's FBI file containing "allegations that were so fantastic as to be utterly unbelievable." Chevalier has quoted the official as saying, "Someone obviously has it in for you."†

Oppenheimer's identification of Chevalier as the mysterious Professor X did not assuage the curiosity of security officials, who continued to ply the physicist with questions about his former students, many of whom were then working at the Radiation Laboratory in Berkeley.

In the first days of 1944, Peer de Silva drove with Oppenheimer from Los Alamos to Santa Fe. The conversation turned to the situation in Berkeley and soon centered on Bernard Peters, the former Oppenheimer student who had been particularly close to his mentor.

Peters' story was a dramatic one. A Bavarian Jew, he had come to study in Munich on the eve of Hitler's ascension to power. He

---

* Roger Robb, who acted as attorney for the Atomic Energy Commission in the Oppenheimer hearing in 1954, and who studied minutely the entire Oppenheimer investigative file, told the author that there was a reasonable explanation for the delay in interrogating Chevalier and Eltenton, but that he could not reveal what it was.

† One of Chevalier's principal later complaints against Oppenheimer was that while the physicist had in fact been responsible for many of Chevalier's career difficulties, he continued to profess ignorance of any such role or responsibility. This complaint is seemingly contradicted by a letter from Chevalier to Oppenheimer, dated December 3, 1943, stating that the OWI job was still hanging fire *"for reasons that you know.* I am investigating all possibilities," wrote Chevalier, "but it is likely that I will find the same obstacles everywhere." (Emphasis added.) This letter suggests that even before Oppenheimer gave his name to General Groves, Chevalier's radical past had already created some security-clearance difficulties, for which Chevalier in no way seemed to hold his friend responsible.

was, of course, bitterly and actively anti-Nazi, as was the German Communist Party. Arrested and sent to a prison camp, Peters was forced to help erect the barbed-wire fence that would later confine thousands of doomed Jews in the dread camp, Dachau.

With the help of a bribe arranged by his mother, Peters was transferred to the Munich city jail and thence escaped and fled to America. In New York, he worked as a longshoreman, met and married a fellow refugee from Nazi Germany, supported them both while his bride, Hannah, went to medical school.

After her graduation, the two moved to the West Coast. Now it was Hannah's turn to support Bernard's education. At Berkeley the young German was spotted by a professor of theoretical physics named Robert Oppenheimer, and although Peters was far from possessing the necessary academic credits, Oppenheimer saw to his enrollment in the graduate school of physics. Peters became one of Oppenheimer's prize protégés: he was selected to make notes on Oppenheimer's lectures on quantum mechanics. This implied enormous dedication on Peters' part and considerable trust on Oppenheimer's. It would bring them into close and frequent contact as they prepared the notes for publication.

But the relationship went far beyond that of student and professor. Hannah Peters, in addition to being a close friend of Jean Tatlock's, occasionally served as Oppenheimer's personal physician.* The Oppenheimers and the Peterses saw a good deal of each other socially, especially in 1941, and frequently exchanged visits at one another's houses.

In late 1942, shortly after he had been named to head the Los Alamos laboratory, Oppenheimer talked with the Peterses about joining him at Los Alamos. As a husband and wife team (he a physicist, she a doctor) they added up to what Oppenheimer later described as "an attractive deal." But, as noted earlier, the Peterses decided not to come.

Now, in early 1944, more than a year later, Bernard Peters became the object of conversation between Peters' former men-

* Years later, the government was to allege that Hannah Peters was organizer of the professional section of the Communist Party of Alameda County, California, and that she was among those who, in the period 1942–45, stated that Robert Oppenheimer was then a member of the Communist Party. Oppenheimer's hearing board confirmed that she had made the statement about him, but made no finding as to whether she was or had been a member of the Communist Party.

tor, Robert Oppenheimer, and security officer Peer de Silva. As Oppenheimer later recalled it, de Silva mentioned the names of four former Oppenheimer students (David Bohm, Joseph Weinberg, Bernard Peters and "somebody else") and asked which of the four Oppenheimer would regard as "dangerous." At first Oppenheimer cited Bohm and Peters—but then said he did not think Bohm's personality and temperament were inherently those of a dangerous person. Peters, on the other hand, he described as "quite a Red," and a "crazy person" whose actions were unpredictable. (It had been only a little over a year since Oppenheimer had asked this "crazy" man, this "Red" to become a member of the Los Alamos staff.)

On March 12, 1944, Robert Oppenheimer was once again in Berkeley, once again under the surveillance of intelligence agents, who carefully recorded the following:

6:05 P.M.: Subject and Frank [Oppenheimer] left hotel, and walked up and down Telegraph Avenue and in front of the hotel. Both engaged in earnest conversation with each other.

6:15 P.M.: David Bohm walked south on Telegraph Avenue and met the Oppenheimers in front of the hotel. J. R. Oppenheimer and Bohm engaged in conversation for five minutes but Frank stood about 10 feet away from them and did not participate in the conversation.

6:20 P.M.: Subject and Frank entered car, license 53692, with Oppenheimers' luggage and drove to Fisherman's Wharf, San Francisco.

David Bohm, at this juncture, was a thoroughly dejected young man. He had, earlier, journeyed from Pennsylvania to the California Institute of Technology, bursting to make discoveries that would unlock the secrets of the universe and counting on Caltech to satisfy this yearning. He was acutely disappointed. All Caltech seemed to care about was getting students past their exams. He went to Berkeley and, like so many others, he fell under the Oppenheimer spell.

Then the war came and snatched his new-found idol away. He

wanted desperately to follow, and Oppenheimer told him he thought he ought to be transferred to Los Alamos. At one point Bohm thought it was all arranged, but then the plan suddenly fell through. Bohm was given to understand that security reasons lay behind the cancellation, but no specifics were offered. And so Bohm stayed on in Berkeley, lonely and depressed.

Thus when his hero visited Berkeley in March of 1944, Bohm again, in the closely watched sidewalk exchange, urgently sought a transfer to Los Alamos. Oppenheimer was noncommittal. He said he would let Bohm know if any opportunities opened up at Los Alamos, but that if Bohm didn't hear from him, he should assume that nothing could be worked out and should forget about a transfer.

Ten days later, back at Los Alamos, Oppenheimer related to security officer de Silva the sidewalk conversation he had had with Bohm and asked if de Silva would have objections to Bohm's transfer to Los Alamos. De Silva said he would. Oppenheimer agreed and said he considered the matter closed.

Unsettling as his brushes with security officers may have been, they represented but a small fraction of the problems confronting Robert Oppenheimer as director of the Los Alamos laboratory— a job which, by unanimous accord, evoked and exploited the ultimate in this extraordinary man's extraordinary gifts. It was as if the man and the job had each been created with the other in mind. He himself later regarded it as a summing up of his earlier years. "In a way," he said, "Los Alamos was a kind of confluence of my highbrow past, my physics, my students, my horses, my ranch, and my slight knowledge of politics."

The combination of ingredients in the man produced, apparently, a near-magical result. "His was a shining example of how to run an institution," his long-time friend and Los Alamos associate, Victor Weisskopf, has said. "The main task of a director is to create a spirit, and to do that you have to be involved in every important detail. You had a feeling at Los Alamos that if you did something important, Oppie would know about it."

But one does not need to turn to Oppenheimer's friends for high praise of his Los Alamos directorship. Edward Teller, who fell into increasing disagreement with Oppenheimer during the war, has attributed the timely development of the atom bomb "to a great extent to [Oppenheimer's] leadership."

Each of his unique qualities was called into play. Perhaps most important was his extraordinary persuasiveness with all manner of men. For under the thirty-nine-year-old physicist were gathered world-renowned names of science: Bohr, Fermi, Segrè, Peierls. That they came to Los Alamos, that they worked in harness, not only with each other but with soldiers and with scientists from other disciplines, was due in large measure to Oppenheimer's charismatic powers. Weisskopf credits Oppenheimer with creating at Los Alamos "a new form of scientific life": the creative collaborative effort of a large mass of scientists. (This became a common phenomenon in the huge research laboratories that grew up after the war.) While there were a few other such enterprises in World War II (e.g., the MIT Radiation Lab), those who were at Los Alamos consider it special. In part this was due to Oppenheimer's insistence (to the intense discomfort of General Groves and his apprehensive security staff) on a full sharing of all the knowledge among all the scientists, through regular weekly "colloquia."

Los Alamos exploited, too, Oppenheimer's supreme quickness to learn and his remarkable capacity to see through to the core of a problem, as if X-raying it. Cyril Smith, top metallurgist at Los Alamos, tells of Oppenheimer's joining the tail end of a prolonged but inconclusive discussion among the metallurgical experts. Oppenheimer was, comparatively speaking, a novice in their field; yet, after listening in silence to the discussion, he spoke up. "It seems to me like this," he said, and in a few sentences opened the eyes of the experts to the answer that had eluded them.*

Even with his quickness of learning, Oppenheimer's detailed knowledge of what was going on "in every corner of the lab" (as Edward Teller put it) came only through an almost superhuman dedication to his work. In his large but austere office was a portrait of Lincoln and a modified version of a famous Lincoln

---

* In another instance, when Smith was troubled by the advice he was receiving from one of his specialists, a brief dinnertime conversation with Oppenheimer made it clear to him that he must, in this instance, follow his instincts and override his more expert subordinate. (He proved right in doing so.)

phrase: "This world cannot exist half slave and half free." Oppenheimer's spirit of commitment permeated the entire laboratory. The whistle that roused its personnel every morning at seven was known as "Oppie's whistle"; no one needed to be told that their director had long since been up and about.

Perhaps the most succinct tribute to the spirit of the community he generated within Los Alamos' barbed-wire enclosure is contained in one phrase of Victor Weisskopf's: "We felt 'the fence' kept the rest of the world from us, not us from them."

The pace at which Oppenheimer lived and worked in those war years was not without its physical cost. At the end of his Los Alamos ordeal his six-foot frame had wasted away to a scant 115 pounds. And yet, Weisskopf has observed, his total absorption in his work seemed to make his personality stronger and more positive than it had ever been before. And this strength, coupled with an arrogant and often abrasive strain in the man, was bound to bring him into conflict with other forceful persons at Los Alamos. Of these, none was more forceful than the brilliant but strong-willed and vain Hungarian physicist, Edward Teller.

As personalities, Teller and Oppenheimer were acutely dissimilar. Teller was voluble and gregarious, Oppenheimer quiet and private; Teller was extravagant in speech and in thought, Oppenheimer more precise in both.

Teller, it has been said, invests a great deal in his friendships and is painfully hurt when he feels rebuffed. The kinship he had felt with Oppenheimer at Berkeley in the summer of 1942 evidently meant much to Teller, and he may well have felt injured when Oppenheimer, in the early days of Los Alamos, selected Hans Bethe rather than him to head the crucial Theoretical Division. At least, many former colleagues think this was the incident that started their feud. Later, the injury was aggravated when Oppenheimer again passed over Teller and named Victor Weisskopf as Bethe's second-in-command.

Moreover, the project that had united them intellectually the previous summer—the thermonuclear superbomb—had been forced by circumstances to take a distinct back seat. Teller had fully expected the "Super" to be a major goal of the Los Alamos effort, but when the problems of producing a fission bomb proved greater than anticipated, the fusion bomb had to be put aside "for the duration." Whatever the reason or reasons, relations between the two men deteriorated badly; and whereas both men could be extremely winning, both could also be cutting, and colleagues remember that even in chance encounters in the Los Alamos corridors, the friction between the two was evident.

Oppenheimer was later to describe Russia and the United States as "two scorpions in a bottle." Some believe this is an apt description of Oppenheimer and Teller at Los Alamos and in the years that followed.

Teller also developed deep differences with Hans Bethe, with whom he had also worked closely in the 1942 Berkeley study group. Teller persisted in his preoccupation with the thermonuclear problem and, as Bethe recalls it, "He did not do the work which he and his group were supposed to do." Bethe has recalled that in late 1943, sensing Teller's dissatisfaction and frustration, he asked the volatile Hungarian to head up the theoretical work on what Bethe thought was the most challenging new problem facing the division: the "implosion" process.* Bethe has recalled that although he pressed Teller over a period of weeks to take on the assignment, Teller flatly refused. Ultimately, he was assigned to a special project of his own, independent of the main line of work in the laboratory, concentrating on the "Super," even though, as Teller himself later observed, "we had to win the war and there was no time for the super."

While work on the bomb proceeded at Los Alamos, Rossi Lomanitz, holder of a master's degree in theoretical physics, continued his national service as a low-ranking soldier (by August, 1944, he had risen to the rank of private, first class). He had been shunted from one division to another, transferred out of each one just before it was about to be sent overseas. He was still anxious that better use be made of his physics training. He again wrote to Oppenheimer, who, on August 14, sent him a "To Whom It May Concern" memorandum. In it, Oppenheimer stated he knew Lomanitz as "an extremely talented student, conscientious, of unusual intelligence [with] a thorough grounding in modern

* Whereby a large energy release, instead of bursting outward, as in an explosion, would be contained and forced inward.

physical theory." Recalling his earlier "high-priority" war work at the Berkeley laboratory, Oppenheimer concluded:

> Here again I can recommend his performance unreservedly, both from the point of view of scruple and energy and from the point of view of its high technical proficiency.
>
>                                        J. R. OPPENHEIMER

But Rossi Lomanitz was destined to remain A.S.N. 39140466 throughout the war. He rose, ultimately, to the rank of corporal.

In some respects it is ironic that a major factor in Robert Oppenheimer's later downfall should have been the charge that he had opposed the development of a hydrogen bomb, for during the war years he was *positively* inclined toward the "Super." Its theoretical aspects had engaged his keen interest in the Berkeley summer study group in 1942, and when, in September of 1944, Washington headquarters requested his views on the character of postwar research in the nuclear field, he responded: "I should like to put in writing at an early date the recommendation that the subject of initiating violent thermonuclear reactions be pursued with vigor and diligence, and promptly." Two weeks later, he followed this with another memorandum to Washington in which he characterized as "worthy of further research" the thermonuclear process, which, he flatly said, "should afford an energy release some ten thousand times greater than those from presently contemplated designs."

Robert Oppenheimer was not alone in his concern with the postwar posture of the United States. Such thoughts were brought vividly to the mind of William Liscum Borden one night in November of 1944. Borden, who, after Yale, had become an Air Corps pilot, was flying his Liberator bomber toward the English coast after a mission to Holland when suddenly the blackness of the night was filled with a bright crimson glare. Overhead passed a German V-2 rocket, streaming red sparks, headed for London. Borden's plane had taken nearly two hours to get from Holland, and was still a half-hour from home base. The rocket, by contrast, had left Holland just four minutes earlier, and struck London within instants.

The experience had a profound effect on Borden. In fact, it provided the "emotional impetus" for a book he was to write upon his discharge from the Air Force, for at that instant "I became convinced that it was only a matter of time until rockets would expose the United States to direct, transoceanic attack."

Later in that same November, 1944, two American scientists made a discovery of great importance. It was a scientific discovery, but not the kind so urgently sought at Los Alamos. The scientists, poring over captured German scientific documents in the newly captured city of Strasbourg, France, pieced together the startling information that the Germans not only had failed to develop an atomic bomb, but were not even within striking distance of success.

The news of this discovery, although classified "Top Secret," is said to have traveled quickly around Allied laboratories. To many atomic scientists who learned of the German nuclear failure, the prime motivation for helping develop this new instrument of devastation had disappeared. In ensuing months, especially in the Chicago atomic laboratory, where the time deadlines were less urgent than at Los Alamos, scientists began to focus increasing attention on long-range atomic problems, as well as the imminent question of how and where to introduce the first atomic bomb to the world.

In early 1945, Peer de Silva, the Army's security officer at Los Alamos, was transferred to a new assignment. Before leaving he did two contradictory things. On the one hand, he made a point of alerting his successor, Lieutenant Thomas O. Jones, to his doubts about Robert Oppenheimer's loyalty. To Oppenheimer himself, however, de Silva addressed the warm, friendly, "Dear Oppie" letter mentioned earlier. It began:

Upon my transfer from duty at the project, I want you to know of my sincere appreciation of the support and encouragement which you have personally given me during my services here. In spite of your many more urgent problems and duties, *your consideration and help* on matters I have brought to you have been gratifying and *have, in fact, contributed much to whatever success my office has had in performing its [security] mission.* [Emphasis added.]

Nine years later, the recipient of that laudatory letter would be adjudged guilty of "a serious disregard for the requirements of the security system," of "a consistent disregard of a reasonable security system," and of a "willful disregard of the normal and proper obligations of security."

De Silva's letter to Oppenheimer was dated April 11, 1945. The next day, Franklin D. Roosevelt died suddenly at Warm Springs, Georgia. One of the first at the Los Alamos laboratory to learn the news, via a telephone call from Washington, was de Silva's successor, Thomas O. Jones. Shocked, Jones dashed out of his office and, on the second-story catwalk that joined the buildings on either side of the often muddy "main street" of Los Alamos, he encountered J. Robert Oppenheimer.

"Is it true, Thomas O.?" the physicist inquired. Jones confirmed that the news was indeed true. For a moment Oppenheimer looked silently at Jones. Then, standing on that pedestrian catwalk, he began talking about FDR. Not many months previously, he had spoken with the President, and now he recalled how gracious FDR had been. There was, in Oppenheimer's voice, an undisguised, authentic admiration.

The conversation was a brief one, but it made a vivid impression on Thomas O. Jones. Later he reflected on it, against the background of Peer de Silva's doubts about Robert Oppenheimer. The more he reflected on the almost awed respect in which the scientist clearly held the office of the American presidency, the more firmly Jones felt that this man was not—in fact, could not be—disloyal to his country.

On Wednesday, April 25, 1945, delegates from forty-six nations met in San Francisco to begin laying plans for a new United Nations Organization to succeed the impotent League of Nations. (Among the French-English interpreters was a former university instructor by the name of Haakon Chevalier.)

At noon that same day, in Washington, Secretary of War Henry L. Stimson and General Groves briefed the new President of the

United States on the atomic weapon under development. Stimson stressed America's "moral responsibility" in creating "the most terrible weapon ever known in human history, one bomb of which could destroy a whole city." President Truman approved the idea of an "Interim Committee" to formulate long-range plans for the use and control of nuclear energy. One of those named to that committee, President James B. Conant of Harvard, well aware of other scientists' growing discomfort about the atom, recommended creation of a Scientific Advisory Panel to the committee, and suggested four names: Ernest O. Lawrence of the Berkeley Radiation Laboratory; Arthur Compton of the Chicago Metallurgical Laboratory (where the scientists' deepest unrest was centered); Enrico Fermi, also of Chicago; and J. Robert Oppenheimer, director of the Los Alamos laboratory.

On the last day of May, the Interim Committee and its Scientific Advisory Panel held an all-day meeting in Washington. Robert Oppenheimer spoke up on at least three topics. First, he favored a free postwar exchange of atomic information, especially on the atom's peaceful uses. Second, he suggested broaching the subject of the bomb with the Russians (who, he said, had always been friendly to science and whose attitudes should not be prejudged).* Third, Oppenheimer argued against the notion of a demonstration test of the A-bomb (as distinct from its actual military use against Japan) as a means of first introducing it to the world. No such demonstration, he said, could be sufficiently spectacular to convince the Japanese to end the war. On the basis of this and other technical arguments, the Interim Committee recommended: (1) using the bomb against Japan; (2) choosing a military target surrounded by a civilian population; and (3) dropping the bomb without prior warning.

But the idea of a demonstration use of the first A-bomb remained stubbornly alive, principally in a report prepared by a group of Chicago nuclear scientists headed by Oppenheimer's former professor, James Franck. The "Franck Report" predicted that any American nuclear monopoly would be short-lived, and

* Oppenheimer received support for this suggestion from General George C. Marshall, who even went so far as to suggest inviting prominent Russians to witness the first U.S. test shot of the atomic device. But this was decisively vetoed by Presidential Assistant James F. Byrnes.

that in the inevitable nuclear arms race the United States, with its population and industry concentrated in huge cities, would be under a decided handicap. Since America's only long-run hope of avoiding such a disadvantage—international control of the atom —would be badly prejudiced by an unannounced first use of the bomb against Japan, the report urged an initial demonstration "in an appropriately selected uninhabited area."

This proposal (although apparently not the actual Franck Report itself) was put before the four members of the Scientific Advisory Panel at a Los Alamos meeting on June 16. The four scientists were in the harshest of dilemmas. On the one hand, they were keenly sympathetic to the apprehensions of the Chicago scientists. On the other, they, unlike the Chicago group, had been advised by the Pentagon that without a direct use of the bomb a costly invasion of Japan was inevitable. Not being military experts, they felt in no position to contradict.

In that troubled weekend of debate at Los Alamos, Oppenheimer's role seems to have been ambivalent. As he later recalled it, "I set forth my anxieties and the arguments . . . against dropping [the bomb] . . . but I did not endorse them." In the end, the last holdout for a desert-island demonstration of the bomb was not Oppenheimer, as his idolators might have expected, but Ernest O. Lawrence, who, ironically, was later to become one of the most zealous advocates of the vastly more devastating hydrogen bomb.

The four ultimately concluded that they could "see no acceptable alternative to direct military use" of the bomb. They ended their report on a modest note: even though as nuclear scientists they had had special opportunity to think about the implications of atomic energy, they could claim no "special competence in solving the political, social and military problems which are presented by the advent of atomic power."

That very attitude was, a month later, the subject of a conversation at Los Alamos between Oppenheimer and Teller, one that rankled with Teller for years to come and may well have been an important factor behind the extremely damaging testimony he was to present against Oppenheimer. The conversation dealt with a petition that scientist Leo Szilard asked Teller to sign and circulate at Los Alamos, urging the President not to use the atomic bomb unless and until U.S. surrender terms had been explained to and rejected by the Japanese. Teller was sympathetic to the petition, but did not want to support or circulate it without conferring with Oppenheimer, whom he considered not only the constituted authority but the natural leader at Los Alamos. As Teller later recounted the conversation, Oppenheimer told him, "in a polite and convincing way that he thought it improper for a scientist to use his prestige as a platform for political pronouncements."

At the time, Teller felt relieved, and decided not to circulate the petition. But four years later, when Oppenheimer opposed the hydrogen bomb largely on what Teller regarded as political grounds, Teller was infuriated. He regarded Oppenheimer's stance as a flagrant violation of the advice he had given Teller in 1945—advice that Teller bitterly regretted following.

The Scientific Panel's recommendation of a direct bomb-drop on Japan was endorsed in Washington by the Interim Committee, but one of its members remained troubled. Ralph A. Bard, the Navy's representative on the committee, felt so strongly that this would prejudice America's position as a great humanitarian nation that he resigned as Under Secretary of the Navy.

To succeed Bard on the committee, Navy Secretary Frank Knox appointed a reserve captain by the name of Lewis Lichtenstein Strauss. Shortly thereafter, the Interim Committee held a meeting in Stimson's office. Both Oppenheimer and Strauss were present. It was the first time the two had met.

At forty-five seconds past 5:29 A.M. of July 16, 1945, the months and years of agonized effort by Robert Oppenheimer and his associates were culminated. "Trinity." The first explosive release of the atom's energy. The dawn of the atomic era.

Oppenheimer's mental association at that blazing instant is, by now, legendary. To the mind of this student of Sanskrit came the words of the Hindu epic, the Bhagavad-Gita:

If the radiance of a thousand suns
Were to burst at once into the sky,
That would be like the splendor of the Mighty One. . . .

And then, an instant later:

I am become Death,
The destroyer of worlds.

In later years, the power that had been unleashed over the Southwestern desert would tear at Oppenheimer's conscience; a decade later, that power would be, in a large sense, a destroyer of Oppenheimer's world. But for the moment, it mainly brought relief and great satisfaction. Within seventy-two hours, laudatory words from Washington would begin to be heaped on Oppenheimer and his colleagues. General Groves called the achievement "a high-water mark of scientific and engineering performance. Your leadership and skill and the loyal and able performance of all your subordinates made it possible." Oppenheimer was later to recall that at the time "it was hard for us in Los Alamos not to share that satisfaction, and hard for me not to accept the conclusion that I had managed the enterprise well and played a key part in its success."

In the ensuing days, however, "the whole community [of Los Alamos] experienced a kind of cathartic shock," according to one authoritative account. "Unfaced issues suddenly loomed large. The scientists now talked of little else but the effect of the bomb upon the postwar world." But for Robert Oppenheimer and the other principals at Los Alamos, there could have been little time for such thoughts: there was still the task of readying the bomb for the drop on Japan. In the early days of August, on his return from the Potsdam Conference aboard the cruiser *Augusta*, Harry S Truman gave the final go-ahead for the drop on Hiroshima.

On August 6, 1945, the world was introduced to the power of the atom.

At Los Alamos, eight thousand miles from the scene of the holocaust, Oppenheimer strode down the aisle of an auditorium. Mounting the podium, he raised his clasped hands above his head, after the manner of the victorious prizefighter. He told his colleagues that the first atomic bomb had successfully detonated over Hiroshima.

Unlike the occasion of "Trinity," there was little exultation at Los Alamos that day. No one, of course, yet knew the ghastly statistics—78,000 killed, 13,000 missing, 37,000 injured, three-fifths of an entire city totally destroyed. None of the scientists had yet heard what their colleague, Philip Morrison, would soon broadcast over the Albuquerque radio station, after his return from a flight over Hiroshima to assess the bomb's effects:

> We circled finally low over Hiroshima and stared in disbelief. There below was the flat level ground of what had been a city, scorched red. . . . But no hundreds of planes had visited this town during a long night. One bomber, and one bomb, had, in the time it takes a rifle bullet to cross the city, turned a city of three hundred thousand into a burning pyre. That was the new thing.

None of this was yet known at Los Alamos. And yet the efforts of a few to assemble a celebratory party proved at best half-hearted. According to one account: "People either stayed away or beat a hasty retreat. Oppenheimer found a level-headed young group leader being sick in the bushes and knew that the reaction had begun."

# 3. *Transition*

On the evening of August 30, 1945—sixteen days after the surrender of Japan—a new organization was born: the Association of Los Alamos Scientists, ALAS for short. It represented a determination on the part of the scientists to act as a group in trying to influence postwar nuclear policy. Twice before they had been dissuaded from such group discussions by Robert Oppenheimer, who had argued there was little the scientists could appropriately do until the war had ended and they were no longer inhibited by the bonds of secrecy. But now that the war was over, there was no reason to wait further. No less than five hundred Los Alamosites answered the call to gather in Theater No. 2 (the largest meeting place at Los Alamos), ALAS was formed, and a committee was named to draft a statement on the postwar significance of atomic energy. Less than a decade later the members of this committee—Hans Bethe, Jerrold Zacharias, Frank Oppenheimer and Edward Teller—would be bitterly divided at the security hearing of J. Robert Oppenheimer. But now they were united in their concern about the implications of the nuclear monster they had helped create.

Isolated on their remote New Mexico mesa, the scientists needed a link with the world of action. Their director, Robert Oppenheimer, seemed ideal for such a role, for he was now meeting regularly with Washington's highest officials, and so the scientists resolved to rely on him. They gave him "The Document" (their statement urging international control of atomic energy), asking him to seek Washington approval for its public release at Los Alamos.

Oppenheimer agreed to do so, but his behavior in ensuing days caused growing resentment among ALAS scientists. At first he told the ALAS group that the "situation looked real good." A few days later he wrote Victor Weisskopf that the government had made the ALAS paper a state document, thus barring its release at Los Alamos. Oppenheimer said he concurred in this action, believing that a group statement was strongly inadvisable. Individual letter-writing was all right, he said, so long as it was discreet and did not smack of group action.

In a teletype message two days later, Oppenheimer urged that public discussion by the scientists await an imminent presidential message to Congress on the postwar atom. He said his consultations "not only with Dr. [Vannevar] Bush, General Groves and [Stimson aide George] Harrison but with the acting Secretary of State and the new Secretary of War" convinced him that there was no basic disagreement with the ALAS memorandum.

That evening, Willie Higinbotham, the new chairman of ALAS, reported all this to the ALAS membership in Theater No. 2. While deploring the suppression of the ALAS document as "a matter of political expediency," Higinbotham told the group: "We have one representative who does know what is going on and knows personally the people involved, that is, Oppie. . . . The [executive] committee [of ALAS] will vouch for his attitude and everyone knows his ability. . . . We still believe and urge you to go along with Oppie and the Administration."

But when the Administration plan for the management of the atomic energy effort was made public some days later, most of the scientists felt they had been badly let down. Their prime goal was to avoid military control over the atom, yet the Administration proposal did not bar military officers from serving either as the full-time administrator of the proposed new Federal atomic agency or on the nine-man overseeing committee. The suggested plan also called for tight government control over atomic research and, even more noxious, the power to bar scientific discussion of matters the government might deem "secret," on pain of heavy fines and jail sentences. And it lacked any provision for sharing research results with scientists from other countries.

The bill stirred a furor among the atomic scientists at the various Manhattan District laboratories, with the Chicago laboratory the center of the storm. Herbert Anderson, a Los Alamos scientist visiting Chicago, wrote a furious letter to Higinbotham, which concluded:

I must confess my confidence in our leaders, Oppenheimer, Lawrence, Compton, and Fermi . . . who enjoined us to have faith in them and not influence this legislation, is shaken. I believe that these worthy men were duped—that they never had a chance to see this bill.

If Oppenheimer was aware of the discontent among his former associates, it was not reflected in his public posture on the new legislation. When Washington sought a public statement of support from the four-man Scientific Advisory Panel so as to counter the growing protest, Oppenheimer promptly dispatched a telegram to the new Secretary of War, on behalf of himself, Lawrence and Fermi:

WE WOULD MOST STRONGLY URGE THE PASSAGE OF THE LEGISLATION NOW BEFORE CONGRESS . . . DELAY WILL COST US HEAVILY IN EFFICIENCY, IN ACCOMPLISHMENT AND IN SPIRIT. . . . WE ASSURE YOU THAT IN OUR OPINION THE LEGISLATION AS PRESENTED REPRESENTS THE FRUITS OF WELL-INFORMED AND EXPERIENCED CONSIDERATION.

But this did not stem the scientists' protest. On the contrary, they began to descend on Washington to make their views known directly to Senators and Congressmen. Many were on hand when, in mid-October, Robert Oppenheimer was questioned by a Senate committee about the new legislation. Those who assumed he had represented them in the drafting of the measure were surprised to hear Oppenheimer tell the Senators that he didn't "know much" about the bill.

Appearing before a House committee the next day, the physicist acknowledged that the authority granted by the bill was too sweeping, but he urged prompt passage so as to avoid further delays in nuclear research and in negotiations for international control. Again he disclaimed participation in the drafting of the measure. Skirting the substantive objections of the scientists, he instead emphasized the stature of those who had shaped it—Drs. Bush and Conant, "with the knowledge and agreement" of Henry L. Stimson. "I think if they liked the philosophy of this bill . . . it is a very strong argument."

On November 2, 1945, an era came to an end—for the Los Alamos laboratory and for Robert Oppenheimer. On that evening, five hundred Los Alamos scientists and their wives gathered in Theater No. 2 to hear their director speak to them for the last time.

There may well have been some bewilderment at Oppenheimer's decision to leave the laboratory so soon, for in recent weeks many of the scientists had been the targets of eloquent pleas by the director about their high duty to stay on, rather than return to their prewar posts. As for Oppenheimer himself, he had told General Groves that he "was the director of an emergency," and would not "be the right person to preside over the [postwar] change or the new effort." Besides, he later recalled, "there was not much left in me at the moment."

Nonetheless, to many a Los Alamosite his speech that evening stands out as one of their most vivid memories of the war. In that moment, Robert Oppenheimer was again one with his scientific brethren, and he spoke as one of them. "We are not only scientists," he told his audience, "we are men, too. We cannot forget our dependence on our fellow men . . . our deep moral dependence, in that the value of science must lie in the world of men. . . . These are the strongest bonds in the world, stronger than those even that bind us to one another; these are the deepest bonds—that bind us to our fellow men."

Among those who felt most bereft—almost betrayed—by Oppenheimer's departure was Edward Teller. Throughout the wartime concentration on the fission bomb, he alone at Los Alamos had remained preoccupied with the problem of the next nuclear step, the development of a thermo-nuclear bomb. Several times he had considered leaving the laboratory, but when Oppenheimer urged him to continue his work on the "Super," he had come to expect that once the fission bomb was proven successful, Oppenheimer and the other scientists would turn to the H-bomb with the same concentrated team effort. But in the wake of Hiroshima Oppenheimer had done a sudden about-face. Rather than urging Teller to stay on at Los Alamos, he advised him to return to his university.

Later that fall, when Oppenheimer visited Los Alamos, the two talked again. Teller appealed to Oppenheimer to support the programs he felt essential for the laboratory—either an intensive testing of fission weapons or a thorough H-bomb research effort.

When Oppenheimer said he was not in a position to do so, Teller said he would leave the laboratory, and Oppenheimer agreed that he should. According to Teller, Oppenheimer closed the subject at a party that evening by saying, "We have done a wonderful job here, and it will be many years before anyone can improve on our work in any way."

The following February, Edward Teller left Los Alamos.

For most of his personal friends, Robert Oppenheimer had vanished when he had left Berkeley, in March, 1943; they knew nothing of Los Alamos. With Hiroshima, he reappeared, as headlines identified him as the director of the laboratory that had fabricated the atomic bomb. Among those who wrote him was his old friend Haakon Chevalier, who could now understand, he said, the "sombre note" of his last few meetings with Oppenheimer. "There is a weight in such a venture which few men in history have had to bear. I know that with your love of men, it is no light thing to have had a part, and a great part, in a diabolical contrivance for destroying them. But in the possibilities of death are also the possibilities of life, and these I know have been uppermost in your mind." Oppenheimer responded with three handwritten pages from "P.O. Box 1663, Santa Fe, New Mexico," the postal address of the Los Alamos laboratory. He described his concern over the death-dealing invention he had helped to create and his determination that some good should come of it. He passed on some family news—about the arrival of a baby girl in the Oppenheimer family. He concluded with good wishes for Chevalier's new novel, expressing the hope that the Oppenheimers and the Chevaliers would be able to celebrate its completion together over some new culinary dishes the physicist had developed during the war years—"the sole sure evidence of achievement."

The reunion of the four friends would have to wait some months, however. By the time Oppenheimer left Los Alamos and returned to teaching at Caltech in Pasadena, Chevalier was some five thousand miles away, in Nuremberg, Germany. Although he had been unable to clear the security-screening net of the FBI and the Office of War Information, he had been engaged (and cleared without question) as an interpreter at the Nazi war crime trials, by the War Department—the very agency that had been in charge of the frenetic wartime probe of the infamous "Chevalier incident."

New Year's Day, 1946, found the Oppenheimers back in Berkeley, visiting the Frank Oppenheimers. Frank had spent the early part of the war at the Oak Ridge atomic facility, and he was credited by many with the important and difficult accomplishment of getting the delicate isotope separators to work in producing the fissionable materials for the A-bomb. Later he helped with the preparations for the first test explosion at Alamagordo. He left the project after the war with a warm letter of praise from General Groves for his wartime work, which Groves termed "an essential factor in our success."

On that New Year's Day, according to the charges later brought against Robert Oppenheimer, he met in Frank's house with two alleged Communist Party members and commented on some matters that one of them hoped to take up at a forthcoming party convention in Sacramento. Oppenheimer later had no recollection of such a meeting, but there were indications (in information apparently possessed and questions asked by the government's attorney in Oppenheimer's security hearing) that the New Year's meeting was the object of close government surveillance.* In any event, Oppenheimer's judges concluded that the meeting had taken place.

When Oppenheimer returned to California from Los Alamos, it was with the hope and intention of devoting full time to his teaching. But he was soon summoned to Washington to help develop a plan for the international control of atomic energy. After two months of intensive work, a report was issued under the names of Under Secretary of State Dean Acheson and TVA Chairman David Lilienthal. But those familiar with it say that it bore the stamp of Robert Oppenheimer more than that of any other single individual. Its plan for international control of the

---

* The government's attorney, Roger Robb, asked Oppenheimer such detailed questions about that meeting as, "Do you recall that Mrs. Oppenheimer . . . was ill that day?" and "You were not staying in the same house as your brother was in, were you?" When Oppenheimer replied, "We were in sort of a barn," Robb said, "That is correct. Don't you recall that Mrs. Oppenheimer was not feeling good, and she stayed in the barn and you went over to your brother's house and talked to [the two alleged Communists]?"

atom—including America's offer to give up its monopoly over the A-bomb—would later be laid before the United Nations by Bernard Baruch as a choice "between the quick and the dead."

One day during his work on the international control report, Robert Oppenheimer accompanied Dean Acheson into the oval White House office of Harry S Truman. The amenities were scarcely over when the scientist, apparently remorseful about his role in the production of the A-bomb, startled the President by blurting out, "Mr. President, I have blood on my hands." If he had set out by design to offend Harry Truman, he could hardly have thought of a more effective device. "Don't you bring that fellow around again," Truman later told Acheson. "After all, all he did was make the bomb. I'm the guy who fired it off."

While Oppenheimer was working on the Acheson-Lilienthal report in Washington, across the country, in Los Angeles, a geophysicist named David Tressel Griggs first became acquainted with the radical background of J. Robert Oppenheimer. Griggs was among the first full-time employees of the RAND Corporation, a newly formed organization conducting research for the Pentagon, and from a RAND associate Griggs learned that at Los Alamos Oppenheimer had been regarded as a definite calculated security risk. Since the information came from a person Griggs respected, he took it seriously. At the time he was not in a position to act on such a report; but later, as Chief Scientist for the United States Air Force, he was to hear similar reports and was to act on them in a way that would significantly affect Robert Oppenheimer.

In 1946, a prescient book was published. Its title: *There Will Be No Time: The Revolution in Strategy*. Its subject: the specter of intercontinental atomic-tipped rockets "fired from within the aggressor's own country" and reaching their destination within an hour's time. Its author: William Liscum Borden, whose tenacious recollection of the fearsome German V-2 rocket speeding toward London had prompted him, a year later, after Hiroshima, to write of his concern that the "honeymoon of military security" had ended at the moment "that rockets and atomic bombs made their appearance." To Borden, the danger of a "rocket Pearl Harbor" demanded drastic steps, such as the amassing of "a whole war's supply of weapons on hand in advance of any fighting" and such as legislation "authorizing the armed forces to act instantly in case of attack, regardless of whether Congress is in session." As he saw it, all domestic problems were "of the most trivial consequence." There was "only one fundamental issue: whether or not the nation will survive."

It was against the background of such an outlook that Borden would later observe, and judge, Robert Oppenheimer's opposition to the hydrogen bomb and other national defense measures that Borden considered essential to the "survival of the nation."

In the late spring of 1946, Robert and Kitty Oppenheimer were reunited with the Haakon Chevaliers for the first time in three years. On their first postwar visit to San Francisco, they drove the twenty miles out to the Chevaliers' cottage at Stinson Beach for a weekend reunion. To Chevalier, just back from Nuremberg, there was a marked change in Oppenheimer's political views since they had last known each other. Oppenheimer had some very uncomplimentary things to say both about the American Communist Party and about the Soviet Union. These jarred Chevalier's ears, but he chose not to get into political debate with his friend.

Shortly thereafter, at noon on a Saturday in early June, Chevalier received a visit from two agents of the Federal Bureau of Investigation. They were anxious to ask him some questions in connection with an investigation they were conducting, and they insistently invited Chevalier to accompany them to the Bureau's San Francisco office. According to Chevalier's later account of the interview, the questioning ultimately focused on his acquaintanceship with and knowledge of George C. Eltenton. Then there were a few references to Robert Oppenheimer. Chevalier began to wonder whether the agents knew of his "kitchen conversation" with Oppenheimer more than three years before, but he volunteered nothing about it, not wanting, he has said, to get either Eltenton or Oppenheimer into trouble.

Finally, he has recalled, one of the FBI agents pulled a folder from a stack of reports he had been fingering. He opened it and said, "I have here three affidavits from three scientists on the atomic bomb project. Each of them testifies that you approached him on three separate occasions for the purpose of obtaining secret information on the atomic bomb on behalf of Russian agents." Chevalier says that he asked for but was denied the names of the three scientists. Ultimately he decided he should relate the truth about Eltenton's conversation with him and his subsequent talk in the Eagle Hill kitchen with Oppenheimer.

The agents, he has said, still insisted that he was holding something back. The questioning dragged on. Finally, they persuaded Chevalier to sign a statement confirming his account of the conversations with Eltenton and Oppenheimer, then drove him back to Stinson Beach. It was around ten that night when he finally arrived home, as he later recalled. He had been with the agents nearly ten hours.

During the marathon interview, Chevalier has said, the telephone in the FBI office rang repeatedly. Also, the principal interrogator would excuse himself from time to time, go into another room, talk briefly on the phone and then return to the questioning. Some time later, Chevalier met George Eltenton at a luncheon party in Berkeley. He mentioned his prolonged interrogation by the FBI; Eltenton said he, too, had been questioned. They compared notes, and established that they had both been interviewed on the same afternoon—Chevalier in San Francisco and Eltenton in Oakland. Eltenton had had the same experience of the repeated telephone interruptions, and the two concluded that the questioners were keeping in constant communication in order to exploit any discrepancies that might arise between the two stories. According to Chevalier, there were none, even though he and Eltenton had not seen each other for years and each had been picked up by the FBI without any warning. This was the first time either had been questioned about the conversation of three years earlier, and Chevalier says that both men wondered how the FBI had gotten wind of it.

Chevalier determined to broach the matter with Oppenheimer. The opportunity came when the Oppenheimers returned briefly to their Berkeley home on Eagle Hill and gave a large cocktail party. Chevalier has recalled that he and his wife were invited to come over before the rest of the guests were to arrive. According to Chevalier, he immediately brought up the matter of the exchange with the FBI; Oppenheimer's face darkened, and he suggested they go outside into the garden. As the two paced back and forth, Chevalier says he told Oppenheimer of recounting to the FBI the Eltenton approach and the "kitchen conversation" with Oppenheimer. The physicist told Chevalier he had been right to do so and said he, too, had had to report it to the authorities. Chevalier says he then questioned Oppenheimer about the alleged approaches to *three* scientists on the atomic project. According to Chevalier, Oppenheimer gave no answer to the question. He seemed "extremely nervous and tense." Twice Kitty came out into the garden to say that the guests were arriving. On the second occasion, Chevalier says, when Kitty became insistent that Robert come inside to greet his friends, the usually mild-mannered Oppenheimer turned on his wife and unleashed "a flood of foul language" to the effect that Kitty should mind her own business and leave him alone. Chevalier has said it was the first time he had ever seen his friend "behave immoderately."

By this time, according to Chevalier, the two men had said all there was to say. Nonetheless, Oppenheimer seemed reluctant to end this "odd, one-sided exchange." Presently, though, the two went into the house and joined the cocktail party.

Three months later, on September 5, 1946, it was Oppenheimer's turn to be questioned by agents of the FBI. Their main interest, it seemed, was Haakon Chevalier and the extent of Oppenheimer's connections with him.

Whatever ambiguities Oppenheimer may have left with General Groves in 1943 concerning his own role in the "kitchen conversation" with Chevalier were now resolved in his interview with the FBI. He explicitly told the agents that his story to Colonels Pash and Lansdale concerning the *three* scientist-contacts in the atomic project had been a fabrication.

But the agents' curiosity extended beyond Haakon Chevalier. Had Oppenheimer, for example, been present at two prewar meetings in the San Francisco area, attended by "persons definitely identified with the Communist Party"? What had been the purpose of these meetings? Who had attended?

Oppenheimer declined to answer these questions, because they seemed to him to have little bearing on the agents' main interest, Haakon Chevalier. Besides, he later recalled, the agents indicated to him that their questions about the meetings were really not of substantive interest to them. Oppenheimer quoted them as saying, "We just do this sort of thing to test your veracity." Nonetheless, it was largely on the basis of Oppenheimer's failure to answer these questions in this 1946 interrogation that the scientist was judged guilty of "a serious disregard for the requirements of the security system."

The agents also asked Oppenheimer about certain of his former students, including Joseph Weinberg and Rossi Lomanitz. Oppenheimer asked what was "wrong" with them, and the agents said there was "a question of their membership in the Communist Party." In his security hearing eight years later he was to swear that this was the first time he had heard more than a rumor about Joseph Weinberg's party membership. But this was contrary to his earlier statement to Colonel Lansdale that he had learned of Weinberg's party status in 1943. Some of Oppenheimer's security judges were to consider this discrepancy evidence of the scientist's untruthfulness.

In the fall of 1946, Oppenheimer took steps to disengage himself from the last "radical" group with which his name remained connected—the Independent Citizens Committee of the Arts, Sciences and Professions (ICCASP), of which he was then listed as a vice chairman. In late September the organization had endorsed an attack by Henry A. Wallace on the Administration's nuclear policies, which Robert Oppenheimer had helped to shape. On October 11 Oppenheimer wrote the ICCASP. "I should not wish to argue," he said gently, "that there was nothing sound in Mr. Wallace's comments, nor for a moment to cast doubt on the validity of his great sense of concern" about international control of the atom. Yet he was convinced that Wallace's call for an immediate nuclear treaty with Russia was of "an illusory nature." He therefore wished to resign, unless he had badly misunderstood the ICCASP position.

The organization made one valiant attempt to persuade Oppenheimer he had misunderstood, but he insisted on resigning, "since the alternative, to make public my dissident views, is repugnant to me and can help neither the ICCASP nor the cause of world peace which is surely our greatest common aim." This time the resignation stuck, and Robert Oppenheimer was out of the organization.

Early in 1946 Winston Churchill, in Fulton, Missouri, introduced the phrase "Iron Curtain" into the political lexicon, and warned of the enmity of the Soviet Union. Increasingly, public attention was focused on the threat of espionage by Soviet agents or even by American Russophiles. In Washington, former Communist Louis Budenz told the Un-American Activities Committee of the links between the American Communist Party and the Soviet Union.

But a more alarming disclosure came from Canada, where in June a Royal Commission revealed that the Soviets had succeeded in establishing an espionage ring that had stolen high military secrets. Igor Gouzenko, the Russian informant, indicated to Canadian authorities that similar activities were being carried on in the United States.

In the U.S. that October, the danger of infiltration was highlighted in a widely publicized report by the United States Chamber of Commerce. Not only did the report allege Communist influence in governmental departments; it charged that Communists or "fellow travelers" had made substantial inroads into nongovernmental groups, especially labor unions. The Chamber's warning flag was up for "Socialists" as well as Communists, since, the Chamber contended, the only essential difference lay in the Socialists' use of constitutional methods to promote their policies.

A similar theme was introduced that fall into the first postwar Congressional elections as anti-Communist Republican candidates sought to emphasize the "radical" character of their liberal Democratic opponents. In southern California, for example, an unknown young lawyer named Richard Nixon was successful in pinning the "radical" label on incumbent Congressman Jerry Voorhis, and in unseating the ten-year Congressional veteran.

Elected with Nixon in a broad Republican sweep of both Houses of Congress were such rabid anti-Communists as Indiana's William Jenner, Ohio's John Bricker, California's William Knowland —and a young judge from Wisconsin by the name of Joseph R. McCarthy.

Both Congress and the Administration responded to the growing public concern about the "Communist problem" and the danger of espionage. Congress acted first, in the dramatic new area of "atomic secrets." An important feature of the Atomic Energy Act of 1946, which transferred the nuclear program from military to civilian hands, was the requirement that each prospective employee of the new Atomic Energy Commission be subjected to a *pre*-employment investigation by the FBI, as a means of appraising employees' "character, associations, and loyalty."

The framework of the atomic security program had originated in Congress, but the Truman Administration was unwilling to leave the initiative on Capitol Hill—especially with Republican legislators now at the head of all Capitol Hill committees (including the House Un-American Activities Committee). Twenty days after the election, Mr. Truman announced the appointment of a President's Temporary Commission on Employee Loyalty—to look into what measures might be necessary to prevent the employment of subversive persons by the government of the United States.

One of the little-noted events of 1946 was the publication of a book by an Austrian physicist, Hans Thirring, later described as "about as good and simple an elucidation of nuclear physics as any ever written." Among other things, Thirring explained "how an atom bomb could be encased in heavy water or some other form of deuterium, the whole surrounded with a tamper to prevent premature explosion." He was, in short, describing for all the world to see the basic process for making a hydrogen bomb.

Just three years later, the subject Thirring was so openly discussing would be surrounded, in official Washington, by an almost obsessive secrecy, which, in retrospect and in light of Thirring's book, seems surprising, if not nonsensical.

At three-fifty on the afternoon of October 28, 1946, the five nominees for the newly created Atomic Energy Commission filed into the White House and, at four o'clock, sat quietly while President Truman announced their names to reporters. Among them was the former naval officer whom Oppenheimer had met briefly during the war, Lewis L. Strauss.

Strauss was also a member of the board of trustees of the Institute for Advanced Study in Princeton, and chairman of a committee charged with choosing a successor for the Institute's retiring director. A member of the Institute faculty had suggested to Strauss five names, headed by that of Robert Oppenheimer. Strauss is said by a close associate to have been cool to the selection of Oppenheimer. If that is so, he expressed no great concern to his colleagues. Instead, he sought and received their assent to tender Oppenheimer the directorship.

Late in 1946 the five prospective members of the Atomic Energy Commission flew out to California to visit the Radiation Laboratory at Berkeley. They were met at the airport by the laboratory's director, Ernest Lawrence, and by Robert Oppenheimer. As the group walked past the hangars, Strauss and Oppenheimer separated from the others, and Strauss relayed the Institute's offer. Oppenheimer said he probably would accept but asked for time to consider the proposal.

The new Atomic Energy Act authorized the President to name a General Advisory Committee of nine persons, to advise the new Commission "on scientific and technical matters." On December 6 the President dispatched letters to his nine nominees, J. Robert Oppenheimer among them. The presidential letter set the stage for the next great phase of Oppenheimer's life.

At 12:01 A.M. of Wednesday, January 1, 1947, the responsibility for the nation's atomic future left the hands of Leslie R. Groves and the United States Army and officially devolved on David E. Lilienthal, Chairman of the Atomic Energy Commission, and his four associates. The Commission's General Advisory Committee held its first meeting two days later. Robert Oppenheimer was delayed in arriving. By the time he entered the meeting he had been elected chairman. Although he tried several times in ensuing years to resign in favor of another member, he was repeatedly and unanimously re-elected. As one GAC committee member later put it, "He was so naturally a leader of our group that it was impossible to imagine that he should not be in the chair."

Oppenheimer's detractors were later to complain of his ubiquitous influence on government policy, owing to the unusual number of Federal advisory committees of which he was not only a member but, often, the chairman.* If he dominated the committees he headed, it was a subtle process. "He did lead and stimulate and inform us and help us in our decisions," one GAC member later said, but "he never dominated nor suppressed contrary or different opinions." Generally, he talked little, and then undogmatically.

But there can be little doubt about the influence exerted by Chairman Oppenheimer: it was rare for a group's conclusions to differ from his. GAC member Cyril Smith, who stood in awe of Oppenheimer's apparent sway over such powerful and independent-minded colleagues as James B. Conant and I. I. Rabi, attributes this to Oppenheimer's consummate lucidity. "Robert would put things so clearly," said Smith, "that after he had spoken no one else felt there was any need to do any thinking."

The physicist's skill at summarizing group discussions has been described as a "miraculous performance." When the GAC would meet with the Atomic Energy Commissioners, Robert Oppenheimer could summarize three entire days of GAC deliberations, giving "the proper weight to the opinion of every member, the proper shade, and it rarely happened that some member would speak up and say, 'This isn't exactly what I meant.'" With such powers of expression and fair synthesis, it is little wonder that many of his committees were only too happy to delegate to him the task of reducing the group's conclusions to writing; their reports would not be couched in the awkward language of group

---

* In postwar years he did chair no less than seven such groups.

composition but in the graceful, eloquent language of J. Robert Oppenheimer.

Oppenheimer was later subjected to the charge that sympathy toward the Soviet Union affected his leadership of the General Advisory Committee. If this was so, such an attitude was certainly not reflected either in his speeches or in his private conversations of early 1947. In a talk with Hans Bethe in Berkeley, for example, he confided that he had abandoned any hope for agreement with the Russians on international control of the atom, since their sole purpose was to deprive America of the weapon that would keep the Soviets out of Western Europe. In a speech at the University of Denver, in February, Oppenheimer warned that while initially Soviet Communism might have been aimed at improving the well-being of the Russian people, "it has [now] given rise to political forms which are deeply abhorrent to us . . . [and] which we are reluctant to see spread into the many areas of the world where there is great lability."

In later years, the General Advisory Committee, and, more particularly, Robert Oppenheimer, were to be criticized for providing advice to the AEC that was neither asked for nor limited to technical and scientific considerations. Indeed, the AEC did consult the GAC on all important policy matters, including such nonscientific questions as the AEC's security program. This was understandable: the original members of the Commission were inexperienced and groping their way through an entirely uncharted field. They welcomed whatever policy advice they could get from the GAC,* many of whose members had played key roles in the wartime atomic effort.

The GAC's preoccupation in its early months was with the nuclear weapons program, and especially with restoring the Los Alamos lab's morale and efficiency, which had deteriorated badly in the uncertain months of debate over national atomic policy. The question of a thermonuclear bomb was discussed sporadically in 1947 and 1948, but with so much to be done in the im-

* Oppenheimer, in fact, nicknamed the GAC the "Jesus Christ Committee," because most of the questions thrown at it by the AEC were so thorny that an appropriate response might have been, "Jesus Christ, why do we have to answer that?"

provement and expansion of existing fission weapons, there was little the GAC could do but point out the cloudiness of the technical prospects for the H-bomb, and to encourage the modest explorations that continued at Los Alamos.

A major problem facing the new Atomic Energy Commission was that of personnel security. General Groves, in handing over the personnel files of the Manhattan District, had warned that some persons had been cleared in the wartime emergency "despite evidence indicating considerable doubt" about their loyalty, and had urged that *all* persons "on whom derogatory information exists . . . be eliminated."

Thus the new AEC started operations with a hot potato in its lap, and the hard-pressed Commissioners spent a considerable amount of their time reviewing personnel files. But with other problems clamoring for attention, it was clear this screening process would have to be delegated, and for this, procedures would have to be established for applying the new atomic law's broad standards. In the shaping of these the Commission's General Counsel, Herbert S. Marks, played a major role. Seven years later, as he sat on the other side of the counsel table as lawyer for Robert Oppenheimer, Marks would find himself confronted with the AEC regulations he had helped to write.

In the government of the United States, Saturday is a day of rest. Most offices are dark and deserted and only urgent business is dealt with. On Saturday, March 8, 1947, two urgent items of business were transacted.

In Washington a special messenger from the FBI appeared at the office of the Chairman of the Atomic Energy Commission to deliver by hand a document and a letter. The document consisted of summaries of the FBI files "relative to Julius Robert Oppenheimer . . . and his brother, Frank Friedman Oppenheimer." The letter was from FBI Director J. Edgar Hoover, and it was the standard letter of transmittal that accompanies most government reports. But in this case the letter had been preceded by a telephone call from Director Hoover himself to Chairman Lilienthal (to Lilienthal's home at night, according to one account) expressing the hope that Lilienthal would give personal attention to the Oppenheimer file that would soon reach him.

On that same March Saturday, one of the subjects of these files, J. Robert Oppenheimer, arrived in New York after an all-night flight from San Francisco. His object was to meet with Frederick Osborn, who only the day before had taken the oath of office to succeed Bernard Baruch as U.S. representative on the United Nations Atomic Energy Commission. Oppenheimer had telephoned Osborn the day before, within hours of Osborn's swearing-in, asking for an early appointment. When Osborn asked for delay of a week or two while he settled into his new job, Oppenheimer insisted the matter would not wait. Could Osborn meet him either in New York or Washington the next day?

Oppenheimer's pressing, self-appointed mission might have surprised some of the FBI's "confidential sources" whose accusations of pro-Russian sympathies on Oppenheimer's part were contained in the investigative file which Hoover had sent David Lilienthal. For what Oppenheimer was bent on conveying to Osborn without delay was his conviction that the Russians would never agree to a world atomic energy control plan that would involve lifting the Iron Curtain. He feared that in order to get agreement UN negotiators might make compromises "which would put the United States in a very dangerous position of not really knowing what was going on in Russia, whereas the Russians would know all about what was going on here." In a weekend of talk at Osborn's country home on the Hudson, Oppenheimer urged that the negotiations be discontinued promptly lest they be used by the Russians as a "medium for propaganda."*

During that weekend AEC Chairman Lilienthal studied the Oppenheimer file. His reaction was that, if true, the allegations of pro-Communist sympathies (which were new to him) "could seriously impeach" the Commission's senior adviser. On Monday morning Lilienthal called his fellow Commissioners to his office to share the material with them. The matter was too important, he said, to be delegated to subordinates; the FBI material must be read by the Commissioners themselves. Page by page, the summary report was passed around the table. The Commission-

* One of those opposing Oppenheimer's view and favoring continued negotiations despite Russian opposition was a conservative former Republican Senator from Vermont, Warren Austin, then United States Ambassador to the United Nations.

ers quickly decided to call in James Conant and Vannevar Bush (for whom Oppenheimer was at the time acting as a consultant), in part to supplement the "derogatory information" in the FBI report with an account of Oppenheimer's positive contributions during the war. The two met with the Commission that afternoon. Neither was familiar with the contents of the FBI report, but they were convinced that Oppenheimer had "clearly demonstrated his loyalty" and "brilliant and driving leadership" at Los Alamos.

Shouldn't Groves be consulted since it had been he who had chosen Oppenheimer initially? David Lilienthal sought to contact the General, but he was en route to Washington by car and could not be reached.

On Tuesday morning the harried Commissioners met for a third time to wrestle with the Oppenheimer matter. While the scientist's public service made his loyalty "prima facie clear," they felt that the questions raised by the FBI summary required a "full and reliable evaluation" and prompt disposition of the case. Moreover, since Oppenheimer's appointment to the General Advisory Committee had come from President Truman, the White House should be advised of the FBI file. Lilienthal and Bush were commissioned to see Clark Clifford, Truman's special counsel, to tell him of the file and to propose a special evaluation panel of distinguished jurists. At a fourth meeting of the Commission late that day, Lilienthal reported that Clifford would take the matter up with the President and advise the AEC further. Meanwhile, the Commissioners learned, the AEC Security Division had begun a detailed analysis of the FBI material.

This was just the beginning of the Commissioners' involvement with the Oppenheimer file. The AEC began to add other FBI material to its initial summary report. All the Oppenheimer material was placed in the custody of Deputy General Counsel Joseph Volpe, and in ensuing weeks Volpe took the material, in turn, to the individual Commissioners, to be read and returned to Volpe at the end of each day. Of the five Commissioners, none was more conscientious about scrutinizing the file than Lewis L. Strauss. As his fellow Commissioner Sumner Pike later recalled, Strauss, with his Navy background in security problems, "took a more direct interest [in such matters] than the rest of us."

The existence of "derogatory imformation" about Oppenheimer was not entirely new to Strauss, for in the months since
Strauss offered Oppenheimer the directorship of the Institute for
Advanced Study, the two had had "a number of conversations,"
and Oppenheimer had told Strauss there existed "derogatory information about me." But now Strauss was confronted with the
FBI reports themselves.* As he delved into the material, he
called Volpe to his office; Volpe found the Commissioner visibly
shaken by what he had been reading. Thereafter Strauss and
Volpe spent many hours, over a period of days, going over the
file document by document, discussing and debating the significance of each major item. Finally, Strauss turned to Volpe
and said, "Joe, what do you think?"

"Well," Volpe replied, "if anyone were to print all the stuff
in this file and say it is about the top civilian adviser to the Atomic
Energy Commission, there would be terrible trouble. His background is awful. But your responsibility is to determine whether
this man is a security risk *now*, and except for the Chevalier incident I don't see anything in this file to establish that he might
be."

Strauss evidently reached the same conclusion, for there is no
record of any dissent to the clearance ultimately voted Oppenheimer by the AEC.

After their individual scrutiny of the file, the AEC Commissioners decided to take the precaution of checking with J. Edgar
Hoover to see if additional facts had come to light and to make
sure that they were "properly construing the facts in the file."
Thus, on March 25, Lilienthal and two aides paid a call on Hoover
in his office. According to an AEC memorandum on the meeting, all those present seemed "keenly alive" to Oppenheimer's
"unique contributions" to national security, both past and presumably, prospective. There seemed "general agreement . . .
that while [Oppenheimer] may at one time have bordered upon
the communistic, indications [were] that for some time he [had]
steadily moved away from such a position."

The crucial question, though, was how Hoover felt about the

* In one of their later conversations concerning the Institute directorship,
Strauss told Oppenheimer that he had "examined [the FBI file] rather carefully" and did not consider it an obstacle to the Institute position.

matter. According to the AEC memo, with the one exception of the "Chevalier incident,"* Hoover appeared to agree with the consensus that Oppenheimer had moved away from his former pro-Communist leanings.

The meeting with Hoover apparently took the matter of Oppenheimer's clearance off the Commission's list of urgent priorities, and for the next three months the problem appears to have been swallowed up in the whirl of other AEC activity. It did not rise to the surface until July 18, when the chief AEC security officer raised the question of whether the Commission had ever reached a formal decision on the Oppenheimer matter.† A check revealed that the AEC had indeed neglected to take any formal action on the clearance. (Joseph Volpe's impression was that the Commission "saw no need for formal action following the meeting . . . with J. Edgar Hoover.") And so the matter was put on the agenda of the August 6 meeting of the Commission, and AEC consideration of the Oppenheimer case seemed about to be concluded.

But, as it turned out, the AEC's action on that August day became one of the minor mysteries of the Oppenheimer affair. The minutes of that meeting show that the AEC Secretary "called the Commission's attention to the fact that [its] decision to authorize the clearance of J. R. Oppenheimer . . . *made in February, 1947*, had not previously been recorded. The Commission directed the Secretary to record [its] approval of security clearance in this case, and to note that *further reports* concerning Dr. Oppenheimer since that date had contained no information which would warrant reconsideration of the Commission's decision." (Emphasis added.)

February? But the Hoover letter and the FBI summary did not reach the Commission until March 8. How could the AEC have

---

* The memorandum reported Hoover as having "one reservation, which he stated with some emphasis, [that] he could not feel completely satisfied in view of J. Robert's failure to report promptly and accurately what must have seemed to him an attempt at espionage in Berkeley."

† By this time there had been developed a "complete investigative file" on the physicist, one of the most recent items of which was a statement volunteered on July 10 by former Manhattan Project security officer, John Lansdale. By then a practicing lawyer in Cleveland, Lansdale said he was "absolutely certain of [Oppenheimer's] present loyalty, despite the fact that he was doubtless at one time at least an avid fellow traveler."

decided to clear Oppenheimer back in February? Under what circumstances? Based on what information? What was meant by "further reports"? And why had the February action not been recorded?

For the moment these questions were unimportant. Oppenheimer had now been formally cleared under the new Atomic Energy Act. On August 11, 1947, the case was laid temporarily to rest by a memorandum noting the Commission's action and requesting that William Uanna, chief of the AEC's personnel Security Division, "make the appropriate entry" of the clearance in his records.

While the Atomic Energy Commission was wrestling with the security clearance of Robert Oppenheimer, the President's Commission on Employee Loyalty rendered its report, and on March 21, 1947, President Truman initiated the nation's first government-wide loyalty screening program.

Because "the presence within the government service of any disloyal or subversive person constitutes a threat to our democratic processes," the President's Executive Order stated, all Federal employees must be of "complete and unswerving loyalty to the United States." Such "loyalty," said the order, could be appraised by investigating a person's background, associations and affiliations. Every Federal employee and job applicant would be subject to investigation. By way of "standards," the Presidential Order listed a variety of "activities and associations" that might provide "reasonable grounds . . . for belief" that an individual was "disloyal." These included sabotage, espionage, or attempts or preparations therefor; knowing association with spies or saboteurs; treason, sedition, or advocacy thereof; advocacy of revolution or violent overthrow of the government; intentional unauthorized disclosure of secrets under circumstances indicating disloyalty; performing his duties so as to serve the interests of another government in preference to the interests of the United States; and membership in, affiliation with, or sympathetic association with any organization designated by the Attorney General as totalitarian, Fascist, Communist or subversive, or having adopted a policy of approving the commission of acts of force or violence to deny others their constitutional rights.

The presidential order also set forth the procedures that Federal agencies should follow in appraising loyalty and in entertaining employee appeals from adverse findings.

While the President's Loyalty Order was hailed by several members of Congress,* it was not universally acclaimed. A month after the order was made public, a group of Harvard law professors listed their misgivings. They were especially concerned about the procedural weaknesses of the screening system, which "fail[ed] to take account of the gravity of the sanctions invoked" —i.e., the loss of all chance of Federal employment and "special difficulties" in securing private jobs. The deficiencies they criticized included: no requirement that loyalty decisions be supported by evidence; no requirement that adverse evidence be introduced in loyalty hearings so as to be challengeable by the "accused"; vague standards of wrongdoing. Such a program, the professors warned, could be so administered "as to miss genuine culprits, victimize innocent persons [and] discourage entry into the public service. . . ."

There was also the danger that the new program could be used to penalize not just subversive *acts* but merely unorthodox *beliefs*. Indeed, some security officials had already demonstrated they were so inclined in their recommendations to the President's Temporary Loyalty Commission. For example, the Navy Department had warned that subversives would seek to penetrate the government "not only overtly to obtain information, but to foment distrust of American practices, ridicule American standards, and breed discontent, dissatisfaction and disaffection." It also cautioned against those who

> masquerade as "protectors of civil liberties" or promoters of the interests of individuals whose level of economy is declared to be substandard. . . . Front organizations, too numerous to name, are ideal for subversive use. . . . The aims of these organizations are couched in lofty terms which belie the actual purpose to which the organizations will be put, and throw off guard the unwary or unsuspecting person.

* The new Senator from Wisconsin, Joseph R. McCarthy, said the order was "definitely needed" since there had, over the years, been "a tremendous number of Communistically inclined employees on the Federal payroll."

Similarly, J. Edgar Hoover warned that among the threats presented by "subversive or disloyal persons" in the Federal employ would be their efforts to "influenc[e] the formation [or execution] of policies of the United States Government . . . so that those policies will either favor the foreign country of their ideological choice or will weaken the United States Government . . . to the ultimate advantage of the above indicated foreign power."

In ensuing years, considerations of policy and of personal belief were injected into security hearings—as illustrated nowhere more vividly than in the security proceeding against J. Robert Oppenheimer.

Among the general public, Robert Oppenheimer was universally and favorably thought of as "the father of the A-bomb." Almost no one was aware of the radical background that so concerned Federal security officials. But it existed, and there was never any telling when one aspect or another might break into the public prints.

It happened twice in 1947. The first instance occurred on July 12, when the Washington *Times-Herald* carried a front-page copyrighted story by reporter James Walter, which began:

Amid official revelation that security of some of this nation's atom secrets has been jeopardized, this newspaper today can reveal that Dr. Frank Oppenheimer, brother of the American scientist who directed development of the atomic bomb at Los Alamos, was a card-carrying member of the Communist Party who worked on the Manhattan project and was aware of many secrets of the bomb from the start.

The story was filled with details clearly indicating that the reporter had been given full access to the FBI file on Frank Oppenheimer. It stated, for example, that in 1937 Frank had held Communist Party membership book No. 56385; in 1938, No. 60439; and in 1939, No. 1001. The records of his Communist affiliation, the story said, had been in the files of "at least one government investigatory agency for a period of six to ten years. And this newspaper can state that Dr. Frank Oppenheimer's participation in Communist Party work has been known to leading

government officials charged with protection of atomic bomb secrets for many months." One official who played a "major role"
in the wartime A-bomb work had told the reporter that "to his
knowledge, Frank Oppenheimer was at Los Alamos in March,
April and August of 1945" and had also "visited" the Oak Ridge
laboratory.

Halfway down the column, the *Times-Herald* interrupted the
story with this italicized insert:

> (*The Times-Herald desires to emphasize that the official re-
> port on Frank Oppenheimer in no way reflects on the loyalty
> or ability of his brother, Dr. J. Robert Oppenheimer.*)

At the time the story broke, Frank Oppenheimer was on the
physics faculty of the University of Minnesota. It was 1:30 in
the morning in Minneapolis when reporter Walter called him
for his comment on the explosive revelation. Whether it was
cloudiness of mind from having been awakened out of a sound
sleep, or an effort to protect his older brother, Frank made a
response he would later be obliged to recant, for while acknowledging having worked in the wartime atomic project, he denied
emphatically ever having been a member of the Communist
Party.

The next day, in Washington, W. A. Higinbotham, a former
Los Alamosite then working for the Federation of American
Scientists, sought to line up legal counsel for Frank. When he
called the physicist in Minneapolis, Frank was clearly distressed
over what he had told reporter Walter. "Oh, dear," he said, "have
you called my brother? If not, you'd better."

Higinbotham called Robert, who surmised that Frank had felt
impelled to deny Communist Party membership because the
Baruch plan for international atomic control, which Robert was
espousing, was in a critical stage in the UN and Frank didn't
want "to louse that up."

"But," said Robert Oppenheimer, "I'm afraid he lied."

On September 17 Oppenheimer again spoke publicly (and
less than flatteringly) about the Soviet Union. In a speech to the
National War College, he said the Russian belief in an inevitable
Soviet-capitalist conflict ("the basis of their state power [in Rus-

sia]") ruled out any agreement on a workable nuclear control plan. "It does not seem to me likely," he said, "that we have found inducements or cajolery or threats which together are adequate to make [the Soviets] take this great plunge" of international cooperation.

On the last day of October, for the second time that year, Robert Oppenheimer's latent "radical" past once again broke into general view—this time more prominently than before, as the "Chevalier incident" became public knowledge for the first time.

It was news enough to command an unusual three-column page-one headline from the *New York Times:*

**FILM INQUIRY REVEALS MOVE BY SOVIET AGENTS TO OBTAIN ATOM RESEARCH DATA IN 1942 . . . EXPERT BALKED IT . . . DR. OPPENHEIMER CALLED STEP "TREASONABLE," INVESTIGATOR SAYS.**

The disclosure was of dubious relevance to the current HUAC inquiry on alleged Communist penetration into the movie industry. The committee had interrupted its parade of Hollywood notables to hear from committee investigator Louis J. Russell, who told the legislators of a chain of contacts leading to Robert Oppenheimer: Soviet Vice Consul Peter Ivanov, to George C. Eltenton, to Haakon Chevalier, to Oppenheimer. But Russell's testimony was highly favorable to the physicist. According to Russell, Oppenheimer had unequivocally told Chevalier that he "would have nothing to do with" such attempts.

There was an indication that the Federal Bureau of Investigation had played an active role in investigator Russell's revelation about Robert Oppenheimer. According to an Associated Press dispatch appearing in the San Francisco *Chronicle,* "a Committee authority said the FBI had approved ahead of time the release of all the information Russell poured out today." Evidently, the FBI's interest was of long standing, for the same committee source said that "the FBI turned the same information over to the Justice Department a year ago for possible action."

Reporters naturally sought out the three available people mentioned in the "incident." George Eltenton, tracked down in

Thornton, England, had no comment except "concerning the committee's work in general, [which] doesn't seem to be sticking very close to facts." Haakon Chevalier, whose resignation had been accepted the previous January by the University of California, said in San Francisco that he had not "approach[ed] Dr. Oppenheimer in order to obtain information of any kind. I merely repeated to him a conversation I had had with Mr. Eltenton.* Dr. Oppenheimer immediately dismissed the subject. That was all there was to it."

In Princeton, Robert Oppenheimer reacted far more cautiously. He issued this written statement:

I would like to withhold comment, either confirmation or denial, of the statements in general or in detail in order not to interfere in any manner with the activities of the agencies of the United States Government concerned.

Fortunately for Oppenheimer, the HUAC revelation of the "Chevalier incident" proved to be a one-day sensation and quickly subsided. Haakon Chevalier went before the California Un-American Activities Committee, but his appearance rated only a squib on page four of the *New York Times*. And no one pressed Oppenheimer for any elaboration of his equivocal "no comment" on the Chevalier episode.

* Some days later, Chevalier added that Eltenton had made no mention of Soviet Consul Ivanov.

## 4. Fame and Influence

Nineteen forty-eight was a year of rising fame and influence for Robert Oppenheimer. He appeared, for example, on the cover of *Time* Magazine and was widely quoted for articulating publicly the deep feeling of guilt he had blurted out privately, two years earlier, to President Truman. "In some sort of crude sense, which no vulgarity, no humor, no overstatement can quite extinguish," he said, "the physicists have known sin; and this is a knowledge which they cannot lose."

Oppenheimer was able to talk freely and unashamedly with the *Time* reporter about his radical past.

"I became a real leftwinger, joined the teachers' union, had lots of Communist friends. It was what most people do in college or late high school. The Thomas [House Un-American Activities] Committee doesn't like this, but I'm not ashamed of it; I'm more ashamed of the lateness. Most of what I believed then now seems complete nonsense, but it was an essential part of becoming a whole man. If it hadn't been for this late but indispensable education, I couldn't have done the job at Los Alamos at all."

Six years later, on trial for his good name, he would not be able to talk of his past in such self-respecting terms.

But Oppenheimer's real fame and standing were within the scientific community, as vividly illustrated in the unusual cover photograph chosen by a new magazine, *Physics Today*, for its inaugural issue, in May. There was no human being in the picture—only a piece of complicated atomic machinery, on which reposed a pork-pie hat. The photograph had no caption, and needed none; that hat could belong to, and symbolize, only one man.

The photograph also suggests the pervasiveness of Oppenheimer's influence on government policy. That influence found expression not only in his committee chairmanships but through his many scientific disciples, who were increasingly called upon to advise the government. One such scientist-adviser later explained the seeming ubiquity of Oppenheimer's power: "Many of us used to feel more comfortable if we had a chance to consult with Oppie before we gave the government our advice. If we didn't have a chance to see him, we'd probably wonder to ourselves, 'I wonder what Oppie would do in a case like this.'"

Oppenheimer's scientific standing also gave him and his persuasive personality access to top-level government officials. This was a source of deep annoyance to some of his former friends from the prewar Berkeley era. One of these past intimates, physicist Philip Morrison, explained it to Haakon Chevalier in a chance sidewalk meeting in New York in 1948. "We no longer speak the same language," Morrison said. "He moves in a different circle." In his most recent meeting with Oppenheimer, Morrison had been mystified by the physicist's references to "George thinks this . . ." and "George says that. . . ." Finally, Morrison asked who "George" was. It turned out to be the much-revered Secretary of State, George C. Marshall. Nearly two decades later, Oppenheimer was to muse that "one could influence foreign policy better from the inside, for a while—with men like George Marshall in power."

Not only was Robert Oppenheimer in the public eye in that year of 1948; he also continued to live under the never-tiring scrutiny of Federal investigators. Ralph Lapp, a scientist and writer, recalls beginning a discussion with Oppenheimer at the physicist's Princeton office, only to be pulled outdoors by Oppenheimer with the observation, "Even the walls have ears." Another friend tells of a time when the Oppenheimers were surprised, in their Princeton garden, by the sudden arrival of several Federal agents. It later developed that the Oppenheimers had, in the course of some new planting, severed a buried wire, and the agents had come to investigate the sudden silence of their eavesdropping machinery inside the house.

Later, Oppenheimer was to observe caustically, "The government paid far more to tap my telephone than they ever paid me at Los Alamos."

In 1948 the development of a hydrogen or "Super" bomb was not considered a matter of urgency. The United States' nuclear monopoly did not appear in imminent danger; Robert Oppenheimer, for example, predicted that year that the Soviets would not have an A-bomb "for a long time to come."\* The Los Alamos weapons laboratory continued its theoretical calculations on the thermonuclear problem, but the approach then being explored did not seem promising. The perfection of existing fission weapons was considered far more urgent.

There was, in 1948, no significant dissent from this low priority assigned to the H-bomb. In fact, two men who later became ardent H-bomb advocates (and who played vital roles in the 1954 proceeding against Oppenheimer)—AEC Commissioner Lewis Strauss and Army nuclear representative Kenneth D. Nichols—both reportedly "joined in recommending that only the current level of effort be maintained in the thermonuclear program."

In June, 1948, William Liscum Borden, now a Justice Department attorney, was on the verge of departing for a European vacation when he received a surprise invitation to lunch with Connecticut Senator Brien McMahon. McMahon had read and been greatly impressed with Borden's book on the prospect of nuclear-armed long-range rockets. When they met, the Senator hardly gave Borden time to remove the napkin from the table before offering him an immediate job in his Senate office. The proposal was tempting; Borden canceled his European trip and went to work on Capitol Hill.

The relationship with McMahon was to grow far closer and would, in just six months' time, bring William Borden into the vortex of atomic energy matters in Washington.

William Borden did not go to Europe that summer, but Robert Oppenheimer did. It was the first time he had left the United

---

\* Years later, Oppenheimer was to acknowledge he had made a "bad guess." But he was far from alone in his erroneously optimistic prediction. In 1945 General Groves had forecast it would take the Russians years to get a bomb, and a government survey of scientists, industrialists and engineers in that same year had yielded estimates ranging from five to twenty years.

States since he had returned from Europe "homesick" nineteen years earlier.

One of his missions on this European trip was to try to repair the rapidly deteriorating atomic relations between America and Britain. During the war the two allies had been full and open partners in atomic research, but in postwar years the United States had become more and more secretive, in part due to the restrictions in the Atomic Energy Act of 1946. Robert Oppenheimer was one of many who favored a relaxation of the secrecy barriers and a rapprochement with the British atomic enterprise.

This view conflicted sharply with that of one AEC Commissioner, Lewis Strauss, who was apprehensive about letting atomic information stray beyond the borders of the United States. His misgivings were particularly keen on the matter of allowing certain radioactive materials to be shipped abroad. On this issue, Strauss split not only with Robert Oppenheimer and the General Advisory Committee but also with his four fellow Commissioners on the AEC. Their repeated intramural debates on the radio-isotope issue became intensely emotional, at least on Strauss' part. Chairman Lilienthal tried hard to avoid the first split vote in the AEC, but Strauss' views were deeply held. He would not compromise. When the matter came to a test in the AEC, he was out-voted four to one. The defeat did not sit easily with him.

But the four-to-one vote was not the only injury Lewis Strauss suffered in those early AEC deliberations on the isotope issue. Whereas Strauss' fellow Commissioners had been at pains to make it clear that they respected his position, even while disagreeing with it, one important AEC figure was not so gentle. J. Robert Oppenheimer, in a meeting with Strauss and the other Commissioners, had simply "dismissed Strauss' objection . . . with a swift rapier thrust, just passing it off as not really worthy of much serious consideration."

This was not the last time the isotope matter was to come between the two men.

While Strauss and Oppenheimer differed on the question of sharing atomic information in 1948, their views of the Soviet Union and her intentions were doubtless far less divergent. Anyone reading Oppenheimer's public utterances on the subject might find it hard to believe that in a few years he would be officially suspected of an affinity for Russia and her policies. In a *Foreign Affairs* article, for example, he again despaired of any hope of any nuclear accord with the Soviets, citing their belief "in the inevitability of conflict—and not in ideas alone, but in force."

Indeed, the possibility of a conflict "in force" with the Soviets seemed nearer at hand in 1948 than at any time since the war. The brutal takeover in Czechoslovakia in February was followed in April by the Berlin blockade. As the Allies mounted their air-lift, and the Soviets threatened to put their fighter aircraft into the same air corridors with Allied planes, the Cold War began to appear imminently much warmer.

If the Communists presented such a clear and present danger in the Berlin air corridors, might they not represent a similar threat within the United States' own borders?

This question was raised with increasing frequency in 1948. Witnesses before the House Un-American Activities Committee testified that in times past Communists had succeeded in infiltrat-ing the highest councils of government and had conveyed secret information to the Soviets. Even the White House had suppos-edly not been immune: ex-Communist Elizabeth Bentley con-tended that one of Franklin Roosevelt's aides, Laughlin Currie, had been among the purveyors of secrets to the Soviets. A Congressman charged that thirteen hundred pounds of uranium compound had been shipped to Russia during the war. CIO Secretary-Treasurer James B. Carey told of Communist inroads into the Electrical Workers' Union. Congressmen Mundt and Nixon proposed mandatory registration of all Communists.

But no event in 1948 gave as much impetus to the "Reds in Government" anxiety as the dramatic accusations and revelations concerning one Alger Hiss, president of the eminently respect-able Carnegie Endowment for International Peace, protégé of an Associate Justice of the United States Supreme Court. If such a man were really guilty of conveying State Department docu-ments to the Soviets, could anyone be wholly free of suspicion?

The entire "Communist" issue was intensified by the politically charged atmosphere of this presidential election year, and Harry

S Truman did nothing to quiet the matter when he denounced the Congressional spy probes as a "red herring" intended to distract attention from the record of the Republican Eightieth Congress. Republican candidate Thomas E. Dewey promised a clean-up of the Communists in government. Nebraska's Senator Kenneth Wherry contended the Red issue was uppermost in the minds of Midwestern voters. Congressman Nixon charged the President with having prevented J. Edgar Hoover from testifying on the Communist issue. Democrat Truman said anyone suggesting he protected Communists in the government was lying.

In mid-campaign, the House Un-American Activities Committee issued a twenty-thousand-word report on "Soviet Espionage Activities in Connection with the Atom Bomb," accusing the Truman Administration of "completely inexcusable" lack of action against atom spies. The committee's report included an account of "the Chevalier incident," which implied that the committee had previously looked into the matter, but had found Robert Oppenheimer blameless. HUAC described it this way:

> Oppenheimer, as previously brought out by the Committee, declined to cooperate with Eltenton in the attempt to secure information regarding the atomic bomb* and told Chevalier that he considered such acts or such attempts to obtain information on this subject as constituting treason.

But this was buried among matters far more sensational, and so went unnoticed.

Harry Truman's astounding upset victory over Thomas E. Dewey was not the only political surprise of 1948. Congressional Democrats who had resigned themselves to continued minority status under "President Dewey" suddenly found themselves in renewed control of Congress and its committees. Connecticut Senator Brien McMahon, for example, took over the chairmanship of the Joint Committee on Atomic Energy. His choice for the post of staff director was twenty-eight-year-old William Liscum Borden.

---

* Testimony in Oppenheimer's security hearing did not claim that Eltenton wanted information on the atomic bomb as such but only "technical information."

There were changes in Harry Truman's cabinet, too—none more controversial than the appointment of Louis A. Johnson, prime Democratic fund-raiser in the presidential campaign, to the post of Secretary of Defense.

Johnson's advent as the Pentagon civilian chief intensified the competition between the military services. This interservice rivalry had already been made acute by the 1947 unification act, which merged the proud service departments into a single Defense Department, and by drastic feast-to-famine cutbacks in military appropriations (from $43 billion to less than $12 billion in the first two postwar years). Moreover, fast-moving, revolutionary changes in weapons made it disconcertingly uncertain as to what the future of each military service would be. The Navy and Air Force were anxiously vying for the dominant role in the long-range atomic-strike "mission," a conflict that President Truman skirted rather than resolved. In 1948 he granted the Navy its dream of a 65,000-ton, $189 million "supercarrier," from which atomic bombers could be launched. At the same time, however, he clamped a $15 billion ceiling on defense spending, so that any increased role for one service had to be at the expense of another. The competitive quest for the suddenly scarce defense dollars became almost desperate, especially between Air Force and Navy partisans.*

In April, 1949, Johnson unceremoniously canceled the Navy's cherished "supercarrier" (without bothering to inform the Navy). The admirals retaliated with an open attack on the efficacy of the Air Force's long-range bomber, the B-36. Later, after further Navy cutbacks by Johnson, the Navy brass mounted an overt attack on the Air Force's strategic-warfare doctrines, even challenging the morality of the Air Force atomic-strike theory of deterrence. Pacific Fleet Commander Arthur W. Radford told a

* The acuteness of interservice sensitivity was illustrated earlier by the Air Force reaction that was stirred when Secretary of Defense James Forrestal casually cited, before a Congressional committee, a favorite Navy statistic: that two-thirds of the globe is covered by water. Air Force Secretary Stuart Symington heatedly protested that Forrestal had dealt the Air Force a "death blow." His passion was dissipated when a Forrestal aide hit upon a diplomatic solution to the crisis: the transcript of the Secretary's testimony would be amended to add that above all the water *and* all the land on earth was *air*. Symington and Air Force generals were delighted with the proffered amendment.

Congressional committee: "The kind of war we plan to fight must fit the kind of peace we want. We cannot look to military victory alone, with no thought to the staggering problems that would be generated by the death and destruction of an atom blitz." Five years later, the introduction of such moral considerations into deliberations on military strategy by Robert Oppenheimer and other scientists was frowned upon by Oppenheimer's judges.

The Navy was not, however, the sole target of the Johnson "economy" crusade. The services had hoped for a $30 billion defense budget, and all felt President Truman's deep 50 percent cut. The Air Force, for example, which had hoped to build toward 70 air groups, was cut back from 55 to 48 groups. In a time of such parsimony, it was little wonder that high Air Force officials reacted so sensitively when Robert Oppenheimer and others suggested military strategies which they feared would diminish the Air Force's role.

The change in the political control of Congress had comparatively little effect on the Communist-hunting zeal of the House Un-American Activities Committee. In the spring of 1949 HUAC began an investigation of alleged Communist penetration of the Berkeley Radiation Laboratory in the early days of the war. Among those summoned before the Committee were many of Robert Oppenheimer's former students, including David Bohm, Rossi Lomanitz and Joseph Weinberg.

Lomanitz was then teaching at Fisk University in Nashville. On his way to testify before HUAC, he stopped off in Princeton to visit David Bohm, who had, with Robert Oppenheimer's help, joined the Princeton physics department. As Bohm and Lomanitz were walking along Nassau Street, they happened on their former mentor returning from a visit to the barbershop. As the pair talked with Oppenheimer, the matter of their forthcoming testimony before the House committee inevitably arose. Oppenheimer advised them to tell the full truth; they assured him they would not lie. The possibility of their "pleading the Fifth"* was not discussed. Later, Oppenheimer had occasion to read the transcripts of their appearances before HUAC. Both witnesses

* The Fifth Amendment, protecting a witness against self-incrimination.

had invoked the Fifth Amendment when asked whether or not they had known Steve Nelson. This worried Oppenheimer. He didn't like it, he later recalled, when people he knew had to plead the Fifth Amendment.

On the morning of Tuesday, June 7, 1949, Oppenheimer himself appeared before a closed-door session of HUAC in Room 226 of the House Office Building.

It was an unusual confrontation. Arrayed around the elevated, semicircular dais, looking down intimidatingly at the witness, were six hard-bitten members of HUAC. At the witness table sat a frail, soft-spoken, highly intellectual professor of theoretical physics. One might have thought this would hardly be a fair match.

And, indeed, in the recollection of one eyewitness, it was not a fair match: the Congressmen never stood a chance. They were as if hypnotized by the scientist before them. According to Joseph Volpe, the AEC's General Counsel, who at the Commission's request sat beside the physicist at the witness table, "Robert seemed to have made up his mind to charm these Congressmen out of their seats." And he succeeded—literally: at the conclusion of the hearing, Volpe has recalled, all six came off the dais to shake the physicist's hand warmly.

Oppenheimer was facing, that day, not only the six Congressmen but also members of the HUAC staff, including senior investigator Louis J. Russell, who had, a year and a half earlier, testified before HUAC about Oppenheimer's role in the "Chevalier incident." But if the physicist was apprehensive about the exposure of his own past, he did not show it.

The questioning was conducted largely by HUAC Counsel Frank S. Tavenner, Jr., who began by explaining politely that the committee had summoned Oppenheimer "to ask your assistance" in the probe of the alleged Communist cell in the Berkeley Radiation Lab, but emphasizing that HUAC was "not seeking to embarrass you" since "your record of loyalty has been vouched for by General Groves."

At the outset, Oppenheimer testified cautiously about his former students. He had only "heard about" the efforts of FAECT, the left-wing technicians' union, to organize scientists and could give the committee little help in identifying its members. He was asked about Joseph Weinberg and Rossi Lomanitz, but his answers were protective of both.

Counsel Tavenner asked about Bernard Peters. Apparently Tavenner had before him a report of Peer de Silva's wartime conversation with Oppenheimer, in which the scientist had called Peters "quite a Red" and a "crazy person" of unpredictable personality. Tavenner asked Oppenheimer about this. The scientist readily remembered what he had told de Silva.

What in Peters' background had prompted Oppenheimer's observations? The physicist replied that on arriving in California in the 1930's Peters had "denounced the Communist Party as being a do-nothing party." Elaborating on this, Oppenheimer said Peters had considered the party "too constitutional and too conciliatory an organization, not sufficiently dedicated to the overthrow of the Government by force and violence." Oppenheimer also cited Peters' background in Germany; he had "fought street battles against the [Nazis] on account of the Communists," had been "placed in a concentration camp," and had "escap[ed] by guile"—all "past incidents not pointing to temperance" on Peters' part. The physicist said that Peters had been a member of the Communist Party in Germany—a fact that was "well known. Among other things," said Oppenheimer, "he told me."

After voicing these opinions about his former protégé and close friend, Oppenheimer faced a new line of questioning:

Counsel Tavenner: "Doctor, you are probably acquainted with the case involving George Charles Eltenton and Haakon Chevalier?"

The scientist parried briefly: "I am familiar with some aspects of it," he replied.

Would he tell the committee about that? Oppenheimer now recounted the "kitchen conversation" with his friend. He described Chevalier as "terribly disturbed" over a prior conversation with Eltenton, who had said he had "facilities for communicating information to the Soviet Government. Dr. Chevalier was clearly embarrassed and confused, and I, in violent terms, told him not to be confused and to have no connection with it. *He did not ask me for information.*" (Emphasis added.)

Oppenheimer was asked what he knew about Chevalier's views on Communism? He replied that he knew "nothing of Chevalier's membership in the Communist Party one way or another. If I may use a phrase that seems accurate to me, he was the prize example of a parlor pink. He had very wide connections with all kinds of front organizations; he was interested in left-wing writers . . . he talked quite freely of his opinions. That is all in the prewar days. I know him quite well."

After a few other questions, counsel Tavenner dropped the matter of "the Chevalier incident."

Later that morning, a committee member, Illinois Congressman Harold Velde, reintroduced the subject, this time probing closer to the heart of Robert Oppenheimer's conduct in the matter, in a surprisingly brief exchange:

MR. VELDE: Did you report [the kitchen conversation] to the security officers?

DR. OPPENHEIMER: I did, first, to the security officers at Berkeley; second, to Colonel Lansdale; and third, to General Groves.

This answer omitted any mention of Oppenheimer's eight-month delay in making his first report. It also passed over the misrepresentations the scientist had made in the accounts he had given Colonels Pash and Lansdale. Congressman Velde, however, seemed to know nothing of this, for, evidently satisfied with Oppenheimer's cryptic answer to his question, he moved on to another subject.

Nor did anyone else in the hearing room press Oppenheimer about the delay or the falsifications. This is in itself a remarkable fact, first, because the FBI already knew of Oppenheimer's lies to the wartime security officers,* and second, because the FBI was apparently working in close cooperation with HUAC.† Yet throughout the hearing, investigator Russell made no protest.

Was the committee ill-informed about the "Chevalier incident" or merely disinclined to press the eminent physicist too hard?

* Oppenheimer himself had told FBI agents all about it in September of 1946 (see p. 94).

† The FBI had given its prior approval to HUAC investigator Russell's earlier "Chevalier incident" revelations (see p. 110).

Evidently the latter was true, as illustrated by the gentle way in which the committee staff questioned Oppenheimer about his younger brother. Asked about Frank's *current* Communist Party membership, Robert readily answered in the negative, "to the best of my knowledge." But then counsel Tavenner posed a more difficult question: had Frank been a member of the party *in the past?*

Robert Oppenheimer ventured a response rarely heard from witnesses before HUAC: "Mr. Chairman . . . I ask you not to press these questions about my brother. If they are important to you, you can ask him. I will answer, if asked, but I beg you not to ask me these questions."

This committee had browbeaten many a witness for similar recalcitrance concerning the Communist affiliations of others. Would it treat Robert Oppenheimer the same, and insist on his answering? Counsel Tavenner was not disposed to do so. "I withdraw the question," he said. Committee Chairman John Wood of Georgia assented with a "Very well," and with that, Tavenner's questions came to an end.

Ultimately, the committee exhausted its curiosity. But before the hearing broke up, one of the committee members asked to be heard. It was Richard M. Nixon, Congressman from California: "Before we adjourn, I would like to say—and I am sure this is the sense of all who are here—I have noted for some time the work done by Dr. Oppenheimer, and I think we all have been tremendously impressed with him and are mighty happy we have him in the position he has in our program."

Chairman Wood joined Nixon in expressing "the deep appreciation of all members of the Committee for the information you have given us and for your sincerity in desiring to help us," and declared the meeting adjourned. Wood, Nixon and the other members of the committee came down from their dais and shook the scientist's hand. It was an atmosphere far different from that which would prevail at Oppenheimer's security hearing. The Oppenheimer who had so charmed these Congressmen was a far more self-possessed witness than the Oppenheimer who would, five years later, confess in anguish that he had lied about the "Chevalier incident" because he was "an idiot."

The June 7 session with HUAC was not the first time that the name of Bernard Peters had been mentioned to Oppenheimer that year. When the American Physical Society had met in Washington, early in May, Oppenheimer had been approached by his long-time friend, physicist Samuel Goudsmit, who was then serving both on an AEC panel reviewing security cases and on the Personnel Security Committee of the Federation of American Scientists. In this latter capacity, Goudsmit was often consulted by scientists with security-clearance problems. One of those had been Bernard Peters, who had just gone through an experience that was as humiliating as it was frightening. Invited to attend and address a European scientific conference in September of 1948, Peters had been furnished with a letter of credentials as a technician for the Office of Naval Research, which at the time was paying half his salary. But when his ship landed at Cherbourg, his passport and other credentials were taken from him by a man who said he was representing the Sûreté Général (police), and who would say only that he was acting on orders from Washington. Peters was obliged, in great embarrassment, to cancel his speech and return to America. There he learned that his work with the Navy was being abruptly terminated. He sought guidance from Goudsmit, saying that he had gone to many important people for letters of endorsement, and that while each had initially assured him they would be glad to help, they had later apologetically withdrawn the offer of assistance.

When Goudsmit looked into the matter, taking advantage of his position as an AEC consultant, he discovered the source of the trouble. There was indeed "derogatory information" in Bernard Peters' file. But, unlike many other cases Goudsmit had seen, the information did not come from some unnamed "informant" or casual acquaintance but from an important and reliable source: J. Robert Oppenheimer. The crucial "derogatory information" consisted of the assessment of Peters that Oppenheimer had given Peer de Silva during the war.

And so, at the American Physical Society meeting in Washington, Goudsmit sought out Oppenheimer to explain the harm his statements had done to his former student and to plead with the scientist to take some corrective action. After all, Goudsmit said, Oppenheimer's statements to de Silva had been made five years before. Did Oppenheimer still have the same doubts about Peters? he asked.

To Goudsmit's surprise, Oppenheimer answered him gruffly and in the affirmative. "Just look at him," he said. "Can't you tell he can't be trusted?"

At 4:30 P.M. of June 8, the day after Oppenheimer's appearance before HUAC, the committee again met in closed session. The witness was Bernard Peters. Considering the gravity of what Robert Oppenheimer had told HUAC about Peters and his background, a tough and detailed probe might have been expected. But the committee had very little to ask Peters. They wanted to know whether he had been a member of the Communist Party in Germany (he said he had not) or in the United States (same reply), or whether his wife had been (answer: no) and whether he had an AEC scholarship fellow under his supervision (answer: yes). After a scant twenty minutes before the committee, Bernard Peters was excused as a witness.

On his way back to Rochester, he stopped in Princeton, to see Oppenheimer. They talked about their respective appearances before the House committee. Peters wondered whether Oppenheimer's testimony had been injurious to him. Oppenheimer's reply: God had guided the committee's questions, and so his testimony had not been hurtful to Peters.* Peters returned to Rochester, doubtless wondering what his former professor would have told the committee if God had not intervened.

But he would not long be in doubt as to precisely what Oppenheimer had told the committee, for a week later a headline in Peters' home-town newspaper, the Rochester *Times-Union*, proclaimed, "DR. OPPENHEIMER ONCE TERMED PETERS 'QUITE RED.'" Verbatim excerpts of Oppenheimer's supposedly secret testimony

---

* Based on question by AEC attorney Roger Robb to Oppenheimer suggesting Robb was quoting an investigative or surveillance report of the Oppenheimer-Peters talk:

Q: Did you see Dr. Peters at Princeton before you saw him at Berkeley?
A: I believe I did.
Q: Did you tell him on that occasion that you had testified but that God had guided the questions so you didn't hurt him?

Oppenheimer flatly denied saying any such thing. But a few questions later, Robb posed the same question, to which Oppenheimer replied that that would not have been an accurate statement and he did not remember making it.

before HUAC had somehow found their way into the hands of the *Times-Union*'s Washington correspondent. Thus Bernard Peters, former prisoner of the Dachau concentration camp, could read how, in the view of his former mentor, he had escaped "by guile" and how he had come to the United States and denounced the American Communist Party as insufficiently dedicated to the overthrow of the government by force and violence.

When Oppenheimer's HUAC testimony became public, a group of his physicist friends were attending a conference on cosmic rays in Idaho Springs, Colorado. Some of them promptly wrote Oppenheimer to convey their displeasure at what he had done. By far the strongest letter came from Bureau of Standards Director Edward U. Condon, who wrote that he had been "shocked beyond description" by the testimony. What particularly outraged Condon was Oppenheimer's use of the word "guile" in describing Peters' escape from Dachau, reportedly through bribery, at a time when many were recoiling in horror at the Nazi atrocities against the Jews. Condon wrote:

> I have lost a good deal of sleep trying to figure out how you could have talked this way about a man whom you have known so long, and of whom you know so well what a good physicist and good citizen he is. One is tempted to feel that you are so foolish as to think you can buy immunity for yourself by turning informer. I hope that this is not true. You know very well that once these people decide to go into your own dossier and make it public that it will make the "revelations" that have been made so far look pretty tame.

Condon simultaneously sent a handwritten letter to his wife, in which, among other things, he recalled how Oppenheimer had befriended Peters and secured his admission to graduate school despite his lack of undergraduate training. "Remember," Condon wrote, "Peters has been on this kind of close personal basis with Oppy for 11 years, that Peters did his Ph.D. thesis under Oppy, that Hannah Peters was Oppy's physician when he had pneumonia, etc."

Naturally, Condon kept no copy of this personal, handwritten letter to his wife. Yet somehow the text of this letter and that of his letter to Oppenheimer were later to come into the hands of Washington newsmen known to have particularly close contacts in the FBI and the House Un-American Activities Committee.*

Later, the Condon letter was to be cited by Robert Oppenheimer's judges as evidence of his "susceptibility to influence" since, they contended, it was this outraged letter that led Oppenheimer to, in effect, publicly recant his HUAC testimony about Peters. But Condon's was by no means the only letter Oppenheimer received. Others wrote, too, including his brother, Frank, Hans Bethe and his old friend Victor Weisskopf. These letters were more regretful than belligerent, and Oppenheimer later recalled that he felt the pressure of these gentle proddings even more than the sulfurous words of Edward Condon—or even the direct appeal of Peters himself.

The confrontation with Peters took place in Berkeley, where Oppenheimer had gone to teach for the summer. According to the physicist's later recollection, Peters wanted to know whether there was any way Oppenheimer could help him keep his teaching job. He said Oppenheimer had misunderstood him about his Communist Party membership in Germany—that he had worked with the Communists there against the Nazis, and was not ashamed of that. But he had not actually been a party member, and no one could prove he had been. Moreover, he said, Oppenheimer had not known his views on the American Communist Party, and should not have quoted him, as he did, in his testimony before HUAC.

In the wake of these protests from his friends and from Peters, Oppenheimer felt he must try to undo the damage his testimony had apparently caused. Accordingly, on June 30 he wrote a letter to the Rochester *Democrat-Chronicle*, which he was careful to have someone show to HUAC. The letter was published July 6, under the heading, "DR. OPPENHEIMER EXPLAINS." In it, Oppenheimer recalled the prewar Peters "not only as a brilliant student, but as a man of strong moral principles and of high ethical standards" who often spoke "without temperance," as would be "not unnatural in a man who had suffered as he had at Nazi hands."

* At the time these letters were published in the newspapers, in 1954, the *New York Times* said there were reports circulating in Washington "that two investigating committees of Congress, and the FBI, had copies."

He said he had never known Peters "to commit a dishonorable act, nor a disloyal one."

He repeated the denial Peters had recently made to him of party membership in Germany. He also acknowledged that it was possible to conclude from his own HUAC testimony that Peters had, in the Thirties, advocated the violent overthrow of the U.S. Government. But, said Oppenheimer, Peters had recently issued "an eloquent denial of this in his published statement. I believe his statement."

As to his 1944 comments to Peer de Silva, Oppenheimer said these had been made "in connection with confidential wartime assignments."

> I wish to make public my profound regret that anything said in the context should have been so misconstrued, and so abused, that it could damage Dr. Peters and threaten his distinguished future career as a scientist.

Oppenheimer concluded his letter with this plea:

> Beyond this specific issue, there is ground for another, more general, and even greater concern. Political opinion, no matter how radical or how freely expressed, does not disqualify a scientist for a high career in science; it does not disqualify him as a teacher of science; it does not impugn his integrity nor his honor. We have seen in other countries criteria of political orthodoxy applied to ruin scientists, and to put an end to their work. This has brought with it the attrition of science. Even more, it has been part of the destruction of freedom of inquiry, and of political freedom itself. This is no path to follow for a people determined to stay free.

Only a few weeks earlier, Oppenheimer had expressed similar thoughts, in a letter to Senator McMahon concerning the screening of candidates for an Atomic Energy Commission fellowship program. "It would be foolish to suppose," he wrote McMahon, "that a young man sympathetic to and associated with Communists in his student days would by that fact alone become disloyal, and a potential traitor. It is basic to science and to democracy alike that men can learn by error."

To what extent had thoughts such as these been in Oppenheimer's mind while he was testifying before HUAC about Bernard Peters, ex-student radical and now gifted professor of physics?

Like a magnet, the personality of Robert Oppenheimer had two distinct poles. Both were displayed in Congressional hearings in the month of June, 1949.

The positive pole—Oppenheimer the charmer, the persuader, at times almost the hypnotizer—was never more conspicuously or successfully displayed than in his June 7 appearance before HUAC. But six days later there was to be another Oppenheimer on view: Oppenheimer the humiliator, the witherer, the arrogant, impatient condescender of intellects lesser than his own. "Robert could make grown men feel like school children," one friend has observed. "He could make giants feel like cockroaches."

Even the scientist's most loyal supporters acknowledge that Robert Oppenheimer's security-risk hearing and his fall from official grace may have been brought on, at least in part, by this negative side of his extraordinary personality. They can recall wincing with embarrassment for many a hapless individual who, during a government committee meeting chaired by Oppenheimer, uttered a less than brilliant observation, only to be shriveled by an acidulous remark that Oppenheimer tossed into the air seemingly without aim, yet clearly, cruelly and efficaciously targeted. Oppenheimer associates recall that some of those who later testified against the physicist in his security hearing, as well as others who played a leading role in that proceeding, had been at one time or another victims of his scorn.

Generally, this Oppenheimer trait was reserved for private occasions. But in June of 1949 it was displayed in full public view. Only a few well-informed AEC "insiders," however, could have identified the target of Oppenheimer's barbs that day. The occasion was another Congressional hearing, just six days after his closed-door testimony before HUAC. While the HUAC meeting was held in secret, with no reporters present, Oppenheimer's appearance on Monday, June 13, was in the cavernous Caucus Room of the Senate Office Building (later to become famous as the scene of the Army-McCarthy hearings) under klieg lights so bright that many of the Congressional committee members wore sunglasses.

The hearing, before the Joint Committee on Atomic Energy, was prompted by charges of Iowa's Republican Senator Bourke Hickenlooper that the Atomic Energy Commission was guilty of "incredible mismanagement." Oppenheimer appeared as chairman of the AEC's General Advisory Committee. The main issue to which he addressed himself was the shipment of radioisotopes to friendly countries abroad—the issue on which the AEC had previously outvoted Lewis Strauss four to one. Since that time Strauss' opposition to such shipments had, if anything, become even more deeply felt.* He was especially concerned about the shipment of an iron isotope to a Norwegian research laboratory. Convinced that the isotope could have only military usefulness, Strauss had sought to block action within the AEC, but to no avail.

Oppenheimer had been asked by the AEC to testify at the hearing because the General Advisory Committee had not only supported the AEC's isotope policy but had even criticized the Commission for being too conservative.

All five AEC Commissioners were present in the hearing room as Oppenheimer began his testimony, and the physicist could hardly have been unaware not only of Chairman Strauss' presence but of his strong feelings on the isotope issue. Nonetheless, when asked to comment on one of Strauss' concerns—the possible military application of the isotopes—Oppenheimer chose words hardly designed to add dignity to Strauss' position.

"No one," he told the committee, "can force me to say that you cannot use these isotopes for atomic energy. You can use a shovel for atomic energy; in fact, you do. You can use a bottle of beer for atomic energy. In fact, you do. But to get some perspective, the fact is that during the war and after the war these materials have played no significant part, and in my own knowledge, no part at all."

With the mention of the bottle of beer, a ripple of laughter

* Strauss' reasoning: first, that such shipments violated the Atomic Energy Act's prohibition against sharing nuclear information for "industrial" purposes; and second, that once a radioisotope had left the country, the U.S. had no way of preventing its being put to an unintended and injurious use.

ran through the hearing room. Even to an observer who had no background on the issues and personalities involved,* it was clear that Oppenheimer was making a fool of someone.

AEC General Counsel Joseph Volpe, seated beside Oppenheimer at the witness table, had no doubt who that someone was. He sneaked a look at Lewis Strauss, seated with the other Commissioners behind Oppenheimer. There was no mistaking Strauss' reaction—it was a familiar one to Volpe. Strauss' eyes narrowed; the muscles of his jaws began to work visibly; color rose in his face. Thereafter, Volpe kept "one eye on Oppenheimer and the Committee and one eye on Strauss."

Presently Senator Knowland of California posed a question: "Is it not true, Doctor, that the over-all national defense of a country rests on more than secret military development alone?"

Oppenheimer replied, "Of course it does. . . . My own rating of the importance of isotopes in this broad sense is that they are far less important than electronic devices, but far more important than, let us say, vitamins, somewhere in between."

Again laughter filled the hearing room, falling upon the sensitive ears of Lewis Strauss, as well as on those of the official verbatim stenographer, so that Oppenheimer's ridiculing of Strauss' arguments became permanently recorded, for all to see, in a single line:

"[Laughter]."

When the hearing ended, Oppenheimer turned to Volpe and said, "Well, Joe, how did I do?"

Volpe, with the image of Strauss' darkened, angry face all too vividly in mind, replied, "*Too* well, Robert. Much too well."

Volpe was not the only person in the Senate Caucus Room that day who was struck by Strauss' reaction. Strauss' colleagues, David Lilienthal and Gordon Dean, were indelibly impressed by the incident, especially the moment at 12:55 P.M. when the hearing adjourned and Strauss left the hearing room. Five years later, Dean was to tell Lilienthal, "I remember clearly . . . the terrible look on Lewis' face." Lilienthal's memory of that instant, even after seventeen years, was equally clear. "There was a look of hatred there that you don't see very often in a man's face."

* By coincidence, the author was present in the hearing room that day.

The occasion for Dean's recollection came in June, 1954, as he and Lilienthal reflected on the security-risk charges brought against Oppenheimer—under the AEC chairmanship of Lewis Strauss. Dean's comment prompted Lilienthal to observe "how much the course of events is affected by wholly *personal* quirks, by what seem at the time little personal things."

The day after Oppenheimer's testimony on the isotope issue, on the other side of Capitol Hill the House Un-American Activities Committee conducted still another hearing on the alleged Communist cell at Berkeley. The witness before them was Robert Oppenheimer's younger brother, Frank.

The circumstances were far different from those of two years earlier when Frank, suddenly awakened by a newspaper reporter, had denied his past Communist Party membership. This time there had been notice and time to prepare the answers he would have to give under oath. And so, testifying behind the committee's closed doors, Frank and his wife told the Congressmen that they had once belonged to the party but that after three and a half years they had quit—"long before" Frank engaged in atomic research.

When the Oppenheimers emerged from the hearing, they handed a statement to reporters, telling how they had joined the party in 1937, "seeking an answer to the problems of unemployment and want in the wealthiest and most productive country in the world." When the party did not prove to be "the vehicle through which to accomplish . . . progressive changes," they had left it. Acknowledging public fears about the security of the atomic program, Frank gave assurances that he had never "engaged in," nor did he know of any instance of, atomic espionage.

Later that day, the Oppenheimers repeated their story in an open committee hearing. Committee investigator Louis Russell brought out that General Groves had known of Frank's past Communist Party membership. Frank countered with a letter Groves had sent him in 1945, praising his work in various phases of the Manhattan Project as "an essential factor in our success" and expressing "grateful thanks for your indispensable part" in the program. That, said Frank Oppenheimer, should be "sufficient testimony of my own loyalty to my country." Investigator Russell also said that "an outstanding scientist" had vouched for Frank's loyalty. Later he told newsmen that the scientist was J. Robert Oppenheimer.

Less than an hour after Frank appeared before HUAC, he learned—not from his employers but from Washington newsmen—that he was no longer an assistant professor of physics at the University of Minnesota. He had offered his resignation three days earlier, but the university had not made its intentions known directly to Frank. Instead, university officials announced their acceptance of his resignation publicly. (Frank had "done the honorable and wise thing," the announcement said.)

Thus began the academic exile of Frank Friedman Oppenheimer, doctor of philosophy in physics. For nearly ten years, the brother of one of America's most respected physicists would be unable to get a teaching job in any university in the United States.

In the latter days of June, 1949, the following events took place:

On Thursday, the twenty-third, the Oakland *Tribune* quoted Robert Oppenheimer as saying that "nuclear power for planes and battleships is so much hogwash." Later, reportedly, this quote would be read by William Borden, staff director of the Joint Congressional Atomic Committee, and he would interpret it as a sign that Oppenheimer was in part responsible for delays in Admiral Hyman Rickover's atomic reactor engine program.

And on Friday, June 24, Lewis Strauss dispatched a lengthy letter to Senator Brien McMahon, chairman of the Congressional Atomic Energy Committee, not mentioning Oppenheimer by name but vigorously rebutting some of the points made by the physicist in his June 13 appearance before the committee. A reading of the letter strongly suggests that Strauss had indeed been disturbed by Oppenheimer's biting testimony on the radio-isotope issue.

For Robert and Kitty Oppenheimer, the summer of teaching in California offered an opportunity to renew the friendship with Haakon and Barbara Chevalier. On Thursday, July 7, 1949, at a friendly reunion dinner, it was arranged that the four of them would share a weekend at the Chevaliers' house at Stinson Beach.

By the time of the appointed weekend, Barbara Chevalier was in the hospital with an eye ailment, but she insisted that her husband keep the date. And so Haakon Chevalier and the Oppenheimers spent a warm, sunny Saturday swimming. After an elegant dinner cooked by Chevalier over his wood stove, Haakon returned to San Francisco to be with Barbara, leaving the Oppenheimers to spend the night at the Chevalier beach house.

# 5. *The H-Bomb Debate*

At the end of that summer, an Air Force B-29 detected unexpected amounts of radioactivity in samples of air collected near Japan. When the samples were analyzed, it was apparent the radioactivity had been caused by an atomic explosion. But since there had been no Allied nuclear tests, there could be but one conclusion: America's monopoly in the nuclear age, now just four years old, had gone up in a Soviet mushroom cloud.

The evidence of a Soviet explosion was substantial, yet President Truman wanted to be absolutely sure that it meant what most of the analysts thought it meant. He appointed a special panel of scientists to assess the evidence. The chairman of the panel was Dr. Vannevar Bush; one of its members was Robert Oppenheimer. The scientists concluded that this was no mere makeshift "device." The Russians had exploded a genuine atomic bomb.

Oppenheimer was quickly drawn into the center of subsequent activity in Washington. The Under Secretary of State asked him to share in deliberations as to whether the President should publicly announce the new development (Oppenheimer favored this); and he was asked to testify, with some other witnesses, before the Joint Committee on Atomic Energy.

On Friday, September 23, President Truman announced the Soviet success to the world. As it happened, the General Advisory Committee was holding one of its regular meetings that weekend, and naturally much of the group's discussions centered upon the dramatic news. I. I. Rabi, just back from Europe, favored making immediate recommendations to the AEC, but Oppenheimer and a majority of the GAC favored "tak[ing] a little while to think what to do."

The Truman announcement set off a chain reaction of its own. In Berkeley, California, at the Radiation Laboratory, chemist Wendell Latimer and physicist Luis Walter Alvarez (an alumnus of Los Alamos) independently came to the same conclusion: that the United States must move quickly on to the next step—the hydrogen bomb. Together they appealed to Ernest Lawrence, director of the Radiation Lab, and Lawrence was stirred to action. As a first step he called Edward Teller. Alvarez and Lawrence were scheduled to go to Washington for a meeting anyway, and they decided to leave a day early and meet with Teller at Los Alamos.

Teller had never lost his abiding interest in thermonuclear reactions. Even after leaving Los Alamos in February of 1946, he had continued his work on the subject at the University of Chicago. In the summer of 1949, in part at the urging of Robert Oppenheimer, he had returned to Los Alamos full time, although he expected to work mainly on improving the existing fission weapons. When the news of the Soviet atomic explosion reached Teller, he had immediately called Oppenheimer. The physicist's reaction was: "Keep your shirt on."

But now, as Teller talked with Lawrence and Alvarez at Los Alamos, he found in them allies who were anxious *not* to keep their shirts on. He told them that a successful thermonuclear project hinged on an ample supply of tritium (a special form of heavy hydrogen). That, in turn, depended on the building of what was called a heavy-water reactor. This reactor project was to become the core of "the plan" the group would press for in the ensuing days.

From Los Alamos, Lawrence and Alvarez proceeded to Washington and threw themselves into a whirlwind effort to win support for their plan. Saturday, October 8th: meeting with certain AEC officials who would likely be sympathetic; Sunday: breakfast with Robert LeBaron, the principal Defense Department expert on atomic energy; Monday: luncheon with key members of the Joint Congressional Atomic Committee, including Chairman McMahon; also, appointments with all five Atomic Energy Commissioners; Tuesday: on to New York to confer with physicist I. I. Rabi. Although Rabi was later a fervid H-bomb opponent, Lawrence and Alvarez then found him "very happy at our plans," applauding the return of the Berkeley scientists and their cyclotron to what he considered important work.

From New York the two scientists went back to California to continue their efforts to enlist the interest of their fellow scientists in their thermonuclear project.

Ernest Lawrence and Luis Alvarez were far from the only ones to conclude that the United States must react decisively to the Russian atomic explosion. Two men in Washington were even more convinced, and more active, than they.

One was William Liscum Borden. His conviction was the result of having tried to place himself in the Russians' shoes as of 1945, when the U.S. moved crucially ahead in the weapons field with its A-bomb. Had Borden been they, he would immediately have launched an all-out effort not merely to catch up with the Americans but to move one step beyond them—i.e., to proceed full speed toward a vastly more powerful A-bomb. Therefore to Borden, certain that this was what the Soviets *had* been doing since 1945, every day lost in launching a U.S. H-bomb program was a day in which the Russians were almost certainly moving ahead critically in their own breakneck rush for the "Super." To him, the course the U.S. *must* follow was undebatably clear.

According to his associates, Borden became totally consumed with this one problem during the fall of 1949. He successfully urged the naming of a special Congressional subcommittee on the matter, and traveled with the group to Los Alamos and Berkeley. He drafted a lengthy letter from Senator McMahon to President Truman refuting arguments raised against the H-bomb. One close colleague has said, regarding the governmental debate and decision on the H-bomb question, "You can't mention that decision and Bill Borden in two breaths. They are part of the same breath; it was almost of his making."

The other official in Washington who reacted quickly and strongly to the Soviet atomic explosion was AEC Commissioner Lewis Strauss. On October 5, just two weeks after the Soviet feat was announced, Strauss addressed a memorandum to his fellow Commissioners calling for a "quantum jump" in American planning. By this he meant

that we should now make an intensive effort to get ahead with the super. By intensive effort, I am thinking of a commitment in talent and money comparable, if necessary, to that which produced the first atomic bomb. That is the way to stay ahead.

Strauss also recommended that the Commission consult "immediately" with Robert Oppenheimer's General Advisory Committee "to ascertain their views as to how we can proceed with expedition."

Strauss' feeling of urgency was not shared by AEC Chairman Lilienthal, who favored proceeding more deliberately and thoughtfully. Lilienthal was influenced to some extent by a long-planned and recently approved weapons-expansion program that would produce a regular fission weapon equivalent to 500,000 tons of TNT—over twenty times more powerful than the Hiroshima bomb, potent enough, he was assured, to take out almost any target in the world. Moreover, Lilienthal later recalled, there was no record at the time of any Defense Department request for a weapon of virtually unlimited power.

Nevertheless, he agreed that the advice of the GAC should be promptly solicited, and on October 11 he wrote Oppenheimer asking that the group be convened "in the very near future," and stating that the AEC would welcome the group's "advice and assistance on as broad a basis as possible." The latitude of this mandate to the GAC took on great importance when, in the course of Oppenheimer's security proceeding, he and the GAC were criticized for commenting on the moral and political considerations involved in an H-bomb program, and were, in effect, accused of trespassing beyond their legitimate role of providing *technical* advice to the AEC.

On the fourteenth, Oppenheimer replied that October 29 and 30 were the earliest his group could gather, and even then one of the nine would be missing: Dr. Glenn Seaborg, who had a long-planned trip to Sweden he could not put off. But, wrote Oppenheimer, Seaborg had agreed to contribute his H-bomb views in writing.

In point of fact, Glenn Seaborg was composing his letter to Oppenheimer on that very day, in California.

Ordinarily Seaborg, a careful and conscientious man, would have written such an important letter with great care, putting it through more than one draft. But, he has since recalled, when he received Oppenheimer's request, he was on the verge of departing for Sweden and thus was obliged to write and dispatch the letter with unaccustomed haste, dictating a single draft and sending it off without revision. This may account, in part, for the tentativeness that pervaded the letter. "I will try to give you my thoughts for what they may be worth," he began, ". . . but I am afraid that there may be more questions than answers." The AEC's assignment for the meeting was very broad, he said, and any conclusions would, he knew, only be reached "after a large amount of give and take discussion at the GAC meeting."

On the crucial question of the H-bomb, Seaborg's tentativeness was especially pronounced. To the extent that he expressed a view as to what the United States should do, it was contained in the following two sentences:

> Although I deplore the prospects of our country putting a tremendous effort into this, I must confess that I have been unable to come to the conclusion that we should not. . . . My present feeling would perhaps be best summarized by saying that I would have to hear some good arguments before I could take on sufficient courage to recommend not going toward such a program.

Seaborg seems to have been aware that the expression of his H-bomb views was less than a model of lucidity, for he closed his letter by saying, "I have great doubt that this letter will be of much help to you, but I am afriad that it is the best that I can do at this time."

Within the Pentagon, proponents of the H-bomb, perhaps aware that the absence of an official military request for such a huge weapon was being used against them, moved to close that loophole. On Thursday, October 13, General Kenneth D. Nichols —later to be General Manager of the AEC during Oppenheimer's security hearings—went to Air Force Chief of Staff Hoyt Vandenberg and urged him, "as the No. 1 bomber man," to express the military's interest in a large nuclear weapon. The next day Vandenberg and the Joint Chiefs of Staff appeared before the Joint Atomic Energy Committee. Vandenberg, speaking for his military colleagues, urged that the superbomb be pushed to completion as soon as possible. "We have built a fire under the proper parties," the General said—meaning that the military's view on the H-bomb was being pressed upon the AEC through established channels.

The H-bomb advocates were also joined by Edward Teller,

who flew East from Los Alamos. One of his stops was Ithaca, New York, where he sought to persuade Hans Bethe to return to Los Alamos and work on the thermonuclear problem. Bethe was torn by internal conflict. On the one hand, Teller seemed to be presenting some new technical ideas that made the "Super" sound more feasible than he had thought it. On the other hand, he did not think that the development of a still bigger bomb would solve any of the problems then confronting the world.

While Bethe and Teller were talking, the phone rang. It was Robert Oppenheimer from Princeton. In the course of the conversation, he invited Bethe and Teller to come and visit him in Princeton, which they did, a few days later.

Bethe hoped for some decisive advice from Oppenheimer, but he was disappointed. He found the former Los Alamos director equally troubled about what should be done. He showed the pair some correspondence from James B. Conant in which, as Teller later recalled it, Conant had said the H-bomb would go forward "'over my dead body.'" The principal argument Teller remembered Oppenheimer making was not against the H-bomb program as such but against surrounding it with the degree of secrecy that had obtained during the Los Alamos wartime effort.

Teller was well aware of Oppenheimer's persuasive powers, and before their Princeton visit he had predicted that Bethe would emerge from the meeting dissuaded from joining the Los Alamos effort. But as they departed from the conversation with Oppenheimer, Teller recalls, Bethe turned to him saying, "You see, you can be quite satisfied. I am still coming."

Two days later, however, Teller received a surprising call from Bethe, saying he had changed his mind and was not going to Los Alamos after all. Contrary to Edward Teller's surmise, Bethe's change of heart had been brought about not by Robert Oppenheimer but by two other scientists, George Placzek and Oppenheimer's close friend, Victor Weisskopf. Bethe later said he conversed with the two while driving from Princeton to New York and reached the conclusion with them that a hydrogen war would leave a world none of them would want to preserve.

In Princeton, Robert Oppenheimer was aware of the pro-H-bomb stirrings of what he termed "two experienced promoters"—Edward Teller and Ernest Lawrence—and their apparent success disturbed him. On October 21 he wrote fellow GAC member James B. Conant about the "very great change . . . in the climate of opinion," both in Congress and among competent physicists, including Bethe, who was "seriously considering" returning to Los Alamos to work on the H-bomb. Technically, he said, he was not sure "the miserable thing will work, nor that it can be gotten to a target except by ox-cart."* But his main worries, he wrote Conant, were not technical:

> What does worry me is that this thing appears to have caught the imagination both of the Congressional and of military people, as the answer to the problem posed by the Russian advance. It would be folly to oppose the exploration of this weapon. *We have always known it had to be done; and it does have to be done. . . .* But that we become committed to it as the way to save the country and the peace appears to me full of dangers.
>
> We will be faced with all this at our meeting and anything that we do or do not say to the President† will have to take it into consideration. I shall feel far more secure if you have had an opportunity to think about it. [Emphasis added.]

By this time Oppenheimer had received Glenn Seaborg's letter, and he told Conant that he had Seaborg's "general views . . . in written form."

On Monday, October 24, with the crucial GAC meeting only five days away, the optimism that Lawrence and Alvarez had begun to feel started to wane. From an AEC conference in Oak Ridge came disturbing reports that a key physicist (a reactor expert named Walter Zinn) was being negative about Lawrence's plan for a heavy-water reactor and that a certain AEC official, once enthusiastic, was now less so. Alvarez was urged to go to Washington to present the reactor plan to the GAC in person. He made plans to do so, deciding to stop off in Princeton on the way, to bring Oppenheimer up to date on developments. But a

---

* In this respect, Oppenheimer was prophetic: the first hydrogen device exploded weighed no less than sixty-five tons.

† In a meeting then contemplated (but apparently never held) for Sunday, October 30, at the conclusion of the GAC deliberations.

conference in Chicago was suddenly called for the same date, and Alvarez had to attend, so he arranged that the visit to Oppenheimer be made instead by Robert Serber, his younger colleague at Berkeley. Serber had been working on the Lawrence-Alvarez plan and, it was assumed, enthusiastically supported it.

Alvarez later recalled being pleased at the change, since Serber was "somewhat closer" to Oppenheimer than he. This was an understatement. Serber had been, in the earlier days, at least, among the inner circle of Oppenheimer's students. Few had been on more intimate terms with "Opje" or had worshipped him more. Apparently it did not occur to Alvarez that Serber might be won over by his former idol. And so Robert Serber proceeded to Princeton.

October 29, 1949. A gray, drizzly morning in Washington. Eight men gathered in Room 213 of the Atomic Energy Commission headquarters building on Constitution Avenue. Before them was this question: Should the United States once again embark on a crash effort to unlock the energy of the atom, this time to produce a weapon that could pulverize not just one Hiroshima but at least twenty such cities—or more?

Six of the eight men who met in Room 213 had played a role in the first furious endeavor that had culminated at Hiroshima four years earlier. None of the eight had lived with the atom more intimately than their chairman, Robert Oppenheimer.

That morning, as usual, their deliberations began with a joint meeting with the five Atomic Energy Commissioners. Then followed assessments of the Soviet explosion and its implications by George F. Kennan of the State Department and by an assortment of military spokesmen headed by General Omar Bradley, Chairman of the Joint Chiefs of Staff. Members of the AEC staff also sat in on this morning session, among them Air Force General James McCormack, head of the AEC's Military Application Division, and, as such, the AEC aide most concerned with the Soviet explosion and the U.S. reaction to it. McCormack assumed that the GAC would reach no firm conclusions about the H-bomb at this first meeting on the subject, and so he felt free to leave Washington. That afternoon he flew to the AEC testing ground on Eniwetok Atoll.

After the briefing session, the eight men went into closed session.

Chairman Oppenheimer began the meeting solemnly. He called first on the leading nuclear physicist of the group, Enrico Fermi, for an appraisal of the technical prospects for a thermonuclear weapon. Fermi did not have to start from first principles with this group, for the "Super" was far from new to the GAC. Thermonuclear research had been proceeding continuously at Los Alamos since World War II, albeit on a small scale, and at most GAC meetings there had been progress reports on this research effort. But the more they had heard, one GAC member recalled later, the more discouraged they had become about the prospects, and the atmosphere of the present meeting was one of gloom. At the time, Fermi later recalled, the chances of success were considered a little better than even, but the outcome was far from a foregone conclusion.

Then Oppenheimer asked each of the men around the table, in turn, to express his own views as to the course the United States should follow.

The seven who now spoke were individuals of varied backgrounds and considerable attainment. They were:

James Bryant Conant, chemist and President of Harvard University; a top administrator of the nation's World War II scientific research effort.

Lee DuBridge, physicist and President of the California Institute of Technology; during the war, director of the radar laboratory at MIT.*

Enrico Fermi, physicist, émigré from Italy, and principal creator of the world's first controlled atomic chain reaction.

I. I. Rabi, physicist, Columbia University professor, and colleague of DuBridge's at the MIT radar lab during World War II.

Hartley Rowe, engineer and vice president of the United Fruit Company, wartime expediter of materials procurement for the Manhattan atomic bomb project.

Cyril Smith, metallurgist, MIT professor, wartime head of the metallurgy division at Los Alamos.

Oliver E. Buckley, former president of the Bell Telephone

* In 1969 DuBridge became Science Adviser to President Nixon.

Laboratories and, during World War II, an expert in the guided-missile program.

In retrospect—after the H-bomb had become a reality rather than a dubious theory, and after the Soviets had produced a "Super" only eight months behind the U.S.—it became difficult to imagine that the question before the eight men of the GAC, on that October 29, 1949, could even have been debatable. But, as their later recollections reveal, when Oppenheimer called on each of his seven colleagues to give his views on the "Super," a great many countervailing considerations were in their minds, if not actually voiced.

As they met, the H-bomb was *not* a reality; it was no more than a theoretical possibility—and, in fact, there was no assurance, then, that it was not a theoretical *im*possibility, a violation of the laws of nature and therefore unachievable.

Moreover, some felt there was not enough knowledge at hand to plan a practical crash research program, for there were few indications as to which avenues might best be explored. Of course, the same ignorance and uncertainties had prevailed in 1942 and 1943, when the all-out quest for the A-bomb was launched. But in 1949 there were serious additional drawbacks to such a spare-no-effort program. First, it would necessarily mean diverting funds and scarce scientific talent from the existing fission-weapon program, slowing its hard-gained momentum, and inhibiting the completion of designs for new and more flexible nuclear weapons. Far more critical and troublesome was the "Super's" potential requirement of prodigious amount of plutonium, then in short supply. Assigning quantities of this precious element to the "Super" would severely curtail the production of the efficient new fission weapons. Did it make sense to put such a crimp in the nation's production of weapons of *known* effectiveness in the search for a weapon of dubious feasibility?

Moreover, how much would a "Super" weapon add to the military strength of the United States, compared with an expansion of the existing arsenal of fission weapons? After all, the development of a fission bomb of 500,000 tons had already been approved. How many targets were there in Russia large enough to require an even more powerful bomb? (Were there not, in fact, far more such targets in the United States—and did not self-interest, therefore, lie in trying to negotiate with the Soviet Union an agreement of mutual forbearance on the development of the "Super" before proceeding with our own program?)

There were other vexing questions. For example, since a "Super" bomb would presumably be used only in retaliation to a nuclear strike by Russia, wouldn't the chances of reaching and striking Soviet targets be greater with several U.S. bombers carrying numerous smaller fission weapons than with one or two aircraft carrying "Super" bombs?

Were there not political risks in a unilateral declaration by the United States that it was embarking on the development of a weapon of theoretically *unlimited* destructive power? What effect would this have on both the friends of the United States and uncommitted nations?

Related to that was the moral problem—most graphically expounded later, in the course of the 1954 Oppenheimer security proceeding, by the businessman member of the GAC, Hartley Rowe—that the use of such a massively destructive weapon could not be realistically confined to strictly military targets.* If businessman Rowe entertained such moral doubts in 1949, it is understandable that these should have been shared in even greater measure by the scientists on the GAC who had participated in the fabrication of the bomb that obliterated two Japanese cities and killed tens of thousands of noncombatant civilians. As Robert Oppenheimer later put it, he had always been bothered by "the employment of these weapons on a master scale against civilizations and cities. . . . I suppose," he said, recalling this 1949 GAC meeting, "that bother is part of the freight I took into the General Advisory Committee."

But Chairman Oppenheimer was careful to be the last to give his views on the "Super." When the other seven GAC members had finished speaking, Oppenheimer found that "there was a surprising unanimity—to me very surprising—that the United States ought not to take the initiative at that time in an all out program."

Then, for the first time in the meeting, he expressed his own

* "You [would be] using it against civilization, and not against the military. . . . I don't like to see women and children killed wholesale because the male element of the human race are so stupid that they can't get out of war and keep out of war."

view. "I am glad you feel this way," one participant has recalled him saying, "for if it had not come out this way, I would have had to resign as chairman."

Oppenheimer spoke of the "surprising unanimity" of the seven other GAC members who were present on that October morning. But what of the missing member, Glenn Seaborg? Hadn't his letter leaned, however tentatively and cloudily, in favor of proceeding with the "Super"? Had Oppenheimer apprised the GAC of that letter, so that Seaborg's view might be considered along with those of the eight members present? Normally, Oppenheimer said later, it would have been his practice to read such a letter not only to the GAC, but to the AEC itself; but in this case, he was obliged to acknowledge, he could not remember having done so. In his security-risk proceeding, he would later be berated for this omission.

Yet it is not entirely clear that he did fail to share the Seaborg letter with his colleagues. One GAC member, Cyril Smith, years later remembered with photographic vividness listening to Oppenheimer read the letter aloud, just prior to convening the opening meeting, Saturday morning, to those committee members who had arrived early and were standing nearby. Smith even remembered going around behind Oppenheimer and reading over his shoulder as Oppenheimer read aloud.

If this did, in fact, occur, Oppenheimer failed to recall it and invoke it in his defense, four and a half years later.

At noon that Saturday, after a long morning's work, the group broke for lunch. As Oppenheimer stepped out of the building, he spotted Luis Alvarez and Robert Serber talking together. He beckoned them to join him for lunch, and the trio went to a small basement restaurant near the AEC building.

Up to that moment Alvarez assumed that Serber had transmitted to Oppenheimer an enthusiastic view of the Lawrence-Alvarez plan to build a heavy-water reactor. In fact, Alvarez rather expected Oppenheimer to report that the GAC had voted to support the plan. And so the luncheon conversation that day carried a double surprise for Luis Alvarez. The first was Oppenheimer's attitude. As Alvarez later recalled it, Oppenheimer opposed a U.S. H-bomb program on the ground that if America didn't build one, the Russians would not. The second surprise was that Serber agreed with Oppenheimer. This stunned Alvarez, since just two or three days earlier Serber had assured Alvarez that he would try to convert Dr. Oppenheimer's lukewarmness into some enthusiasm for the Lawrence-Alvarez plan. Oppenheimer later testified that he had sought neither to encourage nor to discourage Serber from working on the hydrogen project, but at the time Alvarez could only conclude that the physicist had worked his charms on his former student during Serber's overnight stay in Princeton.

Discouraged, convinced his program was dead, Alvarez left for California right after the luncheon.

The GAC spent the balance of its two-day meeting drafting, discussing and rewriting its report to the AEC. The result was a recommendation from the entire group on the fission as well as the thermonuclear program and two separate appendices on the hydrogen bomb.

Although the group as a whole concluded that an "imaginative and concerted attack on the [thermonuclear] problem has a better than even chance of producing the weapon," its report said:

> We all hope that by one means or another, the development of these [thermonuclear] weapons can be avoided. We are all reluctant to see the United States take the initiative in precipitating this development. We are all agreed that it would be wrong at the present moment to commit ourselves to an all-out effort towards its development.

As to the policy the United States should adopt on the H-bomb, the committee split. Two of its members, Enrico Fermi and I. I. Rabi, strongly condemned the H-bomb on moral and ethical grounds:

> The fact that no limits exist to the destructiveness of this weapon makes its very existence and the knowledge of its construction a danger to humanity as a whole. It is necessarily an evil thing considered in any light. For these reasons we believe it important for the President of the United States to

tell the American public and the world that we think it is wrong on fundamental ethical principles to initiate the development of such a weapon.*

These two scientists believed that, just as America had built a moral basis for its postwar development of fission weapons by its offer in 1946 to give up its nuclear monopoly, it should make one final attempt to gain international agreement on foregoing the "Super" before embarking unilaterally on its development. Fermi's view was that if such an effort failed, then the U.S. "should, with considerable regret, go ahead."

The other six members of the committee issued a separate appendix on the H-bomb, written by James B. Conant, which expressed these views:

> We believe a super bomb should never be produced. Mankind would be far better off not to have a demonstration of the feasibility of such a weapon until the present climate of world opinion changes. . . .
>
> It is the opinion of the majority that the super program itself should not be undertaken and that the Commission and its contractors understand that construction of neutron producing reactors [which could or could not be used for thermonuclear research, depending on their design] is not intended as a step in the super program. . . .
>
> In determining not to proceed to develop the super bomb, we see a unique opportunity of providing by example some limitations on the totality of war and thus of eliminating the fear and arousing the hope of mankind.

Later, the first sentence above provoked a controversy revolving around this question: Were Robert Oppenheimer and his

---

* British journalist Norman Moss, in his book on the H-bomb, *Men Who Play God*, contends that despite its "moral tone," the Fermi-Rabi report was intended by its authors "to be . . . more cautious" than the majority report. Moss says Rabi and Fermi were merely arguing that "the United States should not be the first to build a super, but should reserve the right to do so if another power did." Regarding the Rabi-Fermi assertion that it was "wrong on fundamental ethical principles to initiate the development" of the "Super," Moss says that Rabi and Fermi placed prime importance on the word "initiate," although the key phrase was more generally interpreted as "wrong on fundamental ethical principles."

colleagues merely opposing an all-out "crash" development of the "Super" (as Oppenheimer later insisted) or were they opposed to the development of the hydrogen bomb *on any basis*, as indicated by the words, "We believe a super bomb should never be produced"?

After the GAC adjourned on Sunday, Chairman Oppenheimer stayed on in Washington. Twice he conferred with Secretary of State Dean Acheson and evidently repeated the GAC majority's stated hope that if the U.S. would voluntarily forswear the development of the H-bomb, it could "provid[e] by example some limitations on the totality of war." This line of argument deeply troubled Acheson, who told his chief nuclear adviser, "You know, I listened as carefully as I knew how, but I don't understand what Oppie is trying to say. How can you really persuade a hostile adversary to disarm 'by example'?"

Yet the hope that Acheson found so frail was regarded as considerably more substantial by Acheson's principal policy adviser, George F. Kennan. In a 128-page analysis of the problem of reacting to the Soviet atomic explosion, Kennan emphasized the Soviet Union's great reliance on *non*military means of expansion (subversion, political action, economic pressure, etc.). This led Kennan to venture the belief that the Soviets would not proceed with a thermonuclear weapon if the United States did not.

Nor was the morality of nuclear warfare the preoccupation exclusively of Oppenheimer and the members of the GAC in the month of October, 1949. It was also a matter of concern to a career military officer, Rear Admiral Ralph A. Ofstie. Testifying before the House Armed Services Committee on October 11, in opposition to the Air Force's long-range B-36 bomber, Admiral Ofstie said: "We consider that strategic air warfare, as practiced in the past and as proposed for the future, is militarily unsound and of limited effect, is *morally wrong*, and is decidedly harmful to the stability of a post-war world." (Emphasis added.)

Ten days after the GAC meeting, the five AEC Commissioners were unable to arrive at a consensus on a "crash" program for the H-bomb. They decided to submit their views individually to the President. Chairman Lilienthal and Sumner Pike, the salty Maine Republican, were flatly opposed to an all-out H-bomb program. Dr. Henry DeWolf Smyth, the only scientist member of the Commission, favored holding off on any intensive H-bomb program until there had been one more quick try at an agreement with the Soviets on international control. If that should fail, Smyth believed, the U.S. would have to make a firm decision about the H-bomb. Gordon Dean, the newest member of the Commission, favored a "crash" program, but also urged further efforts for an agreement with the Soviets. Only Lewis Strauss said America must proceed on the "Super" without delay.

But Strauss did not restrict the expression of his views to the authorized chain of command. He arranged to see the Secretary of Defense, Louis Johnson. One account of that meeting reports Strauss' approach this way:

> Eager to get to the point, Strauss said abruptly as he entered Johnson's office: "Mr. Secretary, isn't it an American tradition that we will never accept the idea that we will be less armed than our enemies?"
>
> Johnson, a former American Legion Commander, agreed. Strauss continued, "The AEC has just voted to reverse that tradition."

According to the same authors, Strauss' conversation with Johnson, which went on until after nightfall, had a dramatic effect on Johnson, for the next morning he called in his top advisers and

> announced dramatically that there was every reason to believe that the Russians were building an H-bomb, that the U.S. was being sold down the river, and that the U.S. *must proceed with an H-bomb program.* . . .

One officer in the room voiced a doubt that the H-bomb was militarily practical. This was one of the arguments the GAC had found persuasive, but this officer is quoted as expressing it in a manner different from that of the GAC: "The Air Force already has a bomb powerful enough to blow Moscow off the map. Why waste money on the H-bomb?" This question was reportedly answered by Major General James Burns, a special adviser to

Johnson, who said quietly, "It's a fundamental law of defense that you always have to use the most powerful weapons you can produce."

In mid-November, Senator Brien McMahon and other members of his Atomic Energy Committee made plans to visit Los Alamos as part of their further inquiry into the question of the "Super." The AEC had sent McMahon copies of the GAC's report on the H-bomb, and so, in order that key members of the Los Alamos staff would be as informed as the Senator, the AEC General Manager called Dr. John Manley, an associate director of the Los Alamos laboratory and secretary to the GAC, and asked him to show the same report to a select number of Los Alamos officials. Manley carried out the instructions.

In the course of that fall the special Congressional subcommittee on the H-bomb traveled to California to confer with some West Coast scientists. They were accompanied by the committee's executive director, William Borden.

One evening Borden and the subcommittee members were invited to the home of Caltech president Lee DuBridge, a GAC member and long-time friend of Robert Oppenheimer, who was also present. As Borden listened to DuBridge discuss the H-bomb question, he was struck by two things: first, that DuBridge's anti-H-bomb arguments seemed intellectually flabby, based on amorphous moral considerations rather than on the rigorous application of intelligence to the problem; and second, that DuBridge seemed to be speaking virtually as Oppenheimer's puppet, that he was under the spell of Oppenheimer's extraordinarily magnetic personality, speaking his lines as if Oppenheimer expected them of him.

The memory of that evening remained sharp in Borden's mind for years afterward.

Word of Robert Oppenheimer's opposition to the H-bomb program reached, and greatly disturbed, Ernest Lawrence and Luis Alvarez. They could not make any sense out of Oppenheimer's arguments and, indeed, felt he was much too lukewarm in pushing the over-all AEC program.

In one instance, in 1949, they had occasion to discuss this with Vannevar Bush, as they drove Bush back to San Francisco from a visit to Stanford University. In the course of the conversation, Bush expressed surprise that he, and not a nuclear physicist like Oppenheimer, had been named head of the special group of scientists charged with evaluating the data on the Soviet atomic explosion. Lawrence and Alvarez later had differing recollections of just what Bush said. Lawrence remembered him saying that the scientific group had been appointed by Air Force Chief of Staff Hoyt Vandenberg (this was in accord with the historical fact of the matter), and that Vandenberg had named Bush chairman because he lacked trust in Robert Oppenheimer. But as Alvarez recalled it, Bush said that the evaluation panel had been appointed by the President of the United States, and observed, "I think the reason the President chose me is that he does not trust Dr. Oppenheimer. . . ." Alvarez was struck by this, he later recalled, because it "was the first time that I have ever heard anyone in my life say that Dr. Oppenheimer was not to be trusted."

Among those most upset by the GAC's October recommendations against the hydrogen bomb was Air Force General James McCormack, who was both surprised and annoyed upon his return from Eniwetok to learn from Ernest Lawrence that the GAC had indeed reached a decision on this most important weapons matter without giving him, the AEC's chief weapons expert, the courtesy of a hearing. In Washington he expressed his displeasure, and so, when the GAC reconvened in early December, McCormack, joined by AEC research chief Kenneth Pitzer, made a strong personal plea to the GAC to reverse its stand and back the H-bomb program.

This time Glenn Seaborg was present. McCormack's strong pro-H-bomb presentation, as well as the AEC's request for amplification of certain points in the October reports, gave Seaborg two opportunities to voice any disagreement he may have had with the group's October conclusions. If he had any such misgivings, he evidently did not voice them, however, for the minutes show that the GAC stuck to its earlier view of the H-

bomb program, without dissent from Dr. Seaborg.* To all in-
tents and purposes, all nine members of the General Advisory
Committee were now unanimous.

Eight weeks later Oppenheimer was asked by the Joint Congressional Atomic Energy Committee how unanimous the GAC
had been in its opposition to an all-out H-bomb program. Oppenheimer replied that he thought the GAC view had been pretty
unanimous, but that one member, Glenn Seaborg, had been absent when the matter was discussed and had not expressed himself on the H-bomb question.

Had not expressed himself? How could Oppenheimer reconcile this with having solicited, received and noted (in his letter
to Conant) Seaborg's written views on the H-bomb matter? Did
he feel that Seaborg's language had been so cloudy that he had
not really "expressed himself"? Or had the Seaborg letter slipped
from his consciousness, as it would during his security hearing
four years later, to Oppenheimer's acute embarrassment?

* Years later Seaborg recalled feeling diffident, as by far the youngest
member of the GAC (he was at the time only thirty-seven), about speaking
out, especially in disagreement with the unanimous view of his eight older
and more senior colleagues on the committee.

## 6. A Failure to "Enthuse"

In Washington, within the government, discussions about the H-bomb took place under a shroud of the most total, almost obsessive secrecy. The principle of the H-bomb was universally known in the scientific community (*viz.* the description of it, in 1946 in a book on atomic physics [p. 97]), yet the merest mention of a superbomb was, for Washington officialdom, a cardinal sin.* But suddenly, in mid-November, the shroud of secrecy was pierced. This was not the work of any Soviet agent. It was the doing of a United States Senator, and it occurred in the course of a nationwide television interview during which the Senator (a) berated American scientists for blabbing atomic secrets, (b) urged tighter security clamps on the atomic energy program, and (c) divulged what he himself labeled as a "top secret."

The Senator was Edwin C. Johnson of Colorado, a member of the Joint Committee on Atomic Energy. Asked whether atomic secrecy barriers could be relaxed now that the Soviets clearly knew how to make an atomic bomb, Senator Johnson replied, "I'm glad you asked that question, because here's the thing that is top secret." He then proceeded to reveal that ever since Hiroshima American scientists had been "trying to make what is known as a superbomb," and that they had already

> created a bomb that has six times the effectiveness [of the Nagasaki bomb]; and they're not satisfied at all; they want one that has a thousand times [as much power]. . . . And that's the secret, that's the big secret that the scientists in America are so anxious to divulge to the whole scientific world.

If there existed any American scientists who were inclined to

---

* One reporter, Alfred Friendly of the Washington *Post*, who had previously covered the "atomic beat," returned from two years abroad to find that all his former friends and "sources" had suddenly clammed up. No one would say anything; they would merely act mysterious. Friendly's reportorial curiosity was aroused. He began to get wind of some talk about a superbomb. He mentioned it one day to AEC Chairman Lilienthal. Lilienthal blanched. He pleaded with Friendly not to publish anything about the bomb.

divulge this tightly held secret, they no longer needed to do so. Senator Johnson had done it for them.

Just six days after President Truman's sensational announcement about the Soviet A-bomb, the House Un-American Activities Committee issued a "Report on Atomic Espionage." One passage concerned a Katherine Puening, who, the report said, had been befriended by the Communist Steve Nelson after the death of her husband in Spain and had later married "one of the leading physicists engaged in the development of the atomic bomb." The report went on to state that both the Communist Party and the Soviet Government were aware of Nelson's acquaintance with "the physicist," and had "attempted to use this as a medium of infiltration at the Radiation Laboratory at the University of California. . . ." But, significantly, HUAC concluded as follows:

An investigation of the aforementioned scientist disclosed that neither he nor his wife engaged in any subversive activities *and that their loyalty has never been questioned by the government.* Nelson later reported that neither the physicist nor his wife were sympathetic to Communism. [Emphasis added.]

Perhaps "the physicist" in question was too busy to notice the report. If he did, he failed to invoke it in his own defense when, years later, his loyalty *was* "questioned by the government."

On Friday, January 27, 1950, Sir Frederick Hoyer Millar, atomic expert in the British Embassy in Washington, paid a call of extraordinary urgency on Under Secretary of State Robert D. Murphy. A scientist named Klaus Fuchs had been arrested in London, Sir Frederick said, and had confessed to espionage on behalf of the Soviet Union. His information had been gained in the course of his work at the Los Alamos weapons laboratory, continuing into the summer of 1946, when he had participated in—and been an important contributor to—discussions on the state of U.S. knowledge of the thermonuclear bomb.

The Fuchs affair could not have been absent from the minds of three key presidential advisers four days later, when they met to arrive at a final recommendation to President Truman on the H-bomb question. Two of them—Defense Secretary Johnson and

Secretary of State Acheson—favored proceeding with the bomb; only AEC Chairman Lilienthal demurred.

The President quickly accepted the majority recommendation and, a few minutes before one o'clock on January 31, 1950, Press Secretary Charles Ross called in reporters and read them a brief statement:

> It is part of my responsibility as Commander-in-Chief of the Armed Forces to see to it that our country is able to defend itself against any possible aggressor.
>
> Accordingly, I have directed the Atomic Energy Commission to *continue* its work on all forms of atomic weapons, including the so-called hydrogen or super-bomb. [Emphasis added.]

The use of the word "continue," deliberately chosen so as to make the announcement as undramatic as possible, was not disingenuous. In spite of the torment that preceded and the anguish that followed the presidential decision, the moral and philosophical Rubicon had already been crossed. Ever since Hiroshima the U.S. had been proceeding continuously, albeit slowly, with research on the thermonuclear project with the knowledge and agreement of all government officials, including the GAC. The Truman announcement merely meant that work on the "Super" would now proceed with more speed and determination, but this was a difference of degree, not of principle.

But the world did not view the January 31 announcement that way. On the contrary the news commanded world headlines and comment. From a public point of view, the Thermonuclear Age had begun.

So had the public debate about the H-bomb. Thus far (Senator Johnson's television revelation aside) the fate of the hydrogen bomb had been shaped largely in secret. But with the Truman announcement the secrecy lid was off. Scientists reacted quickly. Just five days after the presidential decision, twelve of the nation's leading physicists, including Hans Bethe, spoke out against the superbomb. Though it was theoretically possible, they said, to develop a bomb of unlimited destructive power,

We believe that no nation has the right to use such a bomb, no matter how righteous its cause. This bomb is no longer a weapon of war but a means of extermination of whole populations. . . . We urge that the United States . . . make a solemn declaration that we shall never use this bomb first.

The opposition did not come merely from scientists. Among the first-day reactions to the Truman announcement was that of Congressman Sterling Cole of New York, the senior Republican member of the Congressional Atomic Energy Committee, who spoke against making the bomb. Some churchmen were also disturbed: on the first Sunday following the presidential statement, a prominent Methodist minister, the Reverend Dr. John Sutherland Bonnell, preached of the threat to the world in this new dread weapon. A week later, a statement by Albert Einstein received worldwide attention:

If [the H-bomb] is successful, radioactive poisoning of the atmosphere and hence annihilation of any life on earth has been brought within the range of technical possibilities. . . . In the end there beckons more and more clearly general annihilation.

While Einstein, Bethe and others were willing to voice their criticisms publicly, Robert Oppenheimer was not. Only twice did he refer publicly to the Truman decision. In both instances he refrained from discussing the merits of the new policy, confining his remarks to the way in which the decision had been reached. The first was in a radio interview with Eleanor Roosevelt in mid-February. The hydrogen bomb decision, he said, involved matters which, while technical, "touch the very basis of our morality." In a display of extemporaneous eloquence, he said:

There is grave danger for us in that these decisions have been taken on the basis of facts held secret. This is not because the men who must contribute to the decisions . . . are lacking in wisdom; it is because wisdom itself cannot flourish, nor even truth be determined, without the give and take of debate or criticism. The relevant facts could be of little help to an enemy; yet they are indispensable for an understanding of questions of policy. If we are wholly guided by fear, we shall fail in this time of crisis. The answer to fear cannot always lie in the dissipation of the causes of fear; sometimes it lies in courage.

In the month following the President's hydrogen bomb decision, the name of Haakon Chevalier arose twice to affect the life of his old friend, Robert Oppenheimer. It came up first, unbeknownst to either Chevalier or Oppenheimer, in a secret hearing of the Joint Committee on Atomic Energy, on February 6. The hearing was not principally about Oppenheimer; it was a general review of security matters. But in the course of the discussion mention was made of Haakon Chevalier and his wartime approach to Oppenheimer. It was, according to committee records, the first time the matter of Oppenheimer's security background had been officially brought before it. It was an important occasion for it was this meeting that prompted the committee's staff director, William Borden, to begin his own meticulous review of the massive Oppenheimer file some nine months later.

The "Chevalier incident" rose to the surface a second time that month in an exchange of letters between the two old friends. They had not seen each other since their day together at Stinson Beach the previous summer. In the meantime a newspaper article had appeared reporting Oppenheimer's interrogation by HUAC concerning the Chevalier incident. According to the article, Oppenheimer had told the Congressmen that Chevalier had not approached him to get secret information but to report on a prior conversation with Eltenton. Chevalier thought this something of a public vindication, but he wanted the story straight from Oppenheimer. He wrote his friend that he was "most anxious to get back into academic work" but that Oppenheimer's Congressional testimony about him was "one important issue that is repeatedly raised." He received a prompt reply, dated February 24, 1950. Oppenheimer said he could see how an official account of his testimony would be helpful to Chevalier "in seeking a suitable academic position at this time," but that the committee had ruled that the hearings must be kept secret. Still, he wrote, he could give Chevalier a summary of what he had said:

> I told them that I would like as far as possible to clear the record with regard to your alleged involvement in the atom business. I said that as far as I knew, you knew nothing of the

atom bomb until it was announced after Hiroshima; and that most certainly you had never mentioned it or anything that could be connected with it to me. I said that you had never asked me to transmit any kind of information, nor suggested that I could do so, or that I consider doing so. I said that you had told me of a discussion of providing technical information to the USSR which disturbed you considerably, and which you thought I ought to know about. There were many other points; but these were, I think the highlights; and if this account can be of use to you, I hope that you will feel free to use it.

As you know, I have been deeply disturbed by the threat to your career which these ugly stories could constitute. If I can help you in that, you may call on me.

Sincerely yours,
ROBERT OPPENHEIMER*

Later, Chevalier was to avail himself of Oppenheimer's invitation to make use of the letter, in support of his application for a U.S. passport. He was also to wonder why, when the "Chevalier incident" was in all the headlines in 1947, his friend could not have made "some such statement, and made it public," instead of confining himself to a formal "no comment."

There is, each February, a hiatus in the affairs of the U.S. Congress while its Republican members fan out across the country to make fund- and enthusiasm-raising speeches in observation of the birthday of their party's first President, Abraham Lincoln. It was in the course of this annual political exercise that a little-known Republican Senator from the state of Wisconsin found himself, on February 9, 1950, just nine days after the presidential announcement about the hydrogen bomb, in Wheeling, West Virginia. And it was there that Joseph R. McCarthy began his march to notoriety with his sensational charge that he held in his hand "a list of 205" known Communists who were still working in the State Department.

During the next few days of Lincoln Day stumping, McCarthy

* Oppenheimer accompanied this letter with a personal note to Chevalier, apologizing for the "formality" of the enclosure, saying he did not feel at all formal about the troubles Chevalier was having; and wished he might think of an easy solution to them.

moved fast, and so did his statistics. In Denver, the day after the West Virginia charge, the "Communists" had become "Bad security risks." In Salt Lake City, the following day, the number had shrunk from 205 to "57 card-carrying Communists." By February 20 the figure had changed to 81. The variability of the numbers was facilitated by McCarthy's persistent refusal to attach a name to even one of the alleged subversives, but his charges were sufficiently sensational as to engage the President of the United States in the controversy and to persuade the Senate to dignify the charges with a Foreign Relations Committee investigation of them.

Joseph McCarthy was off and running.

Throughout the spring of 1950, although the development of the H-bomb was now established national policy, scientist opposition to it increased rather than abated. On a national radio broadcast, four physicists caused a furor by discussing the feasibility of a bomb that could wipe out the earth's population by radioactivity alone. One of the four was Oppenheimer's friend, Hans Bethe, who also wrote an anti-H-bomb article for the magazine, *Scientific American*.

Leaders in the so-called "soft sciences" of history and government were also heard from: Harvard Dean McGeorge Bundy, economist J. K. Galbraith and historian Arthur Schlesinger, Jr., were among the signers of an April letter to the *New York Times* warning of a U.S. strategy founded on a "misplaced faith in atomic weapons and strategic bombing" that "seems to impair the moral and political strength" of the United States. They also said that overreliance on The Bomb had left the U.S. "not well equipped to deal with problems of limited aggression," a condition which, they thought, "may invite the extension of techniques of guerrilla warfare . . . in marginal areas, in the confidence that such local activity would incur only local risks." Two months later their apprehensions were substantiated as North Korean ground forces crossed the 38th Parallel, and moved into South Korea.

Although it was now official presidential policy to develop an H-bomb, the question remained: How? Even in the short span of time between the October, 1949, GAC meeting and the presidential announcement in January, 1950, the technical prospects had grown bleaker.

The first order of business was to rebuild the depleted scientific staff at Los Alamos and increase the brain power being applied to the seemingly intractable problems. In the wake of Hiroshima and Nagasaki there had been such a mass exodus of Los Alamos scientists that the lab's Theoretical Division (which would be most engaged in the thermonuclear explorations) fell from fifty scientists with postgraduate degrees in 1945 to only eight in 1946, of whom five were assigned not to the thermonuclear project but to perfecting the crude fission weapons used against Japan. Among them there was not a single scientist of the stature of a Fermi or a Bethe or a Teller. Moreover, it was hard to generate enthusiasm for the building of a bomb that would have one thousand times, or more, the destructive power of the weapons that had wiped out two Japanese cities. As Carson Mark, the postwar head of the Theoretical Division later put it, if his researches had proven the thermonuclear bomb a physical impossibility, he would have found this a happy rather than a sad occasion.

In the immediate postwar years, Edward Teller was almost alone in maintaining not only an intense interest in the thermonuclear bomb but the confidence that it could be achieved. He returned to Los Alamos in 1949, clearly to be the spark plug of the new H-bomb effort. In the spring of 1950 he tried to recruit new talent for the project.

Even before the presidential go-ahead on the bomb, he had sought the help of Robert Oppenheimer regarding a brilliant young physicist named Conrad Longmire, who had just received an appointment to the Institute for Advanced Study and was reluctant to give it up. When called by Teller, Oppenheimer gladly agreed to tell Longmire he could resume his Institute appointment "at any time you want it"—in an "attempt to make the decision easy for him." Longmire joined the Los Alamos staff, where he remained for many years.

Teller had also sought to persuade Oppenheimer himself to return to Los Alamos, but received a sufficiently negative reply that he concluded he should not look to Oppenheimer for any further help on the H-bomb. But in the spring of 1950, at the urging of AEC Commissioner Gordon Dean, Teller once again called Oppenheimer, asking, this time, not for the physicist's direct participation but for his help in recruiting others. Four years later, when Teller testified in Oppenheimer's security hearing, he portrayed the physicist as unenthusiastic and comparatively unhelpful. He quoted Oppenheimer as saying, "You know in this matter I am neutral. I would be glad, however, to recommend to you some very good people . . . at the Institute," and mentioned a few. Teller said all his letters to Oppenheimer's nominees had been to no avail.

That was Teller's recollection, four years later. But at the time he apparently had no hesitation in directing scientists whom he was trying to recruit to Oppenheimer, "who could tell you in more detail than I could just how urgent the situation is." More important, he seemed, at the time, to regard Oppenheimer's role far more favorably than he was later to recall it, for on February 17, 1950, he wrote "Dear Oppi" that he was very grateful indeed for the help Oppenheimer was giving and was going to give in the recruitment effort.

Four years later, the grave charge would be leveled at Robert Oppenheimer that he had been "instrumental in persuading other outstanding scientists not to work on the hydrogen-bomb project." Documentary evidence to support this charge is hard to come by; Edward Teller's official testimony on the subject stops short of that serious claim, and when in 1966 he was asked for names of specific scientists allegedly dissuaded by Oppenheimer, he did not furnish any. The same inquiry was made of others who contended that Oppenheimer had hurt the 1950 recruitment program; not one was able—or willing—to give the name of a single scientist Oppenheimer had steered away from the H-bomb project.

His critics contended that his negative influence was not that specific but flowed more generally from his position of preeminent leadership in the scientific community. Oppenheimer accepted this point, observing, "In that sense, I think that if I had gone out to Los Alamos, even if I had done nothing but twiddle my thumbs, if it had been known that I had gone out to promote the 'Super,' it might have had an affirmative effect on other people's actions." To those who sought his advice on joining the H-bomb project, Oppenheimer recalled, he said that it was "a very interesting program and they should find out about it." His role, he later asserted, was to lend "active support as an adviser to the [AEC] . . . in my job on the General Advisory Committee," but not "active support in the sense that I rolled up my sleeves and went to work." He acknowledged that his anti-H-bomb views prior to the presidential decision were inevitably well known in the community of physicists and that this doubtless contributed to their hesitation. But, he insisted, there were other grounds: a disinclination to leave pure, in favor of applied, research; a reluctance to contend with either the isolation of Los Alamos or the personality of Edward Teller. In view of these other factors, "I don't think," Oppenheimer said, "my lack of enthusiasm . . . would have been either persuasive or decisive."

Interestingly enough, the seriousness of Oppenheimer's dampening effect on 1950 recruitment has been cast into doubt by one of Oppenheimer's strongest detractors, Lewis Strauss. "Contrary to predictions," Strauss wrote, "the [Atomic Energy] Commission experienced no difficulty in finding dedicated scientists who were willing to work on the H-bomb and who supported the decision of the President."

One neutral observer, a brilliant physicist who returned to Los Alamos in 1950 to work on the H-bomb, and an admirer of both Teller and Oppenheimer, assessed Oppenheimer's effect on H-bomb recruitment this way:

> There was a feeling at Los Alamos that Oppenheimer, just by being inert at the time of the Truman decision, had put a damper on the hydrogen program. He could have, had he wanted to, recruited several senior people; also, at the Institute [for Advanced Study], he had access to the best of the junior people coming out of the colleges. The only person with any "clout" at Los Alamos was Teller; but Oppenheimer, with his disciples, had access to maybe ten times as many people as Teller did. So the "crash" program ended up by consisting of Teller and Bethe and about a dozen junior people—that's all.

Where was Oppenheimer in late July, 1941? Oppenheimer himself later recalled being on his ranch in New Mexico—a recollection reinforced by Haakon Chevalier and by Hans Bethe (who vividly remembered the horse-kicking incident).

But in May, 1950, Mrs. Sylvia Crouch, appearing at an Oakland hearing of the California Committee on Un-American Activities, had a different recollection of Oppenheimer's whereabouts in that particular month. The scientist had not been in New Mexico, she told the committee; he had been in Berkeley, California. More specifically, she said, he had been host, in his Berkeley home, to a "session of a top-drawer Communist group known as a special section, a group so important that its makeup was kept secret from ordinary Communists." She knew this, she said, because she herself had been there with her husband, Paul, a former Communist who had now become a paid consultant for the Justice Department.

Of the twenty or so people in the Oppenheimer home Mrs. Crouch said she recognized only a few, among them an Oppenheimer student named Joseph Weinberg. How did Mrs. Crouch know Weinberg had been at that meeting? Her answers to this question were a bit vague. At first she told the committee she had identified Weinberg from a photograph. Later she changed her testimony and said she had seen Weinberg not at Oppenheimer's home but a year earlier at a Washington hearing of the House Un-American Activities Committee.

In Washington, Robert Oppenheimer promptly issued a statement, through the Atomic Energy Commission, saying he had "never been a member of the Communist Party" and had never assembled a party meeting "in my home or anywhere else." He acknowledged that he had formerly known many persons "in left-wing circles" and had belonged to many such organizations, but that the government had known about all these affiliations ever since the beginning of the atomic project. The name "Crouch," he said, did not mean anything to him.

The next day, the California committee heard another witness, an ex-Communist and truck driver by the name of Alfred Barbosa. Mr. Barbosa looked at a photograph of Robert Oppenheimer that convinced him that the scientist had been among the fifty to seventy-five people—"all Communists," he said—who had attended a housewarming at the Berkeley home of Kenneth May

some nine years earlier. Mr. Barbosa's acuity in photograph identification was thrown into some doubt later in the hearing when
he was shown a photograph of one Clarence Hiskey and assured
the committee this was a picture of Joseph Weinberg.

That same day, in Oakdale, California, a young Congressman
was campaigning hard for the Republican nomination for United
States Senator. In a midday speech, he took pains to praise a man
whose name could hardly have been a household word to his
audience in Oakdale (population 4,980). Reacting to the news
story about Sylvia Crouch's accusation, he said, "I have complete
confidence in Dr. Oppenheimer's loyalty." As a member of
HUAC, the Congressman said, he had had frequent occasion to
meet and question the nuclear physicist. "We found him on all
occasions a cooperative witness."

"From these conversations and others," the Congressman said,
"I am convinced that Dr. Oppenheimer has been and is a completely loyal American and, further, one to whom the people of
the United States owe a great debt of gratitude for his tireless and
magnificent job in atomic research." So spoke Representative
Richard M. Nixon on Wednesday, May 10, 1950.

Lieutenant General Leslie R. Groves, U.S. Army (Retired)
apparently felt the same way as Congressman Nixon. Then a
business executive living in South Norwalk, Connecticut, Groves,
too, had read of the accusations of Mrs. Crouch, as well as the
defense of Oppenheimer by Nixon. On May 18 he wrote his
former wartime associate. If Oppenheimer should feel it "wise" at
any time, the General would be "pleased" to have him issue a
statement "of the general tenor of that which follows":

'General Groves has informed me that shortly after he took
over the responsibility for the development of the atomic bomb,
he reviewed personally the entire file and all known information concerning me and immediately ordered that I be cleared
for all atomic information in order that I might participate in
the development of the atomic bomb. General Groves has also
informed me that he personally went over all information concerning me which came to light during the course of operations

of the atomic project and that at no time did he regret his decision.'

The General said he didn't foresee any need to use the statement, but thought Oppenheimer might want to show it "to some individual for his use in handling unpleasant situations, if any arise." After expressing his pleasure at the affirmations of persons such as Congressman Nixon "in whose judgment I have more than average faith," the General observed: "I am sure of one thing, and that is that this type of attack, while it is unpleasant, does not in the end do real damage to one's reputation."

Apparently the Federal Bureau of Investigation did not feel as sure about Robert Oppenheimer as General Groves did. Earlier that month, FBI agents had journeyed twice to Princeton to ask Oppenheimer about the Communist meeting allegedly held in his home in 1941. On their first visit Oppenheimer said he wasn't sure which meeting they might be referring to and asked for more details about the alleged meeting. The more the agents described the purported meeting, the surer Oppenheimer became that the meeting had not occurred. But he promised to talk it over with Kitty Oppenheimer to see if she had any independent recollection of the occasion.

When the agents returned a few days later, Oppenheimer told them he was sure the meeting described by the Crouches had not occurred. Moreover, he said, he had never been to a closed Communist meeting. He did remember someone—possibly Kenneth May—asking him for the use of his house for a meeting of young people. Also, Kitty had reminded him of a meeting at the Chevaliers' house in 1940 or 1941 at which Communist official William Schneiderman had tried to explain what the Communist line was all about. Oppenheimer said that when he had been interrogated previously by the FBI, since the agents had talked only of an "East Bay" meeting, he had neither remembered it nor connected it with Haakon Chevalier (the principal object of their inquiry), and so he had declined to answer. Now that Kitty had reminded him of the meeting, though, he remembered it.

Oppenheimer also took this occasion to reflect upon his past ties with the far left. He told the agents that by the time of the

Russo-Finnish war and the Nazi attack on Russia he had come to realize the tactic of Communist infiltration into anti-Fascist groups, had become fed up with the whole affair and lost what little interest in the party he had had. He had made a big mistake, he said, in not dropping his Communist friends long before he did.*

What about one of those friends, Dr. Thomas Addis? the agents asked. Was that question important to them? Oppenheimer wanted to know. Unless it was, he would not discuss his friend Addis, who was now dead and could not defend himself. The agents said they didn't think the question was important, and the matter was allowed to drop there. (Years later, in the security proceeding, Oppenheimer's judges seem to have regarded his failure to respond about Addis as yet another example of his disrespect for the requirements of security.)

The FBI agents also wanted to hear what Oppenheimer knew about his former student Joseph Weinberg, who had recently been alleged, in Congressional hearings, to be the "Scientist X" of a Soviet spy ring. Oppenheimer replied he hadn't known Weinberg was a Communist until it had become public knowledge. (In saying this, he contradicted what he had told Colonel John Lansdale in 1943.†)

The FBI brought a summary of this conversation and of the Crouch testimony to the attention of AEC Commissioner Gordon Dean. Dean concluded that the AEC should talk directly with Oppenheimer about the allegations made by Sylvia Crouch, but he wanted the scientist approached delicately. General Counsel Joseph Volpe was dispatched to broach the matter with Oppenheimer, and he reported back to Dean Oppenheimer's assurances that while he might possibly have met the Crouches—they had plenty of people around their house in those days—he had never been part of any Communist meetings.

Nonetheless, Gordon Dean proceeded to go through the entire Oppenheimer investigative file. After all, Oppenheimer was the chairman of the Commission's General Advisory Committee, and

---

* When questioned about this at his later security hearing, Oppenheimer said he didn't "recognize" having made such a statement.

† He told Lansdale he learned of Weinberg's party membership in a 1943 visit to Berkeley (see p. 61).

although he had been cleared by the AEC in 1947, this had occurred before Dean became a member of the Commission. He felt
he had better review the file personally. Having done so, he called
Oppenheimer in to see him and discussed with him the Crouch
testimony. The scientist repeated substantially what he had told
Volpe.

On Saturday, June 25, 1950, North Korean forces attacked
South Korea across the dividing 38th Parallel. The Cold War had
suddenly turned hot.

With American forces engaged in ground warfare, the attention of the GAC was suddenly focused on the problem of developing nuclear weapons small enough to be used on the battlefield. A
special panel was named to study the problem. Its report caused
the first of many policy controversies over the use of battlefield
nuclear weapons in defense of Western Europe—one of many
policy areas in which Robert Oppenheimer was to be at odds with
the United States Air Force.

The outbreak of war in Korea also brought about a change of
heart in physicist Hans Bethe, who saw it as the first step toward
a general war, and, despite his previous vocal opposition to the
H-bomb, agreed to apply himself to thermonuclear research, at
Cornell and at Los Alamos.

At this juncture the outlook for the H-bomb had never seemed
darker. To test Edward Teller's current approach to the "Super"
by means of theoretical mathematics, mathematician Stanislaw
Ulam was pitted against a computer in a modern-day John Henry
race. While Ulam won the race (unlike John Henry), both his
calculations and the computer's agreed that Teller was on the
wrong track. Teller was in despair.

The deterioration of the outlook for the H-bomb happened to
coincide with a breakthrough in the fission-bomb program that
had great significance for the military policy disputes in which
Oppenheimer and the Air Force found themselves at odds. Theretofore, fission bombs had required first-grade nuclear materials
that were in critically short supply, so that military planners were
in the habit of assuming acute weapons shortages. To the Air
Force's Strategic Air Command (SAC), which had by far the
largest share of bombs, any new use for nuclear materials (e.g.,

for small battlefield weapons) could take place only at the expense of a reduced SAC allocation.

But in mid-1950 it was discovered that fission bombs could use far lower-grade materials, which were in vastly more plentiful supply. This should have meant a sharp change in military thinking, for rather than an "either/or" tug of war between huge strategic bombs and small battlefield nuclear weapons, it was now possible to have "both/and." But this was an adjustment some SAC proponents were to find difficult to make. Many of them would persist in looking with dark suspicion on such proponents of nuclear weapon diversification as J. Robert Oppenheimer.

Among the charges that were later brought against Oppenheimer was that he "continued to oppose" the H-bomb even after it had become a "matter of national policy." In his defense, Oppenheimer supporters sought to point out that, in contrast to his discreet *public* silence on the matter, prominent scientists such as Einstein, Bethe and former AEC Commissioner Robert Bacher spoke out publicly against the bomb, even after the presidential go-ahead. So did New York's Representative Sterling Cole. Cole was no ordinary Congressman, but the ranking Republican member of the Congressional Atomic Energy Committee, and so his July 17 speech, "The Hydrogen Bomb: A Panacea?," was based on considerable official knowledge and carried great authority. He argued that against huge cities the H-bomb would be no more effective—and against small industrial targets less effective—than numbers of smaller fission bombs, and that the coastal cities of the U.S. were far more vulnerable than Russia's landlocked cities to H-bombs secreted in, say, tramp steamers. The New York Congressman then said: "One might well question just how useful such a weapon as the hydrogen bomb would be. Is it worth the hundreds of millions of dollars needed to produce it?" This high-ranking Congressional atomic expert was speaking nearly six months after the President had determined the H-bomb policy.

The growing importance of the hydrogen project in the work of the AEC, as well as its increasingly bleak prospects during the summer of 1950, made Oppenheimer feel somewhat uncomfortable in continuing to serve as chairman of the General Advisory Committee. Some new men had joined the committee, including chemist Willard Libby (whose views were contrary to Oppenheimer's on the hydrogen bomb, but whom Oppenheimer had nevertheless recommended for the job), and Oppenheimer began to wonder whether he should not step aside as chairman. As he later recalled it, he discussed the matter with a number of scientists, including Edward Teller (Teller didn't remember such a discussion), who urged him to remain on. So did Secretary of State Dean Acheson, who besought Oppenheimer not to "upset the applecart." Even so, in the autumn of 1950 he raised the question with Gordon Dean, then AEC Chairman, and with Commissioner Henry Smyth. Both, he later recalled, forcefully told him that they would be very unhappy if he were to quit as chairman.

And so the GAC chairmanship remained in Oppenheimer's hands.

In the summer of 1950 Haakon Chevalier's marriage broke up. In this difficult moment he turned to Robert Oppenheimer, whom he still looked on as his best friend. Oppenheimer replied warmly to Chevalier's letter: "I share in your sorrow; so does Kitty. Yours was one of the families we knew first and best, and we do not readily accept its end." He invited Chevalier to come and stay with them in Princeton "for a good tranquil visit; it will be more rewarding to all of us than a hit and run. . . ."

Twice that fall Chevalier did visit the Oppenheimers in Princeton. The troubled Chevalier poured out his unhappiness and in return received understanding and affection. During his second visit Chevalier told Oppenheimer of the difficulties he was having securing an American passport. The physicist referred his friend to a Washington lawyer, Joseph Fanelli, whom he had not met but who had represented his brother, Frank, in his 1949 appearance before HUAC.

Chevalier's passport difficulties dragged on; he became nervous, then panicky. He began to imagine Kafkaesque plots against him by "fiendish but impersonal agents in a vast administrative labyrinth." Without even telling lawyer Fanelli, whom he had engaged to help him secure the passport, Chevalier decided to take advantage of his dual citizenship and leave for France using his

French passport. Up to the last minute he was afraid he would not be permitted to leave. Even at the airport in New York, on November 2, there were moments of suspense, as the airline agent who took his passport disappeared into a back room for what seemed like an interminable time. Presently, though, the passport was returned, and as his plane left the runway, Haakon Chevalier breathed a sigh of relief.

William L. Borden had, by now, been executive director of the Joint Committee on Atomic Energy of the Congress for more than a year and a half. During that time he had paid very little attention to a matter in which many members of his committee had a considerable interest and that had been virtually the preoccupation of his predecessor—personnel security. It was about time, he felt, to devote some attention to the subject. He called the Atomic Energy Commission and asked if he might come down and look at the files of ten or a dozen employees whom they considered to be among their most difficult "security cases." An appointment was arranged, and on November 20, 1950, Borden went down to the Atomic Energy Commission offices. He was shown into an office and handed a file, the first of the "tough" security cases selected by the AEC for his review. He opened it. It was the file of Julius Robert Oppenheimer.

That fall Oppenheimer was made chairman of the special Pentagon panel charged with helping the government plan the long-range future of its atomic weapons program.* Chairman Oppenheimer made a point of calling Ernest Lawrence's senior assistant, Luis Alvarez, and inviting him to be on the committee. "I would like to have you on this committee," Oppenheimer told Alvarez, "because I know you represent a point [of view] different from mine, and I think it would be healthy to have you on this committee." Alvarez thought Oppenheimer was being very fair and accepted the appointment.

In the committee's second meeting, the subject of discussion was the development of small nuclear weapons for battlefield use.

* Oppenheimer's appointment, notably, was made by Robert LeBaron, deputy to the Secretary of Defense and one of the most intensely pro-H-bomb government officials.

Some in the group felt that the hydrogen-bomb program was interfering with small-weapons research by siphoning off scarce scientific manpower. Luis Alvarez disagreed: there were enough scientists, he said, for both the H-bomb *and* the small-weapons program.

In the course of that meeting (according to Alvarez' recollection nearly four years later), Oppenheimer made a statement that shocked Alvarez considerably. As Alvarez remembered it, Oppenheimer said, "We all agree that the hydrogen-bomb program should be stopped, but if we were to stop it or to suggest that it be stopped, this would cause so much disruption at Los Alamos and in other laboratories . . . that I feel that we should let it go on, and it will die a natural death with the coming [thermonuclear] tests, when those tests fail. At that time will be the natural time to chop the hydrogen program off."

If Alvarez' recollection was correct, it is little wonder that he was shocked, for not only had the chairman said *he* thought the H-bomb program should be stopped. He had gone so far as to say *"we all agree"* it should be—and clearly Alvarez himself did not agree. Nor was he the sole H-bomb advocate in the group: there were General James McCormack, head of the AEC's Military Application Division; Air Force General Roscoe Charles Wilson; and the Navy's Admiral "Deak" Parsons. Wouldn't at least one of these H-bomb supporters have protested an Oppenheimer assertion that "we all agree" the H-bomb program should be stopped? Alvarez recalls no such protest from any of them.

Did Oppenheimer actually make such a statement? No other member of the group has been found who remembers his doing so. Asked about Alvarez' recollection, Oppenheimer himself felt that at most he may have said that everyone agreed, at that juncture, that the prospects for *success* of the thermonuclear were exceedingly bleak, but he was sure that he had not predicted that the impending thermonuclear test would fail. He did feel —and may well have said—that the so-called "Greenhouse" preliminary test made little technical sense. He may also have observed (he said later) that to stop the Greenhouse test, despite these technical drawbacks, would disrupt the Los Alamos effort.

Alvarez later recalled that when the group held its final meeting to consider a draft of its report, he may have been concerned about catching his return flight to California and therefore may not have given the draft as careful attention as he should have. In any event, he and the other committee members made their suggestions, and departed with the understanding that a final version of the report would be circulated for their approval and signature. According to one member of the group, Chairman Oppenheimer stayed on in Washington to complete the revisions, as an "aid to all of us."

Some time later, Oppenheimer called Alvarez in Berkeley. Would Alvarez mind going down to Pasadena, where a copy of the report was being sent, so that he could go over it with fellow committee members C. C. Lauritsen and Robert Bacher at Caltech? Alvarez agreed, made a one-day trip to Pasadena, reviewed and signed the report, and thought no more about it—for the moment.

Some months thereafter, however, trouble erupted. Edward Teller had seen the report. He approached Alvarez about it. "Luis, how could you have ever signed that report, feeling the way you do about hydrogen bombs?" Alvarez was puzzled; he had seen nothing wrong with the report: it had, he acknowledged, emphasized the small-weapons problem, but since the report had said that the hydrogen bomb was an important long-range program, he had seen no objection to signing it.

Well, said Teller, "you go back and read that report and you will find that [it] essentially says that the hydrogen-bomb program is interfering with the small-weapons program, and it has caused me no end of trouble at Los Alamos. It is being used against our program. It is slowing it down and it could easily kill it."

Upon rereading the report, Alvarez was equally shocked, although when he had considered it on the two previous occasions—in Washington and at Pasadena—he had not perceived its anti-H-bomb implications.

But hadn't Oppenheimer named him to the committee to be, in effect, the "H-bomb spokesman," and to keep a particular eye out to protect the pro-H-bomb interests? Why hadn't he read the sections pertaining to the H-bomb with special care and interest? Alvarez' explanation was that he was not trained "in the legal ways of reading documents." By contrast, Oppenheimer was, by Alvarez' later description, "one of the most skilled document writers" he had ever run across.

How could Alvarez be sure that Oppenheimer had personally written the report? Because, Alvarez later commented, "he always wrote the reports of these committees." The way it generally happened, he said, was that after the long and tiring meetings Oppenheimer would ask his committee how the report should be written, and the response would invariably be, "Oh, you write it, Oppie, you're the best at doing that," and Oppenheimer would agree to write a draft for later circulation to committee members for their approval.

Alvarez also began to have disturbing second thoughts about another Oppenheimer tactic. Why had he asked Alvarez to go all the way down to Pasadena to review and sign the report? Why hadn't he had the AEC courier bring the report up to Berkeley for his signature? At the time of Oppenheimer's call Alvarez had attached no significance to the request, but later he was "forced to the conclusion" that the physicist must have calculated that in Pasadena Alvarez would review the report in the company of staunch Oppenheimer friends and supporters (C. C. Lauritsen and Robert Bacher). On the other hand, if the report had been brought to Berkeley, there would have been a good chance Alvarez would show it to Ernest Lawrence, who would surely have objected to the anti-H-bomb implications in the document.

Reflecting on the incident years later, Alvarez said he saw nothing sinister in this; Oppenheimer was simply giving much more thought than he to the tactics and politics of the situation. "Oppenheimer was, in effect, practicing Political Science 4B, on the post-graduate level, while I was still on Political Science 1A, the freshman course."

Not every member of the long-range study panel took such a benign view of Robert Oppenheimer's conduct as its chairman. One member, Air Force General Roscoe C. Wilson, grew increasingly uneasy as he watched the articulate scientist guide the discussions. His uneasiness turned to a concern deep enough to prompt him, after one of the panel meetings, to go to the Air Force Chief of Intelligence and point out what he felt was a dangerous pattern of action on Oppenheimer's part.

The essential Roscoe Charles Wilson was summed up—by Wilson himself—in two words: "dedicated airman." The Air Force was his life, and had been ever since he had been sent directly from West Point to flying school. In the eyes of General "Bim" Wilson, if something was bad for the Air Force, it was bad, period. General Wilson's view of the military tactics to be used against Russia ("the base of international Communism") was, he acknowledged, an airman's view. Protected by Communist satellites on the West, and with little coastal border, Russia was comparatively invulnerable to attack by land or sea. The only method left was attack by air, preferably with large nuclear bombs. "I am first of all a big-bomb man," he said.

It was this outlook that caused General Wilson to regard the beliefs and activities of Robert Oppenheimer with growing alarm through the postwar years. First, there had been his interest in "internationalizing atomic energy . . . at a time when the United States had a monopoly," which Wilson said was probably "the greatest deterrent to further Russian aggression." Although General Wilson knew that the so-called Baruch plan had been supported by many people of good faith, it was his impression that the original plan of internationalization suggested by Oppenheimer was far looser. (In fact, the opposite was true; it was in part at Oppenheimer's insistence that the Baruch plan had called for an international inspection agency to police any nuclear agreement; but of this General Wilson was unaware.)

The General's doubts about Oppenheimer had been reinforced by the scientist's lack of enthusiasm for two of three devices the Air Force had sought in 1948 for the detection of Soviet atomic explosions. The "overall effect" of this had been to "deny to the Air Force the mechanism which we felt was essential to determine when this bomb went off."

Third, there had been Oppenheimer's opposition to the development of a nuclear-powered aircraft. This, General Wilson acknowledged, was a technical judgment on Oppenheimer's part; yet he found it significant that Oppenheimer had been less strong in his opposition to nuclear-powered *ships* for the Navy. "The Air Force feeling was that at least the same energy should be devoted to both projects."

Finally, there was Oppenheimer's approach to the problem of

the H-bomb. Again, he acknowledged that Oppenheimer's attitude sprang in part from technical objections; yet, said General Wilson, he approached the matter with "more conservatism than the Air Force would have liked."

But it wasn't just these dubious veiws that bothered General Wilson. It was, perhaps even more, the man behind them—as Wilson put it, "the fact that he is such a brilliant man, the fact that he has such a command of the English language, has such national prestige, and such power of persuasion." All of this, the General said, "made me nervous. . . . It was for that reason that I went to the Director of Intelligence to say that I felt unhappy."

This was early in 1951. Although nothing immediate seems to have resulted from General Wilson's troubled report, it was the first sign of badly deteriorating relations between Robert Oppenheimer and the United States Air Force.

In the latter months of 1950, and in early 1951, Edward Teller was living under the most intense personal pressures, and if he bristled at his friend Alvarez' innocent signing of a report that came to be used against the H-bomb project, this is understandable. After all, he, more than any other single individual, had committed his own reputation on the workability of a thermonuclear bomb—against the skepticism and opposition of the entire General Advisory Committee. As the months of 1950 went by, this skepticism seemed more and more justified; by fall Ulam's calculations indicated that Teller's approach to the bomb—then thought to be the most natural and promising approach—could never work.

Under such acute pressure to "produce," Teller became agitated. An associate at Los Alamos has recalled him storming out of meetings in a rage and spending hours conversing on matters that seemed more personal than substantive. Relations with his Los Alamos colleagues, never harmonious at best, deteriorated even further.

But suddenly the outlook brightened dramatically. Mathematician Ulam made some new calculations that suggested an entirely new approach to the thermonuclear problem. He discussed them with Teller; in Teller's mind they struck sparks. By

March the new approach was spelled out in a joint paper by Teller and Ulam.

In May, after much suspenseful uncertainty, a crude thermonuclear device was successfully exploded on Eniwetok Atoll, in the Pacific, proving that the fusion reaction was indeed possible.

In mid-June, Teller's new brain child had its first major unveiling at a two-day conference in Princeton, New Jersey, attended by virtually every scientific luminary in the atomic field and by the top AEC officials. The chairman of the meeting was J. Robert Oppenheimer.

As Teller has recalled, it appeared at first that he was not to be given an opportunity to set forth his new theories, but he went determinedly to the blackboard and began expounding them. As such scientists as Fermi, Bethe, Oppenheimer and Rabi began to apprehend what Teller was unfolding, their excitement grew. Rabi has described it: this, he said, was "an entirely different meeting" from anything previous, "because a new invention had occurred."

AEC Chairman Gordon Dean remembers "leaving that meeting impressed . . . that everyone around that table without exception . . . was enthusiastic now that you had something foreseeable. I remember going out and in four days making a commitment for a new plant [even though] we had no money in the budget to do it. . . . There was enthusiasm right through the program for the first time. The bickering was gone."

What about Oppenheimer's reaction? Dean talked with him after the meeting, "and he was, I could say, almost thrilled, that we had something here that looked as though it might work." Edward Teller, who had come to the meeting expecting that Oppenheimer and the GAC would continue to oppose the project, found that Oppenheimer now "warmly supported this new approach." Teller even understood the physicist to say that if anything of this kind had been suggested initially, he never would have opposed it (an observation later confirmed, in effect, by Oppenheimer himself).

The scientist's changed attitude was summed up in an intriguing and, to some, disturbing phrase. With Teller's new approach, he later said, the H-bomb program became "technically so sweet that you could not argue about that." With such an invention, "you go ahead and do it and you argue about what to do about it only after you have had your technical success."

To some, these did not seem the words of a man who entertained strong moral scruples about the development of this weapon of mass annihilation.

If Gordon Dean believed, at the conclusion of the Princeton meeting, that the bickering had stopped, he was unduly optimistic. It might even be said that the intense feuding over the H-bomb that was later to involve and affect Robert Oppenheimer so deeply had just begun.

There was, for example, the clash between Edward Teller and Los Alamos Director Norris Bradbury. Bradbury and Teller had differed in their approaches to the work of the Los Alamos laboratory ever since 1945, when Teller had insisted on either a strong thermonuclear or a vigorous fission-testing program as a condition for his remaining at the lab. Bradbury had failed to meet the demand, and so Teller had left. When Teller returned to Los Alamos in 1949, his differences with Bradbury persisted. Bradbury felt that Teller wanted to strike out in many different directions at once—many of them of doubtful promise—heedless of existing limitations on manpower and funds. Teller, on the other hand, saw the approach espoused by Bradbury and the GAC—one of going slowly, exploring carefully and testing sparingly—as far too conservative, serving "as a brake rather than encouragement." Now, in the wake of the encouraging Princeton meeting, Bradbury and Teller met head on, on the two questions of a new chief for the thermonuclear program and a timetable for producing and testing the device.

On the matter of the new chief, Teller suggested several persons outside the Los Alamos staff. These Bradbury found unacceptable; instead, he appointed a member of his own staff, Marshall Holloway. Whatever Holloway's other qualities, he was, by general agreement, the least likely to be acceptable to, or to work smoothly with, Edward Teller. The two had clashed openly at meetings.

A split between the two arose immediately on the question of a production and test schedule. Holloway insisted a major test could not be achieved in less than thirteen months. To Teller, that signaled just one thing: Holloway's efforts would be only halfhearted. Teller insisted that the job could be done in nine months, and if the longer schedule was to be adopted, he could not stay and participate in the Los Alamos effort. When Bradbury sided with Holloway, Teller concluded, "This is *not* a crash program. They don't need me—I'm leaving." And he departed for the University of Chicago.

For Robert Oppenheimer the summer of 1951 brought the happy news that his old friend Haakon Chevalier was soon to be married again. Chevalier wrote Oppenheimer from Paris that his fiancée, Carol, was returning to the States, and he hoped she would have a chance to meet Kitty and Robert, either in New York or in Princeton. He received a prompt and warm reply from Oppenheimer inviting Carol to visit them in Princeton, which, he said, would have some of the same qualities of a visit from Chevalier.

One of Carol's recollections of her overnight visit to Olden Manor, the Oppenheimer house in Princeton, was of Kitty Oppenheimer turning to her and asking, "You've got money, haven't you?" Years later Carol Chevalier could vividly describe the dismay clearly shown by both Oppenheimers when she replied in the negative. She surmised, with Haakon, that this was born out of chagrin at the damage the "Chevalier incident" had done to Haakon's career and the hope that he was now marrying into financial security.

# 7. Rumblings in the Pentagon

Throughout 1951 aspects of Robert Oppenheimer's leftist background continued to surface here and there. In January one of his former Berkeley students, David Hawkins, in Congressional testimony, told of his past Communist Party membership. The April issue of the *American Mercury* asserted that the party's choice of Steve Nelson to spearhead the "attack" on the Berkeley Radiation Lab had been dictated by Nelson's former friendship with Kitty Oppenheimer. And in June the California Committee on Un-American Activities reached a somewhat bizarre conclusion concerning Robert Oppenheimer: namely, that Steve Nelson's reports to the Communist Party concerning the Oppenheimers' "uncooperative and unsympathetic [attitude] toward Communism" were really just a ruse to throw U.S. agents off the Oppenheimers' trail, and *really* were an indication of their strong ties to the party.

But these were of minor importance compared with a conversation that took place on August 13 between two men who were to play key roles in the later security hearing of the physicist. The two were Lewis L. Strauss and William L. Borden.

Although the occasion for their meeting is not known, according to a memorandum of the conversation which Borden made at the time, Strauss devoted a good part of the conversation to expressing his concern about Oppenheimer. Borden replied that Strauss was not alone in his feeling about the physicist. Borden suggested that he and others had begun to despair of ever reaching any definite conclusion about Oppenheimer's loyalty. The two men agreed that it would probably be impossible to confirm or dispel their fears through the use of intelligence methods (such as surveillance of movements, telephone conversations and the like). Strauss observed that Oppenheimer and his associates would now be exceedingly careful about what they said over the telephone, since "The Barber" (Strauss' and Borden's nickname for former AEC General Counsel Joseph Volpe, a close friend of Oppenheimer's) was in a position to know that Oppenheimer's phone was tapped and would have passed this information on to Oppenheimer.

Strauss recalled, with some annoyance, the first meeting of the General Advisory Committee he had attended, in January, 1947. At the start of that meeting, Strauss related, James Conant had jumped up to nominate Oppenheimer chairman of the group and had more or less railroaded the nomination through. Strauss also recalled with considerable bitterness a 1940 magazine article by Conant entitled, "Wanted: More Radicals," expressing a liberal viewpoint of which Strauss strongly disapproved.

Strauss told Borden how, shortly after the President had given a go-ahead on the H-bomb, physicist Hans Bethe had said he wanted to go to work full time on the bomb and how, to make that possible, Strauss had promised to make up out of his own pocket any salary cut Bethe would suffer by going to Los Alamos.* They had shaken hands on the deal, but then Bethe visited Oppenheimer in Princeton and shortly thereafter called off the arrangement.

That summer John Walker, a Yale Law School classmate of William Borden's and one of his closest friends, joined the staff of the Atomic Energy Committee. One of Walker's assignments was to keep tabs on the progress of the AEC's H-bomb work, and as he set about educating himself in the thermonuclear field, he found one name to be ubiquitous, that of J. Robert Oppenheimer —chairman of this, consultant on that, expert witness on the other. Walker became disturbed at the omnipresence of Oppenheimer, but even more at the manner in which Oppenheimer seemed to exploit his role. For example, he found that Oppenheimer, as a member of a Pentagon policy group, had argued against declaring a military need for the H-bomb since AEC scientists had not yet declared it technically feasible; however, later on the same day, sitting as an AEC adviser, he had discouraged expansion of technical research on the H-bomb, on the ground that the Pentagon had failed to express any military need for such a weapon.

After a nationwide tour of atomic facilities, Walker concluded that Oppenheimer's apparent influence on the H-bomb pro-

---

* Governmental associates of Strauss say this is by no means the sole instance in which Strauss made such offers.

gram was even greater in the scientific community than it was in government councils. As late as October, 1951, even after the unveiling of Edward Teller's promising new approach to the bomb, Walker could find no more than a dozen important scientists who were in favor of the thermonuclear project.

In ensuing months, Walker and his friend William Borden would spend many hours discussing the remarkable Dr. Oppenheimer, whose security file Borden continued to study.

On September 1, 1951, David Tressel Griggs left his post as professor of geophysics at UCLA to become Chief Scientist for the United States Air Force. Shortly after assuming his new post, he was introduced again to a matter that had come to his attention in 1946 when he had joined the RAND Corporation: the possibility that Robert Oppenheimer was a security risk. This time the doubt was expressed by the Secretary of the Air Force, Thomas K. Finletter. According to Griggs' later testimony, Finletter said "he had serious question as to the loyalty of Dr. Oppenheimer." Griggs also learned that Finletter's misgivings were shared by Air Force Chief of Staff Hoyt Vandenberg. Gradually, as Griggs himself became "informed from various sources" about Oppenheimer's left-wing background and his wartime brushes with security officers, he decided that Finletter and Vandenberg were not dealing in "irresponsible" charges. As the Air Force's Chief Scientist, he felt obliged to "take into consideration" what they had said.

It was not long before Griggs encountered Oppenheimer directly. They were brought together in the course of Project Vista, a large-scale study of how atomic weapons might be adapted to conventional warfare. The study sprang from a concern that the huge Russian armies, never fully demobilized after World War II, could sweep across Western Europe unless NATO had some new battlefield arms—such as small nuclear weapons—to stop them. The large airborne atomic weapons on which America had concentrated were excellent for wiping out whole cities but of little use against enemy soldiers. The problem suddenly took on a new urgency when the Korean War broke out and the Communists chose to wage ground warfare.

What kind of nuclear weapons would be needed on the battlefield? Under what conditions might they be used? To answer such questions, the three military services commissioned a study by scientists at Caltech, in Pasadena. Since Oppenheimer had taught there in spring semesters from 1929 to 1942, it was not surprising that the leaders of the Vista study were either former associates or students of his and generally sympathetic to his view of arms and armaments.

Early in the fall of 1951, after a summer of field trips and conferences, the Caltech scientists set about writing their report, but they found it difficult to sort out the many interrelated points they wished to make. And so they turned to the one man who could help them clarify their presentation, Robert Oppenheimer. At the invitation of Vista chairman (and Caltech president) Lee DuBridge, Oppenheimer journeyed to Pasadena and dug into a mass of documents, drafts and notes. After two days of reading and discussion, he was able to bring previously elusive ideas into clear focus. With the help of some associates, he wrote a new draft of what was later to become the controversial Chapter 5 of the Vista report. Then he left Pasadena.

Meanwhile, in the Pentagon, the Air Force began to hear disquieting things about what was being said and written in Pasadena. Air Force Secretary Finletter was nettled by the slogan reportedly being bandied about in Vista: "Let's bring the battle back to the battlefield"; it seemed to disparage the role of air power. Moreover, he began to get the impression that the Vista report was dealing with such factors as the political disadvantages of strategic warfare—matters, he thought, for the *political* experts in Washington to decide and not for scientists to meddle with.

In mid-November a delegation of officials from Air Force headquarters, including David Griggs, flew out to Pasadena to see for themselves what was going on. There they were shown a draft of the controversial Chapter 5. Its author, they were told, was Robert Oppenheimer.

Griggs found three points in the Vista draft "unfortunate from the standpoint of the Air Force." One was a skeptical view of putting H-bombs to tactical uses. Another was what Griggs, at least, understood to be a recommendation that the U.S. publicly forswear use of the H-bomb against Russian cities except in retaliation against a prior Soviet nuclear attack. But it was the third point that most disturbed the Air Force: namely, a three-way allocation of the precious U.S. supply of fissionable materials. Up to then these materials had gone preponderantly to the Strategic Air Command (SAC). Under the Vista allocation, some nuclear materials would go to SAC, some to smaller tactical weapons and some into a reserve, to be used as evolving technology and battlefield conditions might dictate.

To partisans of SAC, this three-way slicing of the nuclear pie represented a significant restriction of SAC's autonomy. As Griggs later put it, the plan would have "restrict[ed] our military atomic capability." The Air Force feared that Oppenheimer's power of persuasion would make the plan contagious in Washington. One of Thomas Finletter's principal assistants, Garrison Norton, remembers an impressive presentation by Oppenheimer before a plenary session of Vista thinkers. Norton later recalled that one could almost visibly perceive the respect in which Oppenheimer was held by everyone in the room. Norton himself could not help being enthralled by the physicist's eloquence and his brilliant mastery of the subject.

Since the Vista report dealt largely with the defense of Western Europe, its authors felt that they should send representatives to Paris to talk with European Commander Dwight D. Eisenhower and his highest-ranking officers.* But the visit to Eisenhower was somehow slow to come about. Secretary of Defense Robert A. Lovett's office was in favor of the trip, but the Air Force and Army seemed to be teaming up to stymie any Vista presentation in Paris. To elude this opposition, one of Lovett's aides, James Perkins (later president of Cornell), hit upon an idea. He suggested that the Vista delegation go to Eisenhower under the auspices of the Defense Department, as representatives of its Research and Development Board, thus freeing them from the jurisdiction and control of any one military service. Secretary Lovett approved the idea, and Perkins arranged for the

* The idea originated with two occasional participants in the Vista deliberations who later came to be regarded as military "hard-liners": General Albert C. Wedemeyer (who offered to write General Eisenhower to pave the way for the Vista delegation's visit) and John A. McCone, who had just resigned as Under Secretary of the Air Force and was later to become Chairman of the AEC and Director of the Central Intelligence Agency.

Research and Development chairman, Walt Whitman, to accompany the Vista group. Chosen as members of the group were Vista Chairman DuBridge, Caltech scientist Charles C. Lauritsen and J. Robert Oppenheimer.

No sooner was the group airborne for Paris than Perkins received an outraged call from Air Force Secretary Thomas Finletter. Finletter, Perkins has recalled, "went straight through the ceiling"; he contended that Perkins had knifed him in the back with his circumventing tactics. Finletter then summoned General Lauris Norstad, the highest-ranking Air Force officer in the NATO command, for a twenty-four-hour visit to Washington so that he could be fully prepared to counter the DuBridge group's recommendations.

In Paris the Vista representatives had a pleasant conversation with General Eisenhower and then met with General Norstad, freshly returned from his Washington briefings. Almost immediately Norstad treated them to a lengthy and forceful lecture on the virtues of strategic warfare. This disturbed the Vista delegates. They did not regard themselves or their report as opposed to strategic warfare or to SAC. Norstad had given them the impression he was more irritated by the tone of their report than opposed to its substance. Overnight they revised its wording, and the next day they took it back to the General. According to Oppenheimer's later recollection, Norstad told them, "If I am asked, I will tell the Chief of Staff and the Secretary [of the Air Force] that I think this is a fine report and very valuable."

The apparent conversion of Lauris Norstad could hardly have won Robert Oppenheimer and his colleagues any friends among the high command of the Air Force in Washington. In fact, Oppenheimer's role in the Vista study and report was but the first in a chain of events that made it apparent to David Griggs that "there was a pattern of activities, all of which involved Dr. Oppenheimer," a pattern that prompted Griggs and, he has said, Finletter as well to entertain "serious question as to the loyalty of Dr. Oppenheimer."

In the fall of 1951 another issue arose to divide the Air Force and Robert Oppenheimer still further: the question of building a second atomic weapons laboratory.

Although Edward Teller had quit Los Alamos, out of impatience with the slow projected pace of H-bomb work, he was not a man to acquiesce quietly. In fact, he had left Los Alamos in part to be free to espouse the idea of a second weapons lab, to provide the friendly competition with Los Alamos on which he felt scientific progress thrives. And espouse it he did, with great effectiveness, through his most natural ally, the United States Air Force, which was prospectively the principal, if not the only, "customer" for the H-bomb. At one point, Teller spent an entire afternoon arguing his view to Secretary Finletter, and soon thereafter Finletter paid a visit to Los Alamos. There he got what he felt was double-talk and excuses, and he concluded that Teller's second-lab concept offered the only way to speed up the H-bomb work. If the AEC would not start such a lab, maybe the Air Force would have to.

In late 1951 the AEC, beginning to feel pressure from the Pentagon, placed the second-lab issue before its General Advisory Committee. At various times the proposals for such a lab had taken varying forms, ranging from devoting a portion of an existing laboratory to thermonuclear work to building an entirely new integrated lab—in effect a replica of Los Alamos. It was in this latter form that the matter came up in the GAC and the group declined to support such a costly and time-consuming project, by a vote of eight to one (chemist Willard Libby dissenting).

Edward Teller was not fazed. He joined forces with Thomas Murray, the only AEC Commissioner who favored a second laboratory, and they prepared a new proposal that was voted on by the GAC in December, 1951. It, too, was voted down, eight to one.

On Capitol Hill, Senator Brien McMahon, chairman of the Joint Committee on Atomic Energy, had been infuriated by the AEC's opposition to a second lab. He had directed William Borden, the committee's executive director, to prepare a specific Joint Committee recommendation for such a facility. Still the AEC was unmoved, arguing that a second lab would "retard rather than accelerate the development progam." Nonetheless, in February the question was again brought before the GAC for a third vote. Again Oppenheimer's group declined to support a second weapons facility.

At the Pentagon, Air Force officials were becoming increasingly restive. David Griggs went to see his ally at the AEC, Commissioner Thomas Murray, and the talk "confirmed my suspicion . . . that roadblocks [were] being put in the way of this development . . . that the General Advisory Committee, and specifically Dr. Oppenheimer, had been interfering" with the starting of a second lab.

But the Air Force had a trump card up its sleeve—a ruling by its lawyers that it had legal authority to start a weapons lab of its own. And so the Air Force began negotiations with the University of Chicago for the transformation of one of its facilities.

The AEC, hearing of these negotiations, began to cast about for a compromise solution. It soon hit upon a logical place for Edward Teller to work with his long-time friend and supporter, Ernest O. Lawrence: a facility at Livermore, California, that was associated with Lawrence's Radiation Lab and engaged in work of which the AEC and its Advisory Committee had begun to take a sour view. The proposal to convert this into a weapons laboratory for Teller and his associates was put to the GAC and, as Oppenheimer later put it, "This we liked and this we endorsed."

And so, in mid-1952, the Livermore Laboratory began operations. Edward Teller had realized his dream. But after months of pressing for faster schedules, more intense work and utmost speed, he was going to work, not on an overtime, or even on a full-time basis, but on a part-time two-days-a-week schedule.

Other Oppenheimer doings helped form the "pattern of activities" that so disturbed David Griggs and his Air Force associates. One was the report that came to sensitive Air Force ears that (as Griggs later described it) "Oppenheimer and two other colleagues [had] formed an informal committee of three to work for world peace, or some such purpose, as they saw it." This suspect trio, the Air Force heard, "considered that many things were more important than the development of the thermonuclear weapon—specifically, the air defense of the continental United States."

Continental defense was indeed of great interest to two physicist friends of Oppenheimer's, Caltech's Charles C. Lauritsen and MIT's Jerrold Zacharias. Both men had participated in a study of the subject that had resulted in the establishment of the Lincoln Laboratory, near Boston, dedicated to developing techniques of air defense, radar detection and the like. Later, in March, 1952, the two met in Los Angeles and discussed reported advances in Soviet weaponry, advances, they felt, that would require early-warning devices far beyond anything being developed at the Lincoln Lab. After consulting by telephone with Lincoln Lab Director Albert Hill, they decided a second summer study was in order.

The summer study idea was taken up again a few weeks later in the Statler Hotel in Boston. In addition to Albert Hill, four men were present: Jerrold Zacharias, Robert Oppenheimer, I. I. Rabi and Charles Lauritsen.

Zacharias . . . Oppenheimer . . . Rabi . . . Lauritsen—a foursome that would play an intriguing part in the security hearing of Robert Oppenheimer. The latter three were close friends of twenty years' standing; each had high regard for the other two. United in their common fear of an escalating arms race, they had met a few times prior to the Boston Statler Hotel gathering, on occasion gathering for a weekend at Oppenheimer's home in Princeton. In one instance they spent nearly two weeks together there, groping for an approach to U.S.-Soviet relations that might avoid an unlimited arms race. But, contrary to Air Force suspicions, the triumvirate was, then and always, nothing more than an informal confluence of three like-minded men who were comfortable with each other and communicated easily and naturally.

Their Boston discussion with Zacharias and Hill reinforced the earlier conclusion that another summer study of continental defense was called for. Zacharias persuaded Oppenheimer, and Rabi and Lauritsen to lend their names and prestige to the study, as an aid in recruiting other prominent and much-sought-after scientists as participants.

The main task of organizing the summer conference fell to Malcolm Hubbard, an official of the Lincoln Lab. According to Hubbard's later account, he discussed the forthcoming study with David Griggs, and listed those who had agreed to play a role in it. When he came to Oppenheimer's name, Griggs interrupted. "Do you think it's a good idea for Oppenheimer to be involved?"

Hubbard, surprised, replied in the affirmative, and asked why Griggs had raised the question. "Well," said the Air Force scientist, "he's not very dependable, is he?"

Hubbard still did not know what Griggs was referring to, but began checking around. "Didn't you know," Hubbard's colleagues told him, "that Griggs and Teller don't think that Oppie is on the right side of the 'big bomb'?" Still, it never occurred to Hubbard that anyone would entertain any doubts about the discretion or loyalty of Robert Oppenheimer.

Another event that did not escape Air Force attention was Robert Oppenheimer's appointment, in the spring of 1952, to a State Department disarmament advisory panel, together with such other luminaries as Vannevar Bush and Allen Dulles. The minutes of that panel's first meeting found their way into the hands of Air Force Chief Scientist David Griggs. As Griggs later recollected them, they stated that Oppenheimer had "advocated giving up the Strategic Air Force."

On April 30 of that year, a sparkling spring day, a luncheon was held at 1224 Thirtieth Street, N.W., the Washington home of Mr. William A. M. Burden, then personal assistant to Air Force Secretary Finletter. Present were two others from the Air Force— Garrison Norton (Burden's deputy) and David T. Griggs. The other two guests were Lee DuBridge, president of Caltech and more recently the chairman of the Vista project, and I. I. Rabi, a member of the scientific quadrumvirate about which the Air Force came to have misgivings.

The purpose of the luncheon was to expose Norton and Burden to well-informed non-Air Force views on the H-bomb question and on the "second-lab" issue. But before the luncheon ended, it branched into heated disputes about other matters. Three things were said that added to Air Force skepticism about Robert Oppenheimer and his intellectual confreres.

First, Rabi mentioned the discussions he, Oppenheimer and Lauritsen had had on the need for a U.S.-Soviet agreement on limiting arms, and said that the three had communicated their views to the State Department. Second, Rabi is said to have declared that such a rapprochement as well as an increased emphasis on U.S. air defense were both more important than the development of the H-bomb. Third, Griggs charged that the AEC's General Advisory Committee was not doing as much as it could or should under the Truman directive to foster development of the H-bomb.

This latter point triggered an angry discussion. Rabi said Griggs was misinformed about the GAC, and the only way to correct this was to read the GAC minutes. Fine, replied Griggs, but how do I get them? Apparently Rabi said that permission would have to come from the group's chairman, Robert Oppenheimer, and that he would arrange a meeting between himself, Griggs and Oppenheimer in Princeton.*

But when the confrontation took place, some three weeks later, Rabi was ill. So it was that at 3:30 on the afternoon of May 23, 1952, David Griggs and Robert Oppenheimer found themselves alone together for about an hour in Oppenheimer's Princeton office.

Griggs raised the matter of the GAC's attitude toward the H-bomb and asked if he could, as Rabi had suggested, read the pertinent GAC minutes so that he could be authentically informed. According to Griggs' recollection, Oppenheimer did not show him the minutes, but did let him read the majority and minority annexes to the controversial October, 1949, report, in which the GAC members had recommended against the H-bomb. Griggs was surprised Oppenheimer should show him these documents, since they merely confirmed that the GAC had, in fact, recommended the course that Griggs regarded as catastrophic. Oppenheimer then attempted to convince Griggs that, since taking that initial position, the members of the GAC had been doing everything they could, both collectively and as individuals, to foster the development of the H-bomb.

Presently the conversation turned to a stickier subject: a story floating around official Washington that portrayed Air Force Secretary Finletter as having said at a Pentagon briefing that if the United States only had a certain number of H-bombs, it could rule the world. The story, Griggs said, was being spread in such a way as to convey the notion that the Air Force was being run

---

* Griggs interpreted this as meaning the minutes were considered Oppenheimer's personal property. This astounded Griggs.

by irresponsible warmongers, and he wanted to know whether Oppenheimer was playing any part in its propagation. The physicist replied that he had heard the story and in such a way as to pinpoint the controversial H-bomb remark as Finletter's. Griggs countered that he had attended the Pentagon meeting at which the statement was allegedly made, and that Finletter had uttered no such remark. But Oppenheimer would not yield: the story had come to him, he said, from a source he could not question.

The colloquy grew more strained. Oppenheimer asked whether Griggs thought him pro-Russian or merely confused. Griggs responded that he wished he knew. Oppenheimer then asked whether Griggs had ever impugned his loyalty to high officials in the Defense Department. If Griggs did not respond with a simple "yes," he at least said he had heard Oppenheimer's loyalty impugned and had discussed this with Secretary Finletter and General Vandenberg.

Oppenheimer's response to this was to call David Griggs a paranoid.

Griggs and Oppenheimer were to meet again in a few weeks' time. The occasion was a luncheon arranged by Thomas Finletter's two assistants, William Burden and Garrison Norton. The two were aware of the doubts about Oppenheimer entertained by the Air Force high command in general and Secretary Finletter in particular. It was time, they felt, that Finletter and Oppenheimer met face to face for a direct exchange of ideas, rather than communicating third- or fourthhand. The two aides set up a luncheon meeting in Finletter's private dining room at the Pentagon.

But it was not a meal à deux. Also present were Burden and Norton—and David Griggs. (Knowing that the confrontation was scheduled, Griggs had recorded his recollection of his stormy Princeton meeting with Oppenheimer, in a special memorandum for Finletter's "eyes only.")

According to one of the participants, the luncheon was one of the most uncomfortable gatherings he had ever attended. Oppenheimer had been testifying that morning before the Joint Congressional Atomic Energy Committee, and arrived late. When they sat down to luncheon, Finletter, a highly cultivated New

York lawyer, made an extraordinary effort to be gracious, out-going and frank. But, this participant has recalled, he was lit-erally frozen by Oppenheimer's unresponsiveness, which in time became "rude beyond belief." Finletter made overture after over-ture; each was rebuffed by Oppenheimer, whose very manner seemed to exude contempt for everyone in the room. As soon as the painful meal was over, Oppenheimer turned his back and walked out.

After the disastrous luncheon, the would-be peacemakers, Burden and Norton, rather sheepishly followed Finletter back into his office. The Air Force Secretary threw back his head and laughed heartily. "I don't think you fellows have convinced me I should feel any more positively about Dr. Oppenheimer," he told them.

In 1952 the Department of the Air Force was not alone in its interest in Robert Oppenheimer's security background. On Capi-tol Hill that same year, investigators for the Senate Internal Se-curity Subcommittee, headed by Nevada's Senator Pat McCarran and Indiana's Senator William Jenner, were uncovering what was later described as "voluminous information" on the atomic physi-cist. But the subcommittee decided to take no action on the information, contenting itself with turning the data over to "the proper agencies of the government." Why? According to a later explanation, the committee's failure to follow through was due to the "highly sensitive nature" of Oppenheimer's work and "the many ramifications involved in the situation."

In mid-June, 1952, Oppenheimer paid a visit to AEC Chairman Gordon Dean. By now, the physicist said, he had been a member of the General Advisory Committee for nearly six years, and he wanted to reaffirm what he had told Dean earlier: that it was time to pass the baton on to another, and therefore he did not wish his name to be considered for reappointment to the com-mittee.

The matter of Robert Oppenheimer's continued status with the AEC became a matter of widespread interest in Washington. One Commission member recalls heated discussions within the AEC in which questions about not only Oppenheimer's GAC membership but the very continuation of his security clearance were raised and discussed—questions prompted mainly by Commissioner Thomas Murray. On Capitol Hill the possibility of Oppenheimer's reappointment to the GAC was viewed with considerable concern, since many if not most of his views ran contrary to the prevailing opinion of the Joint Atomic Energy Committee. According to one report, William Borden, by then deeply immersed in Oppenheimer's security file, "decided to do everything within his power to prevent Oppenheimer's reappointment." He soon found that others in the Pentagon shared his point of view, among them Air Force Secretary Finletter and Robert LeBaron, the Pentagon's chief atomic energy official.

The Federal Bureau of Investigation was also active in the spring of 1952, sending to the White House a number of special reports on Robert Oppenheimer. Many of these were based on interviews the FBI had conducted with high government officials who were opposed to Oppenheimer's reappointment by the President. But for the President's principal adviser on such matters, Admiral Sidney Souers, these reports were by no means the deciding factor. To him, the question of Oppenheimer's reappointment was not complicated: the scientist had never been a strong supporter of the President's H-bomb decision, and there was no reason why Mr. Truman should not appoint men who were more in tune with his thinking. He so advised the President. Oppenheimer was not reappointed. Neither were his philosophical companions on the GAC, James B. Conant and Lee DuBridge.

On July 3, 1952, Haakon Chevalier and his fiancée were married. On the eve of the wedding, Haakon wrote his friend Robert Oppenheimer to say that "we think of you in an important moment." For a wedding present the Oppenheimers sent a mahogany salad bowl from the Virgin Islands. The card expressed the hope that "perhaps before too long we may have the good luck to have a salad from it. . . ."

In July, 1952, Francis Cotter, an FBI agent formerly stationed at Los Alamos (and therefore familiar with matters atomic) and then a Bureau specialist in Soviet espionage techniques, joined the staff of the Joint Committee on Atomic Energy as security officer. He received his first assignment from William Liscum Borden, who told Cotter he had come to believe from the FBI interviews in London with the Soviet spy Klaus Fuchs that Fuchs must have had an accomplice. Cotter's assignment was to look deeply into the security file of J. Robert Oppenheimer to determine whether Oppenheimer might have been that confederate. And so, just as Borden had done some months earlier, Cotter went to the Atomic Energy Commission and began the laborious job of reading the AEC file. The Oppenheimer case and related matters were to consume a large part of Cotter's time during the next six months.

During that same summer, in Lexington, Massachusetts, the Lincoln Summer Study of U.S. air defense got under way. David Griggs had been concerned about the project ever since he had learned that Robert Oppenheimer was to be involved in it. He feared that recommendations for a vast increase in funds for the Air Defense Command, at the expense of the Strategic Air Command, would be made by persons not fully familiar with SAC's mission or responsibilities, and that the energies of the Lincoln Laboratory would be disproportionately concentrated on developing a continental defense system.

At Secretary Finletter's direction, he conveyed the Air Force's misgivings to President James Killian and Provost Julius Stratton of MIT, the university under whose auspices the study was to take place. Both men promised to look into the matter. For several weeks the preparations for the summer project slowed to a near-halt—causing, according to the project's director, Jerrold Zacharias, a crucial and harmful delay in recruiting top-grade participants. Ultimately, Drs. Killian and Stratton assured Griggs that the study would indeed operate to benefit both the Lincoln Laboratory and the Air Force.

But still Griggs was not satisfied. He was concerned that the results of the summer study would get "out of hand"—i.e., that they might be reported directly to the National Security Council, the top presidential advisory group on military matters. President Killian reassured Griggs that he had taken steps that satisfied him the summer study would be "kept in bounds."

Robert Oppenheimer's participation in the Lincoln project was minimal: he appeared briefly in the first and last weeks of the summer-long study. In the opening days he explained to the participants the technical background of air defense, in the course of which, according to Zacharias' recollection, he left no doubt that he felt the Strategic Air Command was getting far too large a share of defense dollars to permit proper development of an air-defense network.

At the end of an intense summer's work, the Lincoln participants produced a report recommending, among other things, an investment of several billion dollars in an early-warning radar system. That fall the report was presented to the Air Force's Scientific Advisory Board, meeting in Cambridge. There, according to David Griggs' recollection, a significant event occurred. Griggs was later to swear (and Jerrold Zacharias to deny, under oath) that at that Cambridge meeting, before an audience of fifty to a hundred people, Zacharias had written on the blackboard the letters, "Z . . . O . . . R . . . C." It would be some seven months before the term "ZORC" would first appear in public and the Air Force's understanding of its meaning would be explained.

The work of the Lincoln Summer Study group was looked on with deep suspicion not only by David Griggs but by Secretary Finletter as well. As Finletter saw it, the principal effect, if not the aim, of the study was to belittle the Air Force's nuclear bomber force, which Finletter and others viewed as the main deterrent to Soviet expansion.

His suspicions were confirmed—and his ire considerably aroused—by two special articles on "The Air Gap" by columnist Stewart Alsop. These articles appeared in early September in the New York *Herald Tribune* and were widely noted and commented on in Washington. They were crammed with suspiciously authoritative facts and figures. Their gist was that the Russians would soon be in a position both to inflict severe losses on any American air strike against the Soviet Union and to launch a "crippling" atomic attack against the United States. Alsop's conclusion particularly angered Finletter. "The experts believe," wrote Alsop, that the remedy lay in "very early warning devices, ground-to-air guided missiles, new techniques in long-range radar," which, he said, could be developed only through "a great emergency project like the Manhattan District," perhaps involving "an expenditure of $25 billion in a two-to-three-year period."

Knowing that Oppenheimer had close ties to Stewart Alsop's brother Joseph, Finletter entertained few doubts as to the identity of "the experts" cited in the Alsop articles. He vented his anger against Oppenheimer to Charles J. V. Murphy, a former editor of *Fortune* who was serving in the Pentagon as a member of the Air Force Reserve. "Oppenheimer may not be a Communist," he told Murphy, "but he is the cleverest conspirator in America." The full extent of Finletter's apparent doubts was revealed when he reached into a desk drawer, took out some papers and showed them to Murphy. They were excerpts from the security file of Dr. J. Robert Oppenheimer.

While the scientists in the Lincoln Summer Study were studying the air-defense problems, work was proceeding rapidly on the thermonuclear project, and it appeared that the first H-bomb would be ready to test in early November. But in mid-1952 the notion of an indefinite postponement of the test, tied to some mutual anti-H-bomb agreement with the Soviets, began to gain currency in official Washington.

The notion may well have arisen on a summer Saturday afternoon in the billiard room of Washington's prestigious Cosmos Club. On that afternoon the trio of scientists about whom David Griggs was so worried—Robert Oppenheimer, I. I. Rabi and Charles Lauritsen—discussed the imminent H-bomb test and their concern that it would end for all time the possibility of reaching an agreement with the Soviets for a mutual forswearing of the superbomb. Since a thermonuclear test explosion would be so enormous as to be unconcealable from the rest of the world, the scientists concluded that any mutual agreement with the Soviets to refrain from such testing need not depend on mutual trust but would, in effect, be self-policing. Why not, then, bring the hydrogen project up to the point of test readiness and then advise the Russians we would refrain from testing until there was evidence they had tested?

The three decided to phone and ask Vannevar Bush, chairman of the State Department disarmament study panel on which Oppenheimer was then serving, to join them. Bush, too, was worried about the impending H-bomb test, especially since it was to coincide with the 1952 presidential election. Thus a November test would mean that a new and irrevocable step deeper into the atomic jungle would be presented to a new President as a *fait accompli*. This, Bush felt, was utterly improper. Hence, when he joined the three scientists in the Cosmos Club billiard room, he was immediately attracted to their idea for a self-policing test postponement. Two days later, on Monday, Bush laid the proposal before Secretary of State Acheson.

Oppenheimer later recalled that he was not as enthusiastic as Rabi and Lauritsen about the postponement notion. On the contrary, he later said, while he perceived both its advantages and disadvantages, his "candid opinion" was that a delay was "utterly impractical." The Air Force, nevertheless, regarded this suggestion for a test postponement as but another anti-H-bomb move by Robert Oppenheimer and his like-minded colleagues, Rabi and Lauritsen.

In the fall of 1952 reports of the hostility between the Air Force and the AEC so perturbed Defense Secretary Robert Lovett that he asked his aide James Perkins to look into the situation and report to him and to AEC Chairman Gordon Dean in three months time. But it didn't take Perkins three months to discern the trouble. In a matter of weeks he had a clear picture of the manner in which the policies of the Oppenheimer-led GAC were rubbing against raw Air Force nerves. Perkins found a belief in high Air Force echelons that the GAC was under the control of people who were opposed not only to the H-bomb but also to the strategic use of A-bombs.

Perkins met with Lovett and Dean over luncheon to make his report, but before he could begin he was surprised to have the Secretary of Defense ask him, "Have you read Oppenheimer's security file? I've just been through it, and it's a nightmare." Perkins was even more startled to hear the usually mild-mannered, patrician Lovett say, "The quicker we get Oppenheimer out of the country, the better off we'll be."

Perkins demurred. The only notable doubt about Robert Oppenheimer's loyalty, he said, was the Air Force view of the physicist as a threat to Air Force doctrine. Lovett looked at Perkins in a way that clearly meant he would hear no more of such talk. It seemed to Perkins that Lovett had become convinced that Oppenheimer was a real menace. Lovett obviously had no interest in hearing Perkins' full report, and the luncheon meeting was curt and brief.

Perkins has recalled Lovett's mentioning the names of a few people who had expressed concern to him about Oppenheimer. One of them was Lewis L. Strauss.

On November 1, 1952, an entire island was wiped off the face of the earth. The feat was accomplished by the world's first explosion of a hydrogen bomb.

Five years earlier the first atomic bomb, the equivalent of twenty thousand tons of TNT, had incinerated three-fifths of a city. The power of the first H-bomb explosion could have destroyed one hundred and fifty Hiroshimas. Its force was equivalent to three *million* tons of TNT.

In just three months a new President would take office, but the decision to cross the thermonuclear threshold would not be his. The word "megaton" had become a reality. The Hydrogen Age had begun.

Two days later William Borden prepared a memorandum for the files of the Joint Committee on Atomic Energy tracing the history of the committee's dealings with the security case of J. Robert Oppenheimer.

By this time Borden's security specialist, Francis Cotter, had progressed considerably in his reading of the AEC's mountainous file on Oppenheimer, and Borden himself had continued to comb through it. The two men had spent hour upon endless hour discussing its contents and implications. Their conclusions had shifted back and forth as they tried to put the many pieces together, but eventually their opinions began to polarize. Cotter's onetime misgivings about Oppenheimer were allayed. By contrast, William Borden grew more and more convinced that Oppenheimer had been an agent of the Soviet Union—and indeed still was.

A key part of the mandate received by Dwight D. Eisenhower and the Republican Party on November 4, 1952, was to rid the Federal Government of the many "subversives" who had supposedly infiltrated the public payrolls. The party platform that year had promised an "overhaul [of] loyalty and security programs" and had been explicit in pledging that "a Republican President will appoint only persons of unquestioned loyalty." At the Republican Convention where that platform was adopted, Senator Joseph R. McCarthy received an ovation when he called for a "rough" anti-Communist drive. The selection of Richard M. Nixon as the vice-presidential candidate was preceded by nominating speeches stressing the Californian's anti-Communist prowess in Congress, and was followed by a speech by Nixon himself, asserting that "destroying the forces of Communism at home and abroad" was the most important campaign issue.

Dwight Eisenhower himself had emphasized the Communist question, sometimes in florid terms. "We can no longer have in our most sensitive high posts of government a toleration of men who take papers from our secret files and pass them on dark streets to spies from Moscow," he said in a speech in San Antonio on October 14. His campaign was a "crusade"—a crusade, among other things, to "get out of the governmental offices . . . people who have been . . . weak enough to embrace Communism and still have found their way into our government." He applauded the record of his "running mate, Dick Nixon," who had seen the threat of "those who plot against" the American system and had "grabbed a police whistle and [blown] it." By election day he had raised the "Communist issue" in no fewer than thirty separate campaign speeches and was fully committed, with his party, to a thorough anti-Communist house-cleaning.

In early December, 1952, at the instructions of AEC Chairman Gordon Dean, representatives of the Atomic Energy Commission paid a call on Oppenheimer in Princeton. Their purpose was to arrange the removal from Oppenheimer's possession of all the secret papers and documents pertaining to the General Advisory Commission, of which Oppenheimer was no longer a member. In all, some thirty-two feet of files were laboriously inventoried, placed in locked trunks and transported from Princeton to Washington.

This act represented a virtually final severing of Oppenheimer's official ties not only with the AEC but with the United States Government. His one remaining link was a consultant's contract with the AEC, but his services were to be called for, subsequently, on only two occasions. Even before the Republican Administration assumed office, Robert Oppenheimer's days of official power in Washington had ended.

# 8. *New Regime in Washington*

On January 20, 1953, Dwight David Eisenhower took the oath as thirty-fourth President of the United States. New men, with new outlooks on public affairs, took their places in the President's cabinet.

In the senior post, the Secretaryship of State, the aristocratic Dean Acheson, intimate of such illustrious men as Felix Frankfurter and Learned Hand and former mentor of Alger Hiss, was replaced by the dour John Foster Dulles, who lost little time in demanding of his subordinates something he termed "positive loyalty." His department had been the prime target of Senator McCarthy, and to insure the purity of its employees, Dulles soon placed the security division in the hands of an avid McCarthy supporter named Robert W. Scott McLeod.

At the Pentagon, Robert Lovett of Wall Street gave way to Charles E. Wilson of General Motors. Wilson entertained the view that the military establishment must be kept clear of Communists because it was no place to reform them. "They ought," said Wilson, "to have a chance [to reform] somewhere else."

The new Secretary of the Army was a wealthy textile manufacturer by the name of Robert T. Stevens. His aides had arranged one hour of carefully prepared briefings per day, to acquaint him with the many complex matters for which he would be responsible. But, after one or two such sessions, Stevens said, "I don't want any more briefings on this stuff. All I want is a thorough briefing on the Communists in the Army."

The new Attorney General, who as head of the Justice Department would be responsible for most of the government's anti-Communist activities, was Herbert Brownell, Jr., a leading figure in Republican politics. Brownell was later to accuse a former President of the United States of knowingly promoting a Soviet spy.

The Secretary of the Treasury was former Taft supporter George Humphrey, an intensely conservative Ohio industrialist who held the view that this "administration ought to be able to find enough men and women above a shadow of suspicion to fill all the posts that [need] to be filled."

These men had been in office only three days when, at their first cabinet meeting, the subject of Federal employee loyalty arose. There was general agreement on the desirability of broadening the precondition of Federal employment. The mere demonstration of "loyalty" was not thought sufficient. There should be an affirmative showing that the person's employment would serve the "interests of national security." This expanded screening criterion was soon instituted by the new Administration.

The changing of the political guard was not confined to the Executive Branch. At the eastern end of Pennsylvania Avenue the Republicans had taken control of Congress and all its committees. No longer would Senator Joseph R. McCarthy be merely the ranking minority member of the Senate's Investigations Subcommittee. He was now its chairman, with broad power to allocate funds, hire staff—and choose investigative targets.

One of the key government positions that did not immediately change hands when the Eisenhower Administration took office was the chairmanship of the Atomic Energy Commission, since the tenure of the incumbent, Gordon Dean, was not scheduled to expire until June. Even for those few intervening months, however, the President had a personal overseer for the vital atomic energy program. During the 1952 political campaign Dwight Eisenhower had met, and been impressed by, former AEC Commissioner Lewis L. Strauss. Although an ardent Taft supporter against Eisenhower before the Republican Convention, Strauss had helped in the campaign by providing memoranda and speech material on national security issues. On March 9 the President appointed Strauss to a newly created position: special assistant to the President on atomic energy matters. Among the congratulatory letters Strauss received was one from J. Robert Oppenheimer.

The new Administration was not long in acting on the campaign pledges to tighten up the screening of Federal employees. In February, 1953, there were "authoritative" predictions of a sweeping new presidential order that would discard the old loyalty program and substitute more severe screening criteria. In

mid-March the Attorney General pronounced the Truman loyalty program a failure, and said it was being scrapped. On April
23 Vice President Nixon reported to the assembled newspaper
publishers of the nation on the effective way the new Administration was dealing with the loyalty issue, and the next day the
President himself set forth for Republican women the efforts his
Administration was making to eliminate "subversion" in the
Federal Government.

Finally, on April 27, the new presidential security order was
unveiled. Under its terms, a government employee had not only
to be adjudged "loyal" in order to serve his country; his background had to be such that his employment by the government
was "clearly consistent with the interests of national security."
For most Federal agencies, new and broader screening criteria
were put into effect. Security officers were given wider authority
to screen out job-holders and applicants with "derogatory information" in their dossiers. All Federal agencies, including such
nonsensitive departments as Agriculture and Interior, were given
the power summarily to suspend suspected "security risks," a
power formerly reserved to agencies having a connection with
national defense. The cases of some nineteen thousand civil
servants whose "full field" investigations had turned up "derogatory information," but who had been cleared under the old Truman loyalty program, were to be "readjudicated" under the new,
more severe screening standards.

In May of 1953 the word "ZORC" appeared in public print for
the first time. It made its debut in that month's issue of *Fortune*,
in an unsigned article entitled, "The Hidden Struggle for the
H-Bomb: The Story of Dr. Oppenheimer's Persistent Campaign
to Reverse U. S. Military Strategy."

David Lilienthal noted the article in his diary of the time,
describing it as "another nasty and obviously inspired article attacking Robert Oppenheimer, in a snide way." What particularly
annoyed Lilienthal was the anonymity of the article. "Even a
gossip columnist signs his gossip, and takes personal responsibility," was Lilienthal's comment.

What Lilienthal and other readers of *Fortune* did not know
was that the article had been written by an Air Force reservist

who had recently completed a tour of duty in the highest echelons of the United States Air Force: Charles J. V. Murphy. Thus
the article gave an unusually authoritative Air Force view of the
events of the previous four years, for Murphy had been privy to
secret documents and private conversations that would have
been inaccessible to an ordinary reporter.

Years later, Murphy recalled the frame of mind in which he
had written the article. He had seen the policy questions raised
in the Lincoln Summer Study (and aired in the Alsop articles)
as part of the continuing struggle over the nature of American
military strategy. In this struggle, in Murphy's view, Robert Oppenheimer was exercising a potent and damaging influence: he
was using his extremely influential position inside government
councils to evangelize for the "denuclearization" of American
policy. To Murphy, it was urgent that Oppenheimer be removed
from this position of control over policy-making—or, at the least,
that his views be challenged. "And that," Murphy recalled, "is
what I did."

The very first words of Murphy's article—describing a "life-
and-death struggle over national military policy"—made clear
how grave its author considered the issues involved. The article
pictured the military establishment pitted against "a highly
influential group of American scientists" whose motives had an
"important hidden aspect," the discrediting of the "retaliatory-
deterrent" principle of the Strategic Air Command's long-range
nuclear bombing force. The "prime mover" among these scientists
was J. Robert Oppenheimer.

The article recounted the events of the preceding four years:
the GAC's recommendation against the H-bomb; the Truman go-
ahead; Edward Teller's belief "that the AEC, under Oppenheimer's influence, was trying to postpone, if not stifle," a crucial
H-bomb experiment; the second-lab controversy and the AEC's
"capitulation" under threat of an Air Force weapons laboratory.

Murphy then turned to the Vista study, during the course of
which, in the summer of 1951, "the Air Force became conscious
of a change in the atmosphere." The explanation: the Vista group
was conferring with Robert Oppenheimer. The physicist's draft of
one Vista chapter "produced an explosion in the Air Force," in
part, at least, because it had contained a "veiled suggestion that

Air Force doctrine was based on the slaughter of civilians," and suggested that "a substantial part" of the atomic stockpile "should be diverted from SAC." Murphy also said the Vista report recommended the U.S. announce that in the event of war it "would withhold SAC from action." The article then described how Air Force Secretary Finletter, interpreting the report as "a brief for disarming the Nation's strongest weapon" (SAC), set about blocking Pentagon approval of it. This, in turn, prompted the Vista group, "sensing defeat," to send the Oppenheimer delegation to Paris to see Dwight Eisenhower. But, said Murphy, that was a waste of time; Air Force opposition had already doomed the Vista report.

Finally, the article spoke of a "shift in tactics" in the spring of 1952, when "there formed around Oppenheimer a group calling themselves ZORC." What was ZORC? According to the Murphy article, it stood for the initials of four scientists:

Z for (Jerrold) Zacharias.

O for (Robert) Oppenheimer.

R for (I. I.) Rabi.

And the C? The C stood for "Charles"—Charles Lauritsen.

How or why the initials happened to stand for three last names and one first name, the article did not explain, but thereafter it continued to describe "ZORC" as an entity, an organization that acted as a unit with a single objective: to prove there could be an air defense so perfect that the U.S. might become a fortress nation with no need for "an offensive atomic weapon." "Without the knowledge of the Air Force," the article continued, "ZORC" proceeded to test its theory through the Lincoln Summer Study, during which all the military assumptions were "war-gamed . . . with the ZORC strategists masterminding the tactics of the Soviet long-range force and of the [U.S.] defense as well." But later that fall, Murphy reported, the ZORC recommendations were defeated in the National Security Council. "There," said Murphy, "the matter rests. Meanwhile the development of thermonuclear and fission weapons continues apace. And SAC, under General LeMay, retains its mighty mission."

The article concluded by raising a "serious question"—to be revived a year later by Robert Oppenheimer's judges—"of the propriety of scientists trying to settle such grave national issues alone, inasmuch as they bear no responsibility for the successful execution of war plans."

After reading the article, David Lilienthal wondered, "Is this the beginning of a campaign of revenge for the way the Hickenlooper ['incredible mismanagement'] investigation against me fizzled out? Are some of those boys out to try to injure the scientists who . . . differed with Strauss and his pal from Iowa [Senator Hickenlooper]? I hope not; but as Jim Forrestal said [about Strauss]: 'He is a persistent man.'"

Whether or not the Murphy article was designed to attract Congressional attention to the activities of Oppenheimer and his followers, it succeeded in doing so. As South Dakota's Republican Senator Karl Mundt later recalled it, the article prompted a discussion among several Republican members of Senator McCarthy's Senate Investigations Subcommittee. They and a few other Senators met to consider whether the McCarthy group should investigate the H-bomb program. "After a discussion, we decided we were not the committee to go into it. It was not a matter for open hearings, [since] it definitely involved security . . . And," recalled Mundt, *we got some pretty high assurances that it would not be neglected.*" (Emphasis added.)

Senator McCarthy assigned one of his staff members to work on "the Oppenheimer case" for a time, but the Senator refrained from any probe of Oppenheimer or the H-bomb program because, he later recalled, he had *assurances from top Administration officials* that this matter would be gone into in detail." (Emphasis added.) Congressional employees intimate with these affairs were given to understand that the principal "top Administration official" responsible for saving Robert Oppenheimer from a McCarthy investigation was the Vice President of the United States, Richard M. Nixon.

Elsewhere on Capitol Hill, William Borden was preparing to turn over the directorship of the Joint Atomic Energy Committee staff to his successor. While, for the most part, he felt he could take satisfaction in the progress that had occurred in his four and a half years of service, there were some unresolved problems. None was as vexing to Borden as the security status of J. Robert

Oppenheimer. Despite the countless hours he had devoted to studying and discussing the investigative file on the physicist, Borden's view of Oppenheimer shifted continuously—from a firm conviction that he was a foreign agent to an equally firm conviction that he was not. As he prepared to leave his Congressional post, he had not yet been able to arrive at any settled conclusions.

And so, as a means of conveying his misgivings to his successor, Borden decided to pull together all the questions he had about Oppenheimer, his background and his conduct. Many of these did not have to do directly with Oppenheimer, but speculated, more generally, as to why the AEC had acted—or failed to act— in certain ways regarding the H-bomb's development and other related matters. As Borden later recalled it, the purpose of this exercise was not to leave a legacy of political trouble but merely to acquaint the future staff of the Joint Committee with his concerns about Oppenheimer. What the staff did about these questions was up to them.

Before Borden's list was completed, his questions had risen to the impressive total of some four hundred. Having finished this "final work," William Liscum Borden left the employ of the United States Congress and departed for a favorite wilderness haunt near the St. Lawrence River for a month of vacation—and of further fretting over the security status of J. Robert Oppenheimer.


On June 20, 1953, Reorganization Plan No. 6 of the United States Department of Defense took effect. Among other things, Reorganization Plan No. 6 abolished the entire Research and Development Board. This, of course, automatically ended the tenure of all who had been either members of or consultants to the Board. Among those consultants was J. Robert Oppenheimer.

Later, when the security-risk charges against Oppenheimer had been made public, Secretary of Defense Charles E. Wilson was to characterize Reorganization Plan No. 6 as "a real smooth way of doing that one as far as the Defense Department was concerned."


On June 30, 1953, ten days after Reorganization Plan No. 6 took effect, Gordon Dean's term as Chairman of the Atomic

Energy Commission expired. One of his last acts as Chairman was to extend for another twelve months Oppenheimer's contract as Commission consultant—an action he took without conferring with his successor.

On Friday, July 3, 1953, on the eve of a long Fourth of July weekend, Lewis Lichtenstein Strauss became the third chairman of the United States Atomic Energy Commission. He had not been in the office more than an hour when he asked for the Commission's files on the shipping of radioisotopes overseas—the issue on which he had first been outvoted as a member of the AEC, and on which he had been made the object of public ridicule by Robert Oppenheimer. A few days later, Oppenheimer's close friend Herbert Marks was to receive a call from a former associate still employed in the Commission, who knew of the Strauss request. "You'd better tell your friend Oppy to batten down the hatches and prepare for some stormy weather," Marks was told.

Because of the long July Fourth weekend, the first opportunity to conduct further government business did not occur until Tuesday, July 7. On that day, according to an AEC press release, the Commission, "at the request of the chairman . . . initiated steps to organize the removal" of whatever classified Commission documents remained in Oppenheimer's files.

Why did Lewis Strauss make such a move, so soon after his accession to the AEC chairmanship? Years later, Strauss' recollection was that it had nothing to do with Oppenheimer personally, but was taken purely for reasons of economy and tighter security. As a trustee of the Institute for Advanced Study, Strauss knew that the AEC had posted a twenty-four-hour guard to protect the documents in Oppenheimer's possession. He said he also knew that Mrs. Oppenheimer would, on occasion, call upon the guard for tasks that would take him away from the document vault, and that as a result (according to Strauss) the facility was sometimes unguarded during the day. This made him fear there would be a breach of security that would reflect on the good name of the Institute. Moreover, Strauss said, he knew that there were twenty-four-hour government guards nearby, both at the Forrestal Memorial Library (for which he had helped raise funds) and at another AEC facility in Princeton. Therefore, he said, it seemed to him ridiculous to occupy so many guards on a three-shift basis at separate locations, and his action, four days after assuming the AEC chairmanship, was aimed merely at consolidating all secret government documents in the Princeton area in one facility that could be guarded by a single set of security guards. It represented, he said, no reflection on Robert Oppenheimer.

AEC records do not reinforce Strauss' retrospective explanation, especially concerning his aim of consolidating the Oppenheimer papers into a single Princeton facility. At no time was such a step taken. The only change in the security arrangements—removal of the files and the security guards from Oppenheimer's office to a newly constructed facility in the basement of the Institute—was authorized in the spring of 1953, before Strauss became Chairman.

A contemporaneous explanation of Strauss' action, one consistent with AEC records, was contained in the wording of an AEC press release of April, 1954, issued just after it had become public knowledge that Robert Oppenheimer had been charged with being a "security risk." That statement implied that Chairman Strauss was presciently aware of the hazards in Oppenheimer's possessing secret documents.

Apparently to offer further evidence of Strauss' alertness, the press release also cited an order directing that a "preliminary study" be made of the Oppenheimer security file by the AEC and the Department of Justice. The implication of the press release was that Strauss had ordered this study at least several weeks before William Borden brought the Oppenheimer case to the attention of the FBI, in his November letter to J. Edgar Hoover.

Apparently the "preliminary study" was known only to the very highest officials, for AEC files contain no record of such an examination of the Oppenheimer dossier. In any event, the 1954 AEC press statement said that by November of 1953 (the month in which the Borden letter was received) the "study" had reached the point where the case could be "brought up for definitive examination and appraisal."

During those summer months Robert Oppenheimer was engaged in lecturing in South America. While he was away, his security file was under study by still another section of the United

States Government. At approximately the time Lewis Strauss was named to the AEC chairmanship, Pentagon security officers brought the file to the personal attention of Dr. Walt Whitman, who had been, prior to Reorganization Plan No. 6, the Chairman of the Defense Department's Research and Development Board.

Oppenheimer was well known to Walt Whitman. They had first met in 1948, during a study of the feasibility of nuclear-powered flight. Whitman had joined the AEC's General Advisory Committee in 1950 and had served for two years under Oppenheimer's chairmanship. Oppenheimer, in turn, had been a consultant to the Research and Development Board under Whitman's chairmanship.

On a quiet Saturday, in Room 3E1006 of the Pentagon, when no one else was around, Walt Whitman spent several hours reading a fifty-page summary of Robert Oppenheimer's security file. On July 10, one week after Lewis Strauss took office as Chairman of the AEC, Whitman gave his judgment of Oppenheimer:

> I have known for some time of the general nature and salient features of the information contained in this file. It discloses nothing which would cause me to modify my previous confidence in his loyalty.
>
> Based on extensive associations with Dr. Oppenheimer over the past three years . . . I am convinced that he can be of great service as a consultant to the research and development work of the Department of Defense.
>
> I unqualifiedly recommend his reappointment as a consultant.

Dr. Whitman's recommendation was considered and concurred in by a three-man review board. But their advice was not heeded. Oppenheimer was not reappointed as a consultant to the Defense Department.

In that same summer, the points of view of Robert Oppenheimer and of the United States Air Force had their final head-on collision. The vehicles were two magazine articles: one by Oppenheimer, the other by *Fortune* editor Charles J. V. Murphy, avid exponent of the Air Force viewpoint.

Oppenheimer spoke first, in the July issue of the prestigious publication *Foreign Affairs*. As "the atomic clock tick[ed] faster and faster," Oppenheimer was concerned about the prospect of "two Great Powers . . . [each] in a position to put an end to the civilization and life of the other, though not without risking its own. We may be likened to two scorpions in a bottle, each capable of killing the other, but only at the risk of its own life." Oppenheimer proposed three changes in governmental policy: greater candor with the American public concerning atomic peril; greater sharing of atomic information with American allies; and greater emphasis on the defense of the American continent against atomic attack—which, in Air Force eyes, could be achieved only by diverting funds from the strategic bombing force.

Even more provocative to the Air Force was Oppenheimer's recitation of how "a high officer in the Air Defense Command" had said "that it was not really our policy" to attempt to protect American civilians against atomic attack, "for that is so big a job that it would interfere with our retaliatory capabilities." Oppenheimer went on to observe that "Such follies can occur only when even the men who know the facts can find no one to talk to about them, when the facts are too secret for discussion, and thus, for thought."

Murphy replied in the August issue of *Fortune*—this time in a signed article. He was critical both of Oppenheimer's appeal for greater candor and of what he believed to be the scientist's attitude toward the Russians: namely, that if America would relax a bit on its own "rigid" atomic policy, "the Soviet Union *might* respond by intimating that it was prepared to modify its own forces of the same type." The "fatal flaw" in the Oppenheimer view, Murphy said, was that it failed "to allow for the terrible consequences that could ensue if the Kremlin leaders declined to act reasonably."

Murphy concluded his article by calling for a brand of nuclear candor which, he said, "would accord with the American tradition of political 'openness' by which the great body of U.S. citizens, and not Oppenheimer alone, lays store," and "would not involve giving away the last critical magnitudes of national strength."

In his July article in *Foreign Affairs*, Robert Oppenheimer ventured the opinion that "in the field of atomic munitions . . . the U.S.S.R. is about four years behind us." A month later, that assessment was abruptly contradicted. On August 12 the AEC confirmed a four-day-old boast of Soviet Premier Malenkov that the Russians had exploded a thermonuclear device and had joined the Hydrogen Age. It had taken the Russians four years to catch up to America with a fission device. By contrast, on the vastly more complex fusion reaction the Russian success followed America's by a scant nine months.

Now there were indeed two scorpions in a bottle.

With Republicans in charge of the various Congressional investigating committees, anti-Communist probes speckled the headlines throughout 1953. In March the new chairman of HUAC, Harold Velde of Illinois, caused a stir by speculating publicly that his committee might investigate alleged Communist infiltration of the American clergy. In July an investigator for Senator McCarthy, J. B. Matthews, created an uproar with a magazine article charging that the largest single group in the U.S. backing the Communist apparatus was the Protestant clergy. And in the early fall Senator McCarthy and the United States Army began to have their first tangles. McCarthy released a theretofore confidential Army study of "Psychological and Cultural Traits of Soviet Siberia," labeled it Communist propaganda (among other things it cited, in its bibliography, a book by alleged leftist Corliss Lamont) and demanded the names of those responsible for the study. The Army responded by charging that McCarthy had violated the espionage law by making the study public. Later, the Senator moved into a probe of the Army Signal Corps facility at Fort Monmouth, New Jersey, emitting, almost daily, sensational accounts of what had been revealed in the committee's closed-door sessions (e.g., that a Monmouth employee had broken down and agreed to tell all about an alleged Soviet spy ring established there by Julius and Ethel Rosenberg).

In November McCarthy disclosed that a Harvard physics professor (whom he later identified as Wendell Furry) had pleaded the Fifth Amendment in refusing to answer questions about his previous Communist connections and activities. Since Professor

Furry's action affected Harvard's reputation, this matter was of concern to Robert Oppenheimer, as chairman of the Harvard physics department's "Visiting Committee." To various of Furry's colleagues, he expressed "rather strong feelings about the fact that Furry had been for really a . . . long time a member of the Communist Party." To some, including Furry himself, he vigorously deplored the physicist's invoking the Fifth Amendment.*

In mid-September of 1953, Haakon Chevalier, now an interpreter for UNESCO in Paris, upon learning that Robert and Kitty Oppenheimer were soon to be in Europe, wrote Oppenheimer to remind him of his promise to come and share a salad from the fine bowl the Oppenheimers had sent as a wedding present. "There is much to tell," Chevalier wrote, "but it will have to wait until we can share that salad."

When the Oppenheimers finally arrived in Paris in November, Kitty Oppenheimer telephoned the Chevaliers' flat. Haakon was away in Rome, attending a conference, but his wife, Carol, promised to wire him. The Oppenheimers went off to Copenhagen briefly, and by the time they returned to Paris, Haakon Chevalier had arranged for a substitute interpreter at the Rome conference (at some expense to himself) and was back in Paris. It was agreed that on their last night in the city the Oppenheimers would join the Chevaliers for dinner at their flat.

And so, on the evening of December 7, 1953, Robert and Kitty Oppenheimer departed the sumptuous surroundings of the Hotel George V for the far more modest atmosphere of Monmartre, alighting at No. 19 Rue du Mont Cenis, at the foot of the Sacré Coeur Cathedral. In the minuscule cage elevator they mounted to the fourth floor and there, in the Chevaliers' small apartment, the four old friends held their reunion.

It was the first time the Oppenheimers had seen Haakon Chevalier in more than three years, and the first time they had ever met Haakon and Carol as a couple. It was a festive occasion: drinks in the tiny living room; a fine dinner in the even tinier dining alcove that also served as an entrance hall; a salad from the mahogany salad bowl; champagne and toasts over dessert;

* By contrast, at least one of Furry's Harvard associates publicly defended Furry's right to such a constitutional plea.

Robert and Kitty writing their names on the champagne cork afterward. Oppenheimer was in a gay mood; with great skill, he told anecdotes of his Washington experiences, eliciting maximum effect out of every phrase of a story about the haughty former Secretary of State, Dean Acheson. When it came time for Carol to walk the dog, he insisted on accompanying her.

During the course of the evening, Chevalier sought Oppenheimer's advice on a problem that appeared to bother him considerably. On the one hand, he was apprehensive that as an American employee of UNESCO he might be subject to a U.S. Government investigation, and if he failed of security clearance, he might lose his UNESCO employment. On the other hand, he was reluctant to renounce his American citizenship. There may also have been mention of Chevalier's problem concerning a U.S. passport. In any event, Oppenheimer apparently did not proffer his own advice, but, instead, gave Chevalier the name of Jeffries Wyman, an old Harvard friend who was now the science attaché at the American Embassy in Paris and with whom the Oppenheimers had lunched a week or two earlier.

With the exception of some discussion of the trial and execution of convicted atomic spies Julius and Ethel Rosenberg, the conversation stayed away from matters of substance and politics. It was mainly personal, anecdotal and very warm.

Shortly after midnight the Oppenheimers rose to leave. It was a cold night. Haakon Chevalier went and got a scarf he had bought in Rome, intended as a Christmas present for someone else, and gave it to his old friend.

The next day Chevalier had the idea of arranging a meeting between Oppenheimer and another Chevalier hero, the distinguished French writer and philosopher, André Malraux, whose 1937 speech in San Francisco had provided the occasion for the first contact between Chevalier and Oppenheimer. Malraux would also provide the occasion for their last, for after the Chevaliers and the Oppenheimers had driven out to the writer's home in Boulogne for an hour's visit, Haakon and Carol drove their friends back to the George V to prepare for their departure that night. It was the last time Chevalier and Oppenheimer ever saw each other.

The evening before, as Oppenheimer was leaving the Chevalier apartment, he had seemed to his host uneasy—to have great misgivings about his return to America, as if trouble might await him there. Chevalier has recalled the scientist saying, "I certainly don't look forward to the next few months."

When Robert and Kitty Oppenheimer flew back to the United States, in that December of 1953, grave trouble did indeed await them.

# III   THE INDICTMENT

In the weeks following his departure from Washington, William Borden remained deeply troubled about the Oppenheimer matter. He could not dispel the feeling that he had fallen short of his duty in raising questions about Oppenheimer's conduct without stating a conclusion. And so in the summer and early fall of 1953, as he began a new career in the Westinghouse nuclear submarine program, he spent most of his evenings reducing his thoughts to writing, in a letter meant for J. Edgar Hoover. It was a solitary effort, he later recalled. As he wrote, he consulted only one person: his wife.

To this task Borden brought the attitudes that had always governed his outlook. According to close associates, he was a person who constantly imposed the most exacting standards on himself, who considered his public office a sacred trust, who would defend an official secret with his life, if necessary, and who could not help expecting others to comport themselves likewise. Thus, to lie to security officers, as Oppenheimer had done in the "Chevalier incident," or to spend the night with "at least one Communist mistress" would have been to Borden an unthinkably heinous breach of trust.

It was this approach to human conduct that led Borden finally to reach the following conclusions:

*First,* that before the war Oppenheimer had been a disciplined, hard-core Communist.

*Second,* that, though he had cut off his overt party ties the moment he entered government service, in the spring of 1942, he had not really broken with the party, but that, instead, he had merely been conforming with standing party instructions for members to go underground for the duration.

*Third,* that there was no evidence in the record of Oppenheimer's wartime or postwar behavior that he ever did break with the party, and that, on the contrary, the only explanation for his opposition to the H-bomb and other nuclear efforts was that he had never ceased to be "an agent of the Soviet Union."

In mid-October, as Borden was completing his letter setting forth these conclusions, he became concerned about the propriety of using information he had obtained as a Congressional employee. He went to Washington to disclose his intentions to Representative Sterling Cole, new chairman of the Congressional Atomic Energy Committee. Cole raised no objections.

On Monday, November 9, Borden was scheduled to embark on a two-week Westinghouse training course, and he decided he must get the letter off before then. On November 7 he gave it the finishing touches.

Borden arranged the "evidence" in his letter according to four separate time periods:

1. *Oppenheimer's prewar activities and associations:* The evidence indicating that

   "(a) He was contributing substantial monthly sums to the Communist Party;

   (b) His ties with Communism had survived the Nazi-Soviet Pact and the Soviet attack upon Finland;

   (c) His wife and younger brother were Communists;

   (d) He had no close friends except Communists;

   (e) He had at least one Communist mistress;

   (f) He belonged only to Communist organizations, apart from professional affiliations;

   (g) The people whom he recruited into the early wartime Berkeley atomic project were exclusively Communists;

(h) He had been instrumental in securing recruits for the Communist Party; and

(i) He was in frequent contact with Soviet espionage agents."

2. *The circumstances of his 1942 entry into government service:* "The evidence indicating that

(a) In May 1942, he either stopped contributing funds to the Communist Party or else made his contributions through a new channel not yet discovered;

(b) In April 1942 his name was formally submitted for security clearance;

(c) He himself was aware at the time that his name had been so submitted; and

(d) He thereafter repeatedly gave false information to General Groves, the Manhattan District, and the FBI concerning the 1939–April 1942 period."

3. *His conduct during the war:* "The evidence indicating that

(a) He was responsible for employing a number of Communists, some of them nontechnical, at wartime Los Alamos;

(b) He selected one such individual to write the official Los Alamos history;

(c) He was a vigorous supporter of the H-bomb program until August 6, 1945 (Hiroshima), on which day he personally urged each senior individual working in this field to desist; and

(d) He was an enthusiastic sponsor of the A-bomb program until the war ended, when he immediately and outspokenly advocated that the Los Alamos Laboratory be disbanded."

4. *His conduct following the war, especially regarding the H-bomb:* "The evidence indicating that

(a) He was remarkably instrumental in influencing the military authorities and the Atomic Energy Commission essentially to suspend H-bomb development from mid-1946 through January 31, 1950;

(b) He has worked tirelessly, from January 31, 1950, onward, to retard the United States H-bomb program;

(c) He has used his potent influence against every postwar effort to expand capacity for producing A-bomb material;

(d) He has used his potent influence against every postwar effort directed at obtaining larger supplies of uranium raw material; and

(e) He has used his potent influence against every major postwar effort toward atomic power development, including the nuclear-powered submarine and aircraft programs as well as industrial power projects."

Some of Borden's law school contemporaries, who would have expected a person of his conscientiousness and legal training to be precise in the presentation of evidence, have expressed surprise at the manner in which Borden sought to support his drastic accusation against Oppenheimer. Was Borden, for example, relying on factual evidence and precise definitions in stating that in prewar years Oppenheimer had "no close friends except Communists" and had "belonged only to Communist organizations"? And could Borden rigorously document his assertion that Oppenheimer had "used his potent influence against *every* major postwar effort toward atomic power development" and against "*every* postwar effort" to expand uranium procurement and the production of fissionable material for A-bombs? (Emphasis added.) Some have found it hard to believe that so complex a person as Oppenheimer could have behaved in such a categorical manner.

In any event, the "evidence" set forth by Borden led him to express the following conclusions:

(1) Between 1939 and mid-1942, more probably than not, J. Robert Oppenheimer was a sufficiently hardened Communist that he either volunteered espionage information to the Soviets or complied with a request for such information. (This includes the possibility that when he singled out the weapons aspect of atomic development as his personal specialty, he was acting under Soviet instructions.)

(2) More probably than not, he has since been functioning as an espionage agent; and

(3) More probably than not, he has since acted under a Soviet directive in influencing United States military, atomic energy, intelligence and diplomatic policy.

It is to be noted that these conclusions correlate with information furnished by Klaus Fuchs, indicating that the Soviets had

acquired an agent in Berkeley who informed them about electromagnetic separation research during 1942 or earlier.

As Borden saw it, the "central problem" was *not* determining
whether Oppenheimer was ever a Communist (since the evidence
made it "abundantly clear" that he was), but gauging

the degree of likelihood that he in fact did what a Communist
in his circumstances, at Berkeley, would logically have done
during the crucial 1939–42 period—that is, whether he became
an actual espionage and policy instrument of the Soviets. Thus,
as to this central problem, my opinion is that, more probably
than not, the worst is in fact the truth.

In closing, Borden wrote of the torment the matter had caused
him:

I am profoundly aware of the grave nature of these comments.
The matter is detestable to me. Having lived with the Oppenheimer case for years, having studied and restudied all data
concerning him that your agency [the FBI] made available to
the Atomic Energy Commission through May 1953, having
endeavored to factor in a mass of additional data assembled
from numerous other sources, and looking back upon the case
from a perspective in private life, I feel a duty simply to state
to the responsible head of the security agency most concerned
the conclusions which I have painfully crystallized and which
I believe any fairminded man thoroughly familiar with the
evidence must also be driven to accept.

Then he concluded the letter in typical Borden conscientiousness: "The writing of this letter, to me a solemn step, is exclusively on my own personal initiative and responsibility." With a
"very truly yours" and a signature, the letter was complete.

On Saturday night, November 7, William Liscum Borden left
his home at 711 St. James Street, went to the main post office in
Pittsburgh, and mailed two envelopes. One was addressed to
J. Edgar Hoover, the Federal Bureau of Investigation, Washing-
tion, D.C. The other, containing a copy of the Hoover letter, was
directed to the Joint Committee on Atomic Energy, the Capitol,
Washington, D.C. To assure that his grave charges would not

go astray, Borden dispatched both letters registered mail, return receipt requested.

That morning the Pittsburgh *Post-Gazette* had carried banner headlines:

TRUMAN HITS BACK AT CHARGE
HE PROMOTED RED SPY

The news story reported a "sensational charge by Attorney General Herbert Brownell that former President Truman [had] promoted a known Soviet spy to high office." The Attorney General had declared, in a luncheon speech to the Chicago Executives' Club the day before, that Mr. Truman had named Assistant Treasury Secretary Harry Dexter White to a new and allegedly more important post in spite of an FBI report, previously sent to the White House, stating that White was a Soviet spy.

The charge generated immediate controversy, in considerable part because the ammunition for the Attorney General's politically explosive accusation had been drawn from the investigative reports of the FBI, theretofore generally expected to be inviolably confidential and antiseptically nonpolitical. In fact, the accuser, Brownell, became almost as controversial as the accusation itself. Democratic National Chairman Stephen Mitchell berated Brownell for making patently political charges in a matter of such gravity before a luncheon club, and for playing the dual role of Attorney General and "political manager" for the Eisenhower Administration. Some editorial writers criticized the Attorney General for attacking President Truman's loyalty. Both President Eisenhower and Brownell denied there had been any such intention, but the matter remained so touchy that the White House felt obliged, some days later, to try to disassociate the President from any responsibility for the Brownell speech.*

It was in such an atmosphere that William Liscum Borden's letter reached the Justice Department, of which the FBI is a part. The letter posed a potentially acute problem for Herbert

* This was not easy to do, since on the day the talk was delivered reporters had been told that it had been cleared with Eisenhower himself.

Brownell. After all, he had just accused the former Democratic Administration of laxity in ignoring a warning that a highly placed official was a Soviet spy. But here was a similar warning that Brownell's own Administration was maintaining as an AEC consultant a man believed to be "an agent of the Soviet Union." How would Brownell and the Administration look if this letter became public? This was far from an impossibility since a copy had evidently been sent to the Joint Committee on Atomic Energy, and was therefore presumably known to the members of that Congressional committee, of both political parties.\*

According to Washington newsman Warren Unna, in a later article in the *Atlantic Monthly*, Brownell and FBI Director Hoover went to see President Eisenhower about the Oppenheimer matter "and demanded that the physicist be ousted from his position as a consultant to the AEC and that his 'Q' clearance be revoked."†

Meanwhile, FBI agents were looking into Borden's allegations, and on November 30 an inch-thick report, together with the Borden letter, was sent to the White House, with copies to AEC Chairman Lewis L. Strauss and Defense Secretary Charles Wilson.

According to Lewis Strauss' later recollection, he found Borden's letter a "shocker" and was amazed that a lawyer would have written such grave charges. As for the FBI report, Strauss assumed that it consisted essentially of information of which he was already aware. And so (according to Strauss' recollection years later) the acutely security-conscious AEC Chairman merely "put a buck slip" on the FBI document and Borden letter and sent them to his four colleagues on the AEC.‡

---

\* The Borden letter was, in fact, made part of a weekly summary of top-secret events circulated to all members of the Joint Committee.

† Hoover sent the *Atlantic* a vigorous denial of his role in such a visit. "It is true," he said, "that the FBI did refer without recommendation information pertaining to Dr. Oppenheimer to appropriate officials in Washington" but said he "did not go to the President and make any demand that the physicist be ousted in any way, shape or form." Reporter Unna found Hoover's denial slightly ambiguous, failing to make clear "whether he denies going to the President on the Oppenheimer case or whether he denies merely thumping on the President's desk about it."

‡ Strauss' memory differs with that of one of the Commissioners, Henry DeWolf Smyth. Smyth was bedridden with influenza when the FBI report reached the AEC; he recalls learning that Strauss showed the Borden letter and the FBI report to the other three AEC Commissioners on Tuesday,

Late on the afternoon of December 3, Lewis Strauss received a request to come to the White House immediately. Arriving at the President's oval office, he found that a meeting was already in progress.* The President asked Strauss whether he was familiar with this latest FBI report on Oppenheimer (Strauss said he was) and whether any formal hearing had ever been held on the charges against Oppenheimer (Strauss said none had). In that case, the President said, a hearing ought to be ordered, and in the meantime a "blank wall" should be placed between Oppenheimer and any information of a sensitive or classified nature.†

After the meeting the President dispatched a two-paragraph memorandum to the Attorney General directing a thorough study of the entire Oppenheimer file and requesting a recommendation as to what further action should be taken. He also made this entry in his diary:

It is reported to me that this same [security] information, or at least the vast bulk of it, has been constantly reviewed and re-examined over a number of years, and that the over-all conclusion has always been that there is no evidence that implies disloyalty on the part of Dr. Oppenheimer. *However, this does not mean that he might not be a security risk.* . . . [Emphasis added.]‡

Late that day a copy of the Eisenhower directive reached

December 1, at an executive or closed meeting of the AEC. Both men's recollections are at variance with official AEC records, which show that the material was not transmitted from Strauss' office to the other Commissioners until December 11.

* None of the accounts of this meeting explains why Strauss, the head of the Federal agency most directly affected, was invited to the White House at the last minute or why a discussion involving his agency's consultant would have begun without him.

† Later, when the President's "blank wall" order became public, the Washington *Post*'s cartoonist, Herblock, depicted Eisenhower and Strauss separated by a wall from Oppenheimer, the scientist who had created so many of the secrets he was now supposedly being denied—all observed by a puzzled Uncle Sam wondering "Who's Being Walled Off From What?"

‡ Years later, when asked what he had meant, the former President said this probably indicated a question, on his part, as to whether Robert Oppenheimer was "one of those guys who cannot keep his mouth shut"—much like a West Point classmate of Eisenhower's whom he had been obliged to demote, in World War II, for inadvertently blurting out a vital piece of information.

Strauss. The AEC Chairman wanted the other four Commissioners to be informed about the situation, but there was no time to inform them himself. He was scheduled to leave with the President early the next morning for a summit meeting in Bermuda with British and French Prime Ministers Churchill and Laniel. And so he arranged that the other Commissioners should meet the next day in order that the situation could be explained to them.

As Strauss left for Bermuda, the news of the Eisenhower "blank wall" directive was already traveling fast along the government grapevine—hardly surprising inasmuch as copies of the directive had gone not only to the AEC but to the Central Intelligence Agency, the Secretary of Defense and the Chairman of the Joint Chiefs of Staff, as well as to Assistant White House News Secretary Murray Snyder. (It was later reported that the substance of the order was also quickly radioed to Army posts throughout the world and to Navy ships at sea.)

Among those who learned of the "blank wall" order that December 4 was a Rear Admiral in the Navy Department by the name of William S. Parsons, who had won fame by riding in the bomb bay of the *Enola Gay* and arming the world's first atomic bomb while it was being flown toward Hiroshima. "Deak" Parsons (as he was universally called) was irate over the President's action. As head of the Ordnance Division at Los Alamos he had been a key Oppenheimer aide, but the relationship was far more than an official one. Parsons and his vivacious wife, Martha, had been next-door neighbors of the Oppenheimers during those wartime years, and a warm friendship had grown up among the four. It had been kept cordially alive in the postwar years, when on more than one occasion the Parsons had been house guests of the Oppenheimers at Olden Manor in Princeton. Thus Parsons was highly exercised by what amounted to the suspension of Oppenheimer's security clearance. Late that afternoon he joined his wife at a cocktail party. He went directly to her; the distress showed on his face as he told her his news.

At home, later that evening, Parsons couldn't get the Oppenheimer matter off his mind. He decided to see the Secretary of the Navy the next day, to protest the security suspension. "Why not go directly to the President?" Martha asked. "No," said Parsons, "the Secretary of the Navy is my boss. I can't go around him."

But Parsons never had the chance to speak to the Secretary of the Navy or the President or anyone else on behalf of his friend. That night he complained of chest pains. Next morning he went to Bethesda Naval Hospital for a test. Before the doctors could complete their examination, "Deak" Parsons, armer of the world's first atomic bomb and friend of Robert Oppenheimer, was dead of a heart attack.

The following week, on Wednesday, December 9, Lewis Strauss returned to Washington. On Thursday he and his AEC colleagues met to decide what steps should be taken to carry out the Presidential "blank wall" directive on Oppenheimer. Because knowledge of the case was being extremely closely held within the Commission, attendance at the meeting was limited to the five Commissioners, the General Manager and his deputy, and the General Counsel. No one from the AEC's Security Division was present, even though this was a security case. In fact, aside from Deputy General Manager Walt Williams, no one at this crucial meeting had had any experience with AEC security regulations and procedures.

According to Commissioner Joseph Campbell, the meeting voted "unanimously to institute the regular procedures of the Commission to determine the veracity or falsity of the charges" contained in William Borden's November 7 letter to the FBI. But was this the only avenue open to the Commissioners that December 10? Was it necessary to put Oppenheimer and the government as well through the torment of a full-dress security hearing? Apparently not. At least one alternative seems to have been available, according to Commissioner Eugene Zuckert: "merely to allow Oppenheimer's consultant's contract to lapse when it expires on June 30, 1954, and thereafter not use his services."* But evidently the Commission elected not to pursue that course, and its vote set into motion the AEC's security machinery.

The first step was the drafting of a statement of charges against Oppenheimer. This assignment fell to William Mitchell, the

* In his 1954 written opinion on the Oppenheimer security case.

AEC's General Counsel, and he set to work the following day. But Mitchell, who had joined the AEC only nine months earlier, had never dealt first-hand with the details of a security case, and he quickly found himself in deep water in trying to draft the charges. He sought and received permission from Chairman Strauss to bring one additional person into the small circle of AEC personnel privy to the Oppenheimer matter. That person was Harold P. Green, a lawyer on Mitchell's staff. For almost three years Green had been counsel to the AEC's Security Division and as such had been involved in the processing of every security case.

At about five P.M. of Friday, December 11, Mitchell called Green into his office and closed the door. On Mitchell's desk (as on President Eisenhower's desk eight days earlier) sat a large stack of documents: the investigative files on J. Robert Oppenheimer. As Green entered, Mitchell's telephone rang. While answering it, he handed Green a copy of William Borden's letter to read. When Mitchell had completed the call and hung up, Green emitted an exclamatory, "Whew!" Mitchell nodded.

In bringing Green up to date on events since receipt of the Borden letter, Mitchell explained that none of the Commissioners was happy about instituting a formal proceeding against Oppenheimer, but that both the Eisenhower "blank wall" directive and AEC security regulations left no alternative. He said that Chairman Strauss had been particularly troubled by the case and had sought divine guidance as to the proper course of action.

Mitchell then turned to the matter of drafting the statement of charges, showing Green the start he had made. Actually, Green was not a great deal more expert than Mitchell in the writing of such charges, for while he had subjected hundreds of such documents to legal review over the preceding two years, he had never actually drafted one. This was a function invariably performed by the AEC's Division of Security. Yet, in this, the biggest and most important of all security cases, the AEC continued, even at this point, to exclude the Security Division and its experts.

Mitchell relayed to Green one crucial instruction from the Commissioners. Although the most spectacular allegation in the Borden letter had to do with Oppenheimer's opposition to the hydrogen bomb, and although there was some material in the

FBI investigative file supporting that Borden charge, neverthe-less, said Mitchell, the Commissioners did not want the H-bomb matter included in the bill of particulars against Oppenheimer. They thought it would be inappropriate to try the scientist, in effect, for the opinions he had held on a purely policy matter.

Mitchell then explained that Green was now one of the very few persons in the AEC with knowledge of the Oppenheimer case. The Commission, he said, was extremely anxious to keep the matter secret, for fear that if it became known in the scien-tific community there might well be a scientists' strike against the AEC. There was also, he said, some apprehension among the Commissioners that if Borden was right about Oppenheimer be-ing a Soviet agent, the knowledge that the AEC was considering bringing security charges against him might prompt Oppen-heimer to flee to Russia. Therefore, Mitchell said, Green was to use no one except the General Manager's personal secretary in typing up the statement of charges. He also instructed Green to get a separate locked file cabinet of his own, so that Green's of-fice mate could not stumble on anything connected with the Op-penheimer case in the file cabinet the two lawyers usually shared.

Mitchell said that the Commission was anxious to have a draft of the statement of charges ready for its consideration on Mon-day, if at all possible. He was aware, he said, that since it was already late Friday, this would involve a strenuous weekend of work for Green.

At six A.M., Saturday, Harold Green came into an empty Atomic Energy Commission building and began to wade through the several feet of reports in the Oppenheimer dossier. Although he had never looked into this file before, he was aware there was a security question about Oppenheimer. Still, as Green read on through the investigative files before him, he was shocked by their contents. If "derogatory information" such as this were be-ing considered *de novo*, Green thought, there would be more than enough in the files to justify initiating action to revoke Op-penheimer's clearance. On the other hand, he reflected, at this late date—after Oppenheimer had had access to the nation's most closely-held secrets for eleven years—any such proceeding would amount to trying to lock the door against a long-gone horse. And (as Green now recalls it) although he thought there might have been wiser ways to dispose of Oppenheimer, he felt that the AEC's decision to initiate the formal hearing procedure was not unreasonable. He set upon his task with a clear conscience.

During the course of that Saturday morning, Green was interrupted several times by calls from AEC General Manager Kenneth D. Nichols, inquiring as to Green's progress. On two occasions, Nichols asked Green to come to his office to talk about the case. Each time, Green had to stow the bulky files in a safe and afterward laboriously remove them before resuming work. In these conversations, Nichols told Green about his past relationships with Oppenheimer, both during the Manhattan Project (when Nichols had served as General Groves' deputy) and in postwar years (when he had been involved in the Pentagon's atomic energy work). He talked at length about Oppenheimer's miserable attitude toward security; about the poor advice the scientist had given the government; and about his arrogance. Green came away from these talks struck by Nichols' evident zest for this security proceeding and with the clear impression that the purpose of these two conversations was to instill in Green a similar degree of enthusiasm for the chore at hand.

The talks were all the more striking to Green, since he was acutely aware that under AEC regulations, Nichols would make the final decision in the case. It was as if, during a prosecuting attorney's preparation of a criminal case, the prospective trial judge had sought to whet the lawyer's appetite for the impending prosecution. By noon Saturday, Green was beginning to develop qualms about the case.

Harold Green worked on through that Saturday, until about seven o'clock. As he worked, he knew that although the AEC security screening criteria did not specifically make lying an earmark of a security risk, in practice an estimate of an individual's truthfulness was often decisive. So, as he began his drafting, Green deliberately inserted charges designed to test Oppenheimer's veracity.

At six o'clock Sunday morning he was back at his AEC desk.

By noon, the draft was finished. As requested, he called William Mitchell, who arranged to come to AEC headquarters in a couple of hours to review Green's work.

If one tried to pinpoint the most crucial two-hour period in the entire Oppenheimer affair, the hours between twelve noon and two P.M. of Sunday, December 13, 1953, would doubtless be a leading candidate, for what transpired in those two hours profoundly affected the nature and conduct of the Oppenheimer security case. Here was lawyer Green, ensconced in the empty, silent catacombs of the Atomic Energy Commission offices at noon on a cloudy Sunday, with two hours to kill. His thoughts went back to the Commissioners' injunction against including Oppenheimer's opposition to the H-bomb in the statement of charges, for fear of seeming to try a man for his policy opinions. But need the H-bomb charge be drafted in that manner, Green wondered? Might it not portray Oppenheimer's alleged conflicting statements about the H-bomb so as to constitute, instead, a test of Oppenheimer's veracity? With nothing better to occupy his time, Green decided to try his hand at drafting a charge on the H-bomb in this latter vein, just so he and Mitchell could see what it looked like.

By the time Mitchell arrived, Green had completed a paragraph on the hydrogen bomb question that seemed to emphasize the issue of Oppenheimer's veracity. After listing some early Oppenheimer statements indicating he believed the H-bomb feasible, it went on to cite reports that Oppenheimer had, in the fall of 1949 and subsequently, "opposed the development of the hydrogen bomb (1) on moral grounds, (2) by claiming that it was not feasible (3) by claiming that there were insufficient facilities and scientific personnel to carry on the development and (4) that it was not politically desirable." The paragraph also alleged that even after President Truman's decision had made the H-bomb "a matter of national policy," Oppenheimer had continued "to oppose the project," had declined to "cooperate fully" in it, and had been "instrumental in persuading other outstanding scientists not to work on the project." There was also a charge that Oppenheimer, improperly, had distributed the October, 1949, GAC reports among the upper echelons at Los Alamos "for the purpose of trying to turn such top personnel against the development of the bomb."*

Immediately following the listing of the charges, in order to make clear that Oppenheimer's veracity was in issue, Green added a phrase specifically stating that the allegations "raise questions as to your *veracity*, conduct and loyalty."† [Emphasis added.]

The H-bomb allegations and the other charges drafted by Green were reviewed by Mitchell when he reached the building early that afternoon. The entire document met with Mitchell's approval, including Green's addition of the hydrogen-bomb matter. "Let's try it on General Nichols tomorrow," he said. The next day, Green and Mitchell took the draft to Nichols and to each of the Commissioners. All approved the document with virtually no change. No one questioned or even discussed the possibility of eliminating the H-bomb charge.

The inclusion of the H-bomb controversy as part of the Oppenheimer security case—in a sense as a sort of afterthought— had an enormous effect on the nature of the hearing that was to follow. Had it been omitted, the charges would have been confined to Oppenheimer's prewar and wartime "leftist" associations and activities; there would presumably have been no examination into his far-ranging activities as a postwar government advisor and his policy views that had so inflamed the Air Force. In the absence of an H-bomb charge, it is probable that six of the eight witnesses eventually called by the government against Robert Oppenheimer would not have testified, since they had very little knowledge of his prewar association with the radical left.

Would the H-bomb charge have been left out if Harold Green had not decided to try his hand at drafting it during those two

* Green says, in retrospect, that he had no basis at the time for believing that such allegations on the H-bomb question would place Oppenheimer on trial for his policy views. He feels, now, that this would not have resulted if the case had been handled normally before a regular, experienced AEC hearing board; as an inquiry, not a trial; and without a full-fledged prosecution.

† Later, at the suggestion of Commissioner Eugene Zuckert, this latter phrase was amended to read "your veracity, conduct and *even your* loyalty." (Emphasis added.)

idle hours of that mid-December Sunday? No one, of course, can say with certainty, but the chances seem overwhelming that but for what transpired during those two solitary hours in the AEC offices that Sunday, the course of events "in the matter of J. Robert Oppenheimer" would have been profoundly different.

On Monday, December 14, Harold Green received an unusual telephone call that added to his growing disquietude about the manner in which the case was being prepared and would, presumably, be prosecuted. The call was from a special agent of the Federal Bureau of Investigation. He had, he said, been assigned to work with the AEC in the handling of the Oppenheimer case. Was there any information he could obtain for Green, he wanted to know, or any other way he could be of help?

The call struck Green as most unusual. In the ordinary security case, in the infrequent instances where information was needed from the FBI, it was asked for and received at arm's length, strictly through channels—and not without considerable grumbling on the part of the FBI at being bothered. So the FBI's initiative in offering carte blanche cooperation caught Harold Green by surprise. He concluded that the Bureau was giving the Oppenheimer case special handling.

The notification letter having been approved by Nichols and the five Commissioners, all that remained was for Nichols to make the final decision to proceed on the basis of the letter. Just before signing the necessary papers, Nichols paused and said, "Do we really have to go through with this? Why don't we just turn the file over to McCarthy?"

With the statement of charges drafted and approved, it remained now to inform Oppenheimer of the suspension of his security clearance, and of his right to a hearing on the allegations against him. Lewis Strauss called the scientist, who had just returned from Europe and, without specifying the purpose, asked if Oppenheimer would come to Washington to see him. They arranged to meet in Strauss' office on the afternoon of Monday, December 21.

When Oppenheimer met Strauss that day, they were joined by AEC General Manager Kenneth D. Nichols.

At first the three made an effort to exchange amenities; there was a mutual lament over the death of Admiral Parsons, whom all three men had known. Strauss told of a visit he had received that morning from Oppenheimer's close friend, Herbert Marks, who had urgently appealed to Strauss to head off a reportedly impending Senate probe of Oppenheimer's background. Oppenheimer expressed surprise, saying he had heard neither of the Senate investigation nor of Marks' visit.

Oppenheimer began to tell of the semiofficial conversations he had recently had in Europe on atomic energy matters, but Strauss said that could wait: there was something more important. Oppenheimer's security file, Strauss said, had undergone two recent government re-evaluations, because of the new Eisenhower screening criteria and because a former government official had drawn attention to Oppenheimer's record. As a result, he said, the AEC had drafted a letter of charges stating the reasons why Oppenheimer's security status was in question. He handed the physicist a copy. Oppenheimer read it, then observed that many of its observations were correct, others incorrect.*

After Strauss had explained to Oppenheimer his rights under the AEC security procedures, there followed a discussion of the merits of Oppenheimer's resigning rather than going through a hearing. There is an unresolved dispute as to who first broached the matter of resignation. Oppenheimer, in a letter sent next day to Chairman Strauss, stated that it was Strauss who had opened up that subject, by "put[ting] to me as a possibly desirable alternative that I request termination of my contract as a consultant to the Commission, and thereby avoid an explicit consideration of the charges on which the Commission's action would otherwise be based."

Strauss and Nichols, on the other hand, insisted it was Oppenheimer who first "raised the question." In fact, an undated memorandum of the conversation written by General Nichols seemed to go out of its way, in a manner unusual to memoranda of that sort, to specify the *sequence* of the remarks made on the subject,

* Oppenheimer was later reported to have resented the way Strauss presented the charges to him, since the AEC Chairman had known him over a period of years and, moreover, had as an AEC Commissioner in 1947 voted to clear Oppenheimer.

observing that Oppenheimer "raised the question of resigning prior to Mr. Strauss discussing this alternative." During the meeting itself, Oppenheimer commented that Strauss seemed to be pressing him to resign rather than insist on a hearing. Strauss denied this, but then proceeded to confirm Oppenheimer's impression by showing him a memorandum intended to be used to notify AEC laboratory directors in case Oppenheimer chose to relinquish his clearance voluntarily. The drafters of this memo, which the AEC had obviously taken trouble preparing, had even included a sentence ascribing to Oppenheimer the view that the matter of his security status should be kept confidential.

Oppenheimer asked how much time he would have to consider his course of action. Strauss replied that he would be at home that evening after eight o'clock to receive Oppenheimer's answer. But, he said, the Commission must have a reply by the next day at the latest, observing that he had, on his own responsibility, delayed the proceeding for nearly three weeks because of Oppenheimer's absence abroad.* Oppenheimer indicated he was going to consult his friend and sometime attorney, Herbert Marks, and asked if for that purpose he could have a copy of the draft letter of charges. Strauss declined this request on the ground that the letter could not be given him before it had been formally signed, but said that if Oppenheimer elected to go ahead with a hearing it would be sent him promptly.

The scientist asked if "the Hill" (Congress) knew about the security case; Strauss said so far as he was aware it didn't but that since the AEC had a duty to keep the Congressional Joint Committee on Atomic Energy fully informed, it would be impossible to withhold the information from them. Oppenheimer, mindful of Herbert Marks' warning of a Senate investigation and possible hearing on his case, observed it would be bad public relations for him to resign just before such a hearing.

The scientist repeated he was going to consult with Herbert Marks, and at 3:35 the painful confrontation ended. Robert Oppenheimer now knew that the government he had served for nearly twelve years was questioning his loyalty and reliability.

* Actually, only eleven days had elapsed since the Commission had first voted to institute the proceeding.

After leaving the Atomic Energy Commission Building, Oppenheimer did not go to the office of Herbert Marks, as he had indicated to Strauss and Nichols. Instead, he proceeded to 1701 K Street, N.W. There he took the elevator to the sixth floor and, at around four o'clock, entered the law office of Joseph Volpe, former general counsel of the AEC. Soon Herbert Marks joined the two. Oppenheimer told them about his conference with Strauss and Nichols, and for more than an hour the three discussed what measures Oppenheimer should take in his own defense.

Essentially, then, even though Oppenheimer had not yet formally retained Marks or Volpe, this conference represented a relationship which the Supreme Court has since held to be inviolably private, that of lawyer and client.* The Federal investigators, however, evidently did not regard the relationship, or this conference, as inviolable, for, although Volpe, Marks and Oppenheimer were not aware of it, they were not alone in Room 605 of 1701 K Street. Also in the room was a representative of the United States Government—not a human representative, but an electronic device, monitoring and recording every word that was being said between Robert Oppenheimer and his attorneys. To be able to overhear this conference so soon after Oppenheimer left the AEC presented a feat of some agility and speed on the part of the eavesdroppers, since there had presumably been no way of knowing that Oppenheimer would proceed from his AEC conference to Volpe's office; on the contrary, he had told Strauss and Nichols he intended to go to Marks' office.

Late that afternoon, Oppenheimer sat in the Georgetown living room of Herbert and Anne Marks, a drink in his hand, gray and utterly appalled by the events of the day. He had been driven to Georgetown by Anne, who had served as Oppenheimer's personal assistant and secretary at Los Alamos and was a close

---

* In 1966 the Supreme Court ordered a complete new trial in a case where the government had eavesdropped on a lawyer-client conversation, and in 1967 the Court strongly indicated that any such "direct intrusion" into the lawyer-client relationship would be considered "adequate justification" for ordering a new trial. Similarly, a U.S. Court of Appeals stated in 1951 that "It is well established that an accused does not enjoy the effective aid of counsel if he is denied the right of private consultation with him."

friend. Years afterward she said that as they drove to the Marks' home, Oppenheimer commented, "I can't believe what is happening to me!"

Later, looking back on that day, he recalled that "It was like Pearl Harbor—on a small scale. Given the circumstances and the spirit of the times, one knew that something like this was possible and even probable; but still it was a shock when it came." The most graphic measure of the state of his mind, he remembered, was that on that shattering day he absent-mindedly misplaced the pipe from which he was ordinarily inseparable.

Tuesday, December 22. Deadline for Oppenheimer to advise Lewis Strauss of his decision: whether he would relinquish the security clearance without a confrontation or insist on a full-dress hearing on the charges.

At 10 A.M. that Tuesday, Oppenheimer spoke with Joseph Volpe and arranged that he and Kitty would meet Volpe and Herbert Marks late that afternoon, to frame a response to Lewis Strauss. From five until nearly midnight the four debated the alternatives. Volpe argued strongly that Oppenheimer should tell Strauss that he would serve as an AEC consultant only as long as the Commission wished him to, so that his future relationship with the AEC would not hinge on a security hearing but on a simple policy decision by the Commission. But in the end it was decided that Oppenheimer had no alternative to asking for a hearing. Any other course would, as Lewis Strauss later put it, "have left all the charges on the record."

A letter was drafted and dispatched to Strauss. It recapitulated the previous day's meeting and what Oppenheimer understood to be Strauss' suggestion that he voluntarily request the termination of his consultant's contract. "I have thought most earnestly of the alternative suggested," Oppenheimer wrote Strauss. "Under the circumstances this course of action would mean that I accept and concur in the view that I am not fit to serve this Government, that I have now served for some 12 years. This I cannot do."

The next sentence was addressed, by implication, to *two* Lewis Strausses: Strauss the Chairman of the Atomic Energy Commission and Strauss the trustee of the Institute for Advanced Study

who had initially offered Oppenheimer the Institute directorship. "If I were thus unworthy," Oppenheimer wrote, "I could
hardly have served our country as I have tried, or been the
Director of our Institute in Princeton, or have spoken, as on more
than one occasion I have found myself speaking, in the name of
our science and our country."

Noting that he had merely "paged through the letter [of
charges] quite briefly" the day before, Oppenheimer said he
would "now read it in detail and make appropriate response."
Then he signed the letter: "Faithfully yours, ROBERT OPPEN-
HEIMER."

Wednesday, December 23. Again Robert and Kitty Oppenheimer met with Volpe and Marks. Now that it was certain
there would be a full-dress hearing, a decision of cardinal importance was the selection of a lawyer to represent Oppenheimer
in the proceeding. One likely candidate was Joseph Volpe, who
had sat beside the physicist during several important Congressional appearances. Oppenheimer now asked Volpe to represent
him in this new imbroglio, but Volpe demurred, feeling that it
was inappropriate for a former general counsel of the AEC to be
the Commission's adversary in a proceeding of this sort.

On that same day, the AEC sent its 3,400-word letter of
charges to Oppenheimer, setting forth the bases of its case
against him and allowing him thirty days to submit a written response. The letter was signed by AEC General Manager Nichols.
It presented some twenty-four allegations, the first twenty-three
of which dealt with Oppenheimer's supposed Communist and
left-wing connections from 1938 to 1946. The dates were significant, for they showed that all the events involved in the first
twenty-three charges had taken place prior to the AEC's meticulous review of the Oppenheimer file and its unanimous
clearance of him in 1947. These charges included Oppenheimer's
prewar membership in organizations later declared "subversive"
(e.g., the Friends of the Chinese People); his association with
Jean Tatlock; the onetime Communist affiliations of Kitty and
of Frank and Jackie Oppenheimer; Robert Oppenheimer's supposed subscription to the *People's Daily World;* his attendance
at various pro-Communist functions, such as the Kenneth May

housewarming in Berkeley in 1941 and the alleged Communist meeting in his own house that same year; his financial contributions to (or through) the Communist Party until his entry into war work in 1942; reports that certain Communists had claimed Oppenheimer as a party member during the war; the physicist's recruitment of supposed Communist sympathizers into the atomic bomb project; his 1946 New Year's meeting with two alleged Communists; and his postwar membership in the Independent Citizens Committee of the Arts, Sciences and Professions, supposedly a "Communist front." Finally, there was the "Chevalier incident": the approach by Chevalier, "either directly or through your brother"; Oppenheimer's delayed and false reporting of the incident to the authorities; and his continued relations with the Chevaliers "in 1946 and 1947."

That completed the "pro-Communist" allegations. But there was a twenty-fourth and final charge—the only one dealing with events that postdated the 1947 AEC clearance. This charge noted early Oppenheimer statements affirming the feasibility of the H-bomb and then cited "reports" that

. . . in the autumn of 1949, and subsequently, you strongly opposed the development of the hydrogen bomb (1) on moral grounds, (2) by claiming that it was not feasible, (3) by claiming that there were insufficient facilities and scientific personnel to carry on the development and (4) that it was not politically desirable.

. . . that you departed from your proper role as an adviser to the [Atomic Energy] Commission by causing the distribution separately and in private, to top personnel at Los Alamos, of the majority and minority reports of the General Advisory Committee on development of the hydrogen bomb for the purpose of trying to turn such top personnel against the development of the hydrogen bomb.

. . . that you were instrumental in persuading other outstanding scientists not to work on the hydrogen-bomb project, and that the opposition to the hydrogen bomb, of which you are the most experienced, most powerful, and most effective member, has definitely slowed down its development.

". . . you strongly opposed . . . you continued to oppose . . .

[you] declined to cooperate fully . . ."—clearly these phrases set the H-bomb charge apart from the other twenty-three regarding Oppenheimer's alleged Communist connections. Those had dealt, for the most part, with actions and events. But the H-bomb charge ventured into quite different areas: Oppenheimer's opinions; the advice these had led him to offer the government as an official consultant; and the extent to which they differed with established "national policy."

Was it proper for a "security-risk" proceeding to delve into a man's opinions? Was it proper for such a deliberation to concern itself with the *merits* of his official advice to the government? These were questions that were to be vigorously raised in the course of the Oppenheimer hearing. In fact, one witness was to argue that Oppenheimer's judges should not have accepted a letter of charges that seemed to consider a man's opinions as relevant to his loyalty or trustworthiness.

But the letter that was mailed that December 23 did deal with Oppenheimer's views and advice on the H-bomb, and in so doing it had a great effect upon the nature of the hearing that was to follow.

On Christmas Eve at his home in Princeton, Oppenheimer was visited by two representatives of the AEC. They presented a letter that said peremptorily that he was "hereby directed to deliver" all the remaining AEC documents in his possession. Arrangements were made for Oppenheimer's secretary to inventory the documents,* and a week later, on New Year's Eve, the AEC aides returned to remove the papers to Washington.

This action would, in at least one instance, place Oppenheimer at a serious disadvantage at the hearing. Not only did it put certain documents in the hands of the government prosecutor; it simultaneously kept Oppenheimer and his attorneys from using those same papers in preparing the physicist's defense.

---

* So numerous were the documents that Katherine Russell, Oppenheimer's devoted secretary, was obliged to work one full week (including thirty-six hours without interruption on December 30 and December 31) to complete the mammoth task—for which the AEC sent her "payment in full for work performed" of $133.23.

As the new year began, the "Communists-in-government" issue, so controversially raised by the Attorney General in November, was taken up by none other than the President himself. In his January 7 State of the Union Message, Mr. Eisenhower told Congress that the new and more stringent security-screening standards he had promulgated in April had brought about the dismissal of more than 2,200 Federal employees.

This sensational claim prompted newsmen to bombard the White House for more information. Did the President mean that 2,200 "subversives" had been found and dismissed? How many of the 2,200 had been "Communists"? How many of them "disloyal"?

At first, the Administration declined to furnish any breakdowns of the dismissals. But soon it did, in a most contradictory and bewildering manner. On February 18 the veil was lifted on 430 of the 2,200 "security risk" firings, only 29 of which were said to involve charges of disloyalty. Yet on February 21 it seemed that there were 41 "loyalty" cases out of some 1,002 dismissals. The figures changed again on March 1, when the Civil Service Commission stated that of 2,224 "security" dismissals, 355 files contained allegations of "subversive" associations. The next day the figures were again altered to show that of 2,427 "security" firings, 383 had been "subversive" cases. With the passage of two more days there was still another change: there had been 2,429 dismissals, of which 422 involved "subversives." These rapidly shifting statistics naturally aroused the Democrats, who claimed the Administration was engaging in a "numbers racket." Senators Stuart Symington and Wayne Morse, as well as former Speaker of the House Sam Rayburn, all excoriated the Administration for its tactics.

With the security-screening program now deeply embroiled in political controversy, Federal departments and agencies came under severe pressure to make good on the Administration's claims of finding and firing large numbers of subversives. For example, when the number of "security risks" reported by the U.S. Information Agency turned out to be small in comparison with other agencies, Vice President Nixon suggested in a January 15 meeting of the President's cabinet that the USIA screening program be reviewed to see why. It was at this same cabinet meeting that Secretary of State John Foster Dulles complained of the cases brought to him alleging nothing more serious than World Federalist membership or the presence of a pacifist in the family.

It was in such an atmosphere that the AEC began readying itself for its examination of J. Robert Oppenheimer.

# IV PREPARATIONS FOR THE HEARING

One of the first problems facing the Atomic Energy Commission was the selection of a three-man board to hear and rule on the charges. This responsibility was assigned to AEC General Counsel William Mitchell. Mitchell and others at the AEC felt that in view of Oppenheimer's stature public confidence in the outcome demanded that his hearing board consist of men of an eminence comparable to his own. And so, in early January, Mitchell began an extensive trip around the country, scouting for potential board members.

As Mitchell later recalled it, the Commissioners had said that the hearing panel should, if possible, contain one person with substantial experience in government service, preferably in the national security area. The man picked to fill that slot was Gordon Gray, president of the University of North Carolina, and in his selection President Eisenhower himself appears to have had a hand. Eisenhower had first come to know Gray in 1947, he as Army Chief of Staff, Gray as an Assistant Secretary of the Army. To Eisenhower, Gray was an ideal choice as head of the Oppenheimer hearing panel. He seemed to the President a sensible man with no ax to grind, who would make an objective study of the case. Moreover, he was a Democrat, and would lend a bipartisan character to the board. The presence of a Democrat might, in part, serve as a buffer at a time when Senator McCarthy's investigative zeal was aimed more at his own party's new Administration than at its Democratic predecessors.

Whether or not the President himself asked Gray to take on the assignment,* Gray was left with no doubt that his selection represented the personal desire of the President of the United States. And so when approached, he agreed to chair Robert Oppenheimer's hearing board.

The AEC's second problem was how the prodigious amount of evidence in the investigative files should be presented to the hearing board, and by whom. Even before a hearing board was picked, it was decided that an outside attorney should be engaged to handle the case for the Commission.

For aid in finding such a person, Lewis Strauss turned to the Department of Justice. There the matter fell largely to Deputy Attorney General William P. Rogers, who, unlike Attorney General Brownell, had previously practiced law in Washington and was therefore well acquainted with the array of local attorneys. Since the case would clearly call for the presentation of a vast amount of information to the board, Rogers sought a man with considerable trial experience, preferably in the role of prosecutor. Prominent among those who seemed to meet Rogers' prerequisites was a native Washingtonian by the name of Roger Robb, who had had seven years of prosecutorial experience as an Assistant United States Attorney. During that time he had tried twenty-three murder cases, obtaining, according to the local newspaper, "an unusually high percentage of convictions," and had won some local renown for his prosecution of Washington gambling czar Sam Beard. Robb had also been the court-appointed attorney for Communist leader Earl Browder in a contempt-of-Congress case, for which he earned Browder's public praise.† William Rogers himself had had occasion to observe

---

* Lewis Strauss recalls that it was he, Strauss, who called Gray about the matter.

† "Despite his pronounced political opinions, which I would call reactionary," Browder wrote in the preface of a book about the trial, Robb pro-

Robb's courtroom talents at first hand, since Robb had been his legal adversary in a libel action against Drew Pearson. (Rogers, who represented Pearson, had emerged victorious on that occasion.)

When Chairman Strauss received Rogers' suggested list of Washington attorneys, Roger Robb was the one he selected to approach first. After one preliminary conversation with Robb, and after obtaining the approval of the other Commissioners, Strauss asked Robb to take on the case.*

Who would be Roger Robb's adversary in the forthcoming hearing? Many people participated in resolving the answer to that question, but none more influentially than Oppenheimer's intimate friend Herbert Marks. A brilliant Washington lawyer, Marks first met Oppenheimer in the course of their work together on the Acheson-Lilienthal report in 1946. An affinity grew between the two as Marks became the first General Counsel and Oppenheimer a senior adviser to the fledgling AEC. Marks developed a worshipful and tenacious attachment to the scientist reminiscent of that felt by many of Oppenheimer's students before the war. After the physicist received the AEC's "security-risk" charges, Marks' private law practice was soon virtually forgotten as he threw himself into the planning and preparations for Oppenheimer's defense.

Marks, like Joseph Volpe, felt that his former association with the AEC barred him from being Oppenheimer's chief counsel, and he sought advice from Supreme Court Justice Felix Frankfurter and the distinguished Washington attorney John Lord O'Brian† on the proper person to serve in his place. Marks believed strongly that Oppenheimer should be represented by an

vided "substantial, not merely formal, assistance," and displayed a high "pride of profession."

* There is a degree of irony in Strauss' personal role in the hiring of Roger Robb as outside counsel for the AEC. Strauss himself was to complain, years later, that a Senate committee's hearing on his own nomination to be Secretary of Commerce was "an inquisition" because "the attorney for the prosecution" had been "brought in by the chief judge" (the committee chairman). Yet as head of the final body to pass on the matter Strauss was to be the "chief judge" in the Oppenheimer case, in which he had personally been responsible for "bringing in" the "attorney for the prosecution."

† Oppenheimer and Marks, in fact, suggested that O'Brian consider taking on the case, but O'Brian was obliged to decline for reasons of health.

attorney as distinguished in the legal field as Oppenheimer was in the scientific arena. Joseph Volpe took a different view: to him, legal stature did not matter as much as skill at courtroom infighting and an appetite for it. Just before the turn of the year he gave Marks the name of the senior partner of a well-known New York law firm, a man with a reputation for tough courtroom tactics. Whether or not his nominee was ever approached, Volpe's advice was not ultimately heeded.

Early in January, in part at the suggestion of John Lord O'Brian, Oppenheimer called Lloyd K. Garrison, a leading New York attorney whom Oppenheimer had come to know the preceding April, when Garrison joined the board of trustees of the Institute for Advanced Study. Garrison came from a distinguished family. His great-grandfather was abolitionist William Lloyd Garrison, his grandfather literary editor of *The Nation*. Garrison himself had been dean of the Wisconsin Law School and a pioneering expert and activist in government labor relations work. As a private practitioner of the law in New York since the war, and as president of the National Urban League and a leader in the American Civil Liberties Union, Garrison had earned a reputation for unimpeachable integrity and enormous dedication to public causes. Lincolnesque in appearance, mild of manner, Garrison sought weekend respite at a country home where he devoted his sparse leisure time to bird-watching and reading philosophy, Greek literature and books on politics.

Oppenheimer and Marks first discussed his security case with Garrison one evening in the attorney's New York apartment. When Garrison had read the AEC's letter of charges, Oppenheimer said, "It looks pretty bad, doesn't it?" Garrison agreed it did.

After discussing the nature of the charges, they turned to the problem of finding counsel to defend the physicist. They concluded it would be no easy matter. With such a long and grave array of charges against Oppenheimer emanating from the respected AEC, and in the atmosphere at the mid-Fifties, even lawyers who were liberals might hesitate to involve themselves. There was, moreover, the near-certainty that Oppenheimer's defense would require any attorney to drop all other concerns and saturate himself in Oppenheimer's past life. Few first-rate law-yers could instantly lay aside their commitments.*

Yet it was urgent (the three men agreed) that work on Oppen-heimer's defense begin immediately, because of the danger that the AEC's charges might at any time become public. Should this occur before Oppenheimer's answers to the charges had been researched and put in writing, there would be nothing that could be quickly distributed to news media to counter the AEC allega-tions, and irreparable harm to his cause might result.

And so it was decided that evening that Lloyd Garrison him-self should begin work immediately on a written rebuttal to the AEC charges and that the search for a permanent chief counsel should be suspended until the written response was complete. With the help of Marks and Oppenheimer, Garrison set about immersing himself in the complex life history of the complex scientist.

On March 4, after many weeks of conferences, interviews, drafting and redrafting, Robert Oppenheimer's reply to the AEC charges was complete, and the search for a chief counsel re-sumed. Garrison's objective, he has recalled, "was not to find just an able lawyer, experienced in litigation, but a statesman and a patriot, a symbol of all that was highest in the profession, whose representation of [Oppenheimer in the security hearing] would in itself carry weight with the Board and, if the matter became public, with people at large. In other words, we said to ourselves that we must find 'a great man.' "†

Garrison went "to such a man," John W. Davis, for whom Gar-rison had, as a young lawyer, campaigned for President in 1924, and to whom he continued to look up "as an advocate of incom-parable ability and as a man of courage and honor." At eighty, intellectually alert but physically frail, Davis said he would be glad to take on the case if the hearing could be held in New York rather than Washington, but the AEC, when approached, said

* In fact, two attorneys mentioned that evening were approached the next day, but proved to be overburdened and unable to take the case.
† This and certain other recollections by Lloyd Garrison are taken from his written answers to questions put to him by the author. The full text of his replies appears on pages 517–66.

that with all the files and documents in Washington a New York hearing would not be feasible.*

Garrison continued his search, but without success. Meanwhile, the prospective date of the hearing was drawing near, and Garrison became more and more involved in the time-consuming process of prehearing interviews of the many friends and associates of Oppenheimer's who were potential witnesses on his behalf. It was finally decided that the search for a chief counsel should be dropped, and that Garrison himself should serve in that capacity.

And so, when the Oppenheimer hearing finally began, on April 12, 1954, the principal opposing counsel were Roger Robb —tough, conservative, experienced in the ways of the prosecutor, and at home in the rough-and-tumble atmosphere of the courtroom—versus Lloyd K. Garrison—mild-mannered, almost saintly, at home in the world of intellect and compassion but a comparative stranger, both by experience and by temperament, to the often merciless world of an adversary courtroom proceeding.

Lloyd Garrison's fears about the danger of the AEC charges becoming public proved well founded. January had not yet ended before they became known to at least one prominent newspaper reporter, and very nearly to the nation at large.

The reporter was James Reston of the *New York Times*, who in mid-January learned of the existence of an AEC letter of charges. After considerable effort, Reston was able to reach Oppenheimer by telephone. Oppenheimer said he "thought it contrary to the national interest" to have the story published and hence would not talk about the matter unless and until it did become public knowledge.

Late in January, Reston called on Garrison. Reston was aware of the attorney's fear that the AEC charges might be disclosed without any Oppenheimer rebuttal. And so he suggested that as soon as a written response was ready, that document as well as the AEC charges be given to the *Times* on the understanding that both charges and reply would be published together—but

* This did not end Davis' association with the case: he was later to lend his name to the legal brief submitted to the AEC on Oppenheimer's behalf.

only at such time as it became evident the story could no longer be kept secret.

Garrison said he would have to take the matter up with his associates in the case. But evidently there was no quick agreement, for on January 31 Garrison told David Lilienthal that Reston was planning to break the story the next day. "So," Lilienthal noted in his diary, "it will be all over the place. Surprising that it hasn't before this."

But the story did not break on February 1, as Garrison had predicted. In fact, Reston was to hold the story for another seventy-two days.

On February 15 a special meeting was held of the trustees of the Institute for Advanced Study. There was only one item on the agenda: the Institute's director wished to advise the trustees of the charges leveled against him by the United States Government, and to proffer his resignation.

The board voted unanimously to voice its complete confidence in its director and to refuse any consideration of his resignation.

Of the fifteen members of the board, two were absent that day: Harold F. Linder and Lewis L. Strauss.

In the early months of 1954 Senator Joseph McCarthy's power to command newspaper headlines and to cow mighty agencies of the United States Government had never seemed greater. It may have reached its acme in February of 1954, when the Senator succeeded in embroiling the Department of the Army in an extensive and highly publicized inquiry as to who was responsible for promoting and then granting an honorable discharge to Irving Peress, an Army Major alleged by McCarthy to have been a Communist. The case soon developed into a major clash between the Senator and the Administration. The Senator demanded the name of every person involved with Peress' discharge and threatened to bring contempt citations against anyone who withheld them. The Army at first refused to allow Peress' commanding officer, General Ralph Zwicker, to appear before McCarthy's committee and then humilatingly backed down—supposedly on orders from a "high Administration" official. It was from this seed that the celebrated nationally televised "Army-McCarthy" hear-

ings later grew, and for eight weeks viewers were virtually trans-
fixed by the spectacle taking place in the Senate Office Building
in Washington. For those who did not live through the agitated
mid-Fifties, it may be hard to believe that such a national tem-
pest could have had its origin in accusations of Communism
against one Irving Peress—a dentist in the Army of the United
States.

As both sides prepared for the hearing, it was generally apparent that the Oppenheimer proceeding, especially because it
involved the H-bomb, would be permeated with matters of the
highest secrecy, to which only those persons enjoying a special
atomic "Q" clearance could be privy. Under the law, a "Q" clearance could only be granted following an extensive "full field"
investigation by the FBI. As a rule this took a minimum of sixty
to ninety days. Where greater speed was needed, there was provision for granting an "emergency Q" clearance on the basis of a
briefer check, valid until the "full field" inquiry could be completed.

The AEC, aware that Roger Robb would be practically ham-
strung without such a clearance, requested an "emergency Q"
clearance for him a week before he was to begin work. In Robb's
case the security machinery worked with unusual speed, and the
emergency clearance was completed in a matter of only eight
days. What is more, the two-to-three-month period usually required for "full field" inquiry and the permanent "Q" clearance
was, in Robb's case, compressed to just twenty-two days.

Lloyd Garrison had an equal need for a "Q" clearance if he
was to have access to all the information that would be available
to Robb. Without it Garrison would be handicapped not only in
getting the facts with which to rebut a charge, but even, in some
cases, in knowing the full basis of the charge itself. Since both he
and Robb were private citizens with no previous connection with
the AEC, presumably (in the absence of contrary evidence) each
should have been equally "clearable," equally trustworthy in
handling secret information. But the treatment which the AEC
accorded the security clearance of the two men was far from
equal.

Garrison first broached the matter on January 18 at a meeting

with Strauss, Nichols and Mitchell. The AEC officials offered to
expedite one application—Garrison's own—should he submit it.
The attorney thanked them but said that Herbert Marks would
be so intimately involved in the work on Oppenheimer's defense
that he would wish clearance for Marks as well. A few days later
he broadened the request to include his law partner, Samuel J.
Silverman, who had been brought into the case. Nonetheless the
AEC's decision was to offer to process a security-clearance request for Garrison alone, but for neither of his associates. In
conveying this to Garrison, AEC General Manager Nichols furnished no supporting reasons, saying merely that the Commission
did "not feel . . . that the granting of clearance to additional
counsel would be warranted." Somewhat gratuitously, he added,
"Your associates may, of course, participate fully in unclassified
aspects of the case."

After much deliberation, Oppenheimer's attorneys decided to
write Strauss that all of them would forgo requesting clearance,
and that they would do the best they could to defend Oppenheimer without access to secret documents.* To do so "as fairly
as possible under the circumstances," Garrison wrote Strauss, "we
shall need—and I am sure we can count on—the Commission's
cooperation" in either declassifying or, alternatively, conveying
the substance of relevant secret documents, such as the minutes
of the GAC's 1949 meeting on the H-bomb.

Nichols, replying for Strauss, said he would be "glad" to cooperate. Yet he rejected Garrison's specific request. Neither declassification nor paraphrase of the 1949 minutes would be
possible. In light of this, Nichols said, Garrison might wish to
reconsider his decision to forgo security clearance.

For some weeks Garrison and his colleagues adhered to their
initial resolve. But eventually some among them became anxious

* Their reasoning: (1) their nonclearance might minimize the amount of
secret material included in the hearing—material that might inhibit whatever
appeal to the courts might later be necessary; (2) if the Gray Board felt free
to delve into secret information about the H-bomb, this might encourage
the board to focus on the *technical* pros and cons of that issue rather than on
what Garrison considered the only relevant factor (Oppenheimer's *motives*);
(3) a security clearance might be of limited value anyway, in view of General Nichols' assertion to Garrison that the government would reserve the
right to decide what documents were relevant, and even what portion of
the relevant documents could be examined by Oppenheimer's attorneys.

lest the unexpected introduction of secret matters into the hearing oblige all of them to leave the hearing room, leaving the scientist "unrepresented and alone." Garrison himself became so troubled by this prospect that on March 26, despite the opposition of his legal associates, he wrote General Nichols requesting security clearance for himself.

Had this request been accorded the same priority given Roger Robb's clearance, there would have been no difficulty in securing at least an "emergency Q" clearance for Garrison in time for the hearing. It had taken only eight days to obtain such a clearance for Robb, and Garrison's request came some seventeen days before the commencement of the hearing. But apparently the AEC's security machinery could not be made to work as rapidly for Lloyd Garrison as it had for Roger Robb, for not only did the Commission fail to process Garrison's request in time for the opening of the hearing; it declared it was "not possible" to clear Garrison before the hearing had ended and the Gray Board had submitted its report—eight weeks after Garrison's initial request.

For Roger Robb, an emergency clearance in eight days; a "full-field" investigation and permanent clearance in twenty-two days. For Lloyd Garrison, not even an emergency clearance in eight weeks' time.

And so Robert Oppenheimer's attorneys, not allowed access to the high secrets that were fully available to Roger Robb, were obliged to defend their client even while legally barred from much of the information on which a judgment would ultimately be based. And Lloyd Garrison's fear did come true: there were, as it developed, at least three occasions in the hearing when he and his colleagues were obliged to leave the hearing room for security reasons, leaving Robert Oppenheimer "unrepresented and alone."

To defend Robert Oppenheimer, Garrison had to immerse himself in the physicist's life history. For weeks, for both Oppenheimer and Garrison, all other activity came to a standstill as they went over every one of the items in the AEC's letter, seeking to relate them to other events in the scientist's life, and to the whole course of his attitude toward governmental and international affairs. At first Garrison commuted daily to Princeton.

Soon, headquarters shifted to Garrison's New York offices and it was Oppenheimer's turn to commute. Notes were taken, memoranda drafted and redrafted.

As Garrison and his associates* sought to piece together the facts and circumstances of the previous twelve years, they found themselves increasingly handicapped by the fact that whereas all of the documents and records were freely available to the AEC lawyers who were preparing the case against them, Garrison and his colleagues had access to virtually none. In part this was because they lacked clearance to see secret materials, but it was also in considerable part because the Commission had recently removed from Oppenheimer's files most of the records he had kept concerning his postwar years as a government consultant. Under these circumstances the hearing was very likely to become a lopsided contest between the Commission's fully documented version of events and Oppenheimer's memory, the latter almost unaided by contemporaneous documents and subject to the frailty of even the most acute of minds.

If this was to be avoided, there would have to be a great willingness on the part of the AEC to furnish the text, or the substance, of as many of the relevant documents as possible. On February 12 Lloyd Garrison and Herbert Marks visited William Mitchell at the AEC. They presented to Mitchell a substantial list of documents they believed were essential to their preparation of Robert Oppenheimer's defense. Mitchell said he would have to place their request under advisement. That very day, however, General Nichols wrote Garrison that in considering whatever requests the attorney might make, the government reserved the right to decide what documents were pertinent to the case, and even what portions of pertinent documents it might be "consistent with the national interest" to permit Garrison to see.

A week later, it became clear that the AEC was going to be extremely severe in making these decisions. General Nichols telephoned Garrison to say that with two exceptions,† every single

* By now the cadre of attorneys engaged in the task had grown to four. In addition to Garrison and Marks, there were Garrison's partner, Samuel J. Silverman, who had had more extensive trial experience than Garrison, and a younger associate in the Garrison firm, Allan B. Ecker.

† The exceptions: a misleadingly paraphrased report of the Commission's minutes on the 1947 clearance of Oppenheimer and the 1949 GAC reports

one of Garrison's requests for documents had been denied. The necessity of being so secretive became highly questionable in the course of the hearing itself, when the government's representative voluntarily introduced into the record certain of the documents requested by (and denied to) Lloyd Garrison.

At the same meeting with AEC General Counsel Mitchell at which Lloyd Garrison requested the documents, Herbert Marks submitted a written list of questions he wished answered in order to clarify certain items in the AEC's letter of charges.†

Marks' questions highlighted another deficiency in security proceedings such as Oppenheimer's: the frequently unspecific character of the "charges." A U.S. Court of Appeals has observed that an "indispensable element [of] due process of law" is that the charges against an individual be "so distinct and specific as clearly to advise him of what he has to meet and to give him a fair and reasonable opportunity to prepare his defense." The courts are not likely to accept, for example, a charge as unspecific as "You made the following seven seditious statements," even if the alleged statements are listed. It would be necessary to state such things as the "time, place, occasion, circumstances, persons present, or any other distinctive earmark," to enable the defendant to "investigate the basis of the charges, to learn . . . who were possible witnesses, and to prepare his defense."

To Herbert Marks, some of the charges contained in General Nichols' December letter seemed excessively vague, and at the meeting with General Counsel Mitchell he sought further specifics. For example, according to the Nichols letter of charges, it had been "reported" that Oppenheimer had been "instrumental in persuading other outstanding scientists not to work on the hydrogen-bomb project." But *which* scientists had Oppenheimer

---

on the H-bomb. The GAC reports, however, could not be seen by Garrison but only by Oppenheimer, and only if Oppenheimer himself would come to AEC headquarters in Washington to see them. Oppenheimer did not avail himself of this opportunity (a point made much of by the AEC in answering Garrison's later charges about the withholding of documents). Garrison has since explained this on the ground that (a) Dr. Oppenheimer looked with distaste upon the prospect of visiting AEC headquarters with a "cloud" hanging over him, and (b) he and Garrison expected that the full story of the 1949 GAC proceedings would be told by the six members of the GAC who would be called to testify in Oppenheimer's behalf.

† See Exhibit A, page 562.

supposedly dissuaded? Marks wanted to know. If he had their names, he could ask them directly about the AEC allegation; but in the absence of any names he and his client were practically helpless to challenge it.

Similarly, the Nichols letter said that "It was further reported that in the autumn of 1949, and subsequently, you [Oppenheimer] strongly opposed the development of the hydrogen bomb. . . ." Marks wanted to know what was meant by the phrase "and subsequently." What were the circumstances of Oppenheimer's alleged opposition? Was it in public speeches, private conversations or what? And how long a period was covered by that open-ended word "subsequently"? Did it extend past June, 1951 (when Oppenheimer heard and was enthusiastic over Edward Teller's new approach to the bomb)?

There were, in all, some nineteen questions that Marks proposed to AEC General Counsel Mitchell at the February 12 conference. The AEC failed to respond to a single one of them.

On February 23 in Paris, Haakon Chevalier decided he would follow up on the matter of his American passport by speaking with Jeffries Wyman, the U.S. science attaché in the Paris Embassy, whose name Oppenheimer had given him. In a letter addressed to Wyman at his home, Chevalier said Oppenheimer had "urged me to get in touch with you [about] a personal problem of mine. . . . I should not have presumed to follow up such a suggestion if it had come from anyone else. But as you know, Opje never tosses off such a suggestion lightly."

A week later, on March 1, Wyman replied cordially, inviting Chevalier to lunch with him at his home. Apparently Wyman was not on as intimate terms with "Opje" as Chevalier: his letter referred to him as "Bob Oppenheimer," a cognomen unheard of to anyone who knew the physicist at all well.

On March 4 Robert Oppenheimer's written reply to the AEC's charges was finally completed and dispatched to the Commission in the form of a letter to AEC General Manager Nichols. Although it filled forty-two typed pages, it was less a point-by-point rebuttal of the government's allegations than an autobiography, in which "comments" (as Oppenheimer put it) on the AEC's bill of particulars were interspersed—almost as incidentals. For the most part, the physicist dealt with details of what was going on both around him and inside him. Some samples:

• I was born in New York in 1904. My father had come to this country at the age of 17 from Germany. He was a successful businessman and quite active in community affairs. My mother was born in Baltimore and before her marriage was an artist and teacher of art. . . .

• In the Spring of 1929, I returned to the United States [from four years of study in Europe]. I was homesick for this country and in fact I did not leave it again for 19 years. I had learned a great deal . . . about the new physics; I wanted to pursue this myself, to explain it and to foster its cultivation. . . .

• I studied and read Sanskrit [in California in the early Thirties]. . . . I read very widely, mostly classics, novels, plays and poetry. . . .

• Beginning in late 1936, my interests began to change. . . . I can discern in retrospect more than one reason for these changes. I had had a continuing, smoldering fury about the treatment of Jews in Germany. I had relatives there. . . . I [also] saw what the depression was doing to my students . . . and through them, I began to understand how deeply political and economic events could affect men's lives. . . .

• In August, 1941, I bought Eagle Hill at Berkeley for my wife, which was the first home we had of our own. We settled down to live in it with our new baby. We had a good many friends, but little leisure. My wife was working in biology. . . .

Oppenheimer explained to General Nichols his reason for using this mode of response. "The items of so-called derogatory information set forth in your letter," he said, "cannot be fairly understood except in the context of my life and my work."

Garrison has observed that the autobiographical nature of Oppenheimer's reply sprang from an apprehension that

given the temper of the times [in 1954] there was grave danger that particular items in the catalogue of the Commission's charges would be wrested out of context and judged in isolation, without regard to the time when they occurred, the prevailing circumstances, the development of Oppenheimer's outlook, the achievements he was to render to his country, and the whole course of his life.

As Garrison saw it, his client's "fate" depended "chiefly" on his ability to persuade the Gray Board and the AEC to judge "the whole man," after the manner of an earlier 1948 AEC security-case ruling. In that instance, the AEC had granted a security clearance to University of North Carolina President Frank P. Graham, despite Graham's associations with vigorously liberal persons and causes, commenting, ". . . *it is the man himself the Commission is actually concerned with* [and his personal] associations are only evidentiary. . . . *Common sense must be exercised* in judging their significance." (Emphasis added.)

It was thus in an effort to portray "the man himself" that Robert Oppenheimer unfolded to the AEC an account of the three main phases of his life (the prewar, wartime and postwar years), ending with these words:

> In preparing this letter, I have reviewed two decades of my life. I have recalled instances where I acted unwisely. What I have hoped was, not that I could wholly avoid error, but that I might learn from it. What I have learned has, I think, made me more fit to serve my country.
>
> Very truly yours,<br>J. Robert Oppenheimer

As March gave way to April, the day on which Julius Robert Oppenheimer was to go on trial for his good name was almost at hand. As with other security-risk hearings, this was not to be a trial in a court of law and, as the chairman of the Oppenheimer hearing panel, Gordon Gray, was to observe, it would not be subject to the strict rules and procedures that govern courtroom trials. Gray's implication was that the comparative informality of a "hearing" worked to the "defendant's" advantage, affording him more flexibility in meeting the charges. Yet Oppenheimer, like other security-risk "defendants," would come to wish that his "hearing" were governed by certain of the rules and procedures of a trial.

For example, when a person is involved in a court trial that may result in the loss of his life, liberty or property, the American legal system offers him the protection of what some lawyers term the "blank pad rule."* By that they mean that when judge and/or jury enters the courtroom at the outset of the trial, they have before them, in effect, a blank pad on which no evidence has as yet been written. Thereafter, the only information that may be recorded on that "pad," and used in judgment, is that permitted by the judge in open court, under established rules of evidence. As a result, both sides are assured equal knowledge of—and equal opportunity to challenge—all the information on which the final verdict will be based. This safeguard is regarded as so essential to a fair trial that any adverse verdict found to be based on evidence not heard in open court, in the defendant's presence, is liable to be nullified by a higher court.

In 1946 the "blank pad rule" was written into a new code of fair procedures for hearings (the Administrative Procedure Act) held not by courts of law, but by government agencies (such as the Federal Trade Commission or the Federal Communications Commission). But while the 1946 law governed *most* administrative hearings, it did not include all of them. At the time of Robert Oppenheimer's hearing, there was no such rule for a person accused of being a "security risk," even though, if found guilty, he might well suffer the loss of his means of livelihood, not to mention public shame and private anguish. In fact, in security cases, the *opposite* of the "blank pad rule" prevailed, for it was the general practice for members of hearing boards to read the investigative file prior to the hearing itself. A person appearing before such a board could be fairly sure that all the basic evidence against him was already in his judges' minds and that the only portions of the adverse evidence that he or his attorney would know about would be reflected in the statement of charges or implied in the board's questions. Thus the chances for a person to be "convicted" on the basis of untrue information were greatly increased.

While Lloyd Garrison had no reason to expect the protection of the "blank pad rule," he could not have anticipated the ex-

---

* Referred to in technical legal parlance as "the exclusivity of the record."

traordinary degree to which its spirit would be flouted in the Oppenheimer case. It would be unthinkable in any trial or hearing where such a rule applied for the judge and/or jury to meet alone with the prosecuting attorney before the trial. But that was precisely what happened in the Oppenheimer case. Garrison, to his surprise and dismay, was advised by the AEC that the members of the hearing board would spend a full week before the hearing studying the investigative materials and talking with Roger Robb, who was to play the role of prosecuting attorney, and other AEC representatives. As Garrison later told the Gray Board, he had experienced "a kind of sinking feeling" at the thought of the board's being exposed to a "week's immersion in FBI files which we would never have the privilege of seeing, and of coming to the hearing with that intense background of study of the derogatory information."

In an effort to counter the effect of this, Garrison asked the Commission to accord him the same privilege as Roger Robb— that is, that it permit him to meet with the board during that week before the hearing so that he could take part in discussions about the contents of the files. The Commission rejected this suggestion; the confidential nature of the files, they said, made any such meetings impractical. Garrison then asked if he might meet informally with the board on the first day of its study of the file (so that their reading of the reports might take place against the background of Garrison's over-all view of the case) and to discuss with the board members the procedures to be followed in the hearings. But this request was also rebuffed. It was the usual practice, Garrison was told, for hearing boards to determine for themselves the way they would conduct a hearing, and their pre-hearing sessions were necessary to give them a thorough mastery of the file ahead of time.

A retrospective question arises: would the Commission have considered it fair if the situation had been reversed—that is, if the Gray Board had spent the week preceding the hearing solely closeted with Lloyd Garrison and exposed only to such information and argumentation favorable to Oppenheimer that he might wish to present, without the presence of Roger Robb or any other representative of the AEC?

The three members of the Gray Board gathered in Washington on April 5, 1954, and spent the ensuing week reading and digesting the government's investigative reports on Robert Oppenheimer. As they studied, Roger Robb, Arthur Rolander and other representatives of the "prosecuting" agency aided them with explanations and elaborations. Neither defendant nor defense counsel was there to offer challenges or counterexplanations to dilute the effect of the adverse evidence.

Lloyd Garrison has said that in retrospect the Gray Board's immersion in the investigative files may have done his client great injury, for it caused

a cloud of suspicion [to hang] over Robert Oppenheimer at the outset which was never quite dissipated in the minds of the majority; even when they became convinced by the testimony that he could not be charged with disloyalty or want of patriotism, we had the impression that an uneasy feeling about him remained which may have been just enough to tip the scales against his clearance.

During the week of the Gray Board's survey of the files, Robert Oppenheimer received a letter from his friend of two decades, Victor Weisskopf, who had learned of Oppenheimer's "predicament." "I would like you to know," Weisskopf wrote,

that I and everybody who feels as I do are fully aware of the fact that you are fighting here our own fight.

Somehow Fate has chosen you as the one who has to bear the heaviest load in this struggle. . . . If I had to choose whom to select for the man who has to take this on, I could not but choose you. Who else in this country could represent better than you the spirit and the philosophy of all that for which we are living.

Please think of us when you are feeling low. Think of all your friends who are going to remain your friends and who rely upon you. . . .

I beg you to remain what you always have been, and things will end well.

During that same week, the headlines were, by coincidence, filled with charges and denials on one of the principal questions with which the Gray Board would have to grapple. The controversy began on the day after the Gray Board first met. In a nationally televised speech, Senator Joseph R. McCarthy of Wisconsin declared that there had been an eighteen-month "deliberate delay" in the development of the hydrogen bomb because of Communists in the United States Government. McCarthy's charge met with bipartisan rebuttal. In Kansas City, former President Truman insisted there had been no delay, and President Eisenhower told a news conference that AEC Chairman Strauss, who kept him fully informed on atomic matters, had not spoken of any such delay.

In the course of that dispute, Lloyd Garrison may well have wondered about the sincerity of the AEC's policy on secrecy and of the reasons it gave in refusing him access to secret documents, for during that week *New York Times* columnist Arthur Krock was allowed to read, and publish the substance of, the anti-H-bomb report that David Lilienthal had made to President Truman in 1949. As Lilienthal noted in his diary, this document was "one that I myself may not now see because it is top secret. Yet it is shown—or parts of it—to a 'friendly newspaperman.' This shows how selective and flexible the concept of 'national security' can be!"

Lilienthal, one of the few Americans who then knew of the AEC charges against Oppenheimer and the imminence of his security hearing, also found a note of irony in the Administration's denials of any H-bomb delay. He wrote in his diary:

. . . the President and the Joint Congressional Committee must know of the charges against Oppenheimer and the hearings about to begin. . . . They will look pretty silly when McCarthy says, as of course he will, in time: "If there was no concern about foul play about the H-bomb, why did you, the Commission, (with the knowledge of the Joint Congressional Committee and the President) make the charges, suspend the clearance of the chief scientist of the H-bomb? If there was nothing to what I have said, why did you do that . . . ?"

"This thing," Lilienthal commented, "gets more and more insane."

# V  THE "TRIAL"

## 1. *The First Week*

On the cool, bright morning of Monday, April 12, 1954, Robert Oppenheimer entered the rear door of a two-story building near the Washington Monument. It was the Atomic Energy Commission Building T-3, one of those depressing, dilapidated "temporary" government structures that had become semipermanent fixtures in Washington. Its Room 2022, a standard Government-Issue executive's office formerly occupied by the AEC's Director of Research, had been transformed into a miniature courtroom.

Entering this broad, oblong room from the corridor, one found oneself facing a row of windows through which one could look across Constitution Avenue and onto the grassy ellipse just south of the White House. Paralleling the short right-hand wall stood a table, with three chairs, for the hearing board members—the "judges" in the case. At right angles to it, forming the stem of a "T," were two longer tables, parallel to the windows. On either side of these tables were to sit the respective attorneys: to the judges' right, with their backs to the windows, Roger Robb and Arthur Rolander, representing the Atomic Energy Commission; to the judges' left, facing the windows, Lloyd Garrison and his colleagues, on behalf of Robert Oppenheimer. At the base of the "T," facing the board members, there was a lone chair: the "witness box." Behind it, against the left-hand wall of the room, was a leather sofa, on which Oppenheimer would sit (when not in the witness chair), puffing incessantly on a pipe or cigarette.

It was in this setting that Robert Oppenheimer would spend four weeks watching the details of his life chopped fine, being probed, sifted and analyzed.

Some time before 10 A.M. that first day, the three members of the hearing board entered Room 2022 and took their places. Before each of them lay, not a "blank pad," but a thick black notebook: material from the government files and investigative reports they had been studying throughout the previous week.

At the center of the board's table sat its chairman, Gordon Gray, the forty-five-year-old president of the University of North Carolina. Gray, like Oppenheimer, had been born into comfortable circumstances. His grandfather had been a banker in the town of Winston, later Winston-Salem, and his father had become president of the mammoth R. J. Reynolds Tobacco Company when Gordon was fifteen. Like Oppenheimer, Gray excelled academically—he was first in his prep school class, Phi Beta Kappa at college and a member of the *Law Journal* at Yale Law School. (He is said to have taken to heart a remark made to him by a cousin—"Now remember, Gordon, you never earned a cent of the money you are about to enjoy"—and to have determined to make for himself a record that money couldn't buy.) And, like the physicist he was about to judge, Gray had achieved distinction and responsibility at a relatively early age.

But in the judgment Gray was about to make of Oppenheimer, the differences between their lives and backgrounds were to prove more significant than the similarities. Whereas Oppenheimer's early education was at New York's Ethical Culture School, peopled largely by the children of German-Jewish intellectuals, Gordon Gray prepared at the hyperexclusive Woodberry Forest School in Virginia, which has been called "the Groton of the South." In the early Thirties, when Robert Oppenheimer was teaching physics, reading poetry and learning Sanskrit in California, Gordon Gray was in New York practicing law with a prominent old-line law firm and entertaining gracefully in a bachelor apartment manned by his own butler. By 1937, the year Oppenheimer met Haakon Chevalier and began to become actively involved in left-wing causes, Gordon Gray had moved to Winston-Salem and put over a million dollars of his inheritance into the Piedmont Publishing Company. The company acquired two newspapers in Winston-Salem and one of the radio stations, and at twenty-eight Gordon Gray became its president. ("I consider myself a trustee for the community," he said at the time.)

In 1938, at age twenty-nine, Gray was elected to the state senate; at age thirty-two he shunned an immediate officer's commission and enlisted as a private in the infantry. ("The life of a private [was] one of the happiest periods of my life," *Time* magazine quoted him as saying, "I never was called upon to make a decision.") The year Robert Oppenheimer became director of the Los Alamos laboratory, Gray became a commissioned officer; he rose to the rank of captain.

In 1947 Oppenheimer became Director of the Institute for Advanced Study and Gray was named an Assistant Secretary of the Army. Just two years later, shortly after his fortieth birthday, he took the oath as Secretary of the Army. Before he had turned forty-one he had been made a special assistant to President Truman, to undertake a review of the government's foreign economic policies, and had been elected president of the University of North Carolina, to take office as soon as he completed that review. "I have decided to devote the rest of my life to public service," he said, "and I would rather do it in North Carolina than anywhere else."

Perhaps the greatest contrast between the lives and backgrounds of Gordon Gray and Robert Oppenheimer lay in their social backgrounds. If there exists such a thing as an American aristocracy, Gordon Gray may be said to be a full-fledged member. Wherever he went in life, he belonged to the best social clubs: in New York, the Brook Club; in Winston-Salem, the Old Town, Twin-City and Forsyth country clubs; in Washington, the Metropolitan Club, and the Chevy Chase and Burning Tree clubs; and, in Augusta, Georgia, the National Golf Club, where the *crème de la crème* of American industry and finance gather.

Oppenheimer had no interest in such social organizations—and if he had had, he would, as a Jew, have found it difficult, if not impossible, to gain admission to them.

Robert Oppenheimer and his chief judge had both had a role in postwar government policy-making. But their experiences and perceptions in the other critical periods that would be under the Gray Board's microscope had been radically different. Especially was this true of the prewar days of Oppenheimer's active involvement with the causes of the radical left, with which Gordon Gray, at the time an affluent young lawyer and then a young publishing tycoon, could have had, at best, only scant contact.

On Gray's right, in Room 2022, sat one of his two fellow hearing-board members, Thomas Alfred Morgan. Morgan's background was as different from Robert Oppenheimer's as was Gray's; yet the difference lay in an opposite direction. Whereas Oppenheimer was born into comfortable urban surroundings, Thomas Morgan was the son of an impoverished North Carolina tobacco farmer. As a boy Morgan performed farm chores, became an expert coon and 'possum hunter, walked three miles to public grade school, and worked his way through high school as spare-time carpenter, telephone linesman and traveling salesman. After high school he enlisted in the Navy and there encountered the opportunity that changed his life. Trained by the Navy as an electrician, he came to the assistance of Elmer Sperry, inventor of the gyrocompass, by twice dismantling and remedying the defects of the compass during a trial of the new device on the battleship *Delaware*. Sperry invited Morgan to join his company, and Morgan became a salesman extraordinary of Sperry equipment in Europe (despite the fact that few Europeans could fathom his North Carolina accent). He rose steadily through the ranks to become company president, a post he was to occupy for a decade and a half, including the period of World War II, when Sperry produced more than a billion and a half dollars' worth of equipment for the armed forces. Morgan's talents also won him directorships in a number of top-flight companies and banks, including the investment banking firm of Lehman Brothers and the Bankers Trust Company.

As he ascended into the corporate stratosphere, he began to move in much the same social circle as Gordon Gray. They both belonged to the Brook Club of New York and to the Metropolitan of Washington. In 1941 Morgan married Celeste Walker Page, daughter of the late Walter Hines Page, renowned journalist and diplomat, and America's Ambassador to Great Britain during World War I. In 1952, at age sixty-five, Morgan retired as board chairman of Sperry. At the time of the Oppenheimer hearing he was devoting his time mainly to service on the boards of various corporations and to his civic interests, which included the chairmanship of the United Negro College Fund drive in New York City.

The third and final member of the hearing board, seated on Gordon Gray's left, was a chemistry professor named Ward V. Evans, a man of intractable political conservatism. A staunch Republican, he once remarked, "The closest I ever came to being a Communist was voting for Franklin Roosevelt in 1932." Born in modest circumstances in rural Pennsylvania, made to be self-reliant at an early age (at the age of five he was required to buy his own shoelaces), Evans had worked hard for everything he had ever attained and felt everyone else should do likewise. To him the New Deal was synonymous with the dole.

He began his career at a private boys' school near Poughkeepsie, teaching math and coaching football. When the school needed a chemistry teacher, he delved into the subject, became fascinated, went back to college and worked his way through to a Ph.D. in chemistry at Columbia. During World War I he became an expert for the Bureau of Mines on the effects of explosions. After the war he went to Northwestern University, where he rose to be chairman of the chemistry department.

"Doc" Evans has been described both by family and by friends as a "character." Short and bowlegged, with a large nose, a chin that jutted up to meet it, and conspicuously protruding ears, he looked, someone has said, like "an elderly gnome." He affected outrageous clothes—a never-pressed gray-black suit, a hopelessly crushed hat, a thin black necktie. But in this gnome-like man lived a forceful and gregarious personality. A surprisingly strong voice carried his outspoken thoughts and his well-told tales. "He was a guy who made an impression," one long-time acquaintance has said.

Colleagues remember him as an exceptional teacher (although they don't rate him as high as a scientist). Students loved him; his freshman chemistry course was famous. But his political conservatism carried over into his scientific outlook. In contrast to Robert Oppenheimer, who was instrumental in introducing "the new physics" to America, Evans had no use for newfangled notions such as the quantum theory, and, as the chairman of the Northwestern chemistry department, he is said to have retarded its modernization by many years.

To Evans, the give-and-take and the drama of the courtroom were both familiar and enjoyable. His expertise in explosives made him a much-sought-after witness in explosion-accident cases.* He is said to have been an extraordinarily adroit witness, with an instinct for appealing to a jury. On campus, he was also a shrewd cross-examiner, sensing when students were guilty of cheating on their exams, and eliciting confessions from them with remarkable frequency.

Evans is also said to have been at ease with power and with the powerful. A good campus politician, he gained membership on most of the important committees and had a significant impact on university policy. His role as an expert consultant and witness on explosions also brought him into contact with prominent industrialists. Thus, when Ward Evans came to Washington in the spring of 1954, he found his two ex-businessmen colleagues, Gordon Gray and Thomas Morgan, men of the type with whom he was comfortable.

"The hearing will come to order."

With these words, Chairman Gordon Gray opened the proceeding, under Section 10(b) (5) (B) (i–iii) of the Atomic Energy Act of 1946, "in the matter of J. Robert Oppenheimer."

For nearly an hour those in Room 2022 heard nothing but the soft North Carolina accents of Gordon Gray as he patiently read into the record the three-thousand-word AEC letter of charges and Robert Oppenheimer's novella-length reply. Then the chairman ventured some personal observations on the nature and

---

* After his testimony in one case resulted in a resounding defeat for a gas utility, the company quickly put him on retainer so as to be sure to have him as a *favorable* witness.

ground rules of the proceeding, some of which were to take on added significance as the hearing progressed.

First, Gray said, he wanted to "remind everyone concerned that *this proceeding is an inquiry, and not in the nature of a trial.* We shall approach our duties in that atmosphere and in that spirit." (Emphasis added.)

The chairman's words, which he was to reiterate frequently in the course of the hearing, were taken almost verbatim from the AEC regulations governing security hearings. But what did Gordon Gray mean by "an inquiry, not a trial"? A clue was contained in a remark he made, later in the proceeding, where he talked of allowing "very considerable latitude" to Oppenheimer and his attorneys and of "not trying to conform to rigid court procedures." Apparently, as Gray viewed them, these "rigid" procedures were more an encumbrance than a protection to the defendant, and the connotation of his remark was that in "an inquiry" of this sort the "defendant" would be accorded *more* leeway, not *less,* than would be true in a regular trial.

That seems to be what Lloyd Garrison took Gray's remark to mean, for he remarked to the chairman, "I should suppose that *a fortiori,* what is proper in a court of law would be accorded to us here in an inquiry." As it developed, however, the exact opposite was the case.

In another portion of his opening remarks, Chairman Gray admonished those present that the proceedings "are regarded as strictly confidential" between the AEC and Oppenheimer, and that the AEC "will not take the initiative in public release of any information relating to the proceeding before this board." Just two months and four days later, however, the AEC would contravene Gray's statement (which he repeated to virtually all of the forty witnesses who appeared before the board) by making public the entire verbatim transcript of the proceeding.

But the AEC was not alone in violating Gray's stricture. Even at the time of Gray's admonition, Lloyd Garrison and Robert Oppenheimer had already vouchsafed to *New York Times* correspondent Reston the AEC charges and the Oppenheimer reply on condition he not print them unless convinced that someone else had the story and was about to break it first.* In the opening moments of the hearing, before Gray's word of warning about confidentiality, Garrison had asked to be excused; he left the hearing room and phoned Reston to see how much longer the story could be held. Reston advised him that the news was about to break at any moment. When Garrison returned to the hearing room, he told the board, off the record, that while he was trying to keep his finger in the dike, it might be necessary for him within a matter of hours to release the AEC charges and the Oppenheimer reply (so that, in fairness to Oppenheimer, both could appear simultaneously). But he did *not* tell the board that as of that moment Reston had already had the documents in his possession for more than seventy-two hours.†

When Gray had completed his opening comments, he offered Lloyd Garrison an opportunity to make an opening statement to the board. From his very first words, this gentle man demonstrated beyond doubt that he was not, either by experience or temperament, the hard-bitten, tough, litigatory lawyer that Joseph Volpe had so urgently recommended for Oppenheimer's defense. In his opening remarks, as throughout the hearing, Garrison spoke as if convinced that if he could just avoid any abrasive actions that might offend the board members he would be able to persuade them to use the rule of reason in judging "the whole Oppenheimer" and find in his favor.

"Mr. Chairman, members of the board," Garrison began, "I would like to say at the outset that far from having thought of challenging any member of the board [as Oppenheimer had the right to do], we appreciate very much the willingness of men of your standing and responsibilities to accept this exacting and onerous job in the interests of the country. I express my appreciation to you."

Garrison went on to raise in his understated, almost gingerly manner, the matter of the Gray Board's week of prehearing

* Late in the preceding week Reston had learned that the scientist's security hearing was about to begin, had met with Oppenheimer and Garrison in New York and had, finally, persuaded them to give him the documents the previous Friday.

† During the luncheon recess that day Garrison again called Reston and authorized the release of the documents and the story.

briefings and examination of FBI files which Garrison was not allowed to see. Of this grievous disadvantage to himself and his client, visibly symbolized by the black notebooks that lay before each of the judges, Garrison merely said he was "confident" that the board members' minds were "open to receive the testimony that we shall submit." As to his greater apprehension—the existence, in the FBI files, of allegations troublesome to the board but which Garrison, in his ignorance of them, could not rebut—the attorney could only say, almost wistfully, that he knew he could "count on you to bring those to our attention so that we may have an adequate opportunity to reply to them."

Chairman Gray assured Garrison he "need have no concern on that score."

Garrison went on to outline his hope that the Gray Board would render its judgment on the basis of "the whole man," balancing the undisputed facts about the scientist's early leftist involvement not only against his wartime service to his country but also against the fact that, the H-bomb episode aside, the AEC alleged no "suspect" activities on his part over the past eight years. During that latter period, he said, Oppenheimer had devoted half his working time to the voluntary service of the government. As to the H-bomb charge, which stood "all by itself," Garrison said he would show that his client's conduct was "an exercise of the most honest judgment done in the best interests of the country."

Garrison said he would be calling some twenty-seven witnesses, and offered to furnish the board with a list of them. Chairman Gray readily accepted this offer, which he termed "helpful."

At 2:15 P.M. of Monday, April 12, after a luncheon recess, Oppenheimer took his place in the witness chair in Room 2022. He would, in the course of the next four weeks, spend a total of some twenty-seven hours in that chair. Some of them would be among the most excruciating of his life.

But that agony would come later. Now, responding to the friendly questions of Lloyd Garrison, he told of his service to his country, beginning with the spring of 1942, when he first became part of the nuclear research project. For nearly an hour and a quarter he held forth, interrupted sporadically by questions from

Garrison, telling of the chaotic beginnings of Los Alamos, the frenzied race for the A-bomb, the ultimate success at Hiroshima, and his entrance onto the stage of postwar high-level policy-making as a consultant on the Acheson-Lilienthal report on atomic energy.

It was at this point, in midafternoon of the very first day of the hearing, that Roger Robb first showed that he, for one, did not regard this as any Marquis of Queensberry "inquiry." The clue came when Garrison voluntarily handed Robb, in accordance with courtroom custom, a copy of the excerpts he was reading into the record of a 1946 memorandum from Oppenheimer to David Lilienthal. Robb interrupted. Could he be furnished not just with excerpts, but with the original copy of the full Oppenheimer memorandum "so that we can see the end of these sentences?" The clear implication was that Robb mistrusted the fairness of Garrison's excerpts, and that material helpful to Robb's case had been omitted. Robb's request was entirely normal in ordinary courtroom combat. But was it appropriate for "an inquiry"? It stood in contrast to his refusal, later in the hearing, to honor a comparable bid by Garrison, who asked to see certain government documents Robb was using in questioning Oppenheimer but was met with a resentful and peremptory rebuff.

Apparently, Gordon Gray considered it of some importance that the Board know in advance the identity of the witnesses Garrison was planning to call, for just before the hearing adjourned for the day, he reminded Garrison of his offer to supply a list. Garrison obligingly displayed on a large chart for all—including Roger Robb—to see, not only the names of the witnesses he planned to bring but also the sequence and timing of their appearance. Later in the hearing there were signs that Roger Robb had derived an important benefit from this information, for his cross-examination of Garrison's witnesses often indicated careful advance research on matters on which they were likely to testify. Yet when Garrison later asked for the reciprocal courtesy —for advance notice of Robb's adversary witnesses—Robb, backed by Gray, refused.

At 5:13 P.M., following a discussion of witness schedules, the first day of the security proceeding against J. Robert Oppenheimer came to an end.

As members of the Gray Board made their way home that evening, linotype operators at the *New York Times* were setting into type the texts of the AEC letter of charges, the Oppenheimer reply and a news story by James Reston. A few hours later, this story was on the street, occupying the most prominent position on the *Times* front page. Above the two-column picture of a meditative, pipe-smoking Oppenheimer in his Princeton study were the headlines:

**DR. OPPENHEIMER SUSPENDED BY A.E.C. IN SECURITY REVIEW; SCIENTIST DEFENDS RECORD; HEARINGS STARTED; ACCESS TO SECRET DATA DENIED NUCLEAR EXPERT—RED TIES ALLEGED.**

Reporter Reston explained how the *Times* had obtained the AEC letter and the Oppenheimer reply. The newspaper had received a report of the case and had sought verification from Chairman Strauss and JCAE Chairman Sterling Cole as well as from Oppenheimer. "In view of the fact that the *Times* was in possession of most of the facts in the case," Reston wrote, "Dr. Oppenheimer made the statement of charges and his reply available to the *Times* so that the record of the case could be written from the actual documents."

The *Times'* coverage of the affair contained far more than the Reston story. Also published were detailed accounts of such related events as the AEC's 1947 clearance of Oppenheimer and the General Advisory Committee's hush-hush 1949 meeting on the H-bomb (complete even to the detail of Glenn Seaborg's absence)—stories that evidently involved extensive research and interviewing on the part of *Times* reporters. And so to interested and informed readers (such as Gordon Gray) it was evident that Oppenheimer's transmission to Reston of the AEC's letter and his reply had not been a last-minute decision, but had occurred some days before the Gray Board began its hearing.

Not surprisingly, the *Times* story was the first item to be taken up when the Gray Board reconvened at 9:30 the next morning. Chairman Gray was clearly irritated.* He reminded the partici-

---

* He had been determined, he recalled years later, that this case should not be tried in the public press.

pants of his previous warnings about confidentiality and said the
board viewed the Reston story "with very deep concern." He had
to assume, he said, that the Nichols and Oppenheimer letters had
been "given to the *New York Times.*"

"It says so in the paper," Oppenheimer interjected.

Gray wanted to know who had given the documents to the
*Times*. Garrison and Oppenheimer now told of having given them
to Reston the previous Friday. This infuriated Gray: "So that you
knew when you made the statement here yesterday morning that
you were keeping the finger in the dike that these documents
. . . were already in the possession of the *New York Times?*"

"Indeed we did," answered Oppenheimer.

Gray's annoyance was principally directed at Lloyd Garrison,
who, he said, had failed to "indicate to me in any way" that he
had handed the documents to Reston. Nor was this a temporary
irritation. On two separate occasions later in the hearing, Gray
alluded sarcastically to the *Times'* news break, once in a way
that indicated he held Garrison responsible not only for leaking
the AEC letter but also for helping furnish the *Times* with the
details of the AEC's 1947 clearance of Oppenheimer.

As the second day of the hearing wore on, Gray's irascibility
toward Garrison grew, and even extended to impugning the
attorney's veracity.* It also showed itself in his statement that
Garrison's witnesses would be heard at times suited "to the
convenience of this board, and not the convenience of the witnesses, as would be true in most [judicial] proceedings in the
American tradition." He even went so far as to "warn" Garrison
that any Oppenheimer witness who wished to be heard at a
particular time would probably be asked to state under oath
that this was the only time he could appear.

That morning Garrison had asked the board to interrupt the
taking of Oppenheimer's testimony to hear from Dr. Mervin J.
Kelly, president of the Bell Telephone Laboratory in New York,
and presently Kelly was duly sworn as the first of thirty-one pro-

---

* Gray insisted on knowing who had excerpted the Oppenheimer writings
read into the record the day before. When Garrison said this had been done
by his associate, Allan Ecker, seated beside him at the counsel table, Gray
complained that none of Oppenheimer's lawyers had been able to answer
certain questions about the excerpts and said, "It is apparent that someone
else [other than Ecker] had prepared them."

Oppenheimer witnesses. Kelly had served on a Pentagon advisory group on atomic energy which, in late 1949, under Oppenheimer's chairmanship, had made a study of the long-range future of nuclear weapons development. Questioned by Garrison, Kelly described how Oppenheimer had stayed on "in Washington between meetings and beyond meetings" to draft the group's report himself. That, said Kelly, "was an aid to all of us."

When Garrison finished his questions, those in the hearing room were given their first glimpse of Roger Robb as cross-examiner. Robb subjected Kelly to a technique that was to become familiar as the inquiry progressed. Armed with top-secret government documents not available to Kelly or to Oppenheimer's lawyers, he proceeded to test (with the apparent aim of impeaching) Kelly's unrefreshed memory of events now more than three years past. Robb first asked the witness whether the H-bomb had been discussed by the long-range study panel in 1950–51. No, said Kelly, because the H-bomb was not, at the time, sufficiently developed as a weapon. Had it been discussed in the panel's *report?* Kelly said he would "feel confident" it had not, since it had not been a part of the panel's deliberations.

Robb had set his trap. Now he was prepared to spring it. "Mr. Chairman," he said, "I would like to read the witness something from the report, which is classified."

At this point, Lloyd Garrison's failure to obtain security clearance came into play for the first time (but not the last) as Chairman Gray asked that those not enjoying "Q" clearance be excused from the room. Garrison said he had hoped this would not happen, but, he said, if the board considered it important to pursue the matter, "it is entirely acceptable to us, and we shall withdraw." For the next few minutes Robert Oppenheimer was in effect denied the right, guaranteed by AEC regulations, to be represented by counsel.*

When Garrison returned, Kelly explained that during the classified discussion it had become apparent that his memory of

---

* In the retrospective view of Oppenheimer, nothing of substance was discussed during this and the three other occasions on which he was temporarily deprived of counsel. But even if Oppenheimer's view was correct, this fortuitous fact does not lessen the violation of the right to counsel supposedly assured by AEC regulations.

events more than three years in the past had been faulty, and that the H-bomb had indeed been discussed in the panel report. He assumed, therefore, that "it must have been discussed" in the course of the panel's deliberations, although Kelly insisted he had no recollection of it.

When Robb finished his cross-examination, Chairman Gray posed his first substantive questions of the hearing. He wondered about Mervin Kelly's inability to remember any discussion of the H-bomb in the course of the study panel's deliberations, inasmuch as the report later written by Robert Oppenheimer definitely discussed the subject. "Is it possible," Gray asked, "that this report could have reflected discussions which the committee did not actually engage in?" The clear implication of this question was that the scientist, in writing his report, had, as Oppenheimer said, "sneaked [in] a conclusion that had not been thoroughly hashed out" in panel discussions.

The importance of the "blank pad rule"—and of its absence in the Oppenheimer hearing—now showed itself. For here was the "chief judge," in the second day of the proceeding, implying a profound suspicion of deviousness in Robert Oppenheimer. What was the source of this apparent doubt? If the board had been observing the "blank pad rule," Gray's impressions of Oppenheimer could have come only from evidence taken in the hearing itself. Yet thus far in the proceeding the board had not heard one word of testimony suggesting that Oppenheimer was a deceitful man. Therefore, Gray's suspicions must have had another origin. Could it be in the undisclosed material contained in those black notebooks the board had studied the previous week? Might it lie in something Roger Robb had said to Gray during that week?

When Kelly was excused as a witness, Oppenheimer resumed the witness stand. First he protested the insinuations of bad faith in Chairman Gray's questions to Mervin Kelly. Then he picked up the threads of his autobiographical testimony.

Oppenheimer's account soon reached the crucial 1949 GAC meetings on the H-bomb, and in testifying about the GAC's written reports on those deliberations, he became involved in an apparent conflict of testimony. Had he and the GAC opposed the "Super" *per se?* Or had they merely been against a "crash" development program? Roger Robb had made available to Oppenheimer, not the complete GAC reports, but selected "extracts," and from these the scientist read a statement in the 1949 report to which all eight members of the GAC had agreed:

> We all hope that by one means or another, the development of these weapons [the H-bomb] can be avoided. We are all reluctant to see the United States take the initiative in precipitating this development. We are all agreed that it would be wrong at the present moment to commit ourselves *to an all-out effort towards its development.* [Emphasis added.]

On its face, this passage, which Oppenheimer told the Gray Board was "the crux of it," seemed to argue more against a crash program for the H-bomb than against the bomb itself.

At this time Oppenheimer had before him only those extracts of the 1949 GAC reports that Robb had provided him. Lloyd Garrison, of course, was not allowed to see even the extracts. Neither of them, therefore, could know what Robb knew*— namely, that the so-called "majority annex" of the GAC report, which Oppenheimer and five others had signed, contained this passage:

> *We believe a super bomb should never be produced.* Mankind would be far better off not to have a demonstration of the feasibility of such a weapon until the present climate of world opinion changes. [Emphasis added.]

Robb waited until the final days of the four-week hearing to unveil this excerpt—to the complete surprise of both Oppenheimer and Garrison.

While Oppenheimer was testifying secretly in Room 2022, official Washington was reacting publicly to the *New York Times'* revelation of his security suspension. From the Atomic Energy Commission came a nine-hundred-word statement that sketched the history of Oppenheimer's involvement with the atomic energy program, taking care to note that his initial wartime security clearance long antedated the birth of the Commission, and also

---

* And hinted at, ominously, at the time, saying, "I might say that later on we might want to come back to this report."

carefully avoiding any mention of the 1947 renewal of his clearance, in which Lewis Strauss had painstakingly participated and to which he had assented.

The AEC statement went on to note, with seeming pride, the close juxtaposition of the dates of two events having to do with Chairman Strauss: his assumption of the AEC chairmanship on July 3 and the initiation, "at the request of the chairman," just four days later, of "steps to organize the removal of [AEC] classified documents" from Oppenheimer's direct possession. The clear implication was that the new AEC Chairman had been alert to the risk of leaving secret papers in the scientist's care, and had moved swiftly to pluck the documents from danger. But according to AEC records, nothing of the sort occurred. As we have seen, for nearly six months after Strauss assumed the AEC chairmanship such secret papers as Oppenheimer still possessed remained exactly where they had been. Not until after William Borden had written his letter to the FBI and formal security-risk charges had been conveyed to Oppenheimer did AEC representatives go to Princeton to arrange for the removal of the papers to Washington.

The AEC press statement then described how Oppenheimer's security file had undergone "preliminary study" by the AEC and the Department of Justice and that "by November it had been brought up for definitive examination and appraisal" and sent to the President, whereupon the "blank wall" had been ordered and Oppenheimer's "Q" clearance suspended. There was not one word about the Borden letter.

On Capitol Hill, the two senior members of the Joint Committee on Atomic Energy, Congressman Sterling Cole and Senator Bourke Hickenlooper, assured the public that the committee had definitely not been asleep at the switch. On the contrary, the legislators said, it had "maintained long and continuing interest in the matters involving Robert Oppenheimer, and is fully acquainted with the circumstances leading to the present hearing. . . . This case, as it has developed *over the past several years*, deserves and has received the closest study and consideration by the Joint Committee." (Emphasis added.)

Senator Joseph McCarthy in Phoenix, Arizona, recuperating from a virus infection, was not to be outdone. The suspension of

Robert Oppenheimer, he said, was "long overdue—it should have been taken years ago. . . . I think it took considerable courage to suspend the so-called untouchable scientist—Oppenheimer. . . . I gave [Chairman] Strauss credit for that." The case, McCarthy insisted, was not new to him, either. He had, he said, started his own H-bomb investigation in the spring of 1953, but had decided after a "dinner meeting with two White House aides" not to hold public hearings for reasons "which cannot be told fully at this time." He reaffirmed a statement by Senator Mundt that he and other Senators were greatly influenced by receiving "assurances . . . from top administration officials that this matter would be gone into in detail."

Scientists also reacted to the news of Oppenheimer's suspension. Most were shocked by the action, and many, including Albert Einstein, came vigorously to Oppenheimer's defense. So did Harry Truman. And in Darien, Connecticut, retired General Leslie Groves said he had "learned nothing" from the AEC letter of charges to indicate he had been mistaken in choosing Oppenheimer to head the supersecret Los Alamos laboratory.

At 9:30 the next morning—Wednesday, April 14—Robert Oppenheimer was back in the witness chair in Room 2022. Lloyd Garrison asked him about his relationship with his brother Frank; about his knowledge of Frank's membership in the Communist Party; about the allegation that a closed party meeting had been held at the Oppenheimer home in Berkeley in July of 1941 (which Oppenheimer now denied categorically); and about his 1946 resignation from the leftist Independent Citizens Committee of the Arts, Sciences and Professions.

This done, Lloyd Garrison said he had completed his questions, to which Chairman Gray responded, "I think . . . we will suggest that counsel for the board put to Dr. Oppenheimer the questions he may have in mind."

Roger Robb had many questions in mind—enough, in fact, to keep Robert Oppenheimer in the witness chair for some twelve hours over the next three days.

Until 10:30 that morning, when Robb stood to confront the scientist, the two men had led totally nonintersecting lives. Oppenheimer's career had been devoted largely to the laboratory and the classroom, Robb's to the courtroom. Robb's professional skill lay in toe-to-toe combat, Oppenheimer's in intellectuality and soft persuasiveness. Oppenheimer was often preoccupied with the distant past and future; Robb, in his career, dealt mainly with the here-and-now. The gulf between the two was epitomized on two occasions that day: when Oppenheimer made references to Friedrich Engels and Niels Bohr, Robb in both instances was obliged to ask, "Who?" Now their lives had intersected: the consummate intellectual was face to face with the master cross-examiner.

Robb quickly established himself as an exacting interrogator. With his very first questions, he sought to manacle Oppenheimer to everything he had said in his lengthy letter of reply to the AEC charges, presumably so that any errors that might later be proven would appear more like deliberate lies than inadvertent mistakes.

Q:  Dr. Oppenheimer, did you [with the assistance of counsel] prepare your letter of March 4, 1954, to General Nichols?
A:  Yes.
Q:  In all events, you were thoroughly familiar with the contents of it?
A:  I am.
Q:  And have read it over very carefully, I assume?
A:  Yes.
Q:  Are all the statements which you make in that letter the truth, the whole truth and nothing but the truth?
A:  Yes.

Robb then asked about a year-by-year biographical sketch that Lloyd Garrison had given the board. That, said Oppenheimer, had been prepared by his secretary, and he hadn't even read it over very carefully, whereupon Robb, in true prosecutorial style, demanded, "Are you, or are you not prepared to vouch for [its] accuracy?"

Oppenheimer would merely say it was accurate so far as he knew.

Then emerged Roger Robb the bulldog: fiercely tenacious; once set upon a line of questions, impossible to shake off with elliptical answers.

Why, during World War II, had Oppenheimer considered *current* (as distinct from past) Communist Party membership as incompatible with secret war work? Robb inquired. Was it because party members were expected, if so ordered, to commit espionage? "I was never told that," replied Oppenheimer.

Robb was not satisfied. He wanted a direct answer. It required four separate forays, but ultimately he prevailed:

Q:  [*First probe*] Doctor, let me ask you a blunt question. Don't you know, and didn't you know certainly by 1943, that the Communist Party was an instrument or a vehicle of espionage in this country?

A:  I was not clear about it.

Q:  [*Second probe*] Didn't you suspect it?

A:  No.

Q:  [*Third probe*] Wasn't that the reason why you felt that membership in the party was inconsistent with the work on a secret war project?

A:  I think I have stated the reason about right.

Q:  [*Fourth probe*] I am asking you now if your fear of espionage wasn't *one of the reasons* why you felt that association with the Communist Party was inconsistent with work on a secret war project. [Emphasis added.]

A:  Yes.

Q:  [*Success. Now, nail it down*] Your answer is that it was?

A:  Yes.

Soon Robb was to catch Oppenheimer in another contradiction. When, he asked, had the physicist been a "fellow traveler"?

A:  From late 1936 or early 1937, and then it tapered off, and I would say I traveled much less fellow after 1939 and very much less after 1942.

Then, this exchange:

Q:  How long after 1942 did you continue as a fellow traveler?

A:  After 1942 I would say not at all.

Q:  But you did continue as a fellow traveler until 1942?

A:  Well, now, let us be careful.

Q:  I want you to be, Doctor.

A: I had no sympathy with the Communist line about [U.S. intervention in] the war between the spring of 1940 and when they changed [from isolationism to interventionism]. . . .

Q: Did you cease to be a fellow traveler at the time of the Nazi-Russian [nonaggression] Pact in 1939?

A: I think I did, yes.

Q: [After one intervening question] Are you now amending your previous answer that you were more or less a fellow traveler until 1942?

A: *Yes, I think I am.* [Emphasis added.]

This was not a consequential matter—at worst, it was a bit unsettling for the witness—and when Lloyd Garrison jumped in to emphasize that Oppenheimer had talked of "tapering off" rather than ceasing his "fellow traveling," Robb did not press the point.

Some twenty minutes later, however, Robb neatly led his witness into still another carefully constructed trap. The subject at hand was Oppenheimer's guarded 1943 letter to Colonel Lansdale about getting the Army to assign Private Giovanni Rossi Lomanitz to the Radiation Laboratory at Berkeley. From Robb came this inviting question: "Of course, you would not have written that letter if you had known Lomanitz was an [active] Communist, would you?"

Unsurprisingly, the answer was a flat "No." But Robb wanted to be very sure his trap contained no escape routes: "In all events, you didn't know then, did you?" Again, an unqualified "No."

Robb let the matter drop, for the moment. Then, later that day, he asked Oppenheimer when he had first learned of the Communist Party membership of another former student, Joseph Weinberg. The scientist replied, "At the time of the 1946 interview with the FBI, the agents told me. . . ."

Oppenheimer's answers were, of course, based on unaided memory. Robb's questions were not. Unbeknown to the physicist, Robb had in his possession a tape recording of Oppenheimer talking with security officers in 1943. The tape was made three weeks before he wrote the letter about Lomanitz and three years before the 1946 FBI interview, and it revealed him as saying: "I know for a fact, I know, I learned on my last visit to Berkeley, that both Lomanitz and Weinberg were members [of the Communist Party]."

In mistaking the time he learned of Lomanitz' and Weinberg's party membership, had Oppenheimer merely been prey to a faulty memory? Or had he lied to the Gray Board?

Later that afternoon Robb set one more trap. He brought up the name of Rudy Lambert, and then asked casually:

Q:   By the way, was Lambert a member of the Communist Party?
A:   Yes.
Q:   What was his function?
A:   I never knew.
Q:   You knew he was a member?
A:   I knew he was a member and, in fact, had an official job.
Q:   How often did you see Lambert?
A:   Half a dozen times.
Q:   In what connection?
A:   Different ones. Affairs like this: I had lunch with him once or twice with Folkoff. I saw him at a Spanish party.
Q:   What was the purpose of those luncheons?
A:   This was one of the times when they were telling me about why I needed to give them money.
Q:   Money to what?
A:   To them for use in Spain.

One or two questions about Folkoff (a party official), and then the trap:

Q:   Can you describe Lambert to us?
A:   A lean, rather handsome man, moderate height, rather an effective speaker in conversation.

Like Robb's questions about Lomanitz and Weinberg, this one was not drawn from the blue; it was based on the transcript of the Oppenheimer-Lansdale conversation ten and a half years earlier. Lansdale, querying Oppenheimer about a list of suspected Party members, had first asked about William Schneiderman, whom Oppenheimer identified as secretary of the Communist Party. Lansdale then touched fleetingly on Rudy Lambert, and moved quickly to the other names on his list, in this exchange:

LANSDALE: Do you know a fellow named Rudy Lambert?
OPPENHEIMER: *I'm not sure, do you know what he looks like?*
LANSDALE: No, I've never seen him. He's a member of the party. Do you know a Dr. Hannah L. Peters?
OPPENHEIMER: *Yes; I know her quite well. . . .* [Emphasis added.]

How could Oppenheimer have provided a detailed description of Lambert in 1954 and yet have not known what he looked like in 1943, as he professed to Lansdale?

What must Robert Oppenheimer have felt at these and similar moments during Robb's interrogation? The defendant sits in the witness chair, facing first the prospect and then the reality of being pummeled by skillful, relentless and hostile questions from a tough, adroit trial attorney. The heart pounds; the blood rises into the face. . . .

*How much does the prosecutor know? . . . What will he ask? . . . What is he getting at with this question or that? . . . Is he leading me into a trap? . . . Is my memory correct? . . . Can I outguess him? . . . Is he closing in on me? . . . Has he outsmarted me? . . .* Emotion rises; and as it does, reason and intellect recede. Common sense flees. The interrogator appears more and more omniscient; the beleaguered witness feels growingly impotent. It is, at best, an intimidating experience; at worst, it is terrifying.

Particularly must this have been true for Robert Oppenheimer. Aware that for eleven years his daily life had been under the Federal Government's most high-powered investigative microscope, he nevertheless must have been appalled, as he testified, to realize the full extent of the government's scrutiny. As the hearing proceeded, it became clear that the secretly made tape recordings of the Pash and Lansdale interrogations were only the beginning of the intimate, mysteriously gathered information that Robb had in his possession. Pitted against Robb's hidden reports, in the struggle to recapture the truth about events, peo-

ple and places after more than a decade's passage of time, was
the naked memory of J. Robert Oppenheimer, prey not only to
the toll that time itself exacts, but also to the tendency of all
humans to permit their recollections to be cosmetically altered
by their wishes. As Oppenheimer himself put it, in the Gray
Board hearing, "I don't want to remember more than I do remember."

Of course, this was not the first time Oppenheimer had been
interrogated about his past. He had been questioned many times
—by security officers, FBI agents and, once, by the Congressmen
of the House Un-American Activities Committee. In those previous encounters he had, by and large, acquitted himself well—
never better than in his 1949 appearance before HUAC, when he
had quite captivated the committee members. But witnesses to
that prepossessing HUAC performance would not have recognized the Robert Oppenheimer who now sat in the witness chair
in Room 2022, often anguished, sometimes surprisingly inarticu-
late, frequently apologetic about his past and even self-castigat-
ing. Perhaps this was because his previous questioners had been
less well informed than Roger Robb. Perhaps it was because the
McCarthy era and the fears that accompanied it were now at
their height. Perhaps it was because on previous occasions he had
always spoken as the awesome statesman and man of science.
Never before had he been the prisoner in the dock. Above all,
never before had he been locked in an encounter with the likes
of Roger Robb.

Robb now turned to the most sensitive matter of all, the
"Chevalier incident." Robb wanted to know more about Oppen-
heimer's relationship with George C. Eltenton, the British scien-
tist who Chevalier said had approached him on behalf of the
Soviets. Oppenheimer had already recalled one instance when
Eltenton had come to his house. Had there been other visits?
Robb inquired. "I am quite sure not," was the reply.

Evidently, Robb was not seeking information. His subsequent
questions indicated that he already knew the answer in discon-
certing detail—knew not only of the *fact* of another Eltenton
visit, but, thanks to government investigators, knew what had
been said *inside* Oppenheimer's home.

q: Did [Eltenton] come to your house in 1942 on one occasion to discuss certain awards which the Soviet Government was going to make to certain scientists?

a: If so, it is news to me. I assume you know that this is true, but I certainly have no recollection of it.

q: You have no recollection of it?

a: No.

q: Let me see if I can refresh your recollection, Doctor. Do you recall him coming to your house to discuss awards to be made to certain scientists by the Soviet Government and you suggesting the names of Bush, Morgan, and perhaps one of the Comptons?

a: There is nothing unreasonable in the suggestions. . . . But I really don't remember.

Now the prosecutor turned to Oppenheimer's delay in reporting the "Chevalier incident" to security officers, and to the "cock and bull" story the scientist had invented in telling Colonel Boris Pash about the "kitchen conversation." Robb minced no words, spared no feelings.

"Now, let us go back to your interview with Colonel Pash. Did you tell Pash the truth about this thing?"

"No."

"You lied to him?"

"Yes." . . .

"Didn't you say that X [Chevalier] had approached three people?"

"Probably."

"Why did you do that, Doctor?"

The anguished witness emitted an answer that was, a few months hence, to make headlines:

"Because I was an idiot."

Roger Robb later recalled this instant as perhaps the turning point of the hearing. Oppenheimer, he recalled, was "hunched over, wringing his hands, white as a sheet. I felt sick. That night when I came home I told my wife, 'I've just seen a man destroy himself.'"

But if Robb felt squeamish at the sight of Robert Oppenheimer's agony, he did not permit this to inhibit him in pressing his advantage. He confronted the physicist with passage after passage of the secretly tape-recorded interview. Time after time, Robb forced Oppenheimer to go back over the various false details that went to make up the single "cock and bull story."

Q:   And your testimony now is that was a lie?
A:   Right.

*And again:*

Q:   Was that true?
A:   No.

*And still again:*

Q:   That wasn't true?
A:   That is right. This whole thing was a pure fabrication except for the one name, Eltenton.

Robb's technique of interrogation thus elicited separate admissions of lies about each aspect of Oppenheimer's interview with Pash, and set the stage for Robb to administer the *coup de grâce.*

ROBB: Isn't it a fair statement today, Dr. Oppenheimer, that according to your testimony now you told not one lie to Colonel Pash, *but a whole fabrication and tissue of lies?* [Emphasis added.]
OPPENHEIMER: Right.

But had Oppenheimer told a whole series of lies or, essentially, just *one lie:* the entirety of his "cock and bull" story about the Chevalier incident? Later in the hearing, Lloyd Garrison was to lament his earlier failure to raise that precise question. "It lies heavy on my conscience," he told the Gray Board, "that I did not at that time object to the impression that was trying to be conveyed to this board of a whole series of lies when in fact there was one story which was told." But Garrison's lament did not occur until five days after the damaging Robb tactic. At the time the injury was inflicted, Garrison sat silent.

There were occasions when Garrison did enter protests. But in contrast to the assertive tone Robb used in addressing the board,

Garrison's complaints frequently sounded apologetic. He wanted, for example, to make sure that in reading excerpts from the Pash and Lansdale interviews Robb was not omitting passages favorable to Oppenheimer. Garrison couched his request in these terms:

> Mr. Chairman, could I just make a short request at this point? . . . I appreciate the existence of the rule under which we cannot ask for access to the file and I am not going to protest that rule. I wonder, however, if it would be within the proprieties of this kind of proceeding when counsel [Robb] reads from a transcript for us to be furnished with a copy of the transcript as he reads from it. This, of course, is orthodox in a court of law. . . . I don't want to make an argument. I put the question to you.

Robb jumped in to deny that courtroom rules entitled Garrison to see the transcript,* but said that in any event it was "presently marked 'Secret' so I could not make it available to Mr. Garrison at this time."

It was not the attorney, Garrison, but, ironically, the client, Oppenheimer, who pointed out the logical fallacy of Robb's argument. While Robb was contending he could not make the "secret" document available to Garrison, he was reading portions of the paper aloud in the hearing room for all, including Garrison, to hear.

Even after his manifold admissions of having lied to Pash and Lansdale, Oppenheimer's ordeal was not ended. There was one added indignity to be suffered that day. It had to do with his visit to Jean Tatlock in Berkeley in June, 1943—in the third year of his marriage to Kitty.

Robb wanted to know why Oppenheimer had felt he "had" to see Miss Tatlock. Oppenheimer replied that she "was undergoing psychiatric treatment. She was extremely unhappy."

Robb was not satisfied. "Did you find out why she had to see you?"

"Because she was still in love with me."

---

* It was a controversial legal point; practices vary from one American legal jurisdiction to another.

"Where did you see her?"

"At her home."

"Where was that?"

"On Telegraph Hill."

"When did you see her after that?"

"She took me to the airport, and I never saw her again."

But Robb wanted every aspect of the visit explicitly spelled out.

"You spent the night with her, didn't you?"

"Yes."

"That is when you were working on a secret war project?"

"Yes."

"Did you think that consistent with good security?"

Oppenheimer's answer was blurred and stumbling: "It was as a matter of fact. Not a word—it was not good practice."*

Would a man be likely to devote part of such a night to talking of atomic secrets? At the time, in 1943, the man principally responsible for atomic security, thought not. Although Colonel John Lansdale had immediately learned of the occurrence, he had concluded that Oppenheimer's "interest was more romantic than otherwise." Yet persons familiar with how the AEC arrived at its decision in the Oppenheimer case say that his night with Jean Tatlock was a significant factor in the negative vote of more than one of the Commissioners.

It was by now four o'clock. Robert Oppenheimer had been on the witness stand since 9:30 that morning, with but one major break, at midday. Weary but wary, he began asking Robb, who was obviously better informed, to fill him in where his memory was vague.

After another half-hour of questioning, Robb pressed again,

* Earlier in the hearing he had given a far more emphatic answer: yes, he admitted, his visit with Jean Tatlock might be thought "potentially dangerous; conceivably dangerous." But then, apparently slightly annoyed, he added: "Look: I have had a lot of secrets in my head a long time. It does not matter who I associate with. I don't talk about those secrets. Only a very skillful guy might pick up a trace of information as to where I had been or what I was up to. Passing the time of day with a Communist—I don't think it is wise, but I don't see that it is necessarily dangerous if the man is discreet and knows what he is up to."

in a manner appropriate to a district attorney trying to wrest a confession from a suspected criminal. Had Oppenheimer told General Groves that Frank Oppenheimer had belonged to the Communist Party? The witness wasn't sure what he *had* told Groves, but he felt he *should not* have told the General any such thing about his own brother.

Might he have told Groves he didn't *know* anything about his brother's membership—and if so, wouldn't that have been another lie? Oppenheimer acknowledged that it would have.

Q: Would you now deny that you made that statement to General Groves?
A: Oh, I couldn't.
Q: In other words, you *might* have told General Groves something that was not true?
A: Well, I hope I didn't.
Q: You might have; is that correct?
A: I hope I didn't.
Q: But might have; might you not?
A: Obviously I might have.

Having scored this one last point, Robb was satisfied. "It is half-past four, Mr. Chairman."

And thus ended the third day of what Chairman Gray had insisted was "an inquiry, and not a trial."

As the Gray Board reconvened on Thursday morning, Lloyd Garrison put Major General Leslie Richard Groves, now retired, on the witness stand. Groves unhesitatingly reaffirmed his wartime decisions to choose, grant clearance to and retain Robert Oppenheimer as head of Los Alamos. In that capacity, the General said, Oppenheimer had had Groves' complete confidence. Groves said he would be "amazed" if Oppenheimer would ever commit a disloyal act.

What about the scientist's delay in reporting the "Chevalier incident," and his refusal to reveal Chevalier's identity until ordered to do so? General Groves said he had shrugged this off as "the typical American school boy attitude that there is something wicked about telling on a friend." Groves added he had always been confident that Oppenheimer had done the essential thing: he had revealed the name of Eltenton, the "source of danger."*

Under Robb's questioning, the helpfulness of Groves' testimony was considerably blunted. Robb noted that Groves had ordered Oppenheimer cleared because he was "absolutely essential to the [wartime A-bomb] project." But would the General do the same today? General Groves had anticipated this question and had looked up the screening criteria listed in the Atomic Energy Act after his responsibility for the program had ended. As he understood the new criteria, they did not permit the "common sense" standard he himself had used in 1943 in weighing Robert Oppenheimer's importance to the atomic work against the risks indicated by his radical background. As Groves saw it, the law now demanded that clearance be denied, no matter "how important the man is, if there is any possibility other than a tortured one that his associations or his loyalty or his character might endanger" the common defense or security. Largely on the basis of Oppenheimer's prewar associations, Groves said, he "would not clear Dr. Oppenheimer today" under his interpretation of the new security standards.

Late that morning, while a rainstorm beat against Temporary Building 3, General Groves was excused from the stand, and Robert Oppenheimer faced the renewed questioning of Roger Robb.

Once again Robb focused on Oppenheimer's prewar affiliations with the far left. Once again there was evidence of the thoroughness with which the United States Government had probed into the life of its most prominent atomic scientist. Robb asked what Oppenheimer's income had been in the prewar days when he had been making contributions to and/or through the Communist Party. But, as before, Robb showed he was not really looking for information, for he told Oppenheimer he had already "looked at your [California] income tax return for, I think, 1942 and [your income] seemed to me to be about $15,-000." Robb, of course, offered no explanation of how a *state* in-

---

* Years later, in an interview, Groves recalled that the only reason he had ultimately ordered Oppenheimer to reveal Chevalier's name was to fend off any further agitation from his security officers.

come tax return, especially of such ancient vintage, had come to repose in a *Federal* investigative dossier.

In midafternoon, Robb resumed reading selected portions of the transcript of the Lansdale interview, including one that revealed the apparent error of Oppenheimer's earlier testimony about the Communist Party membership of Rossi Lomanitz and Joseph Weinberg. Lloyd Garrison rose again to object to Robb's choosing selectively from the transcript without any chance for Oppenheimer's lawyers to follow the entire document to be sure the excerpts were being fairly chosen. But Robb's retort showed that without the "blank pad rule" Garrison was hopelessly disadvantaged no matter which way he turned:

I resent [Garrison's] statement that I am trying to be unfair. . . . Were I trying to be unfair, I would not ask this witness any of these questions, *but would leave it [the full transcript] in the file for the board to read.* I am giving this witness a chance to make whatever explanation he wishes to make. [Emphasis added.]

For Garrison, which was the lesser of the evils: to hear, and allow Oppenheimer to explain, portions of the transcript, even though risking a biased selection of the excerpts? Or to hear none of the transcript, and allow the Gray Board to use it in judgment without *any* explanations or rebuttals by Oppenheimer? Garrison was damned if he protested and damned if he remained silent.

Later in the hearing, Garrison's dilemma was even more harshly revealed when he protested Robb's use of an unsigned, unidentified AEC memorandum, of "whose purpose, nature, origin, [and] authenticity," Garrison said, "we have no knowledge at all."* Robb's angry reply:

*This board . . . is to base its decision . . . upon the whole file before it.* If [Garrison] does not want to hear this, *and wants the board to go ahead and consider it without him hearing it,* that is all right with me. . . . *This report is before the board in*

---

* Such a memorandum would have been inadmissible in a court of law, as hearsay evidence.

*its entirety.* I can't see why putting a portion in the record seems to be such a horrible step to take. [Emphasis added.]

In one sense Robb was right: the essential "horrible step"—the absence of the "blank pad" principle and the board's use, in arriving at a judgment, of evidence Lloyd Garrison could neither see nor challenge—was already built in, an inherent part of this security proceeding and others of that era.

As to the possibility that Robb would unfairly excerpt the Lansdale transcript, Chairman Gray said he had no worry. "I do not think that it is the purpose of counsel to develop anything beyond what the facts are in this case. At least," said Gray, "that is my interpretation."

"That is my endeavor, Mr. Chairman," said Roger Robb.

And the hearing proceeded.

Robb had already closed the trap on Oppenheimer regarding the Communist Party membership of Lomanitz and Weinberg. Now he proceeded to do the same about Rudy Lambert, whom Lansdale had asked Oppenheimer to identify, only to have the scientist ask, "Do you know what he looks like?"

"You knew what Rudy Lambert looked like, didn't you?" asked Robb.

"Sure," replied Oppenheimer.

"Why did you ask Lansdale what he looked like?"

Oppenheimer dodged. "I don't know that I did."

"If you did, Doctor, would it mean that you were ducking the question?"

No escape now. "I would think so," was the answer.

Robb now turned to the matter of Oppenheimer's testimony in 1949 before HUAC about Bernard Peters, and the letter Oppenheimer later wrote to the Rochester newspaper in an effort to undo the damage of what he had told the Committee.* In trying to explain the discrepancy between his public letter (in which he said Peters had recently told him he had not been a Communist Party member in Germany) and his categorical statement to HUAC that Peters "was a member of the German Na-

* See p. 121.

tional Communist Party," Oppenheimer's testimony took on a disingenuous tone:

Q: You would not have said that [to HUAC] would you, had you not been absolutely sure it was true?

A: I was convinced it was true, or I wouldn't have said it. . . .

Q: And yet when Peters came to see you and you received a letter from Dr. Condon, you in effect repudiated that testimony, didn't you?

A: Does it [the letter] say that I don't believe he was a member of the party? . . . [After rereading the letter] I don't say [in the letter] I believe his denial. I just say he denied it.

This may well have seemed to Robb like hair-splitting, for if Oppenheimer had *dis*believed Peters' denial, would he have included it in his letter? Robb pressed on in his quest for a straight explanation:

Q: Very well. Isn't the implication of your letter that you were wrong in believing that he had been a member of the party?

A: I think it leaves the matter open.

Q: Was it your intention to convey that impression when you wrote the letter?

A: I think the sum total of my intention was not to get this guy fired . . . because of intemperate remarks I made before the House Committee. . . .

Q: You thought the truth was intemperate?

A: I think the phrasing of it was intemperate.

Q: Was it intemperate for you to testify, believing it to be true, that Peters had told you he had been a member of the Communist Party?

A: No.

Q: Wasn't it your intention in writing this letter . . . to convey to the public the impression that you had been mistaken . . . ?

A: I simply gave his own statement.

Q: I know you did. But wasn't it your intention to give the

public through the press the impression that you were
mistaken?

A:  I had no specific intention.

This was not the only instance in which Oppenheimer's testimony seemed evasive to the point of disingenuousness. For example, the next day, Robb asked him about a statement he had
made in a letter to James B. Conant shortly before the 1949 GAC
meeting on the H-bomb in which he attributed a "change of
climate" about the bomb to the fact that "two experienced promoters have been at work, i.e., Ernest Lawrence and Edward
Teller. The project has long been dear to Teller's heart; and
Ernest has convinced himself that we must learn from Operation
Joe [the initial Soviet A-bomb explosion] that the Russians will
soon do the super, and that we had better beat them to it." The
exchange between Robb and Oppenheimer went this way:

Q:  Would you agree, Doctor, that your references to Dr.
Lawrence and Dr. Teller and their enthusiasm for the super
bomb . . . are a little bit belittling?

A:  Dr. Lawrence came to Washington. He did not talk to the
[Atomic Energy] Commission. He went and talked to
[Congressmen] and to members of the Military Estab-
lishment. I think that deserves some belittling.

Q:  So you would agree that your references to those men in
this letter were belittling?

A:  No. I pay my great respects to them as promoters. I don't
think I did them justice.

Q:  You used the word "promoters" in an invidious sense,
didn't you?

A:  I promoted lots of things in my time.

Q:  Doctor, would you answer my question? When you used
the word "promoters" you meant it to be in a slightly invidious sense, didn't you?

A:  I have no idea.

Q:  When you use the word now with reference to Lawrence
and Teller, don't you intend it to be invidious?

A:  No.

Q:  You think that their work of promotion was admirable, is
that right?

A: I think they did an admirable job of promotion.

Oppenheimer's behavior in the Peters case deeply disturbed Chairman Gray. It seemed to him to expose a tendency in Oppenheimer to be caught up in a "conflict between loyalty to [and] a desire to protect [an individual friend] . . . and a broader obligation" to his country. Wasn't this the same conflict that had prevented him from reporting the "Chevalier incident" promptly and truthfully? Gray asked Oppenheimer. The physicist acknowledged such a conflict might have been present in the case of the Chevalier incident. As to Peters, however, "I do not believe I violated a broader obligation in writing the letter. . . . He was a good scientist doing according to everyone's account no political work of any kind, doing no harm, whatever his views. . . . It was for the public interest that I wrote [the letter]."

On November 23, 1953, slightly less than five months before the Oppenheimer security hearing began, the President of the United States said, in a speech:

I was . . . raised in a little town . . . called Abilene, Kansas. . . . Now, that town has a code, and I was raised as a boy to prize that code. It was: "Meet anyone face to face with whom you disagree." . . . In this country, if someone . . . accuses you, he must come up in front. He cannot hide behind the shadow. He cannot assassinate you or your character from behind.

The "Abilene Code," as it was called by the press at the time of the President's speech, was in fact a restatement of the right guaranteed by the Sixth Amendment to the United States Constitution: the right of a citizen accused of a crime "to be confronted with the witnesses against him." But for Robert Oppenheimer, and all other security-risk "defendants" of his day, neither the "Abilene Code" nor the Sixth Amendment was applicable.* At the time the President spoke, accusing witnesses

---

* The Sixth Amendment, which applies to criminal proceedings, need not, strictly speaking, apply to security hearings where no criminal offense is alleged. Yet the findings of such hearings may have consequences for the defendant that are just as severe as do the sentences of criminal courts. (For example, one $18,000-a-year executive who was judged a security risk

were carefully hidden "behind the shadow" of anonymity, able to "assassinate . . . character from behind" without fear of challenge to their veracity in general or in the particular case.

In the Gray Board hearing the evils of this practice were vividly demonstrated in Roger Robb's failure to call Paul Crouch to the witness stand. Crouch and his wife, Sylvia, were an important source of the AEC's charge that Oppenheimer had attended the closed meeting of the Communist Party at his Berkeley residence in July, 1941. An active party member in the San Francisco area in those days, Crouch presumably could have provided considerable detail about Oppenheimer's prewar involvements with the Communist Party. Yet Robb apparently preferred to have Crouch's testimony reach the Gray Board via the investigative file rather than in person.

From Robb's point of view, this was a wise tactic, for had Crouch appeared, he would have been subject to cross-examination by Lloyd Garrison and his colleagues, and through cross-examination they might have drawn the following profile of this important witness against Robert Oppenheimer:

• In 1925 Crouch wrote a letter to a newspaper explaining his habit of "writing letters to my friends and imaginary persons, sometimes to kings and other foreign persons in which I place myself in imaginary positions." He said he did this "to develop my imaginative powers."

• As an Army enlistee in Hawaii, he was court-martialed and sentenced to forty years in a Federal penitentiary for his efforts to foment revolution both in an Army garrison and among the civil population in Hawaii.

• After his sentence was commuted to three years, he left Alcatraz, joined the American Communist Party and went to Russia; there, he said, he conferred with high officers of the Red Army General Staff, who told the twenty-four-year-old ex-Army private the detailed plans "they [had] formulated for penetration of the American Armed Forces."

• In postwar years Crouch became a paid "consultant" to the

---

found that, as a result, the best job he could get was as a $4,400-a-year draftsman.) In that sense, the fair-trial principle to which the Sixth Amendment addresses itself is relevant to such hearings.

U.S. Department of Justice, testifying as a government witness in cases against persons alleged by the United States to be current or past members of the Communist Party.

• In one such case, against one Armand E. Scala, Crouch told HUAC: "I do not know of my own knowledge what his party affiliations are." Yet, ten days later, Crouch told a Senate committee he had "every reason" to know Scala was a "very active Communist." Crouch also wrote a series of articles for the Hearst papers naming Scala as "the chief courier for the [Communist] Party in Latin America"—a libel for which Scala later won $5,000 in a damage suit. (Crouch told the Senate committee that the story of Scala as a Communist "courier" came from "many references which I have heard around the office.")

• In the government's deportation case against Chicago cartoonist Jacob Burck, Crouch testified that he and Burck had worked in the Communist Party for many years and had often attended "closed [party] meetings" together. Yet, when asked to identify Burck in a hearing room, Crouch pointed not to Burck but to the photographer for the Chicago *Tribune*.

It was in considerable part on the word of such a man that the AEC had based its charge that Oppenheimer had participated in a closed Communist meeting in his own home. This was a vital part of the charges for, if true, it would contradict Oppenheimer's persistent denials of actual party membership and cast crucial doubt on his veracity. But Paul Crouch was permitted to avoid the cross-examination that could have brought his reliability forcibly into question. Conceivably, Lloyd Garrison could have asked the Gray Board to call Crouch as a witness, and, assuming the board followed usual AEC procedures, it would have complied. But in this as in other instances, the absence of the "blank pad rule" deprived Garrison of the information on which to base such a risky decision. Having no way of appraising either the gravity or the persuasiveness of the Crouch testimony in the board's secret file, he could not estimate how much credence the board might be giving Crouch's reports.

Did Gordon Gray and his colleagues know that Crouch was the informant? If so, how much did they know about him? Aside from Crouch's faulty identification in the Burck case and one other similar instance cited by Garrison in his written brief to the board, there is no record that any of the adverse information came to the board's attention.

Friday, April 16, the fifth day of the Gray Board hearing and the third and last day of Robert Oppenheimer's cross-examination by Roger Robb, was a day of constant thunderstorms outside AEC Building T-3 but of comparative calm within Room 2022. For three hours Robb questioned Oppenheimer, but less aggressively than on the first two days. At one point, when the witness anticipated the question Robb was about to ask and answered it in advance, the attorney said, "Doctor, you and I are getting along fine." In only one major instance did Robb elicit a significant contradiction in testimony. When the verdicts in the case were all in, it was clear that the prosecutor has scored a major point.

Robb wanted more detail on Oppenheimer's earlier testimony that there had been "surprising unanimity" against the H-bomb among the members of the General Advisory Committee at their October, 1949, meeting. Had everyone on the committee expressed himself on the question? Robb asked. Yes, said Oppenheimer, and then added that Glenn Seaborg had been absent, in Sweden.

Q: So you didn't know how he felt about it [the H-bomb]?
A: We did not.
Q: You didn't know either how he felt about it. He just was not there.
A: He was in Sweden, *and there was no communication with him*. . . .
Q: You didn't poll him by mail or anything?
A: This was not a convenient thing to do. [Emphasis added.]

The exposure of a gap in Robert Oppenheimer's memory—a grievous gap, in this instance—began in a manner by now all too familiar to the witness, as Robb said, "I am going to show you a letter taken from your files at Princeton . . . dated October 14, 1949, signed Glenn Seaborg. . . ."

Oppenheimer evidently realized his predicament, for he

quickly replied: "I am going to say before I see that that I had no recollection of it."

Oppenheimer's forgetfulness about the Seaborg letter after five years, while embarrassing, might have been understandable. But now Robb proceeded to show that the letter had dropped from Oppenheimer's mind only a few *months* after its receipt, for the scientist had failed to recall it in his testimony before the Joint Atomic Energy Committee in January, 1950. To compound Oppenheimer's embarrassment, Robb then produced yet another document he had found in the files plucked away from Princeton, which confirmed Oppenheimer's awareness of the Seaborg communication. It was Oppenheimer's October 21 letter to "Uncle Jim" Conant, in which he specifically mentioned having received Seaborg's "general views . . . in written form."

Oppenheimer told Robb that it "would have been normal practice for me" to have read a letter from an absent member such as Seaborg not only to the members of the GAC but also to the Atomic Energy Commission, when the two groups met together. But, he said, "having no recollection of the Seaborg letter, I cannot say that I did this." He also pointed out that at a subsequent meeting of the GAC, in December, 1949, Glenn Seaborg *had* been asked "how he felt about it [the H-bomb], and he said he would prefer not to express his views."

Oppenheimer told the Gray Board that at the time of his testimony before the Joint Atomic Energy Committee he had "known for a fact" that the government's pro-H-bomb decision "had been taken,"* and so his testimony "was not an attempt to persuade" the Committee, but merely to explain the reasoning of the GAC. "So this was not a piece of advocacy. It was a piece of exposition."

Here again Robert Oppenheimer's judges were confronted with the question: Was the scientist's initial statement to the Gray Board that there had been "no communication" from Seaborg a simple matter of forgetfulness or was it a lie?

Roger Robb had gone to considerable effort to portray Robert Oppenheimer's testimony to the Joint Committee about the Sea-

---

* Strictly speaking, Oppenheimer was not correct; his testimony was on January 30, and it was not until the next day that the matter was finally brought before President Truman for decision.

borg letter as an outright and important falsehood. This was the exchange:

Q: . . . didn't you tell the Joint Committee that Dr. Seaborg had not expressed himself on this subject prior to the meeting of October 29, 1949?

A: I would have to see the transcript [of the Joint Committee hearing]. I don't remember that question and the answer.

Q: If you did make that statement, it was not true, was it?

A: It is clear that we had an expression, not unequivocal, from Seaborg, before the meeting of October 29.

Q: Doctor, did you hear my question?

A: I heard it, but I have heard that kind of question too often.

Q: I am sure of that, Doctor, but would you answer it nevertheless?

As Oppenheimer sought to make clear, the extent of his misstatement before the Joint Committee would depend greatly on just what the committee had asked him. If, as Robb implied, the committee had inquired directly as to whether or not Glenn Seaborg had expressed himself on the H-bomb question prior to the October meeting, then Oppenheimer's negative answer would have been a serious misrepresentation of the facts. But suppose that the question merely concerned the degree of the GAC's *unanimity* on the H-bomb question without particular reference to Seaborg. In that event, Oppenheimer's statement that the GAC had been unanimous would be, at most, a minor misstatement of the facts, since the eight members present at the October meeting had indeed been unanimous, and Seaborg's written views had been expressed in equivocal terms.

Just what question *had* the Joint Committee asked Oppenheimer? Lloyd Garrison tried to find out but was once again confronted by a curtain of secrecy: any release of the verbatim transcript of those questions would, Robb said, require a special vote of the Joint Committee. That seemed strange to Garrison, for weren't Robb's own questions derived from the hearing transcript? And if so, had its release to Robb been specially voted by the Joint Committee? Chairman Gray replied that Robb's questions had not been based on the verbatim transcript, but merely on what the board understood about the hearing "from a source it believes to be reliable."* And so Garrison was powerless to combat factually Roger Robb's implied charge that Oppenheimer had lied to the Joint Committee.

Thus the secrecy weapon was potent, even as a single-edged instrument. But in the hands of Roger Robb it was two-edged, to be wielded as might suit his advantage. In the case of the Seaborg letter, where it was Garrison who needed a Joint Committee transcript, the material was held to be unobtainable because of the implied impossibility of getting the committee's permission. Later, however, when it was Robb who needed a Joint Committee transcript (so that *his* witness, Air Force General Roscoe C. Wilson, could read excerpts into the Gray Board record), Robb was able to declare, almost casually: "I might say, Mr. Chairman, that [transcript] has been released by formal action of the Joint Committee, confirmed to [AEC General Manager] Nichols by letter which we received this morning."

This was by no means the only instance where secrecy seemed governed by a double standard. Lloyd Garrison was at first barred from seeing the full transcripts of the Pash and Lansdale interrogations of Oppenheimer because Robb said they bore a secret classification, yet Robb seemed to feel at liberty to read aloud such portions of those supposedly secret documents as he saw fit to introduce into the hearings.

Similarly, other documents Garrison asked to see (e.g., a memorandum of the private luncheon held in William Burden's Georgetown home†) were denied him on grounds of secrecy, yet secret documents that Roger Robb wished to inject into the record could, it seemed, be made nonsecret on the spot. For example, on the next to last day of the hearing, when Robb suddenly introduced a wartime letter of Oppenheimer's, he said to Oppenheimer's attorneys that he was "trying to get this unclassified so I can hand you a copy of it." But it developed that an on-the-spot declassification was not necessary. That had already been accomplished on the second day of the Oppen-

---

* Gray's statement indicated that the board had received the information from the Joint Committee and had passed it on to Robb—implying a close cooperation between Oppenheimer's prosecutor and his judges.

† See p. 189.

heimer hearing—especially, it seemed, for the purpose of aiding Robb's presentation.

In late morning, April 16, Robb said, at long last, "That is all [the questions] I have at the moment, Mr. Chairman." Garrison suggested a brief recess, but Oppenheimer, hearing that the board members still wanted to question him, said, "Let us get that over with."

For nearly half an hour Gordon Gray plied him with questions. The topics that interested Gray: Oppenheimer's reasoning at the time of his 1949 opposition to the H-bomb; the point in time at which Oppenheimer, the fabricator of the first A-bomb, had developed "strong moral convictions" against the H-bomb; and the apparent conflict in Oppenheimer between his loyalty to friends (such as Chevalier and Bernard Peters) and his allegiance to the security system.

Board member Thomas Morgan, who, like Gray, had sat through more than four days of Oppenheimer's testimony, had not a single question to ask the witness. Ward Evans wanted further information about the role Edward Condon's irate letter had played in prompting Oppenheimer's "retraction letter" about Bernard Peters, and about Oppenheimer's 1949 estimate of the mathematical feasibility of the H-bomb.

Then, at 12:15, Oppenheimer was excused from the witness chair he had occupied for a total of more than twenty hours.

While the Gray Board was in recess for luncheon that day, a man who in the early press reports was identified only as "a high administration official," gave an off-the-record address to the American Society of Newspaper Editors. He had just returned from a tour of Asia, and for nearly an hour he held the editors spellbound with a lucid, extemporaneous account of his findings. It was an oratorical tour de force, and the editors responded with a prolonged standing ovation. Flushed with his success, the "high official" agreed to accept questions. Among them was a request for his views on the Oppenheimer case.

Still speaking off the record, the official said he had been familiar with the case since the late 1940's, when he had been a member of a House committee that had questioned the scientist.

He had, he said, found Oppenheimer "cooperative, impressive and responsive" as a witness. He had seen the full Oppenheimer file, he continued, and while it presented "an extremely difficult problem," still, "on the evidence I have seen, Dr. Oppenheimer in my opinion is a loyal American" who, if "he is not subject to blackmail, should have a right to work for the government."

No man so prominent in Washington can utter such newsmaking remarks and expect them to remain off the record, and the next day this "high Administration official" found his words making headlines. A day later, his identity was revealed. The speaker had been Vice President Richard M. Nixon.

Back in Room 2022 that Friday, there began the long parade of additional pro-Oppenheimer witnesses that would occupy the attention of the Gray Board for the next seven days of the hearing. It was a luminous array of men who came to testify to the character and loyalty of Robert Oppenheimer: major figures of national or world renown in the fields of science (Nobel laureates Fermi and Rabi, and Hans Bethe), of statesmanship (John J. McCloy and George Kennan), of scientific administration (James B. Conant and Vannevar Bush) and of atomic energy (two former AEC Chairmen; three former AEC Commissioners).

Before the luncheon recess there had been brief appearances by former AEC Commissioner T. Keith Glennan and Karl T. Compton, the former MIT president and wartime government consultant on atomic energy matters.

After the luncheon break, the witness chair was assumed by General Groves' former security officer, John Lansdale, the only witness in the hearing whose courtroom experience equaled Roger Robb's, and to whom, therefore, Robb's prosecutorial tactics were neither new nor intimidating. The witness was unfazed, for example, when Robb asked some abrupt questions about something Lansdale said: that the Oppenheimer case was a "manifestation" of the "current hysteria of the times."

Q: You think this inquiry is a manifestation of hysteria?
A: I think—
Q: Yes or no?
A: I won't answer that question "Yes" or "No." . . . If you

will let me continue, I will be glad to answer your question.

Faced with such firmness, Robb backed off. "All right," he said, and permitted Lansdale to answer the question in his own manner.

A few minutes later, Robb sought to pit Lansdale's charitable view of Oppenheimer against that of Los Alamos security officer Peer de Silva, who, he said, "was certainly more of a professional than you were, wasn't he, Colonel [Lansdale]?"

A:   In what field?

Q:   The field he was working in, security.

A:   No.

Q:   No?

A:   No.

Q:   He was a graduate of West Point, wasn't he?

A:   Certainly. I am a graduate of VMI, too. You want to fight about that?

John Lansdale's demeanor in the face of Robb's questions was sharply different from Robert Oppenheimer's as he made his abashed confession to having been "an idiot." And, by consequence, Robb's conduct was correspondingly different. His answer to Lansdale's challenging question was: "No, sir. I don't want to fight with you." Then he changed the subject.

When John Lansdale was excused from the witness chair and the Gray Board made ready to adjourn for the weekend, Chairman Gray answered an earlier Garrison inquiry as to when he might expect to receive his copy of the first week's hearing transcripts, which were essential to his preparation for the further defense of his client. Apparently Robb was receiving each day's transcript within a day, as is normal in courtroom trials. Yet not even the *first day's* transcript had reached Garrison. Chairman Gray's explanation of the delay was that the typed copies of the proceedings had to be reviewed by security officials from many government agencies so that "sensitive" matters could be excised.* Garrison said he had wanted to begin his study of the

* Gray did not explain why such a review was necessary before giving the transcripts to Garrison, inasmuch as Garrison had already heard virtually everything contained in them.

transcripts that very afternoon but he had to be content with a promise that he would receive them the next day.

With that, at 4:35 on the afternoon of Friday, April 16, the first week of the proceeding "in the matter of J. Robert Oppenheimer" came to a close, and the Gray Board recessed for the Easter weekend.

During that week the three members of the Gray Board had spent a great deal of time together, often dining together after the day's hearing had ended. Gordon Gray and Thomas Morgan were appalled at some of the dinner table utterances of their colleague, Ward Evans, for they found Evans' comments shockingly prejudiced against Robert Oppenheimer and the case he was presenting to the board. Gray and Morgan sought to caution Evans against making such injudicious remarks, even to his fellow judges, but Evans' prejudicial comments persisted, so that Gordon Gray, the only lawyer on the panel, felt obliged to begin making memoranda of the mealtime conversations, for his own record.

At the end of each day, Oppenheimer and Garrison and his colleagues had repaired to the Georgetown home of Randolph Paul, Garrison's law partner, where the Oppenheimers were staying so as to be free of the ever-inquisitive press corps.* There they had spent each evening discussing the day's proceedings and planning for the return to battle the next morning. As Paul listened to these daily deliberations, it became increasingly clear to him that while Gordon Gray insisted that this was "an inquiry and not a trial," both Gray and Roger Robb were treating it much as though it were a criminal prosecution in a courtroom, with the respective attorneys pitted against each other in an adversary posture. Yet the hearing clearly lacked the procedural protections usually associated with such an "adversary proceeding."

On the evening of Easter Sunday, April 18, therefore, Randolph Paul invited former AEC General Counsel Joseph Volpe to his home to meet with the Oppenheimers and their trial attorneys. Slowly, Paul coaxed from Garrison and his colleagues a

---

* They were successful in concealing their whereabouts for the impressive period of one week.

description of the prosecutorial atmosphere of the first week's proceedings. When the account was completed, Volpe strongly urged that if there should be a repetition of the tactics he had heard described, Oppenheimer and Garrison should, without further comment, pick up their papers and leave the hearing, advising the members of the Gray Board to dispose of the case in any way they might see fit.

The evening broke up without any firm decision being reached.

The following day, David Lilienthal visited the Atomic Energy Commission, over which he had presided for more than three years. The purpose of his visit was to review the AEC's files on the 1947 clearance of Oppenheimer and on the 1949 meeting of the General Advisory Committee concerning the H-bomb, so that his testimony before the Gray Board, scheduled for the following day, would be based on contemporaneous records rather than on his unrefreshed memory. He had called General Manager Nichols, who, according to Lilienthal's later recollection, had hesitated at first about allowing him to see the files, then assented. When Lilienthal arrived at the AEC, he was given the files he had requested and an office in which to read them. And so he proceeded to leaf through the folders, confident they contained all the documents he would need, unaware that there were missing certain crucial papers that were to bear directly on his own testimony.

## 2. *The Second Week*

While Lilienthal was in the main AEC building, the Gray Board itself had returned to Building T-3 to take up the second week of its hearing.

The first hour and a half were devoted to an effort at comparing the often indistinct tape recording of the Pash-Oppenheimer interrogation in 1943 against the written transcript Roger Robb had used in questioning Oppenheimer. The fears that had prompted Lloyd Garrison to insist on having a verified copy of the transcript were soon justified. A substantive error was found in the Robb transcript, which had quoted Oppenheimer as telling Pash, "To put it quite frankly, I would feel friendly to the idea of the Commander in Chief informing the Russians, who are working on this [atomic bomb] problem." To Lloyd Garrison, this statement, which implied that Oppenheimer knew what the Russians were doing in the nuclear field, sounded "as if there were something sinister about it." Actually, no such implication was warranted, for the recording itself showed that Oppenheimer had, in fact, spoken of "informing the Russians that *we were working* on this problem." [Emphasis added.]

Whether or not Garrison was correct in contending that this inaccuracy had significantly affected his client's answer to Robb's questions, the error was one not of peripheral detail but of substance. Yet neither Robb nor Chairman Gray seemed greatly concerned by it. If Garrison felt his client had been wronged, Gray said, he could correct the error when Oppenheimer returned to the stand later in the hearing.

Former AEC Chairman Gordon Dean now took the witness chair, and gave Robert Oppenheimer an unqualified vote of confidence.

Roger Robb's first question, on cross-examination, was a tendentious one. "Mr. Dean," he began, "Dr. Oppenheimer has testified before this board in substance . . . that when interviewed about [the Chevalier incident] by intelligence officers of the

United States Army, he told these officers a fabrication and tissue of lies." This last phrase, which Robb seemed to be representing as a direct quote from Oppenheimer, had, of course, been Robb's own phrase, and it brought Lloyd Garrison to his feet to object "in the strongest terms to the form of the question which counsel has put." It "gives an utterly false summation of what actually happened in the total Chevalier incident, which is the only way it can be looked at."

While this controversy was quickly smoothed over, another soon arose as Robb, again using secrecy to his own advantage, read a sentence from a classified memorandum. Garrison rose to ask that either he or the witness be allowed to see the document from which Robb was reading selectively. Robb was furious. He had, he said, refrained from objecting to Lloyd Garrison's questions, on the understanding that this was "not a court proceeding. But if Mr. Garrison is going to stick on technicalities and turn this into a proceeding according to the strict rules of evidence, I think we ought to have it understood here and now."

Garrison, too, was angry. His only objection, he said, was to "cross-examination which at times in this room has taken on the atmosphere of a prosecution." Specifically, Garrison objected to Robb's reading of "a scrap of a document" which, as Robb's use of the transcript of the Pash recording had shown, could easily contain error or be taken out of context. "This to me is rather elementary and not a technical matter."

Chairman Gray suggested that Robb go ahead and put his question about the unseen and secret memorandum he held in his hand, and if Garrison had any objection to the question, "I should like to hear from you." But this suggestion showed that Gray had missed Garrison's point, for without a chance to see and understand the entire document Garrison had no basis for knowing whether or not Robb's questions involved a distortion or some other basis for objection. Nevertheless, Garrison made no further protest, and Robb continued to probe the witness, Gordon Dean, with questions about the still-secret document.

Tuesday, April 20, proved to be the longest and most grueling day of the hearing. The morning began with a discussion of the schedule of witnesses. Garrison listed the twelve remaining witnesses he intended to call on Oppenheimer's behalf, and renewed his request to be told "who [the board's witnesses] are going to be." Chairman Gray sounded amenable. The board had reached no "final conclusion," but, he assured Garrison, "we will give you an indication." It was a pledge that was never carried out.

The day's first witness was George Frost Kennan, then a colleague of Oppenheimer's at the Institute in Princeton, but for many previous years the government's chief Kremlinologist, having been a member of the United States' first diplomatic mission to Moscow in 1933 and later American Ambassador there. Roger Robb asked, at the outset of his cross-examination, "Have you had much experience with Communists . . . are you familiar with Communist dogma or technique?"

"I think I am, sir," Kennan replied. "I have had about twenty years of reading the Soviet press. . . . I feel I have a certain familiarity with it."

Kennan told the board that in the years after the war he had been associated with Oppenheimer in the building of an Allied atomic strength that was clearly, he said, "not in the interests of the Soviet Union." Could Oppenheimer possibly have been "dissembling" in these anti-Russian efforts? Robb asked. ". . . You might just as well have asked Leonardo da Vinci to distort an anatomical drawing," Kennan replied, "as . . . ask Robert Oppenheimer to speak responsibly to the sort of questions we were talking about, and speak dishonestly."

In Chairman Gray's interrogation of Kennan, certain of his questions were as significant as the witness' answers. He asked, for example, about the "friends-versus-fatherland" loyalty conflict that seemed to concern him so deeply about Oppenheimer. Would Kennan think it "important," Gray asked, if there had been "continued association" with leftists "for whom [the individual] would have pity [and] conflicts of conscience"? Kennan balked at the absolutism that was implicit in Gray's question. Leaving aside *steady* associations with suspect persons, must all such friendships, he wondered, be automatically ruled out, whether or not they involve one's official duties? Must old friends be "abruptly or in a cruel way" rejected? Shouldn't people "in senior capacity in government . . . be permitted or conceded maturity of judgment" in their associations, or must there be "schoolboy" regulation of their friendships?

Just before Kennan left the witness chair, Gordon Gray asked a question that indicated high expectations of what the security-screening process could achieve. Kennan had referred to the "special problem" posed by "the really gifted and able people" who may not have led "fully conventional" lives but ones involving a "certain amount of trial and error," presumably including political trial and error. These observations prompted Gray to wonder whether such people could reach a point of "stability" where "there can be absolute predictability as to no further excursions." Kennan was skeptical. He would say only that there could be *enough* predictability about a gifted but unconventional person "to warrant his being accepted by the Government for public service."

Kennan was followed on the witness stand by David Lilienthal, whose testimony was interrupted by the appearance of James Bryant Conant. Since he was to be in the United States only briefly before returning to his post as U.S. High Commissioner for Germany, Conant was allowed to testify immediately. He lost no time in assailing the implication, in the Nichols letter of charges, that Oppenheimer's opposition to the H-bomb made him a security risk. If that were the case, Conant said, "it would apply to me, because I opposed it [the H-bomb] . . . as strongly as anybody else." More relevant to a security proceeding, Conant said, were Oppenheimer's early leftist affiliations, but these were more than offset by his manifold contributions to the building of American military strength against Russia.

Roger Robb, a graduate of Yale, rose for cross-examination and proceeded to lecture the former president of Harvard on the proper way to quote from a document such as the Nichols letter. Then he sought to cast doubt on Conant's judgment of Robert Oppenheimer, using a technique favored by lawyers arguing before a jury:

Q:  Of course, Doctor, you don't know what the testimony before this board has been?

A:  No, I don't.

Q: Nor do you know what the record or file before the board discloses?

A: No. I only know what is in the letter of General Nichols.

Robb's line of questioning apparently persuaded Gray, who explained to Conant that "we, you understand, have to take into account all the material . . . before us, perhaps some of which you are not at all familiar with." Ironically, Robb's question exposed precisely the core of the problem faced by Lloyd Garrison, excluded as he was from seeing three thousand pages of material possessed by the Gray Board.

Garrison, on redirect examination, sought to re-establish the authority of Conant's assessment. He led the witness to comment that his testimony was based not on mere conversations with Oppenheimer but on "having participated with him in what I believe to have been effective actions against the Soviet Union." But the ever-alert Robb promptly drew from Conant the concession that "as a scholar" Conant would have to agree that "any opinion or conclusion which is not based on all the [available] relevant facts . . . and . . . evidence might be fallible."

Following Conant, Enrico Fermi, the brilliant physicist who had fled Italy and had played a key role in American nuclear development, took the stand and testified briefly about the meetings the General Advisory Committee held in 1949 on the H-bomb and about the forgotten Seaborg letter.

Then David Lilienthal resumed the witness chair. Garrison's colleague Samuel Silverman led Lilienthal, too, through the events of those GAC meetings and then said he had no further questions. Robb observed it was already quarter to five and asked the board's pleasure. When Lilienthal said he would like to avoid testifying again the next day, the board agreed to hear him through and called a short recess.

Following the break, Garrison and Silverman were again required to leave the hearing room during the discussion of a classified document. This infuriated Lilienthal. "When I saw what they were doing to Oppenheimer, I was ready to throw chairs," he later recalled. "How can a lawyer defend his client's interests if he isn't even in the hearing room? There hadn't been a proceeding like this since the Spanish Inquisition."

In this frame of mind, David Lilienthal began his confrontation with Roger Robb. There quickly ensued one testy exchange with Robb, another with Gray. About six o'clock, in questioning Lilienthal about the AEC's clearance of Oppenheimer in 1947, Robb began to lay a trap:

Q:  Did you suggest to Mr. Clifford [Presidential Counsel Clark Clifford] that a special board be convened to review this [FBI] material [on Oppenheimer]?
A:  No, we did not.
Q:  Was that ever discussed with Mr. Clifford?
A:  No, I believe not.
Q:  Are you sure about that?
A:  I am not sure, but I have no recollection of it.

Robb left the trap set and, some twenty minutes later, began laying another. "Do you recall," he asked Lilienthal, "whether or not in March of 1947 you had at the AEC the old [wartime] Manhattan District files?" Lilienthal replied with assurance that the AEC was supposed to have them, under the presidential order transferring most Manhattan District property to the AEC.

Robb had his man cold. "Just so we can be clear about that," he said, "I have before me a memorandum dated March 12, 1947." The memorandum proved that the Manhattan District security files had gone not to the AEC but to the FBI. The embarrassed Lilienthal was forced to admit his memory had been faulty.

Robb bore in: "Do you think you ever saw the Manhattan District files, Mr. Lilienthal?"

"I am beginning to doubt it. . . ."

Robb now moved back to the matter of Clark Clifford and the 1947 proposal for a special board of review. "I have before me, *taken from the files*, the original of the [1947] memorandum . . . and I will read it to you." (Emphasis added.)

ROBB:  (*reading*) At 3 P.M. today [March 11], Dr. Bush and the Chairman . . . (*Looking up at Lilienthal*) That was you, wasn't it?

LILIENTHAL: Yes, sir.

ROBB: (*reading*) Dr. Bush and the Chairman met with Mr.
Clifford and . . . discussed with him the desirability of having a review of [the Oppenheimer] case by a board of distinguished jurists or other citizens.

Again Lilienthal had to admit the fragility of his memory.
Robb pressed on. Wouldn't Lilienthal agree that the idea of empaneling a special board to review the Oppenheimer file had
made sufficient sense that the AEC was prepared to recommend
it to the White House? "In other words," Robb asked, "you recommended in 1947 . . . the exact step which is now being taken
[i.e., the empaneling of the Gray Board] [which] did not strike
you as fantastic or unreasonable?" Lilienthal had to agree this
was so.

Robb read still another surprise document from the AEC files
to stimulate Lilienthal's recollection. It was a memorandum
that Lilienthal had dictated about another conversation he had
had with Clifford, this time on the telephone, concerning a special
board of review. By now, Lilienthal was aware of what had happened to him. Although there had been no hint from the AEC
that the files he had read the day before were incomplete, clearly
the crucial documents had been pulled from them, presumably
in the course of Robb's preparation for the Gray Board hearing.

As Robb began taxing Lilienthal for forgetting such a "matter
of grave import," Garrison stepped in to protest Robb's technique, already used devastatingly against Oppenheimer, of impelling witnesses to testify from sheer memory about long-past
events, while secretly holding in reserve memoranda containing
the facts about these events. This device, Garrison said, was
"designed to try to make the witness look to the board in as unfavorable a light as possible, and to make what is a lapse of
memory seem like a deliberate falsification." Recalling Gray's
statement that this was to be "an inquiry, not a trial," Garrison
also observed that this "surprise production of documents . . .
seems to me more like a criminal trial than it does like an inquiry.
. . ." Robb protested indignantly that his "professional integrity
and . . . methods" were being questioned and that his use of
"orthodox, entirely proper and entirely legitimate" methods of

cross-examination had proved Lilienthal's memory "was not infallible." Lilienthal interjected that he would "be the first to insist on that. I am a little confused about the technique," he said. "The board wants the facts, and the facts are in the file, and I asked for the file . . . and it was denied me."

Gray's response did not betray any concern about Robb's technique of producing surprise documents, for he made no comment whatever about that. His remarks did, however, contain a clue as to why Robb had laid such heavy emphasis on Lilienthal's attitude in 1947 about having an inquiry on Oppenheimer. What really seemed to be on Gray's mind, judging from his comments, was the public disparagement of his board's hearing. This had arisen, Gray felt, largely because of the attention paid to a detailed account in the *New York Times* of Oppenheimer's clearance by the AEC in 1947, "the information for which was furnished by [Garrison]," he observed, with seeming bitterness. In the "general and public discussions" of the Oppenheimer case, Gray observed, "it is repeatedly and publicly stated that the Commission and others cleared Oppenheimer at the time, [and] that these [the AEC charges being considered by the Gray Board] were old charges rehashed, and completely considered and evaluated at the time." Against the background of this public discussion, Gray concluded, it "does seem important to me to find out exactly what did take place [in 1947]."

Garrison agreed enthusiastically. But, he said, a "shorter" and "fairer" way of accomplishing this, where documentary evidence existed, would be to "introduce that evidence straightaway," instead of entrapping a witness "by first asking him about things he doesn't remember."

At this point, before the chairman could make any further comment, Robb interrupted. "May I proceed? I have two more questions."

Gray inquired whether Robb intended to "confront the witness with any more documents," but according to the record, Robb acted as if the chairman had not even spoken, for without answering Gray's inquiry, he proceeded with his questioning of the witness. Thus, apparently by sheer assertiveness, Robb had avoided any ruling from the chair on Lloyd Garrison's objection. Since this meant, in effect, that Garrison's protest had been overruled, Robb had pre-empted a power that belonged not to the prosecuting attorney but to the judge. His tactic having evoked no objection, either from Gray or from Garrison, Robb was encouraged to try it again several times in the proceeding, and he got away with it each time.

A half-hour later, at 7:45,* the longest day of the hearing came to an end. To Lloyd Garrison and his colleagues, this day had also been the harshest yet. They had once again been required, for reasons of secrecy, to quit the hearing room, leaving their client temporarily undefended. Chairman Gray had permitted Robb to deal with a former senior official of the United States Government after the manner of a county prosecutor cornering a petty thief.† It was just this sort of tactic that Joseph Volpe, two nights earlier at the home of Randolph Paul, had urged be the trigger for Oppenheimer and Garrison to walk out of the hearing in protest. But the Volpe view did not prevail.

When the hearing reconvened the next morning, a salty Maine Republican was called to the witness chair: Sumner Pike, one of the three Atomic Energy Commissioners who had opposed the H-bomb in 1949. One of the reasons Pike had been cool to a crash program for the H-bomb, he said, was that no one had asserted that there was a *military* need for so enormous a weapon. This statement prompted Gordon Gray to ask, "Do you think it is possible that a military need had not been expressed . . . [in 1949] because the military did not have any reason to believe that it [an H-bomb] was feasible?"

Gray appears to have based his question on what John Walker had learned, upon joining the Joint Committee staff in 1951,‡ namely that Robert Oppenheimer had dissuaded the Pentagon from claiming a military need for the H-bomb by advising the Pentagon it was *not technically feasible,* and then, later the same

---

* Years later, Lilienthal felt he had made a mistake in asking that his testimony be crowded into that one day, for as the hearing dragged into the dinner hour, "everyone got edgy and I myself got awfully tired."

† Gray himself had gone so far as to suggest that the former AEC Chairman was guilty of "perjury"—a grave charge indeed, especially since the matter to which Gray was referring involved an inconsequential contradiction in Lilienthal's testimony.

‡ See p. 181.

day, telling the AEC there was no urgent need to press forward on the H-bomb inasmuch as the Pentagon had expressed no military need for it. If that report was indeed what had prompted Gray's question, the incident symbolized what Lloyd Garrison most feared from the absence of the "blank pad rule" and the presence of the black dossiers: that the judges might be seriously disturbed about some "fact" that Garrison could neither know of nor rebut.

In the cross-examination of Garrison's next witness, Harvard physicist and former Los Alamosite Norman Ramsey, Robb developed a discussion of over-all defense strategy and the allocation of Air Force funds as between the Strategic Air Command, on the one hand, and the tactical forces and air defense, on the other. These questions may have been of intense interest to the more zealous of the H-bomb advocates within the Air Force—who strongly supported SAC and were extremely critical of Oppenheimer—but they had not been mentioned in the AEC's letter of charges. Garrison interrupted in his gingerly way: "Mr. Chairman, I don't want to shut off discussion, and this is all very interesting, but is it relevant to the problem before the board?"

This was to be another of those occasions upon which Robb pre-empted the chairman's authority to rule on Garrison's question. Charging in before Gray could utter a word, Robb observed that *he* had considered the question relevant or he "would not have gone into it," and then he pressed on with his questions as if Garrison had not even spoken. Once again, both Gray and Garrison silently acquiesced.

Garrison's failure to pursue his objection and to insist that the hearing confine itself to the matters contained in the original letter of charges significantly altered the nature of the hearing, for it allowed Robb's witnesses to voice the whole range of Air Force suspicions of Oppenheimer, especially those concerning the so-called "ZORC" quadrumvirate. These matters dealt largely, if not wholly, with Oppenheimer's *policy* differences with the SAC partisans within the Air Force—of considerably greater relevance to Oppenheimer's loyalty to the Air Force than to the United States of America.

Gordon Gray may also have had reason to regret his silent

assent to Robb's excursions beyond the boundaries of the Nichols letter of charges, for he frequently expressed irritation at minor delays and prolongations of the hearing. This failure to restrict Robb added measurably to the length of the proceeding, so extensive was the testimony on such policy matters as "ZORC," the Vista report, the second-laboratory issue and continental defense.

Why did Lloyd Garrison fail to object more strenuously to Robb's forays into irrelevant policy matters? His explanation again illustrates the cruelty of the dilemma he faced in having so large a portion of the evidence hidden from him. "I think our feeling," Garrison has written, "was that since all such matters [as Vista, etc.] were undoubtedly in the Board members' secret dossier and had been read by them, the more they were brought to the surface and answered, the better. Had we been before a jury, who would have knowledge only of what was presented to them in open court, the case would have been quite different."

The final witness that day—Nobel laureate Isidor Isaac Rabi, a long-time friend of Oppenheimer's—pleaded with the Gray Board to consider Oppenheimer's past actions in three broad contexts.

First, Rabi asked the board to bear in mind the times in which these actions occurred. For example, while an approach concerning Soviet espionage would be "horrifying" in 1954, a similar overture in 1943—a time of alliance with Russia and years before the emergence of the Cold War—would not, in Rabi's view, have merited anything more than throwing the man out of the house (that is, would not necessarily have required reporting him to authorities).

Second, Rabi said, Oppenheimer's behavior should be judged against his contributions to the national interest. Here Rabi was at his most graphic:

> There is a real, positive record. . . . We have an A-bomb and a whole series of [them]. . . . What more do you want, mermaids? This is just a tremendous achievement. If the end of that road is this kind of hearing, [I think it is] a pretty bad show.

Third, Rabi urged that Robert Oppenheimer be judged against the background of his whole life, and not merely against selected and isolated incidents. Robb, using his customary technique, had suggested that Rabi's judgment, especially about the Chevalier incident, might be fallible because "perhaps the board may be in possession of information which is not now available to you. . . ." Rabi acknowledged this might be true. "On the other hand," he said, "I am in possession of a long experience with this man, going back to 1929, which is 25 years." Any individual incident in a man's life, such as the Chevalier affair, he said, must be taken "in sum."

> That is what novels are about. There is a dramatic moment in the history of the man, what made him act, what he did, and what sort of person he was. That is what you are really doing here. You are writing a man's life.

Late one afternoon, in the course of the Gray Board hearing, Robert Oppenheimer had a fleeting encounter with a face from his distant past—with a man who had played a minor, though not insignificant, role in the events being recounted in the hearing. The man was Lyall Johnson, the Manhattan Project security officer on the Berkeley campus to whom Oppenheimer had first casually mentioned the "Chevalier incident" and who had arranged Oppenheimer's tape-recorded confrontation with Boris Pash.

Johnson had, after the war, joined the Atomic Energy Commission. His offices were on the second floor of Building T-3 in Washington. At five o'clock one afternoon in the spring of 1954, he was hurrying out to meet the other members of his car pool when he saw a familiar figure in the doorway of the reception room of Room 2022. They were no more than ten feet apart when their eyes met. Oppenheimer's seemed to have a searching "Where-have-I-seen-you-before?" look. Johnson, as he passed, said, "How are you, Dr. Oppenheimer?" The scientist merely nodded a greeting, but Johnson had the feeling that Oppenheimer had, however vaguely, made the connection between him, Lyall Johnson, and the proceeding taking place in Room 2022.

Thursday, April 22, 1954.

On Capitol Hill, under bright klieg lights and before a nation-wide television audience, the Army-McCarthy hearings began. The setting was the cavernous Caucus Room of the Senate Office Building—the same room in which, five years earlier, Robert Oppenheimer had publicly ridiculed Lewis L. Strauss and thus deeply enraged the man who was now Chairman of the AEC.

Sixteen blocks away, in Building T-3 of the Atomic Energy Commission, with no klieg lights or TV cameras, the Gray Board began the ninth day of its hearing "in the matter of J. Robert Oppenheimer."

As the hearing began, at 9:30 that morning, Oppenheimer was in his accustomed spot, on the sofa behind the witness chair. He would be there until 6:10 that evening. It was no different from any of the other days of the Gray Board hearing, yet this was far from an ordinary day in his life. It was Robert Oppenheimer's fiftieth birthday.

Among those who observed the event was Haakon Chevalier, who, unaware of his friend's ordeal, sent a postcard expressing warm wishes for his birthday, for springtime and for Oppenheimer's future.

Is there such a thing as redemption? Can a sin ever be erased, a sinner ever be rehabilitated? These were questions that seemed to preoccupy Gordon Gray throughout the Oppenheimer hearing, but especially in his interrogation, that day, of Hartley Rowe. A vice president of the United Fruit Company who had been a member of the General Advisory Committee in 1949 during its deliberations on the H-bomb, Rowe had testified that he had "no reservation whatever" about Robert Oppenheimer's loyalty. But, wondered Gray, suppose Rowe were convinced that the government's charges about the scientist's involvement with the radical left were true—would his testimony still be the same?

No, Rowe replied, not merely the same: "I would make it just that much stronger," because "I think a man of Dr. Oppenheimer's character is not going to make the same mistake twice. I would say he was all the more trustworthy for the mistakes he made."

Gordon Gray was not satisfied. Was Rowe saying that an ex-

Communist or fellow traveler might have "so completely renounced that that he would not be a security risk in later years?" "Yes, sir; that is what I am trying to say," replied Rowe.

Gray posed the question in still a third form, in a manner that indicated his skepticism about the chances of so complete a "rehabilitation": "You would urge that the Government . . . take *whatever chance there was* . . . with an individual who might have had these associations and who apparently had renounced them?" [Emphasis added.]

Rowe replied that "in a great many instances [a] man would be a better risk knowing more about the Communistic [*sic*] Party."

Perhaps Gray's difficulty in accepting Rowe's viewpoint sprang in part from their different perceptions about the change in political climate since the late Thirties and early Forties. Gray's comments indicated an assumption that in order not to be a security risk, a former Communist or fellow traveler of the Thirties would have to undergo a transformation of personal viewpoint so radical as to strain credulity. But as Hartley Rowe and other pro-Oppenheimer witnesses saw it, the very change in political atmosphere since the Depression could in itself bring about a change of viewpoint, without any miraculous "rehabilitation." Even to businessman Rowe, the radicalism of the Thirties was entirely understandable (he recalled that one characteristic suggestion for solving the unemployment problem in the Depression had been to "arm every other man with a pistol and let him go out and shoot one man, and that would cure the unemployment in very short order"). But Gray seemed to lack Rowe's capacity to project himself back into that desperate atmosphere.

Witness after witness took the stand, and their testimony followed a pattern: each would tell why he was convinced Robert Oppenheimer could be no less than totally loyal to his country. Then Robb, or perhaps Gray, would cite the Chevalier incident or some other Oppenheimer misdeed and ask if this didn't shake the witness' conviction. To this the reply would usually be in the negative; both the times and Robert Oppenheimer had changed, they would say.

There began to be signs that this latter mode of argument

disturbed Gordon Gray. He was dismayed that the witnesses could so casually forgive such transgressions as lying to security officers. To Gray, they were implying that their knowledge of Oppenheimer's achievements "washes out anything that happened in the past." Some witnesses, he commented, "in effect have said, 'I know this man to be loyal; clear him.'"

Almost plaintively he observed that "there is substantial and widespread ignorance about . . . the requirements of the law in these cases," and one could not simply dismiss, out of impatience, the AEC's "procedures and regulations, and things of that sort."

At times Gray seemed to treat these "procedures and regulations" as if they were graven on stone tablets: immutable edicts rather than guidelines for common-sense decision-making. One instance occurred during his questioning of Harry A. Winne, a General Electric official who had known Oppenheimer in the days of the Acheson-Lilienthal report. Gray read to Winne some of the AEC's criteria of what constituted a security risk, one of which involved "the individual or his spouse" having been members of subversive organizations. Hadn't that criterion been met in the Oppenheimer case? Gray asked. Winne promptly completed Gray's line of argument: Since Kitty Oppenheimer had been a member of the Communist Party, he said, "taking the strictly legal interpretation, perhaps you have no alternative there." But Gray had drawn Winne into error. For although Kitty Oppenheimer's past Communist membership *permitted* the Gray Board to conclude that her husband was a security risk, the AEC regulations by no means made such a finding *mandatory,* as Gray seemed disposed to believe.

Gray also tended to treat the AEC regulations as a shield against the criticism of witnesses who felt it absurd to accuse Robert Oppenheimer of being disloyal to his country. For example, when Vannevar Bush found fault with the wording of the Nichols letter of charges, Gray retorted that the Nichols letter had been written according to procedures established under the Atomic Energy Act of 1946—procedures which, Gray declared, "have the effect of law."

Similarly, when John J. McCloy seemed to disparage the security case against Oppenheimer, Gray asked, "When the paramount concern is the security of the country, *which I believe is substantially the language of the Atomic Energy Act,* can you allow yourself to entertain reasonable doubts?" (Emphasis added.)

The implication of Gray's comments and questions was that since some of Oppenheimer's actions and associations seemed to fit the AEC's criteria for judging a man a security risk, the Gray Board had no choice but to find him a security risk. It was as if Gray were saying to his critics, "If we find against Oppenheimer, don't blame us; we are the helpless prisoners of laws and regulations handed to us."

Lloyd Garrison saw clearly the attitude reflected in Gray's questions. He sought to counter it by citing a section of the regulations that Gray had not invoked—especially one provision that stated: "The decision as to security clearance is an overall common-sense judgment, made after consideration of all the relevant information. . . ."

But Gordon Gray apparently was not disposed to hear Garrison's argument. The board's fifteen-thousand-word verdict declared that it had not been "allowed to exercise mature, practical judgment without the rigid circumscription of regulations and criteria established for us."

On Friday, April 23, two important controversies took place in Room 2022.

The first was over the matter of witness lists. Lloyd Garrison, having long since disclosed the names of his witnesses, for the third time made his request for a reciprocal disclosure by Robb. Garrison pointed out that knowing whom Garrison was going to call had allowed Robb to make "substantial preparations" for his cross-examinations. Indeed, there had been evidence just the day before of the extent of Roger Robb's preparations. When Lee DuBridge, president of Caltech, had testified, Robb was instantly able to question him on the basis of a top-secret memorandum about what had transpired at a 1952 luncheon that DuBridge had attended in a private home in Washington.* Robb also had at hand newspaper clippings on a recent Washington gathering, also involving DuBridge, for the purpose of raising funds for

* See p. 189.

Robert Oppenheimer's defense. And there were hints in Robb's questions that he was well briefed on some telephone conversations between DuBridge and Oppenheimer in the weeks preceding the Gray Board hearing.

Robb, however, denied he had gained any special advantage from his knowledge of the pro-Oppenheimer witness list. "In the case of almost all of the witnesses," he said, "my only advance preparation for cross-examination was a thorough knowledge of this case." If this was so, it was a nonadvantage he seemed bent on denying his adversary, for he announced that "unless ordered to do so by the board, we shall not disclose to Mr. Garrison in advance the names of the witnesses we contemplate calling." Why? Because the "names of the witnesses would leak"— just as the Nichols letter and Oppenheimer reply had found their way into the *New York Times*, Robb said pointedly—and "witnesses from the scientific world . . . would be subject to pressure" from "friends and colleagues" as to "what they should or should not say." But if this was Robb's sole motivation, he nevertheless had refused to tell Garrison whether or not he was planning to call Mr. and Mrs. Paul Crouch, who would hardly have been subject to "pressure" from physicists. Moreover, three of Robb's eight witnesses were not from "the scientific world."

In this instance, Chairman Gray did exercise his power as chairman and did make a ruling—in favor of Roger Robb. In explaining his ruling, Gray stripped the Oppenheimer proceeding of any pretense of being "an inquiry and not a trial" and exposed its true character: that of a courtroom adversary proceeding.

Had this been an ordinary security hearing, or "inquiry," the atmosphere would have been far less formal and combative. There would not have been anyone acting in the role of prosecuting attorney and presenting "the government's case" against the applicant, since investigative files were usually far smaller and panel members, having read the file, ordinarily relied on the hearing itself primarily to receive any rebuttal the applicant might have wished to offer to the "charges" against him. It would have been unlikely that a government attorney would be on hand, but even if there had been one, his activity would have been restricted. AEC regulations define his role as merely that of "assist[ing] the board in such manner as to bring out a full and complete disclosure of all [relevant] facts. . . ." Such a person would definitely not have been authorized to call witnesses, a function reserved to (and only rarely used by) the hearing boards themselves.

But as Chairman Gray now proceeded to outline it, the proceeding against J. Robert Oppenheimer would differ sharply from the ordinary security proceeding. The anti-Oppenheimer witnesses, he said, would be called, not by the board, but by Robb, whom Gray now characterized as "the attorney for the Atomic Energy Commission" (rather than as "counsel for the board," as Gray had called him at the outset of the hearing). Gray's new description more closely approximated Robb's actual role in the hearing: the presenter of the *government's* case against Oppenheimer.* (In fact, at one juncture, Gray referred to Robb as "the representative of the government in this case.") Gray reinforced this characterization in explaining why Robb, and not the board, would be calling the adverse witnesses. "I am very anxious," he observed, "that it not appear that this board has called any witness as a board witness who had come here in a sense *on behalf of prosecution*." (Emphasis added.)

As in other instances, Gray did not meet Lloyd Garrison's central objection† but dealt instead with the danger that Garrison might be disadvantaged by testimony "in the nature of surprise." If that occurred, Gray said, Garrison should advise the board. Yet, judging from the embarrassment already suffered by Oppenheimer, David Lilienthal and other witnesses as a result of Robb's "surprise" tactics, any *ex post facto* complaint by Garrison would come too late to undo the worst of the damage. Moreover, if there were, as Gray said, a danger to Oppenheimer from surprise testimony, could not Gray have minimized the risk by letting Garrison know who Robb's witnesses were to be?

* This was consonant with Robb's view that his role was prosecutorial. He later said that Oppenheimer's lawyers "were there to introduce all the favorable things about him and my job was to bring out the evidence on the other side."

† That Garrison needed Robb's witness list not only to prepare for those who would appear, but to avoid the needless labor of engaging in extensive research on potential witnesses (such as Paul Crouch) who would *not* be called.

There was an interchange, too, about Roger Robb's tactic of *first* testing a witness' unaided memory and *then* producing a document demonstrating the fallibility of that memory. Garrison protested that this tactic, designed to make "the witness appear in as poor light as possible," was "not in keeping with the spirit of the regulations," which specifically enjoined interrogators in security proceedings to "avoid the attitude of a prosecutor." Gray replied that all the members of the Gray Board had, with but one exception, been present during every moment of the hearing, had a "very vivid recollection of the circumstances under which the testimony was given," and would take this into account in rendering a judgment. Not only did this bypass Garrison's point about Robb's tactics conflicting with AEC regulations; it also failed to deal with the fact that after the Gray Board had ruled, General Nichols and the five members of the Atomic Energy Commission would also be judging Robert Oppenheimer; they would judge him, in part, on the basis of the Gray Board proceedings but *without* benefit of having viewed at first hand "the circumstances under which testimony was given." And, indeed, as it developed, these judges did concern themselves greatly with the matter of Oppenheimer's veracity— largely on the basis of testimony adduced by Robb's tactics.

Following Gray's ruling on the witness-list question, the board faced its most outspoken critic to date: Vannevar Bush, leader of the nation's scientific mobilization effort during World War II. Bush minced no words in saying that he felt "this board has made a mistake . . . a serious one," that of accepting, as one of the AEC's "security-risk" charges, Oppenheimer's opposition to the hydrogen bomb. The inclusion of this, said Bush, made the AEC's letter of charges

quite capable of being interpreted as placing a man on trial because he held opinions, which is quite contrary to the American system. . . . And as I move about I find . . . discussed today very energetically, that here is a man who is being pilloried because he had strong opinions, and had the temerity to express them. If this country ever gets . . . that near to the Russian system, we are certainly not in any condition to attempt to lead the free world toward the benefits of democracy. Now, if I had been on this board, I most certainly would have refused to entertain a set of charges that could possibly be thus interpreted.

Bush made clear that if the Nichols letter had accused Oppenheimer of "improper motivation" in his advice on the H-bomb, based on "allegiance to another system than that of his own country," he would have interposed no objection. But, he said, the letter contained no such suggestion.

Gordon Gray's comment was characteristically tangential. After all, said Gray, the Nichols letter had been made public by Lloyd Garrison—so "I don't think you can blame the board." But then Bush pointed out that even if the charges could have been kept secret forever, this would not have changed the substance either of the Nichols letter or of Bush's complaint about it, which he summarized, a few minutes later, in his typically salty way:

> I think . . . no board should ever [decide] whether a man should serve his country or not because he expressed strong opinions. If you want to try that case, you can try me. I have expressed strong opinions many times. They have been unpopular opinions at times. When a man is pilloried for doing that, this country is in a severe state.

Bush's criticism of the Gray Board had even greater validity than he was aware, barred as he was from knowledge of any but his own part of the proceeding. For not only had the board members failed to object to the nature of the H-bomb charge in the Nichols letter; they had accepted the notion that Oppenheimer's *policy* views on the H-bomb and other matters of U.S. Air Force concern were relevant to their hearing. The board uncomplainingly heard voluminous testimony about the Vista report, the "second-lab" issue, the Lincoln Summer Study and the whole continental defense question—testimony that dealt largely if not wholly with Oppenheimer's substantive beliefs and not with his motives.

On the H-bomb issue itself, for example, the board's interest in Oppenheimer's policy views is typified in this question to former AEC Weapons Chief James McCormack: "Did you feel at the time that perhaps the GAC might . . . have recommended more of an effort than [its] action of October 1949 seemed to you to suggest?"

An onlooker might have expected Lloyd Garrison to be grateful to Vannevar Bush for coming so strongly to Robert Oppenheimer's defense, and for trying to persuade the Gray Board to confine its consideration of the H-bomb question to the matter of Oppenheimer's *motives*. But Garrison's reaction reflected anything but gratitude. On the contrary, even as Bush sat in the witness chair, a few feet away, Garrison pointedly dissociated himself from Bush's testimony. He wished to "leave no misunderstanding," he said, ". . . that we share [Bush's] view that this board should not have served when asked . . . under the letter [of charges] as written."

# 3. *The Third Week*

As the hearing went into its third week, Garrison called to the stand a Caltech physics professor and onetime Los Alamosite named Robert F. Bacher. Bacher testified that during World War II he had interviewed physicist Philip Morrison about joining the Los Alamos staff. Since Morrison had acknowledged having been a member of the Communist Party before the war, Gray wanted to know whether Bacher had been aware of this at the time Morrison came to Los Alamos. No, Bacher replied; in fact, he said, he had been surprised when he later learned that Morrison had been a Communist.

This prompted Gray to ask, in apparent surprise, "When you interviewed people for the laboratory, this kind of question [about political connections] was not asked?" To this Bacher replied:

> No, I had no relation to that. Any interview by a scientific person was concerned entirely with the question of whether that man would be an appropriate addition to the laboratory on scientific and technical grounds. The question of whether he came to the laboratory or not was left to the security office to pass on.

Gray's question clearly was based on 1954 attitudes about the danger of Communists and the importance of "security"; it once again revealed how little he was inclined to project himself backward in time to 1944, when Russia was a gallant ally, when the Cold War had scarcely been hinted at, when American left-wingers were not under widespread suspicion, and when secrecy and "security" were unfamiliar concepts to most Americans. Further, Gray evidently expected that the atomic scientists in their headlong quest for the bomb should simultaneously have acted as assistant security officers, in effect, constantly on the lookout for signs that their colleagues were disloyal or had held radical political views. If that was Gray's belief, as his question strongly indicated, it would have been easy for him to hold Oppenheimer responsible for the presence of former Communists and fellow travelers at Los Alamos, as alleged by the AEC.

At one point, Roger Robb's questioning of Robert Bacher offered a glimpse into the secret Oppenheimer dossier and gave a sample of the kind of material buried therein. The sample consisted of a memorandum extracted from the AEC files, entitled "Analysis of Report on J. Robert Oppenheimer" and dated March 17, 1947.* It began with this statement: "It is known . . . that subject [Oppenheimer] was *responsible for* the employment on the project at Los Alamos of a number of persons . . . *known to be either Communists or active Communist sympathizers.*" (Emphasis added.)

If this memorandum was typical of the rest of the investigative dossier (and those familiar with such files say it almost surely was), its use by the Gray Board points up one acute disadvantage suffered by "defendants" in security-risk proceedings, compared with those on trial in courts of law. For, as Chairman Gray pointed out, the memorandum was "unsigned . . . and with no identification as to its author." A court of law would have ruled such a memorandum inadmissible as evidence—as "hearsay." In fact, the Supreme Court later ruled against the use of anonymous documents in security-risk proceedings. But this memo did not even pretend to be a firsthand report about Oppenheimer, but was merely a digest of a number of other reports; thus it constituted, in effect, double hearsay. Left unanswered (and unanswerable, since none of those involved could be called as witnesses and subjected to cross-examination) were questions such as these: Did the original reports which this analysis was summarizing represent accurate perceptions or recollections about Oppenheimer? Even if so, did the analysis itself represent an accurate summary of the original reports? Did it constitute a fair summary of the entire Oppenheimer file, digesting the favorable as well as the unfavorable information about the scientist?

If the author of the analysis had been called as a witness in the Oppenheimer hearing, he could have been questioned sharply on various parts of the opening sentence quoted above.

* The date indicated that the "analysis" was made in the course of the AEC's consideration of Oppenheimer's clearance.

What was meant by the allegation that Oppenheimer was "responsible for" the employment of the relevant persons at Los Alamos? In what way "responsible"? Did he recruit them directly? Was he legally responsible for their security investigation and appraisal? What was the basis for the phrase "persons . . . known to be either Communists or active Communist sympathizers"? Wasn't that a conclusion rather than a fact? If so, a defense counsel in a court of law could have objected to such a statement by a witness and had it stricken from the record.

Of course, Garrison and his associates could not subject the memorandum to that sort of challenge. Nonetheless, this analysis and undoubtedly many others like it reposed among the three thousand pages of unseen evidence considered by the Gray Board members in judging Robert Oppenheimer.

Among the supposed "Communists or Communist sympathizers" referred to in the analysis were Robert Serber and his wife, Charlotte, whom Oppenheimer had recruited to come to Los Alamos, he as a physicist (he had been one of Oppenheimer's prize students at Berkeley), she as a librarian. The unsigned analysis had this to say about the Serbers:

> . . . It is known that Charlotte Serber's family is prominent in Communist Party ranks in Philadelphia, Pa.; that she herself was *probably* a party member and *possibly* a member of the Comintern, and that she has always been active in radical activities and front organizations wherever she has lived. Her husband, Robert Serber, *perhaps* under her influence, has been active in the same circles since he married her, although there is *no conclusive evidence* that he is a party member. . . . It is known that [Robert Serber and other Oppenheimer students], *perhaps* influenced by subject [Oppenheimer], were extremely active in Communist activities on the campus at Berkeley. . . . When . . . the Serbers were employed at Los Alamos by [Oppenheimer] . . . all of these people were very close personally to subject and *there is little room to doubt* that he was aware of their sympathies and activities. [Emphasis added.]*

---

* The analysis ended on quite a different note: "In evaluating this information, it must be kept in mind that . . . *Serber [was] technically very well*

Roger Robb handed a copy of this analysis to witness Bacher and then began to ask him questions. Hadn't Bacher given the board a judgment that Robert Oppenheimer was not a security risk? Yes. Was Bacher qualified to give such an opinion? Yes, Bacher thought he was. Well, then, surely he was qualified to give a similar opinion regarding Charlotte Serber, assuming the facts in the analysis to be true. Garrison protested: it was "misleading," he said, to make an analogy between Bacher's opinion of Dr. Oppenheimer, "based on many long years of intimate association in Government work," and an opinion on Charlotte Serber that Bacher would base "on a hypothetical set of facts."

Without waiting for Gordon Gray to rule on Garrison's objection, Robb continued to press Bacher until he extracted the reply that Charlotte Serber should not have been cleared for Los Alamos, assuming the facts in the analysis were true.

But Bacher entered a crucial demurrer. In order to give proper judgment, he said, "I think you need all the facts and not just what you have given me" in the analysis. The comment was entirely consonant with the AEC security regulations, which called for hearing boards to make their decisions on the basis of *all* the evidence.* Yet, despite this specific requirement, Robb had insisted that Bacher, posing as a hearing board, render a judgment solely on the basis of certain items extracted selectively from an unsigned memorandum found in the AEC files.

One fact that Robb had failed to disclose to Bacher was that some time after the memorandum was written, a distinguished hearing board, chaired by the retired admiral, Chester Nimitz, *had* considered "all the factors" concerning Robert Serber, and had voted to grant him one of the jealously-guarded "Q" clearances.

On the afternoon of Tuesday, April 27—the twelfth day of the hearing—there began the portion of the proceeding for which there was neither precedent in AEC security hearings nor provision in AEC regulations: the presentation of "the government's

---

*qualified for the work for which subject wanted* [him], despite [his] youth. . . . Serber . . . is highly regarded." [Emphasis added.]

* "The Board shall carefully consider all material before it . . . and shall render an opinion only after considering all the factors."

case" through witnesses called by a "representative of the government."

The first of these witnesses was Wendell Mitchell Latimer, chairman of the chemistry department at Berkeley and an active associate of Ernest Lawrence's at the Berkeley Radiation Laboratory during the war. Latimer's official connection with the atomic energy program had ceased when the war ended, but this did not prevent him from testifying in the most definite—and, some might say, hyperbolic—terms about what he termed U.S. "thumb-twiddling" in the atomic field in postwar years. Said Latimer:

In the period between 1945 and 1949, we didn't get anywhere in our atomic energy program in any direction. We didn't expand our production of uranium much. We didn't really get going on any reactor program. We didn't expand to an appreciable extent our production of fissionable material. We just seemed to be sitting by and doing nothing.*

Latimer also spoke of Robert Oppenheimer's "amazing" persuasiveness, which, he said, had played a key role in bringing about this supposed standstill. Latimer found evidence of this "amazing" influence in the "mystifying" moral opposition of many scientists to the H-bomb program; in the number of Los Alamos scientists who returned to Berkeley as pacifists, which Latimer "judged" was "due very largely to [Oppenheimer's] influence"; in what Latimer termed Oppenheimer's "complete domination" of the General Advisory Committee; and in "the fact that [Oppenheimer] wanted to disband Los Alamos" after the war. "All these things seemed to fit together to give a certain

* The AEC has subsequently said, in answer to an inquiry about Latimer's statements, that: (a) due to improvements in technology, the 1947–49 production of uranium 235 expanded beyond AEC expectations (and even tended to disrupt the balance between uranium and plutonium production); (b) improvements in the making of plutonium succeeded in raising the output of plutonium "substantially" in the 1947–49 period; and (c) three new plutonium reactors were authorized for construction in that period (although they did not become operational until after 1949). The AEC acknowledges that reactor development in the 1947–49 period was not substantial, but attributes this in large part to "the very primitive state of reactor technology," to "the very limited amount of uranium ore known to exist at that time," and to the "absence of clear goals" for the reactor program after the war.

pattern to his philosophy. . . . All his reactions were such as to give me considerable worry about his judgment as a security risk."

Robb completed his interrogation of Latimer, and turned him over to Garrison's partner, Samuel Silverman, for questioning. Since Gray had let Robb withhold his witness list, Silverman had had no opportunity to prepare his cross-examination. He asked for five minutes to confer with his colleagues and his client and to ready his questions. This was a courtesy that any court of law would have granted him almost automatically, and did not seem to him an excessive request. But Gray did not, apparently, see it that way. "Was there anything said you didn't hear, Mr. Silverman?" he asked. No, replied Silverman. "I think we might as well proceed" without the recess, said Gray. Silverman and Garrison yielded without further protest. "I don't press the point particularly," said Silverman.

The bulk of his cross-examination was devoted to trying to establish just how Wendell Latimer had come into possession of the knowledge on which he based his remarkably positive assertions. In the course of the next hour, the following exchanges occurred (emphasis added throughout):

*Regarding Oppenheimer's "amazing" influence over other people:*

Q:  I am trying to arrive on what you base these personal opinions . . . to what extent objective facts—

A:  I had studied this influence that Dr. Oppenheimer had over men. It was a tremendous thing.

Q:  When did you study this influence?

A:  All during the war and after the war. He is such an amazing man that one couldn't help but try to put together some picture.

Q:  Tell us about these studies that you made. . . .

A:  He has been a most interesting study for years. Unconsciously, I think one tries to put together the elements in a man that make him tick—where this influence comes from, what factors in his personality that give him this tremendous influence. I am not a psychoanalyst. I can't give you how my picture of this thing was developed but to me it was an amazing study just thinking about these factors.

*Regarding Oppenheimer's influence over General Groves:*

Q: You think that General Groves was under Dr. Oppenheimer's influence?

A: Oh, very definitely. . . .

Q: On what do you base [that] judgment . . . ?

A: . . . The statements that I have heard attributed to [Groves] . . . [he] seemed to be following the Oppenheimer line. . . . He was so dependent upon [Oppenheimer's] judgment that I think it is reasonable to conclude that most of his ideas were coming from Dr. Oppenheimer.

Q: How do you know he was so dependent?

A: I don't. I don't know, but I have seen the thing operate.

*Regarding U.S. "thumb-twiddling" and lack of atomic progress:*

Q: Do you know whether there was a sizable growth in the stockpile of fissionable material and of atomic weapons in the period of 1947 to 1950? . . .

A: Those figures are confidential and *I don't have access to them,* but *knowing in general* about what the production capacities were, *one could conclude* that the normal production went on, but there was no reasonable expansion of the program.

Q: And on what do you base your conclusion that there was no reasonable expansion of the program?

A: None of my friends disappeared to work on projects anywhere. If there were any such projects set up, they were kept awfully secret to me.

*Regarding Robert Oppenheimer's wish to "disband" Los Alamos:*

Q: I think you said that Dr. Oppenheimer wanted to disband Los Alamos [after the war]?

A: As I recall it, it was essentially that. . . .

Q: How do you know that he wanted to disband Los Alamos?

A: That impression was built quite a number of years ago, and I am not sure that I remember all the details that went into my knowledge, but it was correct, wasn't it? . . .

Q: Was one of the details that went into your knowledge of Dr. Oppenheimer's decision a conversation with Dr. Oppenheimer on this point?

A: No.

*Regarding the 1949 GAC anti-H-bomb report and Oppenheimer's role in it:*

Q: You don't know now whether you have ever read the GAC 1949 report, or do you?

A: I don't recall. I have talked to a good many men who have seen it. . . . Whether I read it or not, I don't recall, but the essence of it was obvious.

Q: Do you know whether these reasons you have given were stated in the 1949 report of the GAC?

A: I can't at this moment say definitely, but they were, as I recall, approximately the arguments given. . . .

Q: Do you know what the reasons that were given in the GAC report were?

A: I can't at the moment quote the reasons given, but the intent of the report was obvious. . . .

Q: I think you said that you judged that the source of the opposition to the hydrogen bomb [in the GAC] . . . was Dr. Oppenheimer.

A: That is right.

Q: Would you tell us on what you based that judgment?

A: As chairman of the Committee he wrote all the Committee reports, and the decisions became pretty apparent. . . . Surely nobody could conclude it wasn't largely Dr. Oppenheimer's opinion which was being presented.

*Regarding the extent of postwar H-bomb research at Los Alamos:*

Q: Did you know that research [on the H-bomb] continued [at Los Alamos after the war]?

A: Yes, it continued without much pressure on it.

Q: How did you know what was being done?

A: I saw [Edward] Teller occasionally. *I don't suppose I had a very clear idea at that time* except that it is not hard to form an impression of the magnitude of a program from many different sources.

Q:  What I am concerned about is to what extent these sources were matters of which you had some fairly direct personal knowledge.

A:  I don't know what you mean quite by direct personal knowledge. *I was not down to Los Alamos* during that period, and *I didn't talk to the men working on the program* during that period. But our general impressions around the [Berkeley] radiation laboratory, *the general impressions I got* from talking to men in Washington, was that things were not moving ahead.

When Samuel Silverman had completed his cross-examination, it was the board members' turn to interrogate. Although Gordon Gray had had questions to pose to each of the *pro*-Oppenheimer witnesses (with three minor exceptions), not one thing Wendell Latimer had said seemed to have aroused Gray's curiosity. He turned to his colleague Ward Evans, who wanted to know whether Latimer had "known any Communists." This was Latimer's astounding reply:

Yes, I have known Communists. They planted a Communist secretary on me at one time during the war until the FBI discovered her. The Army sent her to me. That is the only intimate connection that I recall.

A few minutes later, Roger Robb's first witness was excused from the stand.

The next day the ordinarily civil Gordon Gray displayed an unusual snappishness toward Lloyd Garrison. Gray had read something into the record, and Garrison had sought clarification of one phrase. Gray cut him off. This was not the time, he said, for "discussion of a material nature." Garrison would have an opportunity later to raise his question. Garrison wanted to know when, and Gray retorted that he did not want to establish a precise time. "I should think, Mr. Garrison," he said testily, "that it would be satisfactory for the chairman to assure you that you will have the opportunity."

First in the witness chair that day was Air Force Major General Roscoe Charles ("Bim") Wilson, who had first come into contact with Robert Oppenheimer as the Air Corps' wartime liaison with General Groves and, in postwar years, as a fellow member of a Pentagon atomic research committee.

General Wilson's explanation of how he came to be in the witness chair portrayed him (doubtless unintentionally) as, in effect, an official spokesman for the United States Air Force. He was there, he took pains to explain, not of his own volition, but on the verbal orders of no less than the Chief of Staff of the Air Force, who had directed him "to report to this committee"—and, in particular, to Roger Robb. ("This is the first time any major general ever reported to me," commented Robb.)

The Air Force could not have asked for a more earnest or passionate spokesman, and General Wilson made no bones about his own viewpoints and biases. "I am a dedicated airman," he explained. Not only that, he told the board; he was also "first of all a big-bomb man."

General Wilson then explained to the Gray Board how his "airman's view" of matters had, in 1951, caused him to become so disturbed by a "pattern of action" on Oppenheimer's part that he had felt obliged to report his concern to the Air Force Chief of Intelligence. Wilson cited the details of the "pattern": Oppenheimer's espousal of the "internationalizing of atomic energy"; his lack of enthusiasm for certain Air Force-backed nuclear detection devices; and his display, on the issue of a nuclear-powered aircraft, of "more conservatism than the Air Force would have liked."

Samuel Silverman, on cross-examination, drew from the General the admission that there were people within the Air Force he disagreed with but still considered "people of good faith." Would General Wilson, a "dedicated airman," be willing to say the same of a "dedicated naval officer" like Admiral Ofstie, who in 1949 had told Congress that long-range strategic bombing was both "militarily unsound" and "morally wrong"? General Wilson slid off the question: he would merely question the Admiral's "good judgment," he said.

At this point Chairman Gray broke in to observe that while he had, up to now, allowed "almost unlimited latitude" in the questioning, he felt that Silverman had successfully made his point about the "good faith" of differing points of view, and prodded

Silverman to continue with his cross-examination. It was the first time in the proceeding that Gray had suggested to an interrogator that he had sufficiently plowed a certain furrow and should move on. Not once in Robb's twelve hours of cross-examination of Oppenheimer, even when Robb had returned to a given subject three or four times, had Gray objected. Yet he now stopped Silverman after less than five minutes of questioning on the "good faith" point.*

Silverman then asked Wilson about the items in the Oppenheimer "pattern of action" that had so upset him in 1951. First, there was what Wilson termed the "internationalizing" of atomic energy:

Q: You did know that many people of good faith, many informed people, were in favor of what came to be known as the Acheson-Lilienthal and later the Baruch plan?

A: I don't think you are speaking of quite the same thing. The Baruch plan had certain safeguards [not contained in] what I believed to be Dr. Oppenheimer's earlier program. It was less general, let us say.

Q: Would it surprise you to learn that there are those who think that it was more general?

A: That is possible. . . .

Q: Had you heard that it was Dr. Oppenheimer's view that inspection [in the international control of atomic energy] is not enough, that you could not be sure that the Russians would not evade inspection, and therefore it was necessary to have an international [inspection] agency . . . ?

A: I didn't know this as a fact, I am sorry.

As to two Air Force-backed nuclear detection devices about

---

* Gray's interruption of Silverman should also be compared with his tolerance of Robb's questioning on one occasion in the final days of the hearing. After Oppenheimer had returned to the stand and had undergone an additional four hours of testimony, Robb began questioning him for the fourth time about his 1943 interview with Colonel Pash on the Chevalier incident. Lloyd Garrison protested that this was "covering ground that has already been gone over this afternoon [as well as in earlier] cross-examination." But Gordon Gray, on the basis of this being "one of the important things in the Commission's letter [of charges]," said, "I think I will ask Mr. Robb to proceed *unless he feels* he is simply covering ground that has already been covered." (Emphasis added.)

which Oppenheimer had supposedly been unenthusiastic, Silverman won from Wilson the acknowledgments: (1) that Oppenheimer's initial coolness toward them sprang solely from their bleak *technical* prospects; (2) that nonetheless Oppenheimer had continuously favored research on them; and (3) that as a result of that research the two had been successfully developed.

But there was a third such device, to which Oppenheimer had given wholehearted support. Silverman posed these questions about it:

Q: Do you know that it was under Dr. Oppenheimer's direction at Los Alamos that the first system for long-range detection of atomic explosions was initiated?

A: I don't know that as a fact, but I am not surprised, sir. . . .

Q: Do you know whether Dr. Oppenheimer directed the first trial of that method?

A: No, sir, I don't.

About Oppenheimer's supposed lack of enthusiasm for nuclear-powered aircraft, this exchange occurred:

Q: With respect to Dr. Oppenheimer's opposition to nuclear-powered flight . . .

A: Perhaps opposition is not the word. . . . I don't think I have ever heard Dr. Oppenheimer doubt that this would be accomplished, but it was always 15 to 20 years . . . away. . . .

Q: Was there not a [recent] statement . . . by a very important official in the Air Force . . . that nuclear-powered flight looked like something we might have in about 20 years?

A: I don't know that, sir, I am sorry.

Wilson was followed in the witness chair by Dr. Kenneth Pitzer, to whom Room 2022 was wholly familiar; it had been his own office when he was Director of Research for the AEC. Pitzer made the striking statement that he was not appearing here voluntarily, but "only at the very specific and urgent request of the General Manager." Since AEC regulations vested the final decision-making power in its General Manager, this was like a prosecution witness in a trial revealing that he had been asked to testify "at the very specific and urgent request" of the judge.

The circumstances of this urgent request, as later recalled by Pitzer, make it clear that the "judge" in question, AEC General Manager Nichols, was following the daily course of the Oppenheimer proceeding with active and not wholly objective interest. He made his personal request of Pitzer only after the Gray Board hearing was well into its second week, when he saw it was necessary to counter one of Garrison's principal arguments: namely, that Oppenheimer's judgment and scientific abilities were so exceptional as to offset the negative things about him. To blunt this argument, Nichols phoned Pitzer and told him that the AEC wanted testimony from scientists who had disagreed with Oppenheimer's policy views (as he knew Pitzer had, especially on the H-bomb), so as to portray the physicist's judgment as something less than infallible.

How insistent had Nichols been that Pitzer testify? "Well," Pitzer has recalled, "if he had merely said to me, 'Would you like to testify?' I would have said 'No.' But his request had more the flavor of, 'We really believe it is your duty to testify.'"

Pitzer was able to comply with Nichols' request in good conscience, for not only did he regard Oppenheimer's judgment as far from infallible; he was also troubled by the thought that Oppenheimer might be cleared while others Pitzer knew of in the AEC, men with far less vulnerable backgrounds than Oppenheimer's, had been denied clearance. To Pitzer, there was a certain egalitarian justice in applying the same strict criteria to Oppenheimer as to the others.

On cross-examination, Silverman questioned Pitzer about his earlier expression of "surprise" that Oppenheimer had failed to disqualify himself from the GAC chairmanship after his anti-H-bomb views were rejected as government policy.

Q: Do you know whether Dr. Oppenheimer did in fact offer to resign from the chairmanship of the General Advisory Committee at that time [the fall of 1950]?

A: I have no information on that.

Q: You have not heard that he offered to the AEC Chairman, Mr. [Gordon] Dean, to resign?

A: I don't believe I heard that, no. . . .

Q: I take it you would be less critical of Dr. Oppenheimer's attitude if . . . he offered to resign and was urged to remain?

A: Certainly so.

Silverman also asked whether Pitzer knew that Oppenheimer had recommended that chemist Willard Libby be appointed to the GAC so that the committee would contain "at least one" H-bomb enthusiast. But the witness said he had "no knowledge of that."

Gordon Gray wanted to know if Pitzer had personal evidence to substantiate the AEC's charge that Oppenheimer had continued to oppose the H-bomb project after the presidential go-ahead. Pitzer replied that he had "no personal knowledge of Dr. Oppenheimer going to Mr. X and saying don't work at Los Alamos" or of having made a harmful technical recommendation. But then Pitzer added this significant caveat:

On the other hand, I have great difficulty believing that the program would have had certain difficulties that it did have if he had enthusiastically urged individuals to participate in the program, because . . . he was a great personal influence among theoretical physicists at that time.

Pitzer viewed Oppenheimer's sin, then, as one not of opposition but merely of a failure to "enthuse." This was a theme that was to be picked up, intact, and given a prominent place in the verdict of the Gray Board majority.

At about four o'clock that afternoon, a heavy-set, beetle-browed man entered the hearing room and stood by the witness chair.

"Would you raise your right hand and give me your full name?"

"Edward Teller."

"Edward Teller, do you swear that the testimony you are to give the board shall be the truth, the whole truth and nothing but the truth, so help you God?"

"I do."

Whereupon, Teller took his seat in the witness chair just in front of the leather sofa on which Oppenheimer was seated and proceeded to give what many regard as the most potent of all the 700,000 words of testimony "in the matter of J. Robert Oppenheimer."

With his very first words Teller made clear his discomfort at appearing as an adverse witness against the man he had once considered his close intellectual companion. "I appear," he told the Gray Board, "because I have been asked to, and because I consider it my duty upon request to say what I think in the matter. I would have preferred not to appear."

What was the background of Teller's reluctant appearance in Room 2022? The beginning of that story is unclear: Teller has declined to tell when, where and from whom he first heard of the proceeding against Robert Oppenheimer (Teller says his informant has never released him from a pledge of secrecy). But, according to *Life* writer Robert Coughlan, who has written the most comprehensive and meticulously researched report of the Oppenheimer-Teller episode, Teller was deeply disturbed at the prospect of the hearing and tried his best to head it off.* As much as he would have liked to see his adversary's influence diminished, says Coughlan, Teller abhorred the implications of disloyalty and dishonor that inevitably accompanied a security-risk proceeding.

Soon after hearing of the AEC charges, Teller happened to meet Oppenheimer at a conference in Rochester, New York. Teller told him he was sorry to hear about his difficulties. The physicist responded with a quizzical look, and asked whether Teller thought there was anything "sinister" in what he (Oppenheimer) had been doing. When Teller replied reassuringly in the negative, Oppenheimer said he would be obliged if Teller would talk with his defense counsel, Lloyd Garrison.

The next time Teller was in New York, he did go to see Garrison and his colleagues, who, Teller later recalled, tried to paint Oppenheimer as "an angel." Teller told of his disagreements with Oppenheimer, and of his belief that in some instances the physicist had been dangerously wrong, especially regarding the H-

---

* Coughlan does not specify how Teller tried to block the hearing.

bomb. But, Garrison felt, while he betrayed "an intense dislike" of Oppenheimer (which dispelled any thought Garrison might have had about calling Teller as a witness), Teller made it clear that he had never entertained doubts about the scientist's patriotism.

That being the case, why, writer Coughlan wonders, did Teller end up testifying on behalf of the government? Coughlan accepts Teller's own explanation: that he had been *asked* to testify for the government. By whom? Here again it was AEC General Manager Nichols who, although he was to be the appelate judge in the case, had stepped in and asked a person to appear as a progovernment witness.

But to say simply that he was testifying "because I have been asked" oversimplified the situation a bit, for Teller had been under pressure from both sides. After the news of the case broke in the press, a petition of protest was circulated among Teller's scientific colleagues at Los Alamos, one of whom had a long talk with him in an effort to persuade him not to testify. Teller seemed torn, the colleague recalls. On the one hand, he agreed that the security-risk proceeding was wrong. On the other, the colleague has recalled him saying, Lewis Strauss had made an extremely strong appeal to him to testify. (Both Strauss and Teller have strongly denied having talked about the case prior to Teller's testimony.) After all, the colleague recalls Teller saying, Strauss, virtually the lone H-bomb supporter in the government at one juncture, had gone to great lengths to back him, and he felt that in this sense, at least, his moral debt to Strauss far outweighed whatever obligation he might have toward Oppenheimer, who had consistently tried to block the H-bomb program.

Reporter Coughlan has presented a similar explanation of Edward Teller's reasons for testifying, which Coughlan characterizes as a composite conclusion, based on many interviews and considerable collection and checking of information over a long period of time. "The first and most evident fact," Coughlan has said, "is that Strauss and top leaders of the Air Force did want Oppenheimer's influence and activities curtailed." A "closely related fact" was Strauss' loyal support of Teller and his causes in the past, and Strauss' even greater power to be of help in the future now that he was Chairman of the AEC. "As for the Air

Force," Coughlan has written, "it was to it that Teller chiefly owed his victory in getting a second nuclear weapons laboratory established where *he* would furnish the example, and ideas, and set the pace for project development . . . free from the pervasive influence of Robert Oppenheimer at Los Alamos."

But an additional factor that may have influenced Teller was this: Oppenheimer's wielding of potent and pervasive influence on a wide range of postwar government policies aroused in Teller a growing bitterness—bitterness because it so flagrantly contradicted what Oppenheimer had said in 1945 when Teller had, at Leo Szilard's urging, brought him a petition against dropping the A-bomb over Japan.* At that time Oppenheimer had berated Szilard for using his position as a scientist to influence matters of *political* policy about which he had insufficient information. Yet, in the postwar years, it had seemed to Teller that Oppenheimer had flouted this precept by the breadth of policy issues on which he constantly advised the government.

In Teller's view, to acquiesce in the withdrawal of one's security clearance without a fight was *not* tantamount to a tacit assent to the government's charges. "If the government didn't want my advice and wanted to withdraw my security clearance for whatever reason," Teller later said, "I would not raise a peep." Thus, as he saw it, there was only one way to interpret Oppenheimer's fight to retain his clearance: it was an effort to protract his influence over government policies.

These were the reasons that prompted Edward Teller to journey to Washington to testify before the Gray Board.

According to Robert Coughlan, Teller was in "a troubled and depressed state of mind" when he arrived in Washington to testify. Not only was there the repugnance of subjecting a person of Oppenheimer's eminence to a security trial; there were his own ambivalent personal feelings toward Oppenheimer: "memories of the early friendship, the later festering grievances, the respect he nevertheless still felt for him in many ways; most of all, with his own victories won and the old skilled antagonist crippled and fighting for his life, he felt a leaden kind of sorrow."

Teller's ambivalence was diminished, however, when, just a

* See p. 81.

few hours before he was to testify, Roger Robb showed him a dossier containing items unfavorable to Oppenheimer.* These consisted in part of digests of material from Oppenheimer's security file and in part of excerpts of the Gray Board hearing. Teller had known of Oppenheimer's left-wing background in a general and undocumented way, but to be suddenly confronted with this quantity of information, without time to study and reflect on it, was unsettling. In particular, there was one excerpt from Robert Oppenheimer's own testimony (which Teller has declined to identify) that he found especially disturbing. Nor was his mind set any more at ease by Robb himself, who, Teller has recalled, sought to paint Oppenheimer as a devil.

And so it was in this troubled frame of mind that Edward Teller began testifying about the eminent man who sat behind him on the leather sofa.

Robb's questions quickly got to the heart of the matter. Did Teller intend to suggest, by anything he was about to tell the board, "that Dr. Oppenheimer is disloyal to the United States?"

Teller replied that while it would be "presumptuous" to try to analyze Oppenheimer's motives, "I have always assumed, and I now assume, that he is loyal to the United States."

Robb's next question was "a corollary of that. Do you or do you not believe that Dr. Oppenheimer is a security risk?" Teller's answer was circuitous:

In a great number of cases, I have seen Dr. Oppenheimer act—I understand that Dr. Oppenheimer acted—in a way which for me was exceedingly hard to understand. I thoroughly disagreed with him in numerous issues and his actions frankly appeared to me confused and complicated. To this extent I feel that *I would like to see the vital interests of this country in hands which I understand better, and therefore trust more.* [Emphasis added.]

The latter portion of this response seemed to assume that the question before the Gray Board was not whether Robert Oppen-

* Robb's later explanation of this action was that he considered Teller a rebuttal witness. "How could he testify without knowing what he was rebutting?"

heimer should be entrusted with the nation's secrets but whether he should or should not be appointed, in the future, to govern-mental advisory posts. Teller's reply also seemed to introduce a new criterion of "security risk" nowhere to be found in AEC rules or regulations: the *understandability* of a person.

Presently Robb asked Teller to be more specific about those Oppenheimer actions that had seemed to him "confused and complicated" and difficult to understand. Among the items Teller listed, partly from his own knowledge and partly from hearsay, were: an Oppenheimer proposal for the sharing of plutonium with other countries; Oppenheimer's opposition to early A-bomb detection devices (which Teller put "definitely in the hearsay category, and I might just be quite wrong on it");* and, finally, the issue of a second weapons laboratory.

With that, Robb turned the witness over to Samuel Silverman for cross-examination. Silverman had methodically pressed each of the previous three Robb witnesses for documentation of their often vague hearsay charges against Oppenheimer, and, at least in the case of Teller's statement about atomic detection devices, here was an opportunity for him to do more of the same. But for some reason Teller was spared the kind of questioning Latimer, Wilson and Pitzer had received. "We have so very few [ques-tions]," Silverman said, "I am almost tempted not to ask them."

It was now nearly six o'clock. Teller had been on the stand for nearly two hours. But in these closing minutes he was to admin-ister what was, in effect, the *coup de grâce* to his former friend, seated behind him.

It came in response to a question by Chairman Gray: "Do you feel that it would endanger the common defense and security to grant clearance to Dr. Oppenheimer?"

"I believe," Teller began, "that Dr. Oppenheimer's character is such that he would not knowingly and willingly do anything that is designed to endanger the safety of this country. To the extent, therefore, that your question is directed toward intent, I would say I do not see any reason to deny clearance."

So far, Teller's response had inflicted no damage. But he was

* He was, in part. See p. 337.

unwilling to leave the matter there. His reply continued, with an important "if": *"If it is a question of wisdom and judgment, as demonstrated by actions since 1945, then I would say one would be wiser not to grant clearance."* (Emphasis added.) Teller went on to say that "I am myself a little bit confused on this issue, particularly as it refers to a person of Oppenheimer's prestige and influence."

But how confused *was* Edward Teller? A moment earlier, Gordon Gray had asked whether he was "familiar with the question which this board is called upon to answer." Teller said he believed so—and years later, asked what he had understood that question to be, he had replied, succinctly: the question was, should Robert Oppenheimer be entrusted with the nation's secrets? If that was indeed Teller's understanding of the question before the board, why had he said that *"if* it is a question of wisdom and judgment [on policy matters]* . . . then I would say one would be wiser not to grant clearance"?

Many regard that statement as a critical blow to Oppenheimer's cause, but it also proved, ironically, to inflict an acutely painful wound on Teller, too, for it was this more than any other single sentence in his testimony that brought down upon this sensitive man the rage and ostracism of many of his fellow scientists.

At ten minutes before six, Edward Teller was excused from the witness chair. According to one account, he rose, turned to the frail man seated behind him on the sofa and offered his hand. Oppenheimer accepted it. Then Teller, looking Oppenheimer full in the eyes, said, "I'm sorry."

Oppenheimer replied in a polite but unbelieving tone: "After what you've just said, I don't know what you mean."

Teller turned and walked slowly from the room.

---

* Teller left no doubt that he was talking about Oppenheimer's "wisdom and judgment" on policy, rather than security, matters, for just before leaving the witness stand he was asked about the danger involved in "Dr. Oppenheimer's having access to restricted data *without regard to the wisdom of his advice."* Teller replied that if he merely assumed that Oppenheimer would have "access to security information," but would *"refrain from all advice in these matters,"* he believed "there is no danger." (Emphasis added.)

The next day, Roger Robb's presentation of the government's case against Robert Oppenheimer was interrupted by the testimony of John J. McCloy, whom Lloyd Garrison had been unable to put on the stand in sequence with his other pro-Oppenheimer witnesses.

To McCloy, the determination of what constituted a "security risk" was far from a single-faceted matter. From his World War II experience in the War Department in Washington, McCloy recalled how the government, desperate to enlist every possible physicist with any nuclear knowledge, had eagerly pressed into service European-born scientists with "queer names." Against this background, when asked whether Robert Oppenheimer was a "security risk," McCloy, in the course of a lengthy reply, said:

> I don't know just exactly what you mean by a security risk.
> . . . I think there is a security risk in reverse. . . . We are only secure if we have the best brains and the best reach of mind.
> . . . If the impression is prevalent that scientists as a whole have to work under such great restrictions and perhaps great suspicion in the United States, we may lose the next step in this [nuclear] field, which I think would be very dangerous for us.*

In his questioning of McCloy, Gordon Gray indicated some difficulty in fully understanding and accepting McCloy's plea for a balancing of assets and liabilities in assessing a man as a security risk.

Q:  Would you take a calculated risk with respect to the security of your bank?†

* McCloy was about to illustrate this point from his own experience as High Commissioner in Germany when Gordon Gray interrupted to "suggest that we not wander too far afield." The author found no instance where Gray interrupted an anti-Oppenheimer witnesses for wandering; in fact, later that same day when David Griggs, testifying against Oppenheimer, became concerned that his answers were going too far afield, Chairman Gray encouraged him to be expansive, saying, "Our procedures are very flexible here" and that "Within limits a witness can say anything he believes to be pertinent to the question asked him, except that he is not supposed to engage in argument." Moreover, when Samuel Silverman sought to object to anti-Oppenheimer witness Alvarez illustrating a point with an example, as McCloy had sought to do, Gray overruled Silverman and insisted that Alvarez continue.

† The Chase National Bank, of which McCloy was then chairman of the board of directors.

A:  I take a calculated risk every day in my bank.

Q:  Would you leave someone in charge of the vaults about whom you have *any doubt* in your mind?

A:  No, I probably wouldn't. [Emphasis added.]

McCloy sought to elaborate on his initial brief answer to the "pat analogy to the bank vault man." If a man in charge of the vaults "knew more about . . . the intricacies of time locks than anybody else in the world, I might think twice before I let him go, because I would balance the risks in this connection." He went on to tell how, as High Commissioner in Germany, he had picked Nazi scientists to send to the United States—men who "a few years before were doing their utmost to overthrow the United States Government by violence," many of whom became key figures in the American guided missile program.

Gray, again groping after an absolute, wondered whether "when the paramount concern is the security of the country" it is permissible to "entertain" even "reasonable doubts."

"I suppose," McCloy said, "other things being equal, you would like to have a perfectly pure, uncontaminated chap, with no background, to deal with these [secret] things, but it is not possible in this world. I think you do have to take risks in regard to the security of the country. . . . You can't avoid the necessity of balancing to some degree. . . ." McCloy concluded by saying he "would accept a considerable amount of political immaturity" in return for the "esoteric" quality of the theoretical scientist on which "we are going to be dependent for the next generation."

McCloy's plea for a weighing of all the factors and a balancing of the favorable with the unfavorable lay at the heart of Lloyd Garrison's defense strategy, and the attorney quickly sought to reinforce the point by citing the requirement, in AEC regulations, that security-risk judgments give "due recognition to the favorable as well as unfavorable information concerning the individual and . . . [balance] the cost to the program of not having his services against any possible risks involved."

Roger Robb apparently perceived, too, the aid and comfort McCloy's "balancing" principle was lending to the Oppenheimer cause. He immediately intervened with the observation that the regulation cited by Garrison "does not refer to this board," but merely applied to security determinations by the AEC General

348     THE OPPENHEIMER CASE

Manager. Chairman Gray agreed: the regulation he said, was "by
no means conclusive as to the duties of this board."

Gordon Gray and Roger Robb were in error on this point for,
as Lloyd Garrison pointed out, the language he had cited was
among the clearance criteria which all AEC hearing boards were
explicitly enjoined to "carefully consider." But there is something
more important in the position taken by Gray and Robb than
mere ignorance or misunderstanding of a *technical* AEC regulation. Far more significant, their stand indicated a tendency—
reflected in the verdict of the Gray Board majority—to judge the
matter of "security risk" solely on the basis of the *liabilities* side
of the investigatory balance sheet, rather than from a *balancing*
of the assets against the liabilities, as urged by John J. McCloy
and as called for by the regulations.

Next to testify was David Tressel Griggs, the former Chief
Scientist of the Air Force, whom Robert Oppenheimer had once
called a "paranoid." By most accounts, Griggs was a man endowed with strong feelings and a capacity for zealous adherence
to causes. Arthur Schlesinger, Jr., has written that "those who
used to know Griggs when he was around Harvard in the late
thirties remember him as a man of violent feelings," and Griggs
himself indicated, in his Gray Board testimony, that he had injected intense emotion into the "pretty violent" policy controversies in which he and his Air Force colleagues found themselves
arrayed against Oppenheimer. But Griggs may have had personal
as well as policy reasons for feeling aggrieved at Oppenheimer.
An eyewitness recalls more than one meeting at which Oppenheimer's acerbic tongue ridiculed and humiliated Griggs.

The interrogation of David Griggs taxed his memory, and occasionally he had difficulty. For example, when Samuel Silverman pressed Griggs for details of his volcanic confrontation with
Oppenheimer at Princeton in 1952, Griggs protested: "I can't tell
you what [Oppenheimer] said. Do you expect me to be able to
remember word for word what he said?"*

* The demands on his memory were surely slight compared with those
imposed on Oppenheimer, earlier in the hearing, by Robb, with questions
about events twelve to fourteen years before: (1) *Regarding an alleged
1940 meeting:* "How many people were present? . . . [Was the meeting]

But the well-prepared Roger Robb came to Griggs' rescue and in the process provided an indication of the high degree of cooperation he seems to have received from the Air Force. Robb quickly produced a copy of a memorandum on the 1952 Princeton conversation that Griggs had prepared at the time and had placed in his files at the Pentagon, whence Robb had apparently retrieved it.

On another subject—the origin of the term "ZORC"—Griggs' recollections were explicit and detailed: at a meeting of the Air Force's Scientific Advisory Board in Cambridge in the fall of 1952, Griggs testified, Oppenheimer's friend Jerrold Zacharias had written on the blackboard the letters "Z . . . O . . . R . . . C" and had explained that these stood for Zacharias, Oppenheimer, Rabi and Charles (Lauritsen). Many who attended the Cambridge meeting (including Zacharias) have emphatically denied that Zacharias ever did any such thing, and Griggs later acknowledged that although he still thought he had seen "ZORC" written on the blackboard, "memories are fallible."*

In many respects, Griggs' testimony resembled that of General Wilson of the Air Force. Like Wilson, Griggs made no effort to conceal his pro-Air Force point of view; his testimony is sprinkled with phrases such as "unfortunate from the standpoint of the Air Force" and "helpful to the Air Force," and he acknowledged that as an Air Force partisan he might "not be fully capable of objectivity." Like General Wilson, he had not known Oppenheimer intimately. Like Wilson, he had become disturbed by a "pattern of activities" on Oppenheimer's part. And, as in the case of General Wilson, Griggs' concern seemed based on a less than

---

in the evening? . . . Do you recall who was there? . . . Was Isaac Folkoff there? . . . Was Dr. Addis there? . . . Do you remember anybody else who was there?" (2) *Regarding a 1941 or 1942 visit to Oppenheimer's home by George C. Eltenton:* "Who had called the meeting? . . . Do you remember who presided? . . . Who was there? . . . You are quite positive Eltenton was there? . . . Had you met Eltenton on many other occasions? . . . Where?"

* The truth of the matter, as indicated both by an Air Force memorandum on the subject and by the vivid recollection of one of the participants, is that "ZORC" *was*, for some unexplained reason, written on a blackboard—not at the Cambridge meeting described by Griggs, but in the course of the Lincoln Summer Study on continental defense.

solid factual understanding of Robert Oppenheimer's activities
and views.

This was the way Griggs described the worrisome "pattern":

> It became apparent to us—by that I mean to Mr. Finletter
> [Secretary of the Air Force], Mr. Burden and Mr. Norton
> [Finletter's two assistants] that there was a pattern of activi-
> ties all of which involved Dr. Oppenheimer. Of these, one was
> the Vista project. . . . We were told that in the late fall, I
> believe, of 1951, Oppenheimer and two other colleagues
> formed an informal committee of three to work for world peace
> or some such purpose, as they saw it. We were also told that in
> this effort they considered that many things were more im-
> portant than the development of the thermonuclear weapon,
> specifically the air defense of the continental United
> States. . . .

How authoritatively could Griggs connect Oppenheimer with
the views Griggs had termed "unfortunate from the standpoint of
the Air Force"? How, for example, had Griggs come to know of
Oppenheimer's supposed opposition to a second nuclear weapons
laboratory? "By hearsay evidence, I formed a firm impression that
he was opposed to it," said Griggs. Griggs also swore that he had
learned of an alleged Oppenheimer proposal that the United
States "give up strategic air power" or "consider giving up strategic missiles." How had he learned of these extreme Oppenheimer recommendations? Griggs said he had acquired his
information in 1951 and 1952 from his readings of the Vista
report and of the minutes of a State Department disarmament
meeting attended by Oppenheimer. Nor was Griggs in doubt
about his recollection of these matters, for when Samuel Silverman pressed him as to "how sure" he was that another alleged
Oppenheimer recommendation—that the President announce
that SAC would be used against Russian cities only in response to
a Soviet attack on American cities—had been contained in the
Vista report, Griggs replied:

> I am as sure as I can be of anything which I studied ex-
> tensively two years ago, and which was of considerable
> concern to me.

Q:  You actually saw this in a document?
A:  Oh, yes.

Later, however, Griggs' "sure" recollections proved to be erroneous. After the conclusion of the Gray Board hearing, but before
the rendering of the board's verdict, Oppenheimer's attorneys
discovered that certain papers relating to Vista and to the 1952
State Department disarmament conference were still in the
scientist's office. When Garrison examined these papers (which
he promptly furnished to the Gray Board), he found that none
of the Oppenheimer views described by Griggs appeared either
in the Vista report or in the State Department papers.

Under Silverman's questioning, Griggs also revealed a less than
precise knowledge of Oppenheimer's stance on another matter:
continental defense. Griggs had testified earlier about his concern
in 1952 that undue optimism about the potential effectiveness of
a Canadian radar-warning net might lead to huge expenditures
for such a net, at the expense of the Strategic Air Command. But,
Silverman wanted to know, had Robert Oppenheimer himself
been one of those who had spread such unwarranted optimism?

Q:  Do you know what Dr. Oppenheimer's views were . . . as
    to the effectiveness of continental air defense . . . ? Did
    you ever talk to him about that?
A:  Yes, I think so [at the beginning of the Lincoln Summer
    Study on air defense].
Q:  Was it his view that you could not have a 100 percent
    defense?
A:  I don't know. . . .
Q:  Do you know what his views were at the end of that study?
A:  I do not.
Q:  Do you know what his views are today?
A:  I do not.
Q:  Did you ever hear Dr. Oppenheimer say that it was possi-
    ble to have a 100 percent continental air defense?
A:  No; I have had no contact with Oppenheimer . . . since
    that first session at the beginning of the Lincoln Summer
    Study.

Before he left the witness stand Griggs told with unusual

candor what had made him doubt Oppenheimer. In part, he said, it was an impression of Oppenheimer's past, which Griggs openly acknowledged he had "pieced together by hearsay evidence." But his misgivings had first been aroused by the reports he had received in 1946, upon joining the RAND Corporation, that Oppenheimer had been considered a calculated security risk during the war.

Q: And thereafter in your contacts with Dr. Oppenheimer you could not help being a little bit on your guard?
A: That is correct.
Q: And perhaps trying a little bit to see what might be beneath the surface of what Dr. Oppenheimer was saying?
A: That is correct. May I amplify this point?
Q: Certainly.

Griggs' amplification vividly illuminated the basis for Vannevar Bush's alarm that the Gray Board had accepted a "security-risk" charge based on a person's *policy* views:

. . . as I testified, I was on the opposite side of a pretty violent controversy from Dr. Oppenheimer. . . . I have been involved in . . . a number of pretty strong controversies in the military, and I think it is a fair general observation that when you get involved in a hot enough controversy, it is awfully hard not to question the motives of people who oppose you. This, I am sure, could not but have colored my views on the subject.

Having said this, Griggs added this somewhat ironic coda:

If it ever comes to the day when we can't disagree and disagree violently in public and on national policy, then of course I feel that it will be a calamity for our democracy. I think perhaps I have said enough.

A few minutes later, Griggs was replaced in the witness chair by Luis Walter Alvarez, professor of physics at Berkeley, devoted disciple of Ernest O. Lawrence and staunch supporter of Edward Teller.

Like two previous "prosecution witnesses"—Kenneth Pitzer and Edward Teller—Luis Walter Alvarez was appearing at the official request of the AEC. But if Pitzer and Teller could be said to have testified, in effect, at the invitation of the intermediate judge in the case (AEC General Manager Nichols), it could in like manner be said that Alvarez was appearing at the entreaty of the "Chief Justice of the Supreme Court." For he was there at the behest of Lewis Strauss, Chairman of the Atomic Energy Commission, which would make the final ruling "in the matter of J. Robert Oppenheimer."

These were the circumstances, as later recalled by Alvarez. A few days before Alvarez' testimony, the directors of the various AEC laboratories had convened at the Oak Ridge Laboratory in Tennessee. Among them was Ernest O. Lawrence, who after leaving Oak Ridge was to go to Washington to testify against Oppenheimer. Understandably, the prime topic at the Oak Ridge dinner table was the Oppenheimer hearing. Oppenheimer was a close friend of many of the lab directors, and indignation ran high. After dinner, one of the directors took Lawrence aside and cautioned him that if he and Alvarez were to testify unfavorably to Oppenheimer, their testimony would be discounted and set down to purely personal differences with the former Berkeley physicist. According to what Lawrence later told Alvarez, he was persuaded by this and concluded, moreover, that the Berkeley Radiation Lab would likewise be hurt if he and Alvarez appeared before the Gray Board.

There was an added complication. While at Oak Ridge, Lawrence was stricken by an attack of the intestinal ailment that was ultimately to cause his death.

The day after his dinner conversation about the Oppenheimer case, Lawrence called Alvarez in Berkeley, recounted his Oak Ridge experiences, told him he was canceling his own plans to testify (in part, Alvarez later believed, to protect his health), and requested Alvarez to do the same. As Alvarez later recalled it, he was only too glad to "get off the hot seat," dispatched a telegram to the AEC and canceled his plane reservation to Washington with a sense of considerable relief.

But around six o'clock that evening the phone rang in Alvarez' home. It was Lewis Strauss in Washington (where it was already nine in the evening). According to Alvarez, the AEC Chairman was clearly disturbed that Lawrence and Alvarez wouldn't testify before the Gray Board, and made it clear to Alvarez that he thought Lawrence had been intimidated by his fellow lab directors; Strauss also said he felt Alvarez was being similarly influenced, and told the scientist this was no way for a responsible citizen to behave. As Alvarez later recalled it, Strauss seemed to be saying, "'How are you going to look at yourself in the mirror if you back out on an important responsibility such as this?'"

Alvarez replied that Ernest Lawrence had for years been his superior, whose judgment he respected enormously, and that since Lawrence had so specifically asked him not to testify, he was in no position to countermand the request. Alvarez remembers that Strauss continued to plead with him, but Alvarez said, "Look. There is nothing I can do. I am sorry to let you down, but that's all there is to it."

Luis Alvarez hung up and sat down to dinner. But he could not rid his mind of Strauss' appeal to his conscience. Especially worrisome was the fact that he could offer the Gray Board some vital documentary evidence: a diary he had kept in the fall of 1949, chronicling the coast-to-coast pro-H-bomb activities of Ernest Lawrence and himself.

And so, Alvarez says, he called Lewis Strauss to say he would testify after all, proceeded to the airport and took the midnight plane to Washington. The next evening he dined with Roger Robb at the fashionable Chevy Chase Club in Washington, and on the following afternoon, found himself in Room 2022, preparing to answer Robb's questions about Robert Oppenheimer.

Alvarez' account of his efforts in 1949 to promote the H-bomb ran through Thursday afternoon and into Friday morning. Finally, it came time for board members to interrogate, and, for the first time, the questions asked by Ward Evans seemed to take a tone favorable to Oppenheimer.* He remarked to Alvarez that

* Theretofore, Evans' questions had seemed either noncommittal or tinged with unfriendliness to Oppenheimer's cause—or, more often, of dubious relevance to the proceeding. Two typical examples:

EVANS [to Nobel Prize-winning physicist I. I. Rabi]: Dr. Rabi, would you tell us something about your early education?

RABI: I am a graduate of Manual Training High School in Brooklyn, a graduate of Cornell University with a degree of bachelor of chemistry—we are fellow chemists.

EVANS: I am glad you had some chemistry. . . . Let me ask you another

"the main thing that we have gotten out of you" is that Oppenheimer was opposed to the H-bomb, and asked, "What does this
mean in your mind, anything?" By itself, said Alvarez, "absolutely
nothing." The point he had been trying to make was that "every
time I have found a person who felt this way, I have seen Dr.
Oppenheimer's influence on that person's mind. I don't think there
is anything wrong with this. . . . I just point out the facts as I
see them."

Evans pressed further: "It doesn't mean that he was disloyal?"

"Absolutely not, sir." It did mean, however, that Oppenheimer
had shown "exceedingly poor judgment."

When Alvarez had been excused from the stand, Lloyd Garrison asked to be advised of what "derogatory information" had
existed in Oppenheimer's security file at the time the AEC
cleared him in 1947. Roger Robb protested that this would violate
the rule prohibiting disclosure of FBI reports. If that be true,
Garrison countered, then the Nichols letter of charges—based,
after all, on FBI reports—must also be a violation of that rule. He
asked merely to be told which of the Nichols charges had and had
not been known to the AEC in 1947. But again Robb protested,
and again he swept along Chairman Gray.

Next on the witness stand was Colonel Boris T. Pash, then
Chief of Counter Intelligence for the Sixth Army in San Francisco. With the aid of numerous memoranda and teletypes that
Robb had exhumed from the files of the Manhattan District, Pash
told the Gray Board of his grave misgivings in 1943 about Robert
Oppenheimer, and of his efforts at the time to persuade Oppenheimer to reveal the name of Haakon Chevalier.

In midafternoon Colonel Pash left the stand, and Robb's final
witness was escorted into Room 2022: a slightly built man whose

---

question that has nothing particularly pertinent to this proceeding. Is
George Pegram still active?
RABI: Wonderfully. He is doing two men's work. . . .
EVANS [to Harvard physics professor Norman Ramsey]: Did you meet Mr.
Flanders down there [at Los Alamos]?
RAMSEY: Yes; he was a mathematician. . . .
EVANS: Did he have his beard?
RAMSEY: He had his beard, and it startled the security guards no end.

356 THE OPPENHEIMER CASE

close-cut, sandy hair and boyish face seemed to deprive him of even the thirty-four years that were his. An observer recalls his demeanor as serious, almost severe, as he raised his right hand to swear that his testimony would be "the truth, the whole truth and nothing but the truth." Whereupon, William Liscum Borden took his seat before the Gray Board.

Borden wanted to make clear he was appearing "under official compulsion" in response to a subpoena. As he told of his growing concern about Robert Oppenheimer, a copy of his letter to the FBI was handed to Garrison and his colleagues. They had, of course, wondered what had served to trigger the proceeding against Oppenheimer. They had heard rumors of the Borden letter, but this was the first time they had actually seen it.

Samuel Silverman scanned the letter quickly. His eye was caught by item (e) on the second page of the letter, charging that Robert Oppenheimer "had at least one Communist mistress," and when Robb asked Borden to read the letter aloud, Silverman protested. "There are statements in this letter, at least one that I see, which I don't think anybody would be very happy to have go into this record. . . . There may be serious question whether anybody will be helped by having this letter in the record."

"I think," Gordon Gray observed dryly, "that you are now raising a question that counsel cannot determine, Mr. Silverman."

Garrison sought to object on another ground: that many of the charges in the Borden letter were outside the scope of the Nichols letter of charges. Gray agreed this was a question the board should consider, and asked that the room be cleared except for the members of the board—and Roger Robb.

Robb's presence during the Gray Board's private deliberations did violence to elemental standards of fairness. What would any courtroom spectator think of the spectacle of the trial judge retiring to his chambers to contemplate a procedural ruling, accompanied by a vigorously arguing prosecuting attorney?

The outcome of the "closed" conference was not surprising: Gordon Gray overruled Garrison's objection, directed that William Borden should proceed to read his letter, and said that even though the letter went beyond the boundary of the original Nichols charges, Borden's testimony would not "in any way . . . broaden the inquiry of the board."

"How can it avoid it, sir?" asked Garrison. "Supposing you should believe the witness" and those of his accusations that were "not dreamed of in this proceeding up to this point, and not mentioned in the [Nichols] letter"?

If Lloyd Garrison had been speaking in a court of law, the judge (or jury) would presumably have known nothing about the contents of the Borden letter, and Garrison's argument would have been entirely logical. But the Gray Board's procedures rendered his point futile, for its members were already thoroughly familiar with the contents of the letter. As Chairman Gray himself pointed out, "copies of this letter have been in the possession of the board along with all other material, and have been read by members of this board." Once again Gray highlighted Garrison's dilemma: "If you prefer not to have Dr. Oppenheimer confronted by a witness and cross-examined . . . with respect to material which you know is in the possession of the board, of course that would be your decision."

Faced with this choice, Garrison had no alternative but to withdraw his objection and allow the letter to be read.

And so William Borden recited to the Gray Board his "exhaustively considered opinion" that, "more probably than not," the man seated a few feet behind him on the leather sofa "is an agent of the Soviet Union . . . [who had] been functioning as an espionage agent . . . under a Soviet directive in influencing United States . . . policy."

When Borden had finished reading, Gray entered an observation that may have made the witness wonder why the government had dragged him all the way from Pittsburgh to testify. Without asking Borden so much as one question to ascertain what evidence lay behind his charges, Gray, on behalf of all three board members, proceeded, in effect, to repudiate the essential points of the Borden letter. There was "no evidence" before the board, Gray said, that Robert Oppenheimer had either volunteered or complied with any request for espionage information, or that he had been functioning under a Soviet directive.

Roger Robb proceeded to ask Borden a few questions, culminating in this:

Q:  Let me see whether or not you feel any hesitation about

answering any questions that either have been or may be
put to you here, because of the presence of Dr. Oppenheimer and his counsel.

A: I do not.

Q: The answer is no?

A: The answer is no.

Q: I think that is all I care to ask.

By now it was 4:30 on Friday afternoon. With the assurance
that Borden would be on hand again on Monday for such cross-
examination as Garrison might wish to undertake (and with the
gratuitous observation that "he [Borden] is not happy to be here
in the first place"), Gordon Gray recessed the hearing, and the
third week of the Oppenheimer ordeal came to an end.

Over the weekend Oppenheimer's lawyers faced an important
question of strategy: Should they subject William Borden to
cross-examination, in the hope of impeaching or weakening his
testimony? Or should they accept Chairman Gray's indication
that the hearing board did not place credence in Borden's conclusions—and let the matter go at that?

On this question, the attorneys were at first of divided mind.
It seemed clear that Borden was a major culprit—perhaps *the*
culprit—in bringing about the government's action against Oppenheimer. Herbert Marks, the attorney with the closest emotional ties to Oppenheimer, argued strongly that Borden should
be brought back and kept on the witness stand for days, if necessary. Samuel Silverman, on the other hand, contended that Borden's letter had not added any significant new factual evidence,
but merely argumentative conclusions that the board did not
seem to accept anyway. Besides, he said, any cross-examining
attorney without access to official documents would be on a
distinctly unequal footing with the well-informed Borden.

With no resolution of the dispute on Saturday, it was agreed
that Herbert Marks should try his hand at developing a useful
line of questions to put to Borden. When the attorneys met again
on Sunday, Marks had reached the conclusion that cross-
examining William Borden would serve no useful purpose.

# 4. The Final Week

When the Gray Board reconvened on Monday for the fourth and final week of the hearing, Lloyd Garrison said he would have no questions for Borden, since these would merely invite argumentation on what amounted merely to Borden's "interpretation" of factual evidence.

Nor were there any questions from members of the hearing board. And so William Borden was excused from the witness stand, his charges apparently disbelieved by Oppenheimer's judges. It was as if the match that had ignited the fire had been snuffed out. Yet the fire burned on.

Later, in retrospect, Borden came to regret that he had not been interrogated at greater length. He wished he had been allowed to present more of the evidence that underlay his charges, "only some pieces of which appear in the published record, or anywhere else, for that matter." There were some pertinent documents, Borden has said, that were never seen, either by the Gray Board or by the AEC in their assessment of Oppenheimer. If he had been able to fill in some of the factual gaps, his letter might have been more fairly judged by readers of the Gray Board record. But at the moment he was excused from the stand, his reaction was one of intense relief. "I was never so glad to leave any place in my life," he later recalled.

With Borden's departure, Robb announced he had concluded the presentation of his witnesses.

Gray now addressed himself to Lloyd Garrison. He wanted to be sure that Garrison understood that the testimony on matters such as Vista, strategic air power, continental defense, etc., was now considered "material" by the board, even though these matters had not been specifically mentioned in the AEC's original letter of charges. Garrison said he understood and entered no protest at the inclusion into this "security risk case" of matters that had exclusively *policy* importance.

Now the board called Oppenheimer back to the stand for

further questioning. Gordon Gray began, and with his first question he sought to probe perhaps the most baffling aspect of the Chevalier incident: if the object of Oppenheimer's false accounts of the incident was to protect a friend whose approach he believed to be innocent, why had he invented a complicated "cock and bull story" for Colonels Pash and Lansdale, one that was far more injurious than the simple truth, both to his friend and to himself?

"Or, to put the question another way," Gray continued, couldn't one fairly infer from the patent illogicality of Oppenheimer's behavior that the explanation was simply that Oppenheimer had really told the *truth* to Pash and Lansdale and had *later* invented a protective version of the incident for the FBI in 1946, and for the Gray Board eight years later?

No, said Oppenheimer, what he had told Pash and Lansdale "was a false story. It is not easy to say that." To some of his judges, at least, Oppenheimer's statement would not be persuasive.

Gray's question had to do with *when* Oppenheimer had lied; there remained the troublesome matter of *why*. On this question the scientist was far from his usually lucid self. The opacity of his testimony suggests that he had never come to a full understanding of his own behavior.

Now, when you ask for a more persuasive argument as to why I did this than that I was an idiot, I am going to have more trouble being understandable. I think I was impelled by two or three concerns at that time. One was the feeling that I must get across the fact that . . . Eltenton was the guy that might very well be involved [in the left-wing union trouble at the Radiation Laboratory] and it was serious. Whether I embroidered the story in order to underline that seriousness or . . . to make it more tolerable that I would not tell the simple facts, namely, Chevalier had talked to me about it, I don't know.

Oppenheimer seemed still convinced of the innocence of Chevalier's approach, for he insisted that he had "correctly communicated" to the Gray Board Chevalier's "sense of not wishing to have anything to do with" the Eltenton approach.

The physicist's next words went to the heart of the doubts that many of his judges could not dispel. He realized now, he said, that he should have reported the incident immediately and "completely accurately." But "it was a matter of conflict for me. . . . I may add one or two things. Chevalier was a friend of mine."

"Did you say is a friend?" Ward Evans asked.

"He was a friend of mine," Oppenheimer replied.

"Today?"

"He was then. We may talk later of our present relations. . . . As far as I know, he had no close relations with anyone else on the [Manhattan] project. . . . He was an unlikely and absurd intermediary [for Eltenton]. I think there are circumstances which indicate that . . . there would not have been such a conspiracy—but I am in any case solemnly testifying that there was no such conspiracy in what I knew and what I know of this matter.

"I wish," he concluded, "I could explain to you better why I falsified and fabricated."

Oppenheimer's exposition raised fundamental questions: May a person in high position entertain the kind of "conflict" Oppenheimer admitted to the Gray Board, a conflict between loyalty to a friend and loyalty to his country? Is he entitled to arrogate to himself, as Oppenheimer had done, the judgment that Chevalier was innocent and an "absurd" choice for a Soviet intermediary? And if Oppenheimer's personality permitted him such a conflict and such an arrogation of judgment in the past, what reason was there to believe he might not indulge himself similarly in the future, if he were to conclude that a request for information by a trusted and innocent friend was in the best interests of the nation?

This was the question that seemed continuingly troublesome to Gordon Gray. The chairman inquired whether Oppenheimer would feel today—in 1954—that he could make his own independent judgment about the trustworthiness of an ex-Communist friend in whose "loyalty, discretion [and] character" he had "the highest degree of confidence."

Oppenheimer replied that "it would not be up to me to determine whether his disengagement from the Communist Party was genuine. I would think that at this time investigation would be called for." Evidently, his attitudes toward security had undergone considerable "rehabilitation" (to use Gray's word) since 1943.

Gray now proceeded to ask Oppenheimer whether the Vista report had at any stage suggested a presidential declaration that American nuclear weapons would not be used against Russian cities except in retaliation.* In doing so, Gray was trespassing not only the boundaries of the Nichols charges, but also the border of proper inquiry which Vannevar Bush had tried to suggest, for Gray's question implied that a man's views on purely policy matters could be relevant to whether he was a "security risk."

The next morning Vannevar Bush himself returned to the stand. The principal object of his renewed testimony was to rebut an allegation that President Truman, out of mistrust for Oppenheimer, had picked Bush rather than Oppenheimer to chair a 1949 scientific panel. Bush insisted that Truman had said no such thing; moreover, he said, the panel in question had been chosen by Air Force Chief of Staff Vandenberg, and not the President. A later affidavit from Ernest Lawrence confirmed this. But the testimony quickly became secondary as Roger Robb scolded the eminent scientist on a matter that boiled down to the question, "When is a paragraph not a paragraph?"

Robb's anger had been sparked by Bush's earlier criticism of the Gray Board for having accepted the charge that Oppenheimer had opposed the H-bomb. Bush had contended that the implication that "this man is being tried because he expressed strong opinions" was heightened because "the fact that he expressed strong opinions stands in a single paragraph by itself."

In the version of the Nichols letter Bush had read—the one published in the *New York Times*—this was perfectly true. The offending sentence *was* a separate paragraph. But, it developed, this was evidently for the typographical convenience of the *Times;* in the original Nichols letter, which Bush had not seen, but which Roger Robb now produced and showed him, the sentence was not separate, but was part of a larger paragraph.

* Oppenheimer's reply was verbose and ambiguous.

Robb treated Bush as if he were guilty of a deliberate deceit rather than of a punctuational misunderstanding:

Q: If you read the original letter would you not have made your point about the separate paragraphs?

A: No.

Q: Because it was not based on fact, was it?

A: It was based on what facts I cited.

Q: Yes, sir. Wouldn't you conclude from that, Doctor, that before making such statements it is well to know all the facts?

Robb seemed wholly uninterested in Bush's essential point— the dangers of "a man being tried for his opinions"—which, as the witness pointed out, was unaffected by the technicality of the paragraphing.

Kitty Oppenheimer came to the witness chair. She had made a brief and uneventful appearance earlier in the hearing, in her husband's defense, and now the board had recalled her for further questioning. Whereas her husband had at one point balked at saying Haakon Chevalier was still a friend, Kitty had no hesitancy in characterizing him as such, notwithstanding that "it has been said that he is [still] a Communist."

As Gordon Gray questioned Kitty Oppenheimer, there were fresh signs of his difficulty in imagining the political mood of the Thirties, when associations with either the Communist Party or its members were regarded far more casually than they became in the Fifties. He asked, for example, about "the mechanics" by which a party member "becomes clearly disassociated." Kitty Oppenheimer replied: "I think that varies from person to person, Mr. Gray. Some people do the bump, like that, and even write an article about it. Other people do it quite slowly. I left the Communist Party. I did not leave my past, the friendships, just like that. Some continued for a while."

Next came a vigorous rebuttal of David Griggs' story about the origin of "ZORC." The witness was MIT physicist Jerrold Zacharias, allegedly the "Z" in ZORC; he was the prime organizer of the 1952 Lincoln Summer Study on continental defense.

Zacharias used forceful terms to describe Griggs' efforts to block the study. He spoke of "Griggs' efforts—let me use a strong word —to sabotage the summer study from a position of power as chief scientist for the Air Force."

*"Efforts to sabotage . . . from a position of power . . ."*—these words closely resembled those used by Griggs himself in describing Robert Oppenheimer's suspect "pattern of activities." But as used by Zacharias, their thrust was quite different, for he carefully explained that even though Griggs' tactics had delayed recruitment for the summer study for several critical weeks, thus diminishing the number and quality of the participants, he merely regarded Griggs' efforts as "unwise, but not subversive. I would not want to bring up Dr. Griggs on charges of being disloyal in his effort to sabotage an effort in which I was the major promoter." Zacharias added somewhat puckishly: "Let me say, rather informally, that it is a bit of a pity that dueling has gone out of style. This is a very definite method of settling differences of opinion between people, [better] than [trying] to bring out all the detail in a hearing."

At 9:30 A.M. of Wednesday, May 5, Robert Oppenheimer, the first witness in the proceeding, also became its last, called to the stand now by his own counsel to rebut the testimony presented against him.

In the course of his renewed cross-examination, Roger Robb initiated a new line of questioning. He began by asking whether Oppenheimer considered himself "to be an expert in war . . . or military matters."

Oppenheimer's answer was intriguing: "Of course not. I pray that there are experts in war."

Soon Robb asked, "Doctor, I am a little curious, and I wish you would tell us why you felt it was your function as a scientist to express views on military strategy and tactics."

"I felt, perhaps quite strongly, that having played an active part in promoting a revolution in warfare, I needed to be as responsible as I could with regard to what came of this revolution."

Robb proceeded to "draw a parallel." Did John Ericsson's designing of the first ironclad warship, the *Monitor*, "qualify him to plan naval strategy"?

Samuel Silverman objected that Robb was arguing with the witness, but Gordon Gray said that for weeks now the board had listened to witnesses probing into Oppenheimer's mind with every conceivable kind of question. Once again Gray ruled in Robb's favor.

Robb continued: "Doctor, do you think now that perhaps you went beyond the scope of your proper function as a scientist in undertaking to counsel in matters of military strategy and tactics?" That would depend, said Oppenheimer. In a study such as Vista, the combined intelligence of military officers and "a lot of bright technical and academic people . . . was precisely what gave value to the project."

Robb's theme (the appropriate limits on a scientist's advice), while bearing little relationship either to the Nichols letter of charges or to the AEC's security-screening criteria, was to play an important part in the Gray Board's verdict on Robert Oppenheimer.

After a few minutes, Robb said he had no further questions. Now at last Oppenheimer's part in this hearing was about to end. For three and a half weeks he had been sitting in the wooden witness chair or on the leather sofa behind it while he and others —some friends, some enemies—engaged in what I. I. Rabi had called "writing a man's life." He had watched the inquiry take on the qualities of a criminal prosecution. He had become the prisoner in the dock while the chief prosecutor, with the Gray Board's assent, had browbeaten him and shamed him and stripped his life bare.

And now, in the wake of all this, he said he wished to "make a comment." "I am," he said, "grateful to, and I hope properly appreciative of the patience and consideration that the board has shown me during this part of the proceedings."

On this note Robert Oppenheimer left the witness stand for the last time. His role in the proceeding was over.

When the transcript of the Gray Board hearing was made public some weeks later, *Time* Magazine observed that "in the list of witnesses against J. Robert Oppenheimer, the most effective was J. Robert Oppenheimer himself." And AEC General Counsel William Mitchell, who sat through the entire Gray Board proceeding, has recalled the sensation of being eyewitness to a Greek tragedy, of observing the downfall of a once-great man.

Why did it happen? What had become of the prepossessing witness who, less than five years earlier, had capitivated the stolid members of the House Un-American Activities Committee? Oppenheimer himself later offered a partial explanation. Often during his ordeal with Roger Robb, he said, he had responded unthinkingly to Robb's pounding questions—"the way a soldier does in combat, I suppose. So much is happening or may be about to happen that there is no time to be aware of anything except the next move." Then he added, perhaps more revealingly, "Like someone in a fight—and this was a fight—I had very little sense of self."

Perhaps this sense of self was what was missing in 1954. Years later the French writer André Malraux, critical of Oppenheimer's performance before the Gray Board, said, "He should have told them, at the very outset, '*Je suis la bombe atomique!*'" And indeed, in his earlier confrontation—with HUAC and with FBI interrogators—Oppenheimer had spoken as the respected internationally known "father of the atomic bomb." Judging from the way he was treated on those earlier occasions, he had worn that mantle naturally and well. It had furnished protection. But now, in 1954, he was no longer "*la bombe atomique.*" He had allowed the mantle to fall away. In retrospect his antagonist, Roger Robb, agreed with *Time*'s appraisal. "It turned out," Robb later recalled, "that Oppenheimer was his own worst witness."

If Oppenheimer failed as a witness to make the most of his case, could the same be said of his attorney, Lloyd Garrison? Some lawyers who have read the transcript of the Gray Board hearing believe that Garrison erred in not being more assertive. Whether or not they are correct, their judgment has all the advantages of hindsight. It was Garrison who was on the firing line.

As Garrison himself has explained his posture in the case, he and his associates had decided before the hearing began that they would not (in Garrison's words) "try to build a record on the basis of which we could appeal to the courts if Robert's clearance were denied." They felt that, at best, an appeal would result in a court order for a further hearing and a further "ordeal" for their client. Having reached that decision, "the question of how far we should go in pressing . . . objections before the board became a practical one"—dependent on the "personalities and temperament of the board members, on their day-to-day reactions to evidence" and the like. "If we protested too much, we might only irritate the board members; if we objected too strongly to a particular line of questioning designed to elicit adverse evidence or admissions, we might only magnify its importance in the eyes of the board.

"We felt from the outset that we were waging an uphill fight in which undue combativeness would be a hindrance rather than a help. How far to go was not something which could be reasoned out; it had to be answered by instinctive on-the-spot judgments. Our sole aim was to bring about a favorable decision by the board and, whatever our mistakes of judgment may have been, we subordinated all other considerations to that end."

At 9:30 on the morning of Thursday, May 6, the participants "in the matter of J. Robert Oppenheimer" gathered in Room 2022 for the last time. It was the nineteenth day of the proceeding.

Shortly after ten o'clock, Lloyd Garrison rose to make his summation to the Gray Board. It was, by all accounts, oratorically stunning. For three full hours, that Thursday morning, Garrison addressed the board. Faced with the formidable task of summarizing three thousand pages of testimony, Garrison spoke only from notes; yet his extemporaneous eloquence would have done credit to a written essay or legal brief that had been brought to a high polish.

He began by recalling that when he and the Gray Board had first met, the board members had already had "a week's immersion in FBI files which we would never have the privilege of seeing," and that he had been denied permission for a prehearing informal presentation of his own case. "We came together, then, as strangers, . . . and we found ourselves rather unexpectedly in a proceeding which seemed to us to be adversary in nature."

Garrison then stated what he considered "the basic acid question before the board"—namely, "whether in the handling of restricted [i.e., secret] data, he [Oppenheimer] is to be trusted." He noted that in the rendering of a judgment the AEC's laws and regulations called on the board to consider three factors: loyalty, character and associations. "Certainly," said Garrison, "loyalty is the paramount consideration. If a man is loyal, if in his heart he loves his country and would not knowingly or willingly do anything to injure its security, then associations and character become relatively unimportant."

Then, to reinforce his argument, Garrison drew on a 1948 security decision of the Atomic Energy Commission. In its favorable ruling on a clearance for Dr. Frank Graham (one of Gordon Gray's predecessors as president of the University of North Carolina), the AEC had said that "it is the man himself" who is being judged, and that "common sense must be exercised" in judging the evidence—all the evidence—as required by AEC regulations. Garrison proceeded to apply this test of "common sense" to the matter of Robert Oppenheimer's trustworthiness with secret data. "It would seem to me," he said, "that in approaching that acid question, the most impelling single fact . . . is that for more than a decade Dr. Oppenheimer has created and has shared secrets of the atomic energy program and has held them inviolable. . . . Now . . . after more than a decade . . . to question his safety in the possession of restricted data seems to me a rather appalling matter. . . . I wish we could dispose of [this case] out of hand on the basis of the fact . . . that for more than a decade Dr. Oppenheimer has been trusted, and that he has not failed that trust."

But it was evident that the AEC's case against Oppenheimer could not be thus disposed of, and Garrison set about dealing with its two principal aspects: the hydrogen-bomb charge and Oppenheimer's history of left-wing associations and activities. As to the H-bomb, Garrison said, the matter—and indeed much of the government's case—came down to an appraisal of Robert Oppenheimer's motives. "The only question you have here," he said, is "whether his own advice [on the H-bomb], unlike that of every other member of the GAC, was motivated by a sinister purpose to injure the United States of America and to help our enemy." And with that Garrison felt compelled to add, "The mere utterance of that proposition is somehow shocking to me." There is "not one scrap of evidence to indicate that he differed in his purposes from the other honorable Americans who served on the [General Advisory] Committee and who went into this matter at such length." Even those witnesses who had disagreed with Oppenheimer about the hydrogen bomb had questioned his wisdom but not his loyalty, Garrison noted.

The question of motivation, he continued, was also paramount with regard to those ancillary policy issues—Vista, the "second lab," the Lincoln Summer Study—that made up an "alleged pattern of opposition" implying "a sinister and un-American attitude" toward national defense. The testimony on these matters had been less than precise and well informed, Garrison said. But even if that had not been the case, these issues had "nothing to do with the question of Dr. Oppenheimer's clearance unless you are willing to believe to me the unthinkable thought . . . that in spite of everything he had done to help this country from 1945 on, he suddenly somehow becomes a sinister agent of a foreign power. It is unthinkable."

Garrison had by now been talking steadily for nearly an hour. After a brief recess he took up the question of Oppenheimer's left-wing associations, all of which, he said, were known to General Groves when he ordered Oppenheimer cleared in July, 1943.

Then Garrison moved to "the Chevalier incident." That episode, he said, had been relived during the hearing in such minute detail that it was as if "we are judging a man for something that has happened almost in our presence." This produced an "illusion of a foreshortening of time . . . which to me is a grisly matter, and very, very misleading. This [incident] happened in 1943 . . . in a wholly different atmosphere from that of today. Russia was our so-called gallant ally. The whole attitude toward Russia, toward persons who were sympathetic with Russia . . . was different from what obtains today." He reminded the board of the undiminished confidence in Oppenheimer displayed in the testimony of the two men who had most closely judged the "Chevalier incident" in the times in which it occurred—Lansdale and Groves. "We cannot here reconstruct Robert Oppenheimer's life and activities in the sense of the time and the pressures under which he was working. . . . That is gone forever. No one can reconstruct that, but Groves and Lansdale have that in their minds and in their memories and they lived with it. . . ."

Next on Lloyd Garrison's agenda was Oppenheimer's clearance by the Atomic Energy Commission in 1947. At that time, he pointed out, all five Commissioners had meticulously reviewed the evidence on all the current charges except the hydrogen-bomb allegation. Garrison did not seek to argue that their review was all-conclusive; but, he said, "if a man is solemnly and seriously and deliberately cleared by responsible men, that ought to have a kind of sticking quality . . . because this business of haling men before security boards is one of the most terrible ordeals that we can subject fellow citizens to." Moreover, he said, "if a man's clearance is taken away from him . . . that is the end of that fellow for the rest of his life. It is the end of the country's chance to use him, too. That can't be redone."

Acknowledging the radical-left character of Oppenheimer's involvements before the war, Garrison sought to focus the board's attention on what he regarded as a far more recent and therefore more relevant period in the scientist's life: the postwar decade. Since 1945, Garrison said, whatever relations the physicist might have had with persons the board might consider suspect had been entirely casual, with three exceptions—Robert Serber (who had been cleared by Admiral Nimitz and an AEC security panel); Mrs. Serber; and Haakon Chevalier. As to Chevalier, Garrison said Oppenheimer had "honored himself in describing him as a friend and in not trying to say that it is just a casual matter. He has his loyalties, Mr. Chairman."

When Garrison had spoken for nearly two hours, he moved toward his conclusion.

"You [have] had three and a half weeks now with the gentleman on the sofa. . . . Here he is now with his life in one sense in your hands . . . his life has been an open book." Acknowledging that "you have a tough job of applying these rather complicated standards, criteria, and so forth," Garrison again asked that this be done as in the AEC's 1948 decision in the Frank Graham case, in which the Commission had said that "it is the man himself" who must be judged. The Commission's verdict in the Graham case, said Garrison, "breathes a kind of air of largeness, of reality, of practicality, in dealing with this problem. The thing that I would most urge you not to do, in addition to not bringing 1943 into 1954, is to get chopped up into little compartments of categories that will give to this case a perfectly artificial flavor of judgment. . . .

"There is more than Dr. Oppenheimer on trial in this room. . . . The government of the United States is here on trial also. Our whole security process is on trial here, and is in your keeping, as is his life—the two things together. . . .

"There is an anxiety abroad [in the country]," Garrison continued, "that these security procedures will be applied artificially, rigidly, like some monolithic kind of a machine that will result in the destruction of men of great gifts. . . . America must not devour her own children, Mr. Chairman and members of this board. If we are to be strong, powerful, electric and vital, we must not devour the best and the most gifted of our citizens in some mechanical application of security procedures and mechanisms.

"You have in Dr. Oppenheimer an extraordinary individual, a very complicated man . . . a gifted man beyond what nature can ordinarily do more than once in a very great while. Like all gifted men, unique, sole, not conventional, not quite like anybody else that ever was or ever will be. . . . Does this mean that you should apply different standards to him than you would to somebody like me or somebody else that is just ordinary? No, I say not. I say that there must not be favoritism in this business. . . .

"But this is the point, that if you are to judge the whole man, as the Commission itself in its regulations and its decisions really lays on you the task of doing, you have then a difficult, complicated man, a gifted man to deal with, and in judging him, you have to exercise the greatest effort of comprehension.

"Some men are awfully simple and their acts are simple. That doesn't mean that the standards are any different for them. The standards should be the same. But this man bears the closest kind of examination of what he really is, and what he stands for, and what he means to the country. It is that effort of comprehension of him that I urge upon you.

"I am confident . . . that when you have done all this, you will answer the blunt and ugly question whether he is fit to be trusted with [secret] data in the affirmative. I believe, members of the board, that in doing so you will most deeply serve the interests of the United States of America, which all of us love and want to protect and further.

"That I am sure of, and I am sure that is where the upshot of this case must be.

"Thank you very much."

Garrison sat down. Gordon Gray clarified a few procedural questions and formally advised Oppenheimer of the next steps in the proceeding and of the notification he would receive of the Gray Board's verdict. Lloyd Garrison then ended his part in the hearing as he had begun it, thanking the Gray Board—"for having borne so patiently with me and for the great consideration you have shown to us throughout the proceedings."

The three members of the board thanked Garrison. "We now conclude this phase of the proceedings," said Gordon Gray.

# VI THE GRAY BOARD DECIDES

By the time of the Gray panel's adjournment on May 6 those in
Room 2022 had been living with the Oppenheimer case for
nearly four weeks. Everyone needed respite. The board members departed for their respective homes—Gordon Gray and
Thomas Morgan to North Carolina, Ward Evans to Illinois. For
ten days they rested and gathered their thoughts. On Monday,
May 17, they reconvened in Washington.

On their way there, Morgan and Gray happened to find themselves on the same plane. They compared notes and found that
they had reached much the same conclusions about the case—
conclusions adverse to Oppenheimer. Remembering their earlier dinnertime conversations with Ward Evans, when he had
shocked them with his strongly anti-Oppenheimer views, they
fully expected that there would be a unanimous decision. But
when they met again with Evans, they were flabbergasted at
what seemed to them a complete turnabout in his attitude during
his ten days in the Midwest.

The three did agree, however, on which points of evidence in
the hearing seemed most important, and they asked Roger Robb
and his assistant, Arthur Rolander, to summarize those points
and the board's conclusions as to each. Then each of the board

members began to write his views on the case. AEC regulations required them to make "findings" as to each of the "charges" contained in the original Nichols letter and to state what they felt to be the "significance of these findings." For ten days they labored, and on May 27 they addressed a fifteen-thousand-word memorandum to AEC General Manager Nichols: "Subject: Findings and Recommendation of the Personnel Security Board in the Case of Dr. J. Robert Oppenheimer."

As the three Gray Board members saw it, they were caught in a dilemma "not easily resolved": how, on the one hand, to assure "the survival of free institutions and of individual rights" against the threat of "repressive totalitarianism," while, on the other hand, "protect[ing], preserv[ing] and defend[ing] those human values for which we exist as a nation, as a government, and as a way of life."

Difficult as they found this dilemma, the board was decisive in resolving it. In the "present peril" of the Cold War, "security" was "central" and some "undue restraints upon freedom of mind and action" were necessary. The "protection of all our people," the board members said, must be "paramount to all other considerations." This line of argument led the board to the almost Orwellian statement that, in some cases, what "may seem to be a denial" of freedom might in fact be a "fulfillment" of that freedom. "For," the board said, "if, in our zeal to protect our institutions against our measures to secure them, we lay them open to destruction, we will have lost them all, and will have gained only the empty satisfaction of a meaningless exercise."

The board members seemed conscious that many eyes were watching them. Echoing what both Gordon Gray and Lloyd Garrison had said during the hearing, they stated, "We are acutely aware that in a very real sense this case puts the security system of the United States on trial." Then the board proceeded to examine the manner in which they had conducted the hearing, and made this arresting assertion: "We believe that it has been demonstrated that the Government can search its own soul and the soul of an individual whose relationship to his Government is in question with full protection of the rights and interests of both."

Historian Arthur Schlesinger, Jr., was struck by the Gray Board's assertion that "the Government can search . . . the soul of an individual." Writing in the *Atlantic,* Schlesinger acknowledged that his friend Robert Oppenheimer was at times an "arrogant" man. "But surely," he said, "no arrogance of Oppenheimer equals the arrogance" of the Gray Board members and their claim to be able "to 'search . . . the soul of an individual.' The government which claims to do this would hardly seem a government for Americans."

The Gray Board's self-appraisal continued: "The Board approached its task in the spirit of inquiry, not that of a trial." (*Did such a spirit characterize the tactics of Roger Robb which the board tolerated throughout the hearing?*)

"Dr. Oppenheimer has been represented by counsel . . . at all times in the course of the proceedings." (*Except when his counsel was excluded from the hearing room for "security" reasons.*)

"[Oppenheimer] has confronted every witness appearing before the Board, with the privilege of cross-examination." (*But what of the nameless witnesses—anonymous, perhaps, even to the Gray Board—who did not appear but who bore witness against Oppenheimer via the secret investigative reports? What, for example, of Paul Crouch?*)

"[Oppenheimer] is familiar with . . . every relevant document . . . except those which under governmental necessity cannot be disclosed." (*But that exception encompassed some three thousand pages of documents—equal in length to the record of the Gray Board hearing itself.*)

"As it considered substance, the Board has allowed sympathetic consideration for the individual [*e.g., Robb's cross-examination of Oppenheimer regarding Jean Tatlock or Robb's entrapment of a former AEC Chairman with surprise documents*] to go hand in hand with . . . a realistic . . . attitude toward subversion."*

This ended the board's introductory remarks.

---

* To buttress their judgment of the hearing's fairness, the board cited the compliments bestowed upon it by Oppenheimer and Garrison in the closing days of the proceeding—in each case embellishing them by adding words that neither Oppenheimer nor Garrison had actually uttered.

The board next explained its findings on the AEC's charges, twenty out of twenty-four of which it found to be either "true" or "substantially true." In some cases the board even went beyond the charges—for example, on the matter of whether Oppenheimer had recruited Communists and fellow travelers for Los Alamos. The board not only found him guilty of *wartime* recruitment but also discussed *postwar* events: his help to David Bohm in securing a teaching post (which, notably, involved no access to secrets); his chance encounter with Bohm and Rossi Lomanitz. The finding even managed to frown on Oppenheimer's statement that he would, if asked, have written a letter of recommendation for Bohm as a competent physicist.\* This implied that the Gray Board expected a man in Oppenheimer's position not only to stand in judgment on the political probity of his brethren but also to refrain from telling the truth if asked to evaluate a colleague's professional competence.

The board also strayed beyond the AEC charge regarding the Chevalier incident. It mentioned Chevalier's use of an Oppenheimer letter in his effort to get a passport (surely not Oppenheimer's responsibility). It also mentioned that Oppenheimer had suggested an attorney to represent Chevalier in his passport request. Neither of these points had been mentioned in the original letter of charges. The finding also noted that the lawyer recommended by Oppenheimer had also represented Joseph Weinberg (the alleged "Scientist X") in a perjury trial†—a guilt-by-association argument more to be expected of a Congressional inquisitor than of an attorney of Gray's caliber.

The board spoke of the visit that Oppenheimer made in December, 1953, to the Chevaliers' apartment and of their meeting, the next day, with "a Dr. Malraux" (*sic*). The board's verdict also cited Chevalier's letter to Jeffries Wyman, science attaché at the U.S. Embassy in Paris, about Chevalier's passport problem, and noted that Oppenheimer had "admitted having lunch" with Wyman. The implication was that the physicist had (or might have) interceded with Wyman on Chevalier's behalf; yet the

---

\* On this point Ward Evans observed, "I think I would have recommended Bohm as a physicist. Dr. Oppenheimer was not asked if he would have added that Bohm was a Communist."

† In which Weinberg was acquitted.

board had heard evidence that ruled out any such possibility. Oppenheimer had sworn that the luncheon occurred a week *before* he had dined with Chevalier and learned of Chevalier's passport difficulties.

One particular finding had more than surface importance. The hearing testimony had left uncertain the date on which Oppenheimer had ended his cash contributions to various causes through the Communist Party. But now the board fixed the date—at April, 1942, the very month in which Oppenheimer formally had entered the government's employ. The effect was to appear to confirm one of William Liscum Borden's main arguments for concluding that Oppenheimer was a Soviet agent: namely, that the simultaneity of the physicist's entry into war work and of his dropping of external Communist Party ties conformed with orders then being issued to party members.

The Gray Board's finding on the H-bomb charge (presented here with interpolations) went roughly as follows: After the presidential go-ahead was made public on January 31, 1950, Oppenheimer "did not oppose the [H-bomb] project in a positive or open manner" (*as had Hans Bethe, Albert Einstein and other leading scientists*), nor did he decline to cooperate in the project (*as Edward Teller had done at Los Alamos during the height of global war, in refusing to work on the projects assigned him by his superiors*). Oppenheimer's sin lay in the supremacy of his personal influence in the scientific community, and in the fact that he "did not make it known that he had abandoned" his well-known anti-H-bomb views. This, the board concluded, "undoubtedly had an adverse effect on recruitment of scientists" for the H-bomb program.

The board's H-bomb finding, remarkably, exonerated Oppenheimer on one after another of the specific charges contained in the Nichols letter. The board was unable to find that the scientist had actively discouraged others from working on the "Super" or that his opposition had "definitely slowed down its development" or that he had caused unauthorized distribution at Los Alamos of the 1949 GAC minutes. The most the board could say was that "enthusiastic support on his part would *perhaps* have encouraged other leading scientists to work on the program"* and that the Oppenheimer-led opposition had delayed initiation of the "concerted effort" that had led to the H-bomb. (Emphasis added.)

Ironically, the H-bomb finding that carried the most weight with the board did not originate with the Nichols letter at all. This finding was that in telling the Gray Board he had merely opposed a crash program for the "Super," but had not opposed the bomb *per se,* Oppenheimer had not been "entirely candid with the Board." The evidence of this: "The record reflects that Dr. Oppenheimer expressed the opinion in writing† that the 'super bomb should never be produced,' and that the commitment to this effect should be unqualified." Apparently the board gave no credence to Oppenheimer's own explanation that in saying the "Super" should never be produced, he and his colleagues meant to exhort all parties—Russia as well as the United States—"never" to fabricate such a destructive device.

Having completed its list of findings, the Gray Board now turned to its duty under the regulations to discuss their significance.

The board divided the twenty-four Nichols charges into two main categories: the single charge concerning the H-bomb and the twenty-three that concerned Oppenheimer's prewar leftist connections. As for the latter, the board stated that, while Oppenheimer had been "deeply involved" with many active Communists, "there is no evidence that he was a member of the party in the strict sense of the word." That finding was later considered especially noteworthy by one counterespionage expert, who was peculiarly aware of the microscopic detail with which intelligence officers before the war were scrutinizing both the movements of Oppenheimer and the activities of the Communist Party in California. This expert found it hard to believe that Oppenheimer could have been the hard-core party-liner William Borden

---

* It was this, more a speculation than a finding, that inspired a cartoon by the Washington *Post*'s Herblock, in which the slogan of a government laboratory had been changed from "THINK" to "ENTHUSE."

† In the "majority annex" to the 1949 GAC report, in which five of Oppenheimer's colleagues joined.

believed him to be and still have left "no evidence," as the Gray Board put it.

Despite the "most serious view" the board took of Oppenheimer's "earlier involvements," it found in them "no indication of disloyalty." Indeed, the board members ended their discussion of these "involvements" with the "conclusion . . . that Dr. Oppenheimer is a loyal citizen."

When the verdict turned to the significance of the H-bomb findings, Ward Evans parted company with his fellow board members. All three men agreed that any implication of disloyalty or of "attachment to the Soviet Union" that might be read into Oppenheimer's opposition to the "Super" was "not supported by any material which the Board has seen." But, to Gray and Morgan, this fact was outweighed by their "conclusion that, whatever the motive, the security interests of the United States" had been "affected."* Thus they rejected Garrison's pivotal thesis regarding the H-bomb charge, that Oppenheimer's motives were the central question.

At this point Gray and Morgan made what many consider their most vulnerable statement. "It must be said," they began half-grudgingly, "that Dr. Oppenheimer seems to have had a high degree of discretion, reflecting an unusual ability to keep to himself vital secrets."

To many, this statement should have ended all question about Robert Oppenheimer's security status. For, having found that in the one respect that is the *raison d'être* of a security system—the safeguarding of secrets—Oppenheimer had not just an average but "an *unusual* ability," how could the board majority still consider him a security risk?

The answer was that they found, in Oppenheimer, "suggestions of a tendency to be coerced, or at least influenced in conduct, over a period of years." In support of this assertion, they cited two incidents. The first was Oppenheimer's intervention in the Army's drafting of Rossi Lomanitz, to which he was "led," according to Gray and Morgan, by "the outraged intercession of Dr. [Edward U.] Condon." The second was Oppenheimer's re-

* Based on their contention that Oppenheimer's lack of enthusiasm for the thermonuclear program had affected other scientists and had put a damper on the development effort.

cantation of his secret HUAC testimony against his former protégé Bernard Peters, "as a result of protestations by Dr. Condon,
by Dr. Peters himself, and by other scientists." Out of the myriad
of detail presented to the board about the life of Robert Oppenheimer covering a twenty-year period, these two incidents were
all the evidence Gray and Morgan adduced to show a "tendency
to be coerced . . . over a period of years."

But then suddenly the board majority shifted ground, contending that whether or not the Condon incidents proved "susceptibility to influence" or merely "very bad judgment," they
"clearly raise the question of Dr. Oppenheimer's understanding,
acceptance, and enthusiastic support of the security system." Beginning with the Chevalier incident, Oppenheimer had "repeatedly exercised an arrogance of his own judgment" about the
reliability of other citizens. Morgan and Gray found evidence of
this in Oppenheimer's failure to answer certain questions about
Chevalier posed by FBI agents in 1946; in the career help he gave
to David Bohm "after he had reason to know of Bohm's security
status";* and, most important, in his recent contacts in Paris with
Chevalier. To the latter, the board majority attached a "high
degree of significance." "It is not important to determine that Dr.
Oppenheimer discussed with Chevalier matters of concern to the
security of the United States," they said. What was important was
that Oppenheimer knew about Chevalier's background. That
being the case, Oppenheimer's "association with him, on what
could not be considered a casual basis, is not the kind of thing
that our security system permits on the part of one who cus-
tomarily has access to information of the highest classification."
What Gray and Morgan were saying, in effect, was that an Oppenheimer and a Chevalier were not permitted to have *any*
association whatever, even if they might confine their conversations to such innocent matters as the weather or old wines.

Finally, Gray and Morgan came to their recommendation "in
the matter of J. Robert Oppenheimer."

First, they felt obliged to lay to rest again any question about

* Morgan and Gray did not mention that all of this assistance to David
Bohm involved positions with private universities, involving no access to
secrets.

Oppenheimer's loyalty. "We have come to a clear conclusion," they said, "that he is a loyal citizen," adding somewhat condescendingly that this "should be reassuring to the people of this country." How much reassurance could the public squeeze out of the declaration that the nation's onetime chief atomic scientist was loyal, but nonetheless could not be trusted with the country's secrets? For that was the majority verdict:

> We have . . . been unable to arrive at the conclusion that it would be clearly consistent with the security interests of the United States to reinstate Dr. Oppenheimer's clearance, and, therefore, do not so recommend.

They then listed the "controlling considerations" behind this verdict:

> 1. We find that Dr. Oppenheimer's continuing conduct and associations have reflected a serious disregard for the requirements of the security system.
> 2. We have found a susceptibility to influence which could have serious implications for the security interests of the country.
> 3. We find his conduct in the hydrogen-bomb program sufficiently disturbing as to raise a doubt as to whether his future participation, if characterized by the same attitudes in a government program relating to the national defense, would be clearly consistent with the best interests of security.
> 4. We have regretfully concluded that Dr. Oppenheimer has been less than candid in several instances in his testimony before this Board.

At this point, having rendered findings, discussed their significance and offered a recommendation, the board had fulfilled the requirements of AEC regulations and procedures, but Gray and Morgan were not satisfied. They felt it appropriate to go further and to discuss the "general considerations" underlying their adverse decision.* Ward Evans, however, felt it was "not

---

* In the printed Gray Board opinion itself, the discussion of these "general considerations" precedes the recommendation. The order of their presentation in this chapter has been altered in the interest of simplicity and clarity.

necessary to go into any philosophical discussion to prove points not found in Mr. Nichols' letter."

Gray and Morgan began with what many regard as the pivotal sentence of the Gray-Morgan verdict:

> It seemed to us that an alternative recommendation [i.e., in Oppenheimer's favor] would be possible, if we were allowed to exercise mature practical judgment without the rigid circumscription of regulations and criteria established for us.

"... *without the rigid circumscription of regulations and criteria established for us.*" That single phrase encapsulated the view so often revealed by Gordon Gray's questions to witnesses: that the Gray Board members had no choice because the AEC's "regulations and criteria" strait-jacketed them. Yet three separate provisions of those regulations stated precisely the contrary:

> The decision as to security clearance is an overall common-sense judgment. . . .
>
> *—United States Atomic Energy Commission*
> *Criteria for Determining Eligibility*
> *for Personnel Security Clearance*

> In considering the material before the Board, the members of the Board, as practical men of affairs, should be guided by the same consideration that would guide them in making a sound decision in the administration of their own lives.
>
> *—Section 4.16, United States Atomic Energy*
> *Commission Security Clearance Procedures*

> Cases must be carefully weighed in the light of all the information, and a determination must be reached which gives due recognition to the favorable as well as unfavorable information concerning the individual and which balances the cost to the program of not having his services against any possible risks involved. . . .
>
> *—United States Atomic Energy Commission*
> *Criteria for Determining Eligibility*
> *for Personnel Security Clearance*

Each of these provisions not only permitted but virtually

directed hearing boards to exercise the "mature, practical judgment"* that Gray and Morgan contended were proscribed to them. Could they have been unaware of the three explicit provisions? It seems unlikely, for Lloyd Garrison had cited all three in his oral summation before the board.

Certain of Gray's and Morgan's "general considerations" came in the form of answers to self-addressed questions, including: "What, within the framework of this case, is meant by loyalty?"

In reply they said in part that "any person whose absolute loyalty to the United States is in question . . . should be rejected for government service." What was meant by the phrase "absolute loyalty"? Taking its words at face value, could it not be argued that aliens cannot, by definition, be endowed with this attribute, since they naturally can be expected to retain some residual loyalty, if only emotional, to their mother country? In the case of Wernher Von Braun—spirited to America in 1945, fresh from his all-out efforts to develop V-2 rockets for the mortal enemy of the United States, and pressed immediately into the service of the U.S. Government—could one be sure, at that instant in 1945, that he had "absolute loyalty" to the United States? Might not that requisite likewise have barred from government service such foreign-born scientists as Edward Teller, Enrico Fermi and Niels Bohr?

The next self-posed question was, in effect: Must one accept the principle that "once a Communist, always a Communist," or is there such a thing as rehabilitation? Considering the matter in the abstract, Gray and Morgan chose the latter alternative, even urging that "this principle [of rehabilitation] should be a part of the security policy of the United States Government."† Despite this categorical endorsement of the principle, Gray and Morgan strikingly failed to apply it in the Oppenheimer case. They did

* Those very words, invoked by the board, appear further on in the third provision cited above.

† In one somewhat ironic sense, it already was: the government had no apparent hesitation in trusting implicitly the anti-Communist testimony of such acknowledged former Communists as Elizabeth Bentley, Whittaker Chambers and, of course, Paul Crouch—even when these individuals had been, in their Communist days, proven or self-confessed liars.

acknowledge a massive shift in national and world opinion since Oppenheimer's leftist involvements. But they made no mention whatever of the changes in the man himself: major shifts in his attitude toward the radical left and its adherents, toward the requirements of the security system and toward the Soviet Union.

The board majority then turned to the question of whether the AEC's clearance of Oppenheimer in 1947 rendered the 1954 hearing a meaningless exercise, a violation of the Constitution's precept that a man once acquitted of a crime may not be tried again for the same offense. In arguing that the security system in general did not violate that precept, Gray and Morgan seemed to favor an extraordinary subordination of the individual to the state. Their reasoning was that the "double jeopardy" principle, as applied in criminal law, "is for the protection of the individual, whereas security measures are for the protection of the country, whose interests should never be foreclosed."

As to the Oppenheimer hearing, Gray and Morgan said, somewhat mysteriously, that "it was necessary to the national security that material information not considered in previous clearances be studied." What "material information"? Unless Morgan and Gray were referring to the H-bomb charge (the only one dealing with events subsequent to the 1947 clearance), could one avoid the implication that the FBI or other intelligence agencies had withheld "material information" from General Groves and the AEC? Nothing in the majority opinion sheds light on that serious question.

At several points in the Gray Board hearing, witnesses like Roscoe Charles Wilson and Wendell Latimer and, to an extent, Edward Teller, had openly voiced their apprehension about Oppenheimer's potent and pervasive influence on government policy. A similar worry ran through the last of the board majority's "general considerations," concerning "The Role of Scientists as Advisors in the Formulation of Government Policy." Gray and Morgan were concerned that, due to the increasingly technical nature of many government decisions, specialists who advised the government had "an exponential amplification of influence which is vastly greater than that of the individual citizen." There was a danger that the "advice of specialists relating to moral, military and political issues" might be given "undue and in some cases decisive weight." That being the case, it was important that the advice of scientists and technicians be kept antiseptically clean of "considerations of an emotional character."

Gray and Morgan said they could understand the "emotional involvement" of scientists who had helped "unleash upon the world a force which could be destructive of civilization," and they acknowledged that Robert Oppenheimer was prime among these scientists. But, they insisted, "emotional involvement in the current crisis, like all other things, must yield to the security of the nation." Responsible government officials must be sure that any advice received from scientists and technicians represented "soundly based conviction . . . uncolored and uninfluenced by considerations of an emotional character."

But the board majority insisted that even if a technical adviser could succeed in transforming himself into this sort of dehumanized robot-computer, he still must pass another test: he would have to hold a "genuine conviction that this country cannot in the interest of security have less than the strongest possible offensive capabilities in a time of national danger." Thus in the mind of the board it seemed impermissible to raise any question whatever about any new weapon if that weapon would increase the "offensive capabilities" of the United States.

Later in its verdict, the board professed the "profound and positive view that no man should be tried for the expression of his opinions." It is not easy to reconcile that with the board's requirement that a specialist's convictions be "soundly based" and that he believe in the "strongest possible offensive capabilities." Judged against these two standards, it is little wonder the board found Oppenheimer wanting and, in a sense, surprising that it did not make some adverse comment about Fermi, Rabi, Conant and Bethe—all of whom were at one time more opposed to the H-bomb than Oppenheimer.

Such were the views of the Gray Board majority. But their verdict was not unanimous. Against their opinion that Oppenheimer's clearance should not be reinstated stood a one-and-a-third-page statement entitled, "Minority Report of Dr. Ward V. Evans."

Whereas the Gray-Morgan majority report was later subjected to sharp criticism, the Evans dissent was warmly praised, by no one more enthusiastically than critic and lecturer John Mason Brown. "No one," said Brown, "has been more concise in showing up the charges against Oppenheimer." After the often "irrelevant or rudderless" questions posed by Evans in the course of the Gray Board hearing, Brown continued, the "jabbing directness" of his dissent "comes as a surprise."

The "jabbing directness" of the dissent is attributable not so much to Evans as to that master of jabbing directness, Roger Robb. This paradox came about in the following way. Tentative versions of the various sections of the Gray Board report, including Ward Evans' draft dissent, were circulated among all members of the board. Reading what Evans had written, Gordon Gray was struck by its lack of clarity. Gray felt that if the Evans dissent was published in that original form, it would be badly received, perhaps even ridiculed. And so Gray assigned Robb to help Evans reshape and sharpen it.

"I have reached the conclusion," Evans began simply, "that Dr. J. Robert Oppenheimer's clearance should be reinstated. . . ."

The chemist noted that the majority's adverse verdict had been based largely on the finding that all but one of the initial AEC charges against Oppenheimer were true or substantially true.* But, said Evans, "most of this derogatory information was in the hands of the [Atomic Energy] Commission when Dr. Oppenheimer was cleared in 1947. They apparently were aware of his associations and his left-wing policies; yet they cleared him. They took a chance on him because of his special talents and he continued to do a good job. Now when the job is done, we are asked to investigate him for practically the same derogatory information."

Gray and Morgan had discussed the question of "rehabilitation" in the abstract, but had declined to apply it specifically to Oppenheimer. Ward Evans, however, was very specific. Oppenheimer, he said,

* The exception was the charge about the alleged Communist meeting in Oppenheimer's home, on which the board found the evidence "inconclusive."

had communistic friends, it is true. He still has some. However, the evidence indicates that he has fewer of them than
he had in 1947. He is not as naïve as he was then. He has more
judgment. . . . He [now] hates Russia. . . . To deny him
clearance now for what he was cleared for in 1947, when we
must know he is less of a security risk now than he was then,
seems to be hardly the procedure to be adopted in a free country. . . . To damn him now and ruin his career and his service,
I cannot do it.

His statements in cross-examination show him to be still
naïve but extremely honest and such statements work to his
benefit in my estimation. All people are somewhat of a security
risk. I don't think we have to go out of our way to point out
how this man might be a security risk.

Then Evans turned to the question of Oppenheimer's veracity
(or, as the board majority had couched it, his "lack of candor").
First, as to his misguided wartime interviews with Colonels Pash
and Lansdale, he had "in one place in his testimony said that he
had told a 'tissue of lies.'* What he had said was not a tissue of
lies; there was one lie."†

In the remaining points in Evans' dissent, he examined certain
of Oppenheimer's actions that had been criticized by the board
majority. But, unlike Gray and Morgan, Evans showed he considered the question of Oppenheimer's *motives* to be central to a
judgment of these actions. Moreover, Evans apparently viewed
Oppenheimer's conduct through far different and more charitable
eyes than did Gray and Morgan. "In recent years he [Oppen-
heimer] went to see Chevalier in Paris. I don't like this," said
Evans, "but I cannot condemn him on this ground. I don't like his
about face in the matter of Dr. Peters, but I don't think it subversive or disloyal."

Evans' views on the H-bomb charge carried the same flavor.

* Even Oppenheimer's defender had become a victim of the misimpression
that the "tissue of lies" phrase was Oppenheimer's, whereas in fact it was
Roger Robb's.
† Evans also dealt with Oppenheimer's misstatement about not having
heard from Glenn Seaborg prior to the GAC's 1949 H-bomb meeting—even
though this had not been raised in the Gray-Morgan majority verdict. This
indicates that the matter of the Seaborg letter had been raised in the Gray
Board's *oral* discussions.

"[Oppenheimer] did not hinder the development of the H-bomb," Evans said unequivocally, "and there is absolutely nothing in the testimony to show that he did. . . . If his opposition to the H-bomb caused any people not to work on it, it was because of his intellectual prominence and influence over scientific people, and not because of any subversive tendencies."

Then Evans delivered a peroration: "I personally think that our failure to clear Dr. Oppenheimer will be a black mark on the escutcheon of our country," he began. Oppenheimer's defenders in the Gray Board hearing constituted the "scientific backbone of our nation" and Evans was worried "about the effect an improper decision may have on scientific development in our country."

> We have taken hold of this new development [atomic energy] in a very great way. There is no predicting where and how far it may go and what its future potentialities may be. I would very much regret any action to retard or hinder this new scientific development.*

"This is my opinion as a citizen of a free country," Evans concluded. "I suggest that Dr. Oppenheimer's clearance be restored."

The Gray Board opinion and Ward Evans' dissent were given to AEC General Manager Kenneth D. Nichols on Thursday, May 27. The following day Nichols composed a letter to Oppenheimer advising him of the outcome and of his right to appeal the decision to the AEC's permanent Personnel Security Review Board. Irrespective of such an appeal, Nichols said, he would submit his own "recommendation" to the five Atomic Energy Commissioners, who would make the "final determination." That sentence, and, in particular, the word "recommendation," were to

---

* The board majority, Gordon Gray and Thomas Morgan, had taken cognizance of this point in their "general considerations," as follows: "We know that scientists, with their unusual talents, are loyal citizens, and, for every pertinent purpose, normal human beings. We must believe that they, the young and the old and all between, will understand that a responsible Government must make responsible decisions. If scientists should believe that such a decision in Government, however, distasteful with respect to an individual, must be applicable to his whole profession, they misapprehend their own duties and obligations as citizens."

prove to have far more significance than Lloyd Garrison and his associates at first accorded them.

That same day, Friday, May 28, AEC General Counsel Mitchell telephoned Lloyd Garrison and broke the news of the Gray Board's unfavorable verdict. He also delivered copies of the Gray Board opinion and the Nichols letter to Herbert Marks, who took them to New York that night.

On Saturday, Robert Oppenheimer and his attorneys gathered to go over the Gray Board opinion and to discuss next steps. They were all "deeply distressed by the outcome," Garrison has recalled, although from the beginning they had felt they faced an uphill fight. But, according to Garrison, they "took some comfort from Dr. Evans' dissent and from the vigor with which the Board had affirmed Robert's loyalty."

In one respect, the situation they faced that Saturday was similar to that which had confronted Oppenheimer and Garrison when they had first met in early January. Once again there existed an AEC paper adverse to Robert Oppenheimer. (In January it had been the Nichols letter of charges; now it was the Gray Board verdict.) Once again there was the danger that the unfavorable document might at any time be made public. If this occurred without any accompanying rebuttal, the news stories might present a one-sided picture. And so on Monday Garrison set about preparing his answer, with the intention of releasing it publicly along with the Gray Board opinion.

Garrison's refutation took the form of a letter to General Nichols containing an uncharacteristically blunt attack on the majority's finding that Oppenheimer should not be trusted with national secrets. This, Garrison observed, "stands in such stark contrast with the Board's findings regarding Dr. Oppenheimer's loyalty and discretion as to raise doubts about the process of reasoning by which the conclusion was arrived at."

Garrison's letter (in which he was joined by attorney John W. Davis) bore the date of Tuesday, June 1. Before the day was out, he had furnished a copy of it to the newspapers, together with a copy of the Gray Board decision and Ward Evans' dissent. Garrison also conveyed a separate memorandum prepared by Garrison's associate, Allan Ecker, drawing attention to those passages of the Gray Board opinion that talked of Oppenheimer's "deep devotion to his country," his "loyalty" and his "high degree of discretion in keeping secrets."

The *New York Times* of Wednesday morning, June 2, devoted its most prominent front-page position to the story of the Gray Board's verdict and the Garrison rebuttal. The *Times* headline accented the internal contradiction in the majority opinion that Garrison had attacked in his letter:

**DR. OPPENHEIMER IS BARRED FROM SECURITY CLEARANCE THOUGH 'LOYAL,' 'DISCREET' . . . SCIENTIST CALLS FINDINGS CONTRADICTORY**

"That was a time of bleak and dreary days for Robert and his family," a close friend has recalled of the period following the Gray Board's decision.

Robert himself was kind of numb and automatically agreed to follow his lawyers' advice and appeal the verdict to the AEC Commissioners. . . . Working with them on the appeal, he was partly frantic and partly dazed; he was like a man running on a treadmill, anxious to get off but not quite knowing how.

In Princeton, the day after the *Times* disclosure, he received a visit of support from Albert Einstein and, of course, persistent requests for comment by newsmen, which he adamantly refused. Yet he did accept a radio telephone call from a reporter in Melbourne, Australia, who quoted him as saying: "Maybe this is the end of the road for me. I have no sympathy for Communism, but I have moral principles from which I will never depart."*

On Sunday, June 6, Lewis Strauss' eye caught two sentences in the *New York Times* "News of the Week in Review" that strongly implied he had had a part in bringing the case against Robert Oppenheimer. The *Times* stated that "last July 7, Strauss ordered a new investigation" of Dr. Oppenheimer, and that he had "removed the Oppenheimer file to the White House."

Ordinarily, Sunday is regarded as a virtually inviolable day of rest both for government officials and for newsmen, but for

---

* Oppenheimer denied, the next day, having made the statement, but the Australian newspaper insisted he had talked with them.

Strauss the denial of these implications could not wait. Now it was his turn to call in reporter Reston for an "exclusive" on the Oppenheimer case.

The Sunday session bore fruit the next day in an extensive report in the *Times*, signed by Reston and liberally quoting "AEC officials." The Reston report contained not only a denial of the "Week in Review" statements but also a rebuttal of some of the barbs aimed at the AEC in Lloyd Garrison's June 1 letter. Most notable was the answer to Garrison's complaint that Oppenheimer had been denied AEC documents he had requested to help refresh his recollection and prepare for his Gray Board testimony. The explanation offered by the "AEC official" was that "one of the issues in the case concerns Dr. Oppenheimer's veracity. Accordingly, we felt it relevant to test his oral statements against the actual documents." This as much as said that Roger Robb had been acting at least with AEC blessing, if not at AEC instructions, in using government documents to cross up Oppenheimer and other witnesses before the Gray Board.

Reston's account appeared on Monday, June 7. That same day the five Atomic Energy Commissioners met and considered for the first time an action that was to play a major role in the unfolding of the Oppenheimer case: the public release of the full transcript of the Gray Board hearing (minus selected passages which might contain "security information").

This was a grave step to contemplate, in view of Gordon Gray's ironclad assurances to almost every witness that the board considered the proceeding a "confidential matter" and that "the [Atomic Energy] Commission will make no public releases." There are indications that some on the Commission felt that when Lloyd Garrison violated the confidentiality stricture by releasing the Gray Board opinion, the Commission was in effect released from Gordon Gray's pledge. In any event, the question was merely discussed but not resolved at this June 7 meeting. It was not to remain dormant for long.

In the wake of James Reston's "authoritative" account of the Strauss view of things, both sides began peeling away the concealing cover of secrecy. On Tuesday, June 8, Oppenheimer re-

leased his letter to Strauss of the previous December 22 in which
he had said it was Strauss, not he, who had suggested the alternative of an Oppenheimer resignation as a means of avoiding a
showdown security hearing. (There was, by then, considerable
controversy in the Washington rumor mill as to who had made
the suggestion.) On the same day General Nichols made public a
letter he had sent to Garrison on June 3, advising Garrison that
the AEC would not hear oral argument, as Garrison had asked,
but would accept a written brief—if Garrison could submit it
within four days' time. In the same letter Nichols commented on
Garrison's protest (public, by now) that the Gray Board had
failed to grant Oppenheimer access to documents that were later
introduced at his security hearing. Nichols said the AEC had
offered to furnish Garrison such requested documents as it might
consider relevant and "consistent with the national interest."* He
also called attention to Oppenheimer's failure to take advantage
of the AEC's offer to let him read the 1949 GAC documents, and
to Lloyd Garrison's failure to request security clearance until it
was too late "to complete the necessary background investigation."†

On the following afternoon, June 9, the marathon Army-Mc-
Carthy hearing, now in its thirtieth day, reached its most decisive
single moment. Senator McCarthy, irritated by the withering
cross-examination that his aide, Roy Cohn, was suffering at the
hands of the Army's special counsel Joseph N. Welch, charged
that one of Welch's young law associates was a former member of
the supposedly pro-Communist Lawyers' Guild. Welch, near
tears, turned on McCarthy, and in words that continued for years
to ring in the ears of many viewers who watched the scene on
television, said, "Until this moment, Senator, I think I never
gauged your cruelty or your recklessness. . . . Let us not assassinate this lad further. You have done enough. Have you no
sense of decency, sir? At long last, have you left no sense of
decency?"

---

* Nichols did not mention the AEC's denial of every document requested
by Garrison on February 12 (see pp. 251–52).

† Nichols did not say anything about the eight-day emergency clearance
the AEC had managed to secure for Roger Robb (see p. 248).

Among those watching that affecting moment was a thirteen-year-old boy in Princeton, New Jersey: Robert Oppenheimer's son, Peter. The boy walked away from the television set and went upstairs to his bedroom. There, on the blackboard that resembled those covering one entire wall of his father's office, he wrote the following:

> The Amican Govermerant is unfair to Acuse Certain People that I know, of being unfair to them. Since this true, I think that Certain People, and may I say, only Certain People in the U.S. govermeant, should go to HELL.
>
> Yours truly,<br>CERTAIN PEOPLE.*

On Friday, June 11, the *New York Times'* James Reston again wrote authoritatively on the origins of the Oppenheimer case, again in a manner that strongly suggested that much of his information had come from Lewis Strauss. Among the intriguing bits of information reported by Reston: the Oppenheimer security file had been "reviewed" late in the summer of 1953—that is, at least two months *before* William Liscum Borden addressed his letter to J. Edgar Hoover. An "authoritative" AEC source had advised Reston that this review of the Oppenheimer dossier was not out of the ordinary, but was merely in compliance with the 1953 Eisenhower loyalty-security order.

That same day Atomic Energy Commissioner Eugene Zuckert was on the train taking his family to Stamford, Connecticut, for the weekend. Since he would soon have to render a judgment on the Oppenheimer case, Zuckert was studying an especially prepared summary of the investigative file and of pertinent portions of the Gray Board hearing. As the train neared Stamford, Zuckert closed up the summary and, he thought, put it in his briefcase. But, instead, the document apparently slipped under the train seat. The next morning, Saturday, Zuckert went to his briefcase to resume work and was horrified to find the secret summary missing. He immediately telephoned the Atomic Energy Commission in Washington.

---

* *Life* reporter Robert Coughlan has also told of "that inevitable day when [Peter] came home from school and told his mother a classmate had taunted him: 'Your father is a Communist.'"

Chairman Lewis Strauss was at his farm at Brandy Station, Virginia, some fifty miles from Washington, when he was notified of the loss. He quickly called a meeting of his colleagues for that evening and drove back to the capital. One of those present recalls that when they met in the AEC building that Saturday night, Strauss was in "a state." Obviously, he told his colleagues, the Gray Board hearing had been compromised, and they could probably expect to see the missing document published in the next edition of the *New York Times*. It was urgent, he said, that the entire transcript be made available to the press immediately. A practical obstacle stood in the way: only a few copies of the massive three-thousand-page typed transcript were on hand, a small fraction of the number required to satisfy the huge Washington press corps. But Strauss had a suggestion to meet that problem: place the few copies of the transcript in a room in AEC headquarters, summon the press and, in order to facilitate their perusal of the mountainous volume of words, mark the passages that they would be likely to find most interesting.

This notion did not appeal to at least one of Strauss' colleagues who sensed on the Chairman's part something other than a feeling of warm friendship for Oppenheimer. He feared that any high-lighting of the Gray Board transcript that might emanate from the AEC might not portray Oppenheimer in the most favorable light. Partly to deflect Strauss' strong pressures for immediate release of the transcript, it was agreed that the typescript of the hearing should be sent to the Government Printing Office to be set in type, so that it could be released quickly if need be. The next day, Sunday, reporter Reston was given to "understand" that Strauss had "proposed" that a security-censored version of the Gray Board testimony "should be published at once." In imparting this information in Monday morning's *Times*, Reston also reported that Strauss had picked up an ally in Gordon Gray, who had written the AEC urging that the transcript be published.

The enterprising Reston also called Lloyd Garrison, told him of the possible AEC release of the transcript, and asked Garrison to give him the transcript immediately, so that the *Times* could publish the hearing in installments, with accompanying stories that would put the facts in their proper perspective. Reston later reported that Oppenheimer himself "tended to favor publication." But his attorneys decided to decline Reston's offer. Not only had they given both the AEC and the Gray Board witnesses their assurance that they would not release the transcript; they still entertained the possibility, however unlikely, that the AEC might find in Oppenheimer's favor, and they did not want to risk disturbing the Commission and prejudicing the outcome.

By the time the Atomic Energy Commissioners met again to consider the question of the transcript's release, the missing Gray Board summary had long since been found and safely returned. At the time of the emergency Saturday night meeting, the professional sleuths of the AEC security forces and the FBI had been scouring the route of Zuckert's travels in an intense effort to locate the missing document. But, as is often the case, the most likely solution was the last to be thought of, and it was not a security officer who hit on it; it was AEC Commissioner Thomas Murray who suggested at the Saturday night meeting that someone check the lost-and-found department at Boston's South Station, the ultimate destination of Zuckert's train. Just as Thomas Murray had thought, the missing summary was there—turned in, apparently, by the railroad cleaning crew. Forty-five minutes after midnight, Saturday, AEC officials were notified that the lost had been found and was on its way back to official safety.

Therefore, when the Commission met on Monday, Lewis Strauss' prime justification for releasing the transcript—the danger that it might be "compromised" by someone's publishing Zuckert's lost summary—had evaporated. Strauss' fear that the transcript would find its way into the public prints had not been realized. Nonetheless, when the matter was put to a vote that day, his view prevailed, four to one. Only Commissioner Henry DeWolf Smyth was unable to reconcile the publication of the transcript with Gordon Gray's promise to each witness that the AEC would "not take the initiative" in publishing the hearing.

Why was Lewis Strauss so eager for the public release of the full Gray Board transcript? *Time* Magazine* may have provided

---

* Whose coverage of the Oppenheimer case was based largely on the reporting of two of its Washington correspondents, James Shepley and Clay

at least a partial explanation. As *Time* saw it, the transcript's release was necessary to correct a "distorted" picture the public had received because Oppenheimer's lawyers, "wise in the ways of press relations," had deliberately handed out the Gray Board's verdict together with their own comments.\* As a result, said *Time*, many news dispatches "gave a portrait seen through the eyes of Counsel for J. Robert Oppenheimer." Since many editors had "lazily . . . followed the lawyers' line," the AEC's release of the full transcript was needed to "set the record straight."

In the two days following the AEC decision to publish the hearing, the Government Printing Office must have resembled an old-fashioned speeded-up newsreel, for it achieved something close to a miracle. In the space of about two days, almost three-quarters of a million words were set into type, proofread† and bound into a 992-page book.

At the AEC, meanwhile, there was a blur of activity in the high command. One major task was to contact the witnesses who had appeared before the Gray Board, to warn them of the imminent breach of the assurance that their testimony would be kept confidential. Throughout Monday and Tuesday, June 14 and 15, General Manager Nichols, General Counsel William Mitchell and Arthur Rolander, the AEC's Deputy Director of

---

Blair, Jr. These two were later to write an ardently pro-Strauss book, *The Hydrogen Bomb.*

\* This referred to Allan Ecker's special memorandum highlighting the Gray Board's praise of Oppenheimer's loyalty and discretion. Lloyd Garrison has observed, in retrospect, that he has "no apology to make for the publication of these basic and offsetting documents. Our overriding responsibility was to preserve, so far as we could, Dr. Oppenheimer's reputation; and though the publication of the charges and the Gray Board report did him much damage, the damage would have been far greater if these documents had leaked out without the offsetting material that accompanied them."

† Considering the speed with which the volume was produced, there were remarkably few typographical errors in the transcript. There was, however, at least one uncaught error of transcription that deserves preservation: Early in the hearing, Robert Oppenheimer, in explaining why he was reluctant to accede to Edward Teller's 1951 request that he return to Los Alamos for a second "tour" as director of the laboratory, made the observation, "I think you can't make an omelet rise twice." Apparently, the court stenographer was not familiar with the figure of speech, for the printed transcript quotes Oppenheimer as saying, "I think you can't make anomalous rise twice."

Security, who had served as Roger Robb's assistant counsel, kept telephone lines busy trying to reach the widely scattered witnesses. By the close of business Tuesday nearly all of them had been contacted. The witnesses were not asked for their consent; they were simply advised of the unilateral action being taken by the United States Government.*

At the same time, a team of security experts was engaged in a frantic line-by-line review of the Gray Board transcript, to try to prevent any damaging disclosures about the rarely-talked-of matters that had been discussed extensively in the Oppenheimer hearing. Meanwhile, in the office of Chairman Strauss, aides selected passages from the massive transcript to be highlighted for the guidance of interested parties. These "highlights" played an important role in the next part of the episode.

At 6 P.M. on Tuesday, June 15, the transcript, fresh from the Government Printing Office, was made available to the press corps,* together with instructions that nothing must be broadcast or printed until noon the following day. Accompanying the thick volumes was a statement from the Atomic Energy Commission explaining that inasmuch as "Dr. Oppenheimer's attorneys, as was their privilege, have issued texts of some documents . . . release of the transcript, within the limits of security, will, in the opinion of the Commission, best serve the public interest." The AEC also noted that the Commissioners would reach a decision on the case later that month and observed that "the wide national interest and concern in the matter make inevitable and desirable close public examination of the final determination."

The release time of noon the following day followed the Washington custom of allowing newsmen time to digest the material and write their stories without the pressures of a competitive race

---

* Lewis Strauss, in his book, *Men and Decisions,* recalls that the "*consent* of all witnesses was obtained" (emphasis added), but an AEC letter, in response to an inquiry, states that Commission officials who telephoned witnesses "notified them that the transcript was about to be released. Our records do not indicate that their consent was requested or secured, although in some cases the witnesses were asked for their comments. We should point out that on this matter our information is based largely on informal work papers."

† The AEC also sent a copy to every member of Congress.

to reach the public. Even so, for the mammoth amount of reading involved, eighteen hours hardly provided enough time.
Nevertheless, one reporter was somehow able to share with the
public an account of the hulking transcript within *one hour* of
its being handed to newsmen. This was broadcaster Fulton Lewis,
Jr., who, on his regular seven o'clock program, gave his listeners
snatches from the thousand closely printed pages, complete with
direct quotations. As a result of the Lewis violation of the release
time, other reporters had to rush into print with what *Time* described as "stories admittedly written after only a shallow skimming of the bulky transcript."

How had Fulton Lewis managed to get on the air so quickly
with selected quotes from the hearing? The answer is suggested
by the fact that accompanying a copy of the printed transcript
that was sent to at least one Strauss acquaintance by a personal
assistant to Strauss, there was a typed list of excerpts and page
numbers evidently designed to guide a reader's attention to a
special list of passages which the AEC high command considered of special importance.

In the first highlighted excerpt Robert Oppenheimer, while
describing Haakon Chevalier as a "fellow traveler," said he still
considered him a friend and told of his December, 1953, visit
with Chevalier in his Paris apartment.

In the second spotlighted passage, a reader could watch Roger
Robb pummeling Oppenheimer into admitting that one after
another of his 1943 statements to Boris Pash had been lies, and
into a final admission that "this whole thing, except for the single
references to Eltenton, I believe to be pure fabrication."

The third excerpt called unmistakable attention to the testimony in which Robb characterized Oppenheimer's interview
with Pash as "a whole fabrication and a tissue of lies," and Oppenheimer had responded, "Right."

The fourth was the excruciating passage in which Robert Oppenheimer told of having spent the night at the home of Jean
Tatlock.*

* Lloyd Garrison said, years later, that if he and his colleagues had anticipated "the way in which the Commission was to present the transcript to
the public, we might have published it first ourselves, through Mr. Reston."
Garrison also argued that there was a distinction between the AEC's list
of highlighted passages from the Gray Board hearing and the similar list

And so it went. Armed with such a list, any experienced and interested newsman such as broadcaster Lewis would have had little trouble preparing his "report" within an hour of being handed the testimony.

Three days later, the name of Fulton Lewis, Jr., was in the news again. On June 18 the Washington *Post* and *Times-Herald* reported that a criminal libel action against Lewis in a rural Maryland county near Washington had ended when a key state witness had refused to testify and the prosecutor had dropped the charge against Lewis. "Throughout the case," the *Post* reported, "Lewis was represented by [attorney] Roger Robb. . . ."*

The release of the Gray Board transcript did not produce splashy headlines in the United States. But the same could not be said for France, where Robert Oppenheimer was idolized. On a Paris street, Haakon Chevalier was stunned by a massive black headline across the entire back page of the *Paris-Presse:* "OPPIE CONFESSE: 'J'ÉTAIS UN IDIOT.'" Chevalier quickly bought a copy and there read Oppenheimer's testimony about the "cock and bull" story he had told Pash and Lansdale about the "Chevalier incident" in order, he said, to protect his friend.

Haakon Chevalier later wrote that this was the first time he realized that it was Oppenheimer who had told the authorities the story that had caused him so much trouble over the years. Chevalier had consistently contended that his objective in the "kitchen conversation" was merely to warn his friend about George Eltenton, and in his view, Oppenheimer had made a "fantastic lie" out of the whole incident. "How could he have gone on seeing me all those years [Chevalier wrote later] . . . without letting me know, without making the slightest effort to put an end to the mischief, or at least to limit to its ravages, by simply

___

previously prepared by Allan Ecker, calling attention to selected pro-Oppenheimer passages of the Gray Board's verdict. The two cases, said Garrison, were "not analogous": the purpose of Ecker's memorandum had been to make sure that the press would be "aware of the offsetting portions of the [Gray] Board's report," whereas the object of the AEC list, focusing solely, as it did, on such damaging material as the "Chevalier incident," "was not to assure a balanced consideration but the exact opposite."

* Robb was joined in the case by Kenneth W. Parkins, also of Washington.

telling the truth?" This was at the heart of Chevalier's grievous complaint about Robert Oppenheimer.

But in 1954, after first reading of "Oppie's confession," he clung to the belief that something had gone awry, that his friend had not wronged him in this way, had not carried on a charade all these years. Each morning, Chevalier would "fever-ishly scan the latest papers, looking for the denial I knew must come, for the explanation that would set everything to rights. . . . But no. There was no denial."

Back in the United States, newsmen on a nationally televised program questioned New York's Representative Sterling Cole, chairman of the Joint Committee on Atomic Energy, about the Oppenheimer case. Was Cole's committee planning any inquiry of its own into the case? Cole said the committee's actions would depend "largely on what the eventual outcome is determined to be." This whetted the newsmen's curiosity. After the program, they pressed him for an elaboration. Well, said Cole, if the AEC were to uphold the Gray Board and find against Oppenheimer, his committee would not look into the matter. But "if the Com-mission reverses itself and clears Dr. Oppenheimer, then we may hold hearings." Newsmen interpreted Congressman Cole's state-ment as a threat, placing pressure on the Atomic Energy Com-mission not to reverse the Gray Board's verdict.

Even leaving aside Cole's unsettling televised observation, the members of the Atomic Energy Commission could not help but be aware, as they headed toward the final stages of their decision, that Congressional eyes would be watching them closely.

# VII GENERAL NICHOLS RECOMMENDS

Growing public attention and Congressional pressure were not the only factors with which the five members of the United States Atomic Energy Commission had to deal as the day of judgment drew nearer. Over the hectic weekend in which the hearing summary had been lost and found, another ingredient had been injected. It was the harsh recommendation of the man to whose views, both by law and by common sense, the Commissioners were bound to give considerable weight: AEC General Manager K. D. Nichols. What sort of man was he?

Kenneth David Nichols grew up in what has been described as a "prosperous middle-class home" in Cleveland, the son of a successful contractor, from whom he inherited a fascination for building things. While he was in high school, his mother, enthralled with a movie that extolled cadet life, arranged for her son's appointment to West Point. Nichols was an enthusiastic cadet. He graduated fifth in his class, persuaded his superiors to permit him to continue his studies, and earned a doctorate, a credential that apparently drew considerable respect from the scientists with whom he was later to work. His first assignment was to the faculty at West Point. After Pearl Harbor, although he wanted a field post, he was given a mysterious assignment with something called the Manhattan Engineering District. He soon became the District Engineer, in administrative charge of the MED, operating from headquarters in Oak Ridge, Tennessee, but under the over-all direction of General Leslie Groves in Washington.*

It was in this capacity that Nichols first came to know Oppenheimer—and learn of his radical past. Since all the MED security officers reported to Nichols, he was fully familiar with their objections to Oppenheimer's appointment and retention as head of the Los Alamos laboratory. But because Oppenheimer had been considered "absolutely essential," Nichols himself had signed the 1943 directive clearing the way for the physicist's appointment.

During the war Nichols and Oppenheimer met periodically, usually with General Groves. Those who saw them together believe that it was in these encounters that the acrimony of Nichols' 1954 recommendation to the AEC may well have had its genesis, for more than once Nichols was the target of Oppenheimer's sharp tongue. Such humiliations must have been especially painful to a man like Kenneth D. Nichols, who, acquaintances say, took himself very seriously.

After the war Nichols stayed close to the atomic field, as a consultant to the Joint Committee on Atomic Energy and, more importantly, as senior Army member on the AEC's Military Liaison Committee. As such, he, like Oppenheimer, incurred the wrath of the Air Force by plumping for diversification of the U.S. atomic arsenal and in strongly backing the development of atomic cannons and other tactical nuclear weapons. But there were also points of sharp disagreement between Oppenheimer and Nichols in those years, on such matters as the extent of nuclear cooperation with Britain and Canada and, more importantly, the hydrogen bomb.

Nichols was appointed General Manager of the AEC in 1953.

* Groves has been extravagant in his praise of Nichols' wartime work. The supremely difficult problem of producing fissionable materials was solved, says Groves, only because of Nichols' "intelligence, persistence and drive. . . . I can think of no one who could have done what he did."

A tough administrator who ran an organization in a manner described as "decisive" and "forceful" by supporters and "ruthless" by detractors, Nichols was regarded as the epitome of the good soldier who would undeviatingly carry out the orders of his superior. In 1954, of course, he was answerable to Strauss.

Nichols began his report by carefully noting that, in obedience to AEC regulations, he had taken into account the positive as well as the negative factors in Oppenheimer's record and had assessed the effect on the AEC's programs of denying him security clearance. He also sought to blunt the double-jeopardy argument by stressing the extraordinary wartime circumstances of Oppenheimer's 1943 security clearance as well as General Groves' testimony that he would not clear Oppenheimer under the new screening standards instituted since the war.

Then Nichols presented his five "security findings":

First, there was the matter of Oppenheimer's "Communist activities." Although no *"direct* evidence"* existed that Oppenheimer had ever given away a secret or was disloyal, Nichols said, yet the record showed that he had been "a Communist in every respect except for the fact that he did not carry a party card." In Nichols' view, Oppenheimer had been no "parlor pink," no mere satisfier of a youthful intellectual curiosity. He had been "deeply and consciously involved with hardened and militant Communists at a time when he was a man of mature judgment. Nor could Nichols find any ground for forgiveness in the fact that Oppenheimer later admitted his Communist connections. These admissions, he said, had too often "followed, rather than preceded," the investigations that unearthed the facts, revealing a disinclination "to disclose the facts spontaneously."

Second, there was "the Chevalier incident." Nichols offered two possible explanations for the conflicting stories Oppenheimer had told: either he had lied to Colonels Pash and Lansdale, in which case he had, by his own admission, committed a felony; or, alternatively, he had told the truth in 1943 and had lied ever since. Nichols chose the latter explanation, and not without compelling reasoning. If, as Oppenheimer claimed, his real mo-

---

* A phrase that invites an inference that there was *indirect* evidence.

tivation in his interviews with Pash and Lansdale had been to protect an innocent friend, why would he have invented a complicated story that "showed that Chevalier was not innocent, but on the contrary was deeply involved in an espionage conspiracy"? "Is it reasonable," Nichols asked, "to believe a man will deliberately tell a lie that seriously reflects upon himself and his friend, when he knows that the truth will show them both to be innocent?"

Then Nichols aimed his severest words at Robert Oppenheimer:

> In my opinion, Dr. Oppenheimer's behavior in connection with the Chevalier incident shows that he is not reliable or trustworthy; his own testimony shows that he was guilty of deliberate misrepresentations and falsifications either in his interview with Colonel Pash or in his testimony before the [Gray] Board; and such misrepresentation and falsifications constituted criminal * * * dishonest * * * conduct.*

Now Nichols introduced for the first time an allegation of great significance: that the "complete record" of the Chevalier incident had not been "considered by the Atomic Energy Commission" when it cleared Oppenheimer in 1947.

What was General Nichols saying—or implying? Had new facts about the "Chevalier incident" come to light since 1947? If so, the Gray Board had not considered them important enough to mention in its verdict. Moreover, the central sin of which Nichols was accusing Oppenheimer, the conflict between his 1943 account of the incident and his later accounts, was—or should have been—known to the AEC when it cleared the physicist in 1947.†

In his third security "finding," Nichols again broached a subject that the Gray Board had left untouched: the question of Robert Oppenheimer's "veracity." This aspect of Nichols' verdict was crucial, for it laid the foundation for the "defects of

---

* These asterisks appear in the printed version of General Nichols' report to the AEC. Apparently Nichols was invoking a phrase from the Eisenhower loyalty-security order of 1953.

† The Gray Board heard evidence that in 1946 (the year *before* the AEC cleared him) Oppenheimer had given FBI agents the same account of the Chevalier incident that he gave the Gray Board, and had told the agents that his reports to Pash and Lansdale had been false.

character" charge on which Lewis Strauss and the AEC majority
were to rely heavily in their judgment of Oppenheimer. Nichols
cited six examples of conflicts or contradictions in statements
made by Oppenheimer, but since four of the six were also cited
in the Strauss opinion, they will be discussed along with that
opinion.*

Next, General Nichols turned to "Dr. Oppenheimer's continued associations after World War II." These, he said, "raise a
serious question as to his eligibility for clearance." What "continued associations" did General Nichols have in mind? He mentioned only four: Haakon Chevalier, whom Oppenheimer had
seen no more than a dozen times in the eight postwar years
and with whom he had corresponded only sporadically, and
Bernard Peters, David Bohm and Rossi Lomanitz, none of whom
Oppenheimer had seen more than a few times in the preceding
decade.

Fifth and finally, Nichols cited what he called Robert Oppenheimer's "obstruction and disregard of security," through "actions"
which had "shown a consistent disregard of a reasonable security
system." As examples he referred to the Chevalier incident;
Oppenheimer's refusal to tell security officers about his relations
with people he knew to be Communists; his repeated exercise
of "an arrogance of his own judgment" regarding his own conduct
and regarding the loyalty and reliability of others. All of this,
said Nichols, was "wholly inconsistent with the obligations necessarily imposed by an adequate security system on those who occupy high positions of trust and responsibility in the Government."

What were these "obligations" of the security system of which
General Nichols spoke? He did not spell them out, perhaps
because, as with the Gray-Morgan requirement of "enthusiastic
support of the system," they were of Nichols' own invention. No
such obligations had then or have since been prescribed by law
or regulation.

Nichols then turned to tidying up one or two final points. The
first was headed, "Finding of Security Risk Is Not Based on Dr.

* See pp. 415-20.

Oppenheimer's Opinions." Here Nichols sought to fend off the accusation that the H-bomb allegations in his original letter of charges had amounted to trying a man for his opinions rather than his actions. Such, said Nichols, was never his intent: "Technical opinions have no security implications unless they are reflections of sinister motives."

Why, then, had Oppenheimer's "technical opinions" become an issue in the hearing? Because, said Nichols, in view of the other allegations concerning his political past, it was necessary to test "the good faith of his technical opinions" in the H-bomb matter. Nichols' own conclusion was that "the evidence establishes no sinister motives" in Oppenheimer's anti-H-bomb stand. The only security implications that raised, in Nichols' view, involved the question of Oppenheimer's veracity.* In this context, Nichols said he found the evidence "disturbing."

Finally, complying with the AEC requirement, Nichols dealt with the question of "Dr. Oppenheimer's Value to Atomic Energy or Related Programs." He found that the physicist's "value" had declined, partly because of the advent of other skilled nuclear physicists and partly "because of his loss of scientific objectivity probably resulting from the diversion of his efforts to political fields and matters not purely scientific in nature." He pointed out that the AEC had called on Oppenheimer's consultative services on just three occasions over the preceding two years. General Nichols said that "other government agencies" and "contractors and study groups" in the atomic field might desire Oppenheimer's services if he were cleared, "as one or two have already indicated." Even so, Nichols concluded, while Oppenheimer "could, of course, make contributions in all those fields," he was "far from being indispensable."†

---

* Regarding the Seaborg letter and on the question of whether Oppenheimer had opposed the H-bomb *per se*, or merely a crash program for its development.

† Not everyone appraised Oppenheimer's services as sparingly as the AEC. On June 4 the chairman of the Science Advisory Committee of the Office of Defense Mobilization, Dr. Lee DuBridge, had written to Lewis Strauss to state that the restoration of Oppenheimer's clearance was of "great importance" since his committee was about to undertake some studies on defense problems "on which Dr. Oppenheimer's knowledge and counsel will be of very critical importance."

Nichols concluded his report to the AEC with these words:

I have conscientiously weighed the record of Dr. Oppenheimer's whole life, his past contributions, and his potential future contributions to the Nation against the security risk that is involved in his continued clearance. In addition, I have given consideration to the nature of the cold war in which we are engaged with communism and Communist Russia and the horrible prospects of hydrogen bomb warfare if all-out war should be forced upon us. From these things a need results to eliminate from classified work any individuals who might endanger the common defense or security or whose retention is not clearly consistent with the interests of national security.

Dr. Oppenheimer's clearance should not be reinstated.

K. D. NICHOLS
*General Manager*

A lower court convicts John Doe of theft. Doe appeals. The intermediate court, in a secret ruling, finds Doe guilty not only of theft but also of perjury, a new charge. It sends its decision to the highest court *without Doe's lawyers' even knowing about the perjury ruling,* much less having an opportunity to rebut or comment on it.

One does not have to be a lawyer to realize that such a procedure is unthinkable in any court in the United States.* Yet the above describes what essentially happened in the security-risk case of J. Robert Oppenheimer. General Nichols, acting in the role of an intermediate tribunal, found Robert Oppenheimer guilty of lying in six separate instances, *most of which had not been mentioned either in Nichols' original "indictment" or in the Gray Board's "lower court" verdict.*

Nichols' ruling was made in secret and secretly forwarded to the AEC, without a word to Lloyd Garrison. Thus Nichols' charges of perjury were to be considered by the five Atomic Energy Commissioners—the highest court, in this case—without

---

* In fact, the Supreme Court, in a case decided April 8, 1968, reversed the disbarment of an attorney that was based on a charge not contained in the original bill of particulars but added only after the legal proceedings had begun.

Garrison's even knowing about them, much less being given an opportunity to cope with them.*

Not one of the five Commissioners—not even Eugene Zuckert, the one lawyer among them—took a single step to see that the Nichols statement, with its new charges, was imparted to Oppenheimer and Garrison. Not only that: they denied Garrison's request to appear in person before them to make an oral argument. Had they permitted such an appearance, they would have had a natural occasion to disclose to Garrison the doubts about Oppenheimer's veracity that Nichols had raised. Later a distinguished Boston attorney, Charles Curtis, made this observation:

> As soon as [the AEC Commissioners] saw General Nichols' report, they knew very well that it had raised new points and new charges against Oppenheimer. . . . The Commission should have shown [Oppenheimer's lawyers] the report at once and asked them to argue at least these new charges. It is joking at justice to say that a man has been represented by counsel when a case is decided on charges which his counsel is not allowed to argue.

* Garrison has recalled that he did not think to ask that the Nichols verdict be shown him because Nichols, in his letter to Garrison conveying the Gray Board opinion, had said only that he would submit a "recommendation" to the AEC. Garrison took this to mean that Nichols would merely forward the Gray Board opinion to the Commissioners with a simple "yea" or "nay" recommendation of his own, not that he would submit an extended written opinion that would require Garrison's rebuttal.

# VIII  THE FINAL JUDGMENT

Now that General Manager Nichols had given his opinion, the final resolution of the case awaited only the judgment of five men:

Lewis L. Strauss, investment banker
Joseph Campbell, business accountant
Thomas E. Murray, industrial engineer
Eugene Zuckert, lawyer
Henry DeWolf Smyth, physicist

Some saw a faint hope for Oppenheimer in the political complexion of the Commission: three of the Commissioners (Murray, Zuckert and Smyth)—a bare majority—had been appointed by a Democratic President, and therefore were thought to have less of a vested interest than might Republican appointees in vindicating the campaign pledge to get rid of Communists in government.

Everyone was well aware that this was to be a short-lived balance, for Zuckert's term was due to expire at midnight of Wednesday, June 30. Moreover, there was a strong feeling that the decision had to be rendered before that date for, by coincidence, Oppenheimer's consultant's contract would also expire on June 30 and the question of his security clearance would become moot. The time for decision was short. As of the date Nichols submitted his recommendation, just eighteen days remained.

Each of the Commissioners went about preparing himself for the judgment of Robert Oppenheimer in his own way. Lewis Strauss had been reading the Gray Board transcripts as they had reached him daily, and so he was comparatively up to date; also, he had the advantage of previous exposure to the Oppenheimer file during his earlier service on the AEC. Eugene Zuckert brought his trained legal mind to his reading and research, and he wrote his own opinion. Joseph Campbell reportedly relied heavily on briefings by AEC staff members, particularly David Teeple, a zealously security-conscious assistant to Lewis Strauss who had once served as a Manhatten District security investigator. Thomas Murray is said to have leaned on personal friends, family and staff.

The most intensive preparation was undertaken by Commissioner Henry DeWolf Smyth. For more than three decades a physics professor at Princeton, Smyth had gained national fame, shortly after Hiroshima, as the author of the first official description of the atomic bomb to be made public. The "Smyth Report" was eagerly snapped up and widely read.

Being a physicist rather than a lawyer, Smyth felt a particular need for assistance in studying the evidence and preparing his opinion. He secured the temporary services of Clark C. Vogel, an ex-TVA attorney who had become head of the legal staff at the AEC Savannah River project in South Carolina.* From the AEC Washington office, Smyth asked for the help of Philip Farley, a career government official with seven years' service in a senior policy post reporting directly to General Manager Nichols. When Commissioner Smyth requested Farley's services, Nichols summoned Farley to his office and gave him to understand that he was joining a lost cause since the revocation of Oppenheimer's clearance was generally recognized to be long overdue.

---

* In a sense, it was odd that Vogel should be assisting Smyth, whom he had never met, rather than Eugene Zuckert, who was such an old and close friend as to be godfather to one of Vogel's children.

Farley later recalled that Nichols made very clear what would happen to Farley's career if he chose to take on this assignment. Farley took the assignment nonetheless. (A few months later he arranged a transfer to the more hospitable atmosphere of the State Department.)

Farley and Vogel waded through the Gray Board transcript and the investigative reports (which, Vogel has recalled, stood in a stack nearly four feet high). They next prepared a summary of the evidence on each allegation in the original Nichols letter of charges, which Smyth then offered to share with his fellow Commissioners. (It was this summary that Zuckert lost on the train in Connecticut.)

Shortly before the Commission was to meet, Smyth called in Farley and Vogel and asked them—Vogel in particular—to play the role of devil's advocate: to state every reason why Robert Oppenheimer should be declared a security risk and to shoot holes in every reason Smyth might offer for not doing so. At the end of the session, Smyth said to each of his assistants: "All right, if each of you had to vote in my place, how would you vote?" Each responded that he would vote to clear Oppenheimer.

When Smyth returned home from the AEC on the afternoon of Tuesday, June 22, he was visibly upset. It had become clear that the Commissioners would vote against Robert Oppenheimer, four to one. Not one other Commissioner had sided with Smyth. He had not expected to be in so lonely a position; he had anticipated that at worst the vote would be three to two. On that Tuesday afternoon the difference between four-to-one and three-to-two seemed much larger than merely one Commissioner's vote.

Based on what the other Commissioners had indicated would be their reasoning in the case, Smyth decided to abandon the draft opinion he had been preparing and to write a shorter, stronger and less philosophic statement. For the balance of that week he devoted long hours each evening and until well after midnight Saturday to the preparation of his dissent. But at midday Sunday, AEC General Counsel Mitchell delivered to the Smyth home the first written version of the majority opinion. Its tenor was strikingly different from what Smyth had been given to understand it would be. Clearly, he would have to recast every-

thing he had been writing. He also resolved to insist on a closed
meeting of the Commission the next morning, with a court reporter present to record his formal request that the final version
of the majority decision be in his hands not less than twenty-four
hours before the time of its public release.

On Monday morning, June 28, just two days before the
expiration of Commissioner Zuckert's term and of Robert Oppenheimer's contract, such a meeting was held. The Commission
voted four to one against Oppenheimer. Smyth's request for a
twenty-four-hour grace period was entered and duly recorded by
a court reporter. That evening, however, while the Smyths, Farley and Vogel were at supper together, Roy Snapp, secretary to
the AEC, drove up to the Smyth house with copies of the other
Commissioners' opinions—and with the unwelcome news that
Smyth's dissent would have to be in the hands of the AEC the
next morning. Even working all night he would have barely half
the twenty-four hours supposedly accorded him.

Once again the character of the majority opinion had changed
sufficiently to compel Smyth to abandon the work he had done on
Sunday and begin afresh. With the help of Farley and Vogel, he
began the final drafting and redrafting of his dissent. At one
point, in the early morning hours, the weary Commissioner
looked up from his work and said, "You know, it's funny I should
be going to all this work for Oppenheimer. I don't even like the
guy very much."

The writing was not completed until 6:30 A.M.

At four o'clock that afternoon, the Commissioners' opinions
were handed to the press, under an "IMMEDIATE RELEASE" date-
line.

There were, in all, five separate opinions or statements. There
was the "majority" opinion, signed by Chairman Strauss, Joseph
Campbell and Eugene Zuckert. This was generally looked upon
as primarily the view of Chairman Strauss (and will hereinafter
be referred to as the "Strauss opinion").* In addition, Campbell
and Zuckert each felt obliged to submit an extensive "concurring"

---

* One close student of the Oppenheimer case, Boston lawyer Charles Curtis,
flatly stated that the majority opinion "was written by Chairman Strauss."
Strauss confirmed this in a 1967 interview.

statement in order to fully express their individual points of view. And finally, there were a separate opinion by Commissioner Murray and Henry DeWolf Smyth's lone dissent.

"The issue before the Commission," Lewis Strauss' opinion began, "is whether the security of the United States warrants Dr. J. Robert Oppenheimer's continued access to restricted data of the Atomic Energy Commission." Later, Strauss was to put this even more emphatically; Oppenheimer's clearance was revoked, he stated, "to safeguard [secret] information . . . *and for no other purpose.*" (Emphasis added.)

If the sole issue was Oppenheimer's secret-keeping capacity, the findings of the Gray Board posed a problem for Lewis Strauss, since Gordon Gray and Thomas Morgan had stated their belief in Oppenheimer's loyalty and in his "unusual" discretion with secrets. If Oppenheimer was neither traitorous nor loose-lipped, what other ground was left for Strauss to oppose the physicist's "continued access to [secret] data?" For Strauss, the answer lay in the basic law governing his agency (the Atomic Energy Act of 1946), and in the duty it imposed on Commissioners to judge "the character, associations and loyalty" of its employees. Under that requirement, said Strauss, it was not necessary to find a man disloyal to disqualify him. "Substantial defects of *character* and imprudent dangerous *associations,*" especially with "known subversives," were also "reasons for disqualification." (Emphasis added.)

Character and associations—these would be the two pegs on which Lewis Strauss would hang his adverse finding.

The question of character he framed in these words:

> On the basis of the record before the Commission, comprising the transcript of the hearing before the Gray Board as well as reports of Military Intelligence and the Federal Bureau of Investigation, we find Dr. Oppenheimer is not entitled to the continued confidence of the government and of the [Atomic Energy] Commission because of the proof of fundamental defects in his "character."

The assertion of "defects of character" was wholly different from anything charged by the AEC or enunciated in the Gray Board

ruling on the case, and it later prompted Harry Kalven, law professor at the University of Chicago, to observe that it would be
"unthinkable" in any court proceeding for a higher court to "af-
firm guilt on grounds not raised in the Trial Court."

It also illustrated one of Lloyd Garrison's prime difficulties in
defending Oppenheimer: the continual shifting of the criteria on
which the scientist was found wanting. For example, the original
Nichols charges said nothing about Oppenheimer's supposed "susceptibility to influence," and so Garrison, in his brief to the Gray
Board, did not try to counter such an allegation. When he learned
that the board had made it one of the principal points in its finding against Oppenheimer, he sought to rebut it in his written
brief to the AEC—only to find (when the AEC opinion was
finally published) that the "susceptibility to influence" point had
been wholly dropped, and an entirely new contention—the "defects of character" charge—had moved to stage center. Since this
matter had not even been suggested in the Gray Board opinion
and since the Nichols verdict had been withheld, Garrison never
had an opportunity to present a rebuttal concerning his client's
"character"—the crux of the Strauss opinion.

Many observers have had difficulty reconciling the Strauss
claim of character defect with his sponsorship, within three
months of issuing his critical security ruling, of Oppenheimer's
continuation as director of the Institute for Advanced Study, of
which Strauss was a trustee. If, in Strauss' view, Oppenheimer's
"defects of character" were so grave as to deprive him of the
"continued confidence" of his government, why could they not
also have foreclosed him from the continued confidence of the
trustees of the Institute?

On the second disqualifying matter—that of "associations"—
Strauss found that Oppenheimer's relationships with "persons
known to him to be Communists" far exceeded "the tolerable
limits of prudence and self-restraint" expectable of one in his
high position and had "lasted too long to be justified as merely
the intermittent and accidental revival of earlier friendships."

Strauss had introduced the criteria of "character" and "associations." But he himself had said, at the outset of his opinion,
that the Atomic Energy Act imposed a "duty" to assess a third

attribute: Oppenheimer's loyalty. Probably the most striking aspect of Strauss' opinion was its total silence on that question— a notable silence in the wake of the Gray Board majority's affirmation of Oppenheimer's "loyalty and love of country"; a silence made even more remarkable by the outright accusation, in the concurring opinion of Commissioner Thomas Murray, that Robert Oppenheimer was "disloyal." Strauss, and those who joined in his opinion, must have known of Murray's charge. They allowed it to pass in silence.

After denying that Oppenheimer's policy views had been a factor in his decision and that the physicist was being subjected to unfair "double jeopardy" (because of his previous AEC clearances), Strauss went on to charge that Oppenheimer's "reliability, self-discipline and trustworthiness," which should have been "exemplary" for one entrusted with such high secrets, had "fallen far short of acceptable standards." But Strauss had even harsher words:

> The record shows that Dr. Oppenheimer has consistently placed himself outside the rules which govern others. He has falsified in matters wherein he was charged with grave responsibilities in the national interest. In his associations he has repeatedly exhibited a willful disregard of the normal and proper obligations of security.

With this by way of prelude, Strauss proceeded to set forth his claimed "proof" of Oppenheimer's "defects of character." It consisted of six instances, four of which had been drawn from the Nichols report.

The first concerned Oppenheimer's "cock and bull" story to Pash and Lansdale about the Chevalier incident, described by Strauss as follows: "In the hearings recently concluded [before the Gray Board] *Dr. Oppenheimer under oath swears* that the story he told Colonel Pash was a '*whole fabrication and tissue of lies.*'" (Emphasis added.) Could any reader interpret the words "whole fabrication" and "tissue of lies" other than as the damning personal confession of Robert Oppenheimer?

Second, when had Robert Oppenheimer lied about the "Chevalier incident"—to Pash and Lansdale in 1943 or to the

Gray Board in 1954, as Nichols had concluded? "It is not clear," Strauss said, which was the truth and which the lie. But to him this was of small import, since either way Oppenheimer was damned: "If Dr. Oppenheimer lied in 1943, as he now says he did, he committed the crime of knowingly making false and material statements to a Federal officer. If he lied to the [Gray] Board, he committed perjury in 1954."

All of this was perfectly true—just as true, in fact, in 1954 as it had been in 1947 when, as a matter of record, the conflict between Robert Oppenheimer's wartime and postwar statements on the Chevalier incident was known to the government, and hence presumably to Lewis Strauss.*

The manner in which Strauss presented two other examples of supposed "character defect" reveals Strauss' character as much as Oppenheimer's. These examples involved the conflict between what Oppenheimer told Colonel Lansdale in 1943 and what he said in postwar years about Rossi Lomanitz' and Joseph Weinberg's alleged Communist Party membership. For the convenience of readers of his opinion, Strauss provided the page numbers in the freshly printed Gray Board transcript on which these discrepancies could be found. A reader taking advantage of Strauss' guided tour would have paused at page 119 (where Oppenheimer told the Gray Board that he would not have written about Lomanitz' draft status in 1943 had he known that Lomanitz was an "active Communist") before being ushered to page 875, where this statement was flatly contradicted by Oppenheimer's 1943 statement to Lansdale: "I know for a fact, I know, I learned on my last visit to Berkeley that both Lomanitz and Weinberg were members [of the Communist Party]."

The Strauss "guided tour" ended there. But the Lansdale interview also contained a passage, a few pages later, that made the apparent discrepancy in Oppenheimer's statements somewhat less stark, at least as to Weinberg. That passage—to which Strauss did *not* call attention—indicated far less certainty about Weinberg's party status in 1943, not only on Oppenheimer's part, but

---

* Strauss has insisted he did *not* know about the Pash-Lansdale "cock and bull story" at the time of the 1947 clearance. Yet Oppenheimer had labeled this story a lie in his interview with FBI agents in 1946—a year earlier.

also on the part of Colonel Lansdale, who had access to all of the investigative reports. It read as follows:

LANSDALE: Of course you now know that Weinberg and Lomanitz are both members of the party and members of the union.

OPPENHEIMER: I didn't know Weinberg was a member.

LANSDALE: Well, as a matter of fact, I don't either.

Again Lloyd Garrison was helpless; he could not point out the omission because he had no way of knowing the Weinberg-Lomanitz episodes would be used against his client.

Nor could Garrison anticipate Strauss' charge that Oppenheimer's seeming retraction of his HUAC testimony about Bernard Peters also constituted a "character defect." True, the Peters episode had been mentioned in the Gray Board's opinion, but in a wholly different context. The board had seen the incident as evidence of a "susceptibility to influence," and it was to this charge that Garrison had addressed himself in his brief to the AEC.

The selectivity of Strauss' "guided tour" and his omission of passages favorable to Oppenheimer raise the question of whether the AEC Chairman was looking at the record objectively. That question also arises in connection with his citation of the "Rudy Lambert incident" as an example of "fundamental defects of character." Oppenheimer's ability to describe Lambert to the Gray Board in 1954 suggested that he had been less than candid with Colonel Lansdale in 1943 when he purported not to know what Lambert looked like. But there was reason to doubt that this had been a deliberate evasion. Lansdale had mentioned Lambert's name in the most fleeting manner, amidst a number of other names,* and after Oppenheimer had been subjected to more than an hour of questions. Moreover, AEC Commissioner Smyth, who examined the record with great care, stated that the Lambert incident was based on a "garbled transcript" of the Lansdale interview. But even if it was a deliberate evasion, could it have been Oppenheimer's intent to give Lansdale a basically

* See pp. 62, 280–81.

distorted picture of his past Communist ties? Evidently not, for he readily answered Lansdale about his acquaintance with other Communists far more important then Rudy Lambert, including William Schneiderman, the West Coast party secretary.

As Commissioner Smyth pointed out, an evaluation of all six examples of "character defect" hinges critically on one's appraisal of Oppenheimer's motives. After all, these six isolated examples were drawn not from a mere handful of facts known about Oppenheimer's adult life but from countless such facts. Moreover, they had to be weighed against "the judgment of responsible persons"*—James B. Conant, John J. McCloy, two former AEC chairmen and others—who had worked closely with Oppenheimer and had found him a man of the highest character.

Commissioner Smyth found that "if the entire record is read objectively," then the six Strauss examples "are shown in their proper light as understandable and unimportant." But, said Smyth, "if one starts with the assumption that Dr. Oppenheimer is disloyal," the six incidents "may arouse suspicion."

Admittedly, the six examples did expose contradictions in what Oppenheimer said at various times. If one assumed the physicist to be of sinister motive and bad faith, these contradictions spelled mendacity and lack of character. On the other hand, if one saw him as well motivated and decent, these same discrepancies might easily be dismissed as mere confirmation of the fragility of human memory.

An example from more recent times will illustrate. In early 1967 Lewis Strauss himself was interviewed in connection with this book about events thirteen to fourteen years in the past (by coincidence approximately the same time lapse Oppenheimer faced in the Gray Board hearing). Like Oppenheimer, Admiral Strauss responded to questions without the aid of supporting documents (although, unlike Oppenheimer, he had not had the advantage of extensive preparation for the questioning). Like Oppenheimer, he felt certain about specific recollections. Yet in at least two instances of substantive importance Admiral Strauss'

---

* To which AEC regulations required Oppenheimer's judges to give weight.

memory may have been in error. The first was his statement that he had neither known of nor talked with any of Roger Robb's witnesses in advance of their Gray Board testimony. This is in direct conflict with Luis Alvarez' clear recollection of Strauss' personal plea that he change his mind and testify against Oppenheimer. The second instance was Strauss' statement that he had seen William Borden on only one occasion (at the funeral of Senator McMahon) between 1950 and 1954. That recollection is contradicted by a memorandum in the files of the Joint Committee on Atomic Energy describing in some detail a 1951 conversation between the two about Oppenheimer.

Did Strauss' apparent errors represent a "lack of veracity" or "defects of character"—or had he simply forgotten about his appeal to Alvarez and his conversation with Borden? Those who view Strauss as an honorable and public-spirited man might forgive these conflicts as innocent and inconsequential. On the other hand, those who might see him as a proud and vindictive man bent on retribution for injuries inflicted by Oppenheimer might take as uncharitable a view of the seeming mistakes as Strauss did of Oppenheimer's in 1954.

The AEC Chairman, however, contended that his charge of "fundamental character defects" did not rest solely on the six instances cited. "The work of Military Intelligence, the Federal Bureau of Investigation and the Atomic Energy Commission—all, at one time or another, have felt the effect of his *falsehoods, evasions and misrepresentations*." (Emphasis added.)

"Falsehoods, evasions and misrepresentations." A harsh charge, especially when aimed at one who had been privy to the nation's most sensitive of secrets, a charge that could not help arousing a curiosity about the chapter-and-verse documentation underlying it. But, aside from Oppenheimer's delay and subsequent mendacity in reporting the Chevalier incident, the Strauss verdict cites no added examples of "falsehoods" or "misrepresentations."

Strauss then turned from questions of "character" to his charge that Oppenheimer had had "persistent and continuing association with Communists." Again he was niggardly in citing specific evidence. Aside from Haakon Chevalier,* whom Oppenheimer saw only about a dozen times in eight postwar years, what were these "persistent and continuing associations"? Strauss listed none. Had Strauss' charge been "carefully weighed," as required by AEC regulations, "in the light of *all* the information"? With whom had the scientist associated more in his post-Los Alamos years—with the ex-radicals of his Berkeley days, or with men like George Marshall, Dean Acheson and John J. McCloy? On this question, some of Oppenheimer's early radical colleagues have no doubt: they are bitter about the way he forsook them for the lofty circle of statesmen with whom he was suddenly on first-name terms.

The concluding portion of Lewis Strauss' verdict had this to say:

> It is clear that for one who has had access for so long to the most vital defense secrets of the Government and who would retain such access if his clearance were continued, Dr. Oppenheimer has defaulted not once but many times upon the obligations that should and must be willingly borne by citizens in the national service.

Some might find it hard to believe that those words applied to a citizen who, during World War II, had driven himself unsparingly; who had voluntarily devoted half of his career in the ensuing years to "the national service," and who, during all that time, had never once compromised one of the vital secrets entrusted to him.

Following the presentation of the majority, or "Strauss," opinion, each of the other Commissioners entered a statement of his own.

The first was that of Eugene M. Zuckert, for whom this was to

---

* About whom, Strauss said, Oppenheimer could only offer a "strong guess" that he was no longer active in Communist Party affairs. If this indicated an assumption on Strauss' part that Chevalier *was* still an active Communist, he offered no evidence to support that notion. On the other hand, Gordon Gray, who had access to all the FBI reports available to Strauss, said during the course of the Oppenheimer hearing, "I don't know whether he [Chevalier] is a member of the Communist Party or not."

be his final task for the AEC. Within thirty-six hours his term would expire and he would become a private citizen. That status would be almost a novel experience for Zuckert, who had spent the bulk of his working life in the government. He had come to Washington in 1937, just four years out of Yale Law School, to take a job with the Securities and Exchange Commission. Toward the end of the war he served as an assistant to Stuart W. Symington, then Assistant Secretary of War for Air. He followed Symington into the newborn Department of the Air Force, where he became an assistant secretary, overseeing, among other things, the security screening of Air Force personnel. A Democrat, he was nominated to membership on the Atomic Energy Commission by President Truman in 1952.

As the lone lawyer on the Commission, Zuckert was in a better position than his colleagues to appraise the Gray Board procedures and to compare them with the protections enjoyed by defendants in courts of law. Zuckert did venture such an appraisal: he found it "reassur[ing]" that the Oppenheimer security hearing had been based on "a course of procedure which gave the most scrupulous attention to our ideas of justice and fair treatment."

He observed, further, that while "individual instances" of untruthfulness or obstruction of the security system "would not have been decisive,"

> when I see such a combination of seriously disturbing actions and events as are present in this case, then I believe the risk to security passes acceptable bounds. All these actions and events and the relation between them make no other conclusion possible . . . than to deny clearance to Dr. Oppenheimer.

Chicago law professor Harry Kalven later chastised Zuckert for being "more concerned with stating general principles than with applying the principle exactingly to the case at hand." What particular "actions" and "events" did Zuckert find "seriously disturbing"? How did these relate to the body of law—the AEC regulations and screening criteria—under which Oppenheimer's case was being judged? Lawyer Zuckert failed to say.

He did state that any connotation of disloyalty in the AEC's finding was not justified by the evidence. But this raised an

intriguing question. If Zuckert was willing to confirm Oppenheimer's loyalty under his own name, why had there been no
such affirmation in the majority opinion, which Zuckert had also
signed? Had Zuckert asked that such a statement be included in
the majority opinion, only to be outvoted by Strauss and Campbell? Or had he failed even to raise the question with his two
colleagues? Whatever the answer, Zuckert's support of Oppenheimer's loyalty made more conspicuous the silence of the Strauss
opinion on this point.

Could Oppenheimer be loyal and at the same time a security
risk? That question brought forth additional generalities from
Zuckert. "Every human being," he said, "is some degree of a security risk . . . so long as there are normal human feelings like
pain, or emotions like love of family. . . ." The judgment, he
said, cannot be precise; but he found in Oppenheimer's case
"factors which tend to increase the chance that security might be
endangered" to an extent sufficient to warrant denial of clearance. Many of these "factors" had, he said, been set forth in the
Strauss opinion. The implication was that Zuckert had in mind
other "factors," but he failed to cite any.

"It is a source of real sadness to me," he concluded, "that my
last act as a public official should be participation in the determination of this matter, involving, as it does, an individual who
has made a substantial contribution to the United States. This
matter certainly reflects the difficult times in which we live."

The next individual opinion was that of Commissioner Joseph
Campbell, former business accountant and vice president of Columbia University. In Campbell's view the Commission had a
very restricted role in reviewing a security case. As a general
proposition, he felt, the recommendations of hearing panels such
as the Gray Board must be "honored in the absence of compelling
circumstances" and the AEC General Manager's decisions "must
be upheld unless there can be shown new evidence, violations of
procedures, or other substantial reasons why they should be reversed." Applying these principles to the Oppenheimer case,
Campbell concluded that "serious charges" had been brought;
Oppenheimer had been "afforded every opportunity to refute
them"; he had failed to do so, in the majority view of a hearing

board "composed of men of the highest honor and integrity"; the General Manager had not only upheld but exceeded that view; and Oppenheimer had failed to show any new evidence or any procedural violations. Ergo, the Gray Board and Nichols' views must be upheld.

Attorney Charles Curtis, in his analysis of the case, called Campbell's opinion "an admirable example of the cookbook school of administrative and judicial procedure, the school of Follow the Recipe. You can't go wrong if you just follow the recipe."

Next came Commissioner Thomas E. Murray, former industrial engineer, inventor and corporation executive, prominent lay Roman Catholic. None of the other opinions rendered in the Oppenheimer case—not even Strauss'—was so fervid as Murray's in its hatred and fear of "the Communist conspiracy," with its "methods of infiltration and intrigue, of deceit and duplicity, of falsehood and connivance." Yet none of the other opinions—not even those of the two dissenting scientists—was so insistent that in meeting the Communist threat the government had no right to intrude on what he called "the internal forum of thought and belief."

Murray went to great lengths to defend Oppenheimer's conduct regarding the hydrogen bomb. While his technical judgments had proved wrong, Murray said, "it would be unwise, unjust and dangerous to admit, as a principle, that errors of judgment . . . can furnish valid grounds for later indictments of a man's loyalty, character, or status as a security risk." Murray was not in the least bothered, as Gray and Morgan had been, by Oppenheimer's infusion of "moral reasons" into the H-bomb debate. The physicist had been "quite right" to advance such reasons, Murray said, for "the scientist is a man before he is a technician. Like every man, he ought to be alert to the moral issues that arise in the course of his work." As to the physicist's alleged "lack of enthusiasm" for the H-bomb program once it had been decided upon, Murray observed that "Government can command a citizen's service in the national interest. But Government cannot command a citizen's enthusiasm for any particular program or policy. . . . Lack of enthusiasm is not a justiciable matter."

Murray talked of the difficulty of insuring, under the requirements of security, "that justice is done to the individual. In this situation it is more than ever necessary to protect at every point the distinction between the external forum of action and omission, and the internal forum of thought and belief. . . . However stringent the need for a security system, [it] cannot be allowed to introduce into American jurisprudence that hateful concept, the 'crime of opinion.'"

The American Civil Liberties Union could not have put more eloquently the case for free thought and spirit.

Having disposed of the hydrogen-bomb charge as a consideration, Murray turned to "the primary question"—the definition of loyalty. It was not enough, he said, to define the word "solely in terms of love" of country. Here he turned etymologist: the word "loyal," he said, comes to the English language from the Latin *legalis*—"according to the law." Webster's definition he also found helpful: to be loyal is to be "faithful to the lawful government." The loyal citizen, therefore, recognizes two premises: first, that "his Government for all its imperfections, is a government under law, of law, by law; therefore he is loyal to it"; second, that this government, being lawful, has "the right and the responsibility to protect itself" from internal subversion. To this end, he said, those holding sensitive government posts are "necessarily subject" to a "special system of law"—the security system. Robert Oppenheimer had been subject to that system and "the measure of his obedience to [its] requirements is the decisive measure of his loyalty to his lawful Government. No lesser test will settle the question of his loyalty."

Murray found that Oppenheimer had "failed the test"—by his "frequent and deliberate disregard of those security regulations which restrict a man's associations." It was useless, in Murray's view, to "plead that Dr. Oppenheimer revealed no secrets to the Communists and fellow travelers with whom he chose to associate"; the fault lay in the "associations themselves, however innocent in fact."

Murray seemed to imply that the higher an official's position, the greater his responsibility to adhere to the security system. In view of Oppenheimer's "position of paramount importance," wrote Murray, it was

reasonable to expect that he would be particularly scrupulous in his fidelity to security regulations [which are] the special test of the loyalty of the American citizen who serves his Government in the sensitive area of the Atomic Energy program. Dr. Oppenheimer did not meet this decisive test. He was disloyal.

I conclude that Dr. Oppenheimer's access to restricted data should be denied.

THOMAS E. MURRAY, Commissioner.

The [security] system . . . is a necessary means to an end. Its sole purpose, apart from the prevention of sabotage, is to protect secrets. If a man protects the secrets he has in his hands and his head, he has shown essential regard for the security system.

These words contained the essence of the lone dissenting opinion of Commissioner Henry DeWolf Smyth. Both his conclusion and his reasoning sprang from this view of the security system. As Smyth saw it, judgments in security cases involved a "look into the future"—a prediction of a man's contribution to the strength of his country balanced against an estimate of the danger that he might allow "important secrets to reach our enemies."

To him, the value to the country of a leading physicist such as Oppenheimer was clear. The only question before the AEC, then, concerned the likelihood that "Dr. Oppenheimer will intentionally or unintentionally reveal secret information" to unauthorized persons. Evidence about character and associations was only important insofar as it bore on that one question.

Viewed in this light, the weighing of the evidence was not, in Smyth's view, a difficult matter. It boiled down to

the fact that there is no indication in the entire record that Dr. Oppenheimer has ever divulged any secret information. The past 15 years of his life have been investigated and reinvestigated. For much of the last 11 years he has been under actual surveillance, his movements watched, his conversations noted, his mail and telephone calls checked.

To his description of this official surveillance, Smyth added a caustic but significant sentence: "This professional review of [Oppenheimer's] actions has been supplemented by enthusiastic amateur help from powerful personal enemies." Smyth later recalled that that sentence was provoked by reports in the Oppenheimer file which he said originated with such avid and skeptical Oppenheimer-watchers as Lewis Strauss, William Borden, David Griggs and, to a lesser extent, Edward Teller.

Having disposed of what he considered the central issue, Smyth went on to discuss particular questions that had been raised either by Nichols or the other Commissioners.

The allegations regarding the H-bomb (which he characterized as "the most important" of the initial AEC charges), Smyth dismissed quickly. "I am not surprised," he said, "to find that the evidence does not support these allegations in any way."

On the question of the Seaborg letter about the H-bomb, Smyth said, later in his opinion, that it was hard to understand how Oppenheimer could have forgotten the letter, "but it is still harder to see what purpose he could have hoped to achieve by intentionally suppressing it—and then turning it over to the Commission in his files." Moreover, said Smyth, official minutes of the AEC showed that Seaborg had been present at the December, 1949, meeting of the General Advisory Committee, when the H-bomb question was again discussed, and had raised no objection; hence, Oppenheimer's characterization of the GAC view as "unanimous" was not a distortion.

Smyth dealt with the "proof" of character defects that had been "cull[ed] from the record of Dr. Oppenheimer's active life over the past 15 years." First, there was Oppenheimer's conduct in the Chevalier incident, which Smyth termed "temporary concealment of an espionage attempt and admitted lying, and inexcusable." But Smyth took pains to note aspects of the Chevalier incident that other of Oppenheimer's judges had chosen to ignore: that General Groves had not, at first, considered Oppenheimer's concealment of Chevalier's name important enough to order him to reveal it; that security officials themselves had permitted two and a half years to elapse before even seeking out and interviewing Chevalier and Eltenton about the incident; and, most important, that the incident had come to the attention of security officers only because Oppenheimer had volunteered it "of his own accord." Had his real motive been the concealment of an espionage attempt, why, Smyth asked, would he ever have mentioned the "kitchen conversation" to the authorities? Oppenheimer's "admitted lying" in the Chevalier incident was inexcusable, Smyth said. But, he continued,

> that was 11 years ago; there is no subsequent act even faintly similar. Dr. Oppenheimer has repeatedly expressed his shame and regret and has stated flatly that he would never again so act. My conclusion is that of Mr. Hartley Rowe, who testified "I think a man of Dr. Oppenheimer's character is not going to make the same mistake twice."

As to Oppenheimer's postwar contacts with Haakon Chevalier, Smyth said they "may have been unwise, but there is no evidence that they had any security significance." On the matter of Oppenheimer's other "associations," Smyth concluded that the physicist's postwar contacts with former radicals, even including his brother Frank, had been "nothing more than occasional incidents in a complex life." The public letter about his HUAC testimony on Bernard Peters was, to Smyth, not so much a repudiation of that testimony as a "manifestation of a belief that political views should not disqualify a scientist from a teaching job. . . . One might disagree with this belief," said Smyth, "without taking it as evidence of untrustworthiness."

As to Strauss' claim that there had been numerous instances besides the Chevalier matter in which Oppenheimer had obstructed the work of security officers, Smyth said he had "sought to identify these other instances" and had found, in the entire record of Oppenheimer's contacts with the FBI and other security officials, only one instance: a refusal, in 1950, to answer questions about Jean Tatlock and Thomas Addis on the ground that both were dead and could not defend themselves. "This reticence to discuss the activities of a friend and a former fiancée years after their deaths may have been an error. But in the circumstances it seems understandable hesitation, and does not indicate a persistent 'willful disregard' of security."

Lewis Strauss had claimed that the "catalog" of Oppenheimer's "falsehoods, evasions and misrepresentations" was not confined to the six specific examples which Strauss had cited, but he had failed to suggest any other examples. Smyth's dissenting opinion provided the most authoritative explanation for Strauss' failure, for after combing the record, with the aid of two assistants, Smyth was able to state flatly that Strauss' six examples

constitute the whole of the evidence extracted from a lengthy record. . . . Any implication that these are illustrations only and that further substantial evidence exists in the investigative files to support these charges is unfounded. With the single exception of the Chevalier incident, the evidence relied upon is thin, whether individual instances are considered separately or in combination. All added together, with the Chevalier incident included, the evidence is singularly unimpressive when viewed in the perspective of the 15 years of active life from which it is drawn. Few men could survive such a period of investigation and interrogation without having many of their actions misinterpreted or misunderstood.

"To be effective," said Smyth, "a security system must be realistic," and to this end, the AEC security criteria called specifically for "overall commonsense judgments" in security cases. Such a judgment of the entire record, Smyth observed, "destroys any pattern of suspicious conduct or catalog of falsehoods and evasions, and leaves a picture of Dr. Oppenheimer as an able, imaginative human being with normal human weaknesses and failings."

Unless one confuses a manner of expression with candor, or errors in recollection with lack of veracity, Dr. Oppenheimer's testimony before the Gray Board has the ring of honesty. I urge thoughtful citizens to examine this testimony for themselves, and not be content with summaries or with extracts quoted out of context.

With respect to the alleged disregard of the security system, I would suggest that the system itself is nothing to worship. It is a necessary means to an end. Its sole purpose, apart from the prevention of sabotage, is to protect secrets. If a man protects the secrets he has in his hands and his head, he has shown essential regard for the security system. . . . I frankly do not understand the charge made by the majority that Dr. Oppenheimer has shown a persistent and willful disregard for the obligations of security. . . . No gymnastics of rationalization allow me to accept this argument.

Smyth concluded his dissent with these words:

In these times, failure to employ a man of great talents may impair the strength and power of this country. Yet I would accept this loss if I doubted the loyalty of Dr. Oppenheimer or his ability to hold his tongue. I have no such doubts.

I conclude that Dr. Oppenheimer's employment "will not endanger the common defense and security." . . . I prefer the positive statement that Dr. Oppenheimer's further employment will continue to strengthen the United States. I therefore have voted to reinstate Dr. Oppenheimer's clearance.

The opinions of the AEC Commissioners were handed to newsmen at 4 P.M., Tuesday, June 29—precisely thirty-two hours before Oppenheimer's consultant's contract (and with it, presumably, the need for his clearance) was due to die a natural death.

At that moment, Washington reporters were privileged to read words about a man who had not even been permitted to see them himself. Robert Oppenheimer had first learned of the negative verdict that morning, not from the AEC but from a reporter who had gotten advance word of it. For several hours he had waited for some official notice, but it was not until shortly before the four o'clock release time that AEC General Manager Nichols called the physicist to inform him of "the nature of the findings." At the moment the verdicts themselves were handed to newsmen, no copy had yet been vouchsafed the accused.

Shortly after four, Congressman Sterling Cole, chairman of the Joint Atomic Energy Committee, broke into a House of Representatives debate on a foreign aid measure to announce the

AEC's decision. The news was greeted by a smattering of applause.

*New York Times* reporter James Reston had, as usual, been able to gain unusual access. Going beyond the formally released words of the AEC Commissioners, he reported that the Chevalier incident had been a particularly damaging factor in the AEC verdict. "Indeed," Reston said, "it can be stated on fairly reliable authority that at least one of the Commission members who voted against [Oppenheimer] would have switched but for this incident." Reston also reported that the Commission had been concerned about one matter not officially discussed, an aspect of Oppenheimer's visit to Chevalier in December of 1953. The Commission, said Reston, was dismayed that Oppenheimer, not being sure that Chevalier was not a Communist, had taken the chance that, like many other nuclear scientists, he might have been "forced at gun-point into a plane and taken behind the Iron Curtain." According to Reston's report, Oppenheimer himself "scoffs at this possibility, pointing out that the United States Government knew where he was."\* But, Reston said, others in Washington "cite this prospect as evidence that [Oppenheimer] was casual about security matters that affected not only his own safety but the safety of the country."

Late that evening, after Oppenheimer had received the texts of the AEC opinions and had conferred with Lloyd Garrison, he issued his formal comment. As to the AEC's verdict, he said merely: "Dr. Henry D. Smyth's fair and considered statement, made with full knowledge of the facts, says what needs to be said."

But Oppenheimer also spoke to a larger matter not directly related to his own fate. The reaction of scientists to his security case had been vehement, and, he later recalled, many "were thinking of quitting government projects." He felt it important

\* This indicated what Lloyd Garrison later confirmed: namely, that Oppenheimer "took it for granted that . . . his movements were shadowed, and that when he and his wife went to a social dinner evening with the Chevaliers in Paris, the government would know of it."

to "say, in effect, 'This case is through. The country needs its scientists. Don't resign or quit or fuss.'"

And so, to his terse comment on the AEC verdict, Robert Oppenheimer added these thoughts:

Without commenting on the security system which has brought all this about, I do have a further word to say. Our country is fortunate in its scientists, in their high skill, and their devotion. I know that they will work faithfully to preserve and strengthen this country. I hope that the fruit of their work will be used with humanity, with wisdom and with courage. I know that their counsel when sought will be given honestly and freely. I hope that it will be heard.

# IX    POSTLUDE

On June 30, 1954, the day the AEC's decision appeared in the newspapers, Lloyd Garrison met with Robert and Kitty Oppenheimer. "It was a painful occasion," Garrison has written. "In view of the way the Commission had presented the transcript to the public, we had expected an adverse decision, but we were not prepared for what seemed to us the one-sided and savage character of the majority opinion. The question now was what, if anything, could be done."

Although an appeal to the courts had been ruled out from the start, they considered appealing the case to the President. But they rejected the notion. It was unthinkable that he would substitute his judgment for that of the Gray Board and the AEC, and any presidential affirmation of those decisions "would simply compound the injury already suffered" by Oppenheimer. All Garrison and his colleagues could think to do was to undertake, for subsequent publication, a detailed critique of the AEC verdict and an exposition of the procedural injustices resulting from the government's tactics. They recognized that by the time such a laborious paper could be prepared, interest in the case would probably have waned, and at best their work would be discounted "as the partisan work of disappointed counsel."

"Still," Garrison said, "we could think of nothing better and so we said we would try our hand at it, knowing full well that nothing we could ever write would undo the damage done to the Oppenheimers. And then, with heavy hearts, we parted. . . .

"So our professional relationship with Robert dwindled to its melancholy end. There remained a lasting friendship. . . ."

The government's involvement with the Oppenheimer matter was now officially over. But the verdict continued to reverberate through the remaining months of 1954.

The day after the AEC decision was announced there were several notable reactions:

At his news conference President Eisenhower was asked to comment on it. The Chief Executive declined. His knowledge, he said, was limited to having read in the newspapers "that the vote was four to one."

In Princeton, Albert Einstein and twenty-five colleagues were not as noncommittal as the President. They were "proud," they said, "to give public expression" to their "confidence in [Oppenheimer's] loyalty and patriotic devotion, [which] remains unimpaired."

The New York Times had said it was "generally assumed" in Washington that Oppenheimer would resign as director of the Institute for Advanced Study. From his office at the Institute, Oppenheimer issued a statement of denial.

And Lewis Strauss, in a letter to a friend about the case, felt obliged to comment on reports in the newspapers that he had been moved by personal animosity. Such reports, he said, were disproven by the fact that as a trustee of the Institute for Advanced Study he had secured for Oppenheimer a 25 percent salary increase. This, he said, was "hardly consonant" with any personal hostility toward Oppenheimer.

Editorial reaction to the AEC decision was almost unanimously favorable to the majority verdict. Even the usually liberal New York Post, two of whose executives had studied the Gray Board hearing record, concluded that "Dr. Oppenheimer is clearly guilty of arbitrariness and deceit." The Post editorial wondered, on the other hand, "whether the kind of exacting, total scrutiny to which Dr. Oppenheimer has been subjected is a test that many men in public life could pass."

A few papers raised their voices on the scientist's behalf. The Louisville *Courier-Journal* commented: "We have never before needed so greatly the benefits of such genius as our nation can command. We have never at the same time been so afraid to make use of genius. We have long been told that this is the age of the Common Man. It is fast becoming the Age of the Common Mind."

The Washington *Post* said:

> It is by no means clear this his services can be discarded without loss to the Nation. He might, indeed, have provided the rare flash of genius that would unlock some future discovery, just as Dr. Edward Teller provided the inspiration that led to the hydrogen bomb. . . . Will the security of the country really be stronger because Dr. Oppenheimer has been excluded from the program to which he has contributed so much?

And columnist Walter Lippmann observed: "A strong government would have known how to use Dr. Oppenheimer's genius, discounting his political advice. A weak government, not trusting its own judgment, and fearing the impact of his brilliance, would be justified in terminating his services."

Three days after the AEC's verdict was made public, Robert Oppenheimer granted an interview to Saul Pett, feature writer for the Associated Press. Pett reported that Oppenheimer's "office was serene. The man in it was not. He chain-smoked and fidgeted —but then he always has."

The scientist volunteered little. Pett got the "impression there was much he wanted to say—especially about his own feelings— but did not because he was reluctant to appear to be seeking sympathy." Did Oppenheimer think he had received a fair hearing? The scientist would merely say he hoped "people will study the record of this case and reach their own conclusions. . . . I think there is something to be learned from it."

What did he think of comments picturing him as a sad figure

caught in a Greek tragedy? "In some dramas," he replied cryptically, "a sense of the drama comes from the chorus."

On July 2 the Atomic Energy Commission released a sixty-seven-page booklet containing the *Texts of Principal Documents and Letters* in the case. In addition to publishing the full texts of the Gray Board and AEC opinions, it unveiled, for the first time, Nichols' harsh recommendation to the AEC.

These anti-Oppenheimer documents made up the bulk of the booklet, which was far from a balanced selection of "principal documents and letters" in the case. It did contain Lloyd Garrison's June 1 critique of the Gray Board opinion (and Nichols' rebuttal of it). But it omitted Garrison's surrebuttal of June 9; Garrison's written briefs to the Gray Board and to the AEC;* and two pro-Oppenheimer affidavits that had been added to the Gray Board record, by mutual consent, following the close of the board's hearing.

On July 14 Garrison wrote a letter to Chairman Strauss protesting these omissions and requesting that the AEC publish the omitted documents and distribute them to the same persons to whom it had sent its own pamphlet. He received no reply for nearly four weeks. Finally the answer came, not from Strauss, but from General Manager Nichols. It added little to what was obvious from the pamphlet itself, stating merely that the AEC had "decided to print only the basic findings, recommendations and decisions in the proceedings, together with those letters which had to do with procedures to be followed after the submission of the report of the Personnel Security [Gray] Board." The Nichols letter ended on a somewhat peremptory note: "The Commission contemplates no further action with regard to the matter."

On July 8 the name of Paul Crouch reappeared in the news. The Department of Justice, it seemed, was having second thoughts about its own hired informant ($9,675 had been paid to him in the past two years), and had instituted an investigation of him. Crouch was sufficiently aroused to accuse Attorney Gen-

---

* Garrison had publicly released his brief to the AEC, but not his brief to the Gray Board.

eral Brownell of giving "considerable aid and comfort to the enemies of the United States" and to demand a probe of the loyalty of Brownell's personal aides. He was not alone in his unhappiness: like-minded Congressional staff members were reportedly also dismayed by Brownell's probe of Crouch. According to the *New York Times,* they argued "that his decision would 'discourage informers on whom they as well as the Justice Department depended to a considerable extent.' One official engaged in this work said Mr. Crouch had compiled a fairly large 'blood bank' of paid informers used by the government."

In mid-July, Robert and Kitty Oppenheimer sought respite in the Caribbean. Before he left, the physicist took pains to send a registered letter to FBI Director Hoover. He did not know whether "at this time" Hoover had an interest in his whereabouts, he said, but he thought he "should" report that he was leaving for three or four weeks of rest and sailing in and around Saint Croix "in the U.S. Virgin Islands."

With the completion of the case itself, Lloyd Garrison was able to return to his professional and personal pursuits. For six months, now, he and his associates had devoted themselves almost exclusively to the defense of Robert Oppenheimer's reputation. They had gladly done so without any fee.

The defendant's total costs in a security case such as Oppenheimer's are difficult to reckon. There are the unmeasurable costs: the anguish and anxiety and the prodigious diversion of attention and energy from normal pursuits. But there are measurable costs as well. Oppenheimer's out-of-pocket expenses came to more than $25,000.* But, due to the willingness of Garrison and his colleagues to serve without fee, and to the insistence of almost all the pro-Oppenheimer witnesses on paying their own expenses, the $25,000 represented merely a fraction of the true costs. Garrison and his partners made no effort to record the hours they

* These outlays, for such things as the hearing transcript, printed briefs, lawyers' travel expenses, etc., were over and above the unsolicited contributions Oppenheimer received from hundreds of people whom he did not know, from all parts of the country. Lloyd Garrison has recalled that "the total in dollars was not large, but the generosity of spirit meant more to him than money."

devoted to Oppenheimer's defense, and so it is difficult to arrive at any precise estimate of what the case would have cost Oppenheimer had he been charged ordinary legal fees, but lawyers familiar with such cases say they would not be surprised if the fees would have amounted to $100,000—or perhaps much more.

Oppenheimer's case was exceptionally complex and lengthy. But the legal costs of defending less celebrated security-risk defendants were often substantial. A survey of such cases shows that the defense counsel typically devoted from twenty to fifty working hours to a case. Frequently the time involved was in excess of a hundred working hours. In nearly all the cases surveyed, the defense counsel in effect subsidized the client by charging lower than normal fees—in some cases none at all. This of course did not mean that any of the actual legal costs vanished; it merely meant that they were shifted, in whole or in part, from the "defendant" to his lawyers.

On October 1, 1954, the trustees of the Institute for Advanced Study gathered at the Uptown Club on New York's East Forty-second Street. On the agenda was the question of Robert Oppenheimer's re-election as the Institute's director. Among the trustees in attendance that day was Lewis Strauss, who left the meeting early, brushing hurriedly past reporters. He explained he had to catch a train back to Washington, and referred all questions to Board Chairman Herbert Maass. When the meeting ended, Maass told newsmen that Robert Oppenheimer had been re-elected director. Had the vote been unanimous? Maass replied firmly, "Quite." As it later developed, not only had Strauss voted for the motion to re-elect Oppenheimer; it had been he who proposed it. He saw no inconsistency in this action. "The areas," he wrote years later, "are distinct."

Twice, in the fall of 1954, when the heat of the controversy over the Oppenheimer case was beginning to die, the printed word stirred the coals.

In October two *Time-Life* correspondents, James Shepley and Clay Blair, Jr., published a book entitled, *The Hydrogen Bomb*. It was, to say the least, sparing in its kindness toward Robert Oppenheimer. It enthusiastically expounded the point of view of the

Air Force and of those who had favored the H-bomb. Edward Teller's role in the development of the bomb was so glorified that the scientist, embarrassed by the remarks this was causing among nuclear physicists, set to work on an article giving due credit to the others who had participated in the bomb's birth.

Lewis Strauss, too, was concerned about the perpetuation of the split in the scientific community which this anti-Oppenheimer book might cause—to such an extent that he offered to buy the manuscript with his own funds, so that publication might be deferred "for a period of years during which tempers might cool." The offer was rejected—and later publicized, to Strauss' embarrassment, on a national television program.

The other publication that rekindled the Oppenheimer controversy was an article in *Harper's Magazine* by Joseph and Stewart Alsop, entitled, "We Accuse" (borrowing from Zola's famous tract in the Dreyfus case). Not only did the Alsops assail the AEC decision in the Oppenheimer case; they also accused Strauss of "venting the bitterness of old disputes through the security system" and of having been an instigator of Oppenheimer's security troubles.

As if the Alsop article itself had not hurt the thin-skinned Strauss enough, the Information Division of his own Commission compounded the injury by including a condensation of the Alsop critique in its regular monthly digest of AEC-related magazine articles. There were signs of an angry reaction in the AEC. Columnist-Commentator Fulton Lewis, Jr.* reported that the Commission was cracking down on a "top official" (presumably the AEC's Director of Information) for his "circulation of a highly distorted and critical version of the Oppenheimer investigation." Lewis said the official in question "was brought in [to the AEC] under Lilienthal" and was "a person of decided left-wing tendencies."

To counter the Alsop treatise, Arthur Rolander, the AEC's Deputy Director of Security who had assisted Roger Robb before the Gray Board, prepared a thirty-page rebuttal. The left half of each page quoted "What the Article States"; beside each excerpt, the right half of the page presented "The Facts." Among

---

* Whose clean scoop on the AEC's release of the Gray Board transcript had already indicated he was on friendly terms with the AEC high command.

the items used to rebut the Alsops was a verbatim quote from the minutes of the October 23, 1953, meeting of the trustees of the Institute for Advanced Study—of which Lewis Strauss was a member.*

Nor was Strauss entirely divorced from the distribution of the Rolander rebuttal. His personal assistant sent two copies to New York *Herald Tribune* columnist Roscoe Drummond, noting that the Alsop material was soon due to be published in book form and asking that Drummond forward a copy of the Rolander rebuttal "to whoever writes the *Herald Tribune*'s review of the forthcoming book." The AEC also circulated the Rolander memorandum to all those who had received the Commission's monthly periodical digest, with its offending condensation of the Alsop article.

Noting the AEC's unusual interest in the imminent publication of the Alsop book, the *New York Times* observed that "this is the first case in the memory of observers here [Washington] in which an agency of the Federal government involved in a public controversy has sent to book reviewers in advance of publication of a book a statement of its official views."†

In at least one respect the AEC was highly discriminating in its circulation of the Rolander rebuttal, for when author Stewart Alsop called the Commission to request a copy of the now widely circulated document, he was told that it was for "administrative use only" and therefore could not be furnished him.

On December 3, the names of Robert Oppenheimer and Haakon Chevalier were once again linked in the news. The wire services reported that an "Open Letter" from Chevalier to Oppenheimer had appeared in Paris, in *France Observateur.* In it Chevalier accused his erstwhile friend and idol of having lied in December, 1943, in telling General Groves that Chevalier had tried to elicit atomic secrets from him during the "kitchen conversation." The letter said that Oppenheimer had subsequently

---

* Cited in order to prove that it had been Strauss who had offered the motion for an increase in Oppenheimer's salary.

† The *Times* also noted "an additional complication of the problem," namely, "that while the reviewers have received a statement of AEC policy on the points in controversy, the reviewers are not permitted to quote from this document."

retracted this and had stated, instead, that Chevalier's purpose had merely been to warn him about George Eltenton. But, wrote Chevalier, the Atomic Energy Commission had ignored this retraction. Result: the AEC's decision against Oppenheimer was based on a lie.

This open letter was the culmination of a summer of anguished private letters from Chevalier to Oppenheimer and of cooler replies by the physicist. In a letter in late July, Chevalier had poured out the real source of his torment: it was not merely that Oppenheimer had distorted the kitchen conversation about Eltenton and brought "untold havoc" to Chevalier's career. More serious, Oppenheimer had for years dissembled, never acknowledging to Chevalier the fact that he had invented a "cock and bull" story for Pash and Lansdale, but "continu[ing] to show me the signs of an unaltered friendship."

Still, Chevalier was unwilling to believe that his friend had deliberately betrayed him. He clung to the hope that there must be some explanation. "I have loved you as I have loved no other man," he wrote Oppenheimer. "I placed in you an absolute trust. I would have defended you to the death against malice or slander. . . . I am not prepared . . . to make a final judgment purely on the basis of the facts. . . . Before I finally make up my mind . . . I am asking you, as perhaps the last act of friendship, to explain what the mind conceived and to what the heart consented."

Later that summer, upon his return from his Caribbean vacation, Oppenheimer responded. There was, he wrote, nothing he could add to the published record (which Lloyd Garrison had already sent to Chevalier), but he had never done or said anything with the intent of hurting his friend. Oppenheimer said he recognized the depth of Chevalier's affection, but added that it was not clear to him how much his "cock and bull" story to Groves had damaged Chevalier.

Oppenheimer's letter did little to satisfy Chevalier's questions or doubts. And so he composed his open letter.

When reports of Chevalier's letter appeared in American newspapers, Robert Oppenheimer was asked for comment. He had none.

On December 13 Chevalier addressed a final letter to his friend. Again he berated the scientist, both for having lied and for having dissembled. And yet he was, as he later recalled, "still very much under the spell of the Oppenheimer I had known all those years." Later, he would read and reread the Gray Board hearing transcript. He would study the three telegrams sent by General Nichols in December, 1943, after Oppenheimer's first disclosure of the Chevalier name.* He would note that the telegrams still referred to "three contacts" by Chevalier in the atomic project. And he would draw a bitter conclusion: Oppenheimer had not only implicated Chevalier in the "kitchen conversation"; worse than that, he had concealed his own identity as the other party in the conversation by persisting with the "three-contact" story.

But that discovery came later to Haakon Chevalier. Now, in the days before Christmas, 1954, he wrote Oppenheimer:

> . . . I am no longer angry—anger is not a mood to live with . . . and besides, you are so close to me that despite the immensities that separate us, I somehow regard you as almost a part of myself. That affection of which you speak has not wavered. But there are many worrisome things that crowd around it.

He closed the letter with a wish: "May this Christmas be less fraught with anxieties than the last must have been, and may you contribute in the coming year the share that you *can* contribute to the achievement of Peace on Earth."

* See p. 68.

# X  FALLOUT—1

"America must not devour her own children . . .
we must not devour the best and most gifted
of our citizens. . . ."

This was Lloyd Garrison's closing plea to the Gray Board. It accurately foreshadowed the fate of some of the lesser-known
"gifted citizens" who played a part in the Oppenheimer case.

Giovanni Rossi Lomanitz, the brilliant young Oppenheimer
protégé who had been pulled off his important war work and
thrust into the Army despite Oppenheimer's intercessions, was
released from the Army in May, 1946. He returned to the Radiation Lab in Berkeley and with Oppenheimer's help became a
teaching assistant at the University of California. When Oppenheimer joined the Institute for Advanced Study in Princeton,
Lomanitz sought to go too, but Oppenheimer rebuffed him. He
then taught briefly at Cornell before moving, again with assistance from Oppenheimer, to Fisk University in Nashville, Tennessee. In 1949 Lomanitz was summoned before the House Un-
American Activities Committee. He asserted his loyalty to the
United States and said he himself had never acted contrary

to his country's interests, but he invoked the Fifth Amendment in declining to testify about the alleged Communist activities of himself and others.

The day following his HUAC appearance, Lomanitz and Fisk University parted company, and the young professor returned to his native Oklahoma City. There the news of his HUAC testimony made him something of a curiosity, and the press pursued him everywhere. To support himself and his wife Mary, he took a job as a laborer with the Oklahoma Gas and Electric Company, but even at work he could not escape newspaper reporters. In late July the *Daily Oklahoman* published a photograph of a tall water tower, with this caption:

That's not a rivet atop that sizzling water tower. It's Giovanni Rossi Lomanitz, dodging newsmen Friday.

The job foreman berated the reporters. "He's a damn good working man trying to make an honest living. So why don't you leave him alone?"

It would have been hard to believe that Rossi Lomanitz was an unusually well-trained theoretical physicist, for his ensuing occupations were, successively:

- tarring roofs for the Clint Cook Roofing Company;
- loading burlap bags for the Arrow Bag Company;
- placing bearings in boxes for the L & S Bearing Company;
- trimming trees for the Asplundh Tree Expert Company;
- bottling hair oil for the Rossman Products Company.

Wherever Lomanitz went to work, FBI agents would follow. They would drop by ostensibly to ask his employers how he was getting along with the other people in the plant. In some cases this was enough to get him fired. One of his employers told Lomanitz, "The FBI was in. They didn't say anything against you. But we're scared. We've got a lot of government contracts, you know."

Mary Lomanitz also worked, when she could. Once she drew forty dollars in unemployment compensation, and Lomanitz used it to buy lumber with which he built a shack outside of Oklahoma City. There they cooked on a wood stove, pumped their own water and read by a kerosene lamp.

Lomanitz continued to move from job to job. He worked at seventy-five cents an hour for the Standard Paint Company mixing paint and putty, making deliveries and pasting labels on cans. The Capital Steel Company gave him eighty-five cents an hour for painting and loading iron girders.

The chain was interrupted briefly by his indictment for contempt of Congress in December, 1949, and his trial and acquittal in June, 1951.

Early in 1952 he became a railroad section hand, repairing railroad tracks for $1.35 an hour. That lasted until 1954, when the railroads began laying off men. The Lomanitzes moved to Norman, home of the University of Oklahoma, where Rossi set up a tutoring business for students, and Mary resumed her profession of bookkeeping.

Five years later, in late 1959, Rossi Lomanitz' fortunes improved. Stanley Frankel, a former Berkeley colleague, telephoned and asked if he knew anything about superconductivity. The upshot of the conversation was that Frankel hired Lomanitz as a consultant on a contract with the General Electric Company. Soon afterward, a friend who had also been a victim of the "Red scare" encouraged Lomanitz to write to the American Physical Society, the trade association of physicists, for notice of job opportunities. Among the nibbles that resulted was an offer from Whitman College, in the State of Washington, and in the fall of 1960 the Lomanitzes moved there. Once again, after a wasted decade, Lomanitz was accepted into his profession.

But the lost time could never be made up. Gone was the hope of an associate professorship at a major university or a full professorship at a lesser institution. As of this writing, Lomanitz is associate professor at the New Mexico Institute of Mining Technology in Socorro, New Mexico, an institution with 354 students and 37 teachers.

Rossi Lomanitz suffered a ten-year exile from his profession. David Bohm, his close friend at Berkeley before the war, managed to avoid that, but at the price of something approaching exile from his country.

Like Lomanitz, Bohm had been suspected by security officers during the war, and they had blocked his dream of being with his idol, Oppenheimer, at Los Alamos. Like Lomanitz, Bohm rejoined his former mentor in Berkeley after the war. He served as Oppenheimer's research assistant, then followed him to Princeton in 1947. Summoned to appear before the House Un-American Activities Committee in the spring of 1949, he too pleaded the Fifth Amendment, was indicted for contempt of Congress and was tried and acquitted. And, like Lomanitz, he lost his university position: after his acquittal, the president of Princeton allowed his contract to lapse, despite a plea from a group of physics professors that he be kept on.

Bohm made a few inquiries about other teaching jobs in the United States, but no offers resulted. The University of São Paulo, Brazil, proved more hospitable, and so in the fall of 1951 David Bohm left the country of his birth, carrying with him a highly complimentary letter of recommendation from Albert Einstein.

He had been in São Paulo only a few weeks when he received an unexpected call. Would Dr. Bohm mind coming to see the American Consul and bringing his passport? When Bohm asked why, he was told merely that the Consul wanted to see him. A car would pick him up. When he arrived at the consulate, he was immediately relieved of the passport. After a few minutes he was taken in to see the Consul, who explained that the passport would be stamped "VALID ONLY FOR RETURN TO THE UNITED STATES" and would be kept at the consulate. It was made clear that the purpose of this move was to prevent Bohm from traveling to other countries—especially, Bohm guessed, the Soviet Union.* The official apprehension over the possibility that Bohm might escape was again revealed when Bohm needed his passport to get some baggage through Brazilian customs. Taking no chance, the consulate sent a courier to the docks with the passport rather than permit Bohm to handle it even fleetingly.

Confined within Brazil's borders, Bohm became restive. True,

* Bohm later said he had no desire to visit Russia but would very much have liked to visit Europe to exchange information with European scientists, since from a scientific point of view Brazil was comparatively isolated.

his passport was good for return to the United States, but there he was professionally unwelcome, and if the official jitteriness in the São Paulo Consulate reflected Washington policy, there was the strong chance he would not be allowed to leave the U.S. again. There seemed only one other alternative: to establish Brazilian citizenship and get a Brazilian passport. This was the course that David Bohm chose.

In 1955 he left Brazil for Israel, taught for two years in Haifa and then went to England, where he became a full professor at the University of London. In 1960 he received news from Pennsylvania that his father was dying of a brain tumor. He went to the U.S. Embassy in London to apply for a visa, but ran into a wall of uncooperativeness. It was not until relatives in Pennsylvania obtained the intervention of their Congressman that Bohm obtained permission to visit his native land.

In 1961 Brandeis University, in Massachusetts, offered Bohm an attractive position. He was tempted by the prospect. In order to obtain the necessary re-entry permission, he provided the Department of State with a statement about his political views, seeking to make clear that he was not in sympathy with the Communists. After a time, he was given to understand that U.S. immigration laws required of ex-Communists what amounted to a public recantation of former views. Whether or not Bohm's understanding was correct, it was largely on this account that he decided to decline the Brandeis offer.

And so he has remained in England, in effect an exile from the United States. He is considered, in the community of physicists, to be doing important work, and to be endowed with one of the more creative minds in his field. But it is a mind that is apparently forever lost to the United States of America. As one physicist put it, in the case of David Bohm America is a "country without a man."

Also numbered among America's unofficial exiles is Bernard Peters, the refugee from Hitler whom Oppenheimer had befriended and about whom he had testified controversially before HUAC. In 1949 Peters, like Lomanitz and Bohm, had his own confrontation with the House Un-American Activities Committee* but he received much kinder treatment at the hands of his employer than had his former Berkeley friends. Even after the disclosure concerning Oppenheimer's testimony about him, the University of Rochester refused to fire him, pointing out that there were no supported charges of "wrongful action on his part."

At the end of 1949 Peters was invited to India to engage in some nonsecret research, but the State Department denied him a passport. Alan Valentine, president of the university, took up the physicist's cause. "A man's reputation and career," said Valentine, "have been greatly threatened and perhaps even ruined without his being given an opportunity to hear the grounds for such action, to identify and face his accusers and to offer his defense. It was my impression," Valentine observed tartly, "that our government protected its citizens against such practice. In this case the citizen appears to need protection from his own government."

Two years later the State Department reversed its stand, and Peters was able to accept a professorship at the Tata Institute of Fundamental Research in Bombay. And so Bernard Peters left his adopted country. He has not returned since. In 1959 he went to Copenhagen, former home of the great Niels Bohr, and joined the Ionosphere Laboratory of the Technical University there. He now supervises all European cosmic-ray experimentation. His name, like that of David Bohm, fails to appear in *American Men of Science* because his talents, too, have been lost to America.

The name of Frank Oppenheimer does appear in that collection, but in a quick reading of his capsule biography it would be easy to skip over the fact that he, like Rossi Lomanitz, was excluded from his profession for nearly a decade.

Following his "resignation" from the University of Minnesota in 1949, Frank Oppenheimer sought refuge in the mountains of the Southwest, in which he and his brother had spent so many companionable months. In Colorado, about 120 miles from Los Alamos and not far from the old Oppenheimer ranch at Perro Caliente, Frank Oppenheimer, Doctor of Philosophy in physics, became a sheep rancher.

* See p. 125.

The isolation he sought was denied him by the agents of the Federal Bureau of Investigation. From time to time they would wander into the nearby towns and make inquiries of the Oppenheimers and their activities. Their unusual questions might easily have disquieted Oppenheimer's neighbors: Was Frank doing any physics experiments at his ranch? Did he have any radio equipment there? Were the neighbors sure—had they been in *all* the buildings on the ranch?* But Frank's neighbors told the FBI that they did not particularly care about such things. The Oppenheimers, they said, were good neighbors, and that was all that mattered to them.

However much Frank Oppenheimer may have loved the outdoors and the mountains, this was not the life for which he had spent years of study preparing himself. From time to time he made inquiries about jobs in universities, but none was fruitful. After more than seven years he did get back into teaching, at the high school in Pagosa Springs, Colorado (population 1,374). But it was not until 1959 that Frank Oppenheimer was invited to join the physics department at the University of Colorado and permitted to resume the teaching of physics at the college level.

* The relationship between the FBI and the Oppenheimers was not wholly distant. The local agents gradually became friendly—to such an extent that one of them drove to the Oppenheimer ranch to say that he was being transferred and to introduce his replacement.

# XI    FALLOUT—2

After a nuclear explosion, the fallout travels where the winds take it and descends unpredictably. Similarly in the years following the Oppenheimer security case, its corrosive fallout settled not merely on the Bohms, the Peterses, the Lomanitzes, the Frank Oppenheimers, but also on some of the very people who played leading roles in bringing down Robert Oppenheimer.

In June, 1954, Lewis Strauss had sat in judgment on Oppenheimer's "loyalty, character and associations" and his suitability for government service. Just five years later, in June, 1959, Strauss' role was reversed. As the United States Senate deliberated on his nomination to be Secretary of Commerce, Strauss was no longer the judge. It was he who was being judged, he whose future in government service hung in the balance.

Ordinarily, cabinet nominations slide through the Senate without controversy, and no one predicted more than nominal opposition to Strauss from the few Senators whom he had offended during his tenure as AEC Chairman. But the committee hearings on his nomination were only in their second day when Strauss ran into trouble.

It began when the nominee was questioned about an action he

had taken a week earlier, as Acting Secretary of Commerce. Strauss had issued a ruling blocking a sale of iron pipe to the Soviet Union. In so doing he had merely exercised his legal authority to override the objections of the State Department, but when he was questioned about a newspaper criticism of this action, his reply was surprising. The report of State Department opposition, he said, was not true. "There was absolutely no difference between the State Department and the Commerce Department on this," he stated categorically.

Presently, however, the committee unearthed a written statement of objection to Strauss' action from the State Department. Seven members of the committee later concluded that this memorandum "was a matter of record, and Mr. Strauss knew of it when he spoke" before the committee. Then, in language as severe as any Strauss had applied to Robert Oppenheimer, the seven Senators charged that the cabinet nominee had been "guilty of an outright misrepresentation."*

That was only the beginning of Strauss' difficulties. As the hearings dragged on over a two-month period, the nominee began to antagonize committee members who had at first been inclined to support him. His cause was not enhanced by further contradictions in his testimony. For example, at one point what he said to the Senators conflicted with what he had previously told a committee of the House of Representatives. Strauss' explanation: the House hearing record must have been tampered with. But when the stenographic reporter who had taken a verbatim record of Strauss' House testimony was asked to fish out his old notes and retranscribe them, they confirmed that Strauss had indeed made the statement he now sought to repudiate. There had been no tampering with the record.

The Oppenheimer case was introduced into the Strauss hearing by two nuclear scientists, David R. Inglis and David L. Hill, both formerly of the Los Alamos laboratory. Inglis charged that Strauss had been motivated by "personal vindictiveness" that had

---

* Even years afterward, Strauss insisted his "testimony was accurate. The position of the Department of State had been given to me by the Under Secretary of State, Mr. Douglas Dillon. At a much lower level in the State Department, approval of the export license had been favored, but the policy of the State Department was not established at subordinate echelons."

its origin in Oppenheimer's 1949 disagreement with Strauss on the shipment of radioisotopes. Inglis also cited the very words Strauss had used in his 1954 adverse verdict against Robert Oppenheimer, saying to the Senate Committee, "It is he [Strauss] who, because of 'substantial defects of character' . . . is unfit to serve on the President's cabinet."

Hill embroidered on this, asserting that Strauss twice had used the AEC security program as a means of retribution against AEC employees who had disagreed with him. He gave first the example of former AEC General Manager Carroll Wilson, who had often been in conflict with Strauss from 1947 to 1950, when Strauss was a member of the AEC. Wilson's security status, as an official of a private contracting firm which did work for the AEC, came under sudden and intense investigation shortly after Strauss became Chairman of the AEC in 1953. Hill also spoke of scientist Malcolm Henderson, who had likewise disagreed with Strauss on policy matters and whose atomic "Q" clearance was suspended shortly after his departure from the AEC. The Commission claimed this was a routine matter, but witness Hill told the Senate Committee that Henderson had made inquiries and was convinced that the clearance suspension had been taken "through [the] direct and active intervention" of Lewis Strauss.*

These were grave charges to be leveled at a prospective cabinet officer, but they were promptly lent credence by none other than Strauss himself. During Inglis' appearance before the Senate committee, reporter Jack Anderson, Drew Pearson's co-writer of "The Washington Merry-Go-Round" column, was seated a few feet from Strauss. According to Anderson's later testimony, his eye was caught by a folder before Strauss stamped "CONFI-

* Later in the hearing Strauss said that he "did not personally order any investigation of Mr. Wilson so far as I can remember, and there is no reason why I should have. He had never done anything to me." Asked about Hill's charge that Wilson's company—an AEC contractor—had received "a strong indication that Strauss felt he should have been consulted before such a man as Wilson had been hired," Strauss replied, "If there [was] any such, I have no recollection of it." Regarding Malcolm Henderson, Strauss said, "I have no recollection of Mr. Henderson at all." In view of that, he said it was "unlikely" he had talked with National Security Council Secretary Robert Cutler about Henderson. (Hill had charged that a job offer to Henderson with the National Security Council had been "immediately withdrawn" after "Admiral Strauss heard about it.")

DENTIAL" in prominent red letters. "The subject matter," Anderson later told the committee, "was Dr. Inglis. It was not a routine biography because it quoted from the FBI. I saw that much with my own eyes." Anderson said he had subsequently asked a Strauss aide about the report. The aide had acknowledged to Anderson that it was "a dossier on Dr. Inglis," and said he was uncertain about its source but "thought it came from the AEC or the FBI."

Four days later, the "Washington Merry-Go-Round" published Anderson's account of what he had seen. At the May 11 committee hearing Strauss was asked about the report. His reply was absolute: "I have never asked for anything on Mr. Inglis in my life." But again the facts showed that Strauss was, at the least, guilty of extravagant statement. The committee elicited from John McCone, Strauss' successor as Chairman of the AEC, a letter declaring that about April 20 Strauss himself had contacted McCone's office concerning Inglis. Strauss, McCone wrote, said he had learned of the possibility of Inglis' testifying at his confirmation hearing and that "in order to have a general idea as to the area Dr. Inglis might cover, it would be helpful to know whether he was employed by an AEC contractor and, if so, the name of his profession." The following day the AEC told Strauss that Inglis was employed at the AEC's Argonne laboratory in Chicago, and that *American Men of Science* listed Inglis' fields of competence. None of this data was secret.*

Strauss modified his original flat statement. He told the committee that he *had* called the AEC to ask whether Inglis was still an AEC employee, where his security files were kept, whether he still had an atomic "Q" clearance, what kind of job he did and what his qualifications were. While he did not say *why* these matters were of interest to him, Strauss insisted that his call to the

---

* The matter did not stop there. Chairman McCone's assistant ordered the AEC Security Division to review Inglis' security file to see (according to McCone's later explanation) if there was "any public information contained in the record re Dr. Inglis which might suggest whether his general testimony would involve the AEC." Although McCone did not explain why a search of a secret government dossier was necessary to produce "public information," no such information was found in the file, and, said McCone, "no information of any type was furnished directly or indirectly to any person."

AEC had taken place *after* the Pearson-Anderson column was published. This statement was remarkable to some committee members, since it was in direct conflict with John McCone's letter: McCone had stated explicitly that Strauss' call had come two weeks *before* the Pearson column appeared. When one Senator sought to press Strauss on this point, the nominee cut him off abruptly, saying, "I have nothing more to say, Mr. Chairman, on this point."

By the time the hearings ended on May 14 the committee had amassed over a thousand pages of testimony, and Lewis Strauss had amassed eight opponents out of the seventeen members of the Senate Commerce Committee. On May 19 the committee recommended Strauss' confirmation, but by only one vote. Nine members were for, eight against.

The majority's report found Strauss "to be a man of honesty and integrity," the adverse testimony having "in the main . . . stemmed from disagreements [with Strauss] on questions of judgment and philosophy or from inferred affronts to personal or official dignity." "On the question of [Strauss'] competence," said the majority, "there is *no* adverse testimony."

The minority report of the eight Strauss opponents was scathing. Some excerpts from their findings about Lewis Strauss:

Lacking in the sincerity and the tolerance required for confirmation . . . guilty of an outright misrepresentation . . . resorted to unnecessary untruths in what appeared to be an attempt to put himself in the best possible light before the Committee . . . seems unable to confess to error in any way . . . has shown a willingness to seek to fit the facts to his preconceived notions.

Their concluding paragraph was reminiscent of what Strauss and his AEC colleagues had said about Robert Oppenheimer five years earlier:

We have concluded . . . partly on evidence as to his past record, but mostly on the basis of his conduct and demeanor before us—that Lewis L. Strauss is lacking in the degree of integrity and competence essential to proper performance of the duties of the office to which he has been nominated.

The Senators' heavy emphasis on Strauss' "conduct and demeanor before us" suggests that, just as some believed Robert Oppenheimer had been his own worst enemy before the Gray Board, the witness most damaging to Strauss before the Senate committee seems to have been Lewis Strauss himself.

On June 17 the Senate began its debate on Strauss' nomination. At the dramatic hour of midnight, June 18, with ninety-five of the ninety-eight Senators in their seats, the vote began. When the tally was complete, the presiding officer, Senator Prescott Bush of Connecticut, announced the result:

"On this vote the yeas are forty-six and the nays are forty-nine. The advice and consent of the Senate to the nomination of Lewis L. Strauss to be Secretary of Commerce is not agreed to."

At 12:52 the Senate completed its business. A few minutes later, Lewis Strauss emerged from the Department of Commerce Building, where he had been awaiting word of the Senate vote. "I am sure," he told waiting reporters, "that justice will emerge from all of this."

Then he climbed into his limousine and headed for his Shoreham Hotel apartment. Twelve days later he resigned as Acting Secretary of Commerce. At this writing, he has not held public office since.

Both Strauss and Oppenheimer were called to account for their actions. At the outset of their respective "trials," there was considerable expectation of a favorable outcome. Then each man testified in his own behalf. Each, after his testimony, was found less than believable. Each was found wanting on matters of character. In the end, both were brought down. Both were denied further service to their country.

It was five years before the fallout from the Oppenheimer affair reached Strauss. In the case of Edward Teller it came quickly. The setting was the place of Oppenheimer's greatest accomplishments, Los Alamos. The occasion was a large conference of nuclear scientists from all parts of the country. The time was

July, 1954, only a few weeks after the AEC's final pronouncement on Oppenheimer.

A few days earlier, copies of the Gray Board transcript, including Teller's anguished, ambivalent testimony against Oppenheimer, had reached Los Alamos and were beginning to pass from hand to hand among the scientists there.

Teller had arrived early for the conference. He was clearly glad to see his old Los Alamos associates, and at first they seemed to reciprocate. But then there began to be subtle signs of a change: a friend who one day warmly greeted Teller would the next day somehow be looking the other way when he passed. It was not until the opening day of the conference, however, that the full impact struck Teller.

At lunch that day in the dining room of the central Lodge, the atmosphere was one of conviviality as one scientist after another arrived and met old friends. Among the arrivals were two of Oppenheimer's close scientific and personal friends: from Pasadena the towering Robert Christy, from New York the diminutive I. I. Rabi. They sat at a table not fifty feet from where Edward Teller was sitting with his wife and a guest.

Teller went over to Rabi's table, greeting its occupants with a hearty laugh and hand outstretched, quite clearly expecting to share in the camaraderie. But camaraderie was not what awaited him. As the crowded dining room looked on, first Christy, then Rabi, refused Teller's proffered hand. Rabi then proceeded acidly to congratulate Teller on the "brilliance" of his testimony before the Gray Board and "the extremely clever way" he had phrased his reply concerning Oppenheimer as a security risk. "'I would personally feel more secure' without Oppenheimer in the government," Rabi said caustically, "a brilliant way of saying, 'don't restore his clearance.'"

When Teller returned to his table, he could hardly speak. He seemed to be having trouble keeping his face composed, as if he were about to weep. He excused himself and went to his room. There, according to *Life* reporter Robert Coughlan, he permitted the tears to flow. He did not emerge from his room that day, and throughout the remainder of the conference he was cautious in his approaches to other scientists, for fear of risking another humiliating rebuff. Even his wife was coolly received by some of the scientists and many of their wives. It would be nine years before the Tellers would visit Los Alamos again.

The ostracism of Edward Teller did not end at Los Alamos. In Berkeley many of his old friends dropped him; and as he traveled around the country, he could never be sure of the reception he would receive from former colleagues. Robert Coughlan has observed that "for someone of Teller's temperament, a man who enjoys human relationships so much and likes to be liked, such treatment [was] traumatic."

The feeling against Teller was intensified in October of 1954, by the publication of the Shepley-Blair book, *The Hydrogen Bomb*, which extolled Teller's role in the development of the H-bomb, but which had few kind things to say about Robert Oppenheimer. Later he again stirred the enmity of the pro-Oppenheimer scientists by campaigning against the nuclear-test-ban treaty.

The price he paid was heavy. He developed a painful and dangerous form of colitis, a disease believed to be primarily psychological in origin. His gaiety left him; he was often despondent. No one, perhaps, was more painfully affected by the Oppenheimer case than Edward Teller.

William Liscum Borden had always been attracted to Washington and to government service. He had been born and raised in the capital, and, in the view of one intimate, was fascinated by the national power that is concentrated there. For four and a half years, as executive director of the Congressional Joint Committee on Atomic Energy, he had lived amid that power. But in mid-1953, with a Republican Administration newly in office, he had concluded there would not soon be any challenging government jobs open to a liberal Democrat like himself. And so he moved to Pittsburgh—in part, a friend has said, to open up the possibility of running for office—and began working on nuclear submarine reactors for the Westinghouse Corporation. But his new life lacked the rewards of his earlier work. To a friend he spoke of the "transitional difficulties" of "getting used to problems whose dimensions are something less than global in scope."

In November of 1960 the Democrats were voted back into power. John F. Kennedy instructed aides to recruit the ablest possible people for the New Frontier. It was natural that Borden's name should be thrown into the hopper. He had ample Washington experience and great knowledge of military and atomic matters, and he was a loyal Democrat. He also was well known to the man in charge of the Kennedy talent hunt, Sargent Shriver, a Yale contemporary with whom Borden had, as a youth, spent a summer abroad.

For a time Borden was considered for a responsible position in the Pentagon. But then it was recalled not only that it had been he who had triggered the Oppenheimer case with his charge that Oppenheimer was a Soviet agent but also that his accusation had been disbelieved by Oppenheimer's judges, who had examined all the evidence. Did a man who would make such an extreme charge possess the balance and judgment required of a senior government official? The question was debated by the Kennedy aides.

Whether or not the Oppenheimer involvement was the disqualifying factor, William Liscum Borden received no job offer from the Kennedy Administration. He remained in Pittsburgh. In the fall of 1966 he moved to New York as special assistant to the president of Westinghouse International. But New York is not Washington.

"Power appeals to Lic," one intimate has said, "and he is frustrated and disappointed that life has not quite dealt the cards so that he could reach the pinnacles he saw in Washington."

# XII    FALLOUT—3

The security case, of course, wrought significant changes in the life of its central character, Robert Oppenheimer. In one sense his life was far more tranquil than it had been before that tormenting year of 1954. No longer did he need to make frequent trips to Washington and to government laboratories. For the most part, he stayed in Princeton. His large, simple, sunlit office at the Institute was just a three-minute walk across the lawn from Olden Manor, home for the Oppenheimers, their two children and their two horses, Topper and Step-up.

Oppenheimer's name appeared in the news only sporadically now. But when it did, it was usually involved in controversy. In February, 1955, for example, President Henry Schmitz of the University of Washington in Seattle abruptly canceled an invitation for Oppenheimer to lecture there. Scientists and scholars boycotted the university in protest and President Schmitz was hanged in effigy by irate students. (A year later, Oppenheimer helped organize, and attended, a physics conference at the university.)

Early in 1955 the Fund for the Republic offered to make available to colleges and civic organizations a filmed interview with Oppenheimer by Edward R. Murrow.* When the Pleasant-ville, New York, school system sought to show the film, a leading member of the American Legion protested because the film did not mention that Oppenheimer might be a security risk.

On those infrequent occasions when Oppenheimer acceded to newsmen's requests for interviews, he barred any discussion of his security case. But there were two exceptions. One was an interview published in the Minneapolis *Tribune* on June 16, 1957 (exactly three years to the day after the AEC's release of the Gray Board transcript), under the headline, "CAN A SECURITY RISK SURVIVE?" The word "survive" was Oppenheimer's own. It arose in his discussion of the two alternatives that had seemed open to him after the AEC's verdict. One was to appeal the AEC decision ("I didn't think we'd buy ourselves anything by that"); the other was to establish "by other means that what was put out as a final judgment about me wasn't *the* final judgment. And the only way to do this was by surviving."

Robert Oppenheimer discussed the security case even more openly with the author and critic John Mason Brown, who apparently won the confidence of the Oppenheimers to an unusual degree. Brown wrote:

. . . the hearing abides in the Oppenheimer home as a per-manent resident. In Kitty's blood it continues to boil, an under-standable source of indignation. Oppenheimer has tried to put it behind him, explaining, in a phrase large in spirit and Biblical in phrasing, "I cannot sit with anger."

When Brown sought to tell Oppenheimer of the shame he felt, as an American, "because of the dry crucifixion to which he had been subjected," Oppenheimer smiled "the unhappiest of smiles, [and] said, 'You know, it wasn't so very dry. I can still feel the warm blood on my hands.'"

For nearly three years Robert Oppenheimer remained largely out of the news. Then, in the fall of 1957, came Russia's Sputnik I,

---

* The interview appeared initially on nationwide television, and, for the most part, the general public responded ecstatically to this rare public glimpse of Robert Oppenheimer at his mesmeric finest. Even a dozen years later, those who had seen the broadcast still found it vividly memorable.

and with it a sudden outcry for rapid mobilization of the nation's best scientists. Calls began to be heard for Oppenheimer's reinstatement or, at least, a rehearing of his case by the AEC. They came first from friends, soon from Congressmen, finally from a majority of the President's Science Advisory Committee.

Most striking of all was a statement by Oppenheimer's severest judge, former AEC Commissioner Thomas Murray. His 1954 vote against Oppenheimer, he explained, had been made "within the exigencies of the moment"; he was now recommending to the Joint Committee on Atomic Energy a change in the "security-through-secrecy" principle of the 1954 Atomic Energy Act.*

In early January, 1958, a newsman asked AEC Chairman Lewis Strauss whether he felt that the so-called "father of the atomic bomb" should be brought back as an adviser on the government's post-Sputnik scientific speed-up. Strauss reddened at the question. If "substantial new evidence" were brought in, he said, he was sure the AEC would consider it. But, he said, "this has not happened, and I know of no substantial new evidence." Strauss and his legal advisers made it clear that it was up to Oppenheimer to bring in the evidence and reopen the matter.

Two months later, Democratic Congressman Frank Thompson of New Jersey commented, at a hearing of the House Education Committee, that it was "tragic that because of political considerations the country has been deprived of the services of Dr. Oppenheimer." The witness before the committee agreed: the manner of Robert Oppenheimer's dismissal had "hurt the whole scientific community very badly." The witness said he was not in a position to comment on the security aspects of the Oppenheimer case, but he thought "the British would have knighted him."

The speaker was rocket scientist Wernher Von Braun, a principal designer of the Nazi V-2 rocket, whose services the U.S. Government had enlisted immediately after the war. Some found a touch of irony in the fact that Oppenheimer, who had served the United States unstintingly in World War II, was deemed unworthy of access to his nation's secrets, while the bemoaner of

---

* Murray later retreated somewhat, saying he had "no doubt that my verdict [in the Oppenheimer case] was justly rendered" and that his reasons for it "were valid."

that fact, who had devoted *his* total wartime energies to the service of the mortal enemy of the United States, nonetheless enjoyed the full trust of the American Government.

In June, 1958, Lewis Strauss resigned as Chairman of the Atomic Energy Commission, and was replaced by John A. Mc-Cone. Senator Clinton Anderson of New Mexico asked the new Chairman to review the Oppenheimer case. A study was made by AEC General Counsel Loren K. Olson, who found that there was "a messy record from a legal standpoint; that the charges kept shifting at each level of the proceedings; that the evidence was stale and consisted of information that was 12 years old and was known when a security clearance was granted during World War II, and that it was a punitive, personal abuse of the judicial system."

Later, when Olson became an AEC Commissioner, he tried to arrange the restoration of Oppenheimer's clearance, but nothing came of his behind-the-scenes efforts.

If Robert Oppenheimer was no longer an object of public acclaim in his own country, he certainly remained so in France. In the spring of 1958 he delivered a series of lectures at the University of Paris and was treated like a movie celebrity. He was followed in the streets by cars full of reporters and photographers, and his lectures were packed. "Not since the days of Henri Bergson, the famed French philosopher, have so many people crowded into the university's lecture halls," read one American press account.

Back in America, honor of a different sort came to the nuclear physicist: the Bristol, Pennsylvania, Township School Board decided that the new high school in Levittown should be named after him. Again the American Legion protested, and so did the Levittown Civic Association, because of the "stigma" attached to the name. There is today no Oppenheimer High School in Levittown, Pennsylvania.

By 1960, although Oppenheimer's own government would not yet permit him to serve it again, international agencies were beginning to enlist his talents. In July the International Atomic

Energy Agency named him U.S. representative to a multination conference on high-energy physics. The appointment was made by the agency's Director General, former U.S. Congressman W. Sterling Cole, who, as the chairman of the Joint Committee on Atomic Energy in 1954, had threatened an investigation if the AEC cleared Oppenheimer.

In 1961 the Organization of American States invited Oppenheimer to deliver a series of lectures throughout Latin America. This aroused the columnist and broadcaster Fulton Lewis, Jr., whose newsletter proclaimed, "OPPENHEIMER TOURS ON U.S. TAXPAYERS." "The U.S. taxpayer, who pays 60 percent of the OAS budget, is stuck with the major share of Oppenheimer's [travel] bill," Lewis complained.

When John F. Kennedy assumed the presidency, some close friends of Oppenheimer's moved into high policy posts and began to look for some means of restoring the physicist's reputation. But the inclination in politically-sensitive Administration circles was to wait until after the mid-term Congressional elections in the fall of 1962. And so the matter lay temporarily dormant.

In mid-April of 1962 the names of Robert Oppenheimer and Edward Teller were again associated in the news headlines. The occasion was a taped television interview with Teller by Professor Eric Goldman of Princeton. In the course of it Goldman asked if Teller would favor reinstating Oppenheimer's security clearance. The usually voluble Teller was unable to utter a word. He sat silent. Presently, Goldman moved on to another question. Later Teller pleaded with Goldman to have the question about Oppenheimer deleted from the TV tape before broadcast. Goldman obliged, but word got out, and the incident became page-one news.

Two weeks later the White House decided to put its toe into the political water. It announced a formal dinner honoring American Nobel prize winners, and among the names on the guest list was that of J. Robert Oppenheimer.

During the course of the evening AEC Chairman Glenn Seaborg reportedly approached Oppenheimer and asked if he would like to have another security hearing to restore his clearance. Oppenheimer is said to have replied, "Not on your life."

The scientist's attitude posed a problem for those friends who hoped to redress the injury to Oppenheimer's reputation, for it appeared he could not regain his clearance without a new hearing. The best alternative seemed to lie in the annual award given by the AEC in the name of Enrico Fermi. Six distinguished scientists had already received the award. Robert Oppenheimer, the "father of the A-bomb," seemed a natural candidate.

Early in 1963, following its customary practice, the AEC canvassed a broad group of scientists for nominations for the award. Among them was the 1962 award winner, Edward Teller. To him, this appeared an opportunity, at long last, to carry out the wish that Fermi had expressed to him years earlier to heal the deep wound in the scientific community caused by his public feud with Oppenheimer. Teller wrote Oppenheimer's name on his ballot and mailed it in. The nomination was unanimously approved by the AEC's General Advisory Committee and then by the AEC. On April 5, 1963, the White House announced that the 1963 Fermi award would go to J. Robert Oppenheimer.*

It was evident that Oppenheimer was delighted by the honor, although the statement he issued was restrained. "Most of us," he said, "look to the good opinion of our colleagues and to the good will and the confidence of our government. I am no exception."

One question remained unresolved: who would present the award to Oppenheimer? John F. Kennedy himself had bestowed the honor on the previous two recipients, Hans Bethe and Edward Teller. Would he do the same for the hotly controversial Oppenheimer? The answer appeared in the morning newspapers of Friday, November 22, 1963: the President would confer the award on Robert Oppenheimer in a White House ceremony on

* While there was no immediate reaction from Republicans on Capitol Hill, by July the grumbling had begun: California Congressman Craig Hosmer saw in the Fermi award "disturbing indications" that the government might be considering slipping Oppenheimer into a post not requiring Congressional approval. He called on President Kennedy to make it clear that the award "does not condone the recipient's actions which lost him his security clearance." And Iowa's Senator Bourke Hickenlooper said he was going to introduce legislation providing Congressional control over future Fermi awards.

the afternoon of December 2. Less than twelve hours after that news appeared, Kennedy was dead in Dallas.

It had been on December 2, 1942, that Enrico Fermi achieved the world's first nuclear chain reaction. Exactly twenty-one years later, leaders of science and government assembled in the Cabinet Room of the White House for the presentation of an award in Fermi's name. On hand were many who had played important roles in the life of Robert Oppenheimer. There were, of course, Kitty Oppenheimer and the two children, Peter and Katherine, now twenty-two and nineteen. There was their close friend, Martha Parsons, widow of Admiral "Deak" Parsons. There was AEC Chairman Glenn Seaborg, whose 1949 letter to Oppenheimer on the H-bomb had become a factor in the Oppenheimer case. There was Henry DeWolf Smyth, Oppenheimer's lone defender among the five AEC Commissioners who had judged him in 1954. And, in from California especially for the occasion, there was Edward Teller.*

Lyndon Johnson entered the room. After John Kennedy's assassination, some had thought that the AEC should present the award, so as to spare the new Chief Executive any political embarrassment. But Johnson had insisted that the President of the United States confer the prize in the White House, as originally planned.

"One of President Kennedy's most important acts," he said to Oppenheimer, "was to sign [this] award." Then, "on behalf of . . . the people of the United States," he presented to Oppenheimer the citation, a gold medal and, "perhaps least important to you, a $50,000 check from the Treasury of the United States."

Oppenheimer quickly handed the check to Kitty, standing behind him. For a few moments, he stood, silent and reflective, looking down at the citation and the medal. And then, turning to

* Some invitees were not present. The *New York Times* noted that the Republican members of the Joint Atomic Energy Committee were "noticeably absent." Their ranking member, Iowa's Senator Bourke Hickenlooper, had declared that he could not, "in good conscience," attend. "Over the years," Hickenlooper had said, "I have been unable to find convincing evidence of any outstanding contribution to atomic science such as could be attributed to other recipients of the Fermi award that could be credited to Dr. Oppenheimer."

Johnson, he said, "I think it is just possible, Mr. President, that it has taken some charity and some courage for you to make this award today. That would seem to me a good augury for all our futures." The scientist paused and continued: "These words I wrote down almost a fortnight ago. In a somber time, I gratefully and gladly speak them to you."

Afterward there was a reception at which photographers recorded a smiling handclasp of "reconciliation" between Oppenheimer and Teller, with Kitty Oppenheimer, evidently unenchanted, looking on. But the ceremony was over. Robert Oppenheimer had been officially honored in the White House by the President of the United States.

Ten years, minus one day, earlier there had been another gathering in the White House concerning Robert Oppenheimer, the meeting at which another President had decided that a "blank wall" should be placed between Oppenheimer and his nation's secrets.

The day after Robert Oppenheimer received the Fermi award a *New York Times* editorial observed that the White House ceremony had "served to write finis to the controversy surrounding Dr. Oppenheimer." But had it? For, as Robert Oppenheimer emerged from the White House, with his gold medal and his citation and his check, the "blank wall" still stood. Officially he was still deemed unworthy of being entrusted with his country's secrets.

Insofar as the public record shows, the last years of Oppenheimer's life were bittersweet, a mixture of honors, controversy, the opening of old wounds and, finally, illness and pain.

In the spring of 1964 there were two sentimental homecomings, one at Los Alamos, his first public appearance there since the war, the other at Berkeley before an audience of 12,500. In both cases, prolonged, standing ovations; in both cases, a Robert Oppenheimer deeply affected by the outpouring of respect. A former student who heard the Berkeley speech recalls the sight of a tiny figure at the podium of the huge auditorium, "looking so fragile," totally overcome by the response of the enormous audience.

In the fall a play taken largely from the transcript of the Gray

Board hearing and using the real names of Oppenheimer and the other dramatis personae of that hearing, was produced in Germany, first on television, and then, to great acclaim and success, on the stage in Berlin and Munich.* In Princeton, Oppenheimer commented, "The whole damn thing [the Gray Board proceeding] was a farce, and these people are trying to make a tragedy out of it."

The following year a new book about the security case was published. Its author was Haakon Chevalier, and its title was *Oppenheimer: The Story of a Friendship*. For Chevalier, it was the story not only of friendship but of frustration and heartbreak, for he had concluded, from long study of the Gray Board hearing, that Oppenheimer had betrayed him in the most dishonorable fashion, especially in revealing Chevalier's name to General Groves while apparently concealing his own participation in the "kitchen conversation."

This was the second book Chevalier had written on the subject. The first, published in 1959, was a fictionalized version of the same material, under the title, *The Man Who Would Be God*. But it had attracted virtually no attention. The same could not be said for the nonfiction account: it was widely reviewed, and although it was generally passed off as the embittered complaint of a rejected friend, it stirred many of the old controversies and questions.

In 1966 Oppenheimer was stricken with throat cancer. In the spring he resigned as director of the Institute and underwent surgery. By June, although he depended on a cane and a leg brace for support, he was able to attend the Princeton graduation exercises and received an honorary degree. The citation termed him "physicist and sailor, philosopher and horseman, linguist and cook, lover of fine wines and better poetry. . . ."

In an interview with a magazine reporter, he reminisced and ruminated on various subjects: *On the immediate postwar years:* "One could influence policy better from the inside for a while—with men like George Marshall in power." *About the future:* "I'm not very sanguine about the future, but at least the ideas I ex-

* The play, by Heinar Kipphardt, was later translated into English and produced in London and New York.

pressed are no longer radical." *About his own plans:* he hoped to write a history of physics in the twentieth century, but no personal memoir. "I would work with gusto on the former, but I have a complete lack of interest in the latter." *About himself:* a wry anecdote, about a general who was reviewing his troops after a bitter battle, and stopped to ask one soldier what he had done in the engagement. "The soldier," said Oppenheimer, laughing, "replied 'I survived.'"

# XIII  WHAT IS SECURITY?

> We could in good conscience [say that] there can be
> no tampering with the national *security*, which in times
> of peril must be absolute. . . . Any doubts whatsoever
> must be resolved in favor of the national *security*.
> [Emphasis added.]
> —The Gray Board Majority Opinion

> Concern for the defense and *security* of the United
> States requires that Dr. Oppenheimer's clearance
> should not be reinstated. [Emphasis added.]
> —The AEC Majority Opinion

Since it was in the name of security that Robert Oppenheimer's
access to secrets was stripped from him, since it was in the name
of security that he was to die still marked as unworthy of his government's trust, it is appropriate to ask: What is "security"? Is it
the absolute, palpable, definable commodity that Oppenheimer's
judges seemed to consider it? What *is* security?

The following two narratives may help to answer that question.

1

On November 15, 1944, Allied troops moved into Strasbourg, France, home of one of Europe's great universities. Among the first to enter the city was Colonel Boris T. Pash, military head of the Alsos mission, a team of soldiers and scientists charged with determining, from captured German scientists and scientific papers, the status of German war research. Soon Pash's men found papers at the Strasbourg Institute of Physics that described the efforts of German nuclear physicists to produce an atomic bomb. For two days and nights, aided only by candlelight, two Allied scientists studied the papers until their eyes hurt. But in the end the answer was clear: Germany had no atomic bomb. Nor were her scientists even close to developing one. The evidence indicated they were at least two years behind the American atomic program.

In the succeeding months, the scientific leader of the Alsos mission, Samuel Goudsmit, continued his hunt for added clues to the German war research effort. Now he had a new question in mind: *why* had the German nuclear effort failed so miserably?

He began to find some answers.* Right in Strasbourg, he found that the university faculty had been chosen less for their academic prowess than for their loyalty to the Nazi Party. Several faculty members belonged to Himmler's SS, the Elite Guard. At Munich, once "the world's most productive university in theoretical physics," the great professor who had made it such had, upon his retirement, been replaced by a Nazi named Müller, who according to Goudsmit "did not 'believe' in modern physics (probably because he could not grasp its intricacies)." In Heidelberg, Goudsmit found that the foremost physicist was an old man named Lenard, one of the earliest and most rabid Nazis, whose work in physics, once distinguished, had deteriorated as his in-

---

* Which he later reported in his book, *Alsos*, from which many of the quotations below are taken.

terest in politics increased. Goudsmit discovered that Lenard had been responsible for the removal of a Professor Bothe, who, while an outstanding physicist, was a lukewarm Nazi. In Bothe's place, Lenard had appointed a physicist named Wesch, the top Nazi in Heidelberg, whom Goudsmit found to be a "first-rate windbag and second-rate physicist."

Goudsmit soon learned that the favoring of "politically acceptable" scientists was far from accidental. It could be traced in significant part to a Professor Osenberg, whom Hermann Goering had placed in charge of the Planning Office of the Reich's Research Council. Goudsmit found Osenberg to be a man "inspired by a mania for organization and a passion for card indexes." As the boss of the Planning Office—and, more importantly, as a high member of the Gestapo—Osenberg had a great deal of say about the assignment of scientific personnel to various projects. In determining such assignments, Osenberg relied on his extensive personnel files. These he had developed in his capacity as head of that section of the Gestapo charged with enforcing Nazi doctrine at educational and cultural institutions. Osenberg maintained the appropriate orthodoxy at these institutions by means of informers. These spies attended all important scientific conferences and were scattered throughout German laboratories, sometimes in the person of a professor, sometimes a scrubwoman. Attitudes toward Nazi doctrine interested them as much as the quality of the work at the installations. Those judged to be less than enthusiastic in their support of Hitler suffered. Goudsmit discovered, for example, that one famous medical scientist had been downgraded for his political unreliability. Another able young physicist was "accused of having democratic ideals, probably influenced by his Swiss wife."

Goudsmit also pointed out that with the persecution and exiling of all scholars "afflicted with the Jewish 'taint' . . . Germany lost some of the greatest scientists in the world." While other countries might have mitigated such a loss by training the brightest students, Goudsmit learned that the most promising German youth had not gone into such frowned-upon, "non-Aryan" fields as physics.

Many of the answers Goudsmit found, then, had a common denominator: the imposition of politics—or, more precisely, of political dogma—upon science and scientists. For this, the Germans paid a high price. For when Samuel Goudsmit stumbled upon their secret papers in Strasbourg in November, 1944, not only were the Germans "nowhere near" discovering the secret of the atom bomb, "at the rate they were going, and the direction they were taking, it is anybody's guess if they would have arrived at it at all in any practicable period of time."

2

July 20, 1943, Washington, D.C., 4:30 P.M. Jean O'Leary walked into the Pentagon office of her boss and found his hulking body collapsed across his desk. She tried to rouse him. There was no response. General Leslie Richard Groves was dead, the victim of a massive heart attack. His fountain pen still lay in his hand. On the desk, with the first letters of Groves' signature on it, lay an order directing that "clearance be issued for the employment of Julius Robert Oppenheimer without delay, irrespective of the information which you have concerning Mr. Oppenheimer."

The next day, the Army named General Joseph R. Burch to replace General Groves. Like Groves, Burch was a West Pointer and a career Army man. As with Groves, there was no doubt in Burch's mind that the real enemy of the United States was Russia. But his conviction in this regard was even more passionate than Groves'. Burch had come up through the ranks of Army Intelligence and had become an expert in counterintelligence and counterespionage. He had a particular enthusiasm for card-index systems, with which he could detect suspect views or associations. Indeed, it was his passion for security that commended Burch to his superiors, who had in mind President Roosevelt's recent letter on the need for secrecy on the atomic project.*

One of the first matters that occupied General Burch's attention was Groves' unsigned clearance order for Oppenheimer. The general was immediately struck by the words, "irrespective of the

* See p. 45.

information which you have concerning Mr. Oppenheimer."
What information? He ordered the file brought to him.

What he read appalled him. There, before him, was a memorandum to Groves from the security officer in the field recommending that the scientist be "removed completely from the
project and dismissed from employment by the United States
Government." The memorandum noted intelligence reports that
a Soviet cell was being organized in Berkeley. Its key organizer
allegedly had asked Oppenheimer for information. The report
also stated that the scientist had, in the previous month, spent the
night with a woman who was known to be a former Communist.

General Burch now called for and carefully reviewed the full
investigative file on Robert Oppenheimer. Although he had never
met the physicist, the evidence against him seemed overpowering. The General began composing a memorandum to the commanding officer of the Los Alamos laboratory. "Subject: Julius
Robert Oppenheimer."

> The record contains substantial evidence of Dr. Oppen-
> heimer's associations with Communists, Communist function-
> aries, and Communists who have engaged in espionage. He is
> not a mere "parlor pink." His relations with these hardened
> Communists are such that they consider him to be one of their
> number. The record indicates that Dr. Oppenheimer is a Com-
> munist in every respect except for the fact that he does not
> and did not carry a party card.
>
> These facts raise serious questions as to Dr. Oppenheimer's
> eligibility for clearance.
>
> I hereby order and direct, effective immediately, that he be
> dismissed from his post as director of Los Alamos laboratory,
> and from all government employment.
>
> I further order and direct that there be sent to this office im-
> mediately, for my personal review, the security files of all those
> whom Dr. Oppenheimer has recruited for the Los Alamos lab-
> oratory, as well as those on behalf of whose security clearance
> he has intervened.

General Burch's orders were carried out with dispatch. To the
consternation of the scientists at the laboratory, most of whom
had been lured away from other pressing war work only because

of Oppenheimer's mesmeric blandishments, their leader was suddenly spirited out of Los Alamos in an Army car, in the company of the chief security officer. He was not seen again at Los Alamos. He spent the balance of the war teaching at Berkeley. Because General Burch barred him from any type of government position, he was not allowed to participate in the work of the Radiation Laboratory.

But the purge of scientists from the Manhattan Project did not end there. The files of the Oppenheimer associates and recruitees were sent to Washington, where they received the personal attention of General Burch. First, there was the file of a young Hungarian scientist named Edward Teller, whom Oppenheimer had asked to be given security clearance, even though Teller had relatives living in Hungary. Clearly, this made Teller a ready victim for blackmail, and Burch immediately ordered him off the project.

Then came Robert Serber, who had been, in prewar Berkeley days, an intimate of Oppenheimer's and as heavily involved as Oppenheimer in left-wing circles. Although Serber was a valuable group leader in the Theoretical Division at Los Alamos, he was dispatched from the vital weapons laboratory and excluded from all Manhattan Project work.

Assuming full authority to hire, fire and transfer scientists as he might see fit, General Burch reached into other atomic facilities under his command. From the Chicago Metallurgical Laboratory, the brilliant Philip Morrison, formerly a radical and an associate of Oppenheimer's, was quickly dismissed—and was thus prevented from contributing to the war effort an ingenious new reactor he later invented on his own. From the laboratory at Oak Ridge, Tennessee, Robert Oppenheimer's brother, Frank, was expelled—and thus was barred from continuing the essential work in electromagnetic isotope separation in which he was engaged.

Throughout the atomic project, morale plummeted. Nor could it be restored by the man who replaced Robert Oppenheimer at the Los Alamos laboratory, Dr. Horace Williams. The former head of the physics department at the Arizona School of Mining and Metallurgy, Williams was one of the few scientists whose security record seemed to General Burch to be wholly free of "derogatory information." Williams also commended himself to

Burch in that he shared the General's deep suspicions of "leftist" philosophies and appeared to take the degree of interest in security regulations that Burch deemed essential.

With Williams' active cooperation, Burch sprinkled all the atomic laboratories with informants, some of whom posed as janitors or stenographers, some as scientists. Williams also forbade interchanges among personnel working in different nuclear facilities. Even within the Los Alamos laboratory the free exchange of information on which Oppenheimer had insisted was ended. Scientists in the various divisions were issued different-colored badges, and even dinner table conversation between a White Badge and a Red Badge was discouraged.

A year later, General Burch's sharp-eyed security officers detected the presence, at Los Alamos, of two suspicious individuals. One was a bespectacled young sergeant named David Greenglass. The other was a quiet, self-contained German-born physicist who had come to Los Alamos with a British contingent. His name was Klaus Fuchs. Burch's clever surveillance of the two revealed that both were part of an apparatus to convey secret information to the Soviets. Both were arrested and imprisoned.

It is somewhat doubtful, however, that either Greenglass or Fuchs could have given a great deal of help to the Soviets, for there was little information to convey. In the months after the dismissal of Oppenheimer, the purge of the other scientists and the inauguration of General Burch's new secrecy regulations, very little progress had been made, either at Los Alamos or elsewhere in the Manhattan Project. As it finally developed, the atomic bomb was not ready for use in World War II. In fact, America was not able to detonate its first atomic device until March, 1950—six months after the first Russian device was exploded.

The first of these "narratives" is true in every detail. The second, of course, is fictional.* But not entirely. *The first two para-*

* As shown by the many postwar events involving General Groves that are recounted in this book, the untimely "demise" of the General described above is most definitely fictional (General Groves is still alive at this writing, in 1969). General Joseph Burch, Dr. Horace Williams and the Arizona School of Mining and Metallurgy are likewise intended to be entirely fictional.

*graphs of General Burch's memorandum to Los Alamos ordering Robert Oppenheimer's dismissal are taken, word for word, from the 1954 adverse opinion in the Oppenheimer case rendered by Kenneth D. Nichols.\** Nichols was Groves' number two man in the Manhattan Project at the time General Groves ordered Oppenheimer cleared. Thus Nichols might well have stepped into Groves' shoes had the General died in 1943. And so . . .

*What if* the decision on the 1943 clearance of Robert Oppenheimer had been made by a General Burch instead of by Leslie Groves?

*What if* Robert Oppenheimer's request for the clearance of Edward Teller had been rescinded—and Teller had been barred from any later work on the hydrogen bomb?

*What if* the brilliant but radical scientists whom Robert Oppenheimer recruited into the atomic project had been dismissed because their political views made them too risky?

Of course, all these actions would have been taken in the name of security. But would the security of the United States of America *really* have been enhanced?

What *is* "security"?

> The anti-Semitism doctrine of the Nazis was disastrous to German physics [in part] because it brought about the exile of certain notable scientists.
> —SAMUEL GOUDSMIT, in *Alsos*

> Nuclear physics is new in our country. Most of our authorities in this field came from overseas. . . . Dr. Oppenheimer got most of his education abroad.
> —WARD EVANS, dissent in the Oppenheimer case

> We are only secure if we have the best brains and the best reach of mind in this [nuclear] field.
> —JOHN J. McCLOY, before the Gray Board

Two of the "best brains . . . in this field" are those of David

---

\* The facts about the personal contributions to the wartime A-bomb program by Philip Morrison and Frank Oppenheimer are also true.

Bohm and Bernard Peters. Both are now engaged in significant scientific explorations. Both are entirely capable of unlocking a secret of nature that could have great importance to a nation's security. Both are permanent political exiles from America. Has the security of the United States been enlarged by their loss?

> The art [of atomic physics] is still in its infancy, and we still are in need of great imagination in this field.
> —JOHN J. McCLOY, before the Gray Board

It is generally believed that a theoretical physicist is likely to enjoy his most inventive years before the age of thirty. Einstein's greatest discoveries, for example, came before he was twenty-six.

Giovanni Rossi Lomanitz, a young man from Oklahoma who showed enough brilliance in theoretical physics at age twenty-one to take over the war work of far more senior scientists, did not spend those usually creative years in the laboratory or even in the classroom, imparting his knowledge to potential Fermis or Oppenheimers. Instead, he devoted those years to repairing railroad tracks and loading burlap bags and trimming trees and bottling hair oil. Was the security of the United States enhanced?

In the early 1950's an eminent British scientist was invited to visit certain American universities—and with good reason: in his field, the State Department was told, he was "conservatively estimated to be fully two years ahead of his American colleagues." The work he was to observe was wholly nonsecret. Yet he was denied permission to come unless he submitted to American security-clearance procedures. Because time was too short for this, the visit was canceled. American researchers, the State Department was advised, were thereby deprived "of the opportunity of making a two-year forward step in their work."

In a single year, the following occurred:

• The *New York Times* reported that from "20,000 to 50,000 technicians, engineers, scientists and other key industrial employes" were either not working or were marking time, doing nonsecret work, "pending their specific approval for handling [secret] processes or materials."

• Many academicians willing to work at atomic facilities during their summer vacation were prevented from doing so because their security clearance was not granted until the summer was almost at an end.

• The Joint Committee on Atomic Energy reported that nearly 900 persons had withdrawn their applications for clearance because, before it was granted, they had decided to work elsewhere.

These clearances and the investigations attendant upon them were required in the name of security.

> By putting politics first and science second, the Nazis contributed greatly to the deterioration of German scientific teaching and research.
>
> —SAMUEL GOUDSMIT, in *Alsos*

In the early 1950's a roster of experts was canvassed for an important survey of military medical research facilities. The name of one especially qualified doctor came up. It had been reported that he had supported Henry Wallace in the 1948 presidential election. His name was stricken. A second, less qualified man was chosen.*

About that same time a senior scientist in the Federal Government, who himself had recently been the subject of a security-clearance hearing, was obliged to fill a vacancy on his staff. Of two applicants, one was more experienced and more highly reputed. But he had freely voiced opinions which could only be regarded as controversial. The scientist passed him over in favor of the second, less experienced applicant.

> . . . by the infusion of dogma into the body of scientific thought the Nazis tended to bring the whole sub-

---

* The "rather sour cream of this jest," as one observer put it, was that this man was not a Wallace supporter at all, but a staunch backer of the Democratic candidate, Harry S Truman.

ject of modern physics into disrepute, with the result
that the "Jewish science" of physics became unpopular
at the universities. . . . [There was a] prohibition
[against] teaching Einstein's work in Germany.
                                    —SAMUEL GOUDSMIT, in *Alsos*

The effect of a loyalty or security program on the free pursuit
of scientific inquiry is by no means limited to the direct screening
of persons for security clearances. To illustrate: In 1947, at the
time the United States instituted its first government loyalty-
screening program, one of the widely read medical journals in
and around Washington was the *American Review of Soviet
Medicine,* which contained translations of Russian articles on
such matters of universal interest as cancer and tuberculosis. At
that time the readers of this journal included some six hundred
members of the American-Soviet Medical Society (which published it), and there were about 150 subscriptions in Bethesda,
Maryland, locus of the U.S. government's National Institutes of
Health.

By October, 1948, when the journal suspended publication,
not a single subscription in the Bethesda area remained (although
the magazine received numerous requests to receive the journal
in a plain wrapper).

Professor Walter Gellhorn, writing of this occurrence, has commented that "in order to avoid doubt about their loyalty, Federal
medical scientists appear to have felt that they must remain ignorant of Soviet researches that might very possibly have fur-
thered their own work in American laboratories."

Robert Oppenheimer was charged, tried and found wanting in
the name of security. Yet the process by which his loyalty was
tested could not help but involve the very "interference of politicians in the affairs of science" of which Samuel Goudsmit says the
Germans were guilty, and for which, he says, they paid so high a
price.

Could a similar political intrusion into "the affairs of science"
occur in the United States to anything like the degree described
by Samuel Goudsmit in Nazi Germany? Unthinkable.

Or is it? This chapter has presented a fictional narrative describing the 1943 barring of Robert Oppenheimer from government service. In 1943 such an eventuality would have seemed unthinkable. But just eleven years later it came true.

# XIV  SECURITY ON TRIAL

> We are acutely aware that in a very real sense
> this case puts the security system of the
> United States on trial. . . .
> —The Gray Board opinion in the Oppenheimer case

As the Gray Board said, the United States *v.* J. Robert Oppenheimer is more than an isolated security case. It is, in part, the story of a decade in which America was caught up in fear—seemingly a fear of the outside world but actually a fear about itself. An account of the Oppenheimer case is not complete without a look at that era of fear, at the current state of the loyalty program it produced, and at the effects of that program on American society.

In the years immediately following World War II, the government of the United States asserted a power it had never before claimed or exercised on a government-wide basis in peacetime: the power to investigate the private lives and the political beliefs and affiliations of its citizens and, from its findings, to appraise their "loyalty." There had been attempts, during prior crises in American history, to limit freedom of expression, but, notes the distinguished attorney, John Lord O'Brian, this was the first instance since the Alien and Sedition Acts of 1798 of "any attempt . . . to establish [a] peacetime governmental policy aimed at the control of *ideas* thought to be subversive." (Emphasis added.)

The public justification given for the 1947 loyalty program centered around the fear that disloyal Federal employees would compromise secret information. In 1953, with the promulgation of the Eisenhower security program, the protection of secrets became the paramount consideration in the investigation and screening of Federal employees. As recently as 1967 the U.S. Justice Department official in charge of internal security declared that the protection of secrets remained virtually the exclusive purpose of the personnel-security-screening system. Ostensibly it was the central factor in the Oppenheimer case. Both Oppenheimer's harshest critic, Lewis Strauss, and his lone AEC defender, Henry DeWolf Smyth, described the case that way.*

Yet surprisingly little of the testimony taken at the hearing bore directly on Oppenheimer's secret-keeping ability (enough, however, to lead the board to conclude he had "an unusual ability to keep . . . vital secrets"). By contrast, a substantial part of the testimony dealt with Oppenheimer's *opinions*—on such matters as continental defense, the Vista report and the second lab. Those opinions could be considered relevant to Oppenheimer's discretion with secrets only if one entertained a scandalous possibility—that his beliefs sprang from an allegiance to a foreign power, an allegiance that might impel him to betray his country. But the Gray Board verdict ruled out that possibility with its unanimous affirmation of Oppenheimer's loyalty.

There is also this disturbing illogicality: if Oppenheimer did not divulge nuclear secrets when the Russians had *no* bomb (and there was no evidence that he did), why should he do so in 1954, when Russia, like the United States, possessed a *hydrogen* bomb? Moreover, Oppenheimer's judges might revoke his clearance, but many secrets remained in his brain. No hearing board could ex-

---

* Smyth observed that the "sole purpose" of the security system, "apart from the prevention of sabotage, is to protect secrets," and Strauss later observed that the revocation of Oppenheimer's clearance had been "a measure taken to safeguard [secret] information . . . and for no other purpose."

482 THE OPPENHEIMER CASE

tract them and lock them in a vault. That being the case, did
the government indeed bring the security case against Oppenheimer primarily out of a fear that he would give away secrets?

The case prompts this and other questions. For example, would
Oppenheimer have been charged as a security risk if he had not
held controversial opinions; if he had not advocated them with
extraordinary persuasiveness; if he had not aroused (and, on
occasion, sorely offended) persons in high office? But for his
views would anyone have thought it necessary to bring him to
his knees?

The Oppenheimer case was by no means exceptional. Many
others were charged as security risks for reasons having little or
no connection with the protection of secrets. Soon rather bizarre
factors were considered relevant to a person's eligibility for government employment. Here are examples of charges filed against
Federal employees in security cases in the Fifties:

• Belonging to a "radical group" that had been "extremely
critical of the American Legion and of other laws and institutions."

• Seconding a motion at a community meeting that "the Bible
should be burned and start building from there."

• Having "close and continued association with your parents"
—who had belonged to some "radical" organizations.

• Being an editor of a newspaper that "has carried several
editorials and articles expressing radical viewpoints."

• Having purchased books from a certain bookstore that was
not even alleged to be subversive but was cited merely as the
"possible" successor to the Washington Book Shop (cited at one
time as a Communist organization by the Attorney General).

And it wasn't long before representatives of the Federal Government, in loyalty-security inquiries, began asking questions
such as these:

• What do you think of female chastity?
• Is it proper to mix white and Negro blood plasma?
• There is a suspicion in the record that you are in sympathy
with the underprivileged. Is that true?

• In your newspaper reading, what headlines attract your attention? Do you follow the United Nations' activities?

• How many times did you vote for Norman Thomas? How about Henry Wallace?

• What were your feelings at that time concerning race equality?

• Have you ever made statements about the "downtrodden masses" and "underprivileged people"?

In 1952 the Navy Department advised its employees to "seek wise and mature counsel prior to association with persons or organizations of any political or civic nature, no matter what their apparent motives may be, in order to determine the true motives and purposes of the organization."*

Although supposedly concerned in considerable measure with the protection of secrets, the loyalty-security programs encompassed all Federal employees, even those who had not the remotest connection with such secrets. For example, in 1954 a Federal meat inspector was suspended and subjected to a full-dress security hearing, although he had no access whatever to secret material. During the course of the hearing, government representatives raised the possibility that an ill-motivated meat inspector might "walk in there with a needle full of some kind of liquid and stick it into a carcass and it would be contaminated. . . ."

During the 1950's the loyalty-security-screening process quickly spread beyond the Federal realm. States and cities discovered that they, too, had secrets to be protected, or, at any rate, decided that it was important for them to be sure of the loyalty of their employees. The State of New York, for example, classified as "sensitive" the jobs of scientists in the Paleontology Section of the Department of Education, on the ground that they had

* Such advice was not dissimilar to the counsel a lawyer reluctantly gave in the early 1950's to a $3,000-a-year government librarian. She had just been through a security trial and wanted to avoid another. "Drop your Negro friends," said the lawyer, "and express no views whatever on any [government] programs which are not generally accepted as conservative." That such advice should have come from Thurman Arnold, who was regarded as an outspoken liberal, is a significant commentary on the times in which he spoke.

knowledge about the location of certain caves suitable for defense storage purposes. The City of New York suspended a washroom attendant who had been a Communist Party member in the 1930's.* And the Department of Sanitation in New York City was designated a "security agency" on the theory that disease might spread in the event the department failed to do its job.

Loyalty tests were by no means confined to those on public payrolls. The State of Indiana insisted on satisfying itself concerning the loyalty of wrestlers to whom it was issuing licenses; Texas was similarly concerned about pharmacists and the District of Columbia about those receiving licenses as piano dealers.

The measuring of loyalty soon became a nongovernmental activity as well. Private individuals, publications and investigative services† set themselves up as the arbiters over who was loyal enough to merit employment in, for example, the movie or television industry.‡ If loyalty tests were originally intended as a means of safeguarding state secrets, they now were also used to protect the country from the wiles of persons like Dorothy Parker and Ring Lardner, Jr.

The owner of a commercial radio station is neither entrusted with nor disseminates state secrets. Yet in 1954 the Federal Communications Commission sought to deny renewal of a radio license to a man it said had been a member of the Communist Party.¶ The connection between orchestra musicians and state secrets is also remote. Yet in 1956 the U.S. Information Agency canceled a foreign tour by the NBC Symphony Orchestra because of rumors that a few of its members had exhibited Communist sympathies on an earlier Asian trip.

It had begun as a program to protect secrets. But within a

* He was ultimately restored to his job by order of a State Supreme Court justice who had difficulty "visualiz[ing] how a washroom attendant in his official capacity could give aid to his country's enemies."

† The credit rating firm of Dun & Bradstreet established its own Personnel Security Service.

‡ Viz., the testimony of Warner Brothers' Jack Warner regarding his firing of six screen writers: "When I say these people are Communists, . . . it is from hearsay. It was from printed forms I read in the Hollywood Reporter."

¶ An accusation made with the aid of witnesses who later recanted their testimony and accused FCC representatives of inducing them to perjure themselves.

decade one job in every five in America—an estimated 13,500,000 jobs in all—was affected by the blight of loyalty tests.

It would be comforting to dismiss the above as aberrations of a less enlightened time, now passed. But the problem cannot be thus dismissed. The use of the loyalty-security program—and other government powers as well—to penalize unorthodox opinions is not a thing of the past. It is a thing of today.

As of mid-1969, for example, the Small Business Administration persisted in a policy of refusing business loans to members of "subversive" organizations or to persons who had pleaded the Fifth Amendment in declining to testify about "subversive" activities. In such cases the applicant would merely be advised that the loan had been turned down "in the best interests of the United States," and hence he would have no bill of particulars to rebut. Yet nothing in the legislation creating the Small Business Administration authorized it to consider such factors as grounds for disqualification for a business loan.

In June, 1969, *Science* magazine reported that the U.S. Department of Health, Education and Welfare was barring scientists from serving as HEW consultants for security reasons, even though the positions involved no secrets. Some of the scientists who learned that HEW did not trust them were at the same time serving on high-level Defense Department panels; one even had a top-secret "Q" clearance for atomic information. *Science* mentioned a list of thirty-seven scientists whom HEW considered "currently ineligible" to be consultants. In no case have these scientists been presented with any charges or even told the reasons why they weren't cleared.* One of the "unclearable" scientists, Brewster Smith, chairman of the psychology department at the University of Chicago, told *Science* he believes it is because of his membership in a leftist student organization while a sophomore and junior in college. *Science* reported that another, MIT psychology professor Stephan Chorover, suspects it is be-

* According to Dr. James A. Shannon, former director of the National Institutes of Health, which is part of HEW, it is even difficult for agency officials to get a full account of why scientists are rejected. *Science* comments that "if the agency heads do not know what information the security office possesses about a man, they are reluctant to totally commit themselves to try to overturn his rejection."

cause of such activities of his as getting professors in the Boston area to sign anti-Vietnam war statements. (HEW security officials deny that antiwar activity has been used as a disqualifying reason.)

Former HEW executives cite other cases. Dr. Robert H. Felix, director of the National Institute of Mental Health until 1964, told *Science* of "a good scientist, as loyal as George Washington," who was barred from an NIMH panel because he had been arrested after demonstrating to integrate a swimming pool. And Dr. Philip R. Lee, an HEW Assistant Secretary until 1968, told of a scientist who was excluded from an HEW panel because his father-in-law had subscribed to a Jewish Communist newspaper in the time before his daughter was married to the scientist.

The general belief that scientists are barred for political reasons has intimidating effects. One member of an NIMH consultant panel told *Science*, "Knowing what happened to Steve Chorover, I wondered whether I should endanger my career by marching in a Vietnam protest a couple of weeks ago."

In November, 1968, before a U.S. Appeals Court, the government sought to defend the "disenrollment" of a young man named George T. Newell from a college naval-officer training program. The Navy said it had taken this action because of Newell's "admitted activities, associates and expressed opinions," including the following:

(1) He became President of one of the student organizations in which he was active; its interest was then extended to "Race Relations, Poverty, World Peace, and University Reform";

(2) . . . he became interested in "an organization known as Students for a Democratic Society (SDS)." He shared "some of their views concerning the war in Viet Nam," being against our involvement in that armed conflict.

Newell's loyalty was evidently a factor, for while barring him as an officer, the Chief of Naval Personnel insisted that Newell serve out his Navy term as an enlisted man so that he might "with proper counseling and additional experience" be able "by his behavior . . . to put any question as to his loyalty beyond any reasonable doubt."

In 1967 the security clearance of a Navy petty officer was suspended because of "his quick espousing of radical position in any discussion of politics, social norms and world affairs" and because he "deliberately baited those whose views support U.S. government policies." He would enjoy a "better reputation for reliability," said the Navy, were he to assert more vigorously, in his discussions with "his peers," his "loyalty to and support of duly established authority and to the policies of the government."

For the first five months of 1967, the security clearance of a soldier stationed in Japan was suspended for the following reasons:

1. He favored the right of U.S. citizens to travel to Cuba.
2. He was an atheist.
3. He was marrying meerly [*sic*] to obtain additional monetary allowance.

Those reasons had to be extracted from the Army by a Senate committee to which the soldier appealed, since the Army declined to explain to him the basis on which his security clearance was lifted.

Even more ominous, governmental power is increasingly invoked outside of the loyalty-security program to penalize officially unpopular opinions. Critics of the Vietnam war and of the draft are the prime targets for these Federal actions.

In mid-1969, the Navy brought charges of sedition (punishable by death) against a sailor, Roger Priest, for his off-duty writing and publication of an antiwar newspaper highly critical of, among other things, the Chairman of the Joint Chiefs of Staff. So seriously did the Navy take the sailor's activities that it enlisted the aid of the Washington, D.C., Sanitation Department to make a "special pickup" of Priest's trash, for naval inspection, and assigned no less than twenty-five investigators to follow his activities. One investigator acknowledged that at a "workshop" addressed by Priest at an antiwar conference in Cleveland, six of the fifteen persons in attendance were Navy agents.

In late 1968 the Secretary of Health, Education and Welfare barred a prominent critic of the draft from speaking in the HEW building in Washington on the subject, "The Selective Service Bureaucracy—an Administrative Nightmare." (The prohibition was overruled by a Federal court.) In 1967 Selective Service Director Lewis B. Hershey instructed local draft boards that they could cancel the draft deferment of anyone participating in an "illegal" antiwar or antidraft demonstration. In June, 1969, General Hershey refused to circulate to draft boards a Federal court ruling that declared his earlier instruction illegal and probably unconstitutional.

In February, 1969, a court-martial sentenced to six months *at hard labor* a Navy nurse who had participated in an antiwar demonstration in full uniform. (When asked about this incident, she replied, "Well, generals wear their uniforms when they speak out in favor of the Vietnam war, so why can't we?") Also in 1969, a Senate investigating committee sought to subpoena from university administrators the names of students belonging to such antiwar organizations as Students for a Democratic Society. A *New York Times* editorial characterized this as "an intolerable intrusion into freedom of association and opinion," combining "those elements of intimidation and thought control that marked the witchhunting forays of the McCarthy era."

Even without the use of subpoenas, the Senate committee could probably have obtained the desired information from the massive files of the Church League of America, a private organization that sends what it calls "undercover operatives" to antiwar demonstrations and conferences, photographing and collecting the names of the participants and entering the results on three-by-five index cards, which the League boasts now number seven million. The League also tells businessmen that for a donation of twenty-five dollars—tax-deductible—they can get a rundown on any present or prospective employee. "When someone writes in to us and says, 'What've you got on so-and-so?'" says the League's Executive Secretary, "we simply get all of the cards out on that particular individual and then write the report." Thus, says a CBS report on the League, "businessmen can find out who was at the [Hemispheric Conference Against the War in Vietnam in Montreal in 1969] and can find out who disrupted an ROTC drill at Northwestern University."

The abuses of the loyalty-security program are not as frequent or flagrant as they once were. Yet the potential for abuse still exists. The power to probe opinions and affiliations and to appraise loyalty still finds sanction in the laws of the land. That power, built into the program by the men who devised it, came to be exercised in ways they may never have expected or intended. But they had put a genie in a bottle, with little control over its use by future, unknown masters. Can anyone now predict who will summon the genie, or for what purposes? Can there be any guarantee against a future Oppenheimer case?

In 1951 Alan Barth, in his book, *The Loyalty of Free Men*, wrote what he called a "description of an authoritarian society."

Any American hearing of a foreign country in which the police were authorized to search out the private lives of law-abiding citizens, in which a government official was authorized to proscribe lawful associations, in which administrative tribunals were authorized to condemn individuals by star-chamber proceedings on the basis of anonymous testimony, for beliefs and associations entailing no criminal conduct, would conclude without hesitation that the country was one in which tyranny prevailed.

Barth went on to say that this description was in fact a fair likeness of America itself (as the Oppenheimer case dramatically illustrates). It still is. Consider each of the elements of Barth's description:

• A police force *"authorized to search out the private lives of law-abiding citizens"*: The Gray Board hearing revealed how the most intimate aspects of Robert Oppenheimer's life were observed and reported by government investigators. Today the FBI, a national police investigative force, armed with ever more ingenious and inconspicuous surveillance devices, continues to eavesdrop on citizens—even, as revealed in 1969, citizens of such national prominence and stature as Martin Luther King, Jr.

• *"A government official . . . authorized to proscribe lawful associations"*:* This referred to the power of the Attorney Gen-

---

* Part of the dictionary definition of the word "proscribe" is "to condemn . . . as harmful." It is in this sense that Mr. Barth must have used the word

eral to pronounce organizations "subversive." Although not recently invoked, that authority still exists. The courts have yet to strike it down, despite the Supreme Court's recent suggestion that the right to join lawful groups is guaranteed by the freedom-of-assembly provision in the First Amendment.* The House Un-American Activities Committee (recently renamed the House Internal Security Committee) also has its list of "subversive" groups, and Federal agencies continue to consult the committee's files as they screen Federal employees.

• *"Administrative tribunals . . . authorized to condemn individuals by star-chamber proceedings"*: Oppenheimer's security case was heard—and the fate of his reputation decided—in strict secrecy. Security hearings are still held behind closed doors, with the public barred (although the "subject" may later release the transcript of the hearing). In that sense they are still "star-chamber" proceedings.

• *"On the basis of anonymous testimony"*: The Sixth Amendment to the Constitution guarantees to citizens accused of crimes the right to confront and cross-examine their accusers. That guarantee was denied Robert Oppenheimer in his 1954 security proceeding (*viz.*, the failure to call Paul Crouch as a witness). Although the Oppenheimer case was not actually a criminal court case, but an administrative proceeding, the Supreme Court had recognized, five years prior to the Oppenheimer hearing, that the right of confrontation was essential to a fair hearing in administrative proceedings as well as criminal cases. More recently, the Court has said this right applies to all proceedings (administrative as well as judicial) in which the effect of the government's action is to penalize or punish. Today, while confrontation is more widely accorded in selected Federal security programs, the principle of fairness which the Sixth Amendment seeks to guarantee is still not assured most Federal employees.†

---

here, rather than in the sense of outlawing. The Attorney General has no power to outlaw organizations.

* The Supreme Court has said that proscription of "mere knowing membership" in an organization, without "specific intent" to participate in any of its unlawful activities, "run[s] afoul of the Constitution."

† As a consequence of the Supreme Court decision in *Greene* v. *McElroy* (360 U.S. 474 [1959]), the Department of Defense modified its industrial security program (covering employees of private defense contractors) so as

• *"Individuals [condemned] . . . for beliefs and associations entailing no criminal conduct":* Oppenheimer was condemned largely because of noncriminal "beliefs and associations." The laws and regulations that permitted this in 1954 are basically unchanged today. As noted in the cases of recent date, above, those laws are still invoked to penalize opinions and associations whose only offense is their controversiality.

In short, Alan Barth's description seems essentially as apt today as it was at the time of Oppenheimer's ordeal.

There are other ways in which the loyalty-security program has done violence to many of the precepts embodied in the Constitution and laws of the United States for the protection of her citizens. These precepts apply, in general, to persons accused of crimes and therefore are not legally applicable to defendants in security cases. Nonetheless the punishments flowing from such cases can be so severe—often more severe than those meted out in many criminal trials*—that the same kinds of protections ought, in fairness, to apply.

Three hallowed legal principles were violated in the case of J. Robert Oppenheimer. The first is that no man should be twice tried for the same offense. Many others besides Oppenheimer have been first cleared and later recharged for the same offenses.

---

to provide confrontation except where a high-level official certifies that the identification of an informant would be "substantially harmful to the national interest." In practice, this exception has been rarely used. The Atomic Energy Commission security program uses similar procedures, both for its own employees and for contractor personnel. But for the bulk of Federal employees, the only requirement of agencies is that before issuing a letter of charges against an employee or applicant, they consult the Department of Justice for advice as to "the extent to which confrontation and cross-examination of witnesses will be required" to substantiate the charges. (Letter to agencies by Civil Service Commission Chairman John Macy, Nov. 18, 1965.)

* Consider, for example, the "sentence" suffered by William Lewis Greene, an $18,000-a-year vice president of an electronics firm whose principal business was with the Defense Department, who, after being declared a "security risk," could not get a more remunerative job than that of a $4,400-a-year architectural draftsman—and thus suffered a salary loss of nearly $50,000 in a six-year period. Very few criminal sentences involve fines as large even as $10,000, although they can also, of course, involve imprisonment. (This is the case referred to in a footnote on page 293.)

THE OPPENHEIMER CASE

Those subject to the loyalty-security program are still vulnerable to this double jeopardy.

Second, there is the principle that, because of the perishability of evidence and memory, there should be a limit on the amount of time that may elapse between the commission of an offense and the judgment of the man accused of it.* No such limit obtained in the Oppenheimer case.† No such limit obtains in the loyalty-security program today. Persons subject to the program are not only liable to multiple jeopardy; they live in perpetual jeopardy.

Third, there is the principle set forth in Article I, Section 9, of the Constitution that no person should be held accountable for an act that was lawful at the time he engaged in it. That principle, too, was ignored in the Oppenheimer case.‡ For those currently under the loyalty-security programs, proper and innocent beliefs or associations of today could at any time become the security-risk charges of tomorrow. This cannot help but have the "chilling effect" on freedom of belief and association of which the Supreme Court has recently warned.

Americans have prided themselves on their adherence to the concept that a man is presumed innocent until proven guilty. In other words, the burden of proof lies with the prosecution, which must produce evidence and witnesses to support its indictment or charges. In the Oppenheimer hearing the charges were presumed to be true, and it was Oppenheimer who had the burden of disproving them or of mitigating their significance. In loyalty-security hearings today the same unjust procedure prevails.

But all these lapses from ordinary legal practice shrink in significance when compared to the absence of the blank-pad rule. Even if none of these lapses had afflicted the Oppenheimer case, there still could not have been a truly fair hearing, because before

* There are some exceptions to these so-called statutes of limitation: e.g., murder.

† Some of Oppenheimer's alleged transgressions occurred sixteen years prior to his security hearing in 1954. Federal criminal statutes allow a maximum time lapse of five years.

‡ Oppenheimer was charged with membership in organizations that were wholly unexceptionable at the time of his involvement with them, and became questionable only by subsequent government fiat. Specifically, each of the supposedly "tainted" groups to which the physicist belonged acquired its "subversive" label years after he had been a member.

the hearing began and before a single word of evidence had been heard, the Gray Board members had studied the large black notebooks whose contents had been drawn from three thousand pages of secret reports on Oppenheimer. This exposure of the board members to secret evidence rendered Oppenheimer wholly dependent on their fairness. But not even the fairest of men can completely erase from his mind what he has read and assimilated. And, in any case, Oppenheimer's judges were not required to do so. They were expected to use the secret information in rendering their judgment, and they did.

In this respect there has been major progress. Responding to court decisions, the Civil Service Commission in late 1965 instructed Federal agencies that investigative information should not be made available to hearing boards unless it is also made available to the employee or applicant.

Among the more dismaying characteristics of the loyalty program is its reliance on dossiers—the investigative files on millions of Americans that repose in the files of the Federal Government. These dossiers have an enduring quality (not even the death of the "subject" seems to bring about their removal from Federal files*), and they are secret. Many are filled with misinformation that the "subject" has no way of rebutting or correcting, for he has no way of knowing what the file contains or who furnished the information. Nor does he know what persons may have access to the file or what conclusions they may draw.

The number of these secret files has grown explosively over the last two decades. In addition to those of the FBI and the CIA, Columbia Law Professor Alan F. Westin reports that the "Department of Defense has fourteen million life histories in its security files, the Civil Service Commission eight million." Professor Westin also tells of "the largest American private investigative agency," the Retail Credit Company. It "rates persons for a wide variety of purposes including industrial security . . . [and] maintains dossiers on forty-two million people." Moreover, says Westin, "there are investigations and dossiers that people never

---

*Viz., the posthumous use of the file on Harry Dexter White, five years after his death. (See p. 221.)

494 THE OPPENHEIMER CASE

even learn about. For example, the Federal Housing Administration has private agencies conduct investigations of more than a million annual applicants for FHA loans" and receives reports that include assessments of the "marital stability" of applicants. (The theory is that there is more risk of foreclosure when divorce is threatening.)

Since under the Federal security program the kind of "association" a person has is one criterion of measuring his "security risk," investigative dossiers invariably involve, and often incriminate, more than the "subject" himself. Guilt by association is an entrenched part of the security-screening process, and anyone even remotely connected with a questionable person may himself become tainted. Since the compilers of these files appear to be consummately skilled cross-indexers, especially since the advent of the computer, the dossiers often become links in virtually endless chains of guilt.*

There is, it seems, no limit on the use to which these files may be put, save the consciences of those who have access to them, and so these dossiers are, in effect, time bombs. There is no telling when they may detonate or, because they contain so many "related" names, who may be injured when they do explode.

Here follow examples of some of the uses to which these supposedly secret, supposedly nonpolitical files have been put. They may seem all too familiar to persons who have lived under totalitarian governments, which often use secretly acquired information to further the political aims of those in power:

• In a campaign speech he made when he was Vice President, Richard Nixon quoted from a Naval Intelligence security report,

---

* There is, for example, the case of Mr. X, who (according to official charges) became suspect in part because his release from the Coast Guard had been requested by Mr. C, whose file, in turn, had evidently been combed to reveal "information indicat[ing] that [C] was author of [title], a book which was advertised in a Louis Adamic publication; Louis Adamic has been listed as an official of the Progressive Party in Philadelphia in 1948, which has been cited as a Communist Front organization by the California Tenney Legislative Committee." But the chain did not stop there: C was also of questionable reliability because he had listed as references Robert E. Sherwood, Owen Lattimore and [E], "who have been identified as members of Communist Front Groups."

based on data received from the FBI, to discredit and contribute to the defeat of a Democratic Congressman.*

• A secret Army Counter Intelligence investigation of a retired Army brigadier general came to light in the midst of a political campaign, and he was forced to withdraw as Republican candidate for Congress. Shortly after his withdrawal, the general was cleared of "any suspicion of disloyalty." It developed that the Counter Intelligence investigation had been initiated because the Communist newspaper, the *Daily Worker,* had reported one of the general's campaign speeches.

• A previously secret investigative report was used by Attorney General Brownell, a Republican, as the basis for a politically-charged claim that former President Truman had knowingly promoted a Soviet spy in the employ of the United States.†

• During Senate hearings on the nomination of Lewis Strauss for Secretary of Commerce, it came to light that Strauss had called the Atomic Energy Commission for information concerning a scientist he heard was scheduled to testify against him.‡

The above examples tend to confirm the observation made by Alan Barth that the loyalty-security program "fundamentally alters the traditional American relationship of the individual to the State—a relationship that is the key characteristic of a free society."

But the program also affects the relationship of one citizen to another. This becomes grimly obvious when one considers the kind of information that finds its way into the government's investigative dossiers and how that information gets there.

Clues to the sort of data lodged in these secret files are contained in the following charges, which were used in actual security-risk cases:

A reliable source has disclosed that at a meeting held at the

* The political quarantining of that particular Congressman on loyalty grounds was a bipartisan matter. Even before Nixon quoted from the Naval Intelligence report, the Democratic National Chairman announced a withholding of any national party funds or implied endorsement—at a time when the doubts about the Congressman had not progressed beyond the public-rumor stage.

† See p. 221.
‡ See pp. 451–53.

[———] School in [X housing development] during National Brotherhood Week in 1943–44, a motion was made by one Mr. [———] that "the Bible should be burned and start building from there," and that you verbally seconded the motion and discussed it.

Communist literature was observed in the book shelves and Communist art\* was seen on the walls of your residence.

In connection with your study at the University of [X] in the pursuit of a Ph.D. degree . . . you wrote a thesis which was based mainly on material obtained from the Institute of Pacific Relations which has been cited as a Communistic [sic] Front organization by the House Committee on Un-American Activities.

How did the information behind these charges get into government investigative files? Was a government agent present at the National Brotherhood Week meeting back in 1943–44? Was it a Federal investigator who spotted the "Communist art" on the walls of the employee's residence? And do government investigative agencies deploy agents to scrutinize Ph.D. dissertations in search of those that draw from suspect source material?

Frightening as are those possibilities, the more likely alternative is even more disquieting: *Everyman is becoming the government's agent, the eyes and ears of the national police force.* We are becoming a society in which, especially in times of national fear, everyone speaks with a guarded tongue and in which neighbor eyes neighbor with apprehension or mistrust; a society in which everyone becomes the potential prey of the busybody next door who may not approve of the art in his home or the views he expounds at the PTA meeting.

But information flowing into government files does not originate solely with busybodies. Even a Robert Oppenheimer—the antithesis of a gossip—was induced on several occasions to talk to security investigators about the views and activities of former colleagues and intimate friends. One can find tragedy, and irony too, in the thought that such a man permitted himself to become

---

\* The "Communist art" was stated in the investigative report to have been the work of "Picasso, Matisse, Renoir and Moddigliotti [sic]."

the instrument of the very system that brought his downfall. But the significance of his actions to the society as a whole is even more disturbing. For if this once independent, intensely skeptical radical could be made to play the security agent's game, how many can be expected to resist, when fear is at large in the land?

Other clues as to the contents of government investigative files may sometimes be found in the questions asked in security hearings. The following are drawn from hearing transcripts:

Q:  When you were in X's home, did X's wife dress conventionally when she received her guests? Conventionally . . . would you expect [a dinner hostess] to appear in overalls?

Q.  Were there any beds in X's house which had no mattresses on them? Was the interior of their house dirty?

Q:  Did you ever hear it said that X's wife slept on a board in order to keep the common touch?

Beyond the matter of who provided the government with the information underlying those questions (and *why*), other discomforting questions arise: Why should the government interest itself in such wholly private details of citizens' lives as the manner of their dress, the tidiness of their housekeeping or their preference for bed boards over mattresses? Should the government have the right and authority to inquire into such matters? And what happens to the character of society if the state begins to attach some significance, however small, to the fact that X's wife entertains in overalls or sleeps on a board?

Here are further questions asked in security hearings:

Q:  The file indicates that you were quite hepped up over the One World idea . . . [and that] you were a strong advocate of the United Nations. Are you still?

Q:  Do the books in X's home appear to have been purchased from book clubs or individually from book stores?

Q:  How many copies of Howard Fast's novels have you read?

Why should the government take an interest in a citizen's views about One World or the United Nations? Or in where he

THE OPPENHEIMER CASE

purchased his books? Or in how many of Howard Fast's novels he has read? Are there not, in the very *asking* of such questions about behavior and about beliefs by a representative of the state, the seeds of Orwellian thought (and behavior) control?

As the Oppenheimer case showed, the security system permits, if indeed it does not encourage, the equating of disagreement with disloyalty. With the government officially in the business of measuring loyalty, it was only natural for General Roscoe Charles Wilson, after hearing Oppenheimer express his views at a top-secret Pentagon meeting, to scurry to the Air Force Chief of Intelligence to express his doubts about Oppenheimer's allegiance to the United States. And it was also natural that the report of his misgivings became part of the investigative dossier later used in the physicist's security proceeding. How can a Federal employee who today speaks against, say, the antiballistic missile be sure that his views will not likewise find their way into a security dossier that will one day be used against him?

The security system's tendency to blur opinions and motives has spilled over into American politics, with important effects even at the political summit. In the early 1950's for example, powerful men in public life were arguing that China did not fall but was pushed into Communist hands by a few pro-Red China experts. "But for the machinations of the small group [in the Institute of Pacific Relations]," said Senator Pat McCarran of Nevada, "China would today be free." Even ten years later that line of argument still had potent effect. In 1961 President Kennedy privately acknowledged to UN Ambassador Adlai Stevenson that on the merits the American position toward China was "irrational." But he flatly told Stevenson that any major shift of policy at that time would be political disaster, both for him and for Stevenson. He left no doubt that domestic politics was the controlling factor in America's China policy: in mentioning to Stevenson the possibility of a change of position on the matter of letting China into the UN, Kennedy noted that there would be Congressional elections in 1962 and spoke of "delay[ing] the admission of Red China until after the election." At this writing, seven years later, the policy is unchanged. China, with her newly perfected H-bomb, remains isolated.

498

Of graver immediate import, does any American political leader today recommend making concessions to the Communists —about Vietnam or disarmament or any other issue—free of the fear of someday being accused of being "soft on Communism"? That is no hypothetical danger. As recently as the spring of 1968, political representatives of the President of the United States openly argued that a vote for Senator Eugene McCarthy, a critic of the Vietnam war, "will be greeted with cheers in Hanoi." A few months later, in the presidential campaign itself, the Republican vice-presidential candidate, Spiro T. Agnew, accused Democrat Hubert Humphrey of being "soft on Communism" and apparently for "peace at any price." In such an atmosphere political debate and decisions are apt to revolve more around the seeming "anti-Communism" of a given policy than around what is rational. When policy miscalculations carry the possibility of thermonuclear war, there is an urgent pertinence in Justice Brandeis' admonition that "In frank expression of conflicting opinion lies the greatest promise of wisdom in governmental action; and in suppression lies ordinarily the greatest peril."

If the introduction of a massive loyalty-security system has had its price, what has the country *gained* from it? The system was initiated, supposedly, to counter a threat of internal subversion. But what have been the dimensions of that threat? Equally important, has the loyalty-security system been well suited to meet it?

No one put the Communist menace in perspective more succinctly than President Eisenhower. Speaking on the day the Gray Board first met, in April of 1954, he said, "This fear [of Communist infiltration] has been greatly exaggerated. . . . In our country today there are possibly some 25,000 doctrinal Communists. The FBI knows pretty well where they are. . . . Actually, 25,000 out of 160,000,000 people means about one out of 6,000."

Many have sought to create the impression that the Federal payroll was honeycombed with Communists. But it is a reassuring fact that, over the past twenty years, among the millions of Federal employees who have had to swear that they were not members of the Communist Party, not one has been prosecuted for falsifying that denial (a felony punishable by up to five years imprisonment and/or $10,000 fine). Today the FBI estimates the number of Communists at 13,000. In a country of 200,000,000, this means roughly one out of every 15,000 Americans or one six-thousandth of one percent of our population.

Numbers are not, of course, the sole measure of the danger: it would require but a tiny fraction of the 13,000 Communists to form an effective espionage cadre. But that in itself leads to a further question: Was the massive loyalty-screening program the best means of countering a threat of espionage? What have been the results?

Statistics in this area are frustratingly slippery, but the broadest intelligible figures cover the period of the government-wide Truman loyalty program, from its inception in 1947 through mid-1952. In that period the United States Government screened a total of 4,756,705 individuals. In 4,730,469 cases—99.5 percent of the total—not a modicum of evidence nor even any suggestion of disloyalty was found. In only 26,236 cases—one-half of one percent of the total—was there *any* evidence that would raise so much as a question as to loyalty. And of the nearly five million persons screened, in only 560 cases—about one one-hundredth of one percent—were individuals "removed or denied Federal employment on grounds relating to loyalty." It could be said that the population seeking Federal employment turned out to be $99^{99}/_{100}$ percent "pure."

In the process of discovering all these reassuring facts about the "purity" of its applicants and employees, the United States Government has spent, over the last twenty years, between one-half and three-quarters of a *billion* dollars. Given a population more than 99 percent of which is loyal beyond any question, it seems unnecessary to have launched so prodigiously expensive a screening program.*

* It is argued on behalf of the screening program that its very existence has discouraged Communists from applying for Federal employment, and that this accounts, in part at least, for the "purity" of the millions screened. But President Eisenhower gave assurance that the Federal Bureau of Investigation knows pretty well where the Communists are. (FBI Director Hoover was able, in 1950, to provide the Senate Appropriations Committee with a state-by-state head count.) If the domestic Communists are so clearly known to the FBI, would they not in all probability have been spotted if they had happened to apply for Federal employment?

Even as vast and costly as the screening program has been, it has not been foolproof. Since World War II at least eleven persons who were able to pass the screening tests later turned out to be spies. Thus it may, after all, be unrealistic to expect the "absolute predictability" of human behavior that Gordon Gray, in the Oppenheimer hearing, indicated he thought feasible.* As Roger Robb put it, "Future conduct . . . can never be the subject of present proof."

But of even greater relevance to the current governmental opinion-probing powers is the striking fact that in recent years very few of the Americans indicted for espionage have had a left-wing background. The modern spy is apparently a mercenary rather than an ideologue. That being the case, it seems of dubious utility, in spotting would-be spies, to dig into the political backgrounds and beliefs of applicants for Federal jobs. One writer on the loyalty-security system, Professor Ralph Brown of the Yale Law School, comments that "we find no responsible claims that the loyalty-security programs have caught a single known spy."

Another question needs to be asked: To what extent are the secrets supposedly safeguarded by the security system really "keepable"? The fact is that most secrets are far less "keepable" than most people imagine. The American image of secrecy, its importance and efficacy, was hugely magnified by the atomic bomb experience—by the sudden, blinding emergence of a new and terrible weapon developed entirely in secret. There was a tendency, or perhaps a wish, on the part of the general public to believe that if America could just safeguard the atomic secret, no one else would "get" the bomb. There has also been a widespread belief that had it not been for the vital information Klaus Fuchs gave the Russians, the Soviets would never have "gotten" the H-bomb. Fuchs' last contact with the American nuclear program, however, was in 1946, when American physicists were dubious the "Super" was even theoretically possible, and five years before Edward Teller and others conceived the new approach that led to the first American H-bomb. Nonetheless, the Soviets were able to achieve their first thermonuclear explosion a scant eight months

* See p. 308.

after ours, and with a far more sophisticated process, one we later imitated. The subsequent development of H-bombs by the British and even the supposedly backward, agrarian Chinese reinforces the lack of exclusivity in the "secrets of nature." This is, of course, well known to scientists: the phenomena in which those secrets are hidden—atoms, protons, mesons, etc.—exist in nature everywhere. Such objects know no national boundaries; they cannot be locked away in safes or vaults. Their secrets are open to any scientist who has talent and patience—and the freedom to search wherever his mind may lead.

Man-made secrets (such as the strength of a nation's military forces) are of course more keepable; and they can be of great value to an enemy. The lesson to be drawn is not that America should abandon all measures to safeguard secrets but that no one should worship secrecy or expect too much of it. The greatest hazard of all may well lie in an obsession with the safeguarding of existing knowledge, an obsession that could hamper the unfettered search for the yet-undiscovered. By the very act of declaring information secret, a government bars that information not only to the "enemy" but also to its own citizens.*

Since the costs of the loyalty-security program are extensive and the results meager, is it sensible to continue vesting this opinion-probing power in the United States Government?

During the first century and a half of its existence the American Republic experienced panic, depression, riots, a bloody civil war and two global wars. It survived them all without any wide-ranging loyalty-security-screening program. It assumed that Americans were, in general, loyal and that the laws against treason, espionage and other dangerous acts were sufficient either to deter or to punish those who would deliberately do the nation ill.

For over half a century—from 1884 to 1939—the Federal Government hired its personnel not only without the aid of loyalty screening but, on the contrary, under strict limitations on the inquiries it could make of applicants. These limits were contained in the first rule promulgated under the nation's first Civil Service law. Civil Service Rule I of 1884 stipulated that

---

* The subject of secrecy and its implications, moral as well as political, is vexatious and far-reaching enough to deserve a book of its own.

No question in any form of application, or in any examination shall be so framed as to elicit information concerning the political or religious opinions or affiliations of any applicant, nor shall any inquiry be made concerning such opinions or affiliations, and all disclosures thereof shall be discountenanced.

As seen above, the results of the security screening of the past twenty years suggest that Americans are no less "loyal" today than they were during the first century and a half of this country's history. They also suggest that even in a world of new weapons and great enmities it is safe—and the extensive toll suggests it is imperative—to abolish the security system as it now stands and return to the strictures of Civil Service Rule I. The Federal Government should now put a stop to its wholesale investigations of citizens' lives; end its amassing of often-misleading but seemingly imperishable dossiers; and discontinue its efforts to measure citizens' loyalty.

That would not mean barring the government from *all* inquiries concerning prospective employees. Government should of course solicit the kind of information sought by any prudent employer concerning an applicant's industry, honesty, reliability and discretion, so long as "[no] inquiry [is] made concerning [his] political or religious opinions or affiliations," and so long as "all disclosures thereof shall be discountenanced."*

The problem of defining loyalty remains difficult. General William Westmoreland, America's military commander in Vietnam, returned to the United States in 1967 and spoke of peaceful, lawful demonstrations against the Vietnam war as "unpatriotic acts." Was he right? Was the patriotism of the peace marchers suspect? Or could an argument be directed the other way? Could it, for example, be argued that the *General's* efforts to discourage the free expression guaranteed by the Founding Fathers, and by

* Many have argued—the 1946 Presidential Commission on Employee Loyalty among them—that counterintelligence work is more effective than broad-scale superficial personnel investigations in detecting potential spies. The strictures of Civil Service Rule I would not prohibit the government from referring to its counterintelligence files for evidence of *actions* such as espionage or sabotage on the part of an applicant or employee.

the First Amendment, was a profoundly un-American act—and that it is Westmoreland's patriotism that is open to question?

Both arguments are, of course, simplistic—and ridiculous. Loyalty involves *motive* as well as belief, and both are secreted deep within the human person. The Gray Board, in its opinion on the Oppenheimer case, asserted that "the government can search . . . the soul of an individual . . . with full protection of the rights . . . of both." A society that tolerates and accepts such an assertion does so at its peril.

# XV   EPILOGUE

I am become Death,
The destroyer of worlds.

                    —The Bhagavad-Gita

On the night of Saturday, February 18, 1967, at Olden Manor, Princeton, New Jersey, after less than sixty-three years, Robert Oppenheimer's life came to an end.

In Ithaca, New York, physicist Hans Bethe said, "It was as if an older brother had died."

In Berkeley, California, Edward Teller observed, "He made the [Los Alamos] laboratory. I like to remember that he did a magnificent job and a very necessary job."

In Saigon, David Lilienthal said, "The world has lost a noble spirit—a genius who brought together poetry and science."

In Vienna, at the request of U.S. Representative Henry De-Wolf Smyth, the International Atomic Energy Agency interrupted its proceedings to pay tribute to the American nuclear physicist.

Even in Japan, where the bombs created largely out of Oppenheimer's genius had once incinerated two cities, there were tributes. Nobel prize-winning physicist Hideki Yukawa termed

Oppenheimer "a symbol of the tragedy of the modern nuclear scientists." Yukawa speculated that Oppenheimer's "difficulties and differences of opinion with [his] government" might have shortened the life of this "sensitive" man.

Those eulogies came from Oppenheimer's contemporaries, who were aware not only of his extraordinary service to his country but of the role he had played in transforming American physics. But for the post-Hiroshima generation the residual impression of Robert Oppenheimer might be quite different. Most newspaper obituary biographies gave no more attention to his years of service to his government than to the never-reversed finding of "security risk." What connotations will Oppenheimer's name conjure up for those born after the Nuclear Age had begun? "Teacher of physics?" "Father of the A-bomb?" Or "that scientist who got in trouble with the government"?

Why should so debasing a tragedy have befallen so extraordinary a man? Oppenheimer himself took a rather fatalistic view of the matter. Not long after the security case, he said to an interviewer, "I think of this as a major accident—much like a train wreck or the collapse of a building. It has no relation or connection with my life. I just happened to be there."

To some extent, Oppenheimer did just happen to be in the way of external forces that had very little relation to his personal life:

• *The "McCarthy era":* A wave of postwar anxiety and fear of the unorthodox not dissimilar to that which followed World War I. But in the 1950's popular fears were intensified by the emergence of Russia as a hostile power, the revelations of Soviet espionage against Western powers, and by the rise of a superlative and fearsome demagogue—Senator Joseph McCarthy.\*

• *A quirk in timing:* The coincidence in time between William Borden's letter and a political charge by the Attorney Gen-

---

\* McCarthy, unlike other celebrated American demagogues, was not a lone agent. The proven political success of his tactics led his national political party to adopt the exploitation of anti-Communist fears as one of its most potent weapons.

eral that the preceding President had knowingly promoted a Soviet spy. The alarm about the latter made the rigorous prosecution of the Oppenheimer case a political imperative.

• *The bomb itself:* To an extent Oppenheimer was the victim of the very nuclear weapon he helped create, in that it heightened the intensity of intramural struggles over U.S. military policy. To the men involved in these struggles, the debate over the H-bomb was not just another quarrel over, say, an improvement in a weapons system. "This," said a perceptive inside observer, "was an argument over survival, where if you guessed wrong, you might blow the whole game." It is understandable that some who pictured the stakes so high should have doubted the patriotism of those who seemed to them to be "guessing wrong."

• *The emergence of the scientist-as-policy-maker:* Oppenheimer was both the symbol and the victim of a new and perplexing problem in American Government: the sudden transformation of The Scientist from a rumpled, abstracted, ivory-tower figure into a major force in American policy-making. If technology put new tools in the hands of the statesmen and the military, it also made them increasingly dependent on the technical advice of The Scientist. But how does the nonexpert layman who receives such advice distinguish a scientist-adviser's "technical" views from his political, moral or philosophical predilections? For example, when such an adviser gives counsel as to the "technical" feasibility of a new weapon, might not his judgment be clouded—however unconsciously—by his view that the weapon is, say, morally repugnant or, on the contrary, absolutely essential to the survival of the nation?

Statesmen and politicians have long had to wrestle with their reliance, in military matters, on generals and admirals. But the postwar dependence on scientists and their sudden inclusion in the high councils of government was something far newer; and because it was new it was, to many, perplexing. The concern it caused was often reflected in the Oppenheimer proceeding, nowhere more clearly than in the Gray Board's plea that scientist-advisers rely on their "special competence" and their "soundly-based convictions . . . uncolored and uninfluenced by considerations of an emotional character."

• *Pure chance:* Would the Oppenheimer security case have come to pass if William Liscum Borden had not been *who* he was *when* he was? What if Borden had written no letter to J. Edgar Hoover that November 7, 1953?

But Robert Oppenheimer was not solely the victim of external forces. It is too simple to agree with him that he "just happened to be there." For at the time these forces came into play in America there were a number of scientists who were assuming powerful roles in government; many who opposed the H-bomb, even more vociferously, and more publicly, than Robert Oppenheimer; and some who, like Oppenheimer, ruffled the sensitive feathers of politicians and statesmen.

If Robert Oppenheimer was standing in a crowd, why did the lightning happen to strike *him?* The answer seems to have resided within him—and, particularly, in two wholly contradictory qualities: his remarkable persuasive powers and his equally extraordinary capacity to antagonize and injure.

Only rarely did the general public get a glimpse of this latter aspect of Oppenheimer,* but, as we have seen, there were numerous less public instances when other men of fragile sensibilities (such as K. D. Nichols, David Griggs, Luis Alvarez and General Roscoe Charles Wilson) were humiliated by Oppenheimer's withering tongue. Often it seemed that his slashes were entirely gratuitous—that he seemed to go out of his way to antagonize. He could be just as infuriatingly condescending to close acquaintances and loyal defenders as to adversaries. Some who wished to give him sympathy and support found it difficult. As Henry DeWolf Smyth said while working all night preparing his defense of Oppenheimer, "I don't know why I'm going to all this trouble—I don't even like the guy very much."†

But to most who met this soft-spoken, ascetically frail and

---

* One rare exception was his public ridiculing of Lewis Strauss on the isotope issue in a klieg-lit Senate hearing see pp. 130–33).

† In this respect, there is a parallel to the Dreyfus case, for the abrasive French Army Captain was evidently little liked by some of his supporters. When a group of affluent men gathered, one evening, to raise funds for his legal defense, after new evidence had pointed to the guilt of Major Esterhazy, one of the potential benefactors said, as he put on his cloak and prepared to depart, "Ah, if it were only Esterhazy we were defending."

beautiful man, he seemed all gentleness and kindness. Whence sprang the less widely known abrasive side of the man? His friend and Princeton neighbor, George Kennan, ventured an explanation: There was in Robert Oppenheimer, said Kennan, a quality "visible . . . primarily only to his closer friends: a deep yearning for . . . friendship, for companionship, for the warmth and richness of human communication. The arrogance which to many appeared to be a part of his personality masked in reality an overpowering desire to bestow and to receive affection. Neither circumstances nor at times the asperities of his own temperament permitted the gratification of this need in a measure remotely approaching its intensity; and in this too lay a portion of that strong element of tragedy which all who knew him sensed . . . in his situation. Such was the nature of his predicament."

While arrogance and condescension naturally breed enemies and court retribution and misadventure, the contrary quality— the capacity to charm and persuade—is more logically associated with power and success than with misfortune. Yet, strangely, this latter quality in Robert Oppenheimer seems also to have contributed materially to the calamity that befell him.

Why, one must ask, did the United States Government apparently feel bound to bring Robert Oppenheimer forcibly to his knees even though he was already out of power and out of official favor? Why did the government choose the painful course of forcibly revoking his clearance when both he and the government could have been spared this agony simply by allowing his affiliation with the AEC to die a natural death?

AEC General Manager Nichols was entirely candid about it: unless Oppenheimer's security clearance were revoked, other government agencies would continue to seek his counsel; the glow of his influence in government would remain. General Roscoe Charles Wilson of the Air Force put it equally frankly before the Gray Board: "He is such a brilliant man, the fact that he has such a command of the English language, has such national prestige, and such power of persuasion, only made me nervous."*

* Giorgio de Santillana has remarked on the similarity between the trials of Oppenheimer and Galileo. In Galileo's trial for heresy in 1633, one of the

Here, then, was the combination of factors that brought about Oppenheimer's fall from grace:—the persuasive advocacy of policies considered by certain persons to be disastrous to their country, coupled with grievous personal offenses against the sensibilities of those very same persons.

Some students of Oppenheimer's career find a note of irony in his having been faulted (especially by the Gray Board) for his moral qualms about the hydrogen bomb, for they question the real depth of his distaste for the "Super." They do not doubt that he experienced great anguish over his role in creating the world's first atomic bomb. Yet they are troubled by facts such as these:

• In the summer of 1942, during the pre-Los Alamos theoretical studies of nuclear explosions, Oppenheimer spent the bulk of his own time and energy on the vastly more destructive thermonuclear process, which he found more intellectually challenging than the comparatively milder fission process.

• As a member of a four-man scientific advisory group in 1945, Oppenheimer is reported to have favored dropping the first A-bomb on a populated area in Japan itself instead of on a remote island.

• While head of Los Alamos, he proposed a major postwar research effort on the "Super" and later, as chairman of the General Advisory Committee, he sanctioned (or at any rate never opposed) the continuing research work on the H-bomb that took place at Los Alamos, albeit on a minimal basis.

• In the General Advisory Committee's deliberations on the H-bomb in 1949, he did not join Fermi and Rabi in their seemingly stronger statement of moral opposition to the "Super." Rather, he sided with the GAC majority, who seemed more opposed to the crash program for the bomb than to the "Super" itself.

• At the Princeton meeting of mid-1951, Oppenheimer is reported to have been enthusiastic about the H-bomb's develop-

---

astronomer's detractors was nervous because "Galileo wrote exquisitely and had a marvelous capacity for persuading people of whatever he wanted to."

ment after Edward Teller had expounded a vastly more promising technical approach to the problems of the "Super."

• Most doubt-provoking of all, in the minds of many, was the phrase that Oppenheimer used in his testimony before the Gray Board in referring to the new program outlined by Teller in 1951. It was, he said, so "technically sweet" that you "could not argue" about it. Was this phrase—which he uttered not once but twice*—the sort likely to emanate from a man beset by fundamental moral qualms about a new weapon of uncalculated destructiveness?

There are those who saw in Robert Oppenheimer an apparent drive toward self-destruction. One close and admiring friend called him "either a masochistic exhibitionist or an exhibitionistic masochist—take your pick." Was there such a drive within Oppenheimer? Even to speculate on such secrets of the psyche is a hazardous affair. Yet included in the legacy left by this most extraordinary man are some unanswered questions:

If, as Oppenheimer contended, the purpose of his "cock and bull" story to Pash and Lansdale was to protect Haakon Chevalier, why did he invent a story that was far more harmful than the truth—both to Chevalier *and* himself? Why did he see fit voluntarily to reveal an explosively dangerous conversation he could easily have concealed? Moreover, why did so superlatively intelligent a man take such an action without having better thought through its logical consequences?

Why did he implicate his close friends Chevalier and Bernard Peters in a manner that brought as much grief to himself as to his friends?

Since he was already aware of security officers' intense interest in "the Chevalier incident," and since he is said to have *assumed* they were watching his movements in Paris in December, 1953, how could he have been ignorant of the danger in his visit to the Chevaliers' apartment?

* Twice he said "technically sweet." On a third occasion he said: "I have always thought it was a dreadful weapon. . . . Even though from a technical point of view it was a sweet and lovely and beautiful job, I have still thought it was a dreadful weapon."

Why would a man so skilled in persuading others, a man with all the knowledge of human behavior that this implies, have seemed at times to seek out ways to alienate others who might in turn do him great harm? Was Oppenheimer really unaware of Lewis Strauss' vanity, and unaware of the intolerable humiliation to which he was subjecting Strauss by publicly ridiculing him in a Congressional hearing? And when he was invited to a luncheon with Thomas Finletter and was offered an opportunity to ingratiate himself with the powerful Air Force Secretary, what prompted him to be so rude?

When he chose to insist on a full-dress security hearing, in December, 1953, did he imagine that he could avoid exposing his entire past? And once having embarked on such a hearing, what robbed him of the charm and self-possession that had so captivated the hard-bitten members of the House Un-American Activities Committee five years earlier? What deprived him of the self-respect that had enabled him, in 1948, to say of his left-wing past, "I'm not ashamed of it; I'm more ashamed of the lateness [of his political awakening]"? What prompted this man, so often accused of being self-willed, arrogant and disdainful of the views of others, to be so self-contemptuous in his own defense as to call himself an "idiot"?

It was intensely cold on February 25, 1967, the day friends, associates and admirers gathered in Princeton, New Jersey, to pay their final respects to J. Robert Oppenheimer. Virtually every phase of his adult life was represented among the persons who entered the auditorium in Princeton University's Alexander Hall on that gray February afternoon. There was Isador Isaac Rabi, who had shared Oppenheimer's postgraduate years in Europe in the Twenties. From the inner circle of Oppenheimer's students and friends of prewar Berkeley, there were Philip Morrison and Robert Serber. From the Los Alamos era, there were metallurgist Cyril Smith and physicist Donald Hornig (then science adviser to President Lyndon Johnson) and others. Retired General Leslie Richard Groves, now white-haired, had chartered a plane from Washington especially to attend these last services. And John Lansdale had flown in from Cleveland to pay his last respects.

The years of Robert Oppenheimer's postwar government service were represented by John J. McCloy and David Lilienthal, who had chaired the Atomic Energy Commission during the first struggling years of the Nuclear Age.

Shortly after three o'clock Carl Kaysen, Oppenheimer's successor as director of the Institute for Advanced Study, rose to address those assembled in Alexander Hall.

"We are here to remember Robert Oppenheimer, whose death diminishes us all, and to remember each of his careers—as a physicist, as a public servant and as director of the Institute. Any of those careers by itself would be an achievement for a less extraordinary man."

To recall each of these careers, three speakers had been chosen: Hans Bethe, to speak of Oppenheimer as scientist; Henry DeWolf Smyth, to honor Oppenheimer as public servant; and George Kennan to recall the final years, at the Institute in Princeton.

"J. Robert Oppenheimer did more than any other man to make American theoretical physics great," began Bethe. But, said Bethe, his legacy to American science lay less in scientific discoveries that had sprung from his own mind than in the gifted young men that his brain and his extraordinary personality had attracted to the arcane new field of theoretical physics. "His was a truly brilliant mind," concluded Bethe, "best described by his long-time associate Charles Lauritsen: 'This man . . . always gave you the answer before you had time to formulate the question.'"

Next came Henry DeWolf Smyth. Having returned late the night before from an Atomic Energy Agency meeting in Vienna, he had begun writing his eulogy of the physicist just a few hours before. Again, it seemed, as he had nearly thirteen years earlier, he was writing about Robert Oppenheimer under pressure of a deadline.

He recited Robert Oppenheimer's many contributions in his government's service, then turned to the manner in which the government had repaid that service. "Such a wrong can never be righted; such a blot on our history never erased," said Henry Smyth. "We regret that his great work for his country was repaid so shabbily, and that he felt impelled to quote these lines of Shakespeare:

> The sad account . . .
> Which I now pay as if not paid before.

"If he paid heavily, as indeed he did," Smyth concluded, "we hope he knew how greatly his country and the world have been rewarded by his work."

The final speaker, George Kennan, made no effort to gloss over the "disappointments and frustrations" of Oppenheimer's "Princeton years." "On no one," he said, "did there ever rest with greater cruelty the dilemmas evoked by the recent conquest by human beings of a power over nature out of all proportion to their moral strength." Nor was there anyone "who more passionately desired to be useful in averting the catastrophes to which the development of the weapons of mass destruction threatened to lead."

"It was as an American" that he wished to be useful, Kennan emphasized. He told of suggesting to Oppenheimer, in the midst of his security travails, the possibility of his "taking residence outside this country. His answer, given to me with tears in his eyes: 'Damn it, I happen to love this country.'

"The truth is," Kennan continued, "that the U.S. Government never had a servant more devoted at heart than this one, in the sense of wanting to make a constructive contribution; and I know of nothing more tragic than the series of mistakes (in part, no doubt, his own, but in what small part!) that made it impossible for him to render this contribution—that obliged him to spend the last decade and a half of his life eating out his heart in frustration over the consciousness that the talents he knew himself to possess, once welcomed and used by the official establishment of his country to develop the *destructive* possibilities of nuclear science, were rejected when it came to the development of the great positive ones he believed that science to possess. . . .

"His struggle is now over. His possibilities in this respect are ended. The rest of us may well search our consciences to discover those deficiencies of our public life that made it impossible for us to make better use at so crucial a time of a man so talented, and one who so desperately wanted to serve."

The Juilliard String Quartet played Beethoven's C-sharp Minor Quartet, No. 14. Those assembled in Alexander Hall sat in silence. When the music ended, they rose and filed out into the biting cold of that February day, taking their final leave of Julius Robert Oppenheimer.

# Responses by Lloyd K. Garrison
# To Various Questions Asked
# By Philip M. Stern*

PREFATORY STATEMENT

When Philip Stern told me he was writing a book about the Oppenheimer case and asked me to give him material from my files, my first reaction was one of dismay. I did not want to relive the case. The preparation, the hearings and the aftermath had consumed six months of my life. They had been troubled months, filled with strain. I had been wholly committed to Robert's cause. During the long ordeal I had been a constant witness to his suffering. I had shared with him and with his devoted wife the anguish of the outcome. For him the blow was a lasting one, which he took with him to his grave.

Somehow in spite of it he found the courage to write and to speak, not about the case or the injustice done to him, but to advance public

* The author informed Roger Robb, who had in effect been the counsel opposing Garrison in the Oppenheimer hearing, that Lloyd Garrison had responded to a series of questions. Mr. Robb was shown the questions themselves, and was also invited to respond to a comparable list of questions. He declined, saying: "While I appreciate your courtesy . . . I cannot add anything to my previous answers"—i.e., answers he had given to the author in two interviews. —P.M.S.

understanding of modern physics and of the relationship between science as an intellectual activity and the wider culture of our times. The academic community rallied around him, and he received high public honors, including the $50,000 Fermi award, voted by the Atomic Energy Commission in 1963 and conferred upon him in the White House by President Johnson. I feared that a revival of the proceedings in book form might stir up old controversies that had been laid to rest, and for myself I dreaded going back into our files and saturating myself once again in the painful details, freighted as they would be with somber memories and always with the gnawing question: if I, as counsel, had done this or that in a different way, would it perhaps have changed the outcome?

I explained my troubles to Philip Stern very frankly. But he had already studied the case sufficiently to convince himself that an analysis of its procedures, and of its implications both for our national security and for the strength and well-being of our democracy, would be in the public interest. He felt that there might again come a time when men would be persecuted and ostracized for their past associations; when fear would supplant reason, and intellectual freedom and public debate would be stifled by a devouring orthodoxy. It was in such a time that the tragedy of Robert Oppenheimer, among many others less noticed, was enacted; and it could only have been enacted in such a time. Philip Stern expressed to me his hope that public understanding of what had then taken place might help to avoid the onset of another such time and to curb its excesses if it came.

I shared his objectives, but my reluctance to participate, for the personal reasons described above, persisted. Finally, when he had virtually completed the manuscript, he put to me a series of written questions about the procedure in the case. These showed how thorough his study had been, and I began to feel that I had some obligation to answer them as factually as I could, rather than force him to make surmises which might not be wholly accurate. Furthermore, the sincerity of his conviction about the public ends to be served by the book impressed me strongly, and in the end I consented to answer his questions.

I agreed to do this, however, on the express understanding that I would neither read his manuscript before publication nor discuss with him any aspects of the case other than those which he had asked me about in writing and to which I would respond in writing. I wanted the evaluation of the case, and of the conduct of all who had participated in it (including myself), to be wholly his own. This understanding has been adhered to. I do not know what the book will contain, and I assume no responsibility for its judgments.

Some of the questions which he put to me could be answered only from memory. Wherever possible I have answered them by reference to my files. The labor of reconstruction has been heavy. I can only hope that it may prove useful.

I. THE CHOICE AND RELATIONSHIPS OF DR. OPPENHEIMER'S COUNSEL

I first met Robert Oppenheimer at Princeton in April, 1953, when I became a member of the board of trustees of the Institute for Advanced Study, of which he was the director. Before the case arose I saw a good deal of him in connection with the meetings of the trustees, at which he was the central figure. During that period I acquired a great admiration and affection for him.

One evening in early January, 1954, he called me up and asked if he and Herbert Marks, whom I had not met, could see me on a matter of grave urgency. Marks, who was to take a leading part in the case, had been the first general counsel to the Atomic Energy Commission, serving under David Lilienthal's chairmanship from August, 1946, until sometime in 1948, when he went into private practice in Washington. He had earlier been assistant general counsel of the War Production Board under John Lord O'Brian, and after the war was over he had played an important part (as Robert Oppenheimer had) in the preparation of what came to be known as the Acheson-Lilienthal report for the control of atomic energy, which, with a few modifications, Mr. Baruch presented to the United Nations and which the Russians proceeded to veto. Marks had become Robert's most intimate friend. He was a talented lawyer and a warm, resourceful and courageous human being. Although I did not know this at the time, he suffered from migraine headaches, and during the proceedings they became almost unbearable, but he carried on in spite of them. Six years after the case was over he died, at the age of fifty-three. He was a great loss to the profession.

Robert's telephone call did not indicate what he and Herbert Marks wanted to see me about. They came to my apartment in New York and brought with them the letter of charges of December 23, 1953, which they asked me to read.* I had not known of its existence. As soon as I

* In a letter to me dated January 27, 1954, after I had gotten into the case, General Nichols stated that the Commission did not regard the letter of December 23, 1953, "as being a statement of charges, but rather a statement of substantial derogatory information bearing upon his [Dr. Oppenheimer's]

had finished reading it Robert said, "It looks pretty bad, doesn't it?" "Yes," I said.

He said that they had come to consult me about retaining counsel. Herbert Marks felt it would not be appropriate for him, as former general counsel to the Commission, to be the leading counsel for Robert in proceedings before the Commission.

We then discussed briefly the background and nature of the charges. Herbert told me that, except for certain charges relating to Robert's attitude toward a crash program for the H-bomb at a time when the practicality of such a bomb appeared to be remote, the charges were virtually a repetition of those which the members of the Atomic Energy Commission had had before them in 1947 when they granted Robert clearance and engaged him as a consultant. Herbert told me further that the matters relating to the H-bomb consisted merely of honest differences of opinion among the scientific advisers to the government, most of whom shared Robert's conclusions at the time.

We then talked about counsel. We recognized the heavy obstacles which Robert would face in obtaining suitable counsel. To begin with, the charges on their face were very serious. In the atmosphere of those days, in which public accusation of associations, no matter how far back in time, with Communists or Communist-supported causes, was enough to ruin any man's career, even liberally-minded lawyers were hesitant to involve themselves in the defense of persons so accused; and in Robert's case the catalogue of associations was long and formidable. Moreover, the prestige of the Atomic Energy Commission was high, and the average person would be predisposed to credit any charges made by it.

In addition, there was an acute problem of time. Robert was required to answer the charges in writing by January 22, 1954. While counsel might be able to obtain an extension from the Commission, it would probably be a relatively short one, and the job of preparing the answer would require immediate, continuous and protracted attention. A lawyer willing to take this on would have to drop nearly everything else that he was doing and saturate himself in Robert's past life, and afterward devote himself without stint to lengthy hearings. It would be hard to find a first-rate lawyer who could or would on such short notice put aside his other commitments for an undertaking of this magnitude and urgency—especially a lawyer who had not known Robert before.

---

eligibility for AEC security clearance." I have throughout this response to Mr. Stern's question used the word "charges" for short, instead of General Nichols' euphemistic paraphrase.

We talked that evening of two lawyers as possibilities: one a member of a leading downtown law firm, the other my partner, Judge Rifkind. It turned out the next day that both had commitments stretching into the future which would make it impossible for them to take on the case.

There was another difficulty. We realized that the more lawyers we talked to, the greater would be the risk of the story spreading and breaking in the newspapers, and we felt that until Robert's side of the matter could be reduced to writing and adequately presented, a publication of the charges, or of the fact that charges had been filed, could do Robert irreparable harm. Meanwhile, the due date of the answer was approaching, and it was essential for someone to get to work on it immediately.

We reached two conclusions. The first was to ask the Commission for an extension of time within which to file the answer. The second was that we should for the time being stop the search for a chief counsel and that I would undertake, with all the help I could get from Herbert Marks and Robert, to prepare the answer. We felt that once the answer was available it would make easier the task of finding a chief counsel. The basic spadework of preparation would have been done, and the facts set forth in the answer would make clear the true nature of the case. Moreover, the answer would be available for publication in case the charges should leak out.

My partners, to whom I put the question, agreed that I should go ahead on this basis. None of us realized at the time that in the upshot I would be compelled virtually to abandon all other activities for the next six months. We undertook the work as a public service, without charge.

On January 18, 1954, I conferred in Washington with Lewis Strauss, General Nichols and William Mitchell, the General Counsel of the Commission. At that meeting they granted an extension to February 23. The extension was a short one—too short as it turned out; another proved necessary, to March 4. Although hard pressed, we did not wish to prolong the time, for fear that any day the news might break before we had completed the job.

At the outset of the work I went to Princeton and spent the next two weeks there in daily association with Robert, going over every one of the items in the letter of charges and relating them to other events in Robert's life, and to the whole course of his attitude toward government and international affairs. I would make notes as we went along and prepare drafts of statements, which I would go over with Robert.

Later the headquarters shifted to our law office, and Robert would come in nearly every day to work with us.

I had in the meantime obtained the invaluable help of my partner, Samuel J. Silverman, later a Supreme Court Justice of New York and now one of the two surrogates of New York County. He had had the extensive trial experience I lacked; he became more and more absorbed in the case, and during the hearings in Washington he spent the entire time with us and conducted much of the examination of witnesses; later he worked intensively on the briefs. We were assisted by one of our associates, now a partner, Allan Ecker, who attended all the hearings and worked on the briefs. During the preparation of the answer I was in constant communication, and met frequently, with Herbert Marks, whose office was in Washington. He later attended the hearings, and worked with us night and day on the briefs. Unlike myself and Silverman, who were members of a very large firm, he had only one partner who could help out in his absence, and he virtually had to give up his practice for the duration of the case. In spite of his migraine headaches he worked unflinchingly throughout the long ordeal, and his help was indispensable.

I am getting a little ahead of the story, because it was understood that as soon as the answer had been drafted we would try to find a chief counsel who would take over the job from me. Our objective was to find not just an able lawyer, experienced in litigation, but a statesman and a patriot, a symbol of all that was highest in the profession, whose representation of Robert before whatever board the Commission might appoint would in itself carry weight with the board, and, if the matter became public, with people at large. In other words, we said to ourselves that we must find "a great man."

When the answer to the letter of charges was finished, I went to such a man: to John W. Davis, the senior member of a leading New York firm who had been Solicitor General of the United States and Ambassador to Great Britain. As a fledgling lawyer I had campaigned for him for President in 1924, and I had long looked up to him as an advocate of incomparable ability and as a man of courage and honor.

He was by now old and frail, but his intellectual powers were as vigorous as ever. He read the letter of charges and Robert's answer, and without hesitation said that he would be willing to serve as chief counsel, provided I would help him, which of course I would be glad to do, and provided that the hearings could be held in New York City. He explained that physically he did not feel up to shuttling between New York and Washington or to any protracted stay in that city. He authorized me to tell the Commission that he would be glad to represent Robert if the hearings could be shifted to New York.

I then called the Commission in the hope of making such an arrangement. My recollection is that I talked directly with Lewis Strauss, although it may have been with General Nichols. In any event, I received word very shortly, I think the next day, that the hearings would have to be held in Washington because of the need of having ready accessibility to various files, etc. The answer was quite explicit, and there was nothing to be done about it.

My visit to Mr. Davis, however, turned out not to have been completely fruitless, for later on he was to join me in the brief which we presented to the Commission after the Gray Board's adverse majority report.

I then talked with two other eminent members of the Bar. Neither was willing to undertake the case. We canvassed a number of other names without agreeing upon anyone who quite filled our needs. Meanwhile the hearings were drawing near, and I became more and more occupied in interviewing potential witnesses with whom Robert had worked both in and out of government.

This was a very time-consuming process—the list was long—and as the hearings approached, we finally decided that the search for a chief counsel had better be dropped and that I should act in that capacity. While the final responsibility for the conduct of the case was to be mine, it was understood that so far as possible we were to function as a team. This we were able to do, and the harmonious relationship which we established survived all strains.

II. THE QUESTION OF SECURITY CLEARANCE FOR COUNSEL

At that first meeting I had with Messrs. Strauss, Nichols and Mitchell—in Washington on January 18, described above—they thought it possible, if not likely, that some classified documents might be discussed in the case and that some of the testimony might touch upon classified subjects. They told me that they would undertake to expedite clearance for me if I so desired. I accepted their proposal but explained that Herbert Marks would be associated with me in the case and that my relationship with him would be so close that I would wish clearance to be extended to him also. Two days after the conference, when my partner Samuel J. Silverman had been brought into the case, I wrote to General Nichols asking that he, too, be included. Clearance required the filling out of elaborate questionnaires and a field investigation by the security officers.

On January 27, in his letter confirming the extension of time to answer, General Nichols declined my request to grant clearance to Messrs. Marks and Silverman. He wrote:

Although it is not our practice to grant security clearance for attorneys to represent individuals in personnel security cases, on the basis of your representation that you and Dr. Oppenheimer feel that it is essential that you have access to "restricted data," we are prepared to process your papers for a limited clearance for the purposes of this case as soon as we receive the Personnel Security Questionnaire which we furnished you on January 18, 1954. We do not feel, however, that the granting of clearance to additional counsel would be warranted. Your associates may, of course, participate fully in unclassified aspects of the case.

On January 29 I telegraphed General Nichols as follows:

YOUR LIMITATION OF CLEARANCE TO ME RAISES SUCH SERIOUS QUESTIONS CONCERNING THE EFFECTIVE CONDUCT OF THE CASE AND YOUR REFERENCE TO QUOTE LIMITED CLEARANCE UNQUOTE MAY RAISE SUCH SERIOUS QUESTIONS AS TO THE SCOPE OF ACCESS INTENDED THAT I REQUEST EARLIEST POSSIBLE MEETING WITH YOURSELF CHAIRMAN AND GENERAL COUNSEL OF COMMISSION TO DISCUSS THESE PROBLEMS. AM TELEPHONING YOU TO MAKE ARRANGEMENTS FOR SUCH CONFERENCE.

The requested conference was held on February 1, and was attended by Messrs. Strauss, Nichols, Mitchell, Marks and myself, and the Commission's security officer, Mr. Beckerley. My best recollection of the discussion was that the Commission regarded clearance of even one lawyer as exceptional, and that, while they would give consideration to the possibility of clearing two additional lawyers, the probabilities were very much against it.

We then went back to New York and discussed the whole question in further depth. We felt that unless all three of us were given clearance, none of us should be. The scope of the case was so great that we would be working constantly together, and it would be impractical for one of us to be privy to documents and testimony whose nature he would have to conceal from the others.

We then gave further consideration to the implications of obtaining clearance, assuming that the Commission were willing to extend this to each of us. We thought of the possibility that we would deem it necessary at some future time to make the transcript of the hearings public, and that we might find ourselves in insoluble controversies with the Commission over the extent of the classified coverage, particularly in the case of testimony where neat divisions of classified and unclassified could not be made. We also thought that if we had clearance the Personnel Security Board might more readily be drawn into an examination of the technical pros and cons of proceeding with the H-bomb development and with other aspects of defense related to it, and thereby lose the main point, which was that if Dr. Oppenheimer's motives were honorable, his recommendations were irrelevant.

In addition to these difficulties, there were others of a procedural nature which argued against clearance. I set these forth in the following letter to Chairman Strauss dated February 3, explaining why we had concluded not to seek clearance:

DEAR MR. STRAUSS:

First let me thank you for the time and consideration which you and your associates—General Nichols, Mr. Mitchell and Mr. Beckerley—gave to the questions of procedure raised by Mr. Marks and myself at our conference on February 1st.

As a result of that conference, and in the light of our present understanding of the facts, we have concluded to present Dr. Oppenheimer's case as best we can on the basis of unclassified evidence. The proposed restriction of clearance to one attorney would, as I explained at the conference, prove unworkable in view of the magnitude of the case and the necessity for an intimate working relationship among counsel. Even if the privilege were broadened to include more than one attorney—as you indicated might possibly be permitted upon reconsideration of the matter—the delays incident to clearance by the regular process of full field investigation would impair the usefulness of clearance when it was finally granted. Your readiness to try to expedite this process is much appreciated, but it is evident that at best clearance would come too late to be of much use in the preparation of the answer, and the period when clearance was still pending might well run into the midst of the hearings, or beyond. Because of these uncertainties, the initial preparation of the case on a nonclassified basis becomes essential whether clearance is sought or not.

The privilege of clearance would be weakened not merely by the uncertainty of the time of its granting, but by the Commission's reservation (as you described it to us) of the right to decide what documents were relevant and what portions thereof counsel might examine. Finally, though clearance were granted, it would not, as you have described the rules to us, carry with it the privilege which is perhaps the most important of all, namely, that of knowing the facts in the possession of the Personnel Security Board which will be used in the Board's final judgment of Dr. Oppenheimer's case.

For all these reasons we have concluded to go forward now without asking for clearance. As I indicated at our conference, I had hoped that in a case of this sort the client might be permitted at the outset to discuss freely all aspects of the matter with his counsel, and that by special action cutting across the involved procedures of field investigation the Commission would accord to counsel the right of access to documents believed by him and his client to be relevant. I do not, however, wish to reargue these points. I fully appreciate the Commission's heavy responsibilities for the maintenance of security; and in submitting to you the considerations which have moved me as counsel anxious to present on behalf of my client all the facts pertinent to his defense, I have had no thought of calling in question those responsibilities or of urging upon the Commission a procedure inconsistent with the national interest.

To present Dr. Oppenheimer's case on a nonclassified basis as fairly as possible under the circumstances, we shall need—and I am sure we can count on—the Commission's cooperation in declassifying whatever relevant material can properly be declassified, and in formulating statements to be stipulated, or questions to be put to witnesses, upon possibly delicate points, in such a way as not to trench upon security. I shall be in touch with you shortly, and from time to time, upon these matters. Meanwhile, I understand you hope to be able to declassify the greatly needed General Advisory Committee Report of 1949, minus certain deletions of a technical character, and that you should be able to give me word of this within a day or so.

With many thanks to you and your associates for your courtesies to us, I am

LLOYD K. GARRISON

On February 12 I received from General Nichols a reply to the above letter, reading as follows:

DEAR MR. GARRISON:

This is in reply to your letter of February 3, 1954, to the Chairman, relative to the clearance case of Dr. J. Robert Oppenheimer, in which you advised of your decision to proceed in this case on an unclassified basis.

The letter of specifications which was delivered to Dr. Oppenheimer advised him of the issues which may be involved at the hearing. The question of whether or not you request clearance in connection with your representation of Dr. Oppenheimer on these

issues is, of course, one for you to decide. I should like to remind
you, however, that we have been willing to expedite the process
to the extent possible. As we pointed out on January 18th and at
the conference of February 1st, we do not anticipate delay in the
granting of your clearance upon receipt of your personnel security
questionnaire. Insofar as your associates are concerned, as we have
told you, we were willing to consider the question of their clearance
upon the basis of your representations that additional clearances
might be necessary. We are still ready to expedite processing your
clearance, if you feel such action is required to prepare Dr. Oppenheimer's case, and to consider the question of processing your two
associates as well, if you should decide to make such a request.

We have also indicated to you our willingness to make available
to you, insofar as our other responsibilities permit us to do so, documents which you reasonably believe are relevant to the matters in
issue. You will appreciate, however, that the Commission must, in
fulfillment of its responsibilities for the maintenance of the common defense and security, reserve the right to decide whether particular documents to which you request access are relevant and
whether your access to such documents, or parts thereof, would
be consistent with the national interest.

Your decision to present Dr. Oppenheimer's case on the basis of
your being uncleared does not, of course, preclude classified testimony by Dr. Oppenheimer or his witnesses before the Board, on
the understanding that uncleared individuals will be excluded from
the hearing during any such testimony and will not otherwise have
access to classified information.

We will also be glad to cooperate with you in an effort to formulate statements to be stipulated in areas involving sensitive information, so as not to jeopardize security.

We are currently reviewing the General Advisory Committee
Minutes of 1949 and our review to date already indicates that it
probably will be impracticable to declassify sufficiently the content
of these minutes to give you a full sense of the actual language
used. Even with the removal of technical data they would still have
security implications that require classification from a national security point of view. The retention of security classification suggests
that you may wish to reconsider your decision concerning whether
or not you wish to be cleared.

We adhered to our prior decision, and we proceeded to prepare
the case on an unclassified basis. Nothing in Robert's answer to the
charges touched upon, or needed to touch upon, any technical matters

relating to the H-bomb program, or upon anything which could not properly have been made public. In our private discussions with him, of course, we did not inquire into any such matters, nor in answering the charges did it ever seem necessary, either to him or to us, to go into classified areas in order to present his case fully and fairly.

We had, of course, to face the sobering contingency that since the Commission was not willing to tell us in advance of the documents they might use in the hearings, or the nature of the testimony they might seek to adduce, we might be confronted with classified matter which would necessitate our exclusion from the hearings while the material was under discussion, with Robert being left unrepresented and alone. The decision which we had made to risk this contingency in view of the other considerations described above was not an easy one. Some of us had more doubts about its wisdom than others.

As April 12, 1954, the date of the commencement of the hearings, drew nearer, anxiety on this score began to trouble me more and more, to the point where finally on March 26 I wrote to General Nichols requesting clearance for myself, enclosing my completed security questionnaire and asking maximum expedition. I did not renew my earlier requests for clearance for my associates, lest this should result in further controversy and delays. I looked upon the request for my own clearance as a precautionary measure to ensure that at all times there would at least be one person who could be at Robert's side. As to the desirability of making this request, my associates and I were divided; it was one of the few occasions in the course of the proceedings in which we were not all of a like mind.

General Nichols wrote me on March 29 that if I had submitted my security questionnaire in January "it probably would have been possible to have completed the processing by this time. We are processing your clearance as expeditiously as possible, but, under the circumstances, we cannot postpone the hearings." The processing was not, in fact, completed before the hearings ended. But no harm was done. On one occasion during the hearings we were excluded to permit Mr. Dean, former Chairman of the AEC, to answer a question which involved a classified topic, but when we were called back, Mr. Gray informed us that "nothing transpired of consequence in absence of counsel," and the other members of the board concurred (Tr. 316).*
I think that there were one or two other similar instances; I recall Robert indicating to us afterward, without describing what had taken place, that the matters under discussion did not in his view affect the

* Page number of the Gray Board hearing transcript.—P.M.S.

substance of the case. Nothing in the opinion of the Gray Board or the Commission suggested anything to the contrary.

I should quickly add that even if one or more of us had been cleared for the inspection of classified military documents, we would not have been permitted to examine the FBI reports in the Commission's possession. It was made clear to us at the outset that these were to be kept from us. As the case developed, the importance of the FBI reports loomed large, as I shall explain in Section VIII (A) below.

## III. PREPARATIONS FOR DEFENDING THE CASE

In the preparation of the answer to the AEC's charges, our basic effort was to reconstruct Robert's career, and his evolving political orientation, in order to give a picture of "the whole man" and to place in the perspective of history, and in the ambit of surrounding circumstances, the acts enumerated in the letter of charges.

We relied upon the following statement by the Atomic Energy Commission of its policy in security proceedings:

Associations of course have a probative value in determining whether an individual is a good or bad security risk. But it must be recognized that *it is the man himself the Commission is actually concerned with, that the associations are only evidentiary, and that common sense must be exercised in judging their significance.* [Emphasis added.]*

We felt that Robert's fate would depend chiefly on our ability to persuade the Commission to adhere to that criterion of judgment. Given the temper of the times, there was grave danger that particular items in the catalogue of the Commission's charges would be wrested out of context and judged in isolation, without regard to the time when they occurred, the prevailing circumstances, the development of Robert's outlook, the achievements he was to render to his country and the whole course of his life.

In keeping with our effort to put things in perspective, Robert's answer to the charges went extensively into the unfolding of his thought over the years and the nature and development of his intellectual and social activities. Most of what he had to say was drawn from his own recollections. So far as I can remember, while our work may perhaps have been slowed up by the absence of the files which the Commission had taken from Princeton, we had no serious difficulty

* From the "Memorandum of Decision Regarding Dr. F. P. Graham," dated December 18, 1948.

in establishing the essential outlines of Robert's story. We received helpful information and advice from Marks and also from Joseph Volpe, a Washington attorney, who had been Deputy General Counsel to the Atomic Energy Commission, and then General Counsel preceding Marks, and who, like Marks, believed wholeheartedly in Robert's cause. The chief significance of the absence of the files, and the Commission's unwillingness to let us see them, was that we never knew what there might be in them of a derogatory character which could have been rebutted, or of a helpful character which could have been utilized. Robert's memory was naturally not equal to the task of reconstructing all that had gone into the files.

While the preparation of the answer involved a thoroughgoing collaboration between client and counsel, the language of the answer in its final form was Robert's, as befitted a document so intensely personal.

The other main task of preparation consisted of talking with all sorts of people, chiefly scientists and former government officials of one sort or another, who had worked with Robert in the past. I have referred to the long list of witnesses who volunteered to testify on Robert's behalf; in each instance they were shown the letter of charges and Robert's answer, and remained unshaken in their conviction of his loyalty and patriotism. We also succeeded in interviewing all of the men (omitting Admiral Strauss) who had been members of the Atomic Energy Commission in 1947 at the time of Robert's earlier clearance, in our effort to reconstruct the procedure which had been followed and the study which the Commissioners had given to the so-called derogatory material in Robert's file. I shall say more about this later.

The work of interviewing continued even after the hearings had begun. From the start to the finish we were under the heaviest time pressures, and some of the interviewing took place late at night and in the early mornings. Altogether thirty witnesses appeared and testified pursuant to our invitation. In the case of each witness we offered to pay his hotel and travel expense. With but two exceptions, all insisted on bearing the expenses themselves in order to relieve Robert of this additional burden. Nevertheless, his total out-of-pocket expenses exceeded $25,000, including the cost of transcripts of the testimony, printed briefs, disbursements and travel of counsel, etc. As previously stated, my firm served without a fee. He was much touched by the unsolicited contributions which hundreds of people whom he did not know sent in from all parts of the country. The total in dollars was not large, but the generosity of spirit meant more to him than money.

Mr. Stern has asked me several questions about Dr. Teller, whom I interviewed but did not call as a witness. At my request he came to see me in my law office, not very long before the hearings were to begin. He was reluctant to come, and insisted on seeing me alone. I asked him about his associations with Robert and his opinion of Robert's loyalty. His feelings toward Robert were not warm, but he did not challenge his loyalty. He expressed lack of confidence in Robert's wisdom and judgment and for that reason felt that the government would be better off without him. His feelings on this subject and his dislike of Robert were so intense that I finally concluded not to call him as a witness. I do not recall his indicating to me that he would be seeing Mr. Robb, who was later to call him as a witness. In any event, when Dr. Teller did take the stand, his testimony did not depart in any substantial respect from what he had said to me in our interview.

Very early in the case—sometime during the first two weeks of preparation of the answer, when I was shuttling back and forth between New York and Princeton—Scotty Reston of the *New York Times* came to see me at my apartment and told me he had heard about the letter of charges.* Subsequently, Joe Alsop of the New York *Herald Tribune* also learned about it. To the credit of these papers, they decided in fairness to Dr. Oppenheimer and in the public interest not to print the story unless the news should become public or unless there was clear evidence that the story was about to break. We were of course hoping that the existence of the security proceeding might not get out into the press and that Robert might be cleared without the damage to his reputation which publicity would cause.

Reston suggested to me that if we would let him have in strict confidence a copy of the charges and of Robert's proposed answer, as soon as the answer had been put into shape, he would prepare a story about the case together with the full text of the documents, holding the script against the day, if it should come, when the secret could no longer be kept.

We were acutely conscious of the fact that if the charges should

* He did not reveal to me the source of his information. Mr. Stern has asked me whether Reston had learned about the charges in a conversation with Dr. Oppenheimer on a New York–Washington plane trip when they had sat next to each other. I do not recall having heard anything to that effect, and Reston has recently told me, when I asked him about it, that Robert had said nothing to him about the charges, and that he had learned about them from another source.

leak out without the answer, they would create a very damaging impression, and that the release of the answer by us—if it was then ready —might come too late to offset that impression. The arrangement which Reston proposed would leave the timing to us, in the first instance at least; if our own reading of the situation was that the news was about to break, we would authorize the *Times* to release its story, which would then be immediately published with the text of the documents. Reston in turn would keep us informed of developments as he learned about them. If the story broke prematurely, the *Times* would, of course, immediately print its story.

I talked over Reston's suggestion with Robert and my associates. We felt that it was the right, and indeed the only prudent, way in which to proceed. The one question left open was whether, if it became necessary for us to release the charges and Robert's answer, we should give the story to the *Times* exclusively or make a simultaneous release to the other papers. Reston, of course, hoped for an exclusive story, but he did not insist upon it. If he were given the charges and the proposed answer in advance of anyone else and could get everything prepared, then even when the documents were released to all the papers, the *Times* story would be far more complete, and more thoroughly and intelligently worked out, than any of the others. In the end, but only after a good deal of vacillating which went on until the very morning when the hearings were to begin, we decided that the story should be released exclusively through the *Times*.

As the day of the hearings approached, the probability of a leak became stronger and stronger. During the previous two weeks or so, hints had been thrown out by certain columnists that revelations regarding the Communist affiliations of a leading atomic scientist were imminent. Then a few days before the hearings there was a reliable report that Senator McCarthy was slated in the near future to make a major speech in Texas (I have forgotten the exact date of the speech) and that in it he would make detailed charges about an atomic scientist, high in the government, and would accuse him of espionage. All signs indicated that at any moment the news would leak out, and some of us felt that we should release the documents immediately. But in courtesy to the Gray Board I wanted to give them at least a day's notice, and I was reluctant to try to explain the situation to them over the telephone.

At the commencement of the hearings, on the morning of April 12, I told the board that we might within a matter of hours deem it necessary to release the documents. This was our first meeting with the board members, and also with Mr. Robb, the Commission's special counsel, of whose designation by the Commission (Tr. 807) we had not known. The Commission had informed us some two weeks earlier of the board's appointment, about which we had not been consulted.

The board was visibly upset by what I had to say about the imminence of a release. I tried to explain why in fairness to Dr. Oppenheimer we felt we had no other choice.* The release itself—the go-ahead to Reston—was authorized during the lunch hour that day, for publication the next morning. Reston had told us then that it would be impossible to wait any longer, that the news was about to break at any moment. Fortunately the news held until the *Times* story appeared. Later, when McCarthy came to make his speech in Texas, he turned to other subjects.

IV. SURVEILLANCE AND RELATED QUESTIONS

During Dr. Oppenheimer's directorship of the Los Alamos project he had been made aware of the surveillance apparatus which permeated the whole enterprise, and he assumed that during his top-secret work as a government adviser after the war similar precautions prevailed. He took it for granted that when he went abroad with his wife in 1953, his movements were shadowed, and that when he and his wife spent a social dinner evening with the Chevaliers in Paris, the government would know of it, as they did.

From the beginning of our work on the case, we conducted ourselves on the supposition that our telephone wires would be tapped, and, when the hearings began, that listening devices would be concealed in the room assigned to us for work, next to the hearing room. I do not know whether these things occurred, but we felt that the risk was such that we should act as if surveillance were a reality.

When we went to Washington with the Oppenheimers the night before the hearings, we all stayed at a hotel, but the next night the Oppenheimers quietly moved into my partner Randolph Paul's house in Georgetown as guests of the Pauls, and there they stayed throughout the hearings. We used the office provided for us by the government next to the hearing room only for secretarial work and to make notes from transcripts; the Pauls' house was the real center of our work. In the hope of maintaining privacy, the board arranged for us to leave and arrive at the hearings by way of a back entrance; some attempts were made to follow us, but it took the press about a week to discover where we were staying. I must say that once the discovery

---

* My statement was off the record, and does not appear in the transcript of the formal proceedings, but further discussion the next day appears at TR. 54, 55.

was made, and after a little buttonholing, the press were very good about leaving us alone.

## V. EVENTS FROM THE CLOSE OF THE HEARINGS TO THE PUBLIC RELEASE OF THE GRAY BOARD'S REPORT

The hearings closed on May 6, 1954. We immediately went to work on a brief containing a detailed analysis of the testimony. I delivered it personally to the board in Washington on May 18. It was in type-written form and was signed by myself, Marks and Silverman. Later, on May 25, I sent printed copies of the brief to the members of the board.

Three days later, on May 28, General Nichols wrote a letter to Dr. Oppenheimer informing him of the adverse findings and recommendations contained in the report of the Gray Board and giving him until June 7 to request a review by the Commission's Personnel Security Review Board. The letter enclosed a copy of the Gray Board report. Mr. Mitchell, the Commission's General Counsel, called me in New York and told me the news, and copies of the letter and the report were delivered to Herbert Marks in Washington. That evening Herbert came to New York, and the next day we met with Dr. Oppenheimer in my office, went over the report and discussed what to do about it.

We were, of course, deeply distressed by the outcome. Mr. Stern has asked whether we expected it. I think the most accurate answer is that we had felt from the beginning that we faced an uphill fight, especially in the adverse climate of the times, but that we still hoped for the best.

In going over the report we took some comfort from Dr. Evans' dissent and from the vigor with which the board had affirmed Robert's loyalty. We concluded to dispense with the intermediate step of an appeal to the Review Board and to appeal directly to the Commission itself. We also concluded to ask for leave to file a brief with the Commission by June 7, the date specified by the Commission for requesting a review, as noted above. This would give us very little time, but not knowing how soon the Commission would act we felt it essential to present our analysis as soon as possible.

On June 1 I wrote General Nichols a letter setting forth these requests, which he granted on June 3. My letter contained a preliminary critique of the Gray Board report. It was a long letter, and it presented the major arguments which we were later to incorporate into the brief. John W. Davis joined in this letter. I have previously described how Mr. Davis had been prepared, after considering the letter of charges and Robert's answer, to act as chief counsel if the hearings could be held in New York City. After the Commission had ruled out this possibility I had kept Mr. Davis informed about the case and had given him a copy of the brief we had submitted to the Gray Board. He had read this with care, and after going over my proposed letter to General Nichols of June 1 he approved it and authorized me to tell General Nichols that he was joining in it. This I did, and I also told General Nichols that we would make the documents public—his letter to Robert of May 28 transmitting the Gray Board's report, the full text of the report and my reply of June 1. That evening (June 1) we gave these documents to the press.

Mr. Stern had asked whether we told the Gray Board what we were about to do. We did not. There was no reason for doing so. Their labors had been completed, and the case was now in the hands of the Commission.

Mr. Stern has also asked why we made the documents public, especially in view of my statement to the Commission on the second day of the hearings that "it is not our purpose to make any press comments upon this case," and that we did not intend to try the case in the press (Tr. 55). We adhered to this policy throughout the proceedings. We made no press comments, and we did not release the transcript. Like the original letter of charges, however, we concluded that the fact of the Gray Board's adverse decision would inevitably become public, and that, just as the letter of charges had been offset by the simultaneous publication of Robert's answer, so the simultaneous publication of the board's report and our critique of it would be essential for a fair understanding of the case. My letter of June 1 was hurriedly written for that purpose. We could not afford to wait for the completion of our appellate brief to the Commission, since the news of the decision might break prematurely.

I have no apology to make for the publication of these basic and offsetting documents. Our overriding responsibility was to preserve, so far as we could, Dr. Oppenheimer's reputation; and though the publication of the charges and the Gray Board report did him much damage, the damage would have been far greater if these documents had leaked out without the offsetting material that accompanied them.

In making the Gray Board report public, my associate, Mr. Ecker, drew to the attention of the press the page references in the report to Dr. Oppenheimer's "deep devotion to his country," his "loyalty" and his "high degree of discretion" in keeping secrets. These references were also contained in my accompanying letter of June 1 to General Nichols, but in view of the length of that letter and the time pressures afflicting the press, we wished to make sure that these all-important conclusions of the board were not overlooked.

When our brief to the Commission was finished, Mr. Davis went over it and signed it "of counsel." His support was a great tonic for all of us. The other signers were Messrs. Marks, Silverman, Ecker and myself. We filed it on June 7, as arranged.

We did not at that time publish the brief, or our earlier brief to the Gray Board. The Gray Board brief was now outdated in view of the board's report, and since we still clung to the hope that the Commission would act favorably on our appeal, we did not think it would be either fitting or wise to publish our brief to the Commission. Moreover, both briefs contained extracts from, and numerous references to, the transcript of the testimony, which had not yet been published; this seemed to us an additional reason why publication of the briefs would be inappropriate.

VI. PUBLICATION OF THE TRANSCRIPT AND THE BRIEFS

At the opening of the hearings the chairman of the Gray Board stated:

> The proceedings and stenographic record of this board are regarded as strictly confidential between Atomic Energy Commission officials participating in this matter and Dr. Oppenheimer, his representatives and witnesses. The Atomic Energy Commission will not take the initiative in public release of any information relating to the proceeding before this board. [Tr. 20.]

The chairman gave a similar admonition to most of the witnesses, adding in each case that the board hoped that the witnesses would likewise not initiate public releases (e.g.: Tr. 300, 323, 340 *et seq.*).

For our part, I stated to the board on the second day of the hearings that "It is not our purpose to release any transcripts" (Tr. 55).

And we did not do so.

Sometime in early June while our appeal was pending before the Commission—I cannot fix the precise date—Mr. Reston called me from the *New York Times*. He said he had heard that the Commission was going to publish the transcript. He hoped we would make it immediately available to him. His plan was to publish it in installments, with accompanying stories which would put things in their proper perspective. After some discussion among ourselves and with Robert, we declined his request for reasons I shall state later.

Soon after this I received telephone calls from several of the witnesses who had testified for Robert, saying that they had been called up by the Commission and asked whether they would have any personal objection to the release of their testimony. They had replied in substance that while the publication would be distasteful to them, they did not see how they could raise any formal objection to it; they wished, however, to make sure that we knew what was happening.

I do not know whether all our witnesses were thus reached. In any event, within a few days after these calls, Mr. Mitchell, the Commission's counsel, telephoned me at noon on June 15 that the Commission had printed the full text of the transcript and would distribute copies to the press at six o'clock that afternoon for release at noon the next day. He wrote me the same day, enclosing a copy and saying that it conformed to our copy except for a few deletions requested by the classification officer and some corrections. He also enclosed a copy of the formal statement which the Commission had given the press when it distributed the transcript. He did not tell us, and we did not learn until later, that the Commission had also distributed to the press a memorandum highlighting the Chevalier incident and drawing attention to the pages in the transcript containing Robert's admissions that his story about it to the security officers in 1943 had been a "tissue of lies."

Thus this incident of eleven years earlier was wrested out of context and played up as if it were the decisive factor in the case, without any reference to the fact that it was Robert himself who had told the security officers about the approach to Chevalier and the name of the person who had made the approach; that General Groves and Colonel Lansdale, who knew all about the incident, were satisfied that Robert's motivation had been an ill-judged attempt to shield his friend Chevalier, whom he believed innocent; that in the eleven years that had passed since that incident Robert had rendered enormous services to his country; and that men of the highest public stature, who had worked with Robert on top-level government undertakings through the years, had with full knowledge of the Chevalier incident come forward and testified to their faith in Robert's loyalty and patriotism. All these aspects of the case were left out of the picture, nor was any reference made to the fact that this same incident was part of Robert's file which the members of the Atomic Energy Commission had before them and had studied in 1947, when they continued Robert's clearance.

Of course, the press might have ascertained these facts from an analysis of the whole transcript, but many days of labor would have been required to accomplish this, and the press had to get its story out in a hurry.

It may be that the Commission equated its promptings to the press with our earlier release of the Gray Board report, at which time, as I have previously noted, Mr. Ecker gave the press page references in the report to the board's affirmation of Dr. Oppenheimer's loyalty and patriotism. But the two cases were not analogous. We had sought merely, as a matter of simple justice to Robert, to make sure that in announcing the adverse decision the press would be aware of the off-setting portions of the board's report. In the case of the Commission's release of the 992-page transcript and its highlighting of the Chevalier incident, alone among all the matters contained in that vast compilation, the purpose was not to assure a balanced consideration but the exact opposite.

Had we anticipated the way in which the Commission was to present the transcript to the public, we might have published it first ourselves, through Mr. Reston. Mr. Stern has asked me whether, as Reston had indicated to him, Robert had favored the acceptance of Reston's proposal. It may be so, but I have no such recollection of my own. Our decision not to publish was based on several considerations. As stated above, we had at the outset assured the Commission, which had given similar assurances to us and to our witnesses, that we did not intend to release the transcript. The case was now pending on appeal before the Commission. Premature publication might lead to hurried and ill-digested commentaries—like those which were to ensue upon the Commission's singling out of the Chevalier incident for the press. Moreover, we still had to entertain the possibility, however unlikely it might be, that the Commission would find in Robert's favor, and if we were to publish the transcript in advance of the decision, we might disturb the Commission and perhaps prejudice the outcome.

For all these reasons we concluded not to accept Mr. Reston's proposal.

After the Commission had published the transcript, and in the hope of offsetting the damage, we released our two briefs (the one to the Gray Board and the one to the Commission) together with my letter of June 9 to General Nichols containing criticisms of the procedure.* But the press paid no attention to them. The Commission's dramatization of the Chevalier incident crowded out all else.

VII. THE COMMISSION'S DECISION AND ITS AFTERMATH

On June 28 Congressman Robert L. Condon wrote me that all members of Congress had received copies of the printed transcript from the Commission.

* This letter is described in Section VIII (H) below.

On June 29 General Nichols wrote Dr. Oppenheimer, enclosing a copy of the decision. He must at the same time have delivered a copy to Herbert Marks in Washington, for my diary speaks of a conference that day with Dr. Oppenheimer and Messrs. Marks and Silverman, and of a brief statement to the press by Dr. Oppenheimer.

Next morning, June 30, the text of the Commissioners' decision and accompanying opinions appeared in full in the *New York Times*. We met again that day, this time with Mrs. Oppenheimer as well as her husband. It was a painful occasion. In view of the way the Commission had presented the transcript to the public, we had expected an adverse decision, but we were not prepared for what seemed to us the one-sided and savage character of the majority opinion. The question now was what, if anything, could be done.

For the reasons stated in Section VIII below we had concluded, very early in the proceedings, that an appeal to the court in the event of an adverse decision would be fruitless, and we were still of that view. Moreover, Robert's term of office as a consultant to the Commission was about to expire that very day, and the Commission of course would not renew it. The case for a restoration of his clearance would then become moot, and the basis for a court appeal would disappear.

We next considered the possibility of an appeal to the President, but he clearly had no power to reverse a decision of the Commission. Even if he were willing to step in, the most he could do would be to state his own personal view of the matter, and it seemed to us unthinkable that he would undertake to substitute his judgment for that of the combined judgments of the Gray Board and the Commission. He could not possibly devote time to an analysis of the case; he would have to farm the work out to someone else and then arrive at a conclusion based on the new set of recommendations. It seemed to us that the necessities of government would compel a statement upholding the Commission, whatever the merits might be, and that this would simply compound the injury already suffered by Dr. Oppenheimer.

So we dropped the idea of an appeal to him, and when some days later at a press conference (without any communication with us) he indicated that Dr. Oppenheimer could appeal to him if he wished, we did not act on the suggestion.

We then considered by what other means we could present Robert's case to the public. Commissioner Smyth had written an able and eloquent dissenting opinion, and for us to do a more detailed analysis, including a critique of the Commission's procedure (which Commissioner Smyth had not attempted), would be a long and laborious task. By the time of its completion interest in the case would have waned; the publication of such a document would not be likely to attract much interest, and would be heavily discounted as the partisan work of disappointed counsel.

Still, we could think of nothing better and so we said we would try our hand at it, knowing full well that nothing we could ever write would undo the damage done to the Oppenheimers. And then, with heavy hearts, we parted.

In the course of the summer I toiled at the analysis, and my partner Sam Silverman did some work on the procedural aspects of the case, but, as I said earlier, other matters began to press upon us and in the upshot we were too weary and discouraged to continue.

So our professional relationship with Robert dwindled to its melancholy end. There remained a lasting friendship, and it is partly because of that that I have undertaken, in answering Mr. Stern's questions, some portion of the unfinished task described above.

VIII. CRITIQUE OF THE COMMISSION'S PROCEDURE

The most serious aspect of the procedure was the withholding from Dr. Oppenheimer and his counsel of innumerable documents which the Gray Board (and, on appeal, the Commission) had before them in their deliberations. The majority opinions of the Gray Board and of the Commission showed that in arriving at their decisions many of these withheld documents—how many we shall never know—had been relied upon. No one can say what the outcome might have been if Dr. Oppenheimer and his counsel had been given access to the withheld documents and had been able to draw attention to those which were favorable, and to challenge and rebut those which were unfavorable.

At the end of the hearings, in my summing up before the Gray Board, I said that I appreciated very much "the fairness which the members of the board have displayed in the conduct of these hearings, and the sincere and intense effort which I know you have been making and will make to come to a just understanding of the issues" (Tr. 972).

At the time those words were sincerely spoken, but they related to the members of the Gray Board as individuals, and not to the procedure which the Commission had prescribed. Now for the first time, in order to reply to Mr. Stern's questions, I have had to survey the record as a whole and to consider with a fresh eye its prejudicial features.

## A. *The Unavailability of FBI Reports and Other Material*

In its report for July, 1948, on page 53, the Atomic Energy Commission expressed its desire to afford its employees an opportunity in investigative hearings to "confront and cross-examine persons who have furnished information unfavorable to them." The Commission noted that FBI reports would be "the primary source" of such information. The Commission then went on to say that there would be "some cases in which important information comes from a source which the FBI has designated as confidential and which, therefore, the Commission may not properly disclose." The Commission recognized that in such a case the employee would not be able to "confront and cross-examine the person who supplied the information." The Commission hoped, however, that it would be possible "to keep these situations to a minimum, and that the sources of significant information bearing on the case can be available at a local board hearing."

Whatever may have been the practice in 1948, we were informed before and during the hearings that the inflexible rule was not to reveal either the source or the text of any of the FBI reports. This rule had nothing to do with the fact that, for the reasons I have previously stated, counsel for Dr. Oppenheimer had elected not to seek clearance. Clearance would have allowed access to classified documents of a military nature, but not to reports by FBI agents containing so-called "derogatory information." As Mr. Robb said flatly, "Of course, as the chairman has said, the FBI reports under the rules of these hearings may not be made available to counsel for Dr. Oppenheimer or Dr. Oppenheimer" (Tr. 807).

The charges against Dr. Oppenheimer were couched in the briefest terms and did not set forth the actual language of the reports; they were mere shorthand paraphrases of documents which were never to be revealed. Even if the identity of each informant had been suppressed, the language of what was reported, if it had been set forth, might have afforded counsel at least some opportunity to inquire into its meaning. But the rules were adamant. As will be described in Section E below, we were refused even an enumeration of which of the derogatory items in the current charges were before the Commission in 1947 when the Commission cleared Dr. Oppenheimer—refused because of the rule of nondisclosure of FBI reports.

While most of the so-called "derogatory information" in the files presumably consisted of FBI reports, as indicated above, there were other documents such as memoranda, minutes, letters, etc., which we were not privileged to see, but which were included in the dossier given to each board member.

## B. *The Scope and Importance of the Undisclosed Material*

The Gray Board stated in its opinion:

He [Dr. Oppenheimer] is familiar with the contents of every relevant document which was made available to the board, except those which under Governmental necessity cannot be disclosed, such as reports of the Federal Bureau of Investigation. [Page 3.]

The exception bulked large indeed. The board stated in its report that it had heard forty witnesses and had compiled over three thousand pages of testimony "in addition to having read the same amount of file material" (page 2). Thus by its own admission, the board had read some three thousand pages of file material, only a tiny fraction of which was made available to us in the course of the hearings. Until the appearance of this statement by the board we had no idea of the magnitude of the undisclosed material.

While the charges relating to the H-bomb program were the subject of extensive testimony by witnesses, the charges relating to "associations" were supported, if at all, exclusively by undisclosed FBI reports. And although it seemed to us that Dr. Oppenheimer (though gravely handicapped by not knowing what the files contained) had rebutted either the accuracy or the sinister connotations, or both, of each of these charges, the findings of the Gray Board supported most of them, avowedly on the basis of the undisclosed file materials.

The Commission, for its part, did not deem it necessary to go into the H-bomb charges, but rested its whole decision on associations and alleged want of "character," most of which, except for the Chevalier incident, was based on the undisclosed material.

## C. *Our Unsuccessful Effort, Prior to the Hearings, to Obtain Clarifying Information Regarding the Charges*

On February 12, 1954, Herbert Marks and I met with Chairman Strauss, General Nichols and the Commission's General Counsel, Mr. Mitchell, and asked for copies of certain documents which would shed light on what we considered to be the two most important aspects of the case: namely, (1) what advice Dr. Oppenheimer had given and what activities he had engaged in with regard to the proposal for developing the H-bomb; and (2) what "derogatory information" the Atomic Energy Commission had had before it in 1947 when it continued Dr. Oppenheimer's clearance after this clearance had been questioned by J. Edgar Hoover. Our basic position was that the Commission had already considered back in 1947, and ought not to be once again considering, the substance of all the charges contained in General Nichols' letter of December 23, 1953, with the exception of Dr. Oppenheimer's attitude toward the H-bomb program, and that as to this there was nothing sinister in what he said or did but that on the contrary he was serving the government ably and in what he believed to be its best interests.

So we first asked for the minutes and reports of the General Advisory Committee which had been chaired by Dr. Oppenheimer and which had to do with defense matters, including the H-bomb program. On February 19, 1954, Mr. Mitchell wrote me denying this request, but stating that Dr. Oppenheimer could go to the Commission's office and read the minutes of the General Advisory Committee meeting in October, 1949, over which he had presided, if he so wished. This was the crucial meeting at which the Committee had advised against a crash program for the development of the H-bomb. Dr. Oppenheimer did not see fit to examine the minutes, partly, no doubt, because the thought of going into the Commission's office with the cloud of charges hanging over him was, to say the least, distasteful, and partly because he expected that the true story of what happened at the meeting would be developed through the testimony and recollections of various members of the General Advisory Committee—Dr. Conant, Dr. Fermi, Dr. Rabi, Dr. DuBridge, and Messrs. Buckley and Rowe. They testified at length as to the discussions in the October, 1949, meeting and as to the views they held about the H-bomb and why they opposed its development; their testimony amply supported Dr. Oppenheimer's. In the upshot, therefore, the absence of the minutes may not have been a serious handicap.

We also asked for a copy of Dr. Oppenheimer's testimony before the Joint Congressional Committee on Atomic Energy, which related to action taken by the General Advisory Committee on the H-bomb program. And, with regard to the AEC's 1947 meeting at which Dr. Oppenheimer's clearance was affirmed, we asked for: (a) an itemization of the charges in J. Edgar Hoover's letter of March, 1947, to David Lilienthal, who was then Chairman of the Commission; (b) the minutes of the meeting at which the Commission acted on the derogatory items; (c) certain letters about Dr. Oppenheimer's loyalty which had been written to the Commission by Secretary of War Patterson, by General Groves and by James Conant and Vannevar Bush;

and (d) certain memoranda of conferences regarding the action to be
taken.

On February 19, 1954, Mr. Mitchell telephoned and wrote me to
say that none of the requested information could be given to us.* He
declined to show us the minutes of the 1947 meeting at which the
Commission had acted on the derogatory items, but gave instead a
stipulation purporting to describe the action taken. But, as later came
out in the hearings (Tr. 677), the stipulation omitted a significant
portion of the action as recorded in the minutes. This will be discussed
below.

At the meeting of February 12, 1954, at which we asked for the
various documents described above, Mr. Marks also presented a list of
nineteen questions asking for clarification of various items in General
Nichols' letter of charges of December 23, 1953. The Commission did
not see fit to answer any of these questions.

## D. *The Gray Board's Preliminary Immersion in the Secret Files*

When the Gray Board was appointed, we were informed that its
members would meet in the Commission's office for a week before the
hearings began to study the FBI reports and other file material, with
the aid of staff. Having been told that we could not have access to the
files, I then asked the Commission for the privilege of meeting with
the board during the week in question to participate with its members
in discussing the substance of what the files contained. I was told that
this was quite impractical. I then asked if I might meet with the
board at the first of its study sessions to give them informally a picture
of the case as we saw it so that the board might at least have that
picture in their minds as they went about their task. I also asked for a
chance to explore with the board at such a session the procedure that
would be followed. These requests were denied.

I said to the Gray Board in my summation that I remembered "a
kind of sinking feeling that I had at that point"—at the thought of the
board's having "a week's immersion in FBI files which we would never
have the privilege of seeing, and of coming to the hearings with that
intense background of study of the derogatory information" (Tr. 971).

I think we all felt that, as a result of the board's prehearing con-

* Subsequently, but only after David Lilienthal testified about them, special counsel for the board introduced the text of the Patterson, Conant and
Bush letters, which we had asked for (Tr. 375–379); he also introduced five
different letters or memoranda by General Groves in cross-examining the latter (Tr. 169, 170, 179). All of these could and should have been shown to us
before the hearings.

centration on the secret dossier, a cloud of suspicion hung over Robert Oppenheimer at the outset which was never quite dissipated in the minds of the majority; even when they became convinced by the testimony that he could not be charged with disloyalty or want of patriotism, we had the impression that an uneasy feeling about him remained which may have been just enough to tip the scales against his clearance.

E. *Obstacles Placed in the Way of a Full Understanding of the Scope and Significance of the AEC's Clearance of Dr. Oppenheimer in 1947*

As has been stated above, on February 12, 1954, we asked the Commission for a copy of the minutes of the meeting of the Atomic Energy Commission on August 6, 1947, at which meeting Robert's clearance was recorded. In a letter to me dated February 19, 1954, the AEC's General Counsel denied the request but stated that:

> The Commission will be prepared to stipulate as follows for purposes of the hearing: "On August 6, 1947, the Commission recorded clearance of Dr. J. Robert Oppenheimer, which it noted had been authorized in February, 1947."

Later in the hearings, when Mr. Robb was cross-examining Mr. Lilienthal, the Commission's Chairman in 1947, he introduced into the record for the purposes of his cross-examination certain documents which we had never been permitted to see and which convinced us that the stipulation quoted above was not in fact a complete account of the action which had been taken. We persuaded the Gray Board to ask the Commission to give us the full text of the relevant portion of the minutes.

The text revealed the fact that the stipulation by the Commission's counsel had been misleading. The relevant portion of the minutes consisted of two sentences reading as follows:

> Mr. Bellsley called the Commission's attention to the fact that the Commission's decision to authorize the clearance of J. R. Oppenheimer, Chairman of the General Advisory Committee, made in February 1947, had not previously been recorded. The Commission directed the Secretary to record the Commission's approval of security clearance in this case *and to note that further reports concerning Dr. Oppenheimer since that date had contained no information which would warrant reconsideration of the Commission's decision.* [Emphasis added.]

From the above it can be seen that the stipulation was a paraphrase of the first sentence of the minutes, and of half—but only half—the second sentence. The omitted half, italicized above, directed the Secretary "to note that further reports concerning Dr. Oppenheimer since that date" (i.e., February, 1947, when the first clearance of Dr. Oppenheimer was voted but not recorded) "had contained no information which would warrant reconsideration of the Commission's decision." The omission of this half of the sentence had left us without any indication of the fact that about a month after the initial clearance in February, 1947, J. Edgar Hoover had transmitted to Chairman Lilienthal copies of summaries of information contained in the FBI files relating to Dr. Oppenheimer and his brother Frank; that this caused the question of clearance to be reopened; that the views of Mr. Hoover, Dr. Bush, Dr. Conant, General Groves and Secretary of War Patterson were sought and obtained; that the Commissioners read Mr. Hoover's summary, met and discussed the case, saw every report in a complete investigative file on Dr. Oppenheimer, and finally, at the meeting of August 6, 1947, reaffirmed the action taken in February and in addition noted that the further reports since that date "had contained," in the language of the omitted portion of the stipulation, "no information which would warrant reconsideration of the Commission's decision." If we had not ourselves questioned very closely the Commissioners who had voted the clearance in 1947, we would never have discovered the above chain of events.

While we were satisfied, upon a close analysis of the testimony, that the facts were as summarized above, the Gray Board chairman toward the close of the hearings expressed doubts as to what really had been before the Commissioners in 1947. He believed that it had consisted of FBI reports, but when I asked not "for a transcript of the reports or a copy of the reports, but simply for a description of what the Commission acted on," special counsel for the Commission objected that this would "fly right in the face of the rule" against disclosure of the contents of the FBI reports. Then when I asked if it would "fly in the face of the rule if we were limited merely to being told which of the items now before the board were before the Commission in 1947?" special counsel indicated that it would, and the chairman of the board sustained his objection (Tr. 808).

## F. *Arbitrary and Prejudicial Use of Withheld Material*

At no point in the proceeding was any material voluntarily offered to us which might have been helpful to Dr. Oppenheimer's case; helpful material was produced only when we demanded it after we had been made aware of its existence accidentally, by some bit of testimony or by some internal evidence in other documents put into the record by the Commission. In addition, documents which had previously been classified were unclassified, in whole or in part during the proceedings, by the Commission's classification officer, when the board's special counsel wished to use them. This naturally raised the question as to how many classified documents in the board's dossier, which might have been helpful to Dr. Oppenheimer, could readily have been declassified and shown to him.

Finally, witnesses produced by us were frequently examined by special counsel for the Commission on the basis of their recollection, without first being permitted to see the contemporaneous documents which would have established the facts; and after they had testified from recollection, only such documents were produced as might seem to contradict them or show their memories to be fallible—as well they might be on points of detail over such long periods of time.

The following are some examples of these techniques.

CROSS-EXAMINATION RELATING TO THE 1947 CLEARANCE OF
DR. OPPENHEIMER BY THE ATOMIC ENERGY COMMISSION

As previously stated, with regard to the 1947 clearance, two points were in issue: namely, how much "derogatory information" the Commission had before it in 1947 and when or how the Commission in fact acted upon it. Cross-examination by special counsel was particularly directed to an effort to show that all the Commission had before it was a "summary" of the FBI file. Mr. Lilienthal, the Chairman of the Commission in 1947, had sought to avail himself of his privilege under the Commission rules to come down in advance of testimony and to examine relevant papers in the Commission files with which he had been concerned during his tenure of office. He was shown some of the papers, but it appeared on his cross-examination that he had been shown only a small part of the relevant documents. And the documents that were shown to him on cross-examination were not produced in chronological order, but in the order which suited special counsel's purpose of demonstrating "that the memory of the witness was not infallible" (Tr. 421).

Specifically, in his cross-examination special counsel introduced four separate documents which we had never seen before, and from the text of which it appeared that there were other related documents that ought to be disclosed. He then at our request read into the record four more documents which we had likewise not seen before. Irked by the confusion thus created, Mr. Lilienthal stated:

Mr. Chairman, may I make this comment, that in the great multiplicity of things that went on at that time, it is not at all impossible that I should not remember even as important a matter as this, but a simple way to secure the truth and accuracy would have been to have given me these files yesterday, when I asked for them, so that when I came here, I could be the best possible witness and disclose as accurately as possible what went on at that time. I am a little confused about the technique. The board wants the facts, and the facts are in the file, and I asked for the file so I could be a better witness, and it was denied me. So I just have to rely on memory during a very troubled and difficult time on matters that are obviously important, but they are not as important as many other things we were concerned with at that time. It would help me a good deal, and I could be a much better witness if I saw the files that I helped to contribute to make. [Tr. 421.]

In the later cross-examination of Dr. Bacher, who had been a member of the Commission in 1947, special counsel introduced an additional document relating to the events in question (Tr. 622) and read into the record still another one at our request (Tr. 611)—neither of which had been produced during the examination of Mr. Lilienthal, who was the principal witness on what had taken place.

### THE SEABORG LETTER

Prior to the meeting on October 29, 1949, of the General Advisory Committee, at which the committee recommended against the initiation of a crash program for the development of an H-bomb, Dr. Conant wrote a letter to Dr. Oppenheimer dated October 21, 1949, which had been taken from Princeton by the AEC after the suspension of Dr. Oppenheimer's clearance. Dr. Conant's letter stated, among other things, that all members of the Advisory Committee would come to the meeting except Dr. Seaborg, "who must be in Sweden and whose general views we have in written form" (Tr. 242).

Dr. Oppenheimer had forgotten the existence and contents of this letter (Tr. 239), and Dr. Conant likewise could not remember it, even after a copy of it had been shown to him by Dr. Oppenheimer's counsel (Tr. 386). Similarly, Dr. Oppenheimer had forgotten, until it was shown to him on cross-examination (Tr. 238), that Dr. Seaborg had written him a letter on October 14, 1949, which the AEC had also taken from Dr. Oppenheimer's files in Princeton. This letter contained some observations about the forthcoming committee meeting. Dr. Seaborg in his letter said that:

I will try to give you my thoughts for what they may be worth regarding the next GAC meeting, but I am afraid that there may be more questions than answers. Mr. Lilienthal's assignment to us is very broad and it seems to me that conclusions will be reached, if at all, only after a large amount of give and take discussion at the GAC meeting. [Tr. 238.]

He then indicated that the question of proceeding with a large-scale thermonuclear program would undoubtedly come up at the meeting; and Dr. Seaborg expressed his feeling that

Although I deplore the prospects of our country putting a tremendous effort into this, I must confess that I have been unable to come to the conclusion that we should not. Some people are thinking of a time scale of the order of 3 to 5 years which may, of course, be practically impossible and would surely involve an effort of greater magnitude than that of the Manhattan project. My present feeling would perhaps be best summarized by saying that I would have to hear some good arguments before I could take on sufficient courage to recommend not going toward such a program.

This appeared to be no more than an expression of tentative views which he might change upon further discussion, and he was certainly not clear as to either the magnitude or the pace of the suggested effort. Although absent at the October 29, 1949, meeting, Dr. Seaborg did attend the next meeting of the General Advisory Committee on December 3, 1949. At that meeting the question of the H-bomb program was further explored at the AEC's request. Dr. Pitzer and General McCormack, advocates of a strong crash program, were present by invitation and spoke their minds; but Dr. Seaborg preferred to take no position on the question (Tr. 239, 604, 703). In view of this, it is quite understandable that Dr. Oppenheimer should have remembered only Dr. Seaborg's nonparticipation and not his earlier and indecisive letter, and that when asked on cross-examination, prior to the introduction of the letter, whether he had received any expression of Dr. Seaborg's views prior to the October 29, 1949, meeting, he should have replied in the negative (Tr. 237).

DR. OPPENHEIMER'S TESTIMONY BEFORE THE JOINT
CONGRESSIONAL COMMITTEE ON ATOMIC ENERGY REGARDING
DR. SEABORG'S VIEWS

Having been confronted with the Seaborg letter, with the implication that Dr. Oppenheimer had deliberately misled the Gray Board, he was next asked why he had told the Joint Congressional Committee on Atomic Energy, when he testified before it on January 29, 1950, that Dr. Seaborg had not expressed himself on the subject prior to the meeting (Tr. 239).

Dr. Oppenheimer said he would "have to see the transcript. I don't remember that question and the answer." We then asked that this portion of the transcript be read into the record, to which special counsel replied that the transcript "will not be released, as I understand it, without a vote of the committee to do so, Mr. Garrison, which is why I was not able to read Dr. Oppenheimer what he said" (Tr. 240).

Dr. Oppenheimer observed that:

> I think a lot depends on the nature of the question. Had Dr. Seaborg made up his mind, had he concurred with your view, or so on. It is clear from this letter he wanted to hear a discussion about it. That he saw it was a very tough question.

We then asked the chairman whether the board had before it the transcript of the Joint Committee testimony. After a recess the chairman stated that the board did not have before it a complete transcript of the testimony under discussion but that:

> However, I can say to Dr. Oppenheimer and his counsel that the board does understand *from a source it believes to be reliable* that Dr. Oppenheimer was asked a question with respect to the extent of unanimity of the views of the members of the GAC with respect to what we have been describing as the crash program. I am not sure whether it was so referred to in the testimony, but there was this question.
>
> In response to the question Dr. Oppenheimer stated that he thought it was [a] pretty unanimous view, that one member of the committee, Dr. Seaborg, was away when the matter was discussed, and that he had not expressed himself on it, and further saying that the other members will agree with what he has said. [Emphasis added.]

If one had kept in mind that this statement to the committee was made several months after the GAC meeting of October and a month after the December meeting, which Dr. Seaborg *had* attended and at which he did *not* express himself on the subject of the H-bomb program, Dr. Oppenheimer's reply to the question—if it had been put in the form which the chairman outlined—would have been unexceptionable.

I have noted this incident for two reasons. First, had we not asked for the production of the Joint Committee minutes, the misleading character of special counsel's question ("Didn't you tell the Joint Committee that Dr. Seaborg had not expressed himself on this subject prior to the meeting of October 29, 1947?") would have stood on the record with the clear implication that this was in fact what Dr. Oppenheimer had told the committee. Second, when we asked for the transcript, we were given only a paraphrase from an unrevealed source, which, while it should have served to negative the implication contained in special counsel's question, was one more illustration of the difficulty put in Dr. Oppenheimer's path in trying to obtain a full disclosure of source material. It should be observed in this connection that special counsel, later on in the proceeding, apparently had no difficulty in obtaining from the Joint Congressional Committee an excerpt from testimony before it which he then introduced in the record in connection with the examination of one of his own witnesses, General Wilson (Tr. 682–683).

The Gray Board in its decision made no reference to the Seaborg letter. The Atomic Energy Commission, however, in its majority decision cited the Seaborg letter and Dr. Oppenheimer's testimony in connection with it as one of the six instances of Dr. Oppenheimer's alleged "want of character."

OTHER USE OF DOCUMENTS ON CROSS-EXAMINATION

Gordon Dean, who had been Chairman of the Atomic Energy Commission in 1949 to 1953, and who had vigorously testified as to Dr. Oppenheimer's loyalty, was asked on cross-examination a number of questions about the opposition of the General Advisory Committee in the fall of 1951 to the establishment of a second laboratory along the lines of Los Alamos. Two critics of Dr. Oppenheimer (Ernest Lawrence and Edward Teller) had urged such an establishment. After Mr. Dean's recollections had proved inadequate, portions of memoranda which the classification officer permitted to be read into the record were introduced to establish the facts, in an apparent effort to weaken the force of Mr. Dean's testimony on behalf of Dr. Oppenheimer (Tr. 312 *et seq.*).

In the cross-examination of Dr. Bethe, who had been a consultant at Los Alamos, he was asked whether in preparing in May, 1952, a history of thermonuclear development for Chairman Dean, he had done so at anyone else's request and whether Dr. Oppenheimer had discussed the report with him. He replied in the negative to both questions. Subsequently he was shown a letter (marked "Top Secret") which he had written Dr. Oppenheimer prior to the completion of the report, and he then said that it "seems to us that we did talk about it. As far as I remember, it was merely that I reported to him that I was writing such a document. It was certainly not initiated by him and the contents that should be in it were not discussed with him" (Tr. 338).

On the next to the last day of the hearings, special counsel, in further cross-examination of Dr. Oppenheimer about the H-bomb program, introduced into the record two letters which Dr. Oppenheimer had written in the fall of 1944 to Dr. Richard Tolman expressing Dr. Oppenheimer's interest at that time in proceeding with a vigorous exploration of thermonuclear reactions. Both letters had been classified. One was declassified on the spot with a few paraphrases. The other had been unclassified three and a half weeks earlier (Tr. 953–955)— another indication of the probability that much of the material in the board's dossier which had once been classified could have been unclassified and made available to Dr. Oppenheimer and his counsel.

The importance of the availability of documentary evidence was well illustrated in connection with the testimony of Mr. Griggs.

Mr. Griggs testified that in 1951 he had examined a draft of the so-called Vista report, said to have been prepared by Dr. Oppenheimer. This report contained a recommendation for a presidential announcement about the circumstances in which we would or would not use strategic attacks on enemy cities. Mr. Griggs was critical of this recommendation. He also testified that he had read minutes of a meeting of a State Department panel which he said recorded Dr. Oppenheimer as recommending that we give up part of our air power. After the hearings, we discovered that the California Institute of Technology, which was concerned with the Vista project, and the State Department, had not yet picked up from Dr. Oppenheimer's secretary his papers relating to these matters. Dr. Oppenheimer then submitted them to the board. They did *not* contain the items which Mr. Griggs had testified that they did contain. Yet the record shows how much oral testimony there was back and forth about whether these documents did contain these statements (Tr. 748, 749, 759–763). The record also shows how hesitant Dr. Oppenheimer was, without an opportunity to consult the documents, to deny flatly an unequivocal statement made by Mr. Griggs as to what was in the documents—even though Mr. Griggs' testimony did not accord with Dr. Oppenheimer's recollection, and even though Mr. Griggs' testimony on its face appeared to be damaging to Dr. Oppenheimer (Tr. 894).

## G. *Nondisclosure of the Names of the Witnesses to Be Called by the Commission*

At the outset of the hearings we gave the Gray Board the names of twenty-seven witnesses whom we proposed to call (Tr. 24), and later we gave the board some further names (Tr. 352). Special counsel for the Commission, however, was unwilling to give us in advance the names of the witnesses to be called by him. He said that if he gave us the names, he feared there would be leaks and that his witnesses would then be subject to pressure by Dr. Oppenheimer's friends as to "what they should or should not say," and that "the truthful presentation of testimony would be impeded were these witnesses to be identified" (Tr. 538).

The board overruled our protest and declined to order Mr. Robb to furnish us with the names, but stated that the board would hear us if at any time we thought we had been disadvantaged by reason of surprise, and would take appropriate steps to avoid any such disadvantage (Tr. 540).

Mr. Stern has asked me whether in fact we were so disadvantaged. It is a difficult question to answer. In the case of two witnesses, Mr. Borden and Dr. Teller, we suffered no prejudice. I shall speak of these first and then refer to the others.

In the case of Mr. Borden, we had heard rumors during the course of the proceedings that he had written a letter to the FBI about Dr. Oppenheimer, which touched off the bringing of the charges by the Commission (Tr. 835). Neither I nor my associates can recall at what stage of the proceedings we heard these rumors, but I am inclined to think that it was considerably in advance of the time he was called as a witness, which came near the end of the proceedings; he was the last witness called by Mr. Robb. We were never officially informed of his letter, nor were we shown the text of it until Mr. Borden took the stand on Friday afternoon, April 30, 1954. The members of the board had all read the letter, copies of which had been in their dossier (Tr. 836). After Mr. Borden's letter had been introduced in evidence and he had explained how he came to write it, and some colloquy had ensued about the nature of its contents, the board adjourned the hearing until the following Monday afternoon at two o'clock. This gave us adequate time in which to consider whether or not to cross-examine, and in the upshot we concluded not to.* I doubt that we

---

* Mr. Stern has asked why we made this decision. The reasons were as I explained them on Monday afternoon to the board, namely, that "Mr. Borden in his brief testimony stated the letter constituted his conclusions, and that he

would have reached any different conclusion if we had been notified earlier than he was to be called or if we had been supplied with a copy of his letter at the outset of the hearings.

As to Dr. Teller, I have described how I interviewed him before the hearings and concluded not to call him as a witness because of his intense dislike of Dr. Oppenheimer, even though he did not accuse him of disloyalty. We were not surprised when he was called, and, as I have previously noted, the position which he took was virtually the same as that which he had expressed to us.

With regard to the other witnesses, we had no way of knowing who they would be, nor did we have time to make any preparations to meet the possible accusations of persons known to have been critics of Dr. Oppenheimer in the past. We simply had to trust to luck, knowing that Dr. Oppenheimer himself would be apt to know the facts about anything which his critics might bring up and that he would be able to educate us rather speedily as the occasion might require. Mr. Silverman was in charge of the cross-examination of these witnesses, and he has informed me that nothing has come to his attention that would indicate that more could have been done on cross-examination if we had had more notice. Of course, one can never be quite sure that if we had had notice, and time to prepare for each witness, we might not have turned up material which might have been helpful and have avoided the kind of confusion which arose, for example, over the Vista report in Mr. Griggs' testimony.

## H. *The Commission's Refusal to Permit Oral Argument on Our Appeal from the Gray Board's Report*

On June 1, 1954, as already described, we published the Gray Board report and with it my letter of the same day to General Nichols, in which Mr. John W. Davis joined, summarizing our criticisms of the

---

had nothing to add. It is quite clear that the letter consists not of evidence, but of Mr. Borden's opinions arrived at from studying FBI reports and other unspecified data. These opinions relate essentially to the items contained in General Nichols' letter to Dr. Oppenheimer of December 23, 1953, which have been canvassed in the testimony, and the documents before this board. It is apparent that except for Mr. Borden's conclusions about espionage, for which there is no evidence, and as to which the chairman has assured us there is no evidence before the board, Mr. Borden's opinions represent his interpretation of evidentiary matters which this board has been hearing about for the past three weeks from persons who actually participated in the particular events which have been the subject matter of this investigation.

"In view of these considerations, it has seemed to us that if we were now to ask Mr. Borden to develop further his opinions and conclusions, we would merely be inviting argument about the interpretation of evidence" (Tr. 843).

Gray Board report and the procedure at the hearings. In this letter I asked for leave to file a brief with the Commission and to make an oral argument.

In General Nichols' reply of June 3, he stated that while the Commission's rules made no provision for a brief or for oral argument, the Commission would give very careful consideration "to any brief we might file, but would not permit oral argument." He then sought to rebut our criticisms of the procedure, and he made his letter public on June 7. On the same day I telegraphed him protesting the denial of oral argument and urging reconsideration, and on June 9 I wrote him a reply in which I said, with regard to oral argument:

> I repeat the hope, expressed in my telegram to you of June 7, that the Commission will see fit to reconsider this decision. Since the Commission in determining to take the case itself is to that extent departing from usual procedure, we had hoped that it would take the same latitude as its Review Board does in exercising its discretion to grant oral argument. As indicated in my telegram, we asked you to reconsider your decision about oral argument, not because of Dr. Oppenheimer's prominence but because such argument is one of the most important means of arriving at a clear understanding of voluminous and complex records.

In the above letter I also replied at length to General Nichols' apologia for the procedure at the hearings, and enlarged upon our objections.* I sent copies of the letter to Admiral Strauss and the other Commissioners. I did not hear from General Nichols until I received a short note from him dated June 24, in which he merely said that the Commission had weighed my renewed request and had "concluded that further argument, either oral or written, would not be in order." He added that the "other matters stated in your letter will be taken into account in considering the evidence in the case." In all likelihood the Commission's decision had *already* been arrived at, for it was dis-

---

* My letter was omitted from a pamphlet on the case which the Commission published in July, 1954, shortly after its decision, entitled *Text of Principal Documents and Letters of Personnel Security Board, General Manager, Commissioners*. The pamphlet included my letter of June 1 to General Nichols and his letter to me of June 3, but not my reply of June 9. Nor did it include either of our briefs. It also failed to include two affidavits that had been added to the record by consent after the close of the hearings. On July 14 I wrote Admiral Strauss protesting all these omissions and urging their inclusion in a supplementary printing and distribution. On August 9 General Nichols wrote me denying the request. In Exhibit A hereto I have set forth my omitted letter to General Nichols of June 9, my letter to Admiral Strauss of July 14, and General Nichols' letter to me of August 9.

tributed to the press five days later, and the accompanying opinions, especially Commissioner Smyth's detailed and extensive dissent, must have taken longer than that to prepare.

If oral argument had been permitted, an important memorandum dated June 12 which General Nichols had given to the Commission members might have come to light, and we might then have had an opportunity to answer it. It constituted in effect a brief for the prosecution. As I shall point out in the following section, it contained certain new charges that we had not had an opportunity to answer, and it appears to have been heavily relied upon by the majority of the Commissioners. The memorandum was not made known to us until July, when it appeared as part of the *Text of Principal Documents and Letters of Personnel Security Board General Manager, Commissioners,* published by the Commission after the case was over, as described in the previous footnote. As I wrote to Admiral Strauss in my letter of July 14, since the memorandum was deemed appropriate for publication, it could and should have been shown to us before the Commission reached its decision. Even if it had not been shown to us, Commissioners who had read it might have questioned us on portions of it and thereby have given us an opportunity to correct erroneous assumptions and errors of fact, just as the courts frequently question counsel about points in the briefs before them which are troubling them.

I. *Nature and Importance of the Undisclosed Nichols Memorandum*

General Nichols, in his letter to Dr. Oppenheimer of May 28 transmitting the Gray Board report, stated that "upon full consideration of the entire record in the case," including the Gray Board report, "I shall submit to the Commission my recommendation as to whether or not your clearance should be reinstated."

We did not at the time pay much attention to this portion of his letter. We were plunged at once into an analysis of the Gray Board report and the preparation of our brief to the Commission, which we filed on June 7. A few days later we were concerned with the incidents which led to the AEC's publication of the transcript on June 16. The next day, according to our diaries, my partner, Mr. Silverman, talked with me and then with Herbert Marks in Washington about "getting a copy of the General Manager's recommendation." There were similar calls on the following day, June 18.

Neither Mr. Silverman nor I can definitely remember whether Mr. Marks asked for a copy and was denied it, or whether we concluded not to ask for it. A reason for not asking for it might have been our supposition that the recommendation would be a short and simple one, no doubt supporting the Gray Board's conclusions, and that perhaps we would be out of bounds in asking for an internal communication of that sort between General Nichols and the Commission. On the other hand, Mr. Silverman's impression, though he cannot say so with certainty, is that we did ask for it and were turned down; this might account for the second round of calls the next day.

In any event, we did not know that the recommendation had already been submitted to the Commissioners in the form of a lengthy memorandum dated June 12. While reaching the same conclusion as the Gray Board report, the memorandum made only a passing reference to it. "I concur," said General Nichols, "with the findings and recommendation of the majority of the Personnel Security Board and submit them in support of this memorandum. *In addition*, I refer in particular to the following considerations. . . ."* And then followed, without any further references to the report, a detailed analysis of the case which differed in material respects from that contained in the report.

The most important difference was that General Nichols' memorandum gave no inkling of the fact that the Gray Board, after having heard testimony from a long list of leading scientists and military personnel who had been intimately associated with Dr. Oppenheimer over the years in matters affecting the vital interests and defense of the country, had unanimously concluded that Dr. Oppenheimer had rendered "loyal and magnificent service" to his country and had shown "deep devotion" to it; that he was a "loyal citizen" and "had a high degree of discretion reflecting an unusual ability to keep to himself vital secrets."

These unanimous conclusions of the Gray Board were passed over in silence by General Nichols. And although the Gray Board had neither mentioned the names nor summarized the testimony of any of the thirty witnesses called by Dr. Oppenheimer, the board had at least stated the conclusions it had derived from them. General Nichols ignored both the conclusions and the fact of the testimony; the charges were considered in a vacuum, isolated both from Dr. Oppenheimer's unfolding career and from the observations of his conduct and character by the many distinguished men who had known and worked with him.

On top of these omissions, the tone of the Nichols memorandum was such as to leave a cloud hanging over the issue of Dr. Oppenheimer's loyalty. For example, at the outset of General Nichols' presentation

* *Texts of Principal Documents*, etc., p. 44; emphasis added.

of his "Security Findings"—the heart of his memorandum—he stated that:

> The record contains no *direct* evidence that Dr. Oppenheimer gave secrets to a foreign nation or that he is disloyal to the United States. *However,* the record does contain substantial evidence of Dr. Oppenheimer's association with Communists, Communist functionaries, and Communists who did engage in espionage. [Emphasis added.]*

And the memorandum was replete with condemnatory summations of Dr. Oppenheimer's conduct, severer and more sweeping than those in the Gray Board report.

With regard to Dr. Oppenheimer's part in the H-bomb program, the Nichols memorandum first quoted in full from the charges in General Nichols' original letter: (1) that he had "continued to oppose the project" and had "declined to cooperate fully" in it; (2) that he had "departed from his proper role as an adviser to the Commission by causing the distribution, separately and in private, to top personnel at Los Alamos of the majority and minority reports of the General Advisory Committee on development of the hydrogen bomb for the purpose of trying to turn such top personnel against the development of the hydrogen bomb"; and (3) that he had been "instrumental in pursuading other outstanding scientists not to work on the hydrogen bomb projects."†

The Nichols memorandum then noted the Gray Board's finding that if Dr. Oppenheimer had "enthusiastically" supported the H-bomb program, a concerted effort to develop it would have been initiated earlier; but the memorandum did *not* mention the fact that the Gray Board had also absolved Dr. Oppenheimer of all three of the above charges.‡ It is true that the Nichols memorandum found that "the evidence establishes no sinister motives on the part of Dr. Oppenheimer in his attitude on the hydrogen bomb, either before or after the President's decision." But in leaving the above three charges standing without comment, and without any reference to the Gray Board's findings rejecting them, the Nichols memorandum was calculated once again to cast doubt on Dr. Oppenheimer's loyalty and patriotism.

The bulk of the memorandum was devoted to establishing Dr. Oppenheimer's lack of veracity in the Chevalier incident and in six other

* *Texts of Principal Documents,* etc., p. 44.
† Ibid., p. 47.
‡ Ibid., p. 13.

incidents. Only three of these were cited in the Gray Board report. Of the other three, two were based on the transcript of a recorded conversation between Dr. Oppenheimer and Colonel Lansdale in 1943, which Commissioner Smyth in his dissenting opinion characterized as "garbled."* The third incident was based on Dr. Oppenheimer's forgetfulness of a letter written to him by Dr. Seaborg in 1949. The Gray Board evidently considered these three incidents as not worthy of mention. Being ignorant of the Nichols memorandum, we had, of course, no way of knowing that these examples of alleged lack of veracity would be presented to, and adopted by, the Commission.

The Commission's majority opinion* was evidently modeled on the Nichols memorandum. There was the same omission of any references to the Gray Board conclusions about Dr. Oppenheimer's loyalty and discretion in keeping secrets; the same omission of any references to the testimony of those who had worked with him; the same failure to consider the derogatory reports in the framework of Dr. Oppenheimer's life and in the perspective of time; the same sweeping condemnation of Dr. Oppenheimer's associations and character; and the same catalogue of incidents of alleged lack of veracity.‡

I do not mean to suggest that the Commissioners had before them nothing but the Nichols memorandum, or that they had not read the Gray Board report or our briefs. I do think that in view of the similarity between the majority opinion and the Nichols memorandum, both in form and in substance, and in what it omitted as well as in what it contained, the memorandum must have had a strong influence on the outcome. And I venture to believe that if we had been permitted to address ourselves to it, and particularly if we had been permitted to do so on oral argument, we might at least have brought about a more

* *Texts of Principal Documents,* etc. It should be noted that in the course of the hearings a sixteen-page typewritten transcript, which had been introduced in evidence, of a recorded conversation between Dr. Oppenheimer and Colonel Pash on August 27, 1943, was compared by counsel for Dr. Oppenheimer and special counsel for the Commission with the original recording; that counsel stipulated the corrections to be made in the transcript; and that these corrections involved an average of over two passages per page (Tr. 844–871). The Lansdale transcript (Tr. 871–886) could not be so tested. Some of the corrections in the Pash transcript were trivial, but others resulted in a substantial change of meaning.

† Set forth in *Texts of Principal Documents,* etc., pp. 51–54.

‡ Plus one more which not even General Nichols had mentioned, either in his original letter of charges or in his memorandum to the Commission—an incident involving an apparent inconsistency between something Dr. Oppenheimer was said to have told the FBI in 1950 about one Rudy Lambert and something he was reported as having said about him to Colonel Lansdale in the untested transcript of 1943. *Texts of Principal Documents,* etc., p. 53.

humane and balanced opinion, perhaps even a simple affirmation of the Gray Board recommendation without the renewed and intensified attack upon Dr. Oppenheimer's character which the majority, following General Nichols' lead, saw fit to indulge in.

## IX. THE TRIAL TACTICS OF DR. OPPENHEIMER'S COUNSEL DURING THE HEARINGS

Mr. Stern has asked why we did not object to the intrusion into the case of testimony relating to items not specified in the letter of charges of December 23, 1953, such as Mr. Griggs' testimony, referred to in Section VIII above, about the Vista report. I think our feeling was that since all such matters were undoubtedly in the board members' secret dossier and had been read by them, the more they were brought to the surface and answered, the better. Had we been before a jury, who would have had knowledge only of what had been presented to it in open court, the case would have been quite different.

Mr. Stern has also asked me whether Robert's cause would have been better served if his counsel had been more combative in protecting him on cross-examination and in raising procedural issues more sharply before the Gray Board.

What we did or failed to do on that score must be weighed in the light of a policy decision made early in the case before the hearings began. The question was whether we would or would not try to build a record on the basis of which we could appeal to the courts if Robert's clearance was denied. Our decision was to rule out an appeal and to stake everything on success or failure before the board.

There were several reasons for this decision. In the first place, given the existing state of the law and the climate of the times, we did not think an appeal could succeed. At that time the right in an administrative proceeding to be confronted by and to cross-examine the authors of otherwise secret reports, and to inspect relevant documents before their use, had not been clearly established. The rules of the Atomic Energy Commission's hearings in security cases then enjoyed the reputation of being the most liberal of any agency. Public concern over the protection of military secrets, particularly in the atomic field, was particularly acute. Alleged Communist infiltration into government agencies had caused much anxiety, and U.S. relations with Russia were strained. Senator McCarthy and others had been fanning the flames of fear for political ends. We concluded that in such an atmosphere, and in the absence of clear legal precedents, the courts would scarcely be in a mood to reverse a commission charged with so acutely sensitive a role as that which had been assigned to the Atomic Energy Commission.

Finally, we were certain that if a judicial reversal could be obtained it would be on procedural grounds only, which would mean that the case would simply be sent back to the board for further hearings to be conducted in accordance with the court's prescription of due process. The law then was, and still is, that a court will not reverse the findings of an administrative agency if they are supported by "substantial" evidence—not a preponderance of the evidence, but something more than nominal evidence. We had no doubt that the Commission's case would meet that very limited test, and that therefore the best we could possibly expect a court to do would be to send the case back for rehearing because of procedural errors. In that eventuality Robert would have to face the ordeal of another round of hearings, and it seemed to us most unlikely that having previously decided against him the board would after a rehearing reverse itself.

For all these reasons we concluded not to try to build a record of procedural objections for later presentation to a court, but to concentrate our energies exclusively on trying to persuade the board to grant Robert his clearance. Having reached this conclusion, the question of how far we should go in pressing such objections before the board became a practical one. It would depend on the personalities and temperament of the board members, on their day-to-day reactions to the evidence and on other intangibles such as the fact that the board and its counsel shared the same quarters, had before them the same dossier and came and went together. If we protested too much, we might only irritate the board members; if we objected too strongly to a particular line of questioning designed to elicit adverse evidence or admissions, we might only magnify its importance in the eyes of the board. We felt from the outset that we were waging an uphill fight in which undue combativeness would be a hindrance rather than a help. How far to go was not something which could be reasoned out; it had to be answered by instinctive, on-the-spot judgments. Our sole aim was to bring about a favorable decision by the board and, whatever our mistakes of judgment may have been, we subordinated all other considerations to that end.

EXHIBIT A

June 9, 1954

*Major General K. D. Nichols*
*General Manager*
*U.S. Atomic Energy Commission*
*Washington 25, D.C.*

DEAR GENERAL NICHOLS:

Pursuant to my telegram to you of June 7, we filed with you and with the Commissioners yesterday copies of our brief on behalf of Dr. Oppenheimer.

Your letter to me of June 3, which you made public June 7, informed me of the Commission's decision not to hear oral argument, as requested in my letter of June 1. I repeat the hope, expressed in my telegram to you of June 7, that the Commission will see fit to reconsider this decision. Since the Commission in determining to take the case itself is to that extent departing from usual procedure, we had hoped that it would take the same latitude as its Review Board does in exercising its discretion to grant oral argument. As indicated in my telegram, we asked you to reconsider your decision about oral argument, not because of Dr. Oppenheimer's prominence but because such argument is one of the most important means of arriving at a clear understanding of voluminous and complex records.

I regret that you construed my letter of June 1 as having implied that there had been any unjustified delay in the proceedings. I meant only to emphasize our desire for a prompt decision by the Commission consistent with due consideration of the case. I am sure the Commission shares this desire.

Your letter of June 3 also contained a comment on certain procedural difficulties which in my letter of June 1st I said had beset the presentation of Dr. Oppenheimer's case. I regret having to go into this matter further, but I feel that for your understanding of the situation I should make this additional explanation since both you and the Commission may find it relevant and helpful in appraising the testimony of witnesses.

Your letter noted the fact that in an earlier letter from you to us dated February 12 you had reported the Commission's willingness to make available to us documents we reasonably believed to be relevant, reserving the right to decide "whether particular documents to which you request access are relevant and whether your access to such documents or parts thereof would be consistent with the national interest." This offer did not turn out in fact to be of help. Among other things we asked on Dr. Oppenheimer's behalf for the minutes and other papers relating to Dr. Oppenheimer's clearance by the Commission in 1947. This request was denied. The papers and minutes later came out piecemeal in the hearings through Commission counsel in a way which confused both the board and ourselves, and for some time obscured the fact that the Commission had cleared Dr. Oppenheimer after serious consideration of the derogatory material in his file. Indeed, the relevant minutes were supplied only on the thirteenth day of the hearings after the chairman of the board had transmitted to the Commission our urgent request for them, and after it was clear that the story could not be complete without them. We cite this as an example of the difficulties which might have been avoided if relevant documents, about which there was no security problem, had been furnished to us in advance.

In your letter of June 3 you also noted the fact that Dr. Oppenheimer had been granted an opportunity, which he had not exercised, to read the minutes of the October, 1949, GAC meeting, and that counsel had not asked for clearance until too late. Neither of these facts had any relationship to the procedural difficulties described in my letter of June 1. As you know, we decided very early in the proceeding that Dr. Oppenheimer's case could most clearly be understood if it were presented to the board on a nonclassified basis, in lay terms, and without resort to secret data. The board cooperated in this plan, and so far as we know, except for a very few items, counsel for the Commission used in the proceedings no documents which were not declassified. Some of these documents were declassified at the moment of cross-examination and some of them earlier, but we were not told of their existence until they were actually used in cross-examination. Since it was possible to declassify them for use on cross-examination, it is clear that their disclosure in no way involved the national security, and there is no reason why they should not have been made available in advance to Dr. Oppenheimer and other witnesses concerned, in order to refresh their recollections of events of past years before cross-examining them.

In view of the massive volume of Dr. Oppenheimer's file which the government had taken from him last January, and of the quantity of documents in other files, there was no possible way in which Dr. Oppenheimer or his counsel could have anticipated in advance what documents would be so produced and used. Some of them, on the other hand, consisted of letters taken from his files whose existence, if he had remembered them, he would have had no motive in concealing; yet without notice that counsel for the Commission had them before him, Dr. Oppenheimer was questioned about matters referred to in them. The letter from Dr. Seaborg, referred to by Dr. Evans in his minority opinion, is an example.

As a result of these tactics, which were used in the case of certain other witnesses, it is understandable that at some points in the testimony limitations of memory may have been mistaken for disingenuousness.

In my letter of June 1st I pointed out these and related facts about the procedure in order to make as certain as possible that the Commission would be aware of them and would take account of them in weighing the testimony.

I think I should add that besides the findings of fact specifically commented on in our brief to the Commission, there are a number of other findings with which we do not agree, but it has seemed to us that these findings would not substantially affect the result and we have therefore not prolonged the brief by arguing them.

Sincerely yours,
LLOYD K. GARRISON

cc Admiral Lewis L. Strauss
   Mr. Joseph Campbell
   Mr. Thomas E. Murray
   Dr. Henry D. Smyth
   Mr. Eugene M. Zuckert
   William D. Mitchell, Esq.

July 14, 1954

*Admiral Lewis L. Strauss*
*Chairman*
*United States Atomic Energy Commission*
*Washington, D.C.*

DEAR ADMIRAL STRAUSS:

My attention has been directed to a pamphlet published through the Government Printing Office by the Atomic Energy Commission, entitled "In the Matter of J. Robert Oppenheimer. Texts of Principal Documents and Letters of Personnel Security Board, General Manager, Commissioners."

I am troubled by observing that this compilation, which I understand the Commission has distributed generally to the persons on its extensive mailing list, includes General Nichols' letter to me of June 3, 1954, but fails to include my reply of June 9 (which corrected the inaccuracies and misunderstandings in his letter to me). You included my letter to General Nichols of June 1, 1954, and I think that my letter of June 9 ought in all fairness to have been also included, and I request that the Commission now have it printed and distributed to the same mailing list.

It seems to me also that our briefs to the Gray Board and to the Commission (exclusive of appendices) should likewise have been included as among the "principal documents." The Commission in its press release of June 16 said: "The wide national interest and concern in the matter make inevitable and desirable close public examination of the final determination." Publication of the briefs by the Government Printing Office and their distribution to the Commission's mailing list along with the other principal documents could only assist that close public examination which the national interest requires; I accordingly ask that this be done.

I note also that the transcript published by the Commission does not include Dr. Oppenheimer's unclassified affidavit concerning the 1952 State Department panel on international control of armaments. Together with a classified affidavit concerning Chapter V of the Vista Report, this was added to the record by consent after the close of the hearings. To the extent this material can be treated as unclassified, I request that it also be included in the supplemental printing and distribution.

I was surprised by the inclusion in the Commission's compilation of the "Recommendations of the General Manager to the United States Atomic Energy Commission in the Matter of Dr. J. Robert Oppenheimer," dated June 12, 1954. If this document, which Dr. Oppenheimer and his counsel have now read for the first time, was of a sort which could be released at the Commission's pleasure, then it seems to me that it should have been shown to us upon its submission to the Commission so that we might have had an opportunity to submit our comments to the Commission, which obviously would have been relevant to the Commission's own decision.

Very truly yours,
LLOYD K. GARRISON

cc Mr. Joseph Campbell
  Mr. Thomas E. Murray
  Dr. Henry D. Smyth
  General K. D. Nichols
  William Mitchell, Esq.

UNITED STATES
ATOMIC ENERGY COMMISSION
WASHINGTON 25, D.C.

August 9, 1954

DEAR MR. GARRISON:

This will acknowledge receipt of your letter of July 14 to the Chairman, Atomic Energy Commission, in which you refer to the pamphlet entitled "In the Matter of J. Robert Oppenheimer, Texts of Principal Documents and Letters of Personnel Security Board, General Manager, Commissioners."

Before publishing this pamphlet the Commission considered carefully what documents should be included. It was decided to print only the basic findings, recommendations and decisions in the proceeding, together with those letters which had to do with procedures to be followed after the submission of the report of the Personnel Security Board. The Commission contemplates no further action with regard to the matter.

Sincerely yours
K. D. NICHOLS
*General Manager*

Lloyd K. Garrison, Esq.
Paul, Weiss, Rifkind, Wharton & Garrison
575 Madison Avenue
New York 22, New York

8/10/54
Copies to Mr. Marks and Mrs. Russell
L.S.

# Notes and Sources

SOURCES

Following are the major sources for facts and quotations contained in this book other than those obtained by the author from personal interviews—and the abbreviations used to identify them in the notes.

AEC Criteria: *Criteria for Determining Eligibility for Personnel Security Clearance, adopted by the U.S. Atomic Energy Commission,* Nov. 17, 1950.

AEC letter: Letters from AEC historian Richard G. Hewlett in response to specific factual queries put to him by Messrs. Stern and Green.

AEC Procedures; also AEC Regulations: U.S. Atomic Energy Commission Security Clearance Procedures; Code of Federal Regulations, Title 10, Chapter 1, Part 4; adopted Sept. 12, 1950, and filed as F.R. Doc. 508085.

*Alsos:* Samuel A. Goudsmit, *Alsos,* Henry Schuman, Inc., New York, 1947.

Arnold: Thurman Arnold, *The Strengthening of American Institutions,* Cornell University Press, Ithaca, N.Y., 1949.

Barth: Alan Barth, *The Loyalty of Free Men,* The Viking Press, New York, 1951.

Bontecou: Eleanor Bontecou, *The Federal Loyalty-Security Program,* Cornell University Press, Ithaca, N.Y., 1953.

Borden: William Liscum Borden, *There Will Be No Time: The Revolution in Strategy*, The Macmillan Co., New York, 1946.

Brown, John Mason: John Mason Brown, *Through These Men*, Harper & Brothers, New York, 1956.

Brown, Ralph: Ralph S. Brown, Jr., *Loyalty and Security: Employment Tests in the United States*, Yale University Press, New Haven, 1958.

Chevalier: Haakon Chevalier, *Oppenheimer: The Story of a Friendship*, George Braziller, New York, 1965.

Coughlan: Robert Coughlan, "The Tangled Drama and Private Hells of Two Famous Scientists," *Life* Magazine, December 13, 1963, pp. 87A–110.

Curtis: Charles P. Curtis, *The Oppenheimer Case: The Trial of a Security System*, Simon and Schuster, New York, 1955.

*Daily Californian:* The campus newspaper of the University of California at Berkeley.

Donovan: Robert J. Donovan, *Eisenhower: The Inside Story*, Harper & Brothers, New York, 1956.

Eisenhower: Dwight D. Eisenhower, *The White House Years: Mandate for Change*, Doubleday & Co., Garden City, N.Y., 1963.

Garrison: The written responses of Lloyd K. Garrison to questions put to him by the author, appearing at pp. 517–66.

Gellhorn: Walter Gellhorn, *Security, Loyalty, and Science*, Cornell University Press, Ithaca, N.Y., 1950.

Goudsmit: See *Alsos.*

*Journals:* David E. Lilienthal, *The Journals of David E. Lilienthal*, Vol. III, Harper & Row, New York, 1966.

Jungk: Robert Jungk, *Brighter Than a Thousand Suns: The Story of the Men Who Made the Bomb*, Grove Press, New York, 1958.

Kalven: Harry Kalven, Jr., "The Case of J. Robert Oppenheimer before the Atomic Energy Commission," *Bulletin of the Atomic Scientists*, September, 1954.

Lamont: Lansing Lamont, *Day of Trinity*, New American Library, New York, 1965.

*Legacy:* Edward Teller, with Allen Brown, *The Legacy of Hiroshima*, Doubleday & Co., Garden City, N.Y., 1962.

Lilienthal: See *Journals.*

*New World:* Richard G. Hewlett and Oscar E. Anderson, Jr., *The New World, 1939/1946: Volume I of A History of the United States Atomic Energy Commission*, Pennsylvania State University Press, University Park, Pa., 1962.

Princ. Docs.: *In the Matter of J. Robert Oppenheimer: Texts of Principal Documents and Letters of Personnel Security Board, General Manager, Commissioners, Washington, D.C., May 27, 1954, through June 29, 1954,* United States Government Printing Office, Washington, D.C., 1954.

Shepley-Blair: James R. Shepley and Clay Blair, Jr., *The Hydrogen Bomb,* David McKay Co., New York, 1954.

Smith: Alice Kimball Smith, *A Peril and a Hope: The Scientists' Movement in America 1945–47,* University of Chicago Press, Chicago, 1965.

Strauss: Lewis L. Strauss, *Men and Decisions,* Doubleday & Co., Garden City, N.Y., 1962.

Strauss hearing: Hearing on the Confirmation of Lewis Strauss as U.S. Secretary of Commerce; before the Senate Interstate and Foreign Commerce Committee, March–May, 1959.

Strauss Report: *Report of the Senate Interstate and Foreign Commerce Committee on the Nomination of Lewis Strauss to be Secretary of Commerce,* Executive Report No. 4, 86th Congress, 1st Session.

Teller: See *Legacy.*

Tr.: *In the Matter of J. Robert Oppenheimer: Transcript of Hearing Before Personnel Security Board (The Gray Board), Washington, D.C., April 12, 1954, through May 6, 1954,* United States Government Printing Office, Washington, D.C., 1954.

Yarmolinsky: Adam Yarmolinsky, ed., *Case Studies in Personnel Security,* Bureau of National Affairs, Washington, D.C., 1955.

*Note:* Information about the weather conditions obtaining in Washington on any given day or hour is drawn from a monthly publication of the U.S. Weather Bureau, *Local Climatological Data.*

NOTES

Page numbers in italics refer to footnotes.

I. THE TRIGGER

1  *Borden letter quote:* Tr. 837.

2  *Four-and-a-half-foot stack of reports:* Donovan 294.

II. THE OPPENHEIMER STORY

1. *The Prewar Years*

8   The description of JRO's early life and personality is drawn from interviews and correspondence with 14 friends, relatives and colleagues, as well as the following written sources: *Time* Magazine, Nov. 8, 1948, pp. 70–81 (including quotes: "My life as a child . . ." [p. 11]; "no . . . way to be a bastard" [p. 11]; "weren't getting enough to eat or drink" [p. 12]; and "on the point of bumping myself off" [p. 13]; Lincoln Barnett, *Writing on Life*, William Sloane Associates, New York, 1951, pp. 345–383; John Mason Brown, pp. 228–291; Robert Serber, "J. Robert Oppenheimer: The Early Years," paper delivered before American Physical Society, Apr. 24, 1967; and from JRO's reply to AEC charges, esp. at Tr. 8.

8   *JRO's isolation from events:* Tr. 8.

8   *The "J" in Oppenheimer's name: J. Edgar Hoover communications:* Tr. 412; *Nuel Pharr Davis book: Lawrence & Oppenheimer,* Simon and Schuster, New York, 1968, p. 11; *Bernstein review: The New Yorker,* May 10, 1969, p. 142; *New York City Health Department:* letter to author, June 30, 1969. That letter explicitly confirms the spelling "Oppenhiemer" on the birth certificate. A *New York Times* obituary of Dr. Oppenheimer also stated that the "J" stood "for nothing." (Feb. 20, 1967, p. 36.)

15  *JRO quotes: "I was interested in man"; "smoldering fury" about treatment of Jews; "how deeply political and economic events"; and "no framework of political conviction":* Tr. 8.

15  *JRO-Tatlock relationship:* Tr. 8, 153–154.

16  *"Probably belonged to every Communist-front":* Tr. 159.

17  *HUAC's "subversive" label:* Tr. 3.

17  *Conditions of farm workers: People's Daily World,* Jan. 7, 1938.

17  *JRO and teachers' union:* Chevalier 23; Tr. 8, 156, 158–159.

17  *Teachers' pay cut: Daily Californian,* Nov. 29, 1937.

17  *JRO licks stamps, etc.:* Chevalier 32–33.

18  *The Popular Front in America:* Eric F. Goldman, *Rendezvous with Destiny,* Alfred A. Knopf, New York, 1953, p. 354; and Granville Hicks, *Where We Came Out,* Viking Press, New York, 1954, p. 46.

18  *Eighty thousand votes for Communist presidential candidate: Statistical Abstract of the United States, 1968,* p. 365.

18  *Communist activity on Berkeley campus: Daily Californian,* Oct. 7, 1938, Oct. 12, 1936.

18  Acceptability of Earl Browder: *New York Times,* Apr. 29, 1954, p. 30.

19  *"Stalin's Russia cherishes no aggression": New York Times,* Dec. 1, 1931, p. 26, as quoted in Frank A. Warren, III, *Liberals and Communists: The "Red Decade" Revisited,* Indiana University Press, 1966, p. 75.

19  *Observations of Edgar B. Stern:* From privately published letters to friends and family written during 1936 visit to Russia. (Mr. Stern is the author's father.)

19  *Soviet engineers inside Ford plant:* Caroline Bird, *The Invisible Scar,* David McKay Co., New York, 1966, p. 141.

19  *President-General of DAR at Soviet Embassy:* Baltimore Sun, Nov. 8, 1937, as quoted in Goldman, *Rendezvous with Destiny,* p. 354.

20  *Casualty rate in Lincoln Brigade; Madison Square rally:* Murray Kempton, *Part of Our Time,* Simon and Schuster, New York, 1955, pp. 310, 311.

20  *Granville Hicks quote: Where We Came Out,* p. 48.

20  *Letterhead of Spanish Medical Aid Committee; 1939 San Francisco protest: Labor Daily Herald,* Jan. 19, 1939.

20  *American Friends of the Chinese People cited by HUAC: HUAC Guide to Subversive Organizations and Publications,* House Doc. 398, 87th Cong., 2nd Session, 1961, p. 21.

21  *JRO "better read than most":* Chevalier 16.

21  *Party membership held no attraction:* Tr. 10.

21  *JRO-Frank relationship:* Tr. 101.

21  *Frank tells JRO of Communist Party membership:* Tr. 186.

22  *CP membership no "matter of dishonor":* Tr. 187.

22  *"What a sad spectacle":* Tr. 102.

22  *JRO's emotional commitment to Spanish war:* Tr. 9.

22  *JRO-Addis relationship:* Tr. 183–185.

22  *JRO on subscribing to People's World:* Tr. 157.

23  *Jack B. Tenney Message:* Arnold Forster and Benjamin R. Epstein, *Cross Currents,* Doubleday, Garden City, N.Y., 1956, p. 56.

23  *JRO's contribution to Longshoremen's Union:* Tr. 157.

24  *JRO's changing attitude toward Russia:* Tr. 10.

26  *Page-one editorial, People's Daily World:* Aug. 23, 1939.

26  *Communist membership dropped:* Bontecou 4.

26  *JRO's reaction to Nazi-Soviet pact:* Tr. 186; Chevalier, p. 32. The line of argument described by Chevalier is also set forth

in D. F. Fleming, *The Cold War and Its Origins*, Doubleday, Garden City, N.Y., 1961, Vol. I, pp. 96–97.

27   *JRO's relations with Folkoff and Lambert:* Tr. 140, 155 and 185.

27   *Study of prewar concern about employee loyalty:* Library of Congress, Legislative Reference Service, *Federal Loyalty-Security Programs in World War II*, Nov. 6, 1967.

28   *Military agencies and "danger to the national security"; Hatch Act amendment; summary dismissal laws:* Bontecou 11–13.

28   *Groves quote:* Tr. 170.

29   *JRO's reaction to fall of France:* Tr. 10, 327, 441 and 644.

29   *Earlier life of Kitty Oppenheimer:* Tr. 571–574.

31   *Oppenheimers' relations with Chevaliers:* Tr. 10.

31   *Oppenheimers' relations with Bransten:* Tr. 191.

31   *Oppenheimers' relations with Nelson:* Tr. 195, 575.

33   *Chevalier-Oppenheimer June, 1941, visit:* Chevalier 41–42.

33   *People's Daily World quotes:* May 1, June 26, June 28, 1941.

33   *The Chevaliers care for Peter:* Chevalier 42.

33   *JRO's return to Berkeley:* Tr. 17.

34   *Oppenheimer's and Bethe's whereabouts, July 24, 1941:* Tr. 336.

34   *Frank employed at Berkeley; JRO's comment:* Tr. 187.

34   *Kenneth May housewarming:* Tr. 4, 10.

34   *JRO restive:* Tr. 11.

35   *Schenectady conference:* New World 46.

35   *JRO devotes more time to nuclear matters:* Tr. 11.

35   *JRO attends last Spanish War Relief party:* Tr. 9.

35   *When JRO's contributions ended:* Tr. 9, 184, 837; Princ. Docs. 7.

36   *Compton enlists JRO:* New World 103; Tr. 11.

36   *Borden's conclusion:* Tr. 838.

## 2. The War Years

37   *JRO helps in Teller clearance:* Coughlan 90.

38   *JRO's July trip to Compton:* New World 104.

38   *JRO-Teller 1942 relations:* Coughlan 90.

38   *Interchange of atomic information with British:* New World 42–43.

39   *Somervell's selection of Groves:* New World 81.

39   *JRO's idea of a single weapons lab:* Tr. 12.

39   *Groves on JRO selection:* Leslie R. Groves, *Now It Can Be Told: The Story of the Manhattan Project*, Harper & Brothers, New York, 1962, pp. 61–63.

40  *Compton's concern and conclusions re JRO security:* Tr. 11; Washington *Post,* Apr. 19, 1954.

40  *Official concern re JRO associations and relatives:* Tr. 260.

41  *JRO clearance granted Dec. 8, 1942:* AEC letter, Sept. 5, 1967.

41  *Groves picks Oppenheimer:* Tr. 165, 561; Groves, *Now It Can Be Told,* pp. 61–63, 66.

41  *MacArthur praises Red Army: New York Times,* Feb. 23, 1942, p. 3.

42  *Henry C. Alexander, New York Times,* May 24, 1942, p. 36.

42  *Life* Magazine *quote:* Oct. 5, 1942, p. 29.

42  *Herbert Brownell: New York Times,* Nov. 6, 1942, p. 36.

42  *Bernard Baruch gave $100,000: New York Times,* Dec. 24, 1942, p. 1.

42  *Chevalier War Relief party:* Chevalier 49.

42  JRO recruiting efforts: *a gigantic boondoggle:* Tr. 29; *isolation problem:* Tr. 12; *"intellectual sex appeal":* Jungk 132; *Serber:* Tr. 204; *Peterses:* Tr. 120; *Bohm:* Tr. 13; *Hawkins:* Tr. 13, 196; *Morrison:* Tr. 621.

43  *Later admission of prewar Communist Party membership: by Morrison: Hearings,* Senate Committee on Judiciary, International Security Subcommittee, 83rd Congress, 1st session, May 7–8, 1963, p. 899; *by Hawkins: New York Times,* Jan. 28, 1951, p. 23.

44  *1942–43 Federal security program:* Library of Congress, Legislative Reference Service, *Federal Loyalty-Security Programs in World War II,* Nov. 6, 1967.

44  *Groves-Conant letter:* Tr. 28; *New World* 231–232;

44  *JRO's 1943 attitude toward ex-Communists:* Tr. 13.

44  *Accounts of Chevalier kitchen conversation:* Chevalier 52–55; JRO testimony to HUAC, June 7, 1949; JRO letter to Chevalier of Feb. 24, 1950, Tr. 142; JRO testimony, Tr. 14, 130–131, 135.

45  *Eltenton a friend of Chevalier:* Chevalier 52; *a mild acquaintance of JRO:* Tr. 135.

46  *Possible military character of Los Alamos; JRO's attitude:* Tr. 28; *New World* 230–232.

46  *FDR letter to JRO:* Tr. 29–30; *New World* 238–239.

46  *JRO's attitude on Los Alamos security measures:* Tr. 29, 117, 262.

47  *Praise of JRO's attitude toward security:* Tr. 166 (Groves); Tr. 262 (Lansdale); Tr. 961 (de Silva).

47  *Groves on Bohr and Lawrence security infringements:* 166.

48  *Lansdale orders tight surveillance:* Tr. 260.

48   *Surveillance of JRO:* Tr. 260; *New York Times,* Apr. 14, 1954, p. 20.

48   *JRO visit to Tatlock:* Tr. 116, 153–154, 264, 267; Jungk, p. 139.

48   *Pash's investigation of Berkeley and report to Lansdale:* Tr. 811–812, 821–822.

49   *Groves' decision on JRO clearance:* Tr. 165, 168, 170.

50   *Pash's search for "Joe":* Tr. 811.

50   *Lomanitz incident: "wild talk":* Tr. 125.

51   *JRO telegrams:* Tr. 123, 133.

51   *Hershey warning:* Tr. 172.

52   *JRO-Lansdale talk:* Tr. 275–276.

54   *JRO-Pash interview:* Tr. 845–853.

57   *Pash's tedious search of files:* Tr. 815.

57   *Pash's message to General Groves:* Tr. 816.

57   *De Silva report:* Tr. 274–275.

58   *"Dear A" note:* Tr. 824.

58   *JRO-Groves train conversation:* Tr. 277.

58   *Acquittal of Weinberg of perjury charges: New York Times,* Mar. 6, 1953, p. 14; Apr. 13, 1954, p. 17.

59   *JRO and Lansdale had had many conversations:* Tr. 266, 271.

60   *JRO-Lansdale interview:* Tr. 871–886.

65   *JRO-Lomanitz letters:* Tr. 117–118, 134.

66   *Pash report to Washington:* Tr. 819.

67   *JRO-Groves talk:* Tr. 153, 889.

68   *Lansdale talk with Tamm and Whitson:* Tr. 264.

68   *Nichols' three telegrams:* Tr. 152–153.

69   *Chevalier's bitter conclusion:* Chevalier 194.

69   *Failure to interrogate Eltenton until 1946:* Chevalier 68.

70   *Chevalier and OWI:* Chevalier 57–58.

70   *JRO-Peters relationship:* Tr. 120–122.

70   *JRO–de Silva conversation on Peters:* Tr. 150–151.

71   *Government charge against Hannah Peters:* Tr. 5.

72   *Surveillance reports on JRO-Bohm:* Tr. 150.

73   *JRO-Bohm sidewalk conversation:* Tr. 149–150.

73   *JRO on Los Alamos as a "confluence": Time,* Nov. 8, 1948.

73   *Teller on JRO leadership:* Edward Teller, "The Work of Many People," *Science,* Feb. 25, 1955.

74   *Groves' discomfort over weekly "colloquia": New World* 238.

75   *Weisskopf quote:* Victor Weisskopf, paper delivered before American Physical Society, Apr. 24, 1967.

75   *Teller reportedly hurt by rebuffs:* Coughlan 90.

76   *Bethe on Teller's Los Alamos role:* Tr. 325.

76  *Teller: "no time for the super":* Edward Teller, "The Work of
Many People."
77  *JRO on the "Super":* Tr. 954, 956.
77  *Borden views V-2 Rocket:* Borden ix.
78  *Discovery at Strasbourg: Alsos,* p. 71.
78  *News traveled around Allied laboratories:* Jungk 171.
78  *De Silva letter:* Tr. 961.
79  *Judgments on JRO's disregard of security:* Princ. Docs., 21, 46,
52.
80  *Deliberations of Interim Committee and Scientific Panel:* Len
Giovannitti and Fred Freed, *The Decision to Drop the Bomb,*
Coward-McCann, Inc., New York, 1965, p. 49; *New World*
343–345, 356–358; Smith 34–35.
80  *JRO spoke on at least three topics: New World,* 357–358.
80  *Franck Report:* Smith 570–571.
81  *June 16 Los Alamos meeting:* Tr. 236; Smith 48–50.
82  *"In a polite and convincing way": Legacy* 13.
82  *JRO-Strauss first meeting:* Strauss 270.
82  *Trinity and its aftermath:* Lamont 180; Tr. 14, 32; Smith 77.
83  *Aftermath of Hiroshima at Los Alamos:* Smith 77, 115.


3. *Transition*

85  *Birth of ALAS, early JRO contacts:* Smith 115–120.
86  *Administration bill to control atomic energy; JRO testimony:*
Smith 129, 130, 136–140, 142–144, 153, 165–166.
87  *JRO leaves Los Alamos:* Smith 303; Tr. 33, 441.
88  *Teller's reaction to JRO's departure:* Coughlan 91; Tr. 711, 724;
*Legacy* 22–23.
89  *Chevalier's letter to JRO:* Chevalier x.
90  *Groves' praise of Frank Oppenheimer:* Letter to Frank Oppenheimer from Groves, Sept., 1945, quoted in Washington *Times-
Herald,* July 12, 1947.
90  *Meeting in Frank's house with two alleged Communists:* Tr. 187–
188.
90  *JRO's stamp on Acheson-Lilienthal plan:* Smith 460.
91  *Griggs–JRO:* Tr. 768.
91  *Quotes from Borden book:* Borden 219–225.
92  *JRO's 1946 visit to Chevalier:* Chevalier 68–69.
92  *Chevalier FBI interrogation:* Chevalier 61–68.
94  *Chevalier interchange with JRO:* Chevalier 69–70.
94  *JRO FBI interrogation:* Princ. Docs. 64; Tr. 192, 194.

95   *JRO resigns from ICCASP:* Tr. 104–106.

96   *Canadian Royal Commission revelation:* Bontecou 21–22.

96   *Chamber of Commerce Report:* Report of Chamber's Committee on Socialism and Communism, as quoted in *New York Times,* Oct. 10, 1946, p. 1.

97   *Truman Loyalty Commission appointed: New York Times,* Mar. 23, 1947, p. 48.

97   *Thirring quote:* Hans Thirring, *Die Geschichte der Atombombe,* 1946, quoted in *New York Times,* Apr. 18, 1954, Sec. IV, p. 9.

98   *Strauss relayed the Institute's offer:* Strauss 270–271.

98   *JRO named to GAC: New World* 648.

99   *Comments on JRO GAC chairmanship:* Tr. 66, 461, 517–518.

99   *Seven committees chaired by JRO:* Lloyd Garrison's brief to the AEC, June 7, 1954, pp. 91–101.

100  *JRO's 1947 comments on Russia:* Tr. 98, 327.

100  *Early GAC days:* Tr. 18, 69–70, 398.

101  *Groves' warning:* Tr. 168–169.

101  *Nighttime Hoover call to Lilienthal: New York Times,* Apr. 13, 1954, p. 19; also, see Tr. 374.

102  *JRO's call and visit to Osborn:* Tr. 343–344.

102  *AEC consideration of JRO's security clearance:* Tr. 374, 375, 413, 417, 418–419.

103  *Pike on Strauss' interest in security:* Tr. 437.

104  *JRO tells Strauss of "derogatory information":* Tr. 27.

104  *Lilienthal meeting with Hoover:* Tr. 379–381.

105  *Volpe on "no need for formal action":* Tr. 424.

105  *Minutes of AEC meeting:* Tr. 677.

105  *Lansdale statement:* Tr. 425.

106  *Uanna's "appropriate entry":* Tr. 425.

107  *Truman Loyalty Commission Report; McCarthy reactions: New York Times,* Mar. 23, 1947.

107  *Misgivings of Harvard law professors:* Letter from Zechariah Chaffee, Jr., Erwin N. Griswold, Milton Katz, Austin W. Scott, *New York Times,* Apr. 13, 1947, p. 8.

107  *Navy and FBI recommendations:* Bontecou 300, 305.

109  *JRO's September 17 comment on Russia:* Tr. 42.

110  *Chevalier incident: New York Times,* Oct. 31, 1947, p. 1; San Francisco *Chronicle,* Oct. 31, 1947, p. 1; *New York Times,* Nov. 1, 1947, p. 8.

110  *Chevalier on Ivanov: New York Times,* Nov. 7, 1947, p. 4.

111  *JRO's written statement: New York Times,* Oct. 31, 1947, p. 3.

111 *Chevalier's California appearance:* New York Times, Nov. 1, 1947, p. 4.

4. *Fame and Influence*

112 *JRO in Time:* Time, Nov. 8, 1948.

113 *Morrison on JRO and Marshall:* Chevalier 79–80.

113 *JRO on Marshall:* Newsweek, June 27, 1966, p. 64.

114 *Development of "Super" not considered urgent:* Tr. 493.

114 *Predictions about Soviet bomb:* JRO–Tr. 47; Groves–New York Times, Sept. 22, 1945 (quoted at Smith 106).

114 *Strauss and Nichols on H-bomb:* U.S. News & World Report, Dec. 24, 1954, p. 101.

114 *JRO's trip to Europe:* Tr. 41.

114 *Government survey:* Tr. 257–258.

115 *Defeat did not sit easily with Strauss; JRO dismisses Strauss objection:* Journals, Vol. III, p. 522.

115 *JRO's 1948 comments on Russia:* Tr. 43.

116 *Communism as 1948 campaign issue:* New York Times, Sept. 2, p. 1; Sept. 3, p. 1; Sept. 9, p. 24; Sept. 25, p. 8.

117 *HUAC report:* HUAC Bulletin No. 81334, Sept. 28, 1948, p. 182.

118 *Defense cutbacks:* Economic Report of the President, January, 1962, p. 273; Congress and the Nation, 1945–64, Congressional Quarterly, Inc., Washington, D.C., 1965, pp. 251–255.

118 *Radford testimony:* Congress and the Nation, p. 255.

119 *JRO's encounter with Bohm and Lomanitz:* Tr. 151, 180–181.

125 *Rochester Times-Union:* June 15, 1949, quoted at Tr. 210–211.

126 *Condon letter to JRO:* Tr. 212; Washington Post, Apr. 16, 1954.

126 *Condon letter to his wife:* Washington Star, Apr. 15, 1954, p. 1.

127 *Letters more regretful than belligerent:* Tr. 215.

127 *Reports on Congressional committees and FBI:* New York Times, Apr. 16, 1954, p. 9.

127 *JRO's meeting with Peters; his public letter:* Tr. 212–214.

127 *JRO letter shown to HUAC:* Tr. 213.

128 *JRO letter to McMahon:* New Republic, June 6, 1949, p. 8.

130 *JCAE hearing: Investigation into the United States Atomic Energy Project,* by the Joint Committee on Atomic Energy, 1949, pp. 277–315; New York Times, June 16, 1949, p. 20.

130 *Strauss reasoning re isotopes:* Strauss 258.

131 *Lilienthal recollection:* Journals, Vol. III, p. 522.

132 *Frank Oppenheimer's appearance before HUAC:* Washington

*Post,* June 15, 1949; Washington *Star,* June 17, 1949, and June 29, 1949.

133  *Quote from Oakland Tribune:* Shepley-Blair 210.

133  *Strauss letter to McMahon: New York Times,* June 25, 1949, p. 8.

133  *JRO visit to Stinson Beach:* Chevalier 81.


5. *The H-bomb Debate*

135  *Events following Soviet A-explosion:* Tr. 75–76.

135  *GAC majority sides with JRO:* Tr. 76.

136  *JRO tells Teller, "Keep your shirt on":* Tr. 714.

136  *Alvarez-Lawrence activities:* Tr. 659, 714–715, 774–778.

137  *Strauss memorandum on "Quantum jump":* Strauss 217.

138  *Lilienthal's reasoning:* Tr. 400, 422.

138  *Lilienthal's request to GAC:* Tr. 401.

138  *JRO's reply:* Tr. 402.

138  *Seaborg letter:* Tr. 238–239.

139  *Nichols-Vandenberg activities:* Tr. 682–683.

140  *Teller-Bethe-JRO interchange:* Tr. 328, 715.

141  *JRO October 21 letter to Conant:* Tr. 242–243.

141  *Weight of first H-device:* Shepley-Blair 136.

142  *Alvarez sends Serber to JRO:* Tr. 784.

142  Description of GAC meeting: Tr. 19, 77, 228, 241, 247, 462, 519, 895. The reconstruction of the considerations underlying the GAC's negative recommendation on an all-out H-bomb program is based on the testimony before the Gray Board of GAC and AEC members involved with the issue at the time, principally the testimony of GAC members Fermi, Rabi, Rowe, DuBridge, Winne and Buckley; AEC members Lilienthal and Pike; and Los Alamos Director Bradbury.

145  *JRO's views on the "Super":* Tr. 77, 87.

146  *JRO on Seaborg letter:* Tr. 240.

146  *JRO later berated for omission:* Princ. Docs. 46, 53.

146  *JRO-Serber-Alvarez luncheon:* Tr. 246–247, 519, 785–786.

147  *GAC reports:* Tr. 79–80; see also DuBridge accounts, Tr. 519.

148  *Norman Moss statements: Men Who Play God,* Harper & Row, New York, 1968, pp. 20–21.

148  *Fermi testimony:* Tr. 395.

148  *GAC majority appendix:* Tr. 80, 462, 895.

149  *JRO-Acheson meetings; Kennan analysis:* unpublished manuscript by Gordon R. Arneson.

149 *Ofstie testimony: New York Times*, Oct. 12, 1949, p. 34.
149 *H-bomb views of AEC Commissioners:* Shepley-Blair 182–183.
150 *Strauss-Johnson talk; advisers' conference:* Shepley-Blair 80–83.
151 *Manley shows GAC papers at Los Alamos:* Tr. 90.
152 *Alvarez-Lawrence-Bush talk:* Tr. 787, 800, 910, 969.
152 *McCormack-Pitzer appearance before GAC:* Tr. 707.
153 *JRO's testimony before JAEC.:* Tr. 240.

## 6. A Failure to "Enthuse"

154 *Senator Johnson disclosure:* Washington *Post*, Nov. 18, 1949, p. 1.
155 *Hoyer Millar visit to Under Secretary Murphy:* Unpublished manuscript by Gordon R. Arneson.
156 *Statement by twelve leading physicists:* Shepley-Blair 105.
157 *Statements on Truman announcement: by Cole: New York Times*, Feb. 1, 1950, p. 3; *by Bonnell: New York Times*, Feb. 6, 1950, p. 18; *by Einstein:* Shepley-Blair.
157 *JRO's radio statement:* 105–106. Shepley-Blair 106.
159 *Chevalier's use of letter:* Princ. Doc. 11.
159 *Chevalier's later speculation:* Chevalier 83.
159 *McCarthy charges:* J. M. Brown, 243; *New York Times*, Feb. 21, 1950, p. 13; Feb. 26, 1950, p. 26.
160 *Bethe article: Scientific American*, Apr. 1950, p. 21.
160 *Bundy-Galbraith-Schlesinger letter: New York Times*, Apr. 30, 1950, Sec. IV, p. 8.
161 *H-bomb technical prospects bleaker:* Tr. 81.
161 *Teller-JRO exchanges:* Tr. 83, 719.
161 *JRO's offer to Longmire:* Tr. 83.
162 *JRO accepted this point:* Tr. 897.
163 *Strauss on scientist recruitment:* Strauss 274.
164 *Crouch testimony: New York Times*, May 10, 1950, p. 28.
164 *JRO's answering statement:* Washington *Post*, May 10, 1950, p. 1.
164 *Barbosa testimony: New York Times*, May 11, 1950, p. 12.
165 *Nixon speech: New York Times*, May 11, 1950, p. 12.
165 *Groves letter:* Tr. 178.
166 *JRO 1950 interrogations by FBI: Questions re Communist meeting:* Tr. 217–218.
166 *Kitty's reminder:* Tr. 10.
166 *JRO reflects on past ties:* Tr. 5; *big mistake;* based on Robb question, Tr. 210.

167  *Failure to answer re Addis:* Tr. 155; *criticism of failure:* Princ. Docs. 20.

167  *Questions on Weinberg:* Tr. 209, 875; Princ. Docs. 53.

167  *FBI brings summary to Dean; Dean reaction:* Tr. 306.

168  *Special GAC panel named to study small nuclear weapons:* Tr. 787–788, 801.

168  *Bethe's change of heart:* Tr. 329.

168  *Mathematical test of Teller theory:* Legacy 47, Tr. 305.

169  *Cole July 17 speech: Congressional Record,* July 24, 1950, pp. A5316–A5318.

170  *JRO's recommendation of Libby:* Tr. 83, 701, 951.

170  *JRO considers whether to resign:* Tr. 83, 86, 307, 897–898.

170  *Chevalier-JRO exchanges; Chevalier's departure:* Chevalier 83–84; Tr. 142, 889.

171  *Long-range planning committee: LeBaron role:* Tr. 57.

171  *JRO calls Alvarez:* Tr. 787.

172  *JRO's statement at second meeting:* Tr. 788.

172  *JRO: "we all agree":* Tr. 951–952.

173  *JRO's role in revising report:* Tr. 58.

173  *Alvarez signs report:* Tr. 802.

173  *Teller's protest to Alvarez:* Tr. 789.

174  *JRO "most skilled document writer":* Tr. 798.

174  *General Wilson's reaction to JRO:* Tr. 684–685, 689.

177  *Teller-Ulam paper on new H-bomb approach:* Ulam letter to author, Feb. 2, 1967.

177  *Accounts of Princeton meeting on new H-bomb approach: by Teller:* Legacy 52–53, Tr. 720; *by Rabi:* Tr. 456; *by Dean:* Tr. 305; *by JRO:* Tr. 81, 84, 87, 251.

178  *JRO on Teller discovery as "technically so sweet":* Tr. 81, 251; for a third, more qualified JRO use of the phrase, see Tr. 229. Also, see footnote, p. 511.

178  *Teller on Bradbury attitude:* Tr. 721.

179  *Teller departs Los Alamos:* Robert Coughlan, "Dr. Edward Teller's Magnificent Obsession," *Life,* Sept. 6, 1954, p. 70.

179  *Chevalier's fiancée's visit:* Chevalier 85–86.

7. *Rumblings in the Pentagon*

180  *Hawkins admits Communist Party membership: New York Times,* Jan. 28, 1951, p. 23; *American Mercury,* April, 1951, pp. 416–417.

180 *California HUAC conclusion: New York Times,* Apr. 14, 1954.

182 *Griggs on Finletter attitude toward JRO:* Tr. 749.

182 *Vista study: background:* Tr. 521, 584.

183 *JRO to Pasadena:* Tr. 891.

183 *JRO drafts Chapter 5:* Tr. 524.

183 *Air Force delegation visit, reaction:* Tr. 747, 759, 762, 900–901.

184 *Vista group to Europe:* Tr. 521, 584.

185 *Talks with Norstad:* Tr. 892, 905.

185 *Griggs' "serious question":* Tr. 749.

185 *"Second lab" controversy: Teller espousal, GAC negative votes:* Shepley-Blair 139.

186 *Replica of Los Alamos:* Tr. 311.

186 *AEC unmoved by McMahon:* Tr. 313–314.

187 *Air Force reaction:* Tr. 755, Shepley-Blair 143.

187 *AEC compromise solution:* Tr. 85, 314.

187 *Teller part-time work schedule:* Shepley-Blair 146.

188 *Lincoln Summer Study: report reaches Air Force:* Tr. 749.

188 *Genesis of Summer Study:* Tr. 923, 935.

189 *Griggs recollections of disarmament panel:* Tr. 760.

189 *Burden luncheon:* Tr. 525–526, Tr. 751.

190 *Griggs-JRO May 23 confrontation:* Tr. 752–724.

192 *Congressional group considers JRO inquiry: New York Times,* Apr. 16, 1954, p. 9.

192 *New appointments to GAC: JRO on passing the baton:* Tr. 96.

193 *Report of Borden's concern; JRO, Conant, DuBridge not re-appointed:* Shepley-Blair 212; Tr. 307.

194 *Griggs' concern over Lincoln Summer Study:* Tr. 749–751.

194 *Griggs reassured by MIT:* Tr. 764.

194 *Zacharias on delay:* Tr. 925–926.

194 *JRO's role in Summer Study:* Tr. 94.

195 *Radar recommendation:* Shepley-Blair 184–185.

195 *Griggs on "ZORC":* Tr. 750.

195 *Zacharias' denial:* Tr. 600, 922.

195 *Alsop articles:* New York *Herald Tribune,* Sept. 3, 1952, p. 21; Sept. 5, 1952, p. 17.

196 *H-bomb postponement issue:* Tr. 247–248, 562.

197 *Air Force view on H-bomb postponement:* Tr. 927.

198 *Three million tons of TNT:* Shepley-Blair 151.

199 *GOP platform: New York Times,* July 11, 1952, p. 1.

199 *McCarthy, Nixon speeches to Republican Convention: New York Times,* July 10, 1952, p. 21; July 12, 1952, p. 6.

199  *Eisenhower statements on Communism:* San Antonio, Oct. 14, 1952; Joliet, Ill., Sept. 15, 1952.

199  *At the instructions of Gordon Dean:* Tr. 320.


## 8. New Regime in Washington

201  *"Positive loyalty":* New York Times, Jan. 23, 1953, p. 1.

201  *Wilson on Communists in Pentagon:* Tr. 502.

201  *Humphrey on Communist problem:* Donovan 291.

202  *Broadening the precondition of Federal employment:* Donovan 286.

203  *Tightening up of screening of Federal employees:* New York Times of 1953; Feb. 4, p. 10 (sweeping presidential order predicted); Mar. 18, p. 36 (Truman program called a failure); Apr. 24, p. 1 (Nixon report to publishers); Apr. 25, p. 5 (Eisenhower to Republican women); Apr. 28, p. 1 (nineteen thousand civil servants).

203  *Lilienthal comments: Journals,* Vol. III, p. 390–391.

206  *Mundt and McCarthy comments: New York Times,* Apr. 14, 1954, p. 18.

207  *Borden's four hundred questions:* Tr. 839.

207  *Reorganization Plan No. 6:* Tr. 499, 502.

207  *Wilson's comment:* Tr. 502.

208  *Dean extends JRO contract:* Strauss 274–275.

208  *The Commission "initiated steps":* AEC press release of Apr. 13, 1954, as quoted in *New York Times,* Apr. 14, 1954.

209  *AEC records on removal of Princeton files:* AEC letter of Sept. 5, 1967.

209  *AEC press release:* Apr. 13, 1954.

209  *AEC files contain no record of "preliminary study":* AEC letter of Sept. 5, 1967, which stated: "A security facility was established for Dr. Oppenheimer at the Institute for Advanced Studies on July 30, 1947. In October, 1947, security guards were assigned from the New York Operations Office to provide 24-hour security service. In January, 1953, representatives of the Commission visited the facility and recovered about 32 linear feet of classified records. . . . Oppenheimer retained at this time that material which was germane to his consultancy to the Commission as well as letters, memoranda, reports, and staff papers representing information received by Oppenheimer from the time of his association with the project dating back to 1943. In the spring of 1953 a storage area was authorized in the basement

of the same building at the Institute for Advanced Studies. Following completion of this area, the facility in Oppenheimer's office was relocated in the basement and the guard position was moved to that location. No additional changes were made until after all classified documents were removed from this facility in December, 1953."

209 *JRO lecturing in South America:* JRO biography in Garrison brief to the AEC, June 7, 1954, p. 103.

210 *Whitman consideration of JRO file:* Tr. 499, 988.

212 *Republican charges of Communism: by Velde: New York Times,* Mar. 10, 1953, p. 1; *by Matthews: New York Times,* July 3, 1953, p. 1.

212 *McCarthy on Army study on Siberia: New York Times,* Sept. 10, 1953, p. 5.

212 *McCarthy on Monmouth: New York Times,* Oct. 17 ff. 1953.

213 *JRO on Furry:* Tr. 442.

213 *Chevalier writes to JRO:* Sept. 15, 1953.

213 *Oppenheimers' visit to Chevaliers' apartment:* Chevalier 86–87; Tr. 140, 920, 971.

213 *Furry defended by Harvard associates: New York Times,* Dec. 21, 1953, p. 31.

### III. THE INDICTMENT

216 *Borden letter:* Tr. 837–838.

221 *Reaction to Brownell speech of Nov., 1953: New York Times,* Nov. 9, p. 1; Nov. 19, p. 18; Nov. 12, p. 1, Nov. 16, p. 1; Nov. 7, p. 11.

222 *Warren Unna article: Atlantic Monthly,* May, 1957, p. 37.

222 *FBI summary sent to White House:* Donovan 294–295, Eisenhower 311.

222 *Borden letter transmitted to other Commissioners December 11:* AEC letter of July 22, 1968.

222 *Hoover's denial: Atlantic Monthly,* Aug., 1957, pp. 24–25.

223 *December 3 White House meeting:* Strauss 267–268; Donovan 295; Eisenhower 311.

223 *Eisenhower diary entry:* Eisenhower 311.

223 *Herblock cartoon:* Washington *Post* and *Times-Herald,* Apr. 14, 1954, p. 14.

224 *Strauss actions:* Strauss 268–269, 275.

224 *News of JRO case sent to Army posts and Navy ships:* Tr. 54.

225 *Parson's death: New York Times,* Dec. 6, 1953, p. 2.

231 *JRO-Strauss-Nichols meeting:* Strauss 276–277, 443–445; Cough-lan 88; Tr. 22.

232 *JRO's resentment of Strauss: New York Times,* Apr. 15, 1954, pp. 1, 14.

234 *1966 Supreme Court case:* Black v. U.S., 385 U.S., 26, 28–29; *1967 case:* Hoffa v. U.S., 387 U.S., 231, 233; *Court of Appeals in 1951:* Coplon v. U.S., 191 F.2d. 749, 757.

234 *Bugging of Volpe office:* Reference at Coughlan 101.

235 *JRO Pearl Harbor reaction and loss of pipe:* Coughlan 88.

235 *Strauss on leaving "the charges on the record":* Strauss 277.

235 *JRO letter to Strauss:* Tr. 22.

238 *Documents removed from Princeton:* AEC letter of May 25, 1967.

238 *Payment to JRO's Secretary:* AEC letter of Jan. 8, 1954.

239 *Various 1954 "security risk" claims: New York Times,* Jan. 8, p. 10; Jan. 16, p. 8; Jan. 22, p. 1; Feb. 9, p. 20; Feb. 10, p. 1; Feb. 13, p. 32; Feb. 19, p. 1; Feb. 22, p. 1; Mar. 2, p. 1; Mar. 3, p. 1; Mar. 5, p. 1.

239 *Nixon and Dulles suggestions in cabinet meeting:* Donovan 289–290.

IV. PREPARATIONS FOR THE HEARING

241 *Eisenhower chooses Gray: New York Times,* Apr. 30, 1954, p. 12.

242 *Robb's background:* Undated biography in Washington *Times-Herald.*

242 *Robb's defense of Browder:* Washington *Post,* May 4, 1951.

243 *Strauss' comment about "attorney for the prosecution":* Strauss 382.

244 *Garrison's background: New York Times,* May 4, 1967, p. 66.

245 *Garrison becomes JRO counsel:* Garrison, pp. 520–23.

246 *Reston-JRO telephone conversation:* Tr. 53–54.

247 *Lilienthal diary note: Journals,* Vol. III, p. 467.

247 *Institute for Advanced Study trustees meeting:* In part from *New York Times,* Apr. 14, 1954, p. 19.

247 *McCarthy-Peress controversy: New York Times,* 1954, Feb. 3, p. 1; Feb. 19, p. 1; Feb. 21, p. 1; Feb. 25, p. 1.

248 *Time required for Robb clearance:* AEC letter of June 28, 1966.

248 *Garrison broaches clearance question:* Garrison, p. 524.

249 *Nichols furnished no reasons:* Letter to Garrison, Jan. 27, 1954 (see p. 524).

249 *JRO attorneys decided to write Strauss:* Feb. 3, 1954 (see pp. 525–26).

250 *AEC declares it was "not possible" to clear Garrison:* Nichols letter to Garrison, June 3, 1954; Princ. Docs. 39–40.

250 *JRO "unrepresented and alone":* Tr. 62, 316, 407; also, Lee Du-Bridge, in an interview with the author, had a firm recollection that at one point during his appearance before the Gray Board JRO's lawyers were excused from the room.

250 *Garrison preparations for the hearing:* Garrison, pp. 521–22. Tr. 22.

251 *AEC denial of documents:* Garrison, pp. 543–44. Tr. 677–678, 806. See also Tr. 179, 375, 380, 407, 417–419, 633.

252 *AEC voluntarily introduced documents denied to Garrison:* Tr. 375–378.

252 *Marks' questions to AEC:* Garrison, p. 544.

252 *U.S. Court of Appeals on unspecific character of charges:* Fontana v. U.S., 262 F. 283 (8th Cir., 1919). The Fontana case has never been overruled, although there has since been a trend toward a relaxation of the degree of specificity required of indictments, with more emphasis on supplementary "Bills of Particulars." The principle of requiring specificity was reaffirmed by the Supreme Court as recently as 1962 (*Russell* v. *U.S.*, 369 U.S. 749 [1962]).

253 *Chevalier-Wyman exchange:* Tr. 969.

254 *Excerpts from JRO's reply to AEC charges:* Tr. 7, 8, 11, 20.

254 *Garrison's comment on JRO's reply:* Garrison, pp. 529–30.

256 *"Blank pad rule" written into new code:* Administrative Procedures Act, Section 7 (d).

256 *The general practice of hearing boards:* Bontecou 40.

257 *Garrison on "sinking feeling":* Tr. 971.

257 *Garrison countersuggestions:* Garrison, p. 544.

257 *Board advises Garrison of usual practice:* Tr. 972.

258 *Gray Board meets on April 5:* Princ. Docs. 58.

258 *Garrison:* "a cloud of suspicion": Garrison, p. 545.

258 *Weisskopf letter to JRO:* April 5, 1954.

259 *McCarthy charge of "deliberate delay":* New York Times, Apr. 7, p. 18; *denials:* New York Times, Apr. 8, p. 1.

259 *Krock column, Lilienthal comment:* Journals, Vol. III, pp. 498, 500.

### V. THE "TRIAL"

#### 1. *The First Week*

261 *Gordon Gray background: "never earned a cent": Time,* June 14, 1954, p. 24; *"consider myself a trustee": Current Biography,* 1949; *"the life of a private": Time,* June 20, 1949, p. 15; *"I have decided to devote the rest of my life": Time,* Feb. 6, 1952, p. 64. Other aspects of Gray biography: *Who's Who in America,* 1958–1959, and 1966–1967; *New York Times,* June 18, 1949, p. 15; *Time,* Sept. 12, 1949, p. 65; *Newsweek,* June 20, 1949, p. 20; as well as personal interviews with Gray associates and acquaintances.

263 *Morgan biography: Time,* June 14, 1954, p. 24; *Who's Who,* 1966–1967, p. 1506.

264 *Evans biography:* interviews with family and professional colleagues; also *Time,* June 14, 1954, p. 24.

266 *"An inquiry," and not . . . a trial":* Tr. 20.

266 *Gray on "very considerable latitude":* Tr. 143.

266 *Garrison's "a fortiori" supposition:* Tr. 202.

266 *Gray on confidentiality:* Tr. 20.

267 *Reston learns hearing to begin:* Tr. 54.

267 *Garrison's opening remarks:* Tr. 21–24.

267 *Garrison-Reston exchanges:* Tr. 53–55; Garrison, p. 533.

269 *Robb requests 1946 memorandum:* Tr. 38.

269 *Robb declines Garrison request to see government documents:* Tr. 148.

269 *Gray reminds Garrison of witness list:* Tr. 48.

269 *Garrison later denied reciprocal courtesy:* Tr. 352, 460, 537–542.

270 New York Times *disclosure: New York Times,* Apr. 13, 1954, p. 1.

270 *Gray comments on* Times *story:* Tr. 53–56.

271 *Gray's later annoyance:* Tr. 421, 565.

271 *Gray impugns Garrison's veracity:* Tr. 54.

271 *Witnesses "to the convenience of this board":* Tr. 56.

271 *Robb's questioning of Kelly:* Tr. 62.

272 *Right to counsel assured by AEC regulations:* AEC Security Procedures, Sec. 4.11 (f).

272 *JRO's view that nothing of substance was discussed:* Garrison, p. 528.

273 *Gray poses first substantive questions:* Tr. 64.

273 *JRO testimony on GAC H-bomb reports:* Tr. 77–80.

274 *First GAC extract:* Tr. 79.

274 *"We believe a super bomb should never be produced":* Tr. 895.

274 *AEC nine-hundred-word statement:* Press release of Atomic Energy Commission, Apr. 13, 1954.

274 *Robb hinted:* Tr. 79.

275 *According to AEC records:* AEC letter of Sept. 5, 1967.

275 *Reactions to JRO case: Cole, Einstein, Truman, Hickenlooper: New York Times,* Apr. 14, 1954; *McCarthy, Groves:* Washington *Post,* Apr. 14, 1954.

276 *McCarthy meeting with White House aides:* John Mason Brown, p. 242.

277 *Robb's first questions:* Tr. 108.

278 *Four probes:* Tr. 111.

278 *JRO on "fellow traveling":* Tr. 114.

279 *Robb's questions on Lomanitz:* Tr. 118–119.

279 *Questions on Weinberg:* Tr. 194.

279 *JRO's 1943 statement:* Tr. 875.

280 *Robb's questions on Lambert:* Tr. 139–140.

280 *JRO-Lansdale conversation:* Tr. 877.

281 *Robb armed with secret tape recording:* Tr. 871–886.

282 *JRO: "I don't want to remember":* Tr. 150.

282 *Robb's questions about Eltenton visit:* Tr. 135.

283 *Robb questions "cock and bull" story:* Tr. 137.

283 *Robb's recollection of JRO wringing hands:* Coughlan 102.

284 *Robb: "tissue of lies":* Tr. 146, 149.

284 *Garrison: "It lies heavy":* Tr. 308.

285 *Garrison request to be furnished transcripts:* Tr. 147–148.

285 *Robb's questions on Tatlock:* Tr. 154.

285 *Practices vary from one legal jurisdiction:* Curtis 217.

286 *Lansdale's conclusion:* Tr. 267.

286 *JRO asks Robb to fill him in:* Tr. 156.

286 *JRO's earlier, more emphatic answer:* Tr. 116–117.

287 *Robb's questions on JRO's statements to Groves:* Tr. 159–160.

287 *Excerpts from Groves' testimony:* Tr. 165, 167, 170, 171.

288 *Robb's questions on California tax return:* Tr. 184.

289 *Garrison's objection to selective excerpts; Robb reply:* Tr. 201.

289 *Later example of Garrison's dilemma:* Tr. 619–620.

290 *Robb's questions on Lambert:* Tr. 205.

290 *Robb-JRO interchange on Peters:* Tr. 211–215.

292 *Other examples of evasive JRO testimony:* Tr. 242–243.

293 *Peters case disturbs Gray:* Princ. Docs. 20, 21, 46, 53.

293 *Gray's questions on Peters and conflict of loyalty:* Tr. 252.

## 2. The Second Week

the word 'perjury,' but if at one point of the testimony a witness says one thing and at another point he says directly contrary, at one point the testimony is in error." (Tr. 411.)

314 *Garrison: ". . . is it relevant to the problem":* Tr. 447.

315 *Garrison: "I think our feeling":* Garrison, p. 560.

315 *Rabi testimony:* Tr. 465, 468–470.

317 *Chevalier's postcard:* Tr. 889.

317 *Hartley Rowe testimony:* Tr. 512–513.

319 *Gray: "washes out anything" and "widespread ignorance":* Tr. 555, 559.

319 *Gray-Winne exchanges:* Tr. 554.

319 *Gray-Bush exchange:* Tr. 566.

319 *Gray-McCloy exchange:* Tr. 739.

320 *Garrison cites regulation:* Tr. 558.

320 *Fifteen-thousand-word verdict:* Princ. Docs. 13.

320 *Gray ruling on Robb witness list: Garrison comment:* Tr. 537.

320 *Robb use of top-secret memo, newspaper clipping and telephone conversation:* Tr. 525–528.

321 *Robb's denial of advantage:* Tr. 538.

321 *Gray ruling:* Tr. 540.

322 *Gray characterizes Robb as "attorney for the AEC":* Tr. 539.

322 *Gray refers to Robb as "the representative of the government":* Tr. 540.

323 *Interchange about Robb's tactics:* Tr. 539–540.

323 *Bush testimony:* Tr. 565, 567.

324 *Question to McCormack:* Tr. 640.

325 *Garrison's dissociation from Bush's testimony:* Tr. 566.


## 3. *Third Week*

326 *Gray questions Bacher:* Tr. 625, 626.

327 *Unsigned "Analysis": of March 17, 1947:* Tr. 622–623.

327 *Later Supreme Court ruling against use of anonymous documents:* Greene v. McElroy, 360 U.S. 474 (1959).

329 *Robb questions Bacher about "Analysis":* Tr. 621–622.

329 *AEC regulations on all the evidence:* AEC Security Clearance Procedures, Sec. 4.16 (a) and (b).

329 *Clearance of Serber by Nimitz board:* Tr. 623.

330 *AEC answer to inquiry on Latimer testimony:* Letter to author from AEC Chairman Glenn Seaborg, Feb. 19, 1968.

330 *Latimer testimony excerpts:* Tr. 658–659, 662, 663, 664, 665, 669, 670, 671.

## 4. The Final Week

### VI. THE GRAY BOARD DECIDES

375 *Arthur Schlesinger comment:* Atlantic Monthly, Oct., 1954, p. 36.

376 *Gray Board "findings" on AEC charges:* Princ. Docs. 3–13; specifically: *on JRO's recruitment for Los Alamos:* pp. 8–9; *Evans' observation on Bohm:* p. 22; *on "Chevalier incident":* p. 11; *on JRO's suggesting an attorney for Chevalier:* p. 11; *on end of JRO's cash contributions through Communist Party:* p. 7; *on H-bomb charge:* p. 13.

378 *Herblock cartoon:* Washington *Post*, June 3, 1954.

378 *Gray Board on significance of findings: on JRO's Communist Party membership:* Princ. Docs. 18; *on JRO and H-bomb:* Princ. Docs. 19.

379 *Evans parts company with fellow members:* Princ. Docs. 22.

379 *Gray-Morgan verdict: on JRO's "high degree of discretion":* Princ. Docs. 20; *on JRO's "tendency to be coerced":* Princ. Docs. 20; *on JRO-Chevalier contacts:* Princ. Docs. 20, 21.

381 *Gray-Morgan recommendations:* Princ. Docs. 21.

381 *Gray-Morgan "general considerations":* Princ. Docs. 13–18; specifically: *on "the rigid circumscription of regulations":* p. 13; p. 14; *on "absolute loyalty":* p. 14; *on rehabilitation:* pp. 14, 15; *on 1947 AEC clearance of JRO:* p. 16; *on the "Role of Scientists as Advisors":* pp. 17–18.

383 *Government trust in Bentley, Chambers, and Crouch:* Chambers and Bentley, in their respective books, both relate actions during their period of active Communist Party membership, such as the use of false names to obtain passports and for other purposes. (Whittaker Chambers, *Witness*, Random House, New York, 1952, pp. 352, 356, 726–752; Elizabeth Bentley, *Out of Bondage*, Devin-Adair, New York, 1951, pp. 71, 94.) Crouch, on April 26, 1954, as a witness in *U.S.* v. *Kuzma, et al.*, Criminal No. 17418, U.S. District Court, Eastern District of Pennsylvania, "testified that he had for many years known and worked in the Communist Party with one David Davis, a defendant in the trial. But it turned out that in an earlier trial, Crouch had testified that he did not know Davis." (Tr. of Kuzma trial, pp. 781–788; 792–796.) (See Garrison brief to Gray Board, p. 70n.)

386 *John Mason Brown comment:* Brown 257.

386 *Evans' "Minority Report":* Princ. Docs. 21–23.

388 *Nichols advises JRO of verdict:* Princ. Docs. 27.

389 *Garrison's and JRO's reactions to verdict:* Garrison, pp. 534–36.

389 *Garrison June 1 letter to Nichols:* Princ. Docs. 31–36.

390 *Aftermath of Gray Board verdict: "bleak and dreary days"; JRO "kind of numb":* Coughlan 103; *visit from Einstein: New York*

*Times,* June 3, 1954; *JRO comment to Australian paper: New York Times,* June 4, 1954, p. 19; *JRO's denial: New York Times,* June 5, 1954, p. 6.

392 *Nichols' June 3 letter to Garrison:* Princ. Docs. 39–40.

393 *Peter Oppenheimer's reaction:* John Mason Brown 228–229.

393 *Coughlan report:* Coughlan 104.

394 *JRO favored publication of transcript: New York Times,* June 14, 1954, p. 1.

395 *Return of lost Zuckert document:* AEC letter of Jan. 25, 1967.

395 Time *Magazine quote:* June 28, 1954.

396 *Garrison: "no apology to make":* pp. 535–36.

396 *"You can't make an anomalous rise twice":* Tr. 85.

397 *Strauss recalls: "consent of all witnesses":* Strauss 291; AEC letter of Jan. 25, 1967.

397 *AEC statement accompanying transcript: New York Times,* June 16, 1954.

398 *"Shallow skimming" of transcript:* Time, June 28, 1954, p. 23.

398 *Garrison said, years later:* Garrison, p. 538.

399 *Chevalier's reaction:* Chevalier 97–98, 101.

400 *Cole television interview: New York Times,* June 14, 1954; June 17, 1954.

VII. GENERAL NICHOLS RECOMMENDS

401 *Nichols biography:* Drawn principally from Louis Cassels, "Brilliant Boss of Atom's Future," *Nation's Business,* Mar. 1954, p. 38 ff.

402 *Nichols himself had signed 1943 directive:* Princ. Docs. 44.

403 *Nichols verdict:* Princ. Docs., 43–48.

403 *Nichols on JRO's "Communist activities":* p. 44.

403 *Nichols on the "Chevalier incident":* pp. 45–46.

404 *Nichols' quote: "he is not reliable or trustworthy":* p. 45.

405 *Nichols on JRO's "associations":* p. 46.

405 *Nichols on JRO's "disregard of security":* pp. 46–47.

405 *Nichols on relevance of JRO's opinions to the case:* p. 47.

406 *Nichols on JRO's value to AEC program:* pp. 47–48.

406 *Nichols' conclusion:* p. 48.

407 *Supreme Court reverses disbarment of attorney: In re Ruffalo,* 390 U.S. 544, 549 (1968).

408 *Garrison on why he did not ask that Nichols' verdict be shown him:* Garrison, p. 557.

408 *Curtis observation:* Curtis 255, 256.

VIII. THE FINAL JUDGMENT

*412 Curtis statement: majority opinion written by Strauss:* Curtis 239.

*413 Strauss on reasons for revocation of JRO's clearance:* Strauss 295.

*413 Strauss' opinion on character and associations:* Princ. Docs. 51.

*414* Kalven comment: Kalven 261.

*414 Strauss' sponsorship of JRO:* Strauss 295.

*415 JRO placing self "outside the rules":* Princ. Docs. 52.

*415 Strauss' proof of JRO's "defects of character"; on "cock and bull story":* Princ. Docs. 52.

*416 Strauss on conflict in JRO testimony on Lomanitz and Weinberg:* Princ. Docs. 53.

*416 Strauss did not know about "cock and bull story":* Strauss 294; contradicted by JRO labeling it a lie in 1946: Item XIV, AEC memorandum of Oct. 25, 1954, prepared by C. A. Rolander, Jr., in rebuttal of Joseph and Stewart Alsop article, "We Accuse," U.S. News & World Report, Dec. 24, 1954, p. 94.

*417 Smyth on garbled transcript on Lambert:* Princ. Docs. 65.

*418 Smyth observation on Strauss' six examples:* Princ. Docs. 67.

*418 AEC regulations on "judgment of responsible persons":* AEC Criteria, p. 120.

*419 "The work of Military Intelligence":* Princ. Docs. 53.

*419 Strauss' opinion on JRO's association with Communists:* Princ. Docs. 54.

*420 Concluding portion of Strauss' verdict:* Princ. Docs. 54.

*421 Zuckert statement:* Princ. Docs. 54–57.

*421 Kalven chastises Zuckert:* Kalven 264.

*422 Campbell opinion:* Princ. Docs. 57–60.

*423 Curtis comment on Campbell's opinion:* Curtis 266.

*423 Murray opinion:* Princ. Docs. 60–63.

*425 Smyth dissenting opinion:* Princ. Docs. 63–67.

*429 Cole breaks into House debate; Reston reports: New York Times,* June 30, 1954, p. 1.

*430 Garrison confirms JRO's assumption of surveillance:* Garrison, p. 533. *JRO's comment on AEC verdict: New York Times,* June 30, 1954, p. 1.

*431 JRO's later reflections:* Minneapolis *Tribune,* June 16, 1957, p. 1.

IX. POSTLUDE

432 *Garrison account of aftermath of case:* Garrison, pp. 538–40.

433 *Eisenhower press conference: New York Times,* July 1, 1954, p. 10.

433 *Einstein statement:* New York *Herald-Tribune,* July 1, 1954.

433 *JRO statement of denial: New York Times,* June 30, 1954, p. 10.

433 New York *Post editorial:* July 1, 1954.

434 Louisville *Courier-Journal editorial:* July 2, 1954.

434 Washington *Post editorial:* July 1, 1954.

434 *Walter Lippmann quote:* Louisville *Courier-Journal,* July 2, 1954.

434 *Saul Pett interview: New York Times,* July 4, 1954, p. 15.

435 *Crouch reappears in the news: New York Times,* July 9, 1954, p. 7.

437 *A survey of such cases:* Yarmolinsky, *Case Studies in Personal Security.*

437 *Institute trustees' meeting: New York Times,* Oct. 2, 1954, p. 1; Strauss 295.

438 *Teller article on H-bomb origin:* "The Work of Many People," *Science* Magazine, Feb. 25, 1955.

438 *Strauss offers to buy Shepley-Blair manuscript:* Strauss 294.

438 *"We Accuse": Harper's,* October, 1954.

438 *Fulton Lewis report:* Nov. 8, 1954.

438 *Rolander rebuttal: U.S. News & World Report,* Dec. 24, 1954, pp. 86–103.

439 *Strauss' assistant to Drummond:* Letter from Everett Holles to Drummond, Nov. 10, 1954.

439 New York Times *observations: New York Times,* Dec. 20, 1954, p. 26.

439 *Chevalier open letter: New York Times,* Dec. 3, 1954, p. 17; Chevalier 110.

440 *Chevalier July letter to JRO:* Chevalier 107–108.

441 *Chevalier pre-Christmas letter to JRO:* Chevalier 109–111.


X. FALLOUT—1

442 *"America must not devour her own children":* Tr. 990.

443 *Lomanitz atop water tower: Daily Oklahoman,* July 23, 1949, p. 2.

447 *Rochester refuses to fire Peters:* Memorandum from University

of Rochester President Alan Valentine dated Sept. 28, 1948, and June 1, 1950.

447 *State Department denies Peters passport:* Statement of Mar. 22, 1950, by University of Rochester President Alan Valentine.

XI. FALLOUT—2

450 *Strauss' denial of State-Commerce difference:* Strauss hearing, p. 44.

450 *Senators charge Strauss of "misrepresentation":* Strauss Report, p. 12.

450 *Contradictions in Strauss' testimony:* Strauss hearing, p. 976, 978, 982–983; Strauss report, p. 15.

450 *Inglis testimony:* Strauss hearing, p. 369.

450 *Strauss' later insistence his "Testimony was accurate":* Strauss 395.

451 *Hill testimony:* Strauss hearing, pp. 730, 732.

451 *Jack Anderson testimony:* Strauss hearing, p. 840.

451 Strauss replies: *about Wilson:* Strauss hearing, p. 824; *about Henderson:* Strauss hearing, pp. 825, 826.

452 *Strauss' denial of Anderson allegation:* Hearing, p. 827.

452 *Letter from McCone:* Hearing, p. 844.

452 *Strauss modifies original statement:* Hearing, p. 842.

452 *McCone's assistant orders AEC to review Inglis file:* Hearing, p. 844.

453 *Minority report of Strauss opponents:* Strauss report, pp. 8–20.

454 *Senate vote:* New York Times, June 19, 1959.

455 *Teller-Rabi confrontation:* in part from Coughlan 104, 107.

456 *Teller's illness and despondency:* Coughlan 107, 109.


XII. FALLOUT—3

459 *Pleasantville American Legion leader protests:* New York Times, Mar. 23, 1955, p. 23.

459 *John Mason Brown quote: Through These Men,* p. 288.

460 *Murray statements on revival of JRO case:* New York Times, Dec. 9, 1957.

460 *Strauss 1958 comment:* Washington Post, Jan. 9, 1958; *New York Times,* Jan. 9, 1958.

460 *Von Braun testimony:* Washington Post, Mar. 15, 1958.

461 *Olson efforts to review JRO case:* New York Times, Apr. 5, 1963, p. 1.

461  *JRO in Paris, 1958:* Washington *Post*, Apr. 25, 1958.

461  *Levittown High School to be named after JRO:* New York *Post*, Aug. 20, 1958.

461  *JRO named to IAEA post:* New York Times, July 30, 1960.

462  *Fulton Lewis attack:* New York *Mirror*, July 5, 1961.

462  *Teller-Goldman interview:* New York Times, Apr. 16, 1962, p. 1.

462  *JRO's invitation to White House dinner:* New York Times, Apr. 30, 1962, p. 1; *his "not on your life" comment:* New York Times, Apr. 5, 1963, p. 1.

463  *Consideration of JRO for Fermi award;* New York Times, Apr. 5, 1963, p. 1.

463  *Teller mails in ballot:* Coughlan 109.

463  *JRO comment on Fermi award:* New York Times, Apr. 4, 1963.

463  *Grumbling Congressional reaction:* New York Times, Apr. 6, 1963; Washington *Post*, July 4, 1963; New York *Herald Tribune*, July 7, 1963.

464  *Fermi award ceremony:* New York Times, Dec. 3, 1963, p. 1; White House Press Release, Dec. 2, 1963; Coughlan 88–89, 109.

465  New York Times *editorial:* Dec. 3, 1963.

465  *Play about JRO:* Heinar Kipphardt, *In the Matter of J. Robert Oppenheimer.*

466  *JRO's reaction:* Washington *Post*, Nov. 13, 1964.

466  *JRO's 1966 appearance at Princeton, interview with magazine reporter:* Newsweek, June 27, 1966, p. 64–65.


XIII.  WHAT IS SECURITY?

468  *Quotes from Gray Board and AEC majority opinions:* Princ. Docs. 13, 54.

469  *Alsos findings: on discovery of papers:* Alsos, pp. 67, 70–71; *on replacement of scientists in Strasbourg:* p. 73, *in Munich:* p. 235, *in Heidelberg:* pp. 83–84; *on Osenberg:* pp. 187–190; *on student antipathy toward "non-Aryan" fields:* p. 235; *"it is anybody's guess":* p. ix.

472  *Burch memorandum drawn from Nichols' 1954 opinion:* Princ. Docs. 44 ("word for word" except for minor change of tense in first paragraph).

473  *Philip Morrison's invention:* Tr. 196; *Frank Oppenheimer's work:* letter to author from K. T. Bainbridge, Dec. 12, 1966.

475  *Quote from Evans' dissent:* Princ. Docs. 23.

475  *Quotes from McCloy testimony:* Tr. 736.

476  *British scientist barred from visit:* Gellhorn, p. 112.

477 *Difficulties in obtaining clearances for scientists:* Gellhorn, pp. 93, 123, 220. (*Note:* These events took place in 1949.)

477 *Rejection of supposed Wallace voter; passing over of "controversial" scientist; Soviet medical journal:* Gellhorn, pp. 123–124, 161–162.


XIV. SECURITY ON TRIAL

481 *John Lord O'Brian quote: National Security and Individual Freedom,* Godkin Lectures, Harvard University, Apr. 27 and 28, 1955, Harvard University Press, pp. 56–57.

481 *Smyth and Strauss on purpose of JRO case: Smyth:* Princ. Docs. 67; *Strauss:* Strauss 295.

482 *Factors considered relevant to employment eligibility:* All from Yarmolinsky; specifically: *on American Legion:* Yarmolinsky, p. 3; *seconding Bible-burning motion:* p. 1; *close association with parents:* pp. 45–47; *editing paper with "radical viewpoints":* p. 1; *having purchased books, etc.:* p. 33.

482 *Questions asked in security hearings: on mixing blood plasma and "sympathy with the underprivileged":* Thurman Arnold, pp. 67–68; others from Yarmolinsky at, respectively, pages 12, 51, 58, 89, 91.

483 *Navy advice about joining organizations:* Ralph Brown 191.

483 *Federal meat inspector suspended:* Yarmolinsky, pp. 158–176.

483 *Loyalty probes: in Paleontology Section, Department of Education:* Ralph Brown 107; *of washroom attendant:* New York Civil Liberties Union, "The Case Against the New York Security Law," Jan., 1957, p. 5; *in Department of Sanitation:* Ralph Brown 107; *among wrestlers, pharmacists and piano dealers:* Ralph Brown 118 and 118n.

483 *Lawyer's advice to government librarian:* Thurman Arnold, pp. 65–66.

484 *Dorothy Parker:* Ralph Brown 174–175.

484 *FCC radio station license:* The case of Edward Lamb: Ralph Brown 371–372.

484 *Cancellation of NBC Symphony Tour:* Ralph Brown 374.

484 *Dun & Bradstreet:* Ralph Brown 145.

484 *Jack Warner testimony:* Thurman Arnold, pp. 59–60.

485 *13,500,000 jobs:* Brown 181. This included 1.6 million in the "professions," including teachers; 7.2 million in "government and military"; 4.5 million in "manufacturing, construction, transport, utilities"; and 300,000 "managers."

485 *Small Business Administration policy:* American Civil Liberties Union memoranda to Members of Congress, Aug. 18, 1967, Oct. 7, 1968.

485 *Department of Health, Education and Welfare barring of scientists: Science,* June 27, 1969, pp. 1499–1504 (by Bryce Nelson).

486 *Newell case: Newell* v. *Ignatius,* Civil Action 756–768, U.S. District Court for the District of Columbia—"Defendant's Statement of Material Facts in Support of Motion for Summary Judgment," pp. 4, 8.

486 *1967 case of Navy petty officer:* Letter of May 3, 1967, from Captain A. H. Berndtson, Assistant Chief for Performance, Bureau of Naval Personnel, to Rep. Jeffery Cohelan.

487 *Suspension of soldier stationed in Japan:* Statement of Capt. Donald E. Taber (soldier's commanding officer) to Major William G. Carpenter (security investigator), Sept. 29, 1966.

487 *Sedition charges brought against Roger Priest:* Washington *Star,* July 22, 1969; Washington *Daily News,* July 23, 1969; *sedition punishable by death:* U.S. Code, Title 10, Sec. 894.

487 *Barring of draft critic from speaking:* Washington *Post,* Nov. 21, 1968.

488 *Hershey instructions to local draft boards:* Letter to all members of Selective Service from Lt. Gen. Lewis B. Hershey, Oct. 26, 1967, as quoted in *New York Times,* Nov. 9, 1967, p. 2.

488 *Hershey's refusal to circulate 1969 decision:* Washington *Post,* June 15, 1969, p. 30.

488 *Navy nurse sentenced to hard labor:* Washington *Post,* Feb. 4, 1969.

New York Times *editorial:* June 11, 1969.

488 *Church League of America operations:* CBS Morning News, June 18, 1969.

489 *Quote from Alan Barth:* Barth 129.

489 *The FBI continues to eavesdrop: New York Times,* Feb. 12, 1969, p. 1.

489 *Wiretap of Martin Luther King:* Washington *Post,* June 5, 1969.

490 *Supreme Court on "Mere knowing membership": Elfbrandt* v. *Russell,* 384 U.S. 11, 18 (1966).

490 *Federal agencies continue to consult committee's files: 1966 Hearings before Joint Committee on the Organization of Congress,* p. 2252.

490 *Right of confrontation essential: Reilly* v. *Pinkus,* 338 U.S. 269, 275 (1949).

490 *Ruling where effect is to punish: Kennedy* v. *Mendoza-Martinez,* 372 U.S. 144, 165–8 (1962).

491 *Many cleared and later recharged:* Examples may be found at Yarmolinsky 14, 28, 48, 54, 60, 70, 85, 158.

491 *Case of William Lewis Greene: Greene* v. *McElroy,* 360 U.S. 474 (1959).

492 *Statute of limitations in Federal Criminal Laws:* 18 U.S. Code 3282.

492 *Supreme Court warning of "chilling effect": Dombrowski* v. *Pfister,* 380 U.S. 479, 487 (1965).

493 *Quotes from Alan F. Westin: Privacy and Freedom,* Atheneum, New York, 1967, p. 159.

494 *Vice President Nixon quotes Naval Intelligence report:* Ralph Brown 360, citing *New York Times* Oct. 27 and 28, 1954.

494 *The case of Mr. X:* Yarmolinsky 32.

495 *Retired brigadier general forced to withdraw:* Brown 360.

495 *Barth quote:* Barth 128–129.

495 *Excerpts from security-risk charges:* Yarmolinsky; specifically, *on National Brotherhood Week:* p. 1; *on "Communist literature and art":* pp. 143, 146; *on Ph.D. thesis:* p. 32.

497 *Questions drawn from hearing transcripts: on wife's dress, lack of mattresses, wife sleeping on board: Greene* v. *McElroy,* 360 U.S. 474, at 489; *on One World idea:* Yarmolinsky 91; *on books in X's home and Howard Fast novels:* Thurman Arnold 67–68.

498 *Senator McCarran on China:* Ralph Brown 366.

498 *Kennedy to Stevenson on China Policy:* Arthur Schlesinger, Jr., *A Thousand Days,* Houghton Mifflin, Boston, 1966, pp. 479, 483.

499 *Political representatives of the President openly argued:* Manchester, N.H., *Union Leader,* Mar. 8, 1968, p. 4; *New Hampshire Sunday News,* Mar. 10, 1968, p. 6.

499 *GOP Vice Presidential Candidate Agnew: New York Times,* Sept. 11, 1968, p. 1.

499 *Justice Brandeis quote: Gilbert* v. *Minnesota,* 254 U.S. 325 (1920), quoted at Barth 232.

499 *Eisenhower on number of Communists: New York Times,* Apr. 6, 1954, p. 16.

500 *FBI estimate on number of Communists:* Testimony of FBI Director to House Subcommittee on Appropriations, Feb. 23, 1968.

500 *Truman loyalty program statistics:* Civil Service Commission, 1953 Annual Report (1954), p. 32, quoted in Ralph Brown 55. These statistics do not include some 8,020 cases where some "derogatory information" was found but where the proceeding

was not completed, usually because the individual withdrew his Federal application before a final judgment was reached. But even assuming that an adverse ruling had been arrived at in each of those 8,000 cases, the total of such rulings would amount to less than two-tenths of one percent of the total number screened.

500 *The government has spent one-half to three-quarters of a billion dollars:* The only calculation of the total cost to the government of the security program was for Fiscal 1955, when the cost to 69 Federal agencies was set at $37,413,267. (*Senate Post Office and Civil Service Subcommittee Hearings on Administration of Federal Employees' Security Program,* May, 1956, p. 964.) If that were typical, the cost of the program, over twenty years, would be $750 million. But allowance has to be made for the fact that security-screening activity was probably at its height in the mid-Fifties.

500 *1950 state-by-state Communist statistics:* Quoted at Barth 36.

501 *Gray on "absolute predictability":* Tr. 372.

501 *Robb on "future conduct":* Speech at Amherst College, Mar. 14, 1955, published in *U.S. News & World Report,* Apr. 1, 1955.

501 *Ralph Brown: "We find no responsible claims:* Brown 36n.

501 *Re sophistication of Soviet H-bomb:* The first American thermonuclear device used liquid materials and hence was so heavy as to be impractical as a transportable weapon. By contrast, the first Soviet bomb used materials in a solid state and was of the kind necessary for use in a rocket warhead. The Americans lagged behind the Russians in solid-state H-bombs.

502 *Even the supposedly backward Chinese:* Letter to author from AEC Chairman Glenn Seaborg, May 2, 1968.

503 *Westmoreland on "unpatriotic acts":* New York Times, Apr. 25, 1967, p. 1.

503 *1946 Presidential Commission: Report of the President's Temporary Commission on Employe Loyalty* (1947), pp. 21–22.

504 *"Government can search . . . the soul of an individual":* Princ. Docs. 2.


XV. EPILOGUE

505 *Comments on JRO's death by Bethe, Teller, Lilienthal, Yukawa: New York Times,* Feb. 20, 1967, p. 20; *by Smyth:* Letter to author from Mrs. Henry DeWolf Smyth, Mar. 8, 1967.

507 *Scientists' advice "uncolored and uninfluenced":* Princ. Docs. 18.

509 *General Wilson's statement to Gray Board:* Tr. 685.

509 *Giorgio de Santillana remarks:* "Galileo and J. Robert Oppen-heimer," *The Reporter*, Dec. 26, 1957, p. 16.

510 *JRO's attitudes toward H-bomb: favored dropping A-bomb on Japan:* Smith 35, 49; New World 358; *sided with GAC majority in 1949:* Tr. 79; *enthusiastic at Princeton meeting:* Tr. 305; *"technically sweet" comment:* Tr. 81, 251.

512 *JRO on his left-wing past: Time,* Nov. 8, 1948.

# INDEX

NOTE: *This index does not encompass the Garrison responses to questions put to him by the author (pp. 517–66)*

Robb, Roger (*cont'd*)
Gen. Groves, 287–88; fails to call Paul Crouch, 294; advantage from exclusive access to secret documents, 299, 305, 310, 311, 320–21, 343; questions John Lansdale, 301–02; receives hearing transcripts more promptly than Garrison, 302, 305; his questioning of Gordon Dean, 305–06, of Kennan, 307, of Conant, 308–09, of Lilienthal, 310–11, of Ramsey, 314, Rabi, 315–16, of Bacher, 326–27, 329, of Wilson, 334–35, of Teller, 343–44, of Griggs, 348–49, of Pash, 355, of Borden, 356–57, of Bush, 362–63; dines with Alvarez before Alvarez testifies, 353; says Oppenheimer was "own worst witness," 366; helps with Evans' dissent, 388; represents Fulton Lewis, Jr., 399
Robeson, Paul, 20
Rochester *Democrat-Chronicle*, 127
Rochester *Times-Union*, 125
Rogers, William P., 242–43
Rolander, Arthur, 258, 438
Roosevelt, Mrs. Eleanor, 157
Roosevelt, Franklin D., 25, 46, 79
Ross, Charles, 156
Rowe, Hartley, 143, 145, 317–18, 427
Russell, Katherine, 238n
Russell, Louis J., 110, 120, 122, 132
Russia, *see* Soviet Union

San Francisco *Chronicle*, 110
San Francisco *Examiner*, 25–26
Scala, Armand E., 295
Schlesinger, Arthur, Jr., 160, 348, 375
Schmitz, Henry, 458
Schneiderman, William, 31, 166, 280, 418

*Science*, 485–86
*Scientific American*, 160
Seaborg, Glenn, 138–39, 141, 146, 152, 153, 270, 296–98, 426, 462, 464
Security clearance, Oppenheimer, 35, 40, 41n, 49, 104, 105–06, 166, 193, 209, 211, 231, 232–33, 259, 274, 275, 286, 403; *AEC 1947 clearance*, 251–52n, 270, 271, 274, 304, 310, 312, 355, 370, 384, 404
Security procedures, regulations (AEC), 226, 228, 232, 238, 255–56, 266, 289, 307, 327, 329, 371, 381–82, 385
Security system, 374, 379, 380, 381, 405, 425, 428, 468, 475–77, 480–81, 482–504
Segrè, Emilio, 74
Serber, Mrs. Charlotte, 61, 328–29, 370
Serber, Robert, 43, 142, 146–47, 328, 329, 370, 512
Shannon, Dr. James A., 485n
Shepley, James, 395n, 437, 456
Sherwood, Robert E., 494n
Shriver, Sargent, 457
Silverman, Samuel J., 249, 251n, 309, 331–34, 335–36, 338–39, 344, 346n, 348, 350–51, 356, 358, 365
Sixth Amendment, 293–94, 490
Small Business Administration, 485
Smith, Brewster, 485
Smith, Cyril, 74, 99, 143, 146, 512
Smyth, Henry DeWolf, 150, 170, 222n, 395, 409, 410–13, 417–18, 430, 464, 481, 505, 508; minority report, 425–30
Snapp, Roy, 412
Somervell, Brehon, 39
Souers, Sidney, 193
Soviet Union, 19–21, 24, 25–26, 27, 32, 41–42, 100, 102, 109, 114, 116, 135, 136, 137, 142, 144,

# ABOUT THE AUTHOR

PHILIP M. STERN is a Phi Beta Kappa Harvard graduate, with varied experience in government, politics and journalism. He was, successively, reporter and editorial writer for the New Orleans *Item;* legislative assistant to Congressman Henry M. Jackson of Washington and Senator Paul H. Douglas of Illinois; campaign aide to Adlai E. Stevenson; Director of Research for the Democratic National Committee; cofounder, editor and then publisher of the *Northern Virginia Sun* in Arlington, Virginia; and Deputy Assistant Secretary of State. Mr. Stern in 1964 wrote *The Great Treasury Raid,* a book about tax loopholes that became a bestseller. He is also author of *The Shame of a Nation,* a photographic essay on American poverty, with photographs by George de Vincent; and coauthor, with his artist-sculptor wife, of *O, Say Can You See, by Dawn's Urban Blight,* a book contrasting the tourist's view of their home city, Washington, D.C., with the neglected aspects of the capital. At the 1968 Democratic National Convention, he nominated Channing E. Phillips, the first black man in history to be placed in nomination for the presidency at a major party convention. In addition to writing, Mr. Stern presides over two foundations and a family of five children.

HAROLD P. GREEN is Professor of Law and Director of the Law, Science and Technology Program at The George Washington University National Law Center. He has had substantial experience in dealing with Government security problems as Government attorney, private practitioner and author.